DATABASE SYSTEM CONCEPTS

SECOND EDITION

HENRY F. KORTH
ABRAHAM SILBERSCHATZ
University of Texas at Austin

McGraw-Hill, Inc.
New York St. Louis San Francisco Auckland Bogotá
Caracas Lisbon London Madrid Mexico Milan
Montreal New Delhi Paris San Juan Singapore
Sydney Tokyo Toronto

DATABASE SYSTEM CONCEPTS

890 AGM AGM 998765

ISBN 0-07-044754-3

The editors were David M. Shapiro and Joseph F. Murphy;
the production supervisor was Kathryn Porzio.
Arcata Graphics/Martinsburg was the printer and binder.

Library of Congress Cataloging-in-Publication Data

Korth, Henry F.
  Database system concepts / Henry F. Korth, Abraham Silberschatz.—
  2nd ed.
      p. cm.
  Includes bibliographical references and index.
  ISBN 0-07-044754-3
  1. Data base management. I. Silberschatz, Abraham. II. Title.
QA76.9.D3K67 1991
005.74—dc20   90-20826

This book is printed on acid-free paper.

In memory of my father Joseph Silberschatz,
and my grandparents Stepha and Aaron Rosenblum.

Avi Silberschatz

To my wife, Joan, and my parents.

Hank Korth

Contents

Appendix A   Network Model

Appendix B   Hierarchical Model

Preface

Database management has evolved from a specialized computer application to a central component of a modern computing environment. As such, database systems have become an essential part of a computer science education. Our purpose in this text is to present the fundamental concepts of database management. These include aspects of database design, database languages, and database system implementation.

This text is intended for a first course in databases at the junior, senior or first-year graduate level. We assume only a familiarity with basic data structures, computer organization, and a high-level (Pascal-like) programming language. Concepts are presented using intuitive descriptions, many of which are based on our running example of a bank enterprise. Important theoretical results are covered, but formal proofs are omitted. The bibliographic notes contain pointers to research papers in which results were first presented and proved. In place of proofs, figures and examples are used to suggest why one should expect the result in question to be true.

The fundamental concepts and algorithms covered in the book are often based upon those used in existing commercial or experimental database systems. Our aim is to present these concepts and algorithms in a general setting not tied to one particular database system.

In this, the second edition of *Database System Concepts*, we have retained the overall style of the first edition while reflecting the evolution of database management. Increased emphasis is placed on the relational data model, the SQL query language, and transaction processing. A new chapter on object-oriented databases is also included. Every chapter has been edited, and most have been modified extensively. We shall describe the changes in more detail shortly.

Organization

Chapter 1 provides a general overview of the nature and purpose of database systems. We explain how the concept of a database system has developed, the common features of database systems, what a database system does for the user, and how a database system interfaces with operating systems. We also introduce an example database application: a banking enterprise consisting of multiple bank branches. This example is used as a running example throughout the book. This chapter is motivational, historical, and explanatory in nature.

Chapter 2 presents the entity-relationship model. This model provides a high-level view of the issues in database design and the problems encountered in capturing the semantics of realistic applications within the constraints of a data model.

Chapters 3 and 4 present the fundamentals of the relational model. Chapter 3 focuses on the model itself, the relational algebra, and the relational calculus. Chapter 4 focuses on user-oriented relational languages, with a primary emphasis on SQL. These two chapters cover data manipulation: queries, updates, insertions, and deletions. Algorithms and design issues are deferred to later chapters. Thus these chapters are suitable for those individuals or lower-level classes who want to learn what a database system is, without getting into the details of the internal algorithms and structure.

Chapters 5 and 6 discuss database constraints. Chapter 5 presents constraints from the standpoint of database integrity, while Chapter 6 shows how constraints can be used in the design of a relational database. Functional dependencies and referential integrity are presented in Chapter 5 as are mechanisms for integrity maintenance, such as triggers and assertions. The theme of this chapter is the protection of the database from accidental damage. Chapter 6 provides an introduction to the theory of relational database design. Such topics as normalization and data dependencies are covered with emphasis on the motivation for each normal form and the intuitive meaning of each type of data dependency.

Chapters 1 through 6, as a group, are suitable for a course on the use and design of a database, while Chapters 7 through 9, cover the internal structure of database systems. Chapter 7 deals with file and system structure and the mapping of relational data to a file system. A variety of data access techniques are presented in Chapter 8, including hashing, B-tree indices, and secondary key indices. Chapter 9 addresses optimization, both from the standpoint of physical organization and the standpoint of query modification.

Chapters 10 through 12 cover transaction management. This is a broad area involving concurrency control, recovery from failure, deadlock, and data consistency. Chapter 10 focuses on transaction *atomicity* and recovery from failure. The primary techniques for ensuring correct transaction execution despite system crashes and disk failures are presented. These include logs, shadow pages, checkpoints, and database dumps. In Chapter 11, our focus is on concurrency control. The concept of *serializability* is presented, and several techniques for ensuring serializability are covered including locking, timestamping, and optimistic (validation) techniques. Chapter 12 ties together the failure-recovery concepts of Chapter 10 and the concurrency-control concepts of Chapter 11, and addresses some of the practical issues of designing a transaction processing system.

Chapter 13 covers object-oriented databases. It introduces the concepts of object-oriented programming and shows how these concepts form the basis for a data model. No prior knowledge of object-oriented systems is assumed.

Chapter 14 introduces two extensions to the relational model: logic databases and nested relations. This chapter extends the concepts of Chapters 3 and 4 to include recursive queries, a Prolog-like query language (Datalog), and a SQL-like language for hierarchically structured objects.

Chapter 15 revisits the issues discussed in Chapters 1 through 12 in order to address the problems encountered if the database is distributed over several computers. In particular, the issues of transaction management, concurrency, and deadlock detection and recovery are addressed. Special techniques for optimizing queries in a distributed system are also presented.

Chapter 16 deals with the protection of the data from accidental and malicious abuse.

Chapter 17 overviews several influential academic and commercial database systems. It also includes a description of application programming using embedded SQL.

Older database texts (including the first edition of this text) have included coverage of the network and hierarchical data models. These data models, though still in use, are now of lesser importance for most applications. Most new database applications use either the relational model or the object-oriented model. However, since there is still a substantial community of users of systems based on the network and hierarchical models, we include detailed coverage of them in Appendix A and Appendix B, respectively.

The Second Edition

Many comments and suggestions were forwarded to us concerning the first edition. These, together with our own observations while teaching at the University of Texas and IBM, have prodded us to produce this second edition. Our basic procedure was to rewrite the material in each chapter, bringing some of the older material up-to-date, improving the exercises, and adding new references. We have also restructured the organization of parts of the book. For the benefit of those familiar with the first edition, we explain the main changes below.

Relational Databases

Coverage of the relational model has been expanded. The old Chapter 3 has been split into two (the new Chapters 3 and 4). Chapter 3 now covers the relational model itself, plus the formal relational languages: the relational algebra and the relational calculus. We have extended the relational algebra to include an explicit assignment operator. This allows us to simplify some examples by creating temporary relations. We then use this syntax to introduce database modification in Section 3.5 using the relational algebra. The concept of view definition is introduced using the relational algebra in Section 3.6. Since the theta join operator is used infrequently, its coverage has been moved into an exercise (Exercise 3.9). We have made a minor change in our notation for the tuple relational calculus which leads to a major simplification of the concept of safety. Specifically, our new notation requires explicit specification of the domain of every existentially or universally quantified tuple variable. This modified notation has been tested in our courses at the University of Texas and IBM and has worked well. We have also added the use of the logical implication operator in the relational calculus. Using the implication operator, we have been able to make several of our examples easier to understand.

Chapter 4 covers SQL, QBE, and Quel. The coverage of each language has been expanded over the first edition. As before, we do not present a complete users' guide for each language, but focus on the main concepts. Our SQL coverage is based primarily on ANSI standard SQL. Since SQL has become the dominant database language, we have included SQL syntax for data definition, index creation, authorization, and transactions in the chapters that cover those subjects.

The old Chapter 6 covered data dependencies and relational database design. This chapter has been split into two (the new Chapters 5 and 6). Chapter 5 is concerned with integrity constraints. It covers referential integrity, functional dependencies, triggers, and assertions. Database design issues and normal forms are covered in Chapter 6. This chapter, as before, presents normalization using functional dependencies, multivalued dependencies, and join dependencies. Discussion for atomic values and first normal form has been moved to Chapter 14. This is a new chapter in which recent extensions to the relational model are presented. A logic-based data model is presented in Section 14.1 using the recursive query language Datalog. The coverage of atomic values and first normal form from the old Chapter 6 has been expanded into Section 14.2 of the new edition. This section covers the nested relational model for non-first normal form relational databases. Section 14.3 introduces expert database systems.

Transaction Processing

Another major change in the second edition is the expansion of coverage of transaction processing (new Chapters 10 through 12). Chapter 10 is similar to the old Chapter 10. Coverage of deadlock and recovery in the old Chapter 11 has been moved into Chapter 12. The new Chapter 11, as did the old, covers the concepts of schedules and serializability, and concurrency control protocols. Section 11.2 on testing for serializability has been revised significantly. A new section (11.8) addresses insertions and deletions and the resulting *phantom* phenomenon.

Chapter 12, a new chapter, covers issues of recovery and concurrency. The deadlock coverage from the old Chapter 11 appears in Section 12.3. New sections address weaker notions of consistency than serializability, concurrent access to index structures, and long-duration interactive transactions.

Object-Oriented Databases

We have expanded our coverage of object-based logical models by including the object-oriented model. We have also improved our coverage of the entity-relationship model.

Chapter 2 in the new edition is similar to the old Chapter 2. We have added coverage of design issues in an E-R database design. Design issues are discussed throughout the chapter, and addressed in particular in a new section (2.10). We have dropped coverage of specialization in Section 2.7 and now cover only generalization. Specialization is introduced in Exercise 2.12 and covered in detail in Chapter 13.

Chapter 13 is a new chapter on object-oriented databases. It is a major expansion of the coverage in the old Chapter 14. It introduces the concepts of object-oriented programming and shows how these concepts form the basis for a data model. No prior knowledge of object-oriented systems is assumed.

Minor Changes

The old Chapters 4 and 5 on the network and hierarchical models have been moved to appendices. The coverage of the mapping of networks and hierarchies to files, which appeared in the old Chapter 7, have been included in the respective appendices, as has been the coverage of network and hierarchical databases systems from the old Chapter 15. This change was made since less emphasis is being placed on these models. For those who would like to cover these models, however, all of the material from the first edition can be found in the appendices.

Chapters 7 through 9 have been refined from their first-edition counterparts. Section 7.5 includes material that was formerly in Section 8.2.1. The coverage of dynamic hashing in Chapter 8 has been extensively modified to clarify the exposition. Chapter 9 now includes a section on parallel join algorithms.

Chapter 15, on distributed databases, is similar to old Chapter 12. We have added coverage of three-phase commit to the section on commit protocols (15.7). Also, we have added a new section on the topic of heterogeneous distributed database systems (multidatabase systems).

Chapter 16, on security, is similar to the old Chapter 13. Chapter 17 (Case Studies) is based on the old Chapter 15.

Acknowledgments

This edition is based on the first, so we would like to thank once again the many people who helped us with the first edition: Don Batory, Haran Boral, Robert Brazile, Sara Strandtman, Won Kim, Anil Nigam, Bruce Porter, Carol Kroll, Jim Peterson, Fletcher Mattox, Ron Hitchens, Alberto Mendelzon, and Henry Korth (father of Henry F.) The idea of using ships as part of the cover concept was originally suggested to us by Bruce Stephan. The cover concept was formulated by the authors. Anne Green of McGraw-Hill was the cover artist for the first edition. Portions of Sections 11.8. 12.8, and 12.9 of the first edition were based upon *Operating System Concepts*, by Peterson and Silberschatz, 1985. This material is reprinted with permission of Addison-Wesley Publishing Company. Gio Wiederhold's on-line bibliography helped us in locating several of the bibliographic references.

Since the publication of the first edition, numerous people have written or spoken to us about the book and offered suggestions and comments. Although we cannot mention all of these people here, we would like especially to thank Alan Fekete, Hyoung-Joo Kim, Keith Marzullo, Mark Roth, Greg Speegle. Ted Van Ryn of IBM Canada provided us with SQL/DS manuals. Greg Speegle and Dawn Bezviner helped us prepare the instructor's manual for the first edition. Their work has served as the basis for the new instructor's manual for the second edition. Hank's dad read the entire manuscript (again!), offered comments, and pointed out sections that needed clarification. The numerous students who have used the first edition in our classes at the University of Texas and at IBM have helped us with both their useful comments and occasional blank stares.

Boyd Merworth assisted us with typesetting. Sara Strandtman and Karen Shaffer typed our text and prepared it for typesetting. The new cover, an evolution of the cover of the first edition, was drawn by Anne Green of McGraw-Hill.

We have endeavored to eliminate typos, bugs, and the like from the text. But, just like most new releases of software, some bugs probably remain. We would appreciate any comments you, the reader, may offer. Correspondence should be addressed to Avi Silberschatz, Department of Computer Sciences, University of Texas, Austin TX 78712-1188, U.S.A. Internet electronic mail should be addressed to avi@cs.utexas.edu or hfk@cs.utexas.edu.

Finally, Avi would like once again to thank his wife, Haya, and his children, Aaron, Lemor, and Sivan, for their patience and support during the revision of this book. Hank would like to thank Avi for being patient when an ultimate frisbee injury caused a delay in the completion of this edition. (Hank continues to play ultimate despite Avi's advice to the contrary.) Most especially, Hank would like to thank his wife Joan for her love and understanding.

H. F. K.
A. S.

DATABASE SYSTEM CONCEPTS

1

Introduction

A *database management system* (DBMS) consists of a collection of interrelated data and a set of programs to access that data. The collection of data, usually referred to as the *database*, contains information about one particular enterprise. The primary goal of a DBMS is to provide an environment that is both *convenient* and *efficient* to use in retrieving and storing database information.

Database systems are designed to manage large bodies of information. The management of data involves both the definition of structures for the storage of information and the provision of mechanisms for the manipulation of information. In addition, the database system must provide for the safety of the information stored, despite system crashes or attempts at unauthorized access. If data is to be shared among several users, the system must avoid possible anomalous results.

The importance of information in most organizations, and hence the value of the database, has led to the development of a large body of concepts and techniques for the efficient management of data. In this chapter, we present a brief introduction to the principles of database systems.

1.1 Purpose of Database Systems

Consider part of a savings bank enterprise that keeps information about all customers and savings accounts in permanent system files at the bank. In addition, the system has a number of application programs that allow the user to manipulate the files, including:

- A program to debit or credit an account.
- A program to add a new account.
- A program to find the balance of an account.
- A program to generate monthly statements.

These application programs have been written by system programmers in response to the needs of the bank organization.

New application programs are added to the system as the need arises. For example, suppose that new government regulations allow the savings bank to offer checking accounts. As a result, new permanent files are created that contain information about all the checking accounts maintained in the bank, and new application programs may need to be written. Thus, as time goes by, more files and more application programs are added to the system.

The typical *file-processing system* described above is supported by a conventional operating system. Permanent records are stored in various files, and a number of different application programs are written to extract records from and add records to the appropriate files. This scheme has a number of major disadvantages

- **Data redundancy and inconsistency**. Since the files and application programs are created by different programmers over a long period of time, the files are likely to have different formats and the programs may be written in several programming languages. Moreover, the same piece of information may be duplicated in several places (files). For example, the address and phone number of a particular customer may appear in a file that consists of savings account records and in a file that consists of checking account records. This redundancy leads to higher storage and access cost. In addition, it may lead to data inconsistency — that is, the various copies of the same data may no longer agree. For example, a changed customer address may be reflected in savings account records but not elsewhere in the system. Data inconsistency results.

- **Difficulty in accessing data**. Suppose that one of the bank officers needs to find out the names of all customers who live within the city's 78733 zip code. The officer asks the data processing department to generate such a list. Since this request was not anticipated when the original system was designed, there is no application program on hand to meet it. There is, however, an application program to generate the list of *all* customers. The bank officer has now two choices: Either get the list of customers and extract the needed information manually, or ask the data processing department to have a system programmer write the necessary application program. Both alternatives are obviously unsatisfactory. Suppose that such a program is actually written and that, several days later, the same officer needs to trim that list to include only those customers with an account balance of $10,000 or more. As expected, a program to generate such a list does not exist. Again, the officer has the preceding two options, neither of which is satisfactory.

  The point here is that conventional file-processing environments do not allow needed data to be retrieved in a convenient and efficient manner. Better data retrieval systems must be developed for general use.

- **Data isolation**. Since data is scattered in various files, and files may be in different formats, it is difficult to write new application programs to retrieve the appropriate data.

- **Concurrent access anomalies**. In order to improve the overall performance of the system and obtain a faster response time, many systems allow multiple users to update the data simultaneously. In such an environment, interaction of concurrent updates may result in inconsistent data. Consider bank account A, with $500. If two customers withdraw funds (say $50 and $100 respectively) from account A at about the same time, the result of the concurrent executions may leave the account in an incorrect (or inconsistent) state. In particular, the account may contain either $450 or $400, rather than $350. In order to guard against this possibility, some form of supervision must be maintained in the system. Since data may be accessed by many different application programs which have not been previously coordinated, supervision is very difficult to provide.

- **Security problems**. Not every user of the database system should be able to access all the data. For example, in a banking system, payroll personnel need only see that part of the database that has information about the various bank employees. They do not need access to information about customer accounts. Since application programs are added to the system in an ad hoc manner, it is difficult to enforce such security constraints.

- **Integrity problems**. The data values stored in the database must satisfy certain types of *consistency constraints*. For example, the balance of a bank account may never fall below a prescribed amount (say, $25). These constraints are enforced in the system by adding appropriate code in the various application programs. However, when new constraints are added, it is difficult to change the programs to enforce them. The problem is compounded when constraints involve several data items from different files.

These difficulties, among others, have prompted the development of database management systems. In what follows, we shall see the concepts and algorithms that have been developed for database systems to solve the abovementioned problems. For most of this book, we use a bank enterprise as a running example of a typical data processing application found in a corporation.

In Chapters 12–14, we consider a different class of database applications, interactive design applications. Most current interactive design applications are built as a collection of files and application programs. There is a substantial amount of research and development work underway to provide database systems that are both sufficiently powerful and sufficiently flexible to manage these applications. The concepts used in this work are based upon those we shall see in earlier chapters of the book.

1.2 Data Abstraction

A database management system is a collection of interrelated files and a set of programs that allow users to access and modify these files. A major purpose of a database system is to provide users with an *abstract* view of the data. That is, the system hides certain details of how the data is stored and maintained. However, in order for the system to be usable, data must be retrieved efficiently. This concern has led to the design of complex data structures for the representation of data in the database. Since many database systems users are not computer-trained, the complexity is hidden from them through several levels of abstraction in order to simplify their interaction with the system.

- **Physical level**. The lowest level of abstraction describes *how* the data are actually stored. At the physical level, complex low-level data structures are described in detail.

- **Conceptual level**. The next-higher-level of abstraction describes *what* data are actually stored in the database, and the relationships that exist among the data. Here the entire database is described in terms of a small number of relatively simple structures. Although implementation of the simple structures at the conceptual level may involve complex physical-level structures, the user of the conceptual level need not be aware of this. The conceptual level of abstraction is used by database administrators, who must decide what information is to be kept in the database.

- **View level**. The highest level of abstraction describes only part of the entire database. Despite the use of simpler structures at the conceptual level, some complexity remains because of the large size of the database. Many users of the database system will not be concerned with all of this information. Instead, such users need only a part of the database. To simplify their interaction with the system, the view level of abstraction is defined. The system may provide many views for the same database.

The interrelationship among these three levels of abstraction is illustrated in Figure 1.1.

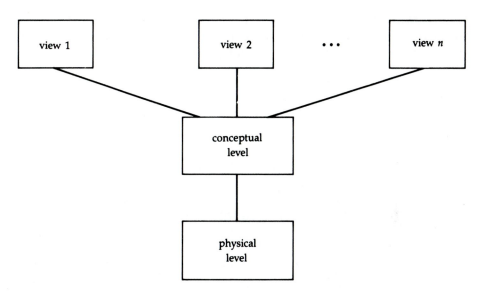

Figure 1.1   The three levels of data abstraction.

An analogy to the concept of data types in programming languages may clarify the distinction among levels of abstraction. Most high-level programming languages support the notion of a record type. For example, in a Pascal-like language we may declare a record as follows:

> **type** *customer* = **record**
> > *name* : string;
> > *street* : string;
> > *city* : string;
> **end**;

This defines a new record called *customer* with three fields. Each field has a name and a type associated with it. A banking enterprise may have several such record types, including:

- *account*, with fields *number* and *balance*.

- *employee*, with fields *name* and *salary*.

At the physical level, a *customer*, *account*, or *employee* record can be described as a block of consecutive storage locations (for example, words or bytes). At the conceptual level, each such record is described by a type definition, illustrated above, and the interrelationship among these record types is defined. Finally, at the view level, several views of the database are defined. For example, tellers in a bank see only that part of the database that has information on customer accounts. They cannot access information concerning salaries of employees.

1.3 Data Models

Underlying the structure of a database is the concept of a *data model*, a collection of conceptual tools for describing data, data relationships, data semantics, and consistency constraints. The various data models that have been proposed fall into three different groups: object-based logical models, record-based logical models, and physical data models.

1.3.1 Object-Based Logical Models

Object-based logical models are used in describing data at the conceptual and view levels. They are characterized by the fact that they provide fairly flexible structuring capabilities and allow data constraints to be specified explicitly. There are many different models, and more are likely to come. Some of the more widely known ones are:

- The entity-relationship model.

- The object-oriented model.

- The binary model.

- The semantic data model.

- The infological model.

- The functional data model.

In this book, we examine the *entity-relationship model* and the *object-oriented model* as representatives of the class of the object-based logical models. The entity-relationship model, explored in Chapter 2, has gained acceptance in database design and is widely used in practice. The object-oriented model, examined in Chapter 13, includes many of the concepts of the entity-relationship model, but represents executable code as well as data. It is rapidly gaining acceptance in practice. Below are brief descriptions of both models.

The Entity-Relationship Model

The entity-relationship (E-R) data model is based on a perception of a real world which consists of a collection of basic objects called *entities*, and *relationships* among these objects. An entity is an object that is distinguishable from other objects by a specific set of attributes. For example, the attributes *number* and *balance* describe one particular account in a bank. A *relationship* is an association among several entities. For example, a *CustAcct* relationship associates a customer with each account that she or he has. The set of all entities of the same type and relationships of the same type are termed an *entity set* and *relationship set*, respectively.

In addition to entities and relationships, the E-R model represents certain constraints to which the contents of a database must conform. One important constraint is *mapping cardinalities*, which express the number of entities to which another entity can be associated via a relationship set.

The overall logical structure of a database can be expressed graphically by an E-R *diagram*, which consists of the following components:

- **Rectangles**, which represent entity sets.

- **Ellipses**, which represent attributes.

- **Diamonds**, which represent relationships among entity sets.

- **Lines**, which link attributes to entity sets and entity sets to relationships.

Each component is labeled with the entity or relationship it represents.

To illustrate, consider part of a database banking system consisting of customers and the accounts that they have. The corresponding E-R diagram is shown in Figure 1.2. This example is extended in Chapter 2.

The Object-Oriented Model

Like the E-R model, the object-oriented model is based on a collection of objects. An object contains values stored in *instance variables* within the object. Unlike the record-oriented models, these values are themselves objects. Thus, objects contain objects to an arbitrarily deep level of nesting. An object also contains bodies of code that operate on the object. These bodies of code are called *methods*.

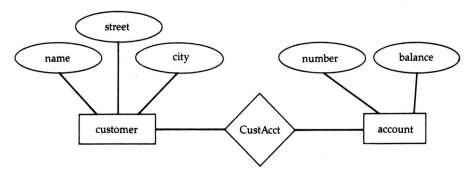

Figure 1.2　A sample E-R diagram.

Objects that contain the same types of values and the same methods are grouped together into *classes*. A class may be viewed as a type definition for objects. This combination of data and code into a type definition is similar to the programming language concept of abstract data types.

The only way in which one object can access the data of another object is by invoking a method of that other object. This is called *sending a message* to the object. Thus, the call interface of the methods of an object defines its externally visible part. The internal part of the object — the instance variables and method code — are not visible externally. The result is two levels of data abstraction.

To illustrate the concept, consider an object representing a bank account. Such an object contains instance variables *number* and *balance*, representing the account number and account balance. It contains a method *pay-interest*, which adds interest to the balance. Assume that the bank had been paying 6 percent interest on all accounts but now is changing its policy to pay 5 percent if the balance is less than $1000 or 6 percent if the balance is $1000 or greater. Under most data models, this would involve changing code in one or more application programs. Under the object-oriented model, the only change is made within the *pay-interest* method. The external interface to the object remains unchanged.

Unlike entities in the E-R model, each object has its own unique identity independent of the values it contains. Thus, two objects containing the same values are nevertheless distinct. The distinction among individual objects is maintained in the physical level through the assignment of distinct object identifiers.

1.3.2 Record-Based Logical Models

Record-based logical models are used in describing data at the conceptual and view levels. In contrast to object-based data models, they are used both to specify the overall logical structure of the database and to provide a higher-level description of the implementation.

Record-based models are so named because the database is structured in fixed-format records of several types. Each record type defines a fixed number of fields, or attributes, and each field is usually of a fixed length. As we shall see in Chapter 7, the use of fixed-length records simplifies the physical-level implementation of the database. This is in contrast to many of the object-based models in which objects may contain other objects to an arbitrary depth of nesting. The richer structure of these databases often leads to variable-length records at the physical level.

Record-based data models do not include a mechanism for the direct representation of code in the database. Instead, there are separate languages that are associated with the model to express database queries and updates. Some object-based models (including the object-oriented model) include executable code as an integral part of the data model itself.

The three most widely accepted data models are the relational, network, and hierarchical models. The relational model, which has gained favor over the other two in recent years, is examined in detail in Chapters 3–6. The network and hierarchical models, still used in a large number of older databases, are described in the appendices. Below we present a brief overview of each model.

Relational Model

The relational model represents data and relationships among data by a collection of tables, each of which has a number of columns with unique names. Figure 1.3 is a sample relational database showing customers and the accounts they have. It shows, for example, that customer Hodges lives on Sidehill in Brooklyn, and has two accounts, one numbered 647 with a balance of $105,366, and the other numbered 801 with a balance of $10,533. Note that customers Shiver and Hodges share account number 647 (they may share a business venture).

Network Model

Data in the network model are represented by collections of *records* (in the Pascal or PL/I sense) and relationships among data are represented by *links*, which can be viewed as pointers. The records in the database are organized as collections of arbitrary graphs. Figure 1.4 presents a sample network database using the same information as in Figure 1.3.

name	street	city	number
Lowery	Maple	Queens	900
Shiver	North	Bronx	556
Shiver	North	Bronx	647
Hodges	Sidehill	Brooklyn	801
Hodges	Sidehill	Brooklyn	647

number	balance
900	55
556	100000
647	105366
801	10533

Figure 1.3   A sample relational database.

Hierarchical Model

The hierarchical model is similar to the network model in the sense that data and relationships among data are represented by records and links, respectively. It differs from the network model in that the records are organized as collections of trees rather than arbitrary graphs. Figure 1.5 presents a sample hierarchical database with the same information as in Figure 1.4.

Differences Between the Models

The relational model differs from the network and hierarchical models in that it does not use pointers or links. Instead, the relational model relates records by the values they contain. This freedom from the use of pointers allows a formal mathematical foundation to be defined.

1.3.3 Physical Data Models

Physical data models are used to describe data at the lowest level. In contrast to logical data models, there are very few physical data models in use. Two of the widely known ones are:

- Unifying model.
- Frame memory.

Physical data models capture aspects of database system implementation that are not covered in this book.

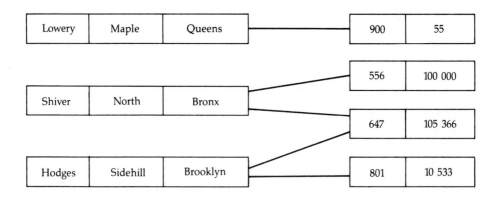

Figure 1.4   A sample network database.

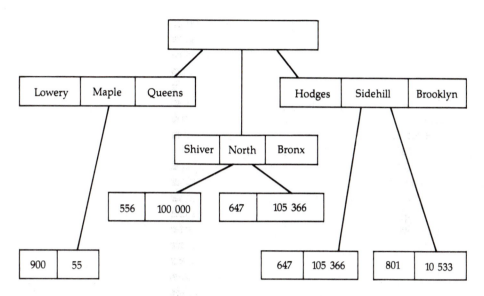

Figure 1.5 A sample hierarchical database.

1.4 Instances and Schemes

Databases change over time as information is inserted and deleted. The collection of information stored in the database at a particular moment in time is called an *instance* of the database. The overall design of the database is called the database *scheme*. Schemes are changed infrequently, if at all.

An analogy to the concepts of data types, variables, and values in programming languages is useful here. Returning to the *customer* record type definition in Section 1.2, note that in declaring the type *customer*, we have *not* declared any variables. To declare such variables in a Pascal-like language, we write:

$$\textbf{var} \quad customer1 : customer;$$

Variable *customer1* now corresponds to an area of storage containing a *customer* type record.

The concept of a database scheme corresponds to the programming language notion of type definition. A variable of a given type has a particular value at a given instant in time. Thus, the concept of the value of a variable in programming languages corresponds to the concept of an *instance* of a database scheme.

Database systems have several schemes, partitioned according to the levels of abstraction discussed in Section 1.2. At the lowest level is the *physical scheme*; at the intermediate level, the *conceptual scheme*; at the highest level, a *subscheme*. In general, database systems support one physical scheme, one conceptual scheme, and several subschemes.

1.5 Data Independence

In Section 1.2, we defined three levels of abstraction at which the database may be viewed. The ability to modify a scheme definition in one level without affecting a scheme definition in the next higher level is called *data independence*. There are two levels of data independence:

- **Physical data independence** is the ability to modify the physical scheme without causing application programs to be rewritten. Modifications at the physical level are occasionally necessary in order to improve performance.

- **Logical data independence** is the ability to modify the conceptual scheme without causing application programs to be rewritten. Modifications at the conceptual level are necessary whenever the logical structure of the database is altered (for example, the addition of money-market accounts in a banking system).

Logical data independence is more difficult to achieve than physical data independence since application programs are heavily dependent on the logical structure of the data they access.

The concept of data independence is similar in many respects to the concept of *abstract data types* in modern programming languages. Both hide implementation details from the users. This allows users to concentrate on the general structure rather than low-level implementation details.

1.6 Data Definition Language

A database scheme is specified by a set of definitions which are expressed by a special language called a *data definition language* (DDL). The result of compilation of DDL statements is a set of tables which are stored in a special file called *data dictionary* (or *directory*).

A data directory is a file that contains *metadata*; that is, "data about data." This file is consulted before actual data is read or modified in the database system.

The storage structure and access methods used by the database system are specified by a set of definitions in a special type of DDL called a *data storage and definition* language. The result of compilation of these definitions is a set of instructions to specify the implementation details of the database schemes which are usually hidden from the users.

1.7 Data Manipulation Language

The levels of abstraction we discussed in Section 1.2 apply not only to the definition or structuring of data but also to the manipulation of data. By data manipulation we mean:

- The retrieval of information stored in the database.
- The insertion of new information into the database.
- The deletion of information from the database.
- The modification of data stored in the database.

At the physical level, we must define algorithms that allow for efficient access to data. At higher levels of abstraction, an emphasis is placed on ease of use. The goal is to provide for efficient human interaction with the system.

A *data manipulation language* (DML) is a language that enables users to access or manipulate data as organized by the appropriate data model. There are basically two types:

- **Procedural** DMLs require a user to specify *what* data is needed and *how* to get it.
- **Nonprocedural** DMLs require a user to specify *what* data is needed *without* specifying how to get it.

Nonprocedural DMLs are usually easier to learn and use than procedural DMLs. However, since a user does not have to specify how to get the data, these languages may generate code which is not as efficient as that produced by procedural languages. This difficulty can be remedied through various optimization techniques, some of which are discussed in Chapter 9.

A *query* is a statement requesting the retrieval of information. The portion of a DML that involves information retrieval is called a *query language*. Although technically incorrect, it is common practice to use the terms *query language* and *data manipulation language* synonymously.

1.8 Database Manager

Databases typically require a large amount of storage space. Corporate databases are usually measured in terms of *gigabytes* or, for the largest databases, *terabytes* of data. A gigabyte is 1000 megabytes (a billion bytes), and a terabyte is a million megabytes (a trillion bytes). Since the main memory of computers cannot store this information, it is stored on disks. Data is moved between disk storage and main memory as needed. Since the movement of data to and from disk is slow relative to the speed of the central processing unit, it is imperative that the database system structure the data so as to minimize the need to move data between disk and main memory.

The goal of a database system is to simplify and facilitate access to data. High-level views help to achieve this. Users of the system should not be burdened unnecessarily with the physical details of the implementation of the system. Nevertheless, a major factor in a user's satisfaction or lack thereof with a database system is its performance. If the response time for a request is too long, the value of the system is diminished. The performance of a system depends on the efficiency of the data structures used to represent the data in the database and on how efficiently the system is able to operate on these data structures. As is the case elsewhere in computer systems, a tradeoff must be made not only between space and time but also between the efficiency of one kind of operation versus that of another.

A *database manager* is a program module which provides the interface between the low-level data stored in the database and the application programs and queries submitted to the system. The database manager is responsible for the following tasks:

- **Interaction with the file manager**. The raw data is stored on the disk using the file system which is usually provided by a conventional operating system. The database manager translates the various DML statements into low-level file system commands. Thus, the database manager is responsible for the actual storing, retrieving, and updating of data in the database.

- **Integrity enforcement**. The data values stored in the database must satisfy certain types of consistency constraints. For example, the number of hours an employee may work in one week may not exceed some specific limit (say, 80 hours). Such a constraint must be specified explicitly by the database administrator (see Section 1.9). The database manager can then determine whether updates to the database result in the violation of the constraint; if so, appropriate action must be taken.

- **Security enforcement**. As discussed above, not every database user needs to have access to the entire content of the database. It is the job of the database manager to enforce these security requirements.

- **Backup and recovery**. A computer system, like any other mechanical or electrical device, is subject to failure. Causes of failure include disk crash, power failure, and software errors. In each of these cases, information concerning the database is lost. It is the responsibility of the database manager to detect such failures and restore the database to a state that existed prior to the occurrence of the failure. This is usually accomplished through the initiation of various backup and recovery procedures.

- **Concurrency control**. When several users update the database concurrently, the consistency of data may no longer be preserved. Controlling the interaction among the concurrent users is another responsibility of the database manager.

Database systems designed for use on small personal computers may not have all the features noted above. For example, many small systems impose the restriction of only one user being allowed to access the database at a time. Others leave the tasks of backup, recovery, and security enforcement to the user. This allows for a smaller data manager, with fewer requirements for physical resources, especially main memory. Although such a low-cost, low-feature approach is sufficient for small personal databases, it is inadequate to meet the needs of a medium- to large-scale enterprise.

1.9 Database Administrator

One of the main reasons for having database management systems is to have central control of both data and programs accessing that data. The person having such central control over the system is called the *database administrator* (DBA). The functions of the database administrator include:

- **Scheme definition**. The original database scheme is created by writing a set of definitions which are translated by the DDL compiler to a set of tables that are permanently stored in the *data dictionary*.

- **Storage structure and access method definition**. Appropriate storage structures and access methods are created by writing a set of definitions which are translated by the data storage and definition language compiler.

- **Scheme and physical organization modification**. Modifications to either the database scheme or the description of the physical storage organization, although relatively rare, are accomplished by writing a set of definitions which are used by either the DDL compiler or the data storage and definition language compiler to generate modifications to the appropriate internal system tables (for example, the data dictionary).

- **Granting of authorization for data access**. The granting of different types of authorization allows the database administrator to regulate which parts of the database various users can access.

- **Integrity constraint specification**. Integrity constraints are kept in a special system structure that is consulted by the database manager whenever an update takes place in the system.

1.10 Database Users

A primary goal of a database system is to provide an environment for retrieving information from and storing new information into the database. There are four different types of database system users, differentiated by the way they expect to interact with the system.

- **Application programmers**. Computer professionals interact with the system through DML calls, which are embedded in a program written in a *host* language (for example, Cobol, PL/I, Pascal, C). These programs are commonly referred to as *application programs*. Examples in a banking system include programs that generate payroll checks, that debit accounts, that credit accounts, that transfer funds between accounts, and so on.

    Since the DML syntax is usually quite different from the host language syntax, DML calls are usually prefaced by a special character so that the appropriate code can be generated. A special preprocessor, called the DML *precompiler*, converts the DML statements to normal procedure calls in the host language. The resulting program is then run through the host language compiler, which generates appropriate object code.

    There are special types of programming languages which combine control structures of Pascal-like languages with control structures for the manipulation of a database object (for example, relations). These languages, sometimes called *fourth-generation languages*, often include special features to facilitate the generation of forms and the display of data on the screen. Most major commercial database systems include a fourth-generation language.

- **Sophisticated users**. Sophisticated users interact with the system without writing programs. Instead, they form their requests in a database query language. Each such query is submitted to a *query processor* whose function is to take a DML statement and break it down into instructions that the database manager understands.

- **Specialized users**. Some sophisticated users write specialized database applications that do not fit into the traditional data processing framework. Among these are computer-aided design systems, knowledge-base and expert systems, systems that store data with complex data types (for example, graphics data and audio data), and environment-modeling systems. Some of these are covered in Chapters 13 and 14.

- **Naive users**. Unsophisticated users interact with the system by invoking one of the permanent application programs that have been written previously. For example, a bank teller who needs to transfer $50 from account *A* to account *B* would invoke a program called *transfer*. This program would ask the teller for the amount of money to be transferred, the account from which the money is being transferred, and the account to which the money is to be transferred.

1.11 Overall System Structure

A database system is partitioned into modules that deal with each of the responsibilities of the overall system. In most cases, the computer's operating system provides only the most basic services and the database system must build on that base. Thus, the design of a database system must include consideration of the interface between the database system and the operating system.

The functional components of a database system include:

- **File manager**, which manages the allocation of space on disk storage and the data structures used to represent information stored on disk.

- **Database manager**, which provides the interface between the low-level data stored in the database and the application programs and queries submitted to the system.

- **Query processor**, which translates statements in a query language into low-level instructions that the database manager understands. In addition, the query processor attempts to transform a user's request into an equivalent but more efficient form, thus finding a good strategy for executing the query.

- DML **precompiler**, which converts DML statements embedded in an application program to normal procedure calls in the host language. The precompiler must interact with the query processor in order to generate the appropriate code.

- DDL **compiler**, which converts DDL statements to a set of tables containing *metadata*, or "data about data".

In addition, several data structures are required as part of the physical system implementation, including:

- **Data files**, which store the database itself.

- **Data dictionary**, which stores metadata about the structure of the database. The data dictionary is used heavily. Therefore, great emphasis should be placed on developing a good design and efficient implementation of the dictionary.

● **Indices**, which provide for fast access to data items holding particular values.

Figure 1.6 shows these components and the connections among them.

1.12 Summary

A database management system (DBMS) consists of a collection of interrelated data and a collection of programs to access that data. The data contains information about one particular enterprise. The primary goal of a DBMS is to provide an environment which is both *convenient* and *efficient* to use in retrieving and storing information.

Database systems are designed to manage large bodies of information. The management of data involves both the definition of structures for the storage of information and the provision of mechanisms for the manipulation of information. In addition, the database system must provide for the safety of the information stored, despite system crashes or attempts at unauthorized access. If data is to be shared among several users, the system must avoid possible anomalous results.

A major purpose of a database system is to provide users with an abstract view of the data. That is, the system hides certain details of how the data is stored and maintained. This is accomplished by defining three levels of abstraction at which the database may be viewed: the *physical level*, the *conceptual level*, and the *view level*.

Underlying the structure of a database is the *data model*, a collection of conceptual tools for describing data, data relationships, data semantics, and data constraints. The various data models that have been proposed fall into three different groups: *object-based logical* models, *record-based logical* models, and *physical data* models.

Databases change over time as information is inserted and deleted. The collection of information stored in the database at a particular moment in time is called an *instance* of the database. The overall design of the database is called the database *scheme*. The ability to modify a scheme definition in one level without affecting a scheme definition in the next-higher level is called *data independence*. There are two levels of data independence: physical data independence and logical data independence.

A database scheme is specified by a set of definitions which are expressed by a *data definition language* (DDL). DDL statements are compiled into a set of tables which are stored in a special file called the *data dictionary* which contains *metadata*.

A *data manipulation language* (DML) is a language that enables users to access or manipulate data. There are basically two types: procedural DMLs,

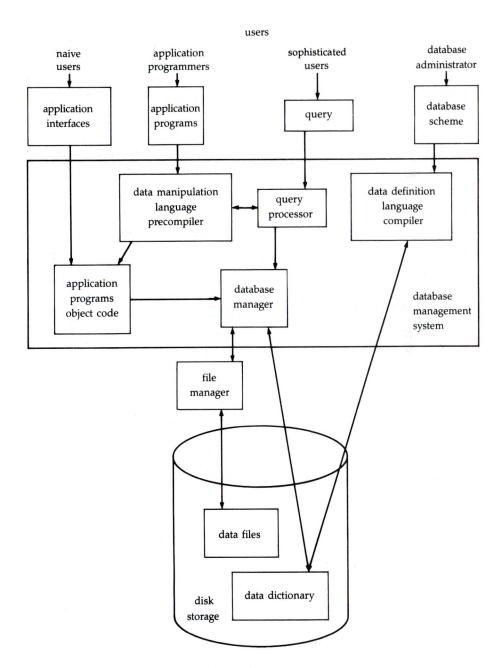

Figure 1.6   System structure.

which require a user to specify what data is needed and how to get it, and nonprocedural DMLs, which require a user to specify what data is needed without specifying how to get it.

A database manager is a program module which provides the interface between the low-level data stored in the database and the application programs and queries submitted to the system. The database manager is responsible for interaction with the file manager, integrity enforcement, security enforcement, backup and recovery, and concurrency control.

Exercises

1.1 What are the main differences between a file-processing system and a database management system?

1.2 This chapter has described some of the major advantages of a database system. What are the disadvantages?

1.3 Explain the difference between physical and logical data independence.

1.4 List the responsibilities of the database manager. For each responsibility, explain those problems that would arise if the responsibility were not met.

1.5 What are the main functions of a database administrator?

1.6 List several different programming languages which are (a) procedural, and (b) nonprocedural. Which group is easier to learn and use?

1.7 List the major steps that need to be taken in setting up a database for a particular enterprise.

1.8 Consider a two-dimensional integer array of size $n \times m$ which is to be used in your favorite programming language. Illustrate the difference (a) between the three levels of data abstraction, and (b) between a scheme and instances.

Bibliographic Notes

Discussions concerning the evolution of database management systems and the development of database technology are offered by Fry and Sibley [1976] and Sibley [1976].

The three levels of data abstraction were introduced in the CODASYL DBTG report [CODASYL 1971]. A similar proposal was put forward in the

ANSI/SPARC report, in which these levels were termed *internal, conceptual,* and *external* [ANSI 1975]. Additional discussions concerning the ANSI/SPARC proposal are offered by Tsichritzis and Klug [1978] and Jardine [1977].

The entity-relationship, object-oriented, relational, network, and hierarchical models are covered in great detail in other chapters. Detailed discussions of these models can be found in Tsichritzis and Lochovsky [1982]. Surveys discussing various types of data models are offered by Kerschberg et al. [1976] and Senko [1977]. Detailed discussions of various object-based logical data models can be found in Tsichritzis and Lochovsky [1982]. More extensive bibliographic references are provided in later chapters of this book.

The binary data model was proposed by Abrial [1974]. Additional discussions are offered by Deheneffe et al. [1974], Hainaut and Lecharlier [1974], Senko [1975], and Bracchi et al. [1976].

The semantic data model is based on the semantic network data models that were initially developed in connection with artificial intelligence. Discussion concerning the various models can be found in Roussopoulos and Mylopoulos [1975], Woods [1975], Mylopoulos et al. [1976], Bachman and Daya [1977], Hayes [1977], Hendrix [1977], Wong and Mylopoulos [1977], Brachman [1979], Levesque and Mylopoulos [1979] and Hammer and McLeod [1981]. A survey of semantic data models is provided by Hull and King [1987] and Peckham and Maryanski [1988].

The infological data model was first introduced by Langefors [1963, 1977, 1980]. Additional discussions are offered by Sundgren [1974, 1975].

The functional data model was proposed by Sibley and Kerschberg [1977] and has been extended by Shipman [1981]. Several functional query languages have been proposed, including FQL [Buneman and Frankel 1979] and DAPLEX [Shipman 1981].

The unifying model was introduced by Batory and Gotlieb [1982]. The frame memory structure was introduced by March et al. [1981].

Discussions concerning data dictionaries can be found in Uhrowczik [1973]. Database administration issues are covered in Weldon [1981]. Discussions concerning the importance of data independence are offered by Stonebraker [1974], Ullman [1988], ElMasri and Navathe [1989], and Date [1990a].

Several books offer a collection of research papers on database management. Among these are Bancilhon and Buneman [1990], Date [1986, 1990b], Kim et al. [1985], Kim and Lochovsky [1989], and Stonebraker [1988]. A review of accomplishments in database management and future research challenges appears in Silberschatz et al. [1990].

Entity-Relationship Model

The entity-relationship (E-R) data model is based on a perception of a real world which consists of a set of basic objects called *entities* and *relationships* among these objects. It was developed in order to facilitate database design by allowing the specification of an *enterprise scheme.* Such a scheme represents the overall logical structure of the database.

2.1 Entities and Entity Sets

An *entity* is an object that exists and is distinguishable from other objects. For example, John Harris with social security number 890-12-3456 is an entity, since it uniquely identifies one particular person in the universe. Similarly, account number 401 at the Redwood branch is an entity that uniquely identifies one particular account. An entity may be concrete, such as a person or a book, or it may be abstract, such as a holiday or a concept.

An *entity set* is a set of entities of the same type. The set of all persons having an account at a bank, for example, can be defined as the entity set *customer*. Similarly, the entity set *account* might represent the set of all accounts in a particular bank.

Entity sets need not be disjoint. For example, it is possible to define the entity set of all employees of a bank (*employee*) and the entity set of all customers of the bank (*customer*). A *person* entity may be an *employee* entity, a *customer* entity, both, or neither.

An entity is represented by a set of *attributes*. Possible attributes of the *customer* entity set are *customer-name*, *social-security*, *street*, and *customer-city*. Possible attributes of the *account* entity set are *account-number* and *balance*. For each attribute there is a set of permitted values, called the *domain* of that attribute. The domain of attribute *customer-name* might be the set of all text strings of a certain length. Similarly, the domain of attribute *account-number* might be the set of all positive integers.

Formally, an attribute is a function which maps from an entity set into a domain. Thus, every entity is described by a set of (attribute, data value) pairs, one pair for each attribute of the entity set. A particular *customer* entity is described by the set {(*name*, Harris), (*social-security*, 890-12-3456), (*street*, North), (*city*, Rye)}, which means the entity describes a person named Harris with social security number 890-12-3456, residing at North Street in Rye.

The concept of an entity set corresponds to the programming language notion of type definition. A variable of a given type has a particular value at a given instant in time. Thus, a variable in programming languages corresponds to the concept of an *entity* in the E-R model.

A database thus includes a collection of entity sets each of which contains any number of entities of the same type. Figure 2.1 shows part of a bank database which consists of two entity sets: *customer* and *account*.

In this chapter, we shall be dealing with five entity sets. To avoid confusion, unique attribute names are used.

- *branch*, the set of all branches of a particular bank. Each branch is described by the attributes *branch-name*, *branch-city*, and *assets*.

- *customer*, the set of all people who have an account at the bank. Each customer is described by the attributes *customer-name*, *social-security*, *street*, and *customer-city*.

- *employee*, the set of all people who work at the bank. Each employee is described by the attributes *employee-name* and *phone-number*.

- *account*, the set of all accounts maintained in the bank. Each account is described by the attributes *account-number* and *balance*.

- *transaction*, the set of all account transactions executed in the bank. Each transaction is described by the attributes *transaction-number*, *date*, and *amount*.

2.2 Relationships and Relationship Sets

A *relationship* is an association among several entities. For example, we may define a relationship which associates customer Harris with account 401. This specifies that Harris is a customer with bank account number 401.

A *relationship set* is a set of relationships of the same type. Formally, it is a mathematical relation on $n \geq 2$ (possibly nondistinct) entity sets. If $E_1, E_2, \ldots, E_n$ are entity sets, then a relationship set R is a subset of

$$\{(e_1, e_2, \ldots, e_n) \mid e_1 \in E_1, e_2 \in E_2, \ldots, e_n \in E_n\}$$

where $(e_1, e_2, \ldots, e_n)$ is a relationship.

Consider the two entity sets *customer* and *account* in Figure 2.1. We define the relationship set *CustAcct* to denote the association between

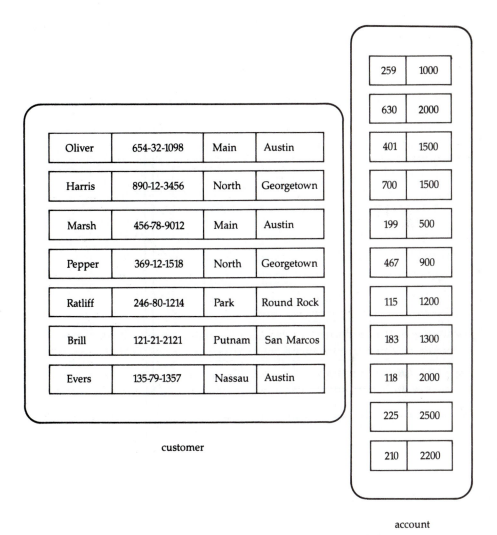

Oliver	654-32-1098	Main	Austin
Harris	890-12-3456	North	Georgetown
Marsh	456-78-9012	Main	Austin
Pepper	369-12-1518	North	Georgetown
Ratliff	246-80-1214	Park	Round Rock
Brill	121-21-2121	Putnam	San Marcos
Evers	135-79-1357	Nassau	Austin

customer

259	1000
630	2000
401	1500
700	1500
199	500
467	900
115	1200
183	1300
118	2000
225	2500
210	2200

account

Figure 2.1   Entity sets *customer* and *account*.

customers and the bank accounts that they have. This association is depicted in Figure 2.2.

The relationship *CustAcct* is an example of a binary relationship set — that is, one which involves two entity sets. Most of the relationship sets in a database system are binary. Occasionally, however, there are relationship sets which involve more than two entity sets. As an example, consider the ternary relationship among the entities corresponding to customer Harris, account 401, and the Redwood branch. This relationship specifies that customer Harris has account 401 at the Redwood branch. It is

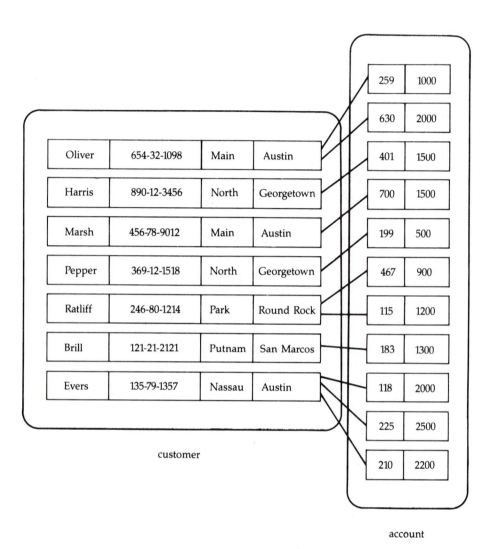

Figure 2.2   Relationship set involving *customer* and *account* entity sets.

an instance of a relationship set *CAB* which involves entity sets *customer*, *account*, and *branch*.

It is always possible to replace a nonbinary relationship set by a number of distinct binary relationship sets. Thus, conceptually, we can restrict the E-R model to include only binary relationship sets. This, however, is not always desirable, as will be shown in Section 2.10.

The function that an entity plays in a relationship is called its *role*. Roles are normally implicit and are not usually specified. However, they are useful when the meaning of a relationship needs clarification. Such is the case when the entity sets of a relationship set are not distinct. For instance, the relationship set *works-for* might be modeled by ordered pairs of *employee* entities. The first employee of a pair takes the role of manager, while the second takes the role of worker. In this way, all relationships of *works-for* are characterized by (manager, worker) pairs; (worker, manager) pairs are excluded.

A relationship may also have descriptive attributes. For example, *date* could be an attribute of the *CustAcct* relationship set. This specifies the last date on which a customer has accessed the account. The *CustAcct* relationship among the entities corresponding to customer Harris and account 401 is described by {(*date*, 23 May 1990)}, which means that the last time Harris accessed account 401 was on 23 May 1990.

2.3 Attributes

Since the notion of an entity set and a relationship set is not a precise one, it is possible to define a set of entities and the relationships among them in a number of different ways. The main difference is in the way we treat the various attributes. Consider the entity set *employee* with attributes *employee-name* and *phone-number*. It can easily be argued that a phone is an entity in its own right with attributes *phone-number* and *location* (the office where the phone is located). If we take this point of view, the *employee* entity set must be redefined as follows:

- The *employee* entity set with attribute *employee-name*.
- The *phone* entity set with attributes *phone-number* and *location*.
- The relationship set *EmpPhn*, which denotes the association between employees and the phones that they have.

What, then, is the main difference between these two definitions of an employee? In the first case, the definition implies that every employee has precisely one phone number associated with him or her. In the second case, however, the definition states that employees may have several phone numbers (including zero) associated with them. Thus, the second definition is more general than the first one, and may more accurately reflect the real world situation.

Even if we are given that each employee has precisely one phone-number associated with him or her, the second definition may still be more appropriate if the phone is shared among several employees.

It would not be appropriate, however, to apply the same technique to the attribute *employee-name*. This is because it is difficult to argue that *employee-name* is an entity in its own right (in contrast to the phone). Thus it is appropriate to have *employee-name* as an attribute of the *employee* entity set.

A natural question thus arises: What constitutes an attribute, and what constitutes an entity set? Unfortunately, there is no simple answer. The distinction mainly depends on the structure of the enterprise being modeled and the semantics associated with the attribute in question.

2.4 Mapping Constraints

An E-R enterprise scheme may define certain constraints to which the contents of a database must conform. One important constraint is *mapping cardinalities*, which express the number of entities to which another entity can be associated via a relationship set.

Mapping cardinalities are most useful in describing binary relationship sets, although occasionally they contribute to the description of relationship sets that involve more than two entity sets. In this section, we shall be concentrating only on binary relationship sets. We shall deal with *n*-ary ($n > 2$) relationship sets later.

For a binary relationship set R between entity sets A and B, the mapping cardinality must be one of the following:

- **One-to-one**. An entity in A is associated with at most one entity in B, and an entity in B is associated with at most one entity in A. (See Figure 2.3.)

- **One-to-many**. An entity in A is associated with any number of entities in B. An entity in B, however, can be associated with at most one entity in A. (See Figure 2.4.)

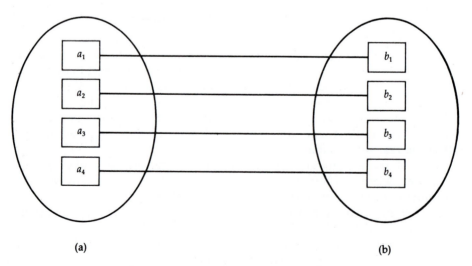

(a)   (b)

Figure 2.3   One-to-one relationship.

- **Many-to-one**. An entity in A is associated with at most one entity in B. An entity in B, however, can be associated with any number of entities in A. (See Figure 2.5.)

- **Many-to-many**. An entity in A is associated with any number of entities in B, and an entity in B is associated with any number of entities in A. (See Figure 2.6.)

The appropriate mapping cardinality for a particular relationship set is obviously dependent on the real world that is being modeled by the relationship set.

To illustrate, consider the *CustAcct* relationship set. If, in a particular bank, an account can belong to only one customer, and a customer can have several accounts, then the relationship set is one-to-many from *customer* to *account*. If an account can belong to several customers (as in joint accounts held by several family members), the relationship set is many-to-many.

Existence dependencies form another important class of constraints. Specifically, if the existence of entity x depends on the existence of entity y, then x is said to be *existence-dependent* on y. Operationally, this means that if y is deleted, so is x. Entity y is said to be a *dominant entity* and x is said to be a *subordinate entity*.

To illustrate, consider the entity sets *account* and *transaction*. We form a relationship set *log* between these two sets which specifies that for a

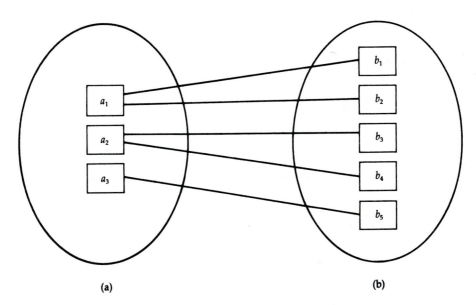

(a)   (b)

Figure 2.4   One-to-many relationship.

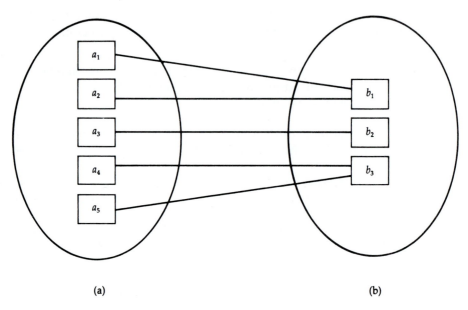

(a)   (b)

Figure 2.5   Many-to-one relationship.

particular account there may be several transactions. This relationship set is one-to-many from *account* to *transaction*. Every *transaction* entity must be associated with an *account* entity. If an *account* entity is deleted, then all of its associated *transaction* entities must be deleted also. In contrast, *transaction* entities can be deleted from the database without affecting any *account*. The entity set *account*, therefore, is dominant and *transaction* is subordinate in the *log* relationship set.

2.5 Keys

It is important to be able to specify how entities and relationships are distinguished. Conceptually, individual entities and relationships are distinct, but from a database perspective the difference among them must be expressed in terms of their attributes. The concept of a *superkey* allows us to make such distinctions. A superkey is a set of one or more attributes which, taken collectively, allow us to identify uniquely an entity in the entity set. For example, the *social-security* attribute of the entity set *customer* is sufficient to distinguish one *customer* entity from another. Thus, *social-security* is a superkey. Similarly, the combination of *customer-name* and *social-security* is a superkey for the entity set *customer*. The *customer-name* attribute of *customer* is not a superkey, as several people might have the same name.

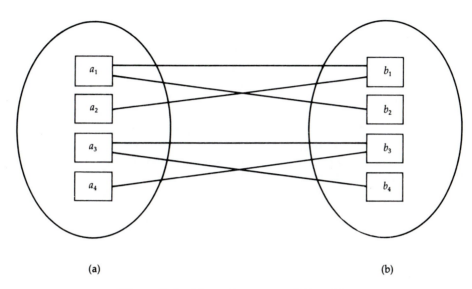

Figure 2.6   Many-to-many relationship.

The concept of a superkey is not sufficient for our purposes, since, as we saw above, a superkey may contain extraneous attributes. If K is a superkey, then so is any superset of K. We are often interested in superkeys for which no proper subset is a superkey. Such minimal superkeys are called *candidate keys*.

It is possible that several distinct sets of attributes could serve as a candidate key. Suppose that a combination of *customer-name* and *street* is sufficient to distinguish among members of the *customer* entity set. Then both {*social-security*} and {*customer-name, street*} are candidate keys. Although the attributes *social-security* and *customer-name* together can distinguish *customer* entities, their combination does not form a candidate key, since the attribute *social-security* alone is a candidate key.

We shall use the term *primary key* to denote a candidate key that is chosen by the database designer as the principal means of identifying entities within an entity set.

It is possible that an entity set does not have sufficient attributes to form a primary key. Such an entity set is termed a *weak entity set*. An entity set which has a primary key is termed a *strong entity set*. To illustrate, consider the entity set *transaction*, which has the three attributes: *transaction-number, date,* and *amount*. Although each *transaction* entity is distinct, transactions on different accounts may share the same transaction number. Thus, this entity set does not have a primary key and is therefore a weak entity set. In order for a weak entity set to be meaningful, it must be part of a one-to-many relationship set. This relationship set should have no descriptive attributes, since any required attributes can be associated with the weak entity set.

The concepts of strong and weak entity sets are related to the existence dependencies introduced in Section 2.4. A member of a strong entity set is by definition a dominant entity, while a member of a weak entity set is a subordinate entity.

Although a weak entity set does not have a primary key, we nevertheless need a means of distinguishing among all those entities in the entity set that depend on one particular strong entity. The *discriminator* of a weak entity set is a set of attributes that allows this distinction to be made. For example, the discriminator of the weak entity set *transaction* is the attribute *transaction-number*, since for each account a transaction number uniquely identifies one single transaction.

The primary key of a weak entity set is formed by the primary key of the strong entity set on which it is existence-dependent, plus its discriminator. In the case of the entity set *transaction*, its primary key is {*account-number, transaction-number*}, where *account-number* identifies the dominant entity of a *transaction*, and *transaction-number* distinguishes *transaction* entities within the same account.

The primary key of an entity set allows us to distinguish between the various entities of the set. We need a similar mechanism to distinguish between the various relationships of a relationship set. To do so, we must explain first how individual relationships are described. Once this is accomplished, we can explain how a primary key for a relationship set is defined.

Let R be a relationship set involving entity sets $E_1, E_2, \ldots, E_n$. Let *primary-key*(E_i) denote the set of attributes which form the primary key for entity set E_i. Assume that the attribute names of all primary keys are unique (if not, use an appropriate renaming scheme). Suppose that R has no attributes. Then the attributes describing individual relationships of the set R, denoted by *attribute*(R), are

$$\text{primary-key}(E_1) \cup \text{primary-key}(E_2) \cup \cdots \cup \text{primary-key}(E_n)$$

In the case that R has descriptive attributes, say $\{a_1, a_2, \ldots, a_m\}$, then the set *attribute*(R) consists of

$$\text{primary-key}(E_1) \cup \cdots \cup \text{primary-key}(E_n) \cup \{a_1, a_2, \ldots, a_m\}$$

To illustrate, consider the relationship set *CustAcct* defined in Section 2.2, which involves the following two entity sets:

- *customer*, with the primary key *social-security*.

- *account*, with the primary key being *account-number*.

Since the relationship set has the attribute *date*, the set *attribute(CustAcct)* consists of the three attributes *social-security*, *account-number*, and *date*.

We can now explain what constitutes the primary key of a relationship set *R*. The composition of the primary key depends on the mapping cardinality, and the structure of the attributes associated with the relationship set *R*.

If the relationship set *R* has no attributes associated with it, then the set *attribute(R)* forms a superkey. This superkey is a primary key if the mapping cardinality is many-to-many. Consider, again, the relationship set *CustAcct*. If the relationship set is many-to-many, then its primary key is {*social-security*, *account-number*}. If the relationship set is many-to-one from *customer* to *account*, then its primary key is {*social-security*}, since a person may have at most one account associated with himself or herself.

If the relationship set *R* has several attributes associated with it, then a superkey is formed as before, with the possible addition of one or more of these attributes. The structure of the primary key depends on both the mapping cardinality and the semantics of the relationship set. To illustrate, consider the entity sets *customer* and *banker* and a relationship set *CustBanker* representing an association between a customer and his or her banker. Suppose that this relationship set has the attribute *type* associated with it, representing the nature of the relationship (such as loan officer or personal banker). If a particular banker can play two different roles in a relationship with a particular customer, then the primary key of *CustBanker* consists of the union of the primary keys of *customer* and *banker*, as well as the attribute *type*. However, if a particular banker can have only one type of relationship with a particular customer, then *type* is not part of the primary key. The primary key in this case is simply the union of the primary keys of *customer* and *banker*.

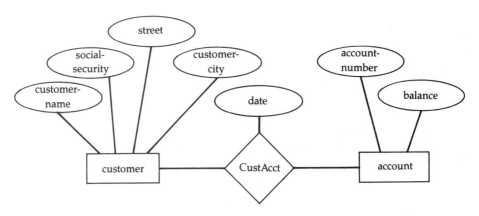

Figure 2.7   E-R diagram.

2.6 Entity-Relationship Diagram

As we saw in Section 1.3, the overall logical structure of a database can be expressed graphically by an *E-R diagram*. Recall that such a diagram consists of the following components:

- **Rectangles**, which represent entity sets.

- **Ellipses**, which represent attributes.

- **Diamonds**, which represent relationship sets.

- **Lines**, which link attributes to entity sets and entity sets to relationship sets.

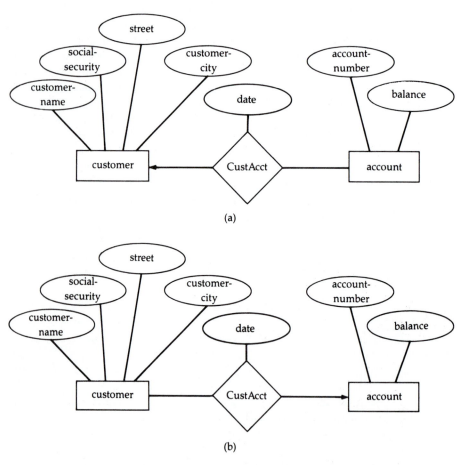

Figure 2.8   One-to-many and many-to-one relationships.

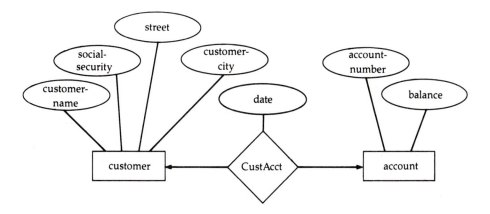

Figure 2.9   One-to-one relationship.

Consider the entity-relationship diagram in Figure 2.7, which consists of two entity sets, *customer* and *account*, related through a binary relationship set *CustAcct*. The attributes associated with *customer* are *customer-name*, *social-security*, *street*, and *customer-city*. The attributes associated with *account* are *account-number* and *balance*.

The relationship set *CustAcct* may be many-to-many, one-to-many, many-to-one, or one-to-one. To distinguish among these, we shall draw either a directed line (→) or an undirected line (—) between the relationship set and the entity set in question. A directed line from the relationship set *CustAcct* to the entity set *account* specifies that *CustAcct* is either a one-to-one, or many-to-one relationship set, from *customer* to *account*; *CustAcct* cannot be a many-to-many or a one-to-many relationship set, from *customer* to *account*. An undirected line from the relationship set *CustAcct* to the entity set *account* specifies that *CustAcct* is either a many-to-many, or one-to-many relationship set, from *customer* to *account*.

Returning to the E-R diagram of Figure 2.7, we see that the relationship set *CustAcct* is many-to-many. If the relationship set *CustAcct* were one-to-many, from *customer* to *account*, then the line from *CustAcct* to *customer* would be directed, with an arrow pointing to the *customer* entity set (Figure 2.8a). Similarly, if the relationship set *CustAcct* were many-to-one from *customer* to *account*, then the line from *CustAcct* to *account* would have an arrow pointing to the *account* entity set (Figure 2.8b). Finally, if the relationship set *CustAcct* were one-to-one, then both lines from *CustAcct* would have arrows, one pointing to the *account* entity set and one pointing to the *customer* entity set (Figure 2.9).

Roles are indicated in E-R diagrams by labeling the lines that connect diamonds to rectangles. Figure 2.10 shows the role indicators *manager* and *worker* between the *employee* entity set and the *works-for* relationship set.

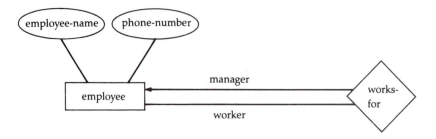

Figure 2.10   E-R diagram with role indicators.

A weak entity set is indicated in E-R diagrams by a doubly outlined box. In Figure 2.11, the weak entity set *transaction* is dependent on the strong entity set *account* via the relationship set *log*.

Nonbinary relationship sets can be specified easily in an E-R diagram. Figure 2.12 consists of three entity sets *customer*, *account*, and *branch*, related through the relationship set *CAB*. This diagram specifies that a customer may have several accounts, each located in a specific bank branch, and that an account may belong to several different customers.

2.7 Reducing E-R Diagrams to Tables

A database which conforms to an E-R diagram can be represented by a collection of tables. For each entity set and for each relationship set in the database, there is a unique table which is assigned the name of the corresponding entity set, or relationship set. Each table has a number of

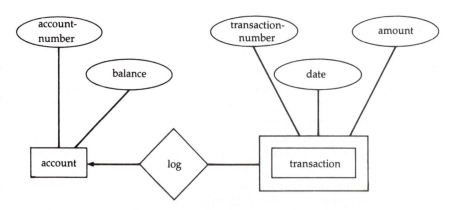

Figure 2.11   E-R diagram with a weak entity set.

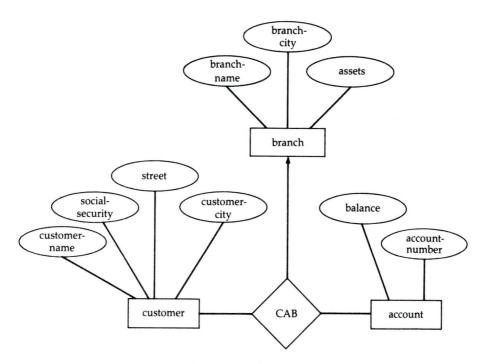

Figure 2.12   E-R diagram with a ternary relationship.

columns which, again, have unique names. We shall present these concepts by considering a tabular representation of the E-R diagram of Figure 2.13.

2.7.1 Representation of Strong Entity Sets

Let E be a strong entity set with descriptive attributes $a_1, a_2, \ldots, a_n$. We represent this entity by a table called E with n distinct columns each of which corresponds to one of the attributes of E. Each row in this table corresponds to one entity of the entity set E.

To illustrate, consider the entity set *account* of the E-R diagram shown in Figure 2.13. This entity set has two attributes: *account-number* and *balance*. We represent this entity set by a table called *account*, with two columns, as shown in Figure 2.14. The row

$$(259, 1000)$$

in the *account* table means that account number 259 has a balance of $1000. We may add a new entity to the database by inserting a row into a table. We may also delete or modify rows.

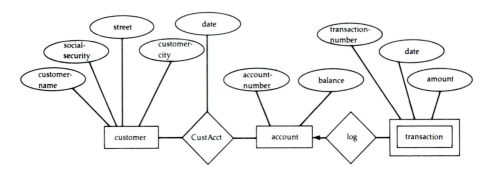

Figure 2.13   E-R diagram.

Let D_1 denote the set of all account numbers and let D_2 denote the set of all balances. Any row of the *account* table must consist of a 2-tuple (v_1, v_2), where v_1 is an account number (that is, v_1 is in set D_1) and v_2 is a balance (that is, v_2 is in set D_2). In general, the *account* table will contain only a subset of the set of all possible rows. We refer to the set of all possible rows of *account* as the *cartesian product* of D_1 and D_2, denoted by

$$D_1 \times D_2$$

In general, if we have a table of n columns, we denote the cartesian product of $D_1, D_2, \ldots, D_n$ by

$$D_1 \times D_2 \times \cdots \times D_{n-1} \times D_n$$

account-number	balance
259	1000
630	2000
401	1500
700	1500
199	500
467	900
115	1200
183	1300
118	2000
225	2500
210	2200

Figure 2.14   The *account* table.

customer-name	social-security	street	customer-city
Oliver	654-32-1098	Main	Harrison
Harris	890-12-3456	North	Rye
Marsh	456-78-9012	Main	Harrison
Pepper	369-12-1518	North	Rye
Ratliff	246-80-1214	Park	Pittsfield
Brill	121-21-2121	Putnam	Stamford
Evers	135-79-1357	Nassau	Princeton

Figure 2.15   The *customer* table.

As another example, consider the entity set *customer* with the four attributes *customer-name*, *social-security*, *street*, and *customer-city*. The table corresponding to *customer* has four columns, as shown in Figure 2.15.

2.7.2 Representation of Weak Entity Sets

Let A be a weak entity set with attributes $a_1, a_2, \ldots, a_r$. Let B be the strong entity set on which A is dependent. Let the primary key of B consist of attributes $b_1, b_2, \ldots, b_s$. We represent the entity set A by a table called A with one column for each attribute of the set:

$$\{a_1, a_2, \ldots, a_r\} \cup \{b_1, b_2, \ldots, b_s\}$$

To illustrate, consider the entity set *transaction* shown in the E-R diagram of Figure 2.13. This entity set has three attributes: *transaction-number*, *date*, and *amount*. The primary key of the *account* entity set, on which *transaction* is dependent, is *account-number*. Thus, *transaction* is represented by a table with four columns labeled *account-number*, *transaction-number*, *date*, and *amount*, as depicted in Figure 2.16.

2.7.3 Representation of Relationship Sets

Let R be a relationship set involving entity sets $E_1, E_2, \ldots, E_m$. Let *attribute(R)* consist of n attributes. We represent this relationship set by a table called R with n distinct columns, each of which correspond to one of the attributes of *attribute(R)*.

To illustrate, consider the relationship set *CustAcct* in the E-R diagram of Figure 2.13. This relationship set involves the following two entity sets:

- *customer*, with the primary key *social-security*.

- *account*, with the primary key *account-number*.

account-number	transaction-number	date	amount
259	5	11 May 1990	+50
630	11	17 May 1990	+70
401	22	23 May 1990	−300
700	69	28 May 1990	−500
199	103	3 June 1990	+900
259	6	7 June 1990	−44
115	53	7 June 1990	+120
199	104	13 June 1990	−200
259	7	17 June 1990	−79

Figure 2.16   The *transaction* table.

Since the relationship set has the attribute *date*, the *CustAcct* table has three columns labeled *social-security*, *account-number*, and *date*, as shown in Figure 2.17.

As a final example, consider the ternary relationship set *CAB* of Figure 2.12. This relationship involves the following three entity sets:

- *customer*, with the primary key *social-security*.

- *account*, with the primary key *account-number*.

- *branch*, with the primary key *branch-name*.

Thus, the *CAB* table has three columns, as shown in Figure 2.18.

social-security	account-number	date
654-32-1098	259	17 June 1990
654-32-1098	630	17 May 1990
890-12-3456	401	23 May 1990
456-78-9012	700	28 May 1990
369-12-1518	199	13 June 1990
246-80-1214	467	7 June 1990
246-80-1214	115	7 June 1990
121-21-2121	183	13 June 1990
135-79-1357	118	17 June 1990
135-79-1357	225	19 June 1990
135-79-1357	210	27 June 1990

Figure 2.17   The *CustAcct* table.

The case of relationship sets linking a weak entity set to its corresponding strong entity set is special. As we noted earlier, these relationships are many-to-one and have no descriptive attributes. Furthermore, the primary key of a weak entity set includes the primary key of the strong entity set. In the example of Figure 2.11, the weak entity set *transaction* is dependent on the strong entity set *account* via the relationship set *log*. The primary key of *transaction* is {*account-number, transaction-number*}, and the primary key of *account* is {*account-number*}. Since *log* has no descriptive attributes, the table for *log* would have two columns, *account-number* and *transaction-number*. The table for the entity set *transaction* has four columns, *account-number*, *transaction-number*, *date*, and *amount*. Thus, the *log* table is redundant. In general, the table for the relationship set linking a weak entity set to its corresponding strong entity set is redundant and need not be present in a tabular representation of an E-R diagram.

2.8 Generalization

Consider the entity set *account* with attributes *account-number* and *balance*. We extend our previous example by classifying each account as being one of the following:

- *savings-account.*

- *checking-account.*

Each of these is described by a set of attributes which include all the attributes of entity set *account* plus additional attributes. For example,

social-security	account-number	branch-name
654-32-1098	259	Downtown
654-32-1098	630	Redwood
890-12-3456	401	Perryridge
456-78-9012	700	Downtown
369-12-1518	199	Mianus
246-80-1214	467	Round Hill
246-80-1214	115	Pownal
121-21-2121	183	North Town
135-79-1357	118	Downtown
135-79-1357	225	Perryridge
135-79-1357	210	Brighton

Figure 2.18 The *CAB* table.

savings-account entities are described further by the attribute *interest-rate*, while *checking-accounts* are described further by the attribute *overdraft-amount*. There are similarities between the *checking-account* entity set and the *savings-account* entity set in the sense that they have several attributes in common. This commonality can be expressed by *generalization*, which is a containment relationship that exists between a *higher-level* entity set and one or more *lower-level* entity sets. In the above example, *account* is the higher-level entity set and *savings-account* and *checking-account* are lower-level entity sets.

In terms of an E-R diagram, generalization is depicted through a *triangle* component labeled ISA, as shown in Figure 2.19. The label ISA stands for "is a" and represents, for example, that a savings account "is an" account.

Generalization is used to emphasize the similarities among lower-level entity types and to hide their differences. The distinction is made through a process called attribute inheritance. The attributes of the higher-level entity sets are said to be *inherited* by lower-level entity sets. For example, *savings-account* and *checking-account* inherit the attributes of *account*. Thus, *savings-account* is described by its *account-number*, *balance*, and *interest-rate* attributes, while *checking-account* is described by its *account-number*, *balance*, and *overdraft-amount* attributes.

There are two different methods for transforming an E-R diagram which includes generalization to a tabular form.

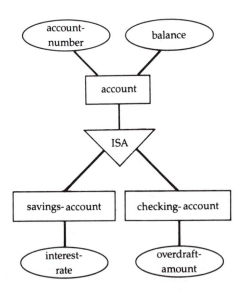

Figure 2.19   Generalization

1. Create a table for the higher-level entity set as described in Section 2.7. For each lower-level entity set, create a table which includes a column for each of the attributes of that entity set plus a column for each attribute of the primary key of the higher-level entity set. Thus, for the E-R diagram of Figure 2.19, we have three tables:

   - *account*, with attributes *account-number* and *balance*.
   - *savings-account*, with attributes *account-number* and *interest-rate*.
   - *checking-account*, with attributes *account-number* and *overdraft-amount*.

2. Do not create a table for the higher-level entity set. Instead, for each lower-level entity set, create a table which includes a column for each of the attributes of that entity set plus a column for *each* attribute of the higher-level entity set. Then for the E-R diagram of Figure 2.19, we have two tables.

   - *savings-account*, with attributes *account-number*, *balance*, and *interest-rate*.
   - *checking-account*, with attributes *account-number*, *balance*, and *overdraft-amount*.

2.9 Aggregation

One limitation of the E-R model is that it is not possible to express relationships among relationships. To illustrate the need for such a construct, consider a database describing information about employees who work on a particular project and use a number of different machines in their work. Using our basic E-R modeling constructs, we obtain the E-R diagram of Figure 2.20. It may appear that the relationship sets *work* and *uses* can be combined into one single relationship set. Nevertheless, they should not be combined, since doing so would obscure the logical structure of this scheme.

The solution is to use *aggregation*. Aggregation is an abstraction through which relationships are treated as higher-level entities. Thus, for our example, we regard the relationship set *work* and the entity sets *employee* and *project* as a higher-level entity set called *work*. Such an entity set is treated in the same manner as any other entity set. A common notation for aggregation is shown in Figure 2.21.

Transforming an E-R diagram which includes aggregation to a tabular form is straightforward. For the diagram of Figure 2.21, using the same procedure as before, we create the following tables:

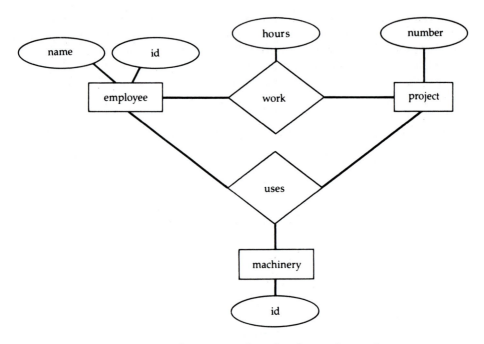

Figure 2.20   E-R diagram with redundant relationships.

- *employee.*
- *project.*
- *work.*
- *machinery.*
- *uses.*

The table for the relationship set *uses* includes a column for each attribute in the primary key of the entity set *machinery* and the relationship set *work*. It also includes a column for the attribute of the relationship set *uses*.

2.10 Design of an E-R Database Scheme

The E-R data model provides a large degree of flexibility in designing a database scheme to model a given enterprise. In this section we consider how a database designer may select from the wide range of alternatives. Among the decisions to be made are:

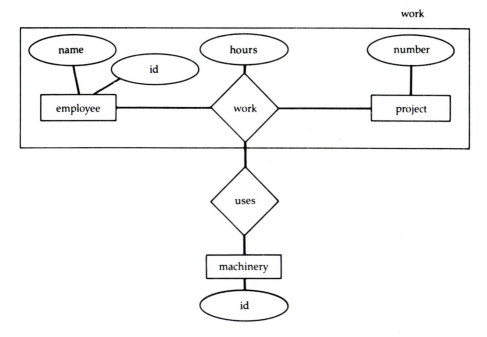

Figure 2.21   E-R diagram with aggregation.

- The use of a ternary relationship versus a pair of binary relationships.

- Whether a real-world concept is best expressed by an entity set or a relationship set.

- The use of an attribute or entity set (as discussed in Section 2.3).

- The use of a strong or weak entity set.

- The appropriateness of using generalization.

- The appropriateness of using aggregation.

We shall see that the database designer needs a good understanding of the enterprise being modeled in order to make these decisions.

2.10.1 Mapping Cardinalities

Consider the ternary relationship set shown in Figure 2.12. This relationship specifies that a customer may have several accounts, each located in a specific bank branch, and that an account may belong to several different customers. This relationship set could be replaced by a pair of relationship sets, as shown in Figure 2.22. Here each account is

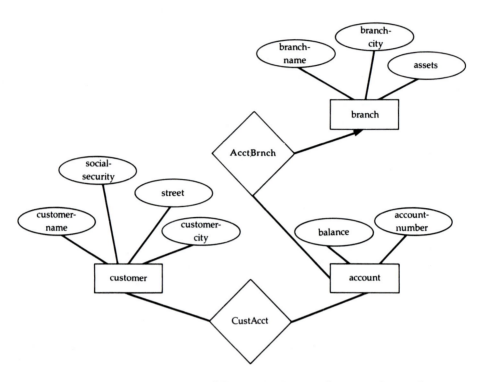

Figure 2.22   Representation of Figure 2.12 using binary relationships.

located at a specific branch. The many-to-many relationship set *CustAcct*
specifies that a customer may have several accounts and an account may
belong to several different customers.

There is a subtle distinction between the E-R diagrams of Figure 2.12
and Figure 2.22. In the former, the relationship between a customer and
account can be represented only if there is a corresponding branch. In the
latter, an account can be related either to a branch with no corresponding
customer, or to a customer with no corresponding branch. For the bank
enterprise, the E-R diagram of Figure 2.12 is more appropriate, since an
account is always expected to relate to both a customer and a branch.

2.10.2 Use of Entity Sets or Relationship Sets

It is not always clear whether an object is best expressed by an entity set
or a relationship set. In both Figures 2.12 and 2.22, a bank account is
modeled as an entity. Figure 2.23 presents an alternative model in which
accounts are represented not as entities but rather as relationships between
customers and branches, with account-number and balance as descriptive

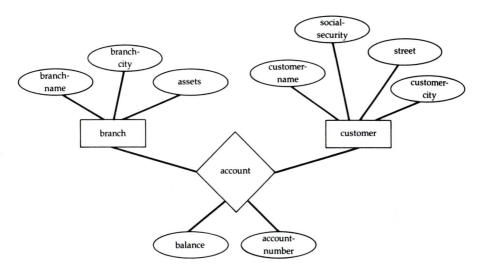

Figure 2.23   E-R diagram with *account* as a relationship set.

attributes. In this database design, a customer may have an account at many branches and a branch may have many customers. Each account is represented by a relationship between a customer and a branch.

The design of Figure 2.23 cannot represent conveniently a situation in which several customers hold an account jointly. A separate relationship must be defined for each holder of the joint account. Each such relationship must, of course, have the same value for the descriptive attributes *account-number* and *balance*. However, if every account is held by exactly one customer, we may find the design of Figure 2.23 satisfactory.

2.10.3 Use of Extended E-R Features

In earlier sections, we illustrated the use of weak entity sets, generalization, and aggregation to model an enterprise in the E-R data model. The designer of an E-R database scheme must decide when these features are appropriate to use. Each of these features contributes to modularity of the design:

- A strong entity set and its dependent weak entity sets may be regarded as a single "object" in the database, since weak entities are existence-dependent on a strong entity.

- Aggregation groups a part of an E-R diagram into a single entity set. It is possible to treat the aggregate entity set as a single unit without concern for the details of its internal structure.

- Generalization, or a hierarchy of ISA relationships, contributes to modularity by allowing common attributes of similar entity sets to be represented in one place in an E-R diagram.

However, excessive use of these features can introduce unnecessary complexity into the design.

2.11 Summary

The entity-relationship (E-R) data model is based on a perception of a real world which consists of a set of basic objects called *entities* and *relationships* among these objects. The model is intended primarily for the database design process. It was developed in order to facilitate database design by allowing the specification of an *enterprise scheme*. Such a scheme represents the overall logical structure of the database.

An *entity* is an object that exists and is distinguishable from other objects. The distinction is accomplished by associating with each entity a set of attributes that describe the object. A *relationship* is an association among several entities. The collection of all entities of the same type is termed an *entity set*, and the collection of all relationships of the same type is a *relationship set*.

Mapping cardinalities express the number of entities to which another entity can be associated via a relationship set. Another form of constraint is *existence dependency*, which specifies that the existence of entity x depends on the existence of entity y.

An important task in database modeling is to specify how entities and relationships are distinguished. Conceptually, individual entities and relationships are distinct, but from a database perspective, their difference must be expressed in terms of their attributes. To make such distinctions, a *primary key* is assigned to each entity set. The primary key is a set of one or more attributes that, taken collectively, allows us to identify uniquely an entity in the entity set and a relationship in a relationship set. An entity set that does not have sufficient attributes to form a primary key is termed a *weak entity set*. An entity set that has a primary key is termed a *strong entity set*.

The overall logical structure of a database can be expressed graphically by an E-R *diagram*. A database which conforms to an E-R diagram can be represented by a collection of tables. For each entity set and for each relationship set in the database, there is a unique table which is assigned the name of the corresponding entity set or relationship set. Each table has a number of columns which, again, have unique names.

Relationship sets among closely related entity sets can be expressed by *generalization*, which is a containment relationship that exists between a higher-level entity set and one or more lower-level entity sets. Generalization is the result of taking the union of two or more disjoint (lower-level) entity sets to produce a higher-level entity set.

One limitation of the E-R model is that it cannot express relationships among relationships. The solution is to use *aggregation*, an abstraction in which relationship sets are treated as higher-level entity sets. Thus, a relationship set and its associated entity sets can be viewed as a higher-level entity that is treated in the same manner as any other entity.

Exercises

2.1 Construct an E-R diagram for a university registrar's office. The office maintains data about each class, including the instructor, the enrollment, and the time and place of the class meetings. For each student-class pair, a grade is recorded.

2.2 Construct an E-R diagram for a car insurance company with a set of customers, each of whom owns a number of cars. Each car has a number of recorded accidents associated with it.

2.3 Construct an E-R diagram for a hospital with a set of patients and a set of medical doctors. A log of the various conducted tests is associated with each patient.

2.4 Construct appropriate tables for each of the E-R diagrams in Exercises 2.1 to 2.3.

2.5 Define the concept of aggregation. Give several examples of where this concept is useful.

2.6 Explain the difference between a weak and a strong entity set.

2.7 Every weak entity set can be converted to a strong entity set by simply adding appropriate attributes. Why, then, do we have weak entity sets?

2.8 Consider an E-R diagram in which the same entity set appears several times. Why is this a bad practice that should be avoided whenever possible?

2.9 Consider a university database for the scheduling of classrooms for final exams. This database could be modeled as the single entity set *exam*, with attributes *course-name*, *section-number*, *room-number*, and *time*. Alternatively, one or more additional entity sets could be defined, along with relationship sets to replace some of the attributes of the *exam* entity set, as:

- *course* with attributes *name, department,* and *c-number.*

- *section* with attributes *s-number* and *enrollment,* and dependent as a weak entity set on *course.*

- *room* with attributes *r-number, capacity,* and *building.*

For these two design alternatives:

a. Show an E-R diagram illustrating the use of all three additional entity sets.

b. Explain what application characteristics would influence a decision to include or not include one or more of the additional entity sets.

2.10 When designing an E-R diagram for a particular enterprise, you have several alternatives from which to choose.

a. What criteria should you consider in deciding on the appropriate choice?

b. Design several alternative E-R diagrams to represent the enterprise. List the merits of each and argue in favor of one of the alternatives.

2.11 An E-R diagram can be viewed as a graph. What do the following mean in terms of the structure of an enterprise scheme?

a. The graph is disconnected.

b. The graph is acyclic.

2.12 Generalization is the result of taking the union of several (lower-level) entity sets to produce a higher-level entity set. An alternative design methodology is to start with a (higher-level) entity set and use *specialization.* Under specialization, a subset of the higher-level entity set is used to form a lower-level entity set. Describe a bank account example where specialization would be appropriate. (*Hint:* Consider a variation of the example of generalization in Figure 2.19.)

Bibliographic Notes

The entity-relationship data model was introduced by Chen [1976]. New research results concerning the E-R model are presented in the various proceedings of the *International Conference on the Entity-Relationship Approach,* which has been held yearly since 1979.

Discussions concerning the applicability of the E-R approach to database design are offered by Chen [1977], Sakai [1980], and Ng [1981]. Modeling techniques based on the E-R approach are covered by Schiffner and Scheuermann [1979], Scheuermann et al. [1979], Dos Santos et al. [1979], Lusk et al. [1980], Casanova [1984], Wang [1984], and Hull and King [1987]. A logical design methodology for relational databases using the extended E-R model is presented by Teorey et al. [1986]. Mapping from extended E-R models to the relational model is discussed by Lyngbaek and Vianu [1987] and Markowitz and Shoshani [1989].

Various data manipulation languages for the E-R model have been proposed. These include CABLE [Shoshani 1978], GERM [Benneworth et al. 1981], GORDAS [ElMasri and Wiederhold 1981], and ERROL [Markowitz and Raz 1983]. A graphical query language for the E-R database was proposed by Zhang and Mendelzon [1983] and ElMasri and Larson [1985]. An algorithm for a general E-R model is presented by Parent and Spaccapietra [1985]. A relationally complete query language for the E-R model is presented by Campbell et al. [1985].

The concepts of generalization, specialization, and aggregation were introduced by Smith and Smith [1977]. Lenzerini and Santucci [1983] have used these concepts in defining cardinality constraints in the E-R model. Logic-based semantics for a variant of the E-R model is given by Di Battista and Lenzerini [1989].

Basic textbook discussions are offered by Tsichritzis and Lochovsky [1982] and ElMasri and Navathe [1989].

3

Relational Model

From a historical perspective, the relational data model is relatively new. The first database systems were based on either the network model (see Appendix A) or the hierarchical model (see Appendix B). Those two older models are tied more closely to the underlying implementation of the database than is the relational model.

In the years following the introduction of the relational model, a substantial theory has developed for relational databases. This theory assists in the design of relational databases and in the efficient processing of user requests for information from the database. We shall examine this theory in Chapters 5 and 6.

The relational model has established itself as the primary data model for commercial data processing applications. Its success in this domain has led to its application outside data processing in systems for computer-aided design and other environments. We shall consider extensions to the relational model for these newer applications in Chapter 14.

3.1 Structure of Relational Databases

A relational database consists of a collection of *tables*, each of which is assigned a unique name. Each table has a structure similar to that presented in Chapter 2, where we represented E-R databases by tables. A row in a table represents a *relationship* among a set of values. Since a table is a collection of such relationships, there is a close correspondence between the concept of *table* and the mathematical concept of *relation*, from which the relational data model takes its name. In what follows, we introduce the concept of relation.

In this chapter, we shall be using a number of different relations to illustrate the various concepts underlying the relational data model. These relations represent part of a banking enterprise. They differ slightly from the tables that were used in Chapter 2 in order to simplify our presentation. We shall discuss appropriate relational structures in great detail in Chapter 6.

3.1.1 Basic Structure

Consider the *deposit* table of Figure 3.1. It has four attributes: *branch-name*, *account-number*, *customer-name*, and *balance*. For each attribute, there is a set of permitted values, called the *domain* of that attribute. For the attribute *branch-name*, for example, the domain is the set of all branch names. Let D_1 denote this set and let D_2 denote the set of all account-numbers, D_3 the set of all customer names, and D_4 the set of all balances. As we saw in Chapter 2, any row of *deposit* must consist of a 4-tuple (v_1, v_2, v_3, v_4), where v_1 is a branch name (that is, v_1 is in domain D_1), v_2 is an account number (that is, v_2 is in domain D_2), v_3 is a customer name (that is, v_3 is in domain D_3), and v_4 is a balance (that is, v_4 is in domain D_4). In general, *deposit* will contain only a subset of the set of all possible rows. Therefore *deposit* is a subset of

$$D_1 \times D_2 \times D_3 \times D_4$$

In general, a table of n columns must be a subset of

$$D_1 \times D_2 \times \cdots \times D_{n-1} \times D_n$$

Mathematicians define a relation to be a subset of a cartesian product of a list of domains. This corresponds almost exactly with our definition of table. The only difference is that we have assigned names to attributes, whereas mathematicians rely on numeric "names," using the integer 1 to denote the attribute whose domain appears first in the list of domains, 2 for the attribute whose domain appears second, and so on. Because tables are essentially relations, we shall use the mathematical terms *relation* and *tuple* in place of the terms *table* and *row*.

In the *deposit* relation of Figure 3.1, there are eight tuples. Let the *tuple variable t* refer to the first tuple of the relation. We use the notation *t*[*branch-name*] to denote the value of *t* on the *branch-name* attribute. Thus,

branch-name	account-number	customer-name	balance
Downtown	101	Johnson	500
Mianus	215	Smith	700
Perryridge	102	Hayes	400
Round Hill	305	Turner	350
Perryridge	201	Williams	900
Redwood	222	Lindsay	700
Brighton	217	Green	750
Downtown	105	Green	850

Figure 3.1 The *deposit* relation.

t[*branch-name*] = "Downtown". Similarly, *t*[*account-number*] = 101, the value of *t* on the *account-number* attribute. *Customer-name* and *balance* follow suit. Alternatively, we may write *t*[1] to denote the value of tuple *t* on the first attribute (*branch-name*), *t*[2] to denote *account-number*, and so on. Since a relation is a set of tuples, we use the mathematical notation of *t* ∈ *r* to denote that tuple *t* is in relation *r*.

We shall require that for all relations *r*, the domains of all attributes of *r* be atomic. A domain is *atomic* if elements of the domain are considered to be indivisible units. For example, the set of integers is an atomic domain, but the set of all sets of integers is a nonatomic domain. The distinction is that we do not normally consider integers to have subparts, but we consider sets of integers to have subparts, namely, the integers comprising the set. The important issue is not the domain itself, but the way we use domain elements in our database. The domain of all integers would be nonatomic if we considered each integer to be an ordered list of digits.

In all our examples, we shall assume atomic domains. In Chapter 14 we shall discuss the *nested relational* data model, which allows nonatomic domains.

3.1.2 Database Scheme

When we talk about a database, we must differentiate between the *database scheme*, or, the logical design of the database, and a *database instance*, which is the data in the database at a given instant in time.

The concept of a relation *scheme* corresponds to the programming language notion of type definition. A variable of a given type has a particular value at a given instant in time. Thus, a variable in programming languages corresponds to the concept of an *instance* of a relation.

It is convenient to give a name to a relation scheme, just as we give names to type definitions in programming languages. We adopt the convention of using lowercase names for relations and names beginning with an uppercase letter for relation schemes. Following this notation, we use *Deposit-scheme* to denote the relation scheme for relation *deposit*. Thus,

Deposit-scheme = (*branch-name, account-number, customer-name, balance*)

We denote the fact that *deposit* is a relation on the scheme *Deposit-scheme* by

deposit (*Deposit-scheme*)

In general, a relation scheme is a list of attributes and their corresponding domains. We shall not be concerned about the precise definition of the domain of each attribute until we discuss integrity constraints in Chapter 5. However, when we do wish to define our domains, we use the notation

> (*branch-name* : string, *account-number* : integer,
> *customer-name* : string, *balance* : integer)

to define the relation scheme for the relation *deposit*.

As another example, consider the *customer* relation of Figure 3.2. The scheme for that relation is

> *Customer-scheme* = (*customer-name*, *street*, *customer-city*)

Note that the attribute *customer-name* appears in both relation schemes. This is not a coincidence. Rather, the use of common attributes in relation schemes is one way of relating tuples of distinct relations. For example, suppose we wish to find the cities where depositors of the Perryridge branch live. We look first at the *deposit* relation to find all depositors of the Perryridge branch. Then, for each such customer, we would look in the *customer* relation to find the city in which he or she lives. Using the terminology of the entity-relationship model, we say that the attribute *customer-name* represents the same entity set in both relations.

It would appear that, for our banking example, we could have just one relation scheme rather than several. That is, it may be easier for a user to think in terms of one relation scheme rather than several. Suppose we used only one relation for our example, with scheme

> *Account-info-scheme* = (*branch-name*, *account-number*, *customer-name*,
> *balance*, *street*, *customer-city*)

customer-name	street	customer-city
Jones	Main	Harrison
Smith	North	Rye
Hayes	Main	Harrison
Curry	North	Rye
Lindsay	Park	Pittsfield
Turner	Putnam	Stamford
Williams	Nassau	Princeton
Adams	Spring	Pittsfield
Johnson	Alma	Palo Alto
Glenn	Sand Hill	Woodside
Brooks	Senator	Brooklyn
Green	Walnut	Stamford

Figure 3.2   The *customer* relation.

Observe that if a customer has several accounts, we must list her or his address once for each account. That is, we must repeat certain information several times. This repetition is wasteful and is avoided by the use of two relations, as in our example.

In addition, if a customer has one or more accounts, but has not provided an address, we cannot construct a tuple on *Account-info-scheme*, since the values for *street* and *customer-city* are not known. To represent incomplete tuples, we must use *null values*. Thus, in the above example, the values for *street* and *customer-city* must be null. By using two relations, one on *Customer-scheme* and one on *Deposit-scheme*, we can represent customers whose address is unknown, without using null values. We simply use a tuple on *Deposit-scheme* to represent the information about the account, and create no tuple on *Customer-scheme* until the address information becomes available.

It is not always possible to eliminate null values. Suppose, for example, that we include the attribute *phone-number* in the *Customer-scheme*. It may be that a customer does not have a phone number, or that the phone number is unlisted. We would then have to resort to null values to signify that the value is unknown or does not exist. We shall see later that null values cause a number of difficulties in accessing or updating the database, and thus should be eliminated if at all possible.

In Chapter 6, we shall study criteria to help us decide when one set of relation schemes is better than another, in terms of information repetition and the existence of null values. For now, we shall assume the relation schemes are given.

For the purpose of this and subsequent chapters, we assume a banking enterprise with the entity-relationship diagram shown in Figure 3.3. The primary keys for the *customer* and *branch* entity sets are *customer-name* and *branch-name*, respectively. The relationship schemes for this enterprise are the same as the tables that might be generated using the method outlined in Section 2.6. The schemes are:

Branch-scheme = (branch-name, assets, branch-city)
Customer-scheme = (customer-name, street, customer-city)
Deposit-scheme = (branch-name, account-number, customer-name, balance)
Borrow-scheme = (branch-name, loan-number, customer-name, amount)

We have already seen an example of a *deposit* relation and a *customer* relation. Figures 3.4 and 3.5 show a sample *borrow* (*Borrow-scheme*) relation and a *branch* (*Branch-scheme*) relation, respectively.

3.1.3 Keys

The notions of *superkey*, *candidate key*, and *primary key*, as discussed in Chapter 2, are also applicable to the relational model. For example, in

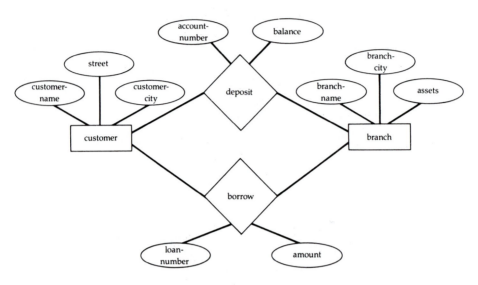

Figure 3.3   E-R diagram for the banking enterprise.

Branch-scheme, {*branch-name*} and {*branch-name*, *branch-city*} are both superkeys. {*branch-name*, *branch-city*} is not a candidate key, because {*branch-name*} ⊆ {*branch-name*, *branch-city*} and {*branch-name*} itself is a superkey. {*branch-name*}, however, *is* a candidate key, which for our purpose will also serve as a primary key. The attribute *branch-city* is not a superkey, since two branches in the same city may have different names (and different asset figures). The primary key for *Customer-scheme* is *customer-name*. We are not using the *social-security* attribute, as was done in

branch-name	loan-number	customer-name	amount
Downtown	17	Jones	1000
Redwood	23	Smith	2000
Perryridge	15	Hayes	1500
Downtown	14	Jackson	1500
Mianus	93	Curry	500
Round Hill	11	Turner	900
Pownal	29	Williams	1200
North Town	16	Adams	1300
Downtown	18	Johnson	2000
Perryridge	25	Glenn	2500
Brighton	10	Brooks	2200

Figure 3.4   The *borrow* relation.

branch-name	assets	branch-city
Downtown	9000000	Brooklyn
Redwood	2100000	Palo Alto
Perryridge	1700000	Horseneck
Mianus	400000	Horseneck
Round Hill	8000000	Horseneck
Pownal	300000	Bennington
North Town	3700000	Rye
Brighton	7100000	Brooklyn

Figure 3.5   The *branch* relation.

Chapter 2, in order to have smaller relation schemes in our running example of a bank database. We expect that in a real world database the *social-security* attribute would serve as a primary key.

Let R be a relation scheme. If we say that a subset K of R is a *superkey* for R, we are restricting consideration to relations $r(R)$ in which no two distinct tuples have the same values on all attributes in K. That is, if t_1 and t_2 are in r and $t_1 \neq t_2$, then $t_1[K] \neq t_2[K]$.

3.1.4 Query Languages

A *query language* is a language in which a user requests information from the database. These languages are typically of a higher level than standard programming languages. Query languages can be categorized as being either *procedural* or *nonprocedural*. In a procedural language, the user instructs the system to perform a sequence of operations on the database to compute the desired result. In a nonprocedural language, the user describes the information desired without giving a specific procedure for obtaining that information.

Most commercial relational database systems offer a query language that includes elements of both the procedural and the nonprocedural approaches. We shall study several commercial languages in Chapter 4. In this chapter, we examine two "pure" languages: The relational algebra is procedural, while the tuple relational calculus and the domain relational calculus are nonprocedural. These query languages are terse and formal, lacking the "syntactic sugar" of commercial languages; but they illustrate the fundamental techniques for extracting data from the database.

Initially, we shall be concerned only with queries. A complete data manipulation language includes not only a query language, but also a language for database modification. Such languages include commands to insert and delete tuples as well as commands to modify parts of existing tuples. We shall examine database modification after we complete our discussion of "pure" query languages.

3.2 The Relational Algebra

The relational algebra is a *procedural* query language. It consists of a set of operations that take one or two relations as input and produce a new relation as their result. The fundamental operations in the relational algebra are *select, project, cartesian product, rename, union,* and *set difference.* In addition to the fundamental operations, there are several other operations, namely, *set intersection, natural join, division,* and *assignment.* These operations will be defined in terms of the fundamental operations.

3.2.1 Fundamental Operations

The select, project, and rename operations are called *unary* operations, since they operate on one relation. The other three operations operate on pairs of relations and are, therefore, called *binary* operations.

The Select Operation

The *select* operation selects tuples that satisfy a given predicate. We use the lowercase Greek letter sigma (σ) to denote selection. The predicate appears as a subscript to σ. The argument relation is given in parentheses following the σ. Thus, to select those tuples of the *borrow* relation where the branch is "Perryridge," we write

$$\sigma_{branch\text{-}name\ =\ \text{"Perryridge"}}\ (borrow)$$

If the *borrow* relation is as shown in Figure 3.4, then the relation that results from the above query is as shown in Figure 3.6.

We may find all tuples in which the amount borrowed is more than $1200 by writing

$$\sigma_{amount\ >\ 1200}\ (borrow)$$

In general, we allow comparisons using $=, \neq, <, \leq, >, \geq$ in the selection predicate. Furthermore, several predicates may be combined into a larger predicate using the connectives *and* ($\wedge$) and *or* ($\vee$). Thus, to find

branch-name	loan-number	customer-name	amount
Perryridge	15	Hayes	1500
Perryridge	25	Glenn	2500

Figure 3.6   Result of $\sigma_{branch\text{-}name\ =\ \text{"Perryridge"}}$ (*borrow*).

customer-name	banker-name
Turner	Johnson
Hayes	Jones
Johnson	Johnson

Figure 3.7   The *client* relation.

those tuples pertaining to loans of more than \$1200 made by the Perryridge branch, we write

$$\sigma_{branch\text{-}name\ =\ \text{``Perryridge''}\ \wedge\ amount\ >\ 1200}\ (borrow)$$

The selection predicate may include comparisons between two attributes. To illustrate, we consider the relation scheme

$$Client\text{-}scheme\ =\ (customer\text{-}name,\ banker\text{-}name)$$

indicating that a customer has a "personal banker." The relation *client* (*Client-scheme*) is shown in Figure 3.7. We may find all those customers who have the same name as their personal banker by writing

$$\sigma_{customer\text{-}name\ =\ banker\text{-}name}\ (client)$$

The relation that results from the above query is shown in Figure 3.8.

The Project Operation

In the above example, we obtained a relation (Figure 3.8) on (*customer-name, banker-name*) in which $t[customer\text{-}name] = t[banker\text{-}name]$ for all tuples t. It seems redundant to list the person's name twice. We would prefer a one-attribute relation on (*customer-name*) which lists all those who have the same name as their personal banker. The *project* operation allows us to produce this relation. The project operation is a unary operation that returns its argument relation, with certain columns left out. Since a relation is a set, any duplicate rows are eliminated. Projection is denoted by the

customer-name	banker-name
Johnson	Johnson

Figure 3.8   Result of $\sigma_{customer\text{-}name\ =\ banker\text{-}name}$ (*client*).

Greek letter pi (Π). We list those attributes that we wish to appear in the result as a subscript to Π. The argument relation follows Π in parentheses.

Suppose we want a relation showing customers and the branches from which they borrow, but do not care about the amount of the loan, or the loan number. We write

$$\Pi_{branch\text{-}name,\ customer\text{-}name}\ (borrow)$$

Let us revisit the query "Find those customers who have the same name as their personal banker." We write

$$\Pi_{customer\text{-}name}\ (\sigma_{customer\text{-}name\ =\ banker\text{-}name}\ (client))$$

Notice that instead of giving the name of a relation as the argument of the projection operation, we give an expression that evaluates to a relation.

The Cartesian Product Operation

The operations we have discussed up to this point allow us to extract information from only one relation at a time. We have not yet been able to combine information from several relations. One operation that allows us to do that is the *cartesian product* operation, denoted by a cross (×). This operation is a binary operation. We shall use infix notation for binary operations and, thus, write the cartesian product of relations r_1 and r_2 as $r_1 \times r_2$. Recall that a relation is defined to be a subset of a cartesian product of a set of domains. From that definition we should already have some intuition about the definition of the relational algebra operation ×. However, we face the problem of choosing the attribute names for the relation that results from a cartesian product.

Suppose we want to find all clients of banker Johnson, as well as the cities in which these clients live. We need the information in both the *client* relation and the *customer* relation in order to do so. Figure 3.9 shows the relation $r = client \times customer$. The relation scheme for r is

(*client.customer-name, client.banker-name, customer.customer-name,*
customer.street, customer.customer-city)

That is, we simply list all the attributes of both relations, and attach the name of the relation from which the attribute originally came. We need to attach the relation name to distinguish *client.customer-name* from *customer.customer-name*. For those attributes that appear in only one of the two schemes, we shall usually drop the relation-name prefix. This

client. customer-name	banker-name	customer. customer-name	street	customer-city
Turner	Johnson	Jones	Main	Harrison
Turner	Johnson	Smith	North	Rye
Turner	Johnson	Hayes	Main	Harrison
Turner	Johnson	Curry	North	Rye
Turner	Johnson	Lindsay	Park	Pittsfield
Turner	Johnson	Turner	Putnam	Stamford
Turner	Johnson	Williams	Nassau	Princeton
Turner	Johnson	Adams	Spring	Pittsfield
Turner	Johnson	Johnson	Alma	Palo Alto
Turner	Johnson	Glenn	Sand Hill	Woodside
Turner	Johnson	Brooks	Senator	Brooklyn
Turner	Johnson	Green	Walnut	Stamford
Hayes	Jones	Jones	Main	Harrison
Hayes	Jones	Smith	North	Rye
Hayes	Jones	Hayes	Main	Harrison
Hayes	Jones	Curry	North	Rye
Hayes	Jones	Lindsay	Park	Pittsfield
Hayes	Jones	Turner	Putnam	Stamford
Hayes	Jones	Williams	Nassau	Princeton
Hayes	Jones	Adams	Spring	Pittsfield
Hayes	Jones	Johnson	Alma	Palo Alto
Hayes	Jones	Glenn	Sand Hill	Woodside
Hayes	Jones	Brooks	Senator	Brooklyn
Hayes	Jones	Green	Walnut	Stamford
Johnson	Johnson	Jones	Main	Harrison
Johnson	Johnson	Smith	North	Rye
Johnson	Johnson	Hayes	Main	Harrison
Johnson	Johnson	Curry	North	Rye
Johnson	Johnson	Lindsay	Park	Pittsfield
Johnson	Johnson	Turner	Putnam	Stamford
Johnson	Johnson	Williams	Nassau	Princeton
Johnson	Johnson	Adams	Spring	Pittsfield
Johnson	Johnson	Johnson	Alma	Palo Alto
Johnson	Johnson	Glenn	Sand Hill	Woodside
Johnson	Johnson	Brooks	Senator	Brooklyn
Johnson	Johnson	Green	Walnut	Stamford

Figure 3.9   Result of *client* × *customer*.

simplification does not lead to any ambiguity. We may now write the
relation scheme for r as

  (client.customer-name, banker-name, customer.customer-name,
  street, customer-city)

Now that we know the relation scheme for $r = client \times customer$, what
tuples appear in r? As you may have suspected, we construct a tuple of r
out of each possible pair of tuples: one from the *client* relation and one
from the *customer* relation. Thus, r is a large relation, as can be seen from
Figure 3.9.

Assume we have n_1 tuples in *client* and n_2 tuples in *customer*. Then
there are $n_1 n_2$ ways of choosing a pair of tuples: one tuple from each
relation; so there are $n_1 n_2$ tuples in r. In particular, note that it may be the
case for some tuples t in r that $t[client.customer\text{-}name] \neq t[customer.customer\text{-}name]$.

In general, if we have relations $r_1(R_1)$ and $r_2(R_2)$, then $r_1 \times r_2$ is a
relation whose scheme is the concatenation of R_1 and R_2. Relation R
contains all tuples t for which there is a tuple t_1 in r_1, and t_2 in r_2 for
which $t[R_1] = t_1[R_1]$ and $t[R_2] = t_2[R_2]$.

Returning to the query "Find all clients of banker Johnson and the city
in which they live," we consider the relation $r = client \times customer$. If we
write

$$\sigma_{banker\text{-}name\,=\,\text{"Johnson"}}\,(client \times customer)$$

then the result is the relation shown in Figure 3.10. We have a relation
pertaining only to banker Johnson. However, the *customer.customer-name*
column may contain customers of bankers other than Johnson. (If you
don't see why, recall that the cartesian product takes all possible pairings
of one tuple from *client* with one tuple of *customer*.) Note that the
client.customer-name column contains only customers of Johnson.

Since the cartesian product operation associates *every* tuple of *customer*
with every tuple of *client*, we know that some tuple in $client \times customer$ has
the address of the banker's customer. This occurs in those cases where it
happens that *client.customer-name = customer.customer-name*. So if we write

$$\sigma_{client.customer\text{-}name\,=\,customer.customer\text{-}name}$$
$$(\sigma_{banker\text{-}name\,=\,\text{"Johnson"}}\,(client \times customer))$$

we get only those tuples of $client \times customer$ that

- Pertain to Johnson.

- Have the street and city of the customer of Johnson.

client. customer-name	banker-name	customer. customer-name	street	customer-city
Turner	Johnson	Jones	Main	Harrison
Turner	Johnson	Smith	North	Rye
Turner	Johnson	Hayes	Main	Harrison
Turner	Johnson	Curry	North	Rye
Turner	Johnson	Lindsay	Park	Pittsfield
Turner	Johnson	Turner	Putnam	Stamford
Turner	Johnson	Williams	Nassau	Princeton
Turner	Johnson	Adams	Spring	Pittsfield
Turner	Johnson	Johnson	Alma	Palo Alto
Turner	Johnson	Glenn	Sand Hill	Woodside
Turner	Johnson	Brooks	Senator	Brooklyn
Turner	Johnson	Green	Walnut	Stamford
Johnson	Johnson	Jones	Main	Harrison
Johnson	Johnson	Smith	North	Rye
Johnson	Johnson	Hayes	Main	Harrison
Johnson	Johnson	Curry	North	Rye
Johnson	Johnson	Lindsay	Park	Pittsfield
Johnson	Johnson	Turner	Putnam	Stamford
Johnson	Johnson	Williams	Nassau	Princeton
Johnson	Johnson	Adams	Spring	Pittsfield
Johnson	Johnson	Johnson	Alma	Palo Alto
Johnson	Johnson	Glenn	Sand Hill	Woodside
Johnson	Johnson	Brooks	Senator	Brooklyn
Johnson	Johnson	Green	Walnut	Stamford

Figure 3.10   Result of $\sigma_{banker\text{-}name\ =\ \text{"Johnson"}}$ $(client \times customer)$.

Finally, since we want only *customer-name* and *customer-city*, we do a projection:

$$\Pi_{client.customer\text{-}name,\ customer\text{-}city}\ (\sigma_{client.customer\text{-}name\ =\ customer.customer\text{-}name}$$
$$(\sigma_{banker\text{-}name\ =\ \text{"Johnson"}}\ (client \times customer)))$$

The result of this expression is the correct answer to our query.

The Rename Operation

In the query considered above, we introduced the convention of naming attributes by *relation-name.attribute-name* in order to eliminate possible ambiguity. Another form of potential ambiguity arises when the same relation appears more than once in a query.

To illustrate, consider the query "Find the names of all customers who live on the same street and in the same city as Smith." We can obtain the street and city of Smith by writing

$$\Pi_{street,\ customer\text{-}city}\ (\sigma_{customer\text{-}name\ =\ \text{"Smith"}}\ (customer))$$

However, to find other customers with this street and city, we must reference the *customer* relation a second time:

$$\sigma_P\ (customer\ \times\ \Pi_{street,\ customer\text{-}city}\ (\sigma_{customer\text{-}name\ =\ \text{"Smith"}}\ (customer)))$$

where *P* is a selection predicate which requires both *street* values and *customer-city* values to be equal. In order to specify to which *street* value we refer, we cannot use *customer.street*, since both *street* values are taken from the *customer* relation. A similar difficulty exists for *customer.city*. This problem is solved using the *rename* operator, denoted ρ. The expression

$$\rho_x\ (r)$$

returns relation *r* under the name *x*. We shall use this to rename one reference to the customer relation and thus reference the relation twice without ambiguity. In the query below, we use the name *customer2* as a second name for the *customer* relation. We refer to *customer2* when computing the street and city of Smith.

$$\Pi_{customer.customer\text{-}name}$$

$$(\sigma_{customer2.street\ =customer.street\ \wedge\ customer2.customer\text{-}city\ =customer.customer\text{-}city}$$

$$(customer\ \times\ (\Pi_{street,\ customer\text{-}city}\ (\sigma_{customer\text{-}name\ =\ \text{"Smith"}}$$

$$(\rho_{customer2}\ (customer))))))$$

The result of this query when applied to the *customer* relation of Figure 3.2 is shown in Figure 3.11.

The Union Operation

Let us now consider a query that might be posed by a bank's advertising department: "Find all customers of the Perryridge branch." That is, find everyone who has a loan, an account, or both. To answer this query, we need the information in the *borrow* relation (Figure 3.4) and the *deposit* relation (Figure 3.1). We know how to find all customers with a loan at the Perryridge branch:

$$\Pi_{customer\text{-}name}\ (\sigma_{branch\text{-}name\ =\ \text{"Perryridge"}}\ (borrow))$$

customer-name
Smith
Curry

Figure 3.11   Customers who live on the same street and city as Smith.

We also know how to find all customers with an account at the Perryridge branch:

$$\Pi_{customer\text{-}name} \left(\sigma_{branch\text{-}name \; = \; \text{``Perryridge''}} (deposit) \right)$$

To answer the query, we need the *union* of these two sets, that is, all customers appearing in either or both of the two relations. This is accomplished by the binary operation union, denoted, as in set theory, by ∪. So the expression the advertising department needs in our example is

$$\Pi_{customer\text{-}name} \left(\sigma_{branch\text{-}name \; = \; \text{``Perryridge''}} (borrow) \right)$$
$$\cup \; \Pi_{customer\text{-}name} \left(\sigma_{branch\text{-}name \; = \; \text{``Perryridge''}} (deposit) \right)$$

The result relation for this query appears in Figure 3.12. Notice that there are three tuples in the result even though the Perryridge branch has two borrowers and two depositors. This is due to the fact that Hayes is both a borrower and a depositor of the Perryridge branch. Since relations are sets, duplicate values are eliminated.

Observe that, in our example, we took the union of two sets, both of which consisted of *customer-name* values. In general, we must ensure that unions are taken between *compatible* relations. For example, it would not make sense to take the union of the *borrow* relation and the *customer* relation. The former is a relation of four attributes and the latter, of three. Furthermore, consider a union of a set of customer names and a set of cities. Such a union would not make sense in most situations. Therefore,

customer-name
Hayes
Glenn
Williams

Figure 3.12   Names of all customers of the Perryridge branch.

for a union operation $r \cup s$ to be valid, we require that two conditions hold:

1. The relations r and s must be of the same arity. That is, they must have the same number of attributes.

2. The domains of the ith attribute of r and the ith attribute of s must be the same.

The Set Difference Operation

The *set difference* operation, denoted by $-$, allows us to find tuples that are in one relation but not in another. The expression $r - s$ results in a relation containing those tuples in r but not in s.

We can find all customers of the Perryridge branch who have an account there but not a loan by writing

$$\Pi_{customer\text{-}name} \ (\sigma_{branch\text{-}name \ = \ \text{``Perryridge''}} \ (deposit))$$
$$- \ \Pi_{customer\text{-}name} \ (\sigma_{branch\text{-}name \ = \ \text{``Perryridge''}} \ (borrow))$$

The result relation for this query appears in Figure 3.13.

Consider the query "Find the largest account balance in the bank." This query can be expressed simply using *aggregate functions* in SQL (see Chapter 4). However, we are able to write this query using only the fundamental operations. Our strategy for doing so is to compute first a temporary relation consisting of those balances that are *not* the largest, and then take the set difference between the relation *deposit* and the temporary relation just computed, to obtain the result. The temporary relation is computed through the expression

$$\Pi_{deposit.balance} \ (\sigma_{deposit.balance \ < \ d.balance} \ (deposit \ \times \ \rho_d \ (deposit)))$$

This expression gives those balances in the *deposit* relation for which a larger balance appears somewhere in the *deposit* relation (renamed as d). The result contains all balances *except* the largest one. This relation is

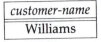

customer-name
Williams

Figure 3.13 Customers with only an account at the Perryridge branch.

balance
500
700
400
350
750
850

Figure 3.14   Result of subexpression $\Pi_{deposit.balance}$
$(\sigma_{deposit.balance\,<\,d.balance}$ $(deposit \times \rho_d\,(deposit)))$.

shown in Figure 3.14. The query can be written by taking the difference between the set of all balances

$$\Pi_{balance}\,(deposit)$$

and the temporary relation computed above. The query is written as follows:

$$\Pi_{balance}\,(deposit)\;-$$

$$\Pi_{deposit.balance}\,(\sigma_{deposit.balance\,<\,d.balance}\,(deposit \times \rho_d\,(deposit)))$$

Figure 3.15 shows the result of this query.

3.2.2 Formal Definition of the Relational Algebra

The operations we have just seen allow us to give a complete definition of an expression in the relational algebra. A basic expression in the relational algebra consists of either one of the following:

- A relation in the database.
- A constant relation.

A general expression in the relational algebra is constructed out of smaller

balance
900

Figure 3.15   Largest account balance in the bank.

subexpressions. Let E_1 and E_2 be relational algebra expressions. Then the following are all relational algebra expressions:

- $E_1 \cup E_2$
- $E_1 - E_2$
- $E_1 \times E_2$
- $\sigma_P(E_1)$, where P is a predicate on attributes in E_1
- $\Pi_S(E_1)$, where S is a list consisting of some of the attributes in E_1
- $\rho_x (E_1)$, where x is the new name for the relation E_1

3.2.3 Additional Operations

The fundamental operations of the relational algebra are sufficient to express any relational algebra query. However, if we restrict ourselves to just the fundamental operations, some common queries are lengthy to express. Therefore, we define additional operations that do not add any power to the algebra, but that simplify common queries. For each new operation, we give an equivalent expression using only the fundamental operations.

The Set Intersection Operation

The first additional relational algebra operation we shall define is *set intersection* ($\cap$). Suppose we wish to find all customers with *both* a loan and an account at the Perryridge branch. Using set intersection, we can write:

$$\Pi_{customer\text{-}name} (\sigma_{branch\text{-}name = \text{``Perryridge''}} (borrow))$$
$$\cap \; \Pi_{customer\text{-}name} (\sigma_{branch\text{-}name = \text{``Perryridge''}} (deposit))$$

The result relation for this query appears in Figure 3.16.

Note, that any relational algebra expression using set intersection can be rewritten by replacing the intersection operation with a pair of set difference operations as follows:

$$r \cap s = r - (r - s)$$

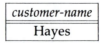

customer-name
Hayes

Figure 3.16   Customers with an account and a loan at the Perryridge branch.

Thus, set intersection is not a fundamental operation and does not add any power to the relational algebra. It is simply more convenient to write $r \cap s$ than $r - (r - s)$.

The Natural Join Operation

It is often desirable to simplify certain queries that require a cartesian product. Typically, a query that involves a cartesian product includes a selection operation on the result of the cartesian product. Consider the query "Find all customers who have a loan at the bank and the cities in which they live." We first form the cartesian product of the *borrow* and *customer* relations, then we select those tuples that pertain to only one *customer-name*. Thus we write

$$\Pi_{borrow.customer-name,\ customer-city}$$
$$(\sigma_{borrow.customer-name\ =\ customer.customer-name}(borrow \times customer))$$

The *natural join* is a binary operation that allows us to combine certain selections and a cartesian product into one operation. It is denoted by the "join" symbol $\bowtie$. The natural join operation forms a cartesian product of its two arguments, performs a selection forcing equality on those attributes that appear in both relation schemes, and finally removes duplicate columns.

Although the definition of natural join is a bit complicated, the operation is applied easily. To illustrate, let us consider again the example "Find all customers who have a loan at the bank and the cities in which they live." This query can be expressed using the natural join as follows:

$$\Pi_{customer-name,\ customer-city}\ (borrow \bowtie customer)$$

Since the schemes for *borrow* and *customer* (that is, *Borrow-scheme* and *Customer-scheme*) have the attribute *customer-name* in common, the natural join operation considers only pairs of tuples that have the same value on *customer-name*. It combines each such pair of tuples into a single tuple on the union of the two schemes (that is, *branch-name, loan-number, customer-name, amount, street, customer-city*). After performing the projection, we obtain the relation shown in Figure 3.17.

We are now ready for a formal definition of the natural join. Consider two relation schemes R and S which are, of course, lists of attribute names. If we consider the schemes to be *sets* rather than lists, we can denote those attributes in both R and S by $R \cap S$, and denote those attributes that appear in R, in S, or in both by $R \cup S$. Note that we refer, here, to union and intersection on sets of attributes, not relations.

customer-name	customer-city
Jones	Harrison
Smith	Rye
Hayes	Harrison
Curry	Rye
Turner	Stamford
Williams	Princeton
Adams	Pittsfield
Johnson	Palo Alto
Glenn	Woodside
Brooks	Brooklyn

Figure 3.17 Result of $\Pi_{customer\text{-}name,\ customer\text{-}city}$ (borrow $\bowtie$ customer).

Consider two relations $r(R)$ and $s(S)$. The natural join of r and s, denoted by $r \bowtie s$ is a relation on scheme $R \cup S$. It is the projection onto $R \cup S$ of a selection on $r \times s$ where the predicate requires $r.A = s.A$ for each attribute A in $R \cap S$. Formally,

$$r \bowtie s = \Pi_{R \cup S} (\sigma_{r.A_1 = s.A_1 \wedge r.A_2 = s.A_2 \wedge \cdots \wedge r.A_n = s.A_n} r \times s)$$

where $R \cap S = \{A_1, A_2, \ldots, A_n\}$.

Because the natural join is central to much of relational database theory and practice, we give several examples of its use below.

- Find the assets and name of all branches which have depositors (that is, customers with an account) living in Stamford.

$$\Pi_{branch\text{-}name,\ assets}$$
$$(\sigma_{customer\text{-}city\ =\ \text{``Stamford''}} (customer \bowtie deposit \bowtie branch))$$

Notice that we wrote customer $\bowtie$ deposit $\bowtie$ branch without inserting parentheses to specify the order in which the natural join operations on the three relations be executed. In the above case, there are two possibilities:

- ○ (customer $\bowtie$ deposit) $\bowtie$ branch
- ○ customer $\bowtie$ (deposit $\bowtie$ branch)

We did not specify which expression we intended because they are equivalent. That is, the natural join is associative. The result relation for this query appears in Figure 3.18.

- Find all customers who have *both* an account and a loan at the Perryridge branch.

$$\Pi_{customer\text{-}name} \left(\sigma_{branch\text{-}name \,=\, \text{"Perryridge"}} (borrow \bowtie deposit) \right)$$

Note that we wrote an expression for this query using set intersection above:

$$\Pi_{customer\text{-}name} \left(\sigma_{branch\text{-}name \,=\, \text{"Perryridge"}} (borrow) \right)$$
$$\cap \ \Pi_{customer\text{-}name} \left(\sigma_{branch\text{-}name \,=\, \text{"Perryridge"}} (deposit) \right)$$

The result relation for this query was shown earlier in Figure 3.16. This example illustrates a general fact about the relational algebra: It is possible to write several equivalent relational algebra expressions that are quite different from each other.

- Let $r(R)$ and $s(S)$ be relations without any attributes in common, that is, $R \cap S = \emptyset$. ($\emptyset$ denotes the empty set.) Then $r \bowtie s = r \times s$.

The Division Operation

The division operation, denoted by $\div$, is suited to queries that include the phrase "for all." Suppose we wish to find all customers who have an account at *all* branches located in Brooklyn. We can obtain all branches in Brooklyn by the expression:

$$r_1 = \Pi_{branch\text{-}name} \left(\sigma_{branch\text{-}city \,=\, \text{"Brooklyn"}} (branch) \right)$$

The result relation for this expression appears in Figure 3.19.

We can find all *customer-name, branch-name* pairs for which the customer has an account at a branch by writing

$$r_2 = \Pi_{customer\text{-}name, \ branch\text{-}name} (deposit)$$

Figure 3.20 shows the result relation for this expression.

branch-name	assets
Round Hill	8000000
Brighton	7100000
Downtown	9000000

Figure 3.18   Result of $\Pi_{branch\text{-}name, \ assets}$
$\left(\sigma_{customer\text{-}city \,=\, \text{"Stamford"}} (customer \bowtie deposit \bowtie branch) \right)$.

branch-name
Brighton
Downtown

Figure 3.19   Result of $\Pi_{branch\text{-}name}$ ($\sigma_{branch\text{-}city\,=\,\text{"Brooklyn"}}$ ($branch$)).

Now we need to find customers who appear in r_2 with *every* branch name in r_1. The operation that provides exactly those customers is the divide operation. The query can be answered by writing

$$\Pi_{customer\text{-}name,\;branch\text{-}name}\;(deposit)$$
$$\div\;\Pi_{branch\text{-}name}\;(\sigma_{branch\text{-}city\,=\,\text{"Brooklyn"}}\;(branch))$$

The result of this expression is a relation that has the scheme (*customer-name*) and contains the tuple (Green).

Formally, let $r(R)$ and $s(S)$ be relations, and let $S \subseteq R$. The relation $r \div s$ is a relation on scheme $R - S$. A tuple t is in $r \div s$ if for every tuple t_s in s there is a tuple t_r in r satisfying both of the following:

$$t_r[S] = t_s[S]$$
$$t_r[R - S] = t[R - S]$$

It may be surprising to discover that the division operation can, in fact, be defined in terms of the fundamental operations. Let $r(R)$ and $s(S)$ be given, with $S \subseteq R$.

$$r \div s = \Pi_{R\,-\,S}\,(r) - \Pi_{R\,-\,S}\,(\,(\Pi_{R\,-\,S}\,(r) \times s) - r)$$

To see that this is true, observe that $\Pi_{R\,-\,S}\,(r)$ gives us all tuples t that

customer-name	branch-name
Johnson	Downtown
Smith	Mianus
Hayes	Perryridge
Turner	Round Hill
Williams	Perryridge
Lindsay	Redwood
Green	Brighton
Green	Downtown

Figure 3.20   Result of $\Pi_{customer\text{-}name,\;branch\text{-}name}$ ($deposit$).

satisfy the second condition of the definition of division. The expression on the right side of the set difference operator,

$$\Pi_{R-S} ((\Pi_{R-S} (r) \times s) - r)$$

serves to eliminate those tuples that fail to satisfy the first condition of the definition of division. Let us see how it does this. Consider $\Pi_{R-S} (r) \times s$. This is a relation on scheme R which pairs every tuple in $\Pi_{R-S} (r)$ with every tuple in s. Thus, $(\Pi_{R-S} (r) \times s) - r$ gives us those pairs of tuples from $\Pi_{R-S} (r)$ and s which do not appear in r. If a tuple t is in

$$\Pi_{R-S} ((\Pi_{R-S} (r) \times s) - r)$$

then there is some tuple t_s in s that does not combine with tuple t to form a tuple in r. Thus, t holds a value for attributes $R - S$ which does not appear in $r \div s$. It is these values that we eliminate from $\Pi_{R-S} (r)$.

The Assignment Operation

It is convenient at times to write a relational algebra expression in parts using assignment to a temporary relation variable. The assignment operation, denoted ←, works in a manner similar to assignment in a programming language. To illustrate this operation, consider the definition of division above. We could write $r \div s$ as

$$temp \leftarrow \Pi_{R-S} (r)$$
$$temp - \Pi_{R-S} ((temp \times s) - r)$$

The evaluation of an assignment does not result in any relation being displayed to the user. Rather, the result of the expression to the right of the ← is assigned to the relation variable on the left of the ←. This relation variable may be used in subsequent expressions.

With the assignment operation, a query can be written as a sequential program consisting of a series of assignments followed by an expression whose value is displayed as the result of the query. For relational algebra queries, assignment must always be made to a temporary relation variable. Assignments to permanent relations constitute a database modification. We discuss this in Section 3.5. It is important to note that the assignment operation does not provide any additional power to the algebra. It is, however, a convenient way to express complex queries.

3.3 The Tuple Relational Calculus

When we write a relational algebra expression, we provide a sequence of procedures that generates the answer to our query. The tuple relational calculus, by contrast, is a *nonprocedural* query language. It describes the desired information without giving a specific procedure for obtaining that information.

A query in the tuple relational calculus is expressed as

$$\{t \mid P(t)\}$$

that is, the set of all tuples t such that predicate P is true for t. Following our earlier notation, we use $t[A]$ to denote the value of tuple t on attribute A, and we use $t \in r$ to denote that tuple t is in relation r.

Before we give a formal definition of the tuple relational calculus, we return to some of the queries for which we wrote relational algebra expressions in the last section.

3.3.1 Example Queries

Find the *branch-name, loan-number, customer-name,* and *amount* for loans of over $1200:

$$\{t \mid t \in borrow \wedge t[amount] > 1200\}$$

Suppose we want only the *customer-name* attribute, rather than all attributes of the *borrow* relation. To write this query in the tuple relational calculus, we need to write an expression for a relation on the scheme (*customer-name*). We need those tuples on (*customer-name*) such that there is a tuple in *borrow* pertaining to that *customer-name* with the *amount* attribute > 1200. In order to express this, we need the construct "there exists" from mathematical logic. The notation

$$\exists \, t \in r \, (Q(t))$$

means "there exists a tuple t in relation r such that predicate $Q(t)$ is true."

Using this notation, we may write the query "Find all customers who have a loan for an amount greater than $1200" as:

$$\{t \mid \exists \, s \in borrow \, (t[customer\text{-}name] = s[customer\text{-}name] \\ \wedge \, s[amount] > 1200)\}$$

In English, we read the above expression as "the set of all tuples t such that there exists a tuple s in relation *borrow* for which the values of t and s for the *customer-name* attribute are equal, and the value of s for the *amount* attribute is greater than $1200."

Tuple variable t is defined only on the *customer-name* attribute, since that is the only attribute for which a condition is specified for t. Thus, the result is a relation on (*customer-name*).

Consider the query "Find all customers having a loan from the Perryridge branch and the cities in which they live." This query is slightly more complex than the previous queries since it involves two relations, namely, *customer* and *borrow*. But as we shall see, all it requires is that we have two "there exists" clauses in our tuple relational calculus expression connected by *and* ($\wedge$). We write the query as follows:

$$\{t \mid \exists\ s \in borrow\ (t[customer\text{-}name] = s[customer\text{-}name]$$
$$\wedge\ s[branch\text{-}name] = \text{``Perryridge''}$$
$$\wedge\ \exists\ u \in customer\ (u[customer\text{-}name] = s[customer\text{-}name]$$
$$\wedge\ t[customer\text{-}city] = u[customer\text{-}city]))\}$$

In English, this is "the set of all (*customer-name, customer-city*) tuples for which *customer-name* is a borrower at Perryridge branch and *customer-city* is the city of *customer-name*." Tuple variable *s* ensures that the customer is a borrower at the Perryridge branch. Tuple variable *u* is restricted to pertain to the same customer as *s*, and *u* ensures that the *customer-city* is the city of the customer. The result of this query is shown in Figure 3.21.

To find all customers having a loan, an account, or both at the Perryridge branch, we used the union operation in the relational algebra. In the tuple relational calculus, we shall need two "there exists" clauses, connected by *or* ($\vee$).

$$\{t \mid \exists\ s \in borrow\ (t[customer\text{-}name] = s[customer\text{-}name]$$
$$\wedge\ s[branch\text{-}name] = \text{``Perryridge''})$$
$$\vee\ \exists\ u \in deposit\ (t[customer\text{-}name] = u[customer\text{-}name]$$
$$\wedge\ u[branch\text{-}name] = \text{``Perryridge''})\}$$

The above expression gives us the set of all *customer-name* tuples such that at least one of the following holds:

- The *customer-name* appears in some tuple of the *borrow* relation as a borrower from the Perryridge branch.

- The *customer-name* appears in some tuple of the *deposit* relation as a depositor of the Perryridge branch.

customer-name	customer-city
Hayes	Harrison
Glenn	Woodside

Figure 3.21   Name and city for all loan customers at the Perryridge branch.

If some customer has both a loan and an account at the Perryridge branch, that customer appears only once in the result because the mathematical definition of a set does not allow duplicate members. The result of this query was shown earlier in Figure 3.12.

If we now want *only* those customers that have *both* an account and a loan at the Perryridge branch, all we need to do is change the *or* ($\lor$) to *and* ($\land$) in the above expression.

$$\{t \mid \exists\, s \in borrow\ (t[customer\text{-}name] = s[customer\text{-}name]$$
$$\land\ s[branch\text{-}name] = \text{``Perryridge''})$$
$$\land\ \exists\, u \in deposit\ (t[customer\text{-}name] = u[customer\text{-}name]$$
$$\land\ u[branch\text{-}name] = \text{``Perryridge''})\}$$

The result of this query was shown in Figure 3.16.

Now consider the query "Find all customers who have an account at the Perryridge branch but do not have a loan from the Perryridge branch." The tuple relational calculus expression for this query is similar to those we have just seen, except for the use of the *not* ($\neg$) symbol.

$$\{t \mid \exists\, u \in deposit\ (t[customer\text{-}name] = u[customer\text{-}name]$$
$$\land\ u[branch\text{-}name] = \text{``Perryridge''})$$
$$\land\ \neg\,\exists\, s \in borrow\ (t[customer\text{-}name] = s[customer\text{-}name]$$
$$\land\ s[branch\text{-}name] = \text{``Perryridge''})\}$$

The above tuple relational calculus expression uses the $\exists\, u \in deposit\ (\cdots)$ clause to require that the customer have an account at the Perryridge branch, and it uses the $\neg\,\exists\, s \in borrow\ (\cdots)$ clause to eliminate those customers who appear in some tuple of the *borrow* relation as having a loan from the Perryridge branch. The result of this query appeared in Figure 3.13.

The query we shall consider next uses implication, denoted $\Rightarrow$ The formula $P \Rightarrow Q$ means "P implies Q;" that is, "if P is true, then Q must be true." Note that $P \Rightarrow Q$ is logically equivalent to $\neg P \lor Q$. The use of implication rather than *not* and *or* often suggests a more intuitive interpretation of a query in English.

Consider the query we used in Section 3.2.3 to illustrate the division operation: "Find all customers who have an account at all branches located in Brooklyn." To write this query in the tuple relational calculus, we introduce the "for all" construct, denoted $\forall$. The notation

$$\forall\, t \in r\ (Q(t))$$

means "Q is true for all tuples t in relation r."

We write the expression for our query as follows:

$$\{t \mid \forall\ u \in branch\ (u[branch\text{-}city] = \text{``Brooklyn''} \Rightarrow$$
$$\exists\ s \in deposit\ (t[customer\text{-}name] = s[customer\text{-}name]$$
$$\wedge\ u[branch\text{-}name] = s[branch\text{-}name]))\}$$

In English, we interpret the above expression as "the set of all customers, (that is, *(customer-name)* tuples *t*) such that for *all* tuples *u* in the *branch* relation, if the value of *u* on attribute *branch-city* is Brooklyn then the customer has an account at the branch whose name appears in the *branch-name* attribute of *u*."

3.3.2 Formal Definition

We are now ready for a formal definition. A tuple relational calculus expression is of the form:

$$\{t \mid P(t)\}$$

where *P* is a *formula*. Several tuple variables may appear in a formula. A tuple variable is said to be a *free variable* unless it is quantified by a $\exists$ or $\forall$. Thus, in

$$t \in borrow \wedge \exists\ s \in customer\ (t[customer\text{-}name] = s[customer\text{-}name])$$

t is a free variable. Tuple variable *s* is said to be a *bound* variable.

A tuple relational calculus formula is built up out of *atoms*. An atom has one of the following forms:

- $s \in r$, where *s* is a tuple variable and *r* is a relation. (We do not allow use of the $\notin$ operation.)

- $s[x]\ \Theta\ u[y]$, where *s* and *u* are tuple variables, *x* is an attribute on which *s* is defined, *y* is an attribute on which *u* is defined, and Θ is a comparison operator ($<, \leq, =, \neq, >, \geq$). We require that attributes *x* and *y* have domains whose members can be compared by Θ.

- $s[x]\ \Theta\ c$, where *s* is a tuple variable, *x* is an attribute on which *s* is defined, Θ is a comparison operator, and *c* is a constant in the domain of attribute *x*.

Formulae are built up from atoms using the following rules:

- An atom is a formula.

- If P_1 is a formula, then so are $\neg P_1$ and (P_1).

- If P_1 and P_2 are formulae, then so are $P_1 \vee P_2$, $P_1 \wedge P_2$, and $P_1 \Rightarrow P_2$.
- If $P_1(s)$ is a formula containing a free tuple variable s, then

$$\exists\, s \in r\ (P_1(s))\ \text{ and }\ \forall\, s \in r\ (P_1(s))$$

are also formulae.

As was the case for the relational algebra, it is possible to write equivalent expressions that are not identical in appearance. In the tuple relational calculus, these equivalences include three rules:

1. $P_1 \wedge P_2$ is equivalent to $\neg\, (\neg P_1 \vee \neg P_2)$.
2. $\forall\, t \in r\ (P_1(t))$ is equivalent to $\neg\, \exists\, t \in r\ (\neg P_1(t))$.
3. $P_1 \Rightarrow P_2$ is equivalent to $\neg P_1 \vee P_2$.

3.3.3 Safety of Expressions

There is one final issue to be addressed. A tuple relational calculus expression may generate an infinite relation. Suppose we wrote the expression

$$\{t \mid \neg\ (t \in borrow)\}$$

There are infinitely many tuples that are not in *borrow*. Most of these tuples contain values that do not even appear in the database! Clearly, we do not wish to allow such expressions.

To assist us in defining a restriction of the tuple relational calculus, we introduce the concept of the *domain* of a tuple relational formula, P. Intuitively, the domain of P, denoted $dom(P)$ is the set of all values referenced by P. These include values mentioned in P itself as well as values that appear in a tuple of a relation mentioned in P. Thus, the domain of P is the set of all values that appear explicitly in P or that appear in one or more relations whose names appear in P. For example, $dom(t \in borrow \wedge t[amount] > 1200)$ is the set of all values appearing in *borrow*. Also, $dom(\neg\ (t \in borrow))$ is the set of all values appearing in *borrow*.

We say that an expression $\{t \mid P(t)\}$ is *safe* if all values that appear in the result are values from $dom(P)$. The expression $\{t \mid \neg\ (t \in borrow)\}$ is not safe. Note that $dom(\neg\ (t \in borrow))$ is the set of all values appearing in *borrow*. However, it is possible to have a tuple t not in *borrow* that contains values that do not appear in *borrow*. The other examples of tuple relational calculus expressions we have written in this section are safe.

3.3.4 Expressive Power of Languages

The tuple relational calculus restricted to safe expressions is equivalent in expressive power to the relational algebra. This means that for every relational algebra expression, there is an equivalent expression in the tuple relational calculus, and for every tuple relational calculus expression there is an equivalent relational algebra expression. We will not prove this fact here, but the bibliographic notes contain references to the proof. Some parts of the proof are included in the exercises.

3.4 The Domain Relational Calculus

There is a second form of relational calculus called *domain relational calculus*. This form uses *domain* variables that take on values from an attribute's domain, rather than values for an entire tuple. The domain relational calculus, however, is closely related to the tuple relational calculus.

3.4.1 Formal Definition

An expression in the domain relational calculus is of the form $\{<x_1, x_2, \ldots, x_n> \mid P(x_1, x_2, \ldots, x_n)\}$ where $x_1, x_2, \ldots, x_n$ represent domain variables. P represents a formula composed of atoms, as was the case in the tuple relational calculus. An atom in the domain relational calculus has one of the following forms:

- $<x_1, x_2, \ldots, x_n> \in r$, where r is a relation on n attributes and $x_1, x_2, \ldots, x_n$ are domain variables or domain constants.

- $x \Theta y$, where x and y are domain variables and Θ is a comparison operator ($<, \leq, =, \neq, >, \geq$). We require that attributes x and y have domains that can be compared by Θ.

- $x \Theta c$, where x is a domain variable, Θ is a comparison operator, and c is a constant in the domain of the attribute for which x is a domain variable.

Formulae are built up from atoms using the following rules:

- An atom is a formula.
- If P_1 is a formula, then so are $\neg P_1$ and (P_1).
- If P_1 and P_2 are formulae, then so are $P_1 \vee P_2$, $P_1 \wedge P_2$, and $P_1 \Rightarrow P_2$.
- If $P_1(x)$ is a formula in x, where x is a domain variable, then

$$\exists\, x\, (P_1(x)) \text{ and } \forall\, x\, (P_1(x))$$

are also formulae.

As a notational shorthand, we write

$$\exists\, a,b,c\ (P(a,b,c))$$

for

$$\exists\, a\ (\exists\, b\ (\exists\, c\ (P(a,b,c))))$$

3.4.2 Example Queries

We now give domain relational calculus queries for the examples we considered earlier. Note the similarity of these expressions with the corresponding tuple relational calculus expressions

- Find the branch name, loan number, customer name, and amount for loans of over $1200:

$$\{<b,l,c,a> \mid\ <b,l,c,a> \epsilon\ borrow \wedge a > 1200\}$$

- Find all customers who have a loan for an amount greater than $1200:

$$\{<c> \mid\ \exists\, b,l,a\ (<b,l,c,a> \epsilon\ borrow \wedge a > 1200)\}$$

Although the second query appears similar to the one we wrote for the tuple relational calculus, there is an important difference. In the tuple calculus, when we write $\exists\, s$ for some tuple variable s, we bind it immediately to a relation by writing $\exists\, s\ \epsilon\ r$. However, when we write $\exists\, b$ in the domain calculus, b does not refer to a tuple, but rather to a domain value. Thus, the domain of variable b is unconstrained until the subformula $<b,l,c,a> \epsilon\ borrow$ constrains b to branch names that appear in the *borrow* relation.

- Find all customers having a loan from the Perryridge branch and the city in which they live:

$$\{<c,x> \mid\ \exists\, b,l,a\ (<b,l,c,a> \epsilon\ borrow \wedge b = \text{``Perryridge''}$$
$$\wedge\ \exists\, y\ (<c,y,x> \epsilon\ customer))\}$$

- Find all customers having a loan, an account, or both at the Perryridge branch:

$$\{<c> \mid\ \exists\, b,l,a\ (<b,l,c,a> \epsilon\ borrow \wedge b = \text{``Perryridge''})$$
$$\vee\ \exists\, b,a,n\ (<b,a,c,n> \epsilon\ deposit \wedge b = \text{``Perryridge''})\}$$

- Find all customers who have an account at all branches located in Brooklyn:

$$\{<c> \mid \forall\, x,y,z\, (\neg\, (<x,y,z> \in branch) \lor z \neq \text{``Brooklyn''}$$
$$\lor\, (\exists\, a,n\, (<x,a,c,n> \in deposit)))\}$$

In English, we interpret the above expression as "the set of all (*customer-name*) tuples $<c>$ such that for all (*branch-name*, *assets*, *branch-city*) tuples, $<x,y,z>$, at least one of the following is true":

- $<x,y,z>$ is not a tuple of the *branch* relation (and, therefore, does not pertain to a branch in Brooklyn).
- z does *not* have the value "Brooklyn."
- The customer c has an account (with account number represented by a and balance represented by n) at branch x.

To say this somewhat more intuitively, "for all names, either the name is not a branch name, the name is the name of a branch not in Brooklyn, or the customer has an account at the named branch."

3.4.3 Safety of Expressions

We noted that in the tuple relational calculus, it was possible to write expressions that may generate an infinite relation. This led us to define *safety* for tuple relational calculus expressions. A similar situation arises for the domain relational calculus. An expression such as

$$\{<b, c, l, a> \mid \neg\, (<b, c, l, a> \in borrow)\}$$

is unsafe because it allows values in the result that are not in the domain of the expression.

For the domain relational calculus, we must be concerned also about the form of formulae within "there exists" and "for all" clauses. Consider the expression

$$\{<x> \mid \exists\, y\, (<x, y> \in r) \land \exists\, z\, (\neg(<x, z> \in r))\}$$

We can test the first part of the formula, $\exists\, y\, (<x, y> \in r)$, by considering only the values in r. However, to test the second part of the formula, $\exists\, z\, (\neg\, (<x, z> \in r))$, we must consider values for z that do not appear in r. Since all relations are finite, an infinite number of values do not appear in r. Thus, it is not possible to test the second part of the formula. Instead, we add restrictions to prohibit expressions like the one above.

In the tuple relational calculus, we restricted any existentially quantified variable to range over a specific relation. Since we did not do so in the domain calculus, we add rules to the definition of safety to deal with cases like the above example. We say that an expression

$$\{<x_1, x_2, \ldots, x_n> \mid P(x_1, x_2, \ldots, x_n)\}$$

is safe if all of the following hold:

1. All values that appear in tuples of the expression are values from $dom(P)$.

2. For every "there exists" subformula of the form $\exists x (P_1(x))$, the subformula is true if and only if there is a value x in $dom(P_1)$ such that $P_1(x)$ is true.

3. For every "for all" subformula of the form $\forall x (P_1(x))$, the subformula is true if and only if $P_1(x)$ is true for all values x from $dom(P_1)$.

The purpose of the additional rules is to ensure that we can test "for all" and "there exists" subformulae without having to test infinitely many possibilities. Consider the second rule in the definition of safety. For $\exists x (P_1(x))$ to be true, we need to find only one x for which $P_1(x)$ is true. In general, there would be infinitely many values to test. However, if the expression is safe, we know that we may restrict our attention to values from $dom(P_1)$. This reduces the number of tuples we must consider to a finite number.

The situation for subformulae of the form $\forall x (P_1(x))$ is similar. To assert that $\forall x (P_1(x))$ is true, we must, in general, test all possible values. This requires us to examine infinitely many values. As above, if we know the expression is safe, it is sufficient for us to test $P_1(x)$ for those values taken from $dom(P_1)$.

All the domain relational calculus expressions we have written in the example queries of this section are safe.

3.4.4 Expressive Power of Languages

When the domain relational calculus is restricted to safe expressions, it is equivalent to the tuple relational calculus restricted to safe expressions. Since we noted earlier that the restricted tuple relational calculus is equivalent to the relational algebra, all three of the following are equivalent:

- The relational algebra.
- The tuple relational calculus restricted to safe expressions.
- The domain relational calculus restricted to safe expressions.

3.5 Modifying the Database

We have limited our attention until now to the extraction of information from the database. We have not shown how to add, remove, or change information. In this section, we address database modification for the relational algebra.

Database modifications are expressed using the assignment operator. Assignments are made to actual database relations using the same notation described in Section 3.2.3 for assignment.

3.5.1 Deletion

A delete request is expressed in much the same way as a query. However, instead of displaying tuples to the user, we remove the selected tuples from the database. We may delete only whole tuples; we cannot delete values on only particular attributes. In relational algebra, a deletion is expressed by:

$$r \leftarrow r - E$$

where r is a relation and E is a relational algebra query.

Below are several examples of relational algebra delete requests.

- Delete all of Smith's accounts.

$$deposit \leftarrow deposit - \sigma_{customer\text{-}name\ =\ \text{"Smith"}} (deposit)$$

- Delete all loans with loan numbers between 1300 and 1500.

$$deposit \leftarrow deposit - \sigma_{loan\text{-}number\ \geq\ 1300\ and\ loan\text{-}number\ \leq\ 1500} (deposit)$$

- Delete all accounts at branches located in Needham.

$$r_1 \leftarrow \sigma_{branch\text{-}city\ =\ \text{"Needham"}} (deposit \bowtie branch)$$
$$r_2 \leftarrow \Pi_{branch\text{-}name,\ account\text{-}number,\ customer\text{-}name,\ balance} (r_1)$$
$$deposit \leftarrow deposit - r_2$$

Note that in the above example, we simplified our expression by using assignment to temporary relations (r_1 and r_2).

3.5.2 Insertion

To insert data into a relation, we either specify a tuple to be inserted or write a query whose result is a set of tuples to be inserted. Obviously, the attribute values for inserted tuples must be members of the attribute's domain. Similarly, tuples inserted must be of the correct arity. In relational algebra, an insertion is expressed by:

$$r \leftarrow r \cup E$$

where r is a relation and E is a relational algebra expression. The insertion of a single tuple is expressed by letting E be a constant relation containing one tuple.

Suppose we wish to insert the fact that Smith has \$1200 in account 9732 at the Perryridge branch. We write:

$$deposit \leftarrow deposit \cup \{(\text{``Perryridge''}, 9732, \text{``Smith''}, 1200)\}$$

More generally, we might want to insert tuples based on the result of a query. Suppose we want to provide all loan customers in the Perryridge branch with a \$200 savings account. Let the loan number serve as the account number for the new savings account. We write:

$$r_1 \leftarrow (\sigma_{branch\text{-}name\, =\, \text{``Perryridge''}} (borrow))$$
$$r_2 \leftarrow \Pi_{branch\text{-}name,\, loan\text{-}number,\, customer\text{-}name} (r_1)$$
$$deposit \leftarrow deposit \cup (r_2 \times \{(200)\})$$

Instead of specifying a tuple as we did earlier, we specify several tuples. Each tuple has the *branch-name* (Perryridge), a *loan-number* (which serves as the account number for the new account), the name of the loan customer who is being given the new account, and the initial balance of the new account (\$200).

3.5.3 Updating

In certain situations we may wish to change a value in a tuple without changing *all* values in the tuple. If we make these changes using deletion and insertion, we may not be able to retain those values that we do not wish to change. Instead, we use the **update** operator δ, which has the form:

$$\delta_{A \leftarrow E} (r)$$

where r is the name of a relation with attribute A, which is assigned the value of expression E. The expression E is any arithmetic expression involving constants and attributes in the scheme of relation r.

To illustrate the use of the δ operator, suppose interest payments are being made, and all balances are to be increased by 5 percent. We write:

$$\delta_{balance \leftarrow balance\, *\, 1.05} (deposit)$$

The above statement is applied once to each tuple in *deposit*.

Let us now suppose that accounts with balances over \$10,000 receive 6 percent interest, while all others receive 5 percent. We write:

$$\delta_{balance \leftarrow balance * 1.06} (\sigma_{balance > 10000} (deposit))$$

$$\delta_{balance \leftarrow balance * 1.05} (\sigma_{balance \leq 10000} (deposit))$$

Note that in the above example the order in which we apply the update expressions is important. If we changed the order, an account whose balance is just under \$10,000 would receive 11.3 percent interest!

3.6 Views

In our examples up to this point, we have operated at the conceptual model level. That is, we have assumed that the collection of relations we are given are the actual relations stored in the database.

It is not desirable for all users to see the entire conceptual model. Security considerations may require that certain data be "hidden" from users. Consider a clerk who needs to know a customer's loan number but has no need to see the loan amount. This clerk should see a relation described, in the relational algebra, by

$$\Pi_{branch\text{-}name,\ loan\text{-}number,\ customer\text{-}name} (borrow)$$

Aside from security concerns, we may wish to create a personalized collection of relations that is better matched to a certain user's intuition than is the conceptual model. An employee in the advertising department, for example, might like to see a relation consisting of the customers of each branch. This relation lists those people who have either an account or a loan at that branch. The relation we would like to create for the employee is

$$\Pi_{branch\text{-}name,\ customer\text{-}name} (deposit)$$
$$\cup\ \Pi_{branch\text{-}name,\ customer\text{-}name} (borrow)$$

Any relation that is not part of the conceptual model but is made visible to a user as a "virtual relation," is called a *view*. It is possible to support a large number of views on top of any given set of actual relations.

Since the actual relations in the conceptual model may be modified, it is not generally possible to store a relation corresponding to a view. Instead, a view must be recomputed for each query that refers to it. In Chapter 9, we shall consider techniques for reducing the overhead of this recomputation. For now, we restrict our attention to the definition and use of views in relational algebra.

When a view is defined, the database system must store the definition of the view itself. Thus, view definition is not a relational algebra expression. Rather, a view definition causes the saving of an expression to be substituted into queries using the view.

3.6.1 View Definition

A view is defined using the **create view** statement. To define a view, we must give the view a name and state the query that computes the view. The form of the **create view** statement is

$$\text{create view } v \text{ as } \text{<query expression>}$$

where <query expression> is any legal relational algebra query expression. The view name is represented by v.

As an example, consider the view consisting of branches and their customers. Assume we wish this view to be called *all-customer*. We define this view as follows:

$$\text{create view } \textit{all-customer} \text{ as}$$
$$\Pi_{branch\text{-}name, \, customer\text{-}name} \, (deposit)$$
$$\cup \; \Pi_{branch\text{-}name, \, customer\text{-}name} \, (borrow)$$

Once we have defined a view, the view name can be used to refer to the virtual relation that the view generates. View names may appear in any place that a relation name may appear. Using the view *all-customer*, we can find all customers of the Perryridge branch by writing:

$$\Pi_{customer\text{-}name} \, (\sigma_{branch\text{-}name \, = \, \text{"Perryridge"}} \, (\textit{all-customer}))$$

Recall that we wrote the same query in Section 3.2.1 without using views.

3.6.2 Updates Through Views and Null Values

Although views are a useful tool for queries, they present significant problems if updates, insertions, or deletions are expressed using views. The difficulty is that a modification to the database expressed in terms of a view must be translated to a modification to the actual relations in the conceptual model of the database.

To illustrate the problem, consider the clerk who needs to see all loan data in the *borrow* relation except *loan-amount*. Let *loan-info* be the view given to the clerk. We define this view as:

$$\text{create view } \textit{loan-info} \text{ as}$$
$$\Pi_{branch\text{-}name, \, loan\text{-}number, \, customer\text{-}name} \, (borrow)$$

Since we allow a view name to appear wherever a relation name is allowed, the clerk may write:

$$loan\text{-}info \leftarrow loan\text{-}info \cup \{(\text{"Perryridge"}, 3, \text{"Ruth"})\}$$

This insertion must be represented by an insertion into the relation *borrow*, since *borrow* is the actual relation from which the view *loan-info* is constructed. However, to insert a tuple into *borrow*, we must have some value for *amount*. There are two reasonable approaches to dealing with this insertion:

- Reject the insertion and return an error message to the user.

- Insert a tuple ("Perryridge", 3, "Ruth", *null*) into the *borrow* relation.

The symbol *null* represents a *null-value* or *place-holder value*. It signifies that the value is unknown or does not exist. All comparisons involving *null* are **false** by definition.

Let us illustrate another problem resulting from modification of the database through views:

> **create view** *branch-city* **as**
> $\Pi_{branch\text{-}name,\ customer\text{-}city}\ (borrow \bowtie customer)$

This view lists the cities in which customers with a loan from the bank live. Consider the following insertion through this view:

$$branch\text{-}city \leftarrow branch\text{-}city \cup \{(\text{"Brighton"}, \text{"Woodside"})\}$$

The only possible method of inserting tuples into the *borrow* and *customer* relations is to insert ("Brighton", *null*, *null*, *null*) into *borrow* and (*null*, *null*, "Woodside") into *customer*. Then we obtain the relations shown in Figure 3.22. The result is unsatisfactory, since the expression for *branch-city*

$$\Pi_{branch\text{-}name,\ customer\text{-}city}\ (borrow \bowtie customer)$$

does *not* include the tuple ("Brighton", "Woodside"). Recall that all comparisons involving *null* are defined to be **false**.

The general problem of database modification through views has been the subject of substantial research. The bibliographic notes mention recent works on this subject.

Another view-related research area of interest is the *universal relation* model. In this model, the user is given a view consisting of one relation. This one relation is the natural join of all relations in the actual relational

branch-name	loan-number	customer-name	amount
Downtown	17	Jones	1000
Redwood	23	Smith	2000
Perryridge	15	Hayes	1500
Downtown	14	Jackson	1500
Mianus	93	Curry	500
Round Hill	11	Turner	900
Pownal	29	Williams	1200
North Town	16	Adams	1300
Downtown	18	Johnson	2000
Perryridge	25	Glenn	2500
Brighton	10	Brooks	2200
Brighton	null	null	null

customer-name	street	customer-city
Jones	Main	Harrison
Smith	North	Rye
Hayes	Main	Harrison
Curry	North	Rye
Lindsay	Park	Pittsfield
Turner	Putnam	Stamford
Williams	Nassau	Princeton
Adams	Spring	Pittsfield
Johnson	Alma	Palo Alto
Glenn	Sand Hill	Woodside
Brooks	Senator	Brooklyn
Green	Walnut	Stamford
null	null	Woodside

Figure 3.22   Tuples inserted into *borrow* and *customer*.

database. The major advantage of this model is that users need not be concerned with remembering what attributes are in which relation. Thus, most queries are easier to formulate in a universal relation database system than in a standard relational database system.

There remain unresolved questions regarding modifications to universal relation databases. Furthermore, a consensus has not yet developed on the best definition of the meaning of certain complex types of universal relation queries.

3.7 Summary

The relational data model is based on a collection of tables. The user of the database system may query these tables, insert new tuples, delete tuples, and update (modify) tuples. There are several languages for expressing these operations. The tuple relational calculus and the domain relational calculus are nonprocedural languages that represent the basic power required in a relational query language. The relational algebra is a procedural language that is equivalent in power to both forms of the relational calculus when they are restricted to safe expressions. The algebra defines the basic operations used within relational query languages.

The relational algebra and the relational calculi are terse, formal languages that are inappropriate for casual users of a database system. Commercial database system have, therefore, used languages with more "syntactic sugar." In Chapter 4 we shall consider the three most influential of the commercial languages: SQL, QBE, and Quel.

Databases may be modified by insertion, deletion, or update of tuples. We used the relational algebra with the assignment operator to express these modifications.

Different users of a shared database may benefit from individualized views of the database. We used relational algebra as an example to show how such views can be defined and used. Views are useful mechanisms for simplifying database queries, but modification of the database through views has potentially disadvantageous consequences. A strong case can be made for requiring all database modifications to refer to actual relations in the database.

Exercises

3.1 Design a relational database for a university registrar's office. The office maintains data about each class, including the instructor, the enrollment, and the time and place of the class meetings. For each student-class pair, a grade is recorded.

3.2 Describe the differences between the terms *relation* and *relation scheme*. Illustrate your answer by referring to your solution to Exercise 3.1.

3.3 Design a relational database corresponding to the E-R diagram of Figure 3.23.

3.4 In Chapter 2, we showed how to represent many-to-many, many-to-one, one-to-many, and one-to-one relationship sets. Explain how primary keys help us to represent such relationship sets in the relational model.

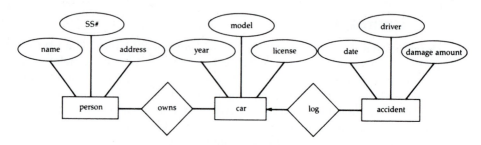

Figure 3.23   E-R diagram.

3.5 Consider the relational database of Figure 3.24. Give an expression in

- the relational algebra
- the tuple relational calculus
- the domain relational calculus

for each of the queries below:

a. Find the name of all employees who work for First Bank Corporation.

b. Find the name and city of all employees who work for First Bank Corporation.

c. Find the name, street, and city of all employees who work for First Bank Corporation and earn more than $10,000.

d. Find all employees who live in the same city as the company they work for.

e. Find all employees who live in the same city and on the same street as their manager.

f. Find all employees who do not work for First Bank Corporation.

> *lives (person-name, street, city)*
> *works (person-name, company-name, salary)*
> *located-in (company-name, city)*
> *manages (person-name, manager-name)*

Figure 3.24   Relational database.

g. Find all employees who earn more than every employee of Small Bank Corporation.

h. Assume the companies may be located in several cities. Find all companies located in every city in which Small Bank Corporation is located.

3.6 Let the following relation schemes be given:

$$R = (A,B,C)$$
$$S = (D,E,F)$$

Let relations $r(R)$ and $s(S)$ be given. Give an expression in the tuple relational calculus that is equivalent to each of the following:

a. $\Pi_A(r)$

b. $\sigma_{B = 17}(r)$

c. $r \times s$

d. $\Pi_{A,F}(\sigma_{C = D}(r \times s))$

3.7 Let $R = (A,B,C)$ and let r_1 and r_2 both be relations on scheme R. Give an expression in the domain relational calculus that is equivalent to:

a. $\Pi_A(r_1)$

b. $\sigma_{B = 17}(r_1)$

c. $r_1 \cup r_2$

d. $r_1 \cap r_2$

e. $r_1 - r_2$

f. $\Pi_{A,B}(r_1) \bowtie \Pi_{B,C}(r_2)$

3.8 Let $R = (A,B)$ and $S = (A,C)$, and let $r(R)$ and $s(S)$ be relations. Write relational algebra expressions equivalent to the following domain relational calculus expressions:

a. $\{<a> | \ \exists \ b \ (<a,b> \ \epsilon \ r \wedge b = 17)\}$

b. $\{<a,b,c> | \ <a,b> \ \epsilon \ r \wedge <a,c> \ \epsilon \ s\}$

c. $\{<b> | \ \forall \ a \ (\neg \ (<a,47> \ \epsilon \ s) \vee <a,b> \ \epsilon \ r)\}$

d. $\{<a> | \ \exists \ c \ (<a,c> \ \epsilon \ s \wedge \exists \ b_1,b_2 \ (<a,b_1> \ \epsilon \ r \\ \wedge <c, b_2> \ \epsilon \ r \wedge b_1 > b_2))\}$

3.9 The *theta join* is a binary operation that allows us to combine the selection and cartesian product into one operation. The theta join is denoted by $\bowtie_\Theta$. Given two relations, r and s, and a predicate Θ,

$$r \bowtie_\Theta s = \sigma_\Theta (r \times s)$$

For the banking enterprise scheme in the text, give an expression in the relational algebra using the theta join operation for the following set of queries:

- a. Find all customers having a loan at the Perryridge branch and the cities in which they live.

- b. Find all clients of Johnson and the cities in which they live.

3.10 Consider the relation of Figure 3.17, which shows the result of the query "Find all customers who have a loan at the bank and the cities in which they live." Observe that customer Jackson does not appear in the result. Note, however, that Jackson does in fact have a loan from the bank, as shown in the *borrow* relation of Figure 3.4.

- a. Explain why Jackson does not appear in the relation of Figure 3.17.

- b. Suppose that it is desired that Jackson appear in the result of queries such that of Figure 3.17. How might the database be modified to achieve this effect?

- c. Suppose that it is desired that to write the query of Figure 3.17 so that Jackson appears in the result without any need to modify the database (as was suggested in part b). The *outer join* is a binary operation that allows us to write such a query easily. The outer join of relations $r(R)$ and $s(S)$ includes not only tuples in $r \bowtie s$, but also those tuples in r that do not join with a tuple in s and those tuples in s that do not join with a tuple in r. These additional tuples are padded with null values to create tuples on the scheme $R \cup S$. Write a relational algebra expression using only σ, Π, $\times$, $\cup$, $\cap$, $-$, and $\bowtie$ to compute the outer join of r and s.

3.11 Consider the relational database of Figure 3.24. Give an expression in the relational algebra for each query below:

- a. Modify the database so that Jones now lives in Newtown.

- b. Give all employees of First Bank Corporation a 10 percent raise.

- c. Give all managers a 10 percent raise.

    d. Give all managers a 10 percent raise unless the salary becomes greater than $100,000. In such cases, give only a 3 percent raise.

    e. Delete all tuples in the *works* relation for employees of Small Bank Corporation.

3.12 List reasons why null values may be introduced into the database.

3.13 Some systems allow *marked* nulls. A marked null $\perp_i$ is equal to itself, but if $i \neq j$, then $\perp_i \neq \perp_j$. One application of marked nulls is to allow certain updates through views. Consider the view *branch-city* (Section 3.5). Show how marked nulls can be used to allow the insertion of the tuple (Brighton, Woodside) through *branch-city*.

Bibliographic Notes

The relational model was proposed by E. F. Codd of the IBM San Jose Research Laboratory in the late 1960s [Codd 1970]. Following Codd's original paper, several research projects were formed with the goal of constructing practical relational database systems, including System R at the IBM San Jose Research Laboratory, Ingres at the University of California at Berkeley, Query-by-Example at the IBM T. J. Watson Research Center, and PRTV (Peterlee Relational Test Vehicle) at the IBM Scientific Center in Peterlee, United Kingdom. System R and Ingres are discussed in Chapter 17. The bibliographic notes of that chapter provide references to those systems. Query-by-Example is described in Zloof [1977] and IBM [1978b]. PRTV is described in Todd [1976].

The original definition of relational algebra is in Codd [1970] and that of tuple relational calculus is in Codd [1972b]. A formal proof of the equivalence of tuple relational calculus and relational algebra can be found in Codd [1972b] and Ullman [1988]. Formal treatment of domain relation calculus is given by Lacroix and Pirotte [1977].

Extensions to the relational model and discussions concerning incorporating null values in the relational algebra (the RM/T model) are offered by Codd [1979]. Codd [1990] is a compendium of E. F. Codd's papers on the relational model.

The problem of updating relational databases through views is addressed by Bancilhon and Spyratos [1981], Cosmadakis and Papadimitriou [1984], Dayal and Bernstein [1978, 1982], Keller [1982, 1985], and Langerak [1990]. The universal relation view is discussed by Sciore [1983], Fagin et al. [1982], and Ullman [1982, 1988]. Several experimental database systems have been built to test the claim that a universal relation view is simpler to use. In such systems, the user views the entire database as one relation and the system translates operations on the universal relation view into operations on the set of relations forming the conceptual scheme. One such system is System/U, which was developed at Stanford University in 1980−1982. System/U is described by Ullman[1982, 1988] and Korth et al. [1984]. Another universal relation system, PITS, is discussed by Maier et al. [1982] and Maier [1983].

Discussions concerning the incorporation of time into the relational data model are offered by Snodgrass and Ahn [1985], Clifford and Tansel [1985], Gadia [1986, 1988], Snodgrass [1987], and Tuzhilin and Clifford [1990].

General discussion of the relational data model appears in most database texts, including Date [1990a], Ullman [1988], ElMasri and Navathe [1989], and Gardarin and Valduriez [1989]. Maier [1983] is a text devoted exclusively to the relational data model.

Relational Commercial Languages

The formal languages described in Chapter 3 provide a concise notation for representing queries. However, commercial database systems require a more "user-friendly" query language. In this chapter, we study three product languages: SQL, QBE, and Quel. We have chosen these languages because they represent a variety of styles. QBE is based on the domain relational calculus; Quel is based on the tuple relational calculus; and SQL uses a combination of relational algebra and relational calculus constructs. All three languages have been influential not only in research database systems but also in commercially marketed systems.

Although we refer to these languages as "query languages," SQL, QBE, and Quel contain many other capabilities besides querying a database. These include features for defining the structure of the data, features for modifying data in the database, and features for specifying security constraints.

It is not our intention to provide a complete users' guide for these languages. Rather, we present their fundamental constructs and concepts. Individual implementations of a language may differ in details, or support only a subset of the full language.

4.1 SQL

There are numerous versions of SQL. The original version was developed at IBM's San Jose Research Laboratory (now the Almaden Research Center). This language, originally called Sequel, was implemented as part of the System R project in the early 1970s. The Sequel language has evolved since then, and its name has changed to SQL (Structured Query Language). Numerous products now support the SQL language. Although the product versions of SQL differ in several language details, the differences are, for the most part, minor.

In 1986, the American National Standards Institute (ANSI) published an SQL standard. IBM has published its own corporate SQL standard, the Systems Application Architecture Database Interface (SAA-SQL). The bibliographic notes provide references to these products and standards, as well as to ongoing standardization work.

SQL has clearly established itself as *the* standard relational database language. In this section, we present a survey of SQL, that draws on features from various implementations, ranging from the original System R version to the latest products.

The SQL language has several parts:

- **Data definition language** (DDL). The SQL DDL provides commands for defining relation schemes, deleting relations, creating indices, and modifying relation schemes.

- **Interactive data manipulation language** (DML). The SQL DML includes a query language based on both the relational algebra and the tuple relational calculus. It includes also commands to insert, delete, and modify tuples in the database.

- **Embedded data manipulation language**. The embedded form of SQL is designed for use within general-purpose programming languages such as PL/I, Cobol, Pascal, Fortran, and C.

- **View definition**. The SQL DDL includes commands for defining views.

- **Authorization**. The SQL DDL includes commands for specifying access rights to relations and views.

- **Integrity**. The original System R Sequel language includes commands for specifying complex integrity constraints. Newer versions of SQL, including the ANSI standard, provide only a limited form of integrity checking. Future products and standards are likely to include enhanced features for integrity checking.

- **Transaction control**. SQL includes commands for specifying the beginning and ending of transactions. Several implementations, including IBM SAA-SQL, allow explicit locking of data for concurrency control.

In this section, we cover only the basic DDL, the interactive DML, and views. In Chapter 5, we discuss SQL's features regarding integrity. Security and authorization are covered in Chapter 16. Transactions are covered in Chapters 10–12. Coverage of embedded SQL is confined to the case studies of Chapter 17.

4.1.1 Basic Structure

The basic structure of an SQL expression consists of three clauses: **select**, **from**, and **where**.

- The **select** clause corresponds to the projection operation of the relational algebra. It is used to list the attributes desired in the result of a query.

- The **from** clause corresponds to the cartesian product operation of the relational algebra. It lists the relations to be scanned in the evaluation of the expression.

- The **where** clause corresponds to the selection predicate of the relational algebra. It consists of a predicate involving attributes of the relations that appear in the **from** clause.

The different meaning of the term "select" in SQL and in the relational algebra is an unfortunate historical fact. We emphasize the different interpretations here to minimize potential confusion.

A typical SQL query has the form:

$$\textbf{select } A_1, A_2, \ldots, A_n$$
$$\textbf{from } r_1, r_2, \ldots, r_m$$
$$\textbf{where } P$$

Each A_i represents an attribute and each r_i a relation. P is a predicate. This query is equivalent to the relational algebra expression

$$\Pi_{A_1, A_2, \ldots, A_n}(\sigma_P (r_1 \times r_2 \times \cdots \times r_m))$$

If the **where** clause is omitted, the predicate P is **true**. The list $A_1, A_2, \ldots, A_n$ of attributes may be replaced with a star (*) to select all attributes of all relations appearing in the **from** clause.

SQL forms the cartesian product of the relations named in the **from** clause, performs a relational algebra selection using the **where** clause predicate, and then projects the result onto the attributes of the **select** clause. In practice, SQL may convert the expression into an equivalent form that can be processed more efficiently. However, we shall defer concerns about efficiency to Chapter 9.

The result of an SQL query is, of course, a relation. Let us consider a very simple query using our banking example, "Find the names of all branches in the *deposit* relation:"

$$\textbf{select } branch\text{-}name$$
$$\textbf{from } deposit$$

4.1.2 Set Operations and Duplicate Tuples

Formal query languages are based on the mathematical notion of a relation being a set. Thus, duplicate tuples never appear in relations. In practice, duplicate elimination is relatively time consuming. Therefore, SQL (and most other commercial query languages) allow duplicates in relations. The above query will, thus, list each *branch-name* once for every tuple in which it appears in the *deposit* relation.

In those cases where we want to force the elimination of duplicates, we insert the keyword **distinct** after **select**. We can rewrite the above query as

> **select distinct** *branch-name*
> **from** *deposit*

if we want duplicates removed.

We note that SQL allows the use of the keyword **all** to specify explicitly that duplicates are not removed.

> **select all** *branch-name*
> **from** *deposit*

Since duplicate retention is the default, we will not use **all** in our examples. In order to ensure the elimination of duplicates in the results of our example queries, we shall use **distinct** whenever it is necessary.

4.1.3 Set Operations

SQL includes the operations **union, intersect,** and **minus,** which operate on relations and correspond to the relational algebra operations $\cup$, $\cap$, and $-$.

Let us demonstrate how the example queries considered in Chapter 3 can be written in SQL. First, we find all customers having an account at the Perryridge branch:

> **select distinct** *customer-name*
> **from** *deposit*
> **where** *branch-name* = "Perryridge"

Next, let us find all customers having a loan from the Perryridge branch:

> **select distinct** *customer-name*
> **from** *borrow*
> **where** *branch-name* = "Perryridge"

To find all customers having a loan, an account, or both at the Perryridge branch we write

> **(select** *customer-name*
> **from** *deposit*
> **where** *branch-name* = "Perryridge")
> **union**
> **(select** *customer-name*
> **from** *borrow*
> **where** *branch-name* = "Perryridge")

Similarly, to find all customers who have both a loan and an account at the Perryridge branch, we write

> (**select distinct** *customer-name*
> **from** *deposit*
> **where** *branch-name* = "Perryridge")
> **intersect**
> (**select distinct** *customer-name*
> **from** *borrow*
> **where** *branch-name* = "Perryridge")

By default, the **union** operation eliminates duplicate tuples. To retain duplicates, we must write **union all** in place of **union**. Note that the default on duplicate elimination for **union** differs from the default on **select**. Because of our use of **select distinct** we have ensured that we do not obtain duplicates in the above intersection.

To find all customers of the Perryridge branch who have an account there but no loan there, we write

> (**select distinct** *customer-name*
> **from** *deposit*
> **where** *branch-name* = "Perryridge")
> **minus**
> (**select** *customer-name*
> **from** *borrow*
> **where** *branch-name* = "Perryridge")

Although the **union** operation is part of ANSI standard SQL, several products do not support it. The **intersect** and **minus** operations were part of the original SQL (Sequel) supported in System R, but they are not included in the standard. It is possible to express these operations using other features of ANSI standard SQL. We shall see these features later in this chapter.

4.1.4 Predicates and Joins

SQL does not have a direct representation of the natural join operation. However, since the natural join is defined in terms of a cartesian product, a selection, and a projection, it is a relatively simple matter to write an SQL expression for the natural join.

Recall that we wrote the relational algebra expression

$$\Pi_{customer-name,\ customer-city}\ (borrow \bowtie customer)$$

for the query "Find the name and city of all customers having a loan at some branch." In SQL, this can be written as

> **select distinct** *customer.customer-name, customer-city*
> **from** *borrow, customer*
> **where** *borrow.customer-name* = *customer.customer-name*

Notice that SQL uses the notation *relation-name.attribute-name*, as does the relational algebra, to avoid ambiguity in cases where an attribute appears in the scheme of more than one relation. We could have written *customer.customer-city* instead of *customer-city* in the **select** clause. However, since the attribute *customer-city* appears in only one of the relations named in the **from** clause, there is no ambiguity when we write *customer-city*.

Let us extend the above query and consider a somewhat more complicated case in which we require also that customers have a loan from the Perryridge branch: "Find the name and city of all customers having a loan at the Perryridge branch." In order to write this query, we shall need to state two constraints in the **where** clause, connected by the logical connective **and**.

> **select distinct** *customer.customer-name, customer-city*
> **from** *borrow, customer*
> **where** *borrow.customer-name* = *customer.customer-name* **and**
>   *branch-name* = "Perryridge"

SQL uses the logical connectives **and, or,** and **not** rather than the mathematical symbols $\wedge$, $\vee$, and $\neg$. It allows the use of arithmetic expressions as operands to the comparison operators. An arithmetic expression may involve any of the operators, $+$, $-$, $*$, and $/$, operating on constants or values from tuples. Many implementations of SQL include special arithmetic functions for particular data types. For example, IBM SAA-SQL includes numerous functions for the *date* data type.

SQL includes a **between** comparison operator in order to simplify **where** clauses that specify that a value be less than or equal to some value and greater than or equal to some other value. If we wish to find the account number of those accounts with balances between $90,000 and $100,000 we may use the **between** comparison to write

> **select** *account-number*
> **from** *deposit*
> **where** *balance* **between** 90000 **and** 100000

instead of

> **select** *account-number*
> **from** *deposit*
> **where** *balance* $\leq$ 100000 **and** *balance* $\geq$ 90000

Similarly, we may use the **not between** comparison operator.

SQL also includes a string-matching operator for comparisons on character strings. Patterns are described using two special characters:

- percent (%). The % character matches any substring.
- underscore (_). The _ character matches any character.

Patterns are case-sensitive; that is, upper-case characters do not match lower-case characters, or vice versa. To illustrate pattern matching, consider the following examples:

- "Perry%" matches any string beginning with "Perry".
- "%idge%" matches any string containing "idge" as a substring, for example, "Perryridge", "Rock Ridge", "Mianus Bridge", and "Ridgeway".
- "_ _ _" matches any string of exactly 3 characters.
- "_ _ _%" matches any string of at least 3 characters.

Patterns are expressed in SQL using the **like** comparison operator. Consider the query "Find the names of all customers whose street includes the substring 'Main'." This query may be written as

> **select** *customer-name*
> **from** *customer*
> **where** *street* **like** "%Main%"

In order for patterns to include the special pattern characters (that is, %, _), SQL allows the specification of an escape character. The escape character is used immediately before a special pattern character to indicate that the special pattern character is to be treated as a normal character. We define the escape character for a **like** comparison using the **escape** keyword. To illustrate, consider the following patterns which use a backslash (\) as the escape character:

- **like** "ab\%cd%" **escape** "\" matches all strings beginning with "ab%cd".
- **like** "ab\\cd%" **escape** "\" matches all strings beginning with "ab\cd".

SQL allows searching for mismatches instead of matches by using the **not like** comparison operator.

4.1.5 Set Membership

SQL draws on the relational calculus for operations that allow testing tuples for membership in a relation. The **in** connective tests for set membership, where the set is a collection of values produced by a **select** clause. The **not in** connective tests for the absence of set membership. To illustrate, reconsider the query "Find all customers who have both a loan and an account at the Perryridge branch." Earlier, we wrote such a query by intersecting two sets: the set of depositors at the Perryridge branch and the set of borrowers from the Perryridge branch. We can take the alternative approach of finding all account holders at the Perryridge branch who are members of the set of borrowers from the Perryridge branch. Clearly, this generates the same results as before, but it leads us to write our query using the **in** connective of SQL. We begin by finding all account holders, and write the subquery:

> (**select** *customer-name*
> **from** *deposit*
> **where** *branch-name* = "Perryridge")

We then need to find those customers who are borrowers from the Perryridge branch and who appear in the list of account holders obtained in the subquery. We do this by embedding the subquery in an outer **select**. The resulting query is

> **select distinct** *customer-name*
> **from** *borrow*
> **where** *branch-name* = "Perryridge" **and**
>   *customer-name* **in** (**select** *customer-name*
>   **from** *deposit*
>   **where** *branch-name* = "Perryridge")

This example shows that it is possible to write the same query several ways in SQL. This is beneficial since it allows a user to think about the query in the way that appears most natural. We shall see that there is a substantial amount of redundancy in SQL.

In the above example, we tested membership in a one-attribute relation. It is possible to test for membership in an arbitrary relation. SQL uses the notation $<v_1, v_2, \ldots, v_n>$ to denote a tuple of arity n containing values $v_1, v_2, \ldots, v_n$. Using this notation, we can write the query "Find all customers who have both an account and a loan at the Perryridge branch" in a third way:

> **select distinct** *customer-name*
> **from** *borrow*
> **where** *branch-name* = "Perryridge" **and**
>   *<branch-name, customer-name>* **in**
>   (**select** *branch-name, customer-name*
>   **from** *deposit*)

We now illustrate the use of the **not in** construct. To find all customers who have an account at the Perryridge branch but do not have a loan at the Perryridge branch, we can write

> **select distinct** *customer-name*
> **from** *deposit*
> **where** *branch-name* = "Perryridge" **and**
>   *customer-name* **not in** (**select** *customer-name*
>   **from** *borrow*
>   **where** *branch-name* = "Perryridge")

4.1.6 Tuple Variables

SQL borrows the notion of tuple variables from the tuple relational calculus. A tuple variable in SQL must be associated with a particular relation. Tuple variables are defined in the **from** clause. To illustrate, we rewrite the query "Find the name and city of all customers having a loan at some branch" as

> **select distinct** *T.customer-name, customer-city*
> **from** *borrow S, customer T*
> **where** *S.customer-name* = *T.customer-name*

Note that a tuple variable is defined in the **from** clause by placing it after the name of the relation with which it is associated, separated by one or more spaces.

In queries that contain subqueries, a scoping rule applies for tuple variables. In a subquery, it is legal to use only tuple variables defined in the subquery itself or in any query that contains the subquery. If a tuple variable is defined both locally in a subquery and globally in a containing query, the local definition applies. This is analogous to the usual scoping rules used for variables in programming languages. When we write expressions of the form *relation-name.attribute-name*, the relation name is, in effect, an implicitly defined tuple variable.

Tuple variables are most useful for comparing two tuples in the same relation. In such cases the relational algebra uses the rename operation. Suppose we want to find all customers who have an account at some branch at which Jones has an account. We write this query as follows:

> **select distinct** *T.customer-name*
> **from** *deposit S, deposit T*
> **where** *S.customer-name* = "Jones" **and**
>   *S.branch-name* = *T.branch-name*

Observe that we could not use the notation *deposit.branch-name*, since it would not be clear which reference to *deposit* is intended.

We note that an alternative way to express this query is

> **select distinct** *customer-name*
> **from** *deposit*
> **where** *branch-name* **in**
>   (**select** *branch-name*
>   **from** *deposit*
>   **where** *customer-name* = "Jones")

4.1.7 Set Comparison

We were able to use the **in** construct in the above query because we were testing for equality between two branch names. Consider the query "Find the names of all branches that have greater assets than some branch located in Brooklyn." We can write the SQL expression:

> **select distinct** *T.branch-name*
> **from** *branch T, branch S*
> **where** *T.assets* > *S.assets* **and**
>   *S.branch-city* = "Brooklyn"

Since this is a "greater than" comparison, we cannot write the expression using the **in** construct.

SQL does, however, offer an alternative style for writing the above query. The phrase "greater than some" is represented in SQL by > **some**. This construct allows us to rewrite the query in a form that resembles closely our formulation of the query in English.

> **select** *branch-name*
> **from** *branch*
> **where** *assets* > **some**
>   (**select** *assets*
>   **from** *branch*
>   **where** *branch-city* = "Brooklyn")

The subquery

> (**select** *assets*
>   **from** *branch*
> **where** *branch-city* = "Brooklyn")

generates the set of all asset values for branches in Brooklyn. The > **some** comparison in the **where** clause of the outer **select** is true if the *assets* value of the tuple is greater than at least one member of the set of all asset values for branches in Brooklyn.

SQL also allows < **some**, ≤ **some**, ≥ **some**, = **some**, and ≠ **some** comparisons. As an exercise, verify that = **some** is identical to **in**. The keyword **any** is synonymous to **some** in SQL. Early versions of SQL allowed only **any**. Later versions added the alternative **some** to avoid the linguistic ambiguity of the word *any* in English.

Now let us modify our query slightly. Let us find the names of all branches that have greater assets than all branches in Brooklyn. The construct > **all** corresponds to the phrase "greater than all." Using this construct, we write the query as follows:

> **select** *branch-name*
> **from** *branch*
> **where** *assets* > **all**
>   (**select** *assets*
>   **from** *branch*
>   **where** *branch-city* = "Brooklyn")

As is the case for **some**, SQL allows < **all**, ≤ **all**, ≥ **all**, = **all**, and ≠ **all** comparisons.

The constructs **in**, > **some**, > **all**, and so on, allow us to test a single value against members of an entire set. Since a **select** generates a set of tuples, we may, at times, want to compare sets to determine if one set contains all the members of some other set. Such comparisons are made in SQL using the **contains** and **not contains** constructs.

Consider the query "Find all customers who have an account at all branches located in Brooklyn." For each customer, we need to see if the set of all branches at which that customer has an account contains the set of all branches in Brooklyn. The query can be written as follows:

> **select distinct** *S.customer-name*
> **from** *deposit S*
> **where** (**select** *T.branch-name*
>   **from** *deposit T*
>   **where** *S.customer-name* = *T.customer-name*)
> **contains**
> (**select** *branch-name*
>   **from** *branch*
>   **where** *branch-city* = "Brooklyn")

The subquery

> (**select** *branch-name*
>   **from** *branch*
>   **where** *branch-city* = "Brooklyn")

finds all the branches in Brooklyn. The subquery

> (**select** *T.branch-name*
> **from** *deposit T*
> **where** *S.customer-name* = *T.customer-name*)

finds all the branches at which customer *S.customer-name* has an account. Thus, the outer **select** takes each customer and tests whether the set of all branches at which that customer has an account contains the set of all branches in Brooklyn.

The **contains** construct was introduced in the original System R Sequel language. It was dropped from later implementations, and it does not appear in the ANSI standard. A likely reason is that processing the **contains** construct is extremely expensive computationally.

4.1.8 Testing for Empty Relations

SQL includes a feature for testing whether a subquery has any tuples in its result. The **exists** construct returns the value **true** if the argument subquery is nonempty. Using the **exists** construct, we can write the query "Find all customers who have both an account and a loan at the Perryridge branch" in still another way:

> **select** *customer-name*
> **from** *customer*
> **where exists** (**select** *
>   **from** *deposit*
>   **where** *deposit.customer-name* =
>   *customer.customer-name* **and**
>   *branch-name* = "Perryridge")
>   **and exists** (**select** *
>   **from** *borrow*
>   **where** *borrow.customer-name* =
>   *customer.customer-name* **and**
>   *branch-name* = "Perryridge")

The first **exists** subquery tests whether the customer has an account at the Perryridge branch. The second **exists** subquery tests whether the customer has a loan from the Perryridge branch.

The nonexistence of tuples in a subquery can be tested by using the **not exists** construct. Returning to an earlier query, we may write "Find all customers of the Perryridge branch who have an account there but no loan there" as follows:

> **select** *customer-name*
> **from** *customer*
> **where exists (select** *
>   **from** *deposit*
>   **where** *deposit.customer-name* =
>   *customer.customer-name* **and**
>   *branch-name* = "Perryridge")
>   **and not exists (select** *
>   **from** *borrow*
>   **where** *borrow.customer-name* =
>   *customer.customer-name* **and**
>   *branch-name* = "Perryridge")

As a final example, consider again the query "Find all customers who have an account at all branches located in Brooklyn." For each customer, we need to see if the set of all branches at which that customer has an account contains the set of all branches in Brooklyn. Using the **minus** construct, we can write the query as follows:

> **select distinct** *S.customer-name*
> **from** *deposit S*
> **where not exists ((select** *branch-name*
>   **from** *branch*
>   **where** *branch-city* = "Brooklyn")
>   **minus**
>   **(select** *T.branch-name*
>   **from** *deposit T*
>   **where** *S.customer-name* = *T.customer-name*))

The subquery

> **(select** *branch-name*
> **from** *branch*
> **where** *branch-city* = "Brooklyn")

finds all the branches in Brooklyn. The subquery

> **(select** *T.branch-name*
> **from** *deposit T*
> **where** *S.customer-name* = *T.customer-name*)

finds all the branches at which customer *S.customer-name* has an account. Thus, the outer **select** takes each customer and tests whether the set of all branches located in Brooklyn minus the set of all branches at which that customer has an account, is empty.

4.1.9 Ordering the Display of Tuples

SQL offers the user some control over the order in which tuples in a relation are displayed. The **order by** clause causes the tuples in the result of a query to appear in sorted order. To list in alphabetic order all customers having a loan at the Perryridge branch, we write

> **select distinct** *customer-name*
> **from** *borrow*
> **where** *branch-name* = "Perryridge"
> **order by** *customer-name*

By default, SQL lists items in ascending order. To specify the sort order, we may specify **desc** for descending order or **asc** for ascending order. Furthermore, ordering can be performed on multiple attributes. Suppose that we wish to list the entire *borrow* relation in descending order of *amount*. If several loans have the same amount, we order them in ascending order by loan number. We express this in SQL as follows:

> **select** *
> **from** *borrow*
> **order by** *amount* **desc**, *loan-number* **asc**

In order to fulfill an **order by** request, SQL must perform a sort. Since sorting a large number of tuples may be costly, it is desirable to sort only when necessary.

4.1.10 Aggregate Functions

SQL offers the ability to compute functions on groups of tuples using the **group by** clause. The attribute or attributes given in the **group by** clause are used to form groups. Tuples with the same value on all attributes in the **group by** clause are placed in one group. SQL includes functions to compute:

- average: **avg**
- minimum: **min**
- maximum: **max**
- total: **sum**
- count: **count**

Operations like **avg** are called *aggregate functions* because they operate on aggregates of tuples. The result of an aggregate function is a single value. To illustrate, consider the query "Find the average account balance at each branch." We write this as follows:

> **select** *branch-name*, **avg** (*balance*)
> **from** *deposit*
> **group by** *branch-name*

The retention of duplicates is important in computing an average. Suppose the account balances at the Brighton branch are $1000, $3000, $2000, and $1000. The average balance is $7000/4 = $1750.00. If duplicates were eliminated, we would obtain the wrong answer ($6000/3 = $2000).

There are cases where duplicates must be eliminated prior to computing an aggregate function. If we do want to eliminate duplicates, we use the keyword **distinct** in the aggregate expression. An example arises in the query "Find the number of depositors for each branch." In this case, a depositor counts only once regardless of the number of accounts the depositor may have. We write this query as follows:

> **select** *branch-name*, **count** (**distinct** *customer-name*)
> **from** *deposit*
> **group by** *branch-name*

At times it is useful to state a condition that applies to groups rather than to tuples. For example, we might be interested only in branches where the average account balance is more than $1200. This condition does not apply to a single tuple. Rather, it applies to each group constructed by the **group by** clause. To express such a query, we use the **having** clause of SQL. Predicates in the **having** clause are applied after the formation of groups, so aggregate functions may be used. We express this query in SQL as follows:

> **select** *branch-name*, **avg** (*balance*)
> **from** *deposit*
> **group by** *branch-name*
> **having avg** (*balance*) > 1200

As another example of the use of aggregate functions, consider the query "Find those branches with the highest average balance." Aggregate functions cannot be composed in SQL. This means that any attempt to use **max** (**avg** (· · ·)) will not be allowed. Instead, our strategy is to find those branches for which the average balance is greater than or equal to all average balances:

> **select** *branch-name*
> **from** *deposit*
> **group by** *branch-name*
> **having avg** (*balance*) $\geq$ **all** (**select avg** (*balance*)
>   **from** *deposit*
>   **group by** *branch-name*)

At times, we wish to treat the entire relation as a single group. In such cases, we do not use a **group by** clause. Consider the query "Find the average balance in all accounts." We write this as follows:

> **select avg** (*balance*)
> **from** *deposit*

The aggregate function **count** is used frequently to count the number of tuples in a relation. The notation for this in SQL is **count** (*). Thus, to find the number of tuples in the *customer* relation, we write

> **select count** (*)
> **from** *customer*

If a **where** clause and a **having** clause appear in the same query, the predicate in the **where** clause is applied first. Tuples satisfying the **where** predicate are then placed into groups by the **group by** clause. The **having** clause is then applied to each group. The groups that satisfy the **having** clause predicate are used by the **select** clause to generate tuples of the result of the query. If there is no **having** clause, the entire set of tuples satisfying the **where** clause is treated as a single group.

To illustrate the use of both a **having** clause and a **where** clause in the same query, consider the query "Find the average balance of all depositors who live in Harrison and have at least 3 accounts."

> **select avg** (*balance*)
> **from** *deposit, customer*
> **where** *deposit.customer-name* = *customer.customer-name* **and**
>   *customer-city* = "Harrison"
> **group by** *deposit.customer-name*
> **having count** (**distinct** *account-number*) $\geq$ 3

The ANSI standard version of SQL requires that **count** be used only as either **count** (*) or **count** (**distinct** $\cdots$). It is legal to use **distinct** with **max** and **min** even though the result does not change. The keyword **all** can be used in place of **distinct** to specify duplicate retention, but since **all** is the default there is no need to do so.

4.1.11 The Power of SQL

SQL is as powerful in expressiveness as the relational algebra (which, as we said earlier, is equivalent in power to the relational calculus). SQL includes the fundamental relational algebra operations. Cartesian product is represented by the **from** clause of SQL. Projection is performed in the **select** clause. Algebra selection predicates are represented in the **where** clause. Both the relational algebra and SQL include union and difference. SQL allows intermediate results to be stored in temporary relations. Thus, we may encode any relational algebra expression in SQL.

We noted that **minus** and **intersect** are not part of the SQL standard. It is still possible to express these operations by the **in** and **not in** constructs of SQL, as we showed in Section 4.1.10.

SQL offers a rich collection of features, including aggregate functions, ordering of tuples, and other capabilities not included in the formal query languages. Thus, SQL is strictly more powerful than the relational algebra.

Many SQL implementations allow SQL queries to be submitted from a program written in a general-purpose language such as Pascal, PL/I, Fortran, C, or Cobol. This embedded form of SQL extends the programmer's ability to manipulate the database even further. Embedded SQL is discussed in Chapter 17.

SQL is not as powerful as a general-purpose programming language. That is, there exist queries that can be expressed in a language such as Pascal, C, Cobol, or Fortran that cannot be expressed in SQL. For such queries, SQL must be embedded within a more powerful language, or an alternative language must be used. In Chapter 14, we discuss the limitations of SQL and other relational languages, and present a more powerful language based on the logic programming paradigm.

4.1.12 Modifying the Database

We have restricted our attention until now to the extraction of information from the database. We show now how to add, remove, or change information using SQL.

Deletion

A delete request is expressed in much the same way as a query. We may delete only whole tuples; we cannot delete values on only particular attributes. In SQL, a deletion is expressed by

$$\textbf{delete } r$$
$$\textbf{where } P$$

P represents a predicate and r represents a relation. Those tuples t in r for which $P(t)$ is true are deleted from r.

We note that a **delete** command operates on only one relation. If we want to delete tuples from several relations, we must use one **delete** command for each relation. The predicate in the **where** clause may be as complex as a **select** command's **where** clause. At the other extreme, we can have an empty **where** clause. The request

delete *borrow*

deletes all tuples from the borrow relation. (Well-designed systems will seek confirmation from the user before executing such a devastating request.)

We give some examples of SQL delete requests

- Delete all of Smith's account records.

delete *deposit*
where *customer-name* = "Smith"

- Delete all loans with loan numbers between 1300 and 1500.

delete *borrow*
where *loan-number* **between** 1300 **and** 1500

- Delete all accounts at branches located in Perryridge.

delete *deposit*
where *branch-name* **in** (**select** *branch-name*
          from *branch*
          where *branch-city* = "Perryridge")

The above **delete** request first finds all branches in Perryridge, and then deletes all *deposit* tuples pertaining to those branches.

Note that although we may delete tuples from only one relation at a time, we may reference any number of relations in a **select-from-where** embedded in the **where** clause of a **delete**.

If the **delete** request contains an embedded **select** that references the relation from which tuples are to be deleted, we face potential anomalies. Suppose we want to delete the records of all accounts with balances below the average. We might write

delete *deposit*
where *balance* < (**select avg** (*balance*)
          from *deposit*)

However, as we delete tuples from *deposit*, the average balance changes! If we reevaluate the **select** for each tuple in *deposit*, the final result will depend upon the order in which we process tuples of *deposit*!

The SQL standard deals with this by simply disallowing delete requests like the one above. An alternative not included in the standard is the following simple rule. During the execution of a **delete** request, we only mark tuples to be deleted; we do not actually delete them. Once we have finished processing the request — that is, once we are done marking tuples — then we delete all marked tuples. This rule guarantees a consistent interpretation of deletion. Thus, our delete request above does, in fact, work the way we would hope and expect.

Insertion

To insert data into a relation, we either specify a tuple to be inserted or write a query whose result is a set of tuples to be inserted. Obviously, the attribute values for inserted tuples must be members of the attribute's domain. Similarly, tuples inserted must be of the correct arity.

The simplest **insert** statement is a request to insert one tuple. Suppose we wish to insert the fact that Smith has $1200 in account 9732 at the Perryridge branch. We write

> **insert into** *deposit*
> **values** ("Perryridge", 9732, "Smith", 1200)

In the above example, the values are specified in the order in which the corresponding attributes are listed in the relation scheme. For the benefit of users who may not remember the order of the attributes, SQL allows the attributes to be specified as part of the **insert** statement. The following are SQL **insert** statements identical in function to the one above:

> **insert into** *deposit (branch-name, account-number,*
> *customer-name, balance)*
> **values** ("Perryridge", 9732, "Smith", 1200)

> **insert into** *deposit (account-number, customer-name,*
> *branch-name, balance)*
> **values** (9732, "Smith","Perryridge", 1200)

More generally, we might want to insert tuples based on the result of a query. Suppose that we want to provide all loan customers in the Perryridge branch with a $200 savings account. Let the loan number serve as the account number for the new savings account. We write

> **insert into** *deposit*
>   **select** *branch-name, loan-number, customer-name,* 200
>   **from** *borrow*
>   **where** *branch-name* = "Perryridge"

Instead of specifying a tuple as we did earlier, we use a **select** to specify a set of tuples. Each tuple has the *branch-name* (Perryridge), a *loan-number* (which serves as the account number for the new account), the name of the loan customer who is being given the new account, and the initial balance of the new account ($200).

The SQL standard prohibits the embedded **select** from referencing the relations into which tuples are being inserted. (Recall what happened earlier in our attempt to delete those accounts with balances below average.) The potential problem here is that a request such as

> **insert into** *deposit*
>   **select** *
>   **from** *deposit*

might insert an infinite number of tuples. Therefore, such insertions are prohibited.

Updates

In certain situations we may wish to change a value in a tuple without changing *all* values in the tuple. For this purpose the **update** statement can be used. As was the case for **insert** and **delete**, we may choose the tuples to be updated using a query.

Suppose interest payments are being made, and all balances are to be increased by 5 percent. We write

> **update** *deposit*
> **set** *balance* = *balance* * 1.05

The above statement is applied once to each tuple in *deposit*.

Let us now suppose that accounts with balances over $10,000 receive 6 percent interest, while all others receive 5 percent. We write two **update** statements:

> **update** *deposit*
> **set** *balance* = *balance* * 1.06
> **where** *balance* > 10000

> **update** *deposit*
> **set** *balance* = *balance* * 1.05
> **where** *balance* ≤ 10000

Note that, as we saw in Chapter 3, the order in which the two **update** statements are written is important. If we changed the order of the two statements, an account whose balance is just under $10,000 would receive 11.3 percent interest.

In general, the **where** clause of the **update** statement may contain any construct legal in the **where** clause of the **select** statement (including nested **selects**). As is the case for **insert** and **delete**, any **select** embedded in the **where** clause of an **update** must not reference the relation that is being updated. To see why this rule is included in SQL, consider the request "Pay 5 percent interest on accounts whose balance is greater than average." We might write this as follows:

> **update** *deposit*
> **set** *balance* = *balance* * 1.05
> **where** *balance* > **select avg** (*balance*)
>   **from** *deposit*

As we saw in earlier examples, this is an ambiguous request. The result would depend on the order in which tuples are processed. Therefore, such updates are disallowed.

4.1.13 Null Values

Our discussion of the **insert** statement considered only examples in which a value is given for every attribute in inserted tuples. It is possible, as we saw in Chapter 3, for inserted tuples to be given values on only some attributes of the scheme. The remaining attributes are assigned a null value denoted by *null*. Consider the request:

> **insert into** *deposit*
>   **values** ("Perryridge", *null*, "Smith", 1200)

We know that Smith has $1200 in an account at the Perryridge branch, but the account number is not known. Consider the query:

> **select** *
> **from** *deposit*
> **where** *account-number* = 1700

Since the account number of Smith's $1200 account at the Perryridge branch is not known, it cannot be determined whether it is equal to 1700.

All comparisons involving *null* are **false** by definition. However, the special keyword **null** may be used in a predicate to test for a null value. Thus, to find all customers who appear in the *borrow* relation with null values for *amount*, we write:

> **select distinct** *customer-name*
> **from** *borrow*
> **where** *amount* **is null**

The predicate **is not null** tests for the absence of a null value.

The existence of null values also complicates the processing of aggregate operators. Assume that some tuples in the *borrow* relation have a null value for *amount*. Consider the following query to total all loan amounts:

> **select sum** (*amount*)
> **from** *borrow*

The values to be summed in the above query include null values, since some tuples have a null value for *amount*. It is not possible to perform addition using *null*. Therefore, we need a special rule for handling aggregate functions when null values occur. Similar problems arise using other aggregate functions. As a result, all aggregate operations except **count** ignore tuples with null values on the argument attributes. It is possible to prohibit the insertion of null values using the SQL data definition language, which we discuss in Section 4.1.15.

4.1.14 Views

A view is defined in SQL using the **create view** command. To define a view, we must give the view a name and state the query that computes the view. The form of the **create view** command is

> **create view** *v* **as** <query expression>

where <query expression> is any legal query expression. The view name is represented by *v*. Observe that the notation we used for view definition in the relational algebra (see Chapter 3) is based on that of SQL.

As an example, consider the view consisting of branch names and the names of customers. Assume we wish this view to be called *all-customer*. We define this view as follows:

> **create view** *all-customer* **as**
>   (**select** *branch-name, customer-name*
>   **from** *deposit*)
>   **union**
>   (**select** *branch-name, customer-name*
>   **from** *borrow*)

View names may appear in any place that a relation name may appear. Using the view *all-customer*, we can find all customers of the Perryridge branch by writing

> **select** *customer-name*
> **from** *all-customer*
> **where** *branch-name* = "Perryridge"

The view update anomaly we discussed in Chapter 3 exists also in SQL. To illustrate, consider the following view definition:

> **create view** *loan-info* **as**
> **select** *branch-name, loan-number, customer-name*
> **from** *borrow*

Since SQL allows a view name to appear wherever a relation name is allowed, we may write

> **insert into** *loan-info*
> **values** ("Perryridge", 3, "Ruth")

This insertion is represented by an insertion into the relation *borrow*, since *borrow* is the actual relation from which the view *loan-info* is constructed. We must, therefore, have some value for *amount*. This value is a null value. Thus the above **insert** results in the insertion of the tuple

> ("Perryridge", 3, "Ruth", *null*)

into the *borrow* relation.

As we saw in Chapter 3, the view update anomaly becomes more difficult to handle when a view is defined in terms of several relations. As a result, many SQL-based database systems impose the following constraint on modifications allowed through views:

- A modification is permitted through a view only if the view in question is defined in terms of one relation of the actual relational database — that is, the conceptual-level database.

Under this constraint, **update**, **insert**, and **delete** operations would be forbidden on the example view *all-customer* that we defined above.

4.1.15 Data Definition

In most of our discussions concerning SQL and relational databases, we have accepted a set of relations as given. Of course, the set of relations in a database must be specified to the system by means of a data definition language (DDL).

The SQL DDL allows the specification of not only a set of relations but also information about each relation, including:

- The scheme for each relation.

- The domain of values associated with each attribute.

- The set of indices to be maintained for each relation.

- Security and authorization information for each relation.

- Integrity constraints.

- The physical storage structure of each relation on disk.

We shall discuss scheme definition here, and defer discussion of the other SQL DDL features to later chapters.

An SQL relation is defined using the **create table** command:

$$\textbf{create table } r\ (A_1\ D_1,\ A_2\ D_2,\ \ldots,\ A_n\ D_n)$$

where r is the name of the relation, each A_i is the name of an attribute in the scheme of relation r, and D_i is the data type of values in the domain of attribute A_i. The **create table** command also includes options to specify certain integrity constraints. We discuss domain types and integrity in Chapter 5.

A newly created relation is empty initially. The **insert** command can be used to load data into the relation. Many relational database products have special bulk loader utilities to load an initial set of tuples into a relation.

To remove a relation from an SQL database, we use the **drop table** command. The **drop table** command deletes all information about the dropped relation from the database. The command

$$\textbf{drop table } r$$

is a more drastic action than

$$\textbf{delete } r$$

The latter retains relation r, but deletes all tuples in r. The former deletes not only all tuples of r but also the scheme for r. After r is dropped, no tuples can be inserted into r unless it is re-created using the **create table** command.

The **alter table** command is used to add attributes to an existing relation. All tuples in the relation are assigned *null* as the value for the new attribute. The form of the **alter table** command is

alter table *r* **add** *A D*

where *r* is the name of an existing relation, *A* is the name of the attribute to be added, and *D* is the domain of the added attribute. The **alter** command appears in some SQL versions, including IBM SAA-SQL, but not in the SQL standard.

4.2 Query-by-Example

Query-by-Example (QBE) is the name of both a data manipulation language and the database system which includes this language. The QBE database system was developed at IBM's T. J. Watson Research Center in the early 1970s. This system is no longer in use, but its data manipulation language is part of IBM's Query Management Facility (QMF). In this section we consider only the data manipulation language. There are two distinctive features of QBE.

- Unlike most query languages and programming languages, QBE has a *two-dimensional* syntax. A query in a one-dimensional language (for example, SQL) *can* be written in one (possibly very long) line. A two-dimensional language *requires* two dimensions for its expression. (There is a one-dimensional version of QBE, but we shall not consider it in our discussion).

- QBE queries are expressed "by example." Instead of giving a procedure for obtaining the desired answer, the user gives an example of what is desired. The system generalizes this example to compute the answer to the query.

Despite these unusual features, there is a close correspondence between QBE and the domain relational calculus.

4.2.1 Basic Structure

Queries in QBE are expressed using *skeleton tables*. These tables show the relation scheme, as presented in Figure 4.1. Rather than clutter the display with all skeletons, the user selects those skeletons needed for a given query and fills in the skeletons with "example rows." An example row consists of constants and "example elements" which are really domain variables. To avoid confusion, in QBE domain variables are preceded by an underscore character (_), as in _ *x*, and constants appear without any

branch	branch-name	assets	branch-city

customer	customer-name	street	customer-city

borrow	branch-name	loan-number	customer-name	amount

deposit	branch-name	account-number	customer-name	balance

Figure 4.1   QBE skeleton tables for the bank example.

qualification. This is in contrast to most other languages, in which constants are quoted and variables appear without any qualification.

4.2.2 Simple Queries

To find all customers having an account at the Perryridge branch, we bring up the skeleton for the *deposit* relation and fill it in as follows:

deposit	branch-name	account-number	customer-name	balance
	Perryridge		P. _ x	

The above query causes the system to look for tuples in *deposit* that have "Perryridge" as the value for the *branch-name* attribute. For each such tuple, the value of the *customer-name* attribute is assigned to the variable x. The value of the variable x is "printed" (actually displayed) because the command P. appears in the *customer-name* column next to the variable *x*. Observe that this is similar to what would be done to answer the domain relational calculus query

$$\{<x> \mid \exists\, b, l, a\ (<b, l, x, a> \in\ deposit \wedge b = \text{``Perryridge''})\}$$

QBE assumes that a blank position in a row contains a unique variable. As a result, if a variable does not appear more than once in a query, it may be omitted. Our previous query could thus be rewritten as:

deposit	branch-name	account-number	customer-name	balance
	Perryridge		P.	

QBE performs duplicate elimination automatically (unlike SQL). To suppress duplicate elimination, the command ALL. is inserted after the P. command.

deposit	branch-name	account-number	customer-name	balance
	Perryridge		P.ALL.	

To display the entire *deposit* relation, we can create a single row consisting of P. in every field. Alternatively, we can use a shorthand notation by placing a single P. in the column headed by the relation name:

deposit	branch-name	account-number	customer-name	balance
P.				

QBE allows queries that involve arithmetic comparisons (for example, >) rather than an equality comparison, as in "Find the account number of all accounts with a balance of more than $1200":

deposit	branch-name	account-number	customer-name	balance
		P.		>1200

Comparisons may involve only one arithmetic expression on the right-hand side of the comparison operation (for example, $> (\_x + \_y - 20)$). The expression may include both variables and constants. The space on the left-hand side of the comparison operation must be blank. The arithmetic operations that QBE supports are $=$, $<$, $\leq$, $>$, $\geq$, and $\neg$.

Note that restricting the right-hand side to a single arithmetic expression implies that we cannot compare two distinct named variables. We shall deal with this difficulty shortly.

As another example, consider the query "Find the names of all branches that are not located in Brooklyn." This query can be written as follows:

branch	branch-name	assets	branch-city
	P.		¬ Brooklyn

The primary purpose of variables in QBE is to force values of certain tuples to have the same value on certain attributes. Consider the query "Find all customers having an account at both the Perryridge branch and the Redwood branch":

deposit	branch-name	account-number	customer-name	balance
	Perryridge		P. _ x	
	Redwood		_ x	

To execute the above query, the system finds two distinct tuples in *deposit* that agree on the *customer-name* attribute, where the value for the *branch-name* attribute is "Perryridge", for one tuple and "Redwood" for the other. The value of the *customer-name* attribute is then displayed.

Contrast the above query with "Find all customers having an account at the Perryridge branch, the Redwood branch, or both," which can be written as:

deposit	branch-name	account-number	customer-name	balance
	Perryridge		P. _ x	
	Redwood		P. _ y	

The critical distinction between these two queries is the use of the same domain variable (x) for both rows in the former query, but, distinct domain variables $(x$ and $y)$ in the latter query. Note that in the domain relational calculus, the former query would be written as

$$\{<x> \mid \exists\, b,a,n\ (<b,a,x,n> \in deposit \land b = \text{"Perryridge"})$$
$$\land \exists\, b,a,n\ (<b,a,x,n> \in deposit \land b = \text{"Redwood"})\}$$

while the latter query would be written as

$$\{<x> \mid \exists\, b,a,n\ (<b,a,x,n> \in deposit \land b = \text{"Perryridge"})$$
$$\lor \exists\, b,a,n\ (<b,a,x,n> \in deposit \land b = \text{"Redwood"})\}$$

As another example, consider the query "Find all customers who have an account at the same branch at which Jones has as account":

deposit	branch-name	account-number	customer-name	balance
	_ x		Jones	
	_ x		P. _ y	

4.2.3 Queries on Several Relations

QBE allows queries that span over several different relations (analogous to cartesian product or natural join in the relational algebra). The connections among the various relations are achieved through variables that force certain tuples to have the same value on certain attributes. To illustrate, suppose we want to find the name and city of all customers who have a loan from the Perryridge branch. This can be written as:

borrow	branch-name	loan-number	customer-name	amount
	Perryridge		_ x	

customer	customer-name	street	customer-city
	P. _ x		P. _ y

To evaluate the above query, the system finds tuples in *borrow* with "Perryridge" as the value for the *branch-name* attribute. For each such tuple, the system finds tuples in *customer* with the same value for the *customer-name* attribute as the *borrow* tuple. The values for the *customer-name* and *customer-city* attributes are displayed.

A technique similar to the one above can be used to write the query "Find the name of all customers who have both an account and a loan at the Perryridge branch":

deposit	branch-name	account-number	customer-name	balance
	Perryridge		P. _ x	

borrow	branch-name	loan-number	customer-name	amount
	Perryridge		_ x	

Let us now consider the query "Find the name of all customers who have an account at the Perryridge branch but do not have a loan from that branch." Queries that involve negation are expressed in QBE by placing a **not** sign (¬) under the relation name and next to an example row.

deposit	branch-name	account-number	customer-name	balance
	Perryridge		P. _ x	

borrow	branch-name	loan-number	customer-name	amount
¬	Perryridge		_ x	

Compare the above query with our earlier query "Find the name of all customers who have both an account and a loan at the Perryridge branch." The only difference is the ¬ appearing next to the example row in the *borrow* skeleton. This difference, however, has a major effect on the processing of the query. QBE finds all *x* values for which

1. There is a tuple in the *deposit* relation in which *branch-name* is "Perryridge" and *customer-name* is the domain variable *x*.

2. There is no tuple in the *borrow* relation in which *branch-name* is "Perryridge" and *customer-name* is the same as in the domain variable *x*.

The ¬ can be read as "there does not exist."

The fact that we placed the ¬ under the relation name rather than under an attribute name is important. Use of a ¬ under an attribute name is a shorthand for ≠. To find all customers who have accounts at two different branches, we write:

deposit	branch-name	account-number	customer-name	balance
	_ y		P. _ x	
	¬ _ y		_ x	

In English, the above query reads "Display all *customer-name* values that appear in at least two tuples, with the second tuple having a *branch-name* different from the first."

4.2.4 The Condition Box

At times it is either inconvenient or impossible to express all the constraints on the domain variables within the skeleton tables, since comparisons may not involve two distinct variables. To overcome this difficulty, QBE includes a *condition box* feature that allows the expression of such constraints. Suppose we modify the above query to "Find all customers not named 'Jones' who have accounts at two different branches." We want to include an "*x* ≠ Jones" constraint in the above query. We do that by bringing up the condition box and entering the constraint "$x \neg=$ Jones":

conditions
$x \neg=$ Jones

To find all account numbers with a balance between $1,300 and $1,500, we write:

deposit	branch-name	account-number	customer-name	balance
		P.		_ x

conditions
_ $x \geq 1300$
_ $x \leq 1500$

As another example, consider the query "Find all branches that have greater assets than some branch located in Brooklyn." This query can be written as:

branch	branch-name	assets	branch-city
	P. _ x	_ y	
		_ z	Brooklyn

conditions
_ $y >$ _ z

QBE allows complex arithmetic expressions to appear in a condition box. The query "Find all branches that have assets that are at least twice as much as the assets of some branch located in Brooklyn" can be written similarly to the above query by modifying the condition box to

conditions
_ $y \geq 2 *$ _ z

QBE also allows logical expressions to appear in a condition box. The logical operators are the words **and** and **or**, or the symbols & and |. To find all account numbers with a balance between $1,300 and $2,000 but not $1,500, we write:

deposit	branch-name	account-number	customer-name	balance
		P.		_ x

conditions
_ x = (≥ 1300 **and** ≤ 2000 **and** ¬ 1500)

QBE includes an unconventional use of the **or** construct to allow comparison with a set of constant values. To find all branches that are located in either Brooklyn or Queens, we write:

branch	branch-name	assets	branch-city
	P.		_ x

conditions
_ x = (Brooklyn **or** Queens)

4.2.5 The Result Relation

The queries we have written thus far have one thing in common: The results to be displayed appear in a single relation scheme. If the result of a query includes attributes from several relation schemes, we need a mechanism to display the desired result in a single table. To accomplish this, we can declare a temporary *result* relation which includes all the attributes of the result of the query. Printing of the desired result is done by including the command P. only in the *result* skeleton table.

To illustrate, consider the query "Find the *customer-name, customer-city,* and *account-number* for all customers having an account at the Perryridge branch." In the relational algebra we would accomplish this as follows:

1. Join *deposit* and *customer*.

2. Project *customer-name, customer-city,* and *account-number*.

To accomplish this in QBE, we:

1. Create a skeleton table, called *result*, with attributes *customer-name, customer-city,* and *account-number*. The name of the newly created skeleton table (that is, *result*) must be different from any of the previously existing database relation names.

2. Write the query.

The resulting query is:

deposit	branch-name	account-number	customer-name	balance
	Perryridge	_z	_x	

customer	customer-name	street	customer-city
	_x		_y

result	customer-name	customer-city	account-number
P.	_x	_y	_z

4.2.6 Ordering the Display of Tuples

QBE offers the user some control over the order in which tuples in a relation are displayed. This can be accomplished by inserting either the command AO. (ascending order) or the command DO. (descending order) in the appropriate column. Thus, to list in ascending alphabetic order all customers who have an account at the Perryridge branch, we write:

deposit	branch-name	account-number	customer-name	balance
	Perryridge		P.AO.	

QBE provides a mechanism for sorting and displaying data in multiple columns. The order in which the sorting should be carried out is specified by including with each sort operator (AO or DO) an integer surrounded by parentheses. Thus, to list all customers of the bank in ascending alphabetic order with their respective account balances in descending order, we write:

deposit	branch-name	account-number	customer-name	balance
			P.AO(1).	P.DO(2).

The command P.AO(1). specifies that the customer name should be sorted first, while the command P.DO(2). specifies that the balances for each customer should be then sorted.

4.2.7 Aggregate Operations

QBE includes the aggregate operators AVG, MAX, MIN, SUM, and CNT. These operators must be postfixed with ALL. to ensure that all the appropriate values are considered (recall that QBE eliminates duplicates by default). Thus, to find the total balance of all the accounts belonging to Jones, we write:

deposit	branch-name	account-number	customer-name	balance
			Jones	P.SUM.ALL.

Suppose that we wish to eliminate duplicates when an aggregate operator is used. Since all aggregate operators must be postfixed with ALL, a new operator, UNQ, must be added to specify that we want duplicates eliminated. Thus, to find the total number of customers having an account at the Perryridge branch, we write:

deposit	branch-name	account-number	customer-name	balance
	Perryridge		P.CNT.UNQ.ALL.	

QBE also offers the ability to compute functions on groups of tuples using the G. operator, which is analogous to SQL's **group by** construct. Thus, to find the average balance at each branch, we may write:

deposit	branch-name	account-number	customer-name	balance
	P.G.			P.AVG.ALL. _ x

The average balance is computed on a branch-by-branch basis. The ALL. in the P.AVG.ALL. entry in the *balance* column ensures that all the balances are considered. If we wish to display the branch names in ascending order, we replace P.G. by P.AO.G.

To find the average account balance at only those branches where the average account balance is more than $1,200, we add the condition box:

conditions
AVG.ALL. _ $x > 1200$

Counting can be used to check for negative information. To find all customers who have an account at the Perryridge branch, but for whom no address is on file, we write:

deposit	branch-name	account-number	customer-name	balance
	Perryridge		P. _ x	

customer	customer-name	street	customer-city
	CNT.ALL. _ x		

conditions
CNT.ALL. _ x = 0

The approach is to count the number of *customer* tuples pertaining to each depositor of the Perryridge branch. If the count is 0 for a depositor, we know that no address is available for that customer.

As a last example, consider the query "Find all customers who have an account at all branches located in Brooklyn":

deposit	branch-name	account-number	customer-name	balance
	CNT.UNQ.ALL. _ y		P.G. _ x	

branch	branch-name	assets	branch-city
	_ y		Brooklyn
	_ z		Brooklyn

conditions
CNT.UNQ.ALL. _ y =
CNT.UNQ.ALL. _ z

The domain variable z can hold the value of names of branches located in Brooklyn. Thus, CNT.UNQ.ALL. _ z is the number of distinct branches in Brooklyn. The domain variable y can hold the value of branches such that both of the following hold:

- The branch is located in Brooklyn.

- The customer whose name is x has an account at the branch.

Thus, CNT.UNQ.ALL. _ y is the number of distinct branches in Brooklyn at which customer x has an account. If CNT.UNQ.ALL. _ y = CNT.UNQ.ALL. _ z, then customer x must have an account at all branches located in Brooklyn. In such a case, x is included in the displayed result (because of the P.).

4.2.8 Modifying the Database

In this section, we show how to add, remove, or change information using QBE.

Deletion

Deletion of tuples from a relation is expressed in much the same way as a query. The major difference is the use of D. in place of P. In QBE (unlike

SQL), we may delete whole tuples as well as values in selected columns. In the case where we delete information in only some of the columns, null values, specified by $-$, are inserted.

We note that a D. command operates on only one relation. If we want to delete tuples from several relations, we must use one D. operator for each relation.

Below are some examples of QBE delete requests.

- Delete all of Smith's account records.

deposit	branch-name	account-number	customer-name	balance
D.			Smith	

- Delete the *branch-city* value of the branch whose name is "Perryridge".

branch	branch-name	assets	branch-city
	Perryridge		D.

Thus, if before the delete operation the *branch* relation contains the tuple (Perryridge, 50000, Brooklyn), the delete results in the replacement of the above tuple with the tuple (Perryridge, 50000, $-$).

- Delete all loans with loan numbers between 1300 and 1500.

borrow	branch-name	loan-number	customer-name	amount
D.		_ x		

conditions
_ x = ($\geq$ 1300 and $\leq$ 1500)

- Delete all accounts at branches located in Brooklyn.

deposit	branch-name	account-number	customer-name	balance
D.	_ x			

branch	branch-name	assets	branch-city
	_ x		Brooklyn

Note that although we may delete tuples from only one relation at a time, we may reference any number of relations in a delete operation.

Insertion

To insert data into a relation, we either specify a tuple to be inserted or write a query the result of which is a set of tuples to be inserted. The insertion is done by placing the I. operator in the query expression. Obviously, the attribute values for inserted tuples must be members of the attribute's domain.

The simplest insert is a request to insert one tuple. Suppose we wish to insert the fact that Smith has $1200 in account 9732 at the Perryridge branch. We write:

deposit	branch-name	account-number	customer-name	balance
I.	Perryridge	9732	Smith	1200

We can also insert a tuple which contains only partial information. To insert into the *branch* relation information about a new branch with name "Capital" and city "Queens" but with a null asset value, we write:

branch	branch-name	assets	branch-city
I.	Capital		Queens

More generally, we might want to insert tuples based on the result of a query. Let us consider again the situation where we want to provide all loan customers in the Perryridge branch with a $200 savings account, with the loan number serving as the account number for the new savings account. We write:

deposit	branch-name	account-number	customer-name	balance
I.	Perryridge	_ x	_ y	200

borrow	branch-name	loan-number	customer-name	amount
	Perryridge	_ x	_ y	

To execute the above insertion request, the system must get the appropriate information from the *borrow* relation, and then use that information to insert the appropriate new tuple in the *deposit* relation.

Updates

There are situations in which we wish to change a value in a tuple without changing *all* values in the tuple. For this purpose we use the U. operator. As was the case for insert and delete, we may choose the tuples to be updated using a query. QBE, however, does not allow users to update the primary key fields.

Suppose we update the asset value of the of the Perryridge branch to $10,000,000. This is expressed as

branch	branch-name	assets	branch-city
	Perryridge	U.10000000	

The blank field of attribute *branch-city* implied that no updating of that value is required.

The above query updates the assets of the Perryridge branch to $10,000,000, regardless of its old value. There are circumstances, however, where we need to update a field value using the previous field value. This must be expressed using two rows: one specifying the old tuples that need to be updated, the other indicating the new updated tuples to be inserted in the database.

Suppose interest payments are being made, and all balances are to be increased by 5 percent. We write:

deposit	branch-name	account-number	customer-name	balance
U.				$\_x * 1.05$
				$\_x$

This query specifies that we retrieve one tuple at a time from the *deposit* relation, determine the balance $\_x$, and update that balance to $\_x * 1.05$.

4.3 Quel

Quel was introduced as the query language for the Ingres database system, developed at the University of California, Berkeley. A commercial version of Ingres was developed by Relational Technology, Inc. (now called Ingres, Inc.). The original academic Ingres system offered only the Quel language. The current commercial Ingres offers both Quel and SQL.

4.3.1 Basic Structure

The basic structure of Quel closely parallels that of the tuple relational calculus. Most Quel queries are expressed using three types of clauses: **range of**, **retrieve**, and **where**.

- Each tuple variable is declared in a **range of** clause. We say

    range of *t* **is** *r*

    to declare *t* to be a tuple variable restricted to take on values of tuples in relation *r*.

- The **retrieve** clause is similar in function to the **select** clause of SQL.

- The **where** clause contains the selection predicate.

A typical Quel query is of the form:

$$\textbf{range of } t_1 \textbf{ is } r_1$$
$$\textbf{range of } t_2 \textbf{ is } r_2$$
$$.$$
$$.$$
$$.$$
$$\textbf{range of } t_m \textbf{ is } r_m$$
$$\textbf{retrieve } (t_{i_1}.A_{j_1},\ t_{i_2}.A_{j_2},\ \ldots,\ t_{i_n}.A_{j_n})$$
$$\textbf{where } P$$

Each t_i is a tuple variable, each is a r_i relation, and each A_{j_k} is an attribute. Quel, like SQL, uses the notation

$$t.A$$

to denote the value of tuple variable t on attribute A. This means the same as $t[A]$ in the tuple relational calculus.

Quel does not include relational algebra operations like **intersect**, **union**, and **minus**. Furthermore, Quel does not allow nested subqueries (unlike SQL). That is, we *cannot* have a nested **retrieve-where** clause inside a **where** clause. These limitations do not reduce the expressive power of Quel. Rather, they provide the user with fewer alternative ways of expressing a query.

4.3.2 Simple Queries

Let us return to our bank example, and write some of our earlier queries using Quel. First, we find the name of all customers having an account at the Perryridge branch:

$$\textbf{range of } t \textbf{ is } deposit$$
$$\textbf{retrieve } (t.customer\text{-}name)$$
$$\textbf{where } t.branch\text{-}name = \text{``Perryridge''}$$

The above query does not eliminate duplicates. Thus, the name of a customer with several accounts at the Perryridge branch will appear several times. To remove duplicates, we must add the keyword **unique** to the **retrieve** clause:

$$\textbf{range of } t \textbf{ is } deposit$$
$$\textbf{retrieve unique } (t.customer\text{-}name)$$
$$\textbf{where } t.branch\text{-}name = \text{``Perryridge''}$$

Although duplicate elimination imposes additional overhead in query processing, we shall specify duplicate elimination when necessary in our examples.

To show a Quel query involving more than one relation, let us consider the query "Find the name and city of all customers having a loan at the Perryridge branch."

> **range of** *t* **is** *borrow*
> **range of** *s* **is** *customer*
> **retrieve unique** (*t.customer-name*, *s.customer-city*)
> **where** *t.branch-name* = "Perryridge" **and**
>   *t.customer-name* = *s.customer-name*

Note that Quel, like SQL, uses the logical connectives **and**, **or**, and **not**, rather than the mathematical symbols ∧, ∨, and ¬, as used in the tuple relational calculus. As in SQL, we need to express the join predicate explicitly. Quel does not have a special notation for natural join. Like SQL, it includes pattern-matching comparisons, but we shall not cover them here.

As another example involving two relations, consider the query "Find the name of all customers who have both a loan and an account at the Perryridge branch."

> **range of** *s* **is** *borrow*
> **range of** *t* **is** *deposit*
> **retrieve unique** (*s.customer-name*)
> **where** *t.branch-name* = "Perryridge" **and** *s.branch-name* = "Perryridge"
>   **and** *t.customer-name* = *s.customer-name*

In SQL, we had the option of writing such a query by using the relational algebra operation **intersect**. As we noted above, Quel does not include this operation.

4.3.3 Tuple Variables

For certain queries we need to have two distinct tuple variables ranging over the same relation. Consider the query "Find the name of all customers who have an account at some branch at which Jones has an account." We write this query as follows:

> **range of** *s* **is** *deposit*
> **range of** *t* **is** *deposit*
> **retrieve unique** (*t.customer-name*)
> **where** *s.customer-name* = "Jones" **and**
>   *s.branch-name* = *t.branch-name*

Since the above query requires us to compare tuples pertaining to Jones with every *deposit* tuple, we need two distinct tuple variables ranging over *deposit*. However, it is often the case that a query requires only one tuple variable ranging over a relation. In such cases, we may omit the **range of** statement for that relation and use the relation name itself as an implicitly declared tuple variable. Following this convention, we rewrite the query "Find the name of all customers who have both a loan and an account at the Perryridge branch" as follows:

> **retrieve unique** (*borrow.customer-name*)
> **where** *deposit.branch-name* = "Perryridge" **and**
> *borrow.branch-name* = "Perryridge" **and**
> *deposit.customer-name* = *borrow.customer-name*

The original academic Quel does not allow the use of implicitly declared tuple variables.

4.3.4 Aggregate Functions

Aggregate functions in Quel compute functions on groups of tuples. However, they take a form different from that of SQL. In SQL, a **group by** clause is part of the query itself. This results in a single grouping of tuples for all aggregate functions in the query. In Quel, grouping is specified as part of each aggregate expression.

Quel aggregate expressions may take the following forms:

> *aggregate function* (*t.A*)
> *aggregate function* (*t.A* **where** *P*)
> *aggregate function* (*t.A* **by** $s.B_1, s.B_2, \ldots, s.B_n$ **where** *P*)

where *aggregate function* is one of **count, sum, avg, max, min, countu, sumu, avgu,** or **any**; *t* and *s* are tuple variables; $A, B_1, B_2,$ and B_n are attributes; and *P* is a predicate similar to the **where** clause in a **retrieve**. An aggregate expression may appear anywhere a constant may appear. The intuitive meaning of **count, sum, avg, max,** and **min** should be clear. We shall explain **any** later in this section. The functions **countu, sumu,** and **avgu** are identical to **count, sum,** and **avg,** respectively, except that they remove duplicates from their operands.

To find the average account balance for all accounts at the Perryridge branch, we write:

> **range of** *t* **is** *deposit*
> **retrieve avg** (*t.balance* **where** *t.branch-name* = "Perryridge")

Aggregates may appear in the **where** clause. Suppose we wish to find all accounts whose balance is higher than the average of all balances at the bank. We write:

> **range of** *u* **is** *deposit*
> **range of** *t* **is** *deposit*
> **retrieve** (*t.account-number*)
> **where** *t.balance* > **avg** (*u.balance*)

The above **avg** (· · ·) expression computes the average balance of all accounts at the bank.

Let us consider a modification to the above query. Instead of using the average balance at the bank, we consider only the Perryridge branch. Thus, we are finding all accounts whose balance is higher than the average balance of Perryridge-branch accounts. We write this as follows:

> **range of** *u* **is** *deposit*
> **range of** *t* **is** *deposit*
> **retrieve** (*t.account-number*)
> **where** *t.balance* > **avg** (*u.balance* **where** *u.branch-name* = "Perryridge")

Let us modify our query further. We now wish to find all accounts whose balance is higher than the average balance at the branch where the account is held. In this case, we need to compute for each tuple *t* in *deposit* the average balance at branch *t.branch-name*. In order to form these groups of tuples, we need to use the **by** construct in our aggregate expression.

> **range of** *u* **is** *deposit*
> **range of** *t* **is** *deposit*
> **retrieve** (*t.account-number*)
> **where** *t.balance* > **avg** (*u.balance* **by** *t.branch-name*
>   **where** *u.branch-name* = *t.branch-name*)

The effect of the **by** construct in Quel differs from that of the **group by** clause in SQL. The primary source of this distinction is the role of tuple variables. The tuple variable *t* used in **by** is the same one that is used in the rest of the query. However, all other tuple variables are local to the aggregate expression even if a variable with the same name appears elsewhere in the query. Thus, in the above Quel query, if we removed "**by** *t.branch-name*" from the expression, we would turn tuple variable *t* into a local variable of the aggregate expression that is not bound to the tuple variable *t* of the outer query.

Let us consider the query "Find the name of all customers who have an account at the Perryridge branch but do not have a loan from the Perryridge branch." In the relational algebra, we wrote this using the set difference operation. We can write this query in Quel using the **count** aggregate operation if we think of the query as "Find the name of all customers who have an account at the Perryridge branch and for whom the count of the number of loans from the Perryridge branch is zero."

> **range of** *t* **is** *deposit*
> **range of** *u* **is** *borrow*
> **retrieve unique** (*t.customer-name*)
> **where** *t.branch-name* = "Perryridge" **and**
>   **count** (*u.loan-number* **by** *t.customer-name*
>   **where** *u.branch-name* = "Perryridge"
>   **and** *u.customer-name* = *t.customer-name*) = 0

Quel offers another aggregate function that is applicable to this example, called **any**. If we replace **count** in the above query with **any**, we obtain 1 if the count is greater than 0; otherwise, we obtain 0. The **any** function allows faster execution of the query in that processing can stop as soon as one tuple is found. The use of a comparison with **any** is analogous to the "there exists" quantifier of the relational calculus. Thus, we may rewrite our query as

> **range of** *t* **is** *deposit*
> **range of** *u* **is** *borrow*
> **retrieve unique** (*t.customer-name*)
> **where** *t.branch-name* = "Perryridge" **and**
>   **any** (*u.loan-number* **by** *t.customer-name*
>   **where** *u.branch-name* = "Perryridge"
>   **and** *u.customer-name* = *t.customer-name*) = 0

As a more complicated example, consider the query "Find the name of all customers who have an account at all branches located in Brooklyn." Our strategy for expressing this query in Quel is as follows: First find out how many branches there are in Brooklyn. Then compare this number with the number of distinct branches in Brooklyn at which each customer has an account. The **count** aggregate function we used earlier counts duplicates. Therefore, we use the **countu** function, which counts unique values.

> **range of** *t* **is** *deposit*
> **range of** *u* **is** *deposit*
> **range of** *s* **is** *branch*
> **range of** *w* **is** *branch*
> **retrieve unique** (*t.customer-name*)
> **where countu** (*s.branch-name* **by** *t.customer-name*
>   **where** *u.customer-name* = *t.customer-name*
>   **and** *u.branch-name* = *s.branch-name*
>   **and** *s.branch-city* = "Brooklyn") =
>   **countu** (*w.branch-name* **where** *w.branch-city* = "Brooklyn")

We use **by** in the first **countu** expression, since we must restrict consideration to a single customer at a time. However, we do not use **by** in the latter **countu** expression, since we are interested in counting all branches in Brooklyn independent of the bindings of tuple variables external to this **countu** expression.

4.3.5 Modifying the Database

Database modification in Quel is similar to modification in SQL, although the syntax differs slightly.

Deletion

The form of a Quel deletion is

> **range of** t **is** r
> **delete** t
> **where** P

The tuple variable t can be implicitly defined. The predicate P can be any valid Quel predicate. If the **where** clause is omitted, all tuples in the relation are deleted.

Below are some examples of Quel delete requests.

- Delete all tuples in the *borrow* relation.

> **range of** t **is** *borrow*
> **delete** t

- Delete all of Smith's account records.

> **range of** t **is** *deposit*
> **delete** t
> **where** t.*customer-name* = "Smith"

- Delete all accounts at branches located in Needham.

> **range of** t **is** *deposit*
> **range of** u **is** *branch*
> **delete** t
> **where** t.*branch-name* = u.*branch-name*
> **and** u.*branch-city* = "Needham"

Insertion

Insertion in Quel takes two general forms: insertion of a single tuple, and insertion of a set of tuples. Quel uses the keyword **append** for insertion. Here are some examples of Quel insert requests

- Insert the fact that Smith has $1200 in account 9732 at the Perryridge branch.

> **append to** *deposit* (*branch-name* = "Perryridge",
> *account-number* = 9732,
> *customer-name* = "Smith", *balance* = 1200)

- Provide all loan customers in the Perryridge branch with a $200 savings account. Let the loan number serve as the account number for the new savings account.

> **range of** *t* **is** *borrow*
> **append to** *deposit* (*t.branch-name, account-number* = *t.loan-number*,
> *t.customer-name, balance* = 200)
> **where** *t.branch-name* = "Perryridge"

Updates

Updates are expressed in Quel using the **replace** command. Examples of Quel update requests follow.

- Pay 5 percent interest. (Increase all account balances by 5 percent.)

> **range of** *t* **is** *deposit*
> **replace** *t* (*balance* = 1.05 * *t.balance*)

- Pay 6 percent interest on accounts with balances over $10,000, and 5 percent on all other accounts.

> **range of** *t* **is** *deposit*
> **replace** *t* (*balance* = 1.06 * *balance*)
> **where** *t.balance* > 10000
> **replace** *t* (*balance* = 1.05 * *balance*)
> **where** *t.balance* ≤ 10000

Recall that the order of these two interest payments matters for amounts with a balance just under $10000.

4.3.6 Set Operations

Let us consider a query for which we used the **union** operation in SQL: "Find the name of all customers who have an account, a loan, or both at the Perryridge branch." Since we do not have a **union** operation in Quel, and we know that Quel is based on the tuple relational calculus, we might be guided by our tuple relational calculus expression for this query:

$$\{t \mid \exists \ s \ \epsilon \ borrow \ (t[customer\text{-}name] = s[customer\text{-}name]$$
$$\wedge \ s[branch\text{-}name] = \text{``Perryridge''})$$
$$\vee \ \exists \ u \ \epsilon \ deposit \ (t[customer\text{-}name] = u[customer\text{-}name]$$
$$\wedge \ u[branch\text{-}name] = \text{``Perryridge''})\}$$

Unfortunately, the above expression does not lead us to a Quel query. The problem is that in the tuple relational calculus query, we obtain customers from *both* tuple variable *s* (whose range is *borrow*) and tuple variable *u* (whose range is *deposit*). In Quel, our **retrieve** clause must be one of the following:

- **retrieve** *s.customer-name*

- **retrieve** *u.customer-name*

If we choose the former, we exclude those depositors who are not borrowers. If we choose the latter, we exclude those borrowers who are not depositors.

In order to write this query in Quel, we must create a new relation and insert tuples into this new relation. Let us call this new relation *temp*. We obtain all depositors of the Perryridge branch by writing

> **range of** *u* **is** *deposit*
> **retrieve into** *temp* **unique** (*u.customer-name*)
> **where** *u.branch-name* = "Perryridge"

The **into** *temp* clause causes a new relation, *temp*, to be created to hold the result of this query. Now we can find all borrowers of the Perryridge branch and insert them in the newly created relation *temp*. We do this using the **append** command.

> **range of** *s* **is** *borrow*
> **append to** *temp* **unique** (*s.customer-name*)
> **where** *s.branch-name* = "Perryridge"

We now have a relation *temp* containing all customers who have an account, a loan, or both, at the Perryridge branch. Our use of the keyword **unique** in both the **retrieve** and **append** requests ensures that any duplicates have been removed.

The strategy of using **append** allows us to perform unions in Quel. To perform a set difference $r - s$ (**minus** in SQL), we create a temporary relation representing r and delete tuples of this temporary relation that are also in s. To illustrate this strategy, let us reconsider the query, "Find the name of all customers who have an account at the Perryridge branch but do not have a loan from the Perryridge branch." We begin by writing the following to create the temporary relation:

> **range of** *u* **is** *deposit*
> **retrieve into** *temp* (*u.customer-name*)
> **where** *u.branch-name* = "Perryridge"

At this point *temp* has all customers who have an account at the Perryridge branch, including those with a loan from that branch. We now delete those customers who have a loan.

> **range of** *s* **is** *borrow*
> **range of** *t* **is** *temp*
> **delete** (*t*)
> **where** *s.branch-name* = "Perryridge" **and**
>   *t.customer-name* = *s.customer-name*

The relation *temp* contains the desired list of customers. We write

> **range of** *t* **is** *temp*
> **retrieve unique** (*t.customer-name*)

to complete our query.

4.3.7 Quel and the Tuple Relational Calculus

To see more clearly the relationship between Quel and the tuple relational calculus, consider the following Quel query

> **range of** t_1 **is** r_1
> **range of** t_2 **is** r_2
> .
> .
> .
> **range of** t_m **is** r_m
> **retrieve unique** $(t_{i_1}.A_{j_1}, t_{i_2}.A_{j_2}, \ldots, t_{i_n}.A_{j_n})$
> **where** P

The above Quel query would be expressed in the tuple relational calculus as:

$$\{t \mid \exists\ t_1 \in r_1,\ t_2 \in r_2,\ \ldots,\ t_m \in r_m\ ($$
$$t[r_{i_1}.A_{j_1}] = t_{i_1}[A_{j_1}] \wedge t[r_{i_2}.A_{j_2}] = t_{i_2}[A_{j_2}] \wedge \cdots \wedge$$
$$t[r_{i_n}.A_{j_n}] = t_{i_n}[A_{j_n}] \wedge P\ (t_1, t_2, \ldots, t_m))\}$$

This expression can be understood by looking at the formula within the "there exists" formula in three parts:

- $t_1 \in r_1 \wedge t_2 \in r_2 \wedge \cdots \wedge t_m \in r_m$. This part constrains each tuple in $t_1, t_2, \ldots, t_m$ to take on values of tuples in the relation over which it ranges.

- $t[r_{i_1}.A_{j_1}] = t_{i_1}[A_{j_1}] \wedge t_{i_2}[A_{j_2}] = t[r_{i_2}.A_{j_2}] \wedge \cdots \wedge t[r_{i_n}.A_{j_n}] = t_{i_n}[A_{j_n}]$. This part corresponds to the **retrieve** clause of the Quel query. We need to ensure that the kth attribute in tuple t corresponds to the kth entry in the **retrieve** clause. Consider the first entry: $t_{i_1}.A_{j_1}$. This is the value of some tuple of r_{i_1} (since range of t_{i_1} is r_{i_1}) on attribute A_{j_1}. Thus, we need $t[A_{j_1}] = t_{i_1}[A_{j_1}]$. We used the more cumbersome notation $t[r_{i_1}.A_{j_1}] = t_{i_1}[A_{j_1}]$ to be able to deal with the possibility that the same attribute name appears in more than one relation.

- $P(t_1, t_2, \ldots, t_m)$. This part is the constraint on acceptable values for $t_1, t_2, \ldots, t_m$ imposed by the **where** clause in the Quel query.

There is no representation of "for all" and "there does not exist" in the relational calculus formulation for the Quel query above. Quel achieves the power of the relational algebra by means of the **any** aggregate function and the use of insertion and deletion on temporary relations.

4.4 Summary

Commercial database systems do not use the terse, formal query languages of Chapter 3. Instead, they use languages based on the formal languages but including much "syntactic sugar." Commercial languages include constructs for update, insertion, and deletion of information as well as for querying the database. We have considered three languages: SQL, QBE, and Quel. SQL has gained wide acceptance in commercial products and a standard for SQL has been defined.

For each of the three languages, we saw how to express queries and modify the database. Modifications to the database may lead to the generation of null values in tuples. We showed how nulls can be introduced in QBE and SQL, and how the SQL query language handles

lives (person-name, street, city)
works (person-name, company-name, salary)
located-in (company-name, city)
manages (person-name, manager-name)

Figure 4.2   Relational database.

queries on relations containing null values. For SQL, we showed how to define relations and create views. Further details on the SQL data definition language appear in Chapters 5 and 16.

Exercises

4.1 Construct the following SQL queries for the relational database of Exercise 3.3.

   a. Find the total number of persons whose car was involved in an accident in 1989.

   b. Find the number of accidents in which the cars belonging to "John Smith" were involved.

   c. Add a new customer to the database.

   d. Delete the car "Mazda" belonging to "John Smith."

   e. Add a new accident record for the Toyota belonging to "Jones."

4.2 Consider the relational database of Figure 4.2. Give an expression in:

   • SQL

   • QBE

   • Quel

For each of the queries below:

   a. Find the name of all employees who work for First Bank Corporation.

   b. Find the name and city of all employees who work for First Bank Corporation.

   c. Find the name, street, and city of all employees who work for First Bank Corporation and earn more than $10,000.

  d. Find all employees who live in the same city as the company they work for.

  e. Find all employees who live in the same city and on the same street as their manager.

  f. Find all employees who do not work for First Bank Corporation.

  g. Find all employees who earn more than every employee of Small Bank Corporation.

  h. Assume the companies may be located in several cities. Find all companies located in every city in which Small Bank Corporation is located.

  i. Find all employees who earn more than the average salary of all employees of their company.

  j. Find the company with the most employees.

  k. Find the company with the smallest payroll.

  l. Find those companies that pay more, on average, than the average salary at First Bank Corporation.

4.3 Consider the relational database of Figure 4.2. Give an expression in:

  • SQL

  • QBE

  • Quel

For each of the queries below:

  a. Modify the database so that Jones now lives in Newtown.

  b. Give all employees of First Bank Corporation a 10 percent raise.

  c. Give all managers a 10 percent raise.

  d. Give all managers a 10 percent raise unless the salary becomes greater than $100,000. In such cases, give only a 3 percent raise.

  e. Delete all tuples in the *works* relation for employees of Small Bank Corporation.

4.4 Let the following relation schemes be given:

$$R = (A,B,C)$$
$$S = (D,E,F)$$

Let relations $r(R)$ and $s(S)$ be given. Give an expression in:

- SQL
- QBE
- Quel

That is equivalent to each of the queries below:

a. $\Pi_A(r)$

b. $\sigma_{B = 17} (r)$

c. $r \times s$

d. $\Pi_{A,F} (\sigma_{C = D}(r \times s))$

4.5 Let $R = (A,B,C)$ and let r_1 and r_2 both be relations on scheme R. Give an expression in:

- SQL
- QBE
- Quel

That is equivalent to each of the queries below:

a. $\Pi_A(r_1)$

b. $\sigma_{B = 17} (r_1)$

c. $r_1 \cup r_2$

d. $r_1 \cap r_2$

e. $r_1 - r_2$

f. $\Pi_{AB}(r_1) \bowtie \Pi_{BC}(r_2)$

4.6 Let $R = (A,B)$ and $S = (A,C)$, and let $r(R)$ and $s(S)$ be relations. Write an expression in:

- SQL
- QBE
- Quel

For each of the queries below:

a. $\{<a> \mid \exists\, b\, (<a,b> \in r \wedge b = 17)\}$

b. $\{<a,b,c> \mid <a,b> \in r \wedge <a,c> \in s)\}$

c. $\{<b> \mid \forall a \ (<a,b> \notin r \lor \exists c \ (<a,c> \in s))\}$

d. $\{<a> \mid \exists c \ (<a,c> \in s \land \exists b_1, b_2 \ (<a,b_1> \in r$
$\land <c, b_2> \in r \land b_1 > b_2))\}$

4.7 Show that in SQL $\neq$ **all** is identical to **not in**.

4.8 Consider the relational database of Figure 4.2. Using SQL define a view consisting of *manager-name* and the average salary of employees working for that manager. Explain why the database system should not allow updates to be expressed in terms of this view.

Bibliographic Notes

The original version of SQL, called Sequel 2, is described by Chamberlin et al. [1976]. Sequel 2 was derived from the languages Square [Boyce et al. 1975] and Sequel [Chamberlin and Boyce 1974]. The American National Standard SQL is described in ANSI [1986] and Date [1989]. The IBM Systems Application Architecture definition of SQL is defined by IBM [1987]. Date [1984] provides a critique of SQL and suggests ways in which the language could be improved.

Several manuals and books consider SQL as implemented in specific commercial products. These include IBM [1982, 1988] and Date and White [1989] for SQL/DS, and Date and White [1988] and Martin et al. [1989] for DB2.

The experimental version of Query-by-Example is described in Zloof [1977], while the commercial version is described in IBM [1978b].

Quel is defined by Stonebraker et al. [1976], Wong and Youssefi [1976], and Zook et al. [1977]. The commercial version of the Ingres database system is described in RTI [1983], Date [1987], and Malamud [1989]. Stonebraker [1986b] provides a collection of research and survey papers related to the Ingres system.

General discussion of the relation data model appears in most database texts, including Ullman [1988], Date [1990a], and ElMasri and Navathe [1989]. Several relational database systems are surveyed in Valduriez and Gardarin [1989]. McFadyen and Kanabar [1991] is a text devoted to SQL.

Integrity Constraints

Integrity constraints provide a means of ensuring that changes made to the database by authorized users do not result in a loss of data consistency. Thus, integrity constraints guard against accidental damage to the database.

We have already seen a form of integrity constraint for the E-R model in Chapter 2. These constraints were in the form of:

- **Key declarations** — the stipulation that certain attributes form a candidate key for a given entity set. The set of legal insertions and updates are constrained to those that do not create two entities with the same value on a candidate key.

- **Form of a relationship** — many-to-many, one-to-many, one-to-one. A one-to-one or one-to-many relationship restricts the set of legal relationships among entities of a collection of entity sets.

In general, an integrity constraint can be an arbitrary predicate pertaining to the database. However, arbitrary predicates may be costly to test. Thus, we usually limit ourselves to integrity constraints that can be tested with minimal overhead.

5.1 Domain Constraints

We have seen earlier that a domain of possible values must be associated with every attribute. In Chapter 4, we saw how such constraints are specified in the SQL DDL. Domain constraints are the most elementary form of integrity constraint. They are tested easily by the system whenever a new data item is entered into the database.

5.1.1 Domain Types

It is possible for several attributes to have the same domain. For example, the attributes *customer-name* and *employee-name* might have the same domain, the set of all person names. However, the domains of *balance* and *branch-name* certainly ought to be distinct. It is perhaps less clear whether *customer-name* and *branch-name* should have the same domain. At the implementation level, both customer names and branch names are character strings. However, we would normally not consider the query "Find all customers who have the same name as a branch" to be a meaningful query. Thus, if we view the database at the conceptual rather than physical level, *customer-name* and *branch-name* should have distinct domains.

From the previous discussion, we can see that a proper definition of domain constraints not only allows us to test values inserted in the database but also permits us to test queries to ensure that the comparisons made make sense.

The principle behind attribute domains is similar to that behind typing of variables in programming languages. Strongly typed programming languages allow the compiler to check the program in greater detail. However, strongly typed languages inhibit "clever hacks" that are often required for systems programming. Since database systems are designed to support users who are not computer experts, the benefits of strong typing often outweigh the disadvantages. Nevertheless, many existing systems allow only a small number of types of domains. Newer systems, particularly object-oriented database systems, offer a rich set of domain types that can be extended easily. Object-oriented databases are discussed in Chapter 13.

5.1.2 Domain Types in SQL

The SQL standard supports a restricted set of domain types:

- Fixed length character string, with user-specified length.

- Fixed point number, with user-specified precision.

- Integer (a finite subset of the integers that is machine-dependent).

- Small integer (a machine-dependent subset of the integer domain type).

- Floating point number, with user-specified precision.

- Floating point and double-precision floating point numbers, with machine-dependent precision.

Several SQL implementations include a *date* type. This type is used to represent dates and allows computations based on dates. For example, if x and y are of type *date*, then $x - y$ is the number of days from date x to date y.

It is often useful to be able to compare values from *compatible* domains. For example, since every small integer is an integer, a comparison $x < y$, where x is a small integer and y is an integer, makes sense. Such a comparison is made by casting small integer x as an integer. A transformation of this sort is called a *type coercion*. Type coercion is used routinely in common programming languages as well as database systems.

Returning to our earlier discussion, we see that in standard SQL, both *branch-name* and *customer-name* would have the domain character string. Although the string lengths might differ, SQL would consider the two domains compatible.

5.1.3 Null Values

In Chapters 3 and 4, we saw that the insertion of incomplete tuples can introduce null values into the database. For certain attributes, null values may be inappropriate. Consider a tuple in the *customer* relation where *customer-name* is null. Such a tuple gives a street and city for an anonymous customer and, thus, does not contain useful information. In cases such as this, we wish to forbid null values, by restricting the domain of *customer-name* to exclude null values.

Standard SQL allows the domain declaration of an attribute to include the specification **not null**. This prohibits the insertion of a null value for this attribute. Any database modification that would cause a null to be inserted in a **not null** domain generates an error diagnostic.

There are many situations where the prohibition of null values is desirable. A particular case where it is essential to prohibit null values is in the primary key of a relation scheme. We note that in our example above of the *customer* relation, *customer-name* is indeed the primary key.

5.2 Referential Integrity

Often we wish to ensure that a value that appears in one relation for a given set of attributes also appears for a certain set of attributes in another relation. This is called *referential integrity*.

5.2.1 Basic Concepts

Consider a pair of relations $r(R)$ and $s(S)$, and the natural join $r \bowtie s$. It may be the case that there is a tuple t_r in r that does not join with any tuple in s. That is, there is no t_s in s such that $t_r[R \cap S] = t_s[R \cap S]$. Such tuples are called *dangling* tuples. Depending upon the entity set or relationship set being modeled, dangling tuples may or may not be acceptable.

Suppose there is a tuple t_1 in the *deposit* relation with $t_1[branch\text{-}name] =$ "Lunartown" but no tuple in the *branch* relation for the Lunartown branch. This would be an undesirable situation. We expect the *branch* relation to list all bank branches. Therefore tuple t_1 would refer to an account at a branch that does not exist. Clearly we would like to have an integrity constraint that prohibits dangling tuples of this sort.

However, not all instances of dangling tuples are undesirable. Assume there is a tuple t_2 in the *branch* relation with $t_2[branch\text{-}name] = $ "Mokan" but no tuple in the *deposit* relation for the Mokan branch. In this case, a branch exists that has no accounts. Although this is not a normal situation, it may arise at the time a new branch is being opened. Thus, we do not want to prohibit this situation.

To see the distinction between these two examples, recall that *branch-name* is the primary key of *Branch-scheme*. Since *branch-name* appears in *Deposit-scheme*, the scheme of *deposit*, tuples of *deposit* reference the primary key of *branch*. We say that the attribute *branch-name* in *Deposit-scheme* is a *foreign key* since *branch-name* is the primary key of a relation scheme other than *Deposit-scheme*. However, the attribute *branch-name* in *Branch-scheme* is not a foreign key since *branch-name* is not the primary key of any other relation scheme.

In the Lunartown example, tuple t_1 in *deposit* has a value on the foreign key *branch-name* that does not appear in *branch*. In the Mokan branch example, tuple t_2 in *branch* has a value on *branch-name* that does not appear in *deposit*, but *branch-name* is not a foreign key. Thus, the distinction between our two examples of dangling tuples is the presence of a foreign key.

Let $r_1(R_1)$ and $r_2(R_2)$ be relations with primary keys K_1 and K_2 respectively. We say that a subset α of R_2 is a *foreign key* referencing K_1 in relation r_1 if it is required that for every t_2 in r_2 there must be a tuple t_1 in r_1 such that $t_1[K_1] = t_2[\alpha]$. Requirements of this form are called *referential integrity constraints*, or *subset dependencies*. The latter term arises from the fact that the above referential integrity constraint can be written as $\Pi_\alpha (r_2) \subseteq \Pi_{K_1} (r_1)$. Note that for a referential integrity constraint to make sense, either $\alpha = K_1$, or α and K_1 must be compatible sets of attributes.

5.2.2 Referential Integrity in the E-R Model

Referential integrity constraints arise frequently. If we derive our relational database scheme by constructing tables from E-R diagrams as we saw in Chapter 2, then every relation arising from a relationship set has referential integrity constraints. Figure 5.1 shows an n-ary relationship set R, relating entity sets $E_1, E_2, \ldots, E_n$. Let K_i denote the primary key of E_i. The attributes of the relation scheme for relationship set R include $K_1 \cup K_2 \cup \cdots \cup K_n$. Each K_i in the scheme for R is a foreign key that leads to a referential integrity constraint.

Another source of referential integrity constraints are weak entity sets. Recall from Chapter 2 that the relation scheme for a weak entity set must include the primary key of the entity set on which it depends. Thus, the relation scheme for each weak entity set includes a foreign key that leads to a referential integrity constraint.

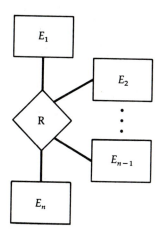

Figure 5.1 An n-ary relationship set.

5.2.3 Database Modification

Database modifications can cause violations of referential integrity. We list below the test that must be made for each type of database modification in order to preserve the following referential integrity constraint:

$$\Pi_\alpha\,(r_2) \subseteq \Pi_K\,(r_1)$$

- **Insert.** If a tuple t_2 is inserted into r_2, the system must ensure that there is a tuple t_1 in r_1 such that $t_1[K] = t_2[\alpha]$. That is

$$t_2[\alpha] \in \Pi_K\,(r_1)$$

- **Delete.** If a tuple t_1 is deleted from r_1, the system must compute the set of tuples in r_2 that reference t_1:

$$\sigma_{\alpha\,=\,t_1[K]}\,(r_2)$$

If this set is not empty, either the delete command is rejected as an error, or the tuples that reference t_1 must themselves be deleted. The latter solution may lead to cascading deletions, since tuples may reference tuples that reference t_1, and so on.

- **Update.** We must consider two cases for update: updates to the referencing relation (r_2), and updates to the referenced relation (r_1).

○ If a tuple t_2 is updated in relation r_2 and the update modifies values for the foreign key α, then a test similar to the insert case is made. Let t_2' denote the new value of tuple t_2. The system must ensure that

$$t_2'[\alpha] \in \Pi_K (r_1)$$

○ If a tuple t_1 is updated in r_1, and the update modifies values for the primary key (K), then a test similar to the delete case is made. The system must compute

$$\sigma_{\alpha = t_1[K]} (r_2)$$

using the old value of t_1 (the value before the update is applied). If this set is not empty, the update is rejected as an error.

5.2.4 Referential Integrity in SQL

The original SQL standard did not include statements to specify foreign keys. A subsequent "integrity enhancement feature" has been approved as an addition to the standard. This feature allows the specification of primary and candidate keys and foreign keys as part of the **create table** statement:

- The **primary key** clause of the **create table** statement includes a list of the attributes that comprise the primary key.

- The **unique key** clause of the **create table** statement includes a list of the attributes that comprise a candidate key.

- The **foreign key** clause of the **create table** statement includes both a list of the attributes that comprise the foreign key and the name of the relation referenced by the foreign key.

We illustrate this feature as well as the domain declarations discussed in Section 5.1 by giving a partial SQL DDL definition of our bank database in Figure 5.2. In the definition of *customer* and *branch* we have used the **not null** specification for the primary key. This is a requirement of SQL. Any attribute that is a member of a candidate key must be declared **not null**. Thus, in the definition of *deposit*, we are required to specify *account-number* and *customer-name* as **not null**. It is allowed to have null values in a foreign key unless that foreign key is a member of a candidate key.

```
create table customer
    ( customer-name  char(20) not null,
      street            char(30),
      customer-city   char(30),
      primary key (customer-name) )
```

```
create table branch
    ( branch-name      char(15) not null,
      assets             integer,
      branch-city      char(30),
      primary key (branch-name) )
```

```
create table deposit
    ( branch-name      char(15),
      account-number char(10) not null,
      customer-name char(20) not null,
      balance           integer,
      primary key (account-number, customer-name),
      foreign key (branch-name) references branch,
      foreign key (customer-name) references customer) )
```

Figure 5.2   SQL data definition for part of the bank database.

5.3 Functional Dependencies

This section focuses on a particular kind of constraint called a *functional dependency*. The notion of functional dependency is a generalization of the notion of *key*, as discussed in Chapters 2 and 3.

5.3.1 Basic Concepts

Functional dependencies are a constraint on the set of legal relations. They allow us to express facts about the enterprise that we are modeling with our database.

In Chapter 2, we defined the notion of a *superkey* as follows. Let R be a relation scheme. A subset K of R is a *superkey* of R if, in any legal relation $r(R)$, for all pairs t_1 and t_2 of tuples in r such that $t_1 \neq t_2$, $t_1[K] \neq t_2[K]$. That is, no two tuples in any legal relation $r(R)$ may have the same value on attribute set K.

The notion of functional dependency generalizes the notion of superkey. Let $\alpha \subseteq R$ and $\beta \subseteq R$. The *functional dependency*

$$\alpha \rightarrow \beta$$

holds on R if in any legal relation $r(R)$, for all pairs of tuples t_1 and t_2 in r such that $t_1[\alpha] = t_2[\alpha]$, it is also the case that $t_1[\beta] = t_2[\beta]$.

Using the functional dependency notation, we say that K is a superkey of R if $K \rightarrow R$. That is, K is a superkey if whenever $t_1[K] = t_2[K]$, it is also the case that $t_1[R] = t_2[R]$ (that is, $t_1 = t_2$).

Functional dependencies allow us to express constraints that cannot be expressed using superkeys. Consider the scheme:

Borrow-scheme = (branch-name, loan-number, customer-name, amount).

If a given loan may be made to more than one customer (for example, to both of a husband/wife pair), then we would not expect the attribute *loan-number* to be a superkey. However, we do expect the functional dependency

loan-number → amount

to hold, since we know that each loan-number is associated with precisely one amount.

We shall use functional dependencies in two ways:

1. To specify constraints on the set of legal relations. We shall thus concern ourselves *only* with relations that satisfy a given set of functional dependencies. If we wish to constrain ourselves to relations on scheme R that satisfy a set F of functional dependencies, we say that F *holds* on R.

2. To test relations to see if they are legal under a given set of functional dependencies. If a relation r is legal under a set F of functional dependencies, we say that r *satisfies* F.

Let us consider the relation r of Figure 5.3 and see which functional dependencies are satisfied. Observe that $A \rightarrow C$ is satisfied. There are two tuples that have an A-value of a_1. These tuples have the same C-value,

A	B	C	D
a_1	b_1	c_1	d_1
a_1	b_2	c_1	d_2
a_2	b_2	c_2	d_2
a_2	b_3	c_2	d_3
a_3	b_3	c_2	d_4

Figure 5.3   Sample relation r.

namely, c_1. Similarly, the two tuples with an A-value of a_2 have the same C-value, c_2. There are no other pairs of distinct tuples that have the same A-value. The functional dependency $C \rightarrow A$ is not satisfied, however. To see this, consider the tuples $t_1 = (a_2, b_3, c_2, d_3)$ and $t_2 = (a_3, b_3, c_2, d_4)$. These two tuples have the same C-value, c_2, but they have different A-values, a_2 and a_3, respectively. Thus, we have found a pair of tuples t_1 and t_2 such that $t_1[C] = t_2[C]$ but $t_1[A] \neq t_2[A]$.

Many other functional dependencies are satisfied by r, including, for example, the functional dependency $AB \rightarrow D$. Note that we use AB as a shorthand for $\{A, B\}$, to conform with standard practice. Observe that there is no pair of distinct tuples t_1 and t_2 such that $t_1[AB] = t_2[AB]$. Therefore, if $t_1[AB] = t_2[AB]$ it must be that $t_1 = t_2$ and, thus, $t_1[D] = t_2[D]$. So, r satisfies $AB \rightarrow D$.

Some functional dependencies are said to be *trivial* because they are satisfied by all relations. For example, $A \rightarrow A$ is satisfied by all relations involving attribute A. Reading the definition of functional dependency literally, we see that for all tuples t_1 and t_2 such that $t_1[A] = t_2[A]$, it is the case that $t_1[A] = t_2[A]$. Similarly, $AB \rightarrow A$ is satisfied by all relations involving attribute A. In general, a functional dependency of the form $\alpha \rightarrow \beta$ is trivial if $\beta \subseteq \alpha$.

In order to distinguish between the concepts of a relation satisfying a dependency and a dependency holding on a scheme, let us return to the banking example. If we consider the *customer* relation (on *Customer-scheme*) as shown in Figure 5.4, we see that *street* $\rightarrow$ *customer-city* is satisfied. However, we believe that, in the real world, two cities can have streets with the same name. Thus, it is possible, at some time, to have an instance of the *customer* relation in which *street* $\rightarrow$ *customer-city* is not satisfied. So,

customer-name	street	customer-city
Jones	Main	Harrison
Smith	North	Rye
Hayes	Main	Harrison
Curry	North	Rye
Lindsay	Park	Pittsfield
Turner	Putnam	Stamford
Williams	Nassau	Princeton
Adams	Spring	Pittsfield
Johnson	Alma	Palo Alto
Glenn	Sand Hill	Woodside
Brooks	Senator	Brooklyn
Green	Walnut	Stamford

Figure 5.4　The *customer* relation.

branch-name	loan-number	customer-name	amount
Downtown	17	Jones	1000
Redwood	23	Smith	2000
Perryridge	15	Hayes	1500
Downtown	14	Jackson	1500
Mianus	93	Curry	500
Round Hill	11	Turner	900
Pownal	29	Williams	1200
North Town	16	Adams	1300
Downtown	18	Johnson	2000
Perryridge	25	Glenn	2500
Brighton	10	Brooks	2200

Figure 5.5   The *borrow* relation.

we would not include *street* → *customer-city* in the set of functional dependencies that hold on *Customer-scheme*.

In the *borrow* relation (on *Borrow-scheme*) of Figure 5.5, we see that *loan-number* → *amount* is satisfied. Unlike the case of *customer-city* and *street*, we do believe that the real-world enterprise that we are modeling requires each loan to have a unique amount. Therefore, we want to require that *loan-number* → *amount* be satisfied by the *borrow* relation at all times. In other words, we require that the constraint that *loan-number* → *amount* hold on *Borrow-scheme*.

In the *branch* relation of Figure 5.6, we see that *branch-name* → *assets* is satisfied, as is *assets* → *branch-name*. We want to require that *branch-name* → *assets* hold on *Borrow-scheme*. However, we do not wish to require that *assets* → *branch-name* hold, since it is possible to have several branches having the same asset value.

branch-name	assets	branch-city
Downtown	9000000	Brooklyn
Redwood	2100000	Palo Alto
Perryridge	1700000	Horseneck
Mianus	400000	Horseneck
Round Hill	8000000	Horseneck
Pownal	300000	Bennington
North Town	3700000	Rye
Brighton	7100000	Brooklyn

Figure 5.6   The *branch* relation.

In what follows, we assume that when we design a relational database, we first list those functional dependencies that must always hold. In the banking example, our list of dependencies includes the following:

- On *Branch-scheme*:

$$branch\text{-}name \rightarrow branch\text{-}city$$
$$branch\text{-}name \rightarrow assets$$

- On *Customer-scheme*:

$$customer\text{-}name \rightarrow customer\text{-}city$$
$$customer\text{-}name \rightarrow street$$

- On *Borrow-scheme*:

$$loan\text{-}number \rightarrow amount$$
$$loan\text{-}number \rightarrow branch\text{-}name$$

- On *Deposit-scheme*:

$$account\text{-}number \rightarrow balance$$
$$account\text{-}number \rightarrow branch\text{-}name$$

5.3.2 Closure of a Set of Functional Dependencies

It is not sufficient to consider the given set of functional dependencies. Rather, we need to consider *all* functional dependencies that hold. We shall see that, given a set F of functional dependencies, we can prove that certain other functional dependencies hold. We say that such functional dependencies are *logically implied* by F.

Suppose we are given a relation scheme $R = (A, B, C, G, H, I)$ and the set of functional dependencies

$$A \rightarrow B$$
$$A \rightarrow C$$
$$CG \rightarrow H$$
$$CG \rightarrow I$$
$$B \rightarrow H$$

The functional dependency

$$A \rightarrow H$$

is logically implied. That is, we can show that whenever our given set of functional dependencies holds, $A \rightarrow H$ must hold also. Suppose that t_1 and t_2 are tuples such that

$$t_1[A] = t_2[A]$$

Since we are given that $A \rightarrow B$, it follows from the definition of functional dependency that

$$t_1[B] = t_2[B]$$

Then, since we are given that $B \rightarrow H$, it follows from the definition of functional dependency that

$$t_1[H] = t_2[H]$$

Therefore, we have shown that whenever t_1 and t_2 are tuples such that $t_1[A] = t_2[A]$, it must be that $t_1[H] = t_2[H]$. But that is exactly the definition of $A \rightarrow H$.

Let F be a set of functional dependencies. The closure of F is the set of all functional dependencies logically implied by F. We denote the *closure* of F by F^+. Given F, we can compute F^+ directly from the formal definition of functional dependency. If F is large, this process would be lengthy and difficult. Such a computation of F^+ requires arguments of the type given above to show that $A \rightarrow H$ is in the closure of our example set of dependencies. There are simpler techniques for reasoning about functional dependencies.

The first technique is based on three *axioms* or rules of inference for functional dependencies. By applying these rules repeatedly, we can find all of F^+ given F. In the rules below, we adopt the convention of using Greek letters (α, β, γ, $\cdots$) for sets of attributes and uppercase Roman letters from the beginning of the alphabet for individual attributes. We use $\alpha\beta$ to denote $\alpha \cup \beta$.

- **Reflexivity rule**. If α is a set of attributes and $\beta \subseteq \alpha$, then $\alpha \rightarrow \beta$ holds.

- **Augmentation rule**. If $\alpha \rightarrow \beta$ holds and γ is a set of attributes, then $\gamma\alpha \rightarrow \gamma\beta$ holds.

- **Transitivity rule**. If $\alpha \rightarrow \beta$ holds, and $\beta \rightarrow \gamma$ holds, then $\alpha \rightarrow \gamma$ holds.

These rules are *sound* because they do not generate any incorrect functional dependencies. The rules are *complete* because for a given set F of functional dependencies, they allow us to generate all of F^+. This collection of rules is called *Armstrong's axioms* in honor of the person who first proposed them.

Although Armstrong's axioms are complete, it is tiresome to use them directly for the computation of F^+. To simplify matters further, we list some additional rules. It is possible to use Armstrong's axioms to prove that these rules are correct (see the exercises).

- **Union rule**. If $\alpha \rightarrow \beta$ holds and $\alpha \rightarrow \gamma$ holds, then $\alpha \rightarrow \beta\gamma$ holds.

- **Decomposition rule**. If $\alpha \rightarrow \beta\gamma$ holds, then $\alpha \rightarrow \beta$ holds and $\alpha \rightarrow \gamma$ holds.

- **Pseudotransitivity rule**. If $\alpha \rightarrow \beta$ holds and $\gamma\beta \rightarrow \delta$ holds, then $\alpha\gamma \rightarrow \delta$ holds.

Let us apply our rules to the example we presented earlier of scheme $R = (A, B, C, G, H, I)$ and the set F of functional dependencies $\{A \rightarrow B, A \rightarrow C, CG \rightarrow H, CG \rightarrow I, B \rightarrow H\}$. We list some members of F^+ below.

- $A \rightarrow H$. Since $A \rightarrow B$ and $B \rightarrow H$ holds, we apply the transitivity rule. Observe that it was much easier to use Armstrong's axioms to show that $A \rightarrow H$ holds than it was to argue directly from the definitions as we did earlier.

- $CG \rightarrow HI$. Since $CG \rightarrow H$ and $CG \rightarrow I$, the union rule implies that $CG \rightarrow HI$.

- $AG \rightarrow I$. Since $A \rightarrow C$ and $CG \rightarrow I$, the pseudotransitivity rule implies that $AG \rightarrow I$ holds.

5.3.3 Closure of Attribute Sets

In order to test if a set α is a superkey, we must devise an algorithm for computing the set of attributes functionally determined by α. We shall see that such an algorithm is useful also as part of the computation of the closure of a set F of functional dependencies.

Let α be a set of attributes. We call the set of all attributes functionally determined by α under a set F of functional dependencies the *closure* of α under F and denote it by α^+. Figure 5.7 shows an algorithm, written in pseudo Pascal, to compute α^+. The input is a set F of functional dependencies and the set α of attributes. The output is stored in the variable *result*.

To illustrate how the algorithm of Figure 5.7 works, let us use the algorithm to compute $(AG)^+$ with the functional dependencies defined

> *result* := α;
> **while** (changes to *result*) **do**
>   **for each** functional dependency β → γ **in** *F* **do**
>   **begin**
>   **if** β ⊆ *result* **then** *result* := *result* ∪ γ;
>   **end**

Figure 5.7   An algorithm to compute α⁺, the closure of α under *F*.

above. We start with *result* = *AG*. The first time we execute the **while** loop to test each functional dependency we find that

- *A* → *B* causes us to include *B* in *result*. To see this, observe that *A* → *B* is in *F*, *A* ⊆ *result* (which is *AG*), so *result* := *result* ∪ *B*.

- *A* → *C* causes *result* to become *ABCG*.

- *CG* → *H* causes *result* to become *ABCGH*.

- *CG* → *I* causes *result* to become *ABCGHI*.

The second time we execute the **while** loop, no new attributes are added to *result* and the algorithm terminates.

Let us see why the algorithm of Figure 5.7 is correct. The first step is correct since α → α always holds (by the reflexivity rule). We claim that for any subset β of *result*, it is the case that α → β. Since we start the **while** loop with α → *result* being true, we can add γ to result only if β ⊆ *result* and β → γ. But then *result* → β by the reflexivity rule, so α → β by transitivity. Another application of transitivity shows that α → γ (using α → β and β → γ). The union rule implies that α → *result* ∪ γ, so α functionally determines any new result generated in the **while** loop. Thus, any attribute returned by the algorithm is in α⁺.

It is easy to see that the algorithm finds all of α⁺. If there is an attribute in α⁺ not yet in *result*, then there must be a functional dependency β → γ for which β ⊆ *result* and at least one attribute in *F* is not in *result*.

It turns out that in the worst case this algorithm may take time quadratic in the size of *F*. There is a faster (though slightly more complex) algorithm that runs in time linear in the size of *F*. The algorithm is presented as part of Exercise 5.17.

5.3.4 Canonical Cover

In order to minimize the number of functional dependencies that need to be tested in case of an update, we restrict a given set *F* of functional dependencies. This is done by combining several functional dependencies into one, where possible, and by eliminating *extraneous attributes*. An attribute is extraneous in a functional dependency if it can be removed without changing the closure of the set of functional dependencies.

Consider a set F of functional dependencies and the functional dependency $\alpha \to \beta$ in F.

- Attribute A is extraneous in α if $A \in \alpha$ and F logically implies $(F - \{\alpha \to \beta\}) \cup \{(\alpha - A) \to \beta\}$.

- Attribute A is extraneous in β if $A \in \beta$ and the set of functional dependencies $(F - \{\alpha \to \beta\}) \cup \{\alpha \to (\beta - A)\}$ logically implies F.

A *canonical cover* F_c for F is a set of dependencies such that F logically implies all dependencies in F_c and F_c logically implies all dependencies in F. Furthermore, F_c must have the following properties:

- No functional dependency in F_c contains an extraneous attribute.

- Each left side of a functional dependency in F_c is unique. That is, there are no two dependencies $\alpha_1 \to \beta_1$ and $\alpha_2 \to \beta_2$ in F_c such that $\alpha_1 = \alpha_2$.

To compute a canonical cover for F, use the union rule to replace any dependencies in F of the form $\alpha_1 \to \beta_1$ and $\alpha_1 \to \beta_2$ with $\alpha_1 \to \beta_1 \beta_2$. Test each functional dependency $\alpha \to \beta$ to see if there is an extraneous attribute in α. For each dependency $\alpha \to \beta$ see if there is an extraneous attribute in β. This process must be repeated until no changes occur in the loop.

Consider the following set F of functional dependencies on scheme (A, B, C):

$$A \to BC$$
$$B \to C$$
$$A \to B$$
$$AB \to C$$

Let us compute the canonical cover for F.

- There are two functional dependencies with the same set of attributes on the left side of the arrow:

$$A \to BC$$
$$A \to B$$

We combine these into $A \to BC$.

- *A* is extraneous in $AB \rightarrow C$ because $B \rightarrow C$ logically implies $AB \rightarrow C$, and thus $(F - \{AB \rightarrow C\}) \cup \{B \rightarrow C\}$ logically implies F_c. As a result of removing *A* from $AB \rightarrow C$, we obtain $B \rightarrow C$, which is already in our set of functional dependencies.

- *C* is extraneous in $A \rightarrow BC$ since $A \rightarrow C$ is logically implied by $A \rightarrow B$ and $B \rightarrow C$.

Thus, our canonical cover is:

$$A \rightarrow B$$
$$B \rightarrow C$$

5.4 Assertions

An *assertion* is a predicate expressing a condition that we wish the database always to satisfy. Domain constraints, functional dependencies, and referential integrity constraints are special forms of assertion. We have paid substantial attention to these forms of assertion because they are easily tested and apply to a wide range of database applications. However, there are many constraints that cannot be expressed using only these three special forms. Examples of such constraints include:

- The sum of all loan amounts for each branch must be less than the sum of all account balances at the branch.

- Every loan customer must maintain an account with a minimum balance of $1000.00.

When an assertion is made, the system tests it for validity. If the assertion is valid, then any future modification to the database is allowed only if it does not cause that assertion to be violated. This testing may introduce a significant amount of overhead if complex assertions have been made.

The high overhead of testing and maintaining assertions has led most system developers to omit support for general assertions. The original proposal for the SQL language included a general-purpose construct called the **assert** statement for the expression of integrity constraints.

An assertion pertaining to a single relation takes the form:

    assert <assertion-name> **on** <relation-name> : <predicate>

For example, if we wish to define an integrity constraint that no account balance is negative we write:

    assert *balance-constraint* **on** *deposit*:
      balance ≥ 0

Of course, we could have written the above assertion as a domain constraint. However, the **assert** statement allows us to specify constraints on a relation that cannot be expressed as domain constraints. The statement

> **assert** *banker-constraint* **on** *client*:
> *customer-name* ≠ *employee-name*

requires that no bank employee may be her or his own personal banker.

Assertions may be restricted to apply only to database modifications as in the case where we wish to prevent the addition of an account (*deposit* tuple) unless the customer's name appears in the *customer* relation. We write the following assertion:

> **assert** *address-constraint* **on insertion to** *deposit*:
> **exists (select ***
>   **from** *customer*
>   **where** *customer.customer-name* =
>   *deposit.customer-name*)

The above assertion is, in fact, a referential integrity constraint.

The most general form of assertion is

> **assert** <assertion-name> : <predicate>

where <predicate> is any valid SQL **where**-clause.

Owing to the high overhead of testing arbitrary assertions, the **assert** statement has disappeared from more recent versions of SQL, including the SQL standard. In place of assertions are the more easily tested constraints, domain constraints, key constraints, and referential integrity constraints that we discussed earlier. However, a proposal exists to include general assertions in a future revision of the SQL standard.

5.5 Triggers

A *trigger* is a statement that is executed automatically by the system as a side effect of a modification to the database.

To design a trigger mechanism, we must:

- Specify the conditions under which the trigger is to be executed.
- Specify the actions to be taken when the trigger executes.

To illustrate this, suppose that instead of allowing negative account balances, the bank deals with overdrafts by setting the account balance to zero and creating a loan in the amount of the overdraft. This loan is given a loan number equal to the account number of the overdrawn account. For the above example, the condition for executing the trigger is an update to the *deposit* relation that results in a negative *balance* value. Let *t* denote the tuple with a negative *balance* value. The actions to be taken are as follows:

- Insert a new tuple *s* in the *borrow* relation with:

$$s[branch\text{-}name] = t[branch\text{-}name]$$
$$s[loan\text{-}number] = t[account\text{-}number]$$
$$s[amount] = -t[balance]$$
$$s[customer\text{-}name] = t[customer\text{-}name]$$

(Note that since *t*[*balance*] is negative, we negate *t*[*balance*] to get the loan amount, a positive number.)

- Set *t*[*balance*] to 0.

The SQL standard does not include triggers, although the original System R SQL proposal included a limited trigger feature. Several existing systems have their own nonstandard trigger features. Below we illustrate how the account overdraft trigger would be written in the original version of SQL:

> **define trigger** *overdraft*
> **on update of** *deposit T*
>   (**if new** *T.balance* < 0
>   **then** (**insert into** *borrow* **values**
>   (*T.branch-name, T.account-number,*
>   *T.customer-name* − **new** *T.balance*)
>   **update** *deposit S*
>   **set** *S.balance* = 0
>   **where** *S.account-number* = *T.account-number*))

5.6 Summary

Integrity constraints ensure that changes made to the database by authorized users do not result in a loss of data consistency. In earlier chapters, we considered several forms of constraints, including key declarations and the declaration of the form of a relationship (many-to-many, many-to-one, one-to-one). In this chapter we considered several additional forms of constraints and mechanisms for ensuring the maintenance of these constraints.

Domain constraints specify the set of possible values that may be associated with an attribute. Such constraints may also prohibit the use of null values for particular attributes.

Referential integrity constraints ensure that a value that appears in one relation for a given set of attributes also appears for a certain set of attributes in another relation.

Functional dependencies are a generalization of key dependencies. They require that the value for a certain set of attributes determines uniquely the value for another set of attributes. Using the formal definition of functional dependencies, we saw how to determine the set of all functional dependencies logically implied by a given set F of functional dependencies. This is called the closure of F. We also saw a way to reduce the size of a set F of functional dependencies without changing the closure. This is called a canonical cover F_c for F.

Domain constraints, referential integrity constraints, and functional dependencies are relatively easy to test. More complex constraints may lead to substantial overhead. We saw two ways of expressing more general constraints. Assertions are declarative expressions stating predicates that we require always to be true. Triggers are procedures to be executed when certain events occur.

Exercises

5.1 Complete the SQL DDL definition of the bank database of Figure 5.2 to include the relations *borrow* and *client*.

5.2 Consider the following relational database:

> *lives (person-name, street, city)*
> *works (person-name, company-name, salary)*
> *located-in (company-name, city)*
> *manages (person-name, manager-name)*

Give an SQL DDL definition of this database. Identify referential integrity constraints that should hold, and include them in the DDL definition.

5.3 Referential integrity constraints as defined in this chapter involve exactly two relations. Consider a database that includes the following relations:

> *salaried-worker (name, ssn, office, phone, salary)*
> *hourly-worker (name, ssn, hourly-wage)*
> *address (name, street, city)*

Suppose we wish to require that every name that appears in *address* appear in *salaried-worker* or *hourly-worker*, but not necessarily both.

    a. Propose a syntax for expressing such constraints.

    b. Discuss the actions that the system must take to enforce a constraint of this form.

5.4 List all functional dependencies satisfied by the relation of Figure 5.8.

5.5 SQL allows specification of candidate keys but not arbitrary functional dependencies. Why do you think this decision was made?

5.6 The rule for preservation of referential integrity allows for cascading deletion. However, the rule does not allow updates to the primary key of a referenced relation to lead to automatic updates to the referencing relations. What practical considerations justify this?

5.7 Why are certain functional dependencies called *trivial* functional dependencies?

5.8 Use the definition of functional dependency to argue that each of Armstrong's axioms (reflexivity, augmentation, and transitivity) are sound.

5.9 Explain how functional dependencies can be used to indicate that:

- A one-to-one relationship set exists between entity sets *student* and *advisor*.

- A many-to-one relationship set exists between entity sets *student* and *advisor*.

5.10 Consider the following proposed rule for functional dependencies: If $\alpha \rightarrow \beta$ and $\gamma \rightarrow \beta$ then $\alpha \rightarrow \gamma$. Prove that this rule is *not* sound by showing a relation r which satisfies $\alpha \rightarrow \beta$ and $\gamma \rightarrow \beta$ but does not satisfy $\alpha \rightarrow \gamma$.

A	B	C
a_1	b_1	c_1
a_1	b_1	c_2
a_2	b_1	c_1
a_2	b_1	c_3

Figure 5.8   Relation of Exercise 5.4

5.11 Use Armstrong's axioms to prove the soundness of the union rule. (Hint: Use the augmentation rule to show that if $\alpha \rightarrow \beta$ then $\alpha \rightarrow \alpha\beta$. Apply the augmentation rule again using $\alpha \rightarrow \gamma$ and then apply the transitivity rule.)

5.12 Use Armstrong's axioms to prove the soundness of the decomposition rule.

5.13 Use Armstrong's axioms to prove the soundness of the pseudotransitivity rule.

5.14 Compute the closure of the following set F of functional dependencies for relation scheme $R = (A, B, C, D, E)$.

$$A \rightarrow BC$$
$$CD \rightarrow E$$
$$B \rightarrow D$$
$$E \rightarrow A$$

List the candidate keys for R.

5.15 Using the functional dependencies of Exercise 5.14, compute B^+.

5.16 Using the functional dependencies of Exercise 5.14, compute the canonical cover F_c.

5.17 Consider the algorithm shown in Figure 5.9 to compute α^+. Show that this algorithm is more efficient than the one presented in the text and that it computes α^+ correctly.

5.18 Write an assertion for the bank database to ensure that the assets value for the Perryridge branch is equal to the sum of all of the amounts loaned by the Perryridge branch.

Bibliographic Notes

Discussions concerning integrity constraints in the relational model are offered by Hammer and McLeod [1975], Stonebraker [1975], Eswaran and Chamberlin [1975], Schmid and Swenson [1975], and Codd [1979].

Functional dependencies were originally defined by Codd [1970]. Armstrong's axioms were introduced by Armstrong [1974]. The theory of functional dependencies is discussed in Maier [1983]. Formal aspects of the concept of a legal relation are discussed by Graham et al. [1986].

The original SQL proposals for assertions and triggers are discussed in Astrahan et al. [1976], Chamberlin et al. [1976], and Chamberlin et al. [1981]. See the bibliographic notes of Chapter 4 for references to ANSI standard SQL.

```
result := α;
/* fdcount is an array whose ith element contains the number
   of attributes on the left side of the ith FD that are
   not yet known to be in α+ */
for i := 1 to | F|  do
   begin
      fdcount [i] := size of left side of ith FD;
   end
/* appears is an array with one entry for each attribute.  The
   entry for attribute A is a list of integers.  Each integer
   i on the list indicates that A appears on the left side
   of the ith FD */
for each attribute A do
   begin
      appears [A] := NIL;
      for i := 1 to | F|  do
         begin
            let β → γ denote the ith FD;
            if A ε β then add i to appears [A];
         end
   end
addin (α);
return (result);

procedure addin (α);
result := result ∪ {A};
for each attribute A in α do
   begin
      if A ∉ result  then
         begin
            for each element  i of appears [A] do
               begin
                  fdcount [i] := fdcount [i] − 1;
                  if fdcount [i] := 0 then
                     begin
                        let β → γ denote the ith FD;
                        addin (γ);
                     end
               end
         end
   end
```

Figure 5.9   An algorithm to compute α^+.

Discussions concerning efficient maintenance and checking of semantics integrity assertion is offered by Hammer and Sarin [1978], Badal and Popek [1979], Bernstein et al. [1980b], Hsu and Imielinsky [1985], and McCune and Henschen [1989]. An alternative to run time integrity checking is to certify the correctness of programs that access the database. This approach is discussed by Sheard and Stemple [1989].

Relational Database Design

This chapter continues our discussion of design issues in relational databases beyond the issues covered in Chapter 5. In general, the goal of a relational database design is to generate a set of relation schemes that allow us to store information without unnecessary redundancy, yet allow us to retrieve information easily. One approach is to design schemes that are in an appropriate *normal form*. In order to determine whether a relation scheme is in one of the normal forms, we shall need additional information about the "real-world" enterprise that we are modeling with the database. We have already seen how functional dependencies can be used to express facts about the data. In this chapter, we define normal forms using functional dependencies and using other types of data dependencies.

6.1 Pitfalls in Relational Database Design

Before we begin our discussion of normal forms and data dependencies, let us look at what can go wrong in a bad database design. Among the undesirable properties that a bad design may have are:

- Repetition of information.
- Inability to represent certain information.
- Loss of information.

Below, we discuss these in greater detail using our banking example, with the following two relation schemes:

> *Branch-scheme* = (*branch-name, assets, branch-city*)
> *Borrow-scheme* = (*branch-name, loan-number, customer-name, amount*)

Figures 6.1 and 6.2 show an instance of the relations *branch* (*Branch-scheme*) and *borrow* (*Borrow-scheme*).

branch-name	assets	branch-city
Downtown	9000000	Brooklyn
Redwood	2100000	Palo Alto
Perryridge	1700000	Horseneck
Mianus	400000	Horseneck
Round Hill	8000000	Horseneck
Pownal	300000	Bennington
North Town	3700000	Rye
Brighton	7100000	Brooklyn

Figure 6.1   Sample *branch* relation.

6.1.1 Representation of Information

Consider an alternative design for the bank database in which we replace *Branch-scheme* and *Borrow-scheme* with the single scheme:

$$Lending\text{-}scheme = (branch\text{-}name, assets, branch\text{-}city, loan\text{-}number,$$
$$customer\text{-}name, amount)$$

Figure 6.3 shows an instance of the relation *lending* (*Lending-scheme*) produced by taking the natural join of the *branch* and *borrow* instances of Figures 6.1 and 6.2. A tuple *t* in the *lending* relation has the following intuitive meaning:

branch-name	loan-number	customer-name	amount
Downtown	17	Jones	1000
Redwood	23	Smith	2000
Perryridge	15	Hayes	1500
Downtown	14	Jackson	1500
Mianus	93	Curry	500
Round Hill	11	Turner	900
Pownal	29	Williams	1200
North Town	16	Adams	1300
Downtown	18	Johnson	2000
Perryridge	25	Glenn	2500
Brighton	10	Brooks	2200

Figure 6.2   Sample *borrow* relation.

- *t[assets]* is the asset figure for the branch named *t[branch-name]*.

- *t[branch-city]* is the city in which the branch named *t[branch-name]* is located.

- *t[loan-number]* is the number assigned to a loan made by the branch named *t[branch-name]* to the customer named *t[customer-name]*.

- *t[amount]* is the amount of the loan whose number is *t[loan-number]*.

Suppose we wish to add a new loan to our database. Assume the loan is made by the Perryridge branch to Turner in the amount of $1500. Let the *loan-number* be 31. In our original design, we would add the tuple

(Perryridge, 31, Turner, 1500)

to the *borrow* relation. Under the alternative design, we need a tuple with values on all the attributes of *Lending-scheme*. Thus, we must repeat the asset and city data for the Perryridge branch and add the tuple

(Perryridge, 1700000, Horseneck, 31, Turner, 1500)

to the *lending* relation. In general, the asset and city data for a branch must appear once for each loan made by that branch.

The repetition of information required by the use of our alternative design is undesirable. Repeating information wastes space. Furthermore,

branch-name	assets	branch-city	loan-number	customer-name	amount
Downtown	9000000	Brooklyn	17	Jones	1000
Redwood	2100000	Palo Alto	23	Smith	2000
Perryridge	1700000	Horseneck	15	Hayes	1500
Downtown	9000000	Brooklyn	14	Jackson	1500
Mianus	400000	Horseneck	93	Curry	500
Round Hill	8000000	Horseneck	11	Turner	900
Pownal	300000	Bennington	29	Williams	1200
North Town	3700000	Rye	16	Adams	1300
Downtown	9000000	Brooklyn	18	Johnson	2000
Perryridge	1700000	Horseneck	25	Glenn	2500
Brighton	7100000	Brooklyn	10	Brooks	2200

Figure 6.3   *branch* ⋈ *borrow* .

the repetition of information complicates updating the database. Suppose, for example, that the Perryridge branch moves from Horseneck to Newtown. Under our original design, one tuple of the *branch* relation needs to be changed. Under our alternative design, many tuples of the *lending* relation need to be changed. Thus, updates are more costly under the alternative design than under the original design. When we perform the update in the alternative database, we must ensure that *every* tuple pertaining to the Perryridge branch is updated, or else our database will show two cities for the Perryridge branch.

The above observation is central to understanding why the alternative design is bad. We know that a bank branch is located in exactly one city. On the other hand, we know that a branch may make many loans. In other words, the functional dependency

$$branch\text{-}name \rightarrow branch\text{-}city$$

holds on *Lending-scheme*, but we do not expect that the functional dependency *branch-name* → *loan-number* holds. The fact that a branch is located in a city and the fact that a branch makes a loan are independent and, as we have seen, these facts are best represented in separate relations. We shall see that functional dependencies can be used for specifying formally when a database design is good.

Another problem with the *Lending-scheme* design is that we cannot represent directly the information concerning a branch (*branch-name, assets, branch-city*) unless there exists at least one loan at the branch. This is because tuples in the *lending* relation require values for *loan-number, amount*, and *customer-name*.

One solution to this problem is to introduce *null values*, as we did in Section 3.6 to handle updates through views. Recall, however, that null values are difficult to deal with. If we are not willing to deal with null values, then we can create the branch information only when the first loan application at that branch is made. Worse, we would have to delete this information when all the loans have been paid. Clearly this is undesirable, since under our original database design, the branch information would be available regardless of whether or not loans are currently maintained in the branch, and we could do so without resorting to the use of null values.

6.1.2 Loss of Information

The above example of a bad design suggests that we should *decompose* a relation scheme with many attributes into several schemes with fewer attributes. Careless decomposition, however, may lead to another form of bad design.

Consider an alternative design in which *Borrow-scheme* is decomposed into two schemes, *Amt-scheme* and *Loan-scheme*, as follows:

$$Amt\text{-}scheme = (amount, customer\text{-}name)$$
$$Loan\text{-}scheme = (branch\text{-}name, loan\text{-}number, amount)$$

Using the *borrow* relation of Figure 6.2, we construct our new relations *amt* (*Amt-scheme*) and *loan* (*Loan-scheme*) as follows:

$$amt = \Pi_{amount, \; customer\text{-}name} \; (borrow)$$
$$loan = \Pi_{branch\text{-}name, \; loan\text{-}number, amount} \; (borrow)$$

We show the resulting *amt* and *loan* relations in Figure 6.4.

Of course, there are cases in which we need to reconstruct the *borrow* relation. For example, suppose that we wish to find those branches from which Jones has a loan. None of the relations in our alternative database contains this data. We need to reconstruct the *borrow* relation. It appears that we can do this by writing:

$$amt \bowtie loan$$

Figure 6.5 shows the result of computing *amt* $\bowtie$ *loan* . When we compare this relation and the *borrow* relation with which we started (Figure 6.2), we notice some differences. Although every tuple that appears in *borrow* appears in *amt* $\bowtie$ *loan*, there are tuples in *amt* $\bowtie$ *loan* that are not in *borrow*. In our example, *amt* $\bowtie$ *loan* has the following additional tuples:

(Downtown, 14, Hayes, 1500)
(Perryridge, 15, Jackson, 1500)
(Redwood, 23, Johnson, 2000)
(Downtown, 18, Smith, 2000)

branch-name	loan-number	amount	amount	customer-name
Downtown	17	1000	1000	Jones
Redwood	23	2000	2000	Smith
Perryridge	15	1500	1500	Hayes
Downtown	14	1500	1500	Jackson
Mianus	93	500	500	Curry
Round Hill	11	900	900	Turner
Pownal	29	1200	1200	Williams
North Town	16	1300	1300	Adams
Downtown	18	2000	2000	Johnson
Perryridge	25	2500	2500	Glenn
Brighton	10	2200	2200	Brooks

Figure 6.4   The relations *amt* and *loan*.

branch-name	loan-number	customer-name	amount
Downtown	17	Jones	1000
Redwood	23	Smith	2000
Perryridge	15	Hayes	1500
Downtown	14	Jackson	1500
Mianus	93	Curry	500
Round Hill	11	Turner	900
Pownal	29	Williams	1200
North Town	16	Adams	1300
Downtown	18	Johnson	2000
Perryridge	25	Glenn	2500
Brighton	10	Brooks	2200
Downtown	14	Hayes	1500
Perryridge	15	Jackson	1500
Redwood	23	Johnson	2000
Downtown	18	Smith	2000

Figure 6.5 The relation *amt* ⋈ *loan*.

Consider the query, "Find those branches from which Hayes has a loan." If we look back at Figure 6.2, we see that Hayes has only one loan, and that loan is from the Perryridge branch. However, when we apply the expression

$$\Pi_{branch\text{-}name} \left(\sigma_{customer\text{-}name = \text{"Hayes"}} \left(amt \bowtie loan \right) \right)$$

we obtain *two* branch names: Perryridge and Downtown.

Let us examine this example more closely. If several loans happen to be in the same amount, we cannot tell which customer has which loan. Thus, when we join *amt* and *loan*, we obtain not only the tuples we had originally in *borrow*, but also several additional tuples. Although we have *more* tuples in *amt* ⋈ *loan*, we actually have *less* information. We are no longer able, in general, to represent in the database which customers are borrowers from which branch. Because of this loss of information, we call the decomposition of *Borrow-scheme* into *Amt-scheme* and *Loan-scheme* a *lossy decomposition*, or a *lossy-join decomposition*. A decomposition that is not a lossy-join decomposition is referred to as a *lossless-join decomposition*. It should be clear from our example that a lossy-join decomposition is, in general, a bad database design.

Let us examine the decomposition more closely to see why it is lossy. There is one attribute in common between *Loan-scheme* and *Amt-scheme*:

$$Loan\text{-}scheme \cap Amt\text{-}scheme = \{amount\}$$

The only way we can represent a relationship between *branch-name* and *customer-name* is through *amount*. This is not adequate because many customers may happen to have loans in the same amount, yet they do not necessarily have these loans from the same branches. Similarly, many customers may happen to have loans from the same branch, yet the amounts of their loans may be unrelated to one another.

Contrast this with *Lending-scheme*, which we discussed earlier. We argued that a better design would result if we decompose *Lending-scheme* into *Borrow-scheme* and *Branch-scheme*. There is one attribute in common between these two schemes:

$$Branch\text{-}scheme \cap Borrow\text{-}scheme = \{branch\text{-}name\}$$

Thus, the only way we can represent a relationship between, for example, *customer-name* and *assets* is through *branch-name*. The difference between this example and the example above is that the assets of a branch are the same regardless of the customer to which we are referring, while the lending branch associated with a certain loan amount *does* depend on the customer to which we are referring. For a given *branch-name* there is exactly one *assets* value and exactly one *branch-city*, while a similar statement cannot be made for *amount*. That is, the functional dependency

$$branch\text{-}name \rightarrow assets\ branch\text{-}city$$

holds, but *amount* does not functionally determine *branch-name*.

The notion of lossless joins is central to much of relational database design. Therefore, we restate the above examples below more concisely and more formally. Let R be a relation scheme. A set of relation schemes $\{R_1, R_2, \ldots, R_n\}$ is a *decomposition* of R if:

$$R = R_1 \cup R_2 \cup \cdots \cup R_n$$

That is, $\{R_1, R_2, \ldots, R_n\}$ is a decomposition of R if for $1 \le i \le n$, each R_i is a subset of R, and every attribute in R appears in at least one R_i. Let r be a relation on scheme R, and let $r_i = \Pi_{R_i}(r)$ for $1 \le i \le n$. That is, $\{r_1, r_2, \ldots, r_n\}$ is the database that results from decomposing R into $\{R_1, R_2, \ldots, R_n\}$. It is always the case that:

$$r \subseteq r_1 \bowtie r_2 \bowtie \cdots \bowtie r_n$$

To see this, consider a tuple t in relation r. When we compute the relations $r_1, r_2, \ldots, r_n$, the tuple t gives rise to one tuple t_i in each r_i, $1 \le i \le n$. These n tuples combine to regenerate t when we compute $r_1 \bowtie r_2 \bowtie \cdots \bowtie r_n$. The details are left as an exercise to the reader. Therefore, every tuple in r appears in $r_1 \bowtie r_2 \bowtie \cdots \bowtie r_n$.

In general, $r \neq r_1 \bowtie r_2 \bowtie \cdots \bowtie r_n$. To illustrate this, consider our earlier example in which:

- $n = 2$.
- $R = $ *Borrow-scheme*.
- $R_1 = $ *Amt-scheme*.
- $R_2 = $ *Loan-scheme*.
- $r = $ the relation shown in Figure 6.2.
- r_1 and $r_2 = $ the relations shown in Figure 6.4.
- $r_1 \bowtie r_2 = $ the relation shown in Figure 6.5.

Note that the relations in Figures 6.2 and 6.5 are not the same.

In order to have a lossless-join decomposition, we need to impose some constraints on the set of possible relations. We found that decomposing *Lending-scheme* into *Borrow-scheme* and *Branch-scheme* is lossless because of the functional dependency *branch-name* → *assets branch-city*. Later in this chapter, we shall introduce other types of constraints besides functional dependencies. We say that a relation is *legal* if it satisfies all rules, or constraints, that we impose on our database.

Let C represent a set of constraints on the database. A decomposition $\{R_1, R_2, \ldots, R_n\}$ of a relation scheme R is a *lossless-join decomposition* for R if for all relations r on scheme R that are legal under C:

$$r = \Pi_{R_1}(r) \bowtie \Pi_{R_2}(r) \bowtie \cdots \bowtie \Pi_{R_n}(r)$$

We shall show how to test whether a decomposition is a lossless-join decomposition in the next sections. A major part of this chapter is concerned with the question of how to specify constraints on the database and how to obtain lossless-join decompositions that avoid the pitfalls represented by the examples of bad database designs that we have seen in this section.

6.2 Normalization Using Functional Dependencies

A given set of functional dependencies can be used in designing a relational database in which most of the undesirable properties discussed in Section 6.1 do not occur. In designing such systems, it may become necessary to decompose a relation to a number of smaller relations. Using functional dependencies, we can define several *normal forms* which represent "good" database designs. There are a large number of normal forms. The ones we will cover here are BCNF (Section 6.2.2) and 3NF (Section 6.2.3).

6.2.1 Desirable Properties of Decomposition

In this subsection, we shall illustrate our concepts by considering the *Lending-scheme* scheme of Section 6.1.1:

$$Lending\text{-}scheme = (branch\text{-}name, assets, branch\text{-}city, loan\text{-}number,$$
$$customer\text{-}name, amount)$$

The set F of functional dependencies that we require to hold on *Lending-scheme* are:

$$branch\text{-}name \rightarrow assets\ branch\text{-}city$$
$$loan\text{-}number \rightarrow amount\ branch\text{-}name$$

As discussed in Section 6.1.1, the *Lending-scheme* is an example of a bad database design. Assume that we decompose it to the following three relations:

$$Branch\text{-}scheme = (branch\text{-}name, assets, branch\text{-}city)$$
$$Loan\text{-}info\text{-}scheme = (branch\text{-}name, loan\text{-}number, amount)$$
$$Customer\text{-}loan\text{-}scheme = (customer\text{-}name, loan\text{-}number)$$

We claim that this decomposition has several desirable properties, which we discuss below.

Lossless-Join Decomposition

In Section 6.1.2, we have argued that it is crucial when decomposing a relation into a number of smaller relations that the decomposition be lossless. We claim that the above decomposition is indeed lossless. To demonstrate this, we must first present a criterion for determining whether a decomposition is lossy.

Let R be a relation scheme and F a set of functional dependencies on R. Let R_1 and R_2 form a decomposition of R. This decomposition is a lossless-join decomposition of R if at least one of the following functional dependencies are in F^+:

- $R_1 \cap R_2 \rightarrow R_1$
- $R_1 \cap R_2 \rightarrow R_2$

We now show that our decomposition of *Lending-scheme* is a lossless-join decomposition by showing a sequence of steps that generate the decomposition. We begin by decomposing *Lending-scheme* into two schemes:

> *Branch-scheme* = (*branch-name*, *assets*, *branch-city*)
> *Borrow-scheme* = (*branch-name*, *loan-number*, *customer-name*, *amount*)

Since *branch-name* → *assets branch-city*, the augmentation rule for functional dependencies (Section 5.3.2) implies that:

$$branch\text{-}name \rightarrow branch\text{-}name \ \ assets \ \ branch\text{-}city.$$

Since *Branch-scheme* ∩ *Borrow-scheme* = {*branch-name*}, it follows that our initial decomposition is a lossless-join decomposition.

Next, we decompose *Borrow-scheme* into:

> *Loan-info-scheme* = (*branch-name*, *loan-number*, *amount*)
> *Customer-loan-scheme* = (*customer-name*, *loan-number*)

This step results in a lossless-join decomposition, since *loan-number* is a common attribute and *loan-number* → *amount branch-name*.

Dependency Preservation

There is another goal in relational database design to be considered: *dependency preservation*. When an update is made to the database, the system should be able to check that the update will not create an illegal relation — that is, one that does not satisfy all of the given functional dependencies. In order to check updates efficiently, it is desirable to design relational database schemes that allow update validation without the computation of joins.

In order to decide whether joins must be computed, we need to determine what functional dependencies may be tested by checking each relation individually. Let F be a set of functional dependencies on a scheme R and let $R_1, R_2, \ldots, R_n$ be a decomposition of R. The *restriction* of F to R_i is the set F_i of all functional dependencies in F^+ that include *only* attributes of R_i. Since all functional dependencies in a restriction involve attributes of only one relation scheme, it is possible to test satisfaction of such a dependency by checking only one relation.

The set of restrictions $F_1, F_2, \ldots, F_n$ is the set of dependencies that can be checked efficiently. We now must ask whether testing only the restrictions is sufficient. Let $F' = F_1 \cup F_2 \cup \cdots \cup F_n$. F' is a set of functional dependencies on scheme R, but, in general, $F' \neq F$. However, even if $F' \neq F$, it may be that $F'^+ = F^+$. If this is true, then every dependency in F is logically implied by F' and if we verify that F' is satisfied, we have verified that F is satisfied. We say that a decomposition having the property $F'^+ = F^+$ is a *dependency-preserving* decomposition. Figure 6.6 shows an algorithm for testing dependency preservation. The

compute F^+;
for each scheme R_i in D **do**
  begin
    $F_i := $ the restriction of F^+ to R_i;
  end
$F' := \varnothing$
for each restriction F_i **do**
  begin
    $F' = F' \cup F_i$
  end
compute F'^+;
if $(F'^+ = F^+)$ **then** return (true)
          else return (false);

Figure 6.6 Testing dependency preservation.

input is a set $D = \{R_1, R_2, \ldots, R_n\}$ of decomposed relation schemes, and a set F of functional dependencies.

We can now show that our decomposition of *Lending-scheme* is dependency-preserving. To see this, we consider each member of the set F of functional dependencies that we require to hold on *Lending-scheme* and show that each one can be tested in at least one relation in the decomposition.

- The functional dependency: *branch-name → assets branch-city* can be tested using *Branch-scheme = (branch-name, assets, branch-city)*.

- The functional dependency: *loan-number → amount branch-name* can be tested using *Loan-info-scheme = (branch-name, loan-number, amount)*.

As the above example shows, it is often easier not to apply the algorithm of Figure 6.6 to test dependency preservation, since the first step, computation of F^+, takes exponential time.

Repetition of Information

The decomposition of *Lending-scheme* does not suffer from the problem of repetition of information that we discussed in Section 6.1.1. In *Lending-scheme*, it was necessary to repeat the city and assets of a branch for each loan. The decomposition separates branch and loan data into distinct relations, thereby eliminating this redundancy. Similarly, observe that if a single loan is made to several customers, we must repeat the amount of the loan once for each customer (as well as the city and assets of the branch). In the decomposition, the relation on scheme *Customer-loan-scheme* contains the *loan-number, customer-name* relationship, and no other scheme does. Therefore, we have one tuple for each customer for a loan only in the relation on *Customer-loan-scheme*. In the other relations involving *loan-number* (those on schemes *Loan-info-scheme* and *Customer-loan-scheme*), only one tuple per loan need appear.

Clearly, the lack of redundancy exhibited by our decomposition is desirable. The degree to which we can achieve this lack of redundancy is represented by several *normal forms*, which we shall discuss in the remainder of this chapter.

6.2.2 Boyce-Codd Normal Form

One of the more desirable normal forms we can obtain is *Boyce-Codd normal form* (BCNF). A relation scheme R is in BCNF with respect to a set F of functional dependencies if for all functional dependencies in F^+ of the form $\alpha \rightarrow \beta$, where $\alpha \subseteq R$ and $\beta \subseteq R$, at least one of the following holds:

- $\alpha \rightarrow \beta$ is a trivial functional dependency (that is, $\beta \subseteq \alpha$).

- α is a superkey for scheme R.

A database design is in BCNF if each member of the set of relation schemes comprising the design is in BCNF.

To illustrate this, let us consider the following relation schemes, and their respective functional dependencies:

- *Branch-scheme = (branch-name, assets, branch-city)*

  branch-name → assets branch-city

- *Customer-scheme = (customer-name, street, customer-city)*

  customer-name → street customer-city

- *Deposit-scheme = (branch-name, account-number, customer-name, balance)*

  account-number → balance branch-name

- *Borrow-scheme = (branch-name, loan-number, customer-name, amount)*

  loan-number → amount branch-name

We claim that *Customer-scheme* is in BCNF. To see this, note that a candidate key for the scheme is *customer-name*. The only nontrivial functional dependencies that hold on *Customer-scheme* have *customer-name* on the left side of the arrow. Since *customer-name* is a candidate key, functional dependencies with *customer-name* on the left side do not violate the definition of BCNF. Similarly, it can be easily shown that the relation scheme *Branch-scheme* is in BCNF.

The scheme, *Borrow-scheme*, however, is *not* in BCNF. First, note that *loan-number* is not a superkey for *Borrow-scheme* since we *could* have a pair of tuples representing a single loan made to two people, as:

(Downtown, 44, Mr. Bill, 1000)
(Downtown, 44, Mrs. Bill, 1000)

Because we did not list functional dependencies that rule out the above case, *loan-number* is not a candidate key. However, the functional dependency *loan-number → amount* is nontrivial. Therefore, *Borrow-scheme* does not satisfy the definition of BCNF.

We claim that *Borrow-scheme* is not in a desirable form since it suffers from the *repetition of information* problem described in Section 6.1.1. To illustrate this, observe that if there are several customer names associated with a loan, in a relation on *Borrow-scheme*, then we are forced to repeat the branch name and the amount once for each customer. We can eliminate this redundancy by redesigning our database so that all schemes are in BCNF. One approach to this problem is to take the existing non-BCNF design as a starting point and decompose those schemes that are not in BCNF. Consider the decomposition of *Borrow-scheme* into two schemes:

Loan-info-scheme = (*branch-name, loan-number, amount*)
Customer-loan-scheme = (*customer-name, loan-number*)

This decomposition is a lossless-join decomposition.

To determine whether these schemes are in BCNF, we need to determine what functional dependencies apply to them. In this example, it is easy to see that

loan-number → amount branch-name

applies to *Loan-info-scheme*, and that only trivial functional dependencies apply to *Customer-loan-scheme*. Although *loan-number* is not a superkey for *Borrow-scheme*, it is a candidate key for *Loan-info-scheme*. Thus, both schemes of our decomposition are in BCNF.

It is now possible to avoid redundancy in the case where there are several customers associated with a loan. There is exactly one tuple for each loan in the relation on *Loan-info-scheme*, and one tuple for each customer of each loan in the relation on *Customer-loan-scheme*. Thus, we do not have to repeat the branch name and the amount once for each customer associated with a loan.

In order for the entire design for the bank example to be in BCNF, we must decompose *Deposit-scheme* in a manner similar to our decomposition

result := {*R*};
done := false;
compute F^+;
while (not *done*) **do**
   if (there is a scheme R_i in *result* that is not in BCNF)
     then begin
          let $\alpha \rightarrow \beta$ be a nontrivial functional dependency that holds
          on R_i such that $\alpha \rightarrow R_i$ is not in F^+, and $\alpha \cap \beta = \varnothing$;
          result := (*result* − R_i) ∪ (R_i − β) ∪ (α, β);
      end
    else *done* := true;

Figure 6.7   BCNF decomposition algorithm.

of *Borrow-scheme*. When we do this decomposition, we obtain the two schemes:

> *Account-info-scheme* = (*branch-name, account-number, balance*),
> *Customer-account-scheme* = (*customer-name, account-number*)

We are now able to state a general method to generate a collection of BCNF schemes. If *R* is not in BCNF, we can decompose *R* into a collection of BCNF schemes $R_1, R_2, \ldots, R_n$ using the algorithm of Figure 6.7 which generates not only a BCNF decomposition but also a lossless-join decomposition. To see why our algorithm generates only lossless-join decompositions, notice that when we replace a scheme R_i with (R_i − β) and (α, β), the dependency $\alpha \rightarrow \beta$ holds, and (R_i − β) ∩ (α, β) = α.

Let us apply the BCNF decomposition algorithm to the *Lending-scheme* scheme that we used earlier as an example of a poor database design.

> *Lending-scheme* = (*branch-name, assets, branch-city, loan-number,*
> *customer-name, amount*)

The set of functional dependencies that we require to hold on *Lending-scheme* are

> *branch-name* → *assets branch-city*
> *loan-number* → *amount branch-name*

A candidate key for this scheme is {*loan-number, customer-name*}.

We can apply the algorithm of Figure 6.7 to the *Lending-scheme* example as follows:

- The functional dependency:

$$branch\text{-}name \rightarrow assets\ branch\text{-}city$$

holds on *Lending-scheme*, but *branch-name* is not a superkey. Thus, *Lending-scheme* is not in BCNF. We replace *Lending-scheme* by

    Branch-scheme = (*branch-name, branch-city, assets*)
    Borrow-scheme = (*branch-name, loan-number, customer-name, amount*)

- The only nontrivial functional dependencies that hold on *Branch-scheme* include *branch-name* on the left side of the arrow. Since *branch-name* is a key for *Branch-scheme*, the relation *Branch-scheme* is in BCNF.

- The functional dependency

$$loan\text{-}number \rightarrow amount\ branch\text{-}name$$

holds on *Borrow-scheme*, but *loan-number* is not a key for *Borrow-scheme*. We replace *Borrow-scheme* by

    Loan-info-scheme = (*branch-name, loan-number, amount*)
    Customer-loan-scheme = (*customer-name, loan-number*)

- *Loan-info-scheme* and *Customer-loan-scheme* are in BCNF.

Thus, the decomposition of *Lending-scheme* results in the three relation schemes *Branch-scheme*, *Loan-info-scheme*, and *Customer-loan-scheme*, each of which is in BCNF. These relation schemes are the same as those used in Section 6.2.1. We have demonstrated in that section that the resulting decomposition is both a lossless-join decomposition and a dependency-preserving decomposition.

Not every BCNF decomposition is dependency-preserving. To illustrate this, consider the relation scheme:

    Banker-scheme = (*branch-name, customer-name, banker-name*)

indicating that a customer has a "personal banker" in a particular branch. The set *F* of functional dependencies that we require to hold on the *Banker-scheme* is

    banker-name → *branch-name*
    customer-name branch-name → *banker-name*

Clearly, *Banker-scheme* is not in BCNF since *banker-name* is not a superkey.

If we apply the algorithm of Figure 6.7, we may obtain the following BCNF decomposition:

Banker-branch-scheme = (*banker-name, branch-name*)
Customer-banker-scheme = (*customer-name, banker-name*)

The decomposed schemes preserve only *banker-name* → *branch-name* (and trivial dependencies) but the closure of {*banker-name* → *branch-name*} does not include *customer-name branch-name* → *banker-name*. The violation of this dependency cannot be detected unless a join is computed.

To see why the decomposition of *Banker-scheme* into the schemes *Banker-branch-scheme* and *Customer-banker-scheme* is not dependency-preserving, we apply the algorithm of Figure 6.6. We find that the restrictions F_1 and F_2 of F to each scheme are as follows (for brevity, we show only a canonical cover):

F_1 = {*banker-name* → *branch-name*}

F_2 = ∅ (only trivial dependencies hold on *Customer-banker-scheme*)

Thus, a canonical cover for the set F' is F_1.

It is easy to see that the dependency *customer-name branch-name* → *banker-name* is not in F'^+ even though it *is* in F^+. Therefore, $F'^+ \neq F^+$ and the decomposition is not dependency-preserving.

The above example demonstrates that not every BCNF decomposition is dependency-preserving. Moreover, it demonstrates that it is not always possible to satisfy all three design goals:

- BCNF.

- Lossless join.

- Dependency preservation.

This is because every BCNF decomposition of *Banker-scheme* must fail to preserve *customer-name branch-name* → *banker-name*.

6.2.3 Third Normal Form

In those cases where we cannot meet all three design criteria, we abandon BCNF and accept a weaker normal form called *third normal form* (3NF). We shall see that it is always possible to find a lossless-join, dependency-preserving decomposition that is in 3NF.

BCNF requires that all nontrivial dependencies be of the form α → β where α is a superkey. 3NF relaxes this constraint slightly by allowing nontrivial functional dependencies whose left side is not a superkey.

A relation scheme R is in 3NF with respect to a set F of functional dependencies if for all functional dependencies in F^+ of the form $\alpha \to \beta$, where $\alpha \subseteq R$ and $\beta \subseteq R$, at least one of the following holds:

- $\alpha \to \beta$ is a trivial functional dependency.

- α is a superkey for R.

- Each attribute A in $\beta - \alpha$ is contained in a candidate key for R.

The definition of 3NF allows certain functional dependencies that are not allowed in BCNF. A dependency $\alpha \to \beta$ that satisfies only the third condition of the 3NF definition is not allowed in BCNF though it is allowed in 3NF. These dependencies are examples of *transitive dependencies* (see Exercise 6.16).

Observe that if a relation scheme is in BCNF, then all functional dependencies are of the form "superkey determines a set of attributes," or the dependency is trivial. Thus, a BCNF scheme cannot have *any* transitive dependencies at all. As a result, every BCNF scheme is also in 3NF, and BCNF is therefore a more restrictive constraint than 3NF.

Let us return to our *Banker-scheme* example (Section 6.2.2). We have shown that this relation scheme does not have a dependency-preserving, lossless-join decomposition into BCNF. This scheme, however, turns out to be in 3NF. To see that this is so, note that {*customer-name, branch-name*} is a candidate key for *Banker-scheme*, so the only attribute not contained in a candidate key for *Banker-scheme* is *banker-name*. The only nontrivial functional dependencies of the form:

$$\alpha \to banker\text{-}name$$

include {*customer-name, branch-name*} as part of α. Since {*customer-name, branch-name*} is a candidate key, these dependencies do not violate the definition of 3NF.

Figure 6.8 shows an algorithm for finding a dependency-preserving, lossless-join decomposition into 3NF. The fact that each relation scheme R_i is in 3NF follows directly from our requirement that the set F of functional dependencies be in canonical form (Section 5.3.4). The algorithm ensures preservation of dependencies by building explicitly a scheme for each given dependency. It ensures that the decomposition is a lossless-join decomposition by guaranteeing that at least one scheme contains a candidate key for the scheme being decomposed. The exercises provide some insight into the proof that this suffices to guarantee a lossless join.

To illustrate the algorithm of Figure 6.8, consider the following extension to the *Banker-scheme* introduced in Section 6.2.2:

Banker-info-scheme = (*branch-name, customer-name, banker-name, office-number*)

let F_c be a canonical cover for F;
$i := 0$;
for each functional dependency $\alpha \rightarrow \beta$ in F_c **do**
if none of the schemes R_j, $1 \le j \le i$ contains $\alpha\ \beta$
   then begin
          $i := i + 1$;
          $R_i := \alpha\ \beta$;
   end
if none of the schemes R_j, $1 \le j \le i$ contains a candidate key for R
   then begin
          $i := i + 1$;
          $R_i :=$ any candidate key for R;
   end
return $(R_1, R_2, \ldots, R_i)$

Figure 6.8   Dependency-preserving, lossless-join decomposition into 3NF.

The main difference here is that we include the banker's office-number as part of the information. The functional dependencies for this relation scheme are:

$$banker\text{-}name \rightarrow branch\text{-}name\ office\text{-}number$$
$$customer\text{-}name\ branch\text{-}name \rightarrow banker\text{-}name$$

The **for** loop in the algorithm causes us to include the following schemes in our decomposition:

Banker-office-scheme = (*banker-name, branch-name, office-number*)
Banker-scheme = (*customer-name, branch-name, banker-name*)

Since *Banker-scheme* contains a candidate key for *Banker-info-scheme*, we are done with the decomposition process.

6.2.4 Comparison of BCNF and 3NF

We have seen two normal forms for relational database schemes: 3NF and BCNF. There is an advantage to 3NF in that we know that it is always possible to obtain a 3NF design without sacrificing a lossless join or dependency preservation. Nevertheless, there is a disadvantage to 3NF. If we do not eliminate all transitive dependencies, it may be necessary to use null values to represent some of the possible meaningful relationships among data items, and there is the problem of repetition of information.

customer-name	banker-name	branch-name
Jones	Johnson	Perryridge
Smith	Johnson	Perryridge
Hayes	Johnson	Perryridge
Jackson	Johnson	Perryridge
Curry	Johnson	Perryridge
Turner	Johnson	Perryridge

Figure 6.9   An instance of *Banker-scheme*.

To illustrate, consider again the *Banker-scheme* and its associated functional dependencies. Since *banker-name → branch-name*, we may want to represent relationships between values for *banker-name* and values for *branch-name* in our database. However, in order to do so, either there must be a corresponding value for *customer-name* or we must use a null value for the attribute *customer-name*.

The other difficulty with the *Banker-scheme* is repetition of information. To illustrate, consider an instance of *Banker-scheme* shown in Figure 6.9. Notice that the information indicating that Johnson is working at the Perryridge branch is repeated redundantly.

If we are forced to choose between BCNF and dependency preservation with 3NF, it is generally preferable to opt for 3NF. If we cannot test for dependency preservation efficiently, we either pay a high penalty in system performance or risk the integrity of the data in our database. Neither of these alternatives is attractive. With such alternatives, the limited amount of redundancy imposed by transitive dependencies allowed under 3NF is the lesser evil. Thus, we normally choose to retain dependency preservation and sacrifice BCNF.

To summarize the above discussion, we note that our goal for a relational database design is:

- BCNF.

- Lossless join.

- Dependency preservation.

If we cannot achieve this, we accept:

- 3NF.

- Lossless join.

- Dependency preservation.

6.3 Normalization Using Multivalued Dependencies

There are relation schemes that are in BCNF which do not seem to be sufficiently normalized in the sense that they still suffer from the problem of repetition of information. Consider again our banking example. Let us assume that in some alternative design for the bank database scheme, we have the scheme:

$$BC\text{-}scheme = (loan\text{-}number, customer\text{-}name, street, customer\text{-}city)$$

The astute reader will recognize this as a non-BCNF scheme because of the functional dependency

$$customer\text{-}name \rightarrow street\ customer\text{-}city$$

that we asserted earlier, and the fact that *customer-name* is not a key for *BC-scheme*. However, let us assume that our bank is attracting wealthy customers who have several addresses (say, a winter home and a summer home). Then, we no longer wish to enforce the functional dependency *customer-name* → *street customer-city*. If we remove this functional dependency, we find *BC-scheme* to be in BCNF with respect to our modified set of functional dependencies. Despite the fact that *BC-scheme* is now in BCNF, we still have the problem of repetition of information that we had earlier.

In order to deal with this, we must define a new form of constraint, called a *multivalued dependency*. As we did for functional dependencies, we shall use multivalued dependencies to define a normal form for relation schemes. This normal form, called *fourth normal form* (4NF), is more restrictive than BCNF. We shall see that every 4NF scheme is also in BCNF, but there are BCNF schemes that are not in 4NF.

6.3.1 Multivalued Dependencies

Functional dependencies rule out certain tuples from being in a relation. If $A \rightarrow B$, then we cannot have two tuples with the same A value but different B values. Multivalued dependencies do not rule out the existence of certain tuples. Instead, they *require* that other tuples of a certain form be present in the relation. For this reason, functional dependencies sometimes are referred to as "equality-generating" dependencies and multivalued dependencies are referred to as "tuple-generating" dependencies.

Let R be a relation scheme and let $\alpha \subseteq R$ and $\beta \subseteq R$. The *multivalued dependency*

$$\alpha \twoheadrightarrow \beta$$

	α		β		$R - \alpha - \beta$	
t_1	a_1 $\cdots$ a_i		a_{i+1} $\cdots$ a_j		a_{j+1} $\cdots$ a_n	
t_2	a_1 $\cdots$ a_i		b_{i+1} $\cdots$ b_j		b_{j+1} $\cdots$ b_n	
t_3	a_1 $\cdots$ a_i		a_{i+1} $\cdots$ a_j		b_{j+1} $\cdots$ b_n	
t_4	a_1 $\cdots$ a_i		b_{i+1} $\cdots$ b_j		a_{j+1} $\cdots$ a_n	

Figure 6.10   Tabular representation of $\alpha \twoheadrightarrow \beta$.

holds on R if in any legal relation $r(R)$, for all pairs of tuples t_1 and t_2 in r such that $t_1[\alpha] = t_2[\alpha]$, there exist tuples t_3 and t_4 in r such that:

$$t_1[\alpha] = t_2[\alpha] = t_3[\alpha] = t_4[\alpha]$$
$$t_3[\beta] = t_1[\beta]$$
$$t_3[R - \beta] = t_2[R - \beta]$$
$$t_4[\beta] = t_2[\beta]$$
$$t_4[R - \beta] = t_1[R - \beta]$$

This definition is less complicated than it appears. In Figure 6.10, we give a tabular picture of t_1, t_2, t_3, and t_4. Intuitively, the multivalued dependency $\alpha \twoheadrightarrow \beta$ says that the relationship between α and β is independent of the relationship between α and $R - \beta$. If the multivalued dependency $\alpha \twoheadrightarrow \beta$ is satisfied by all relations on scheme R, then $\alpha \twoheadrightarrow \beta$ is a *trivial* multivalued dependency on scheme R. Thus, $\alpha \twoheadrightarrow \beta$ is trivial if $\beta \subseteq \alpha$ or $\beta \cup \alpha = R$.

To illustrate the difference between functional and multivalued dependencies, consider again the *BC-scheme*, and the relation *bc* (*BC-scheme*) of Figure 6.11. We must repeat the loan number once for each address a customer has, and we must repeat the address for each loan a customer has. This repetition is unnecessary since the relationship between a customer and his or her address is independent of the relationship between that customer and a loan. If a customer, say Smith, has a loan, say loan number 23, we want that loan to be associated with all of Smith's addresses. Thus, the relation of Figure 6.12 is illegal. To make this relation

loan-number	customer-name	street	customer-city
23	Smith	North	Rye
23	Smith	Main	Manchester
93	Curry	Lake	Horseneck

Figure 6.11   Relation *bc*, an example of redundancy in a BCNF relation.

loan-number	customer-name	street	customer-city
23	Smith	North	Rye
27	Smith	Main	Manchester

Figure 6.12   An illegal *bc* relation.

legal, we need to add the tuples (23, Smith, Main, Manchester) and (27, Smith, North, Rye) to the *bc* relation of Figure 6.12.

Comparing the above example with our definition of multivalued dependency, we see that we want the multivalued dependency

$$customer\text{-}name \twoheadrightarrow street\ customer\text{-}city$$

to hold. (The multivalued dependency *customer-name* $\twoheadrightarrow$ *loan-number* will do as well. We shall soon see that they are equivalent.)

As was the case for functional dependencies, we shall use multivalued dependencies in two ways:

1. To test relations to determine whether they are legal under a given set of functional and multivalued dependencies.

2. To specify constraints on the set of legal relations. We shall thus concern ourselves *only* with relations that satisfy a given set of functional and multivalued dependencies.

Note that if a relation *r* fails to satisfy a given multivalued dependency, we can construct a relation *r'* that does satisfy the multivalued dependency by adding tuples to *r*.

6.3.2 Theory of Multivalued Dependencies

As was the case for functional dependencies and 3NF and BCNF, we shall need to determine all the multivalued dependencies that are logically implied by a given set of multivalued dependencies.

We take the same approach here that we did earlier for functional dependencies. Let *D* denote a set of functional and multivalued dependencies. The closure D^+ of *D* is the set of all functional and multivalued dependencies logically implied by *D*. As was the case for functional dependencies, we can compute D^+ from *D* using the formal definitions of functional dependencies and multivalued dependencies. However, it is usually easier to reason about sets of dependencies using a system of inference rules.

The following list of inference rules for functional and multivalued dependencies is *sound* and *complete*. Recall that *soundness* means that the rules do not generate any dependencies that are not logically implied by D. *Completeness* means that the rules allow us to generate all dependencies in D^+. The first three rules are Armstrong's axioms, which we saw earlier in Chapter 5.

1. **Reflexivity rule**. If α is a set of attributes and $\beta \subseteq \alpha$, then $\alpha \to \beta$ holds.

2. **Augmentation rule**. If $\alpha \to \beta$ holds and γ is a set of attributes, then $\gamma\alpha \to \gamma\beta$ holds.

3. **Transitivity rule**. If $\alpha \to \beta$ holds and $\beta \to \gamma$ holds, then $\alpha \to \gamma$ holds.

4. **Complementation rule**. If $\alpha \twoheadrightarrow \beta$ holds, then $\alpha \twoheadrightarrow R - \beta - \alpha$ holds.

5. **Multivalued augmentation rule**. If $\alpha \twoheadrightarrow \beta$ holds and $\gamma \subseteq R$ and $\delta \subseteq \gamma$, then $\gamma\alpha \twoheadrightarrow \delta\beta$ holds.

6. **Multivalued transitivity rule**. If $\alpha \twoheadrightarrow \beta$ holds and $\beta \twoheadrightarrow \gamma$ holds, then $\alpha \twoheadrightarrow \gamma - \beta$ holds.

7. **Replication rule**. If $\alpha \to \beta$ holds, then $\alpha \twoheadrightarrow \beta$.

8. **Coalescence rule**. If $\alpha \twoheadrightarrow \beta$ holds and $\gamma \subseteq \beta$ and there is a δ such that $\delta \subseteq R$ and $\delta \cap \beta = \emptyset$ and $\delta \to \gamma$, then $\alpha \to \gamma$ holds.

The bibliographic notes provide references to proofs that the above rules are sound and complete. The following examples provide some insight into how the formal proofs proceed.

Let $R = (A, B, C, G, H, I)$ be a relation scheme. Suppose $A \twoheadrightarrow BC$ holds. The definition of multivalued dependencies implies that if $t_1[A] = t_2[A]$ then there exist tuples t_3 and t_4 such that:

$$t_1[A] = t_2[A] = t_3[A] = t_4[A]$$
$$t_3[BC] = t_1[BC]$$
$$t_3[GHI] = t_2[GHI]$$
$$t_4[GHI] = t_1[GHI]$$
$$t_4[BC] = t_2[BC]$$

The complementation rule states that if $A \twoheadrightarrow BC$, then $A \twoheadrightarrow GHI$. Observe that t_3 and t_4 satisfy the definition of $A \twoheadrightarrow GHI$ if we simply change the subscripts.

We can provide similar justification for rules 5 and 6 (see the exercises) using the definition of multivalued dependencies.

Rule 7, the replication rule, involves functional and multivalued dependencies. Suppose that $A \to BC$ holds on R. If $t_1[A] = t_2[A]$ and $t_1[BC] = t_2[BC]$, then t_1 and t_2 themselves serve as the tuples t_3 and t_4 required by the definition of the multivalued dependency $A \twoheadrightarrow BC$.

Rule 8, the coalescence rule, is the most difficult of the eight rules to verify (see Exercise 6.13).

We can simplify the computation of the closure of D by using the following rules, which can be proved using rules 1 to 8 (see the exercises).

- **Multivalued union rule.** If $\alpha \twoheadrightarrow \beta$ holds and $\alpha \twoheadrightarrow \gamma$ holds, then $\alpha \twoheadrightarrow \beta\gamma$ holds.

- **Intersection rule.** If $\alpha \twoheadrightarrow \beta$ holds and $\alpha \twoheadrightarrow \gamma$ holds, then $\alpha \twoheadrightarrow \beta \cap \gamma$ holds.

- **Difference rule.** If $\alpha \twoheadrightarrow \beta$ holds and $\alpha \twoheadrightarrow \gamma$ holds, then $\alpha \twoheadrightarrow \beta - \gamma$ holds and $\alpha \twoheadrightarrow \gamma - \beta$ holds.

Let us apply our rules to the following example. Let $R = (A, B, C, G, H, I)$ with the following set of dependencies D given:

$$A \twoheadrightarrow B$$
$$B \twoheadrightarrow HI$$
$$CG \to H$$

We list some members of D^+ below:

- $A \twoheadrightarrow CGHI$: Since $A \twoheadrightarrow B$, the complementation rule (rule 4) implies that $A \twoheadrightarrow R - B - A$. $R - B - A = CGHI$, so $A \twoheadrightarrow CGHI$.

- $A \twoheadrightarrow HI$: Since $A \twoheadrightarrow B$ and $B \twoheadrightarrow HI$, the multivalued transitivity rule (rule 6) implies that $A \twoheadrightarrow HI - B$. Since $HI - B = HI$, $A \twoheadrightarrow HI$.

- $B \to H$: To show this fact, we need to apply the coalescence rule (rule 8). $B \twoheadrightarrow HI$ holds. Since $H \subseteq HI$ and $CG \to H$ and $CG \cap HI = \emptyset$, we satisfy the statement of the coalescence rule with α being B, β being HI, δ being CG, and γ being H. We conclude that $B \to H$.

- $A \twoheadrightarrow CG$: We already know that $A \twoheadrightarrow CGHI$ and $A \twoheadrightarrow HI$. By the difference rule, $A \twoheadrightarrow CGHI - HI$. Since $CGHI - HI = CG$, $A \twoheadrightarrow CG$.

6.3.3 Fourth Normal Form

Let us return to our *BC-scheme* example in which the multivalued dependency *customer-name* $\twoheadrightarrow$ *street customer-city* holds, but no nontrivial functional dependencies hold. We saw earlier that, although *BC-scheme* is in BCNF, it is not an ideal design since we must repeat a customer's address information for each loan. We shall see that we can use the given multivalued dependency to improve the database design, by decomposing *BC-scheme* into a *fourth normal form* (4NF) decomposition.

A relation scheme R is in 4NF with respect to a set D of functional and multivalued dependencies if for all multivalued dependencies in D^+ of the form $\alpha \twoheadrightarrow \beta$, where $\alpha \subseteq R$ and $\beta \subseteq R$, at least one of the following hold:

- $\alpha \twoheadrightarrow \beta$ is trivial multivalued dependency.

- α is a superkey for scheme R.

A database design is in 4NF if each member of the set of relation schemes comprising the design is in 4NF.

Note that the definition of 4NF differs from the definition of BCNF only in the use of multivalued dependencies instead of functional dependencies. Every 4NF scheme is in BCNF. To see that this is so, note that if a scheme R is not in BCNF, then there is a nontrivial functional dependency $\alpha \rightarrow \beta$ holding on R, where α is not a superkey. Since $\alpha \rightarrow \beta$ implies $\alpha \twoheadrightarrow \beta$ (by the replication rule), R cannot be in 4NF.

The analogy between 4NF and BCNF applies to the algorithm for decomposing a scheme into 4NF. Figure 6.13 shows the 4NF decomposition algorithm. It is identical to the BCNF decomposition algorithm of Figure 6.7 except for the use of multivalued instead of functional dependencies.

If we apply the algorithm of Figure 6.13 to *BC-scheme*, we find that *customer-name* $\twoheadrightarrow$ *loan-number* is a nontrivial multivalued dependency and *customer-name* is not a superkey for *BC-scheme*. Following the algorithm, we replace *BC-scheme* by two schemes:

> *Customer-loan-scheme* = (*customer-name, loan-number*)
> *Customer-scheme* = (*customer-name, street, customer-city*).

This pair of schemes which are in 4NF eliminates the problem we have encountered with the redundancy of *BC-scheme*.

result := {R};
done := false;
compute F^+;
while (**not** *done*) **do**
  if (there is a scheme R_i in *result* that is not in 4NF)
    then begin
        let $\alpha \twoheadrightarrow \beta$ be a nontrivial multivalued dependency that holds
        on R_i such that $\alpha \rightarrow R_i$ is not in F^+, and $\alpha \cap \beta = \varnothing$;
        result := (*result* $- R_i$) $\cup$ ($R_i - \beta$) $\cup$ (α, β);
    end
  else *done* := true;

Figure 6.13   4NF decomposition algorithm.

As was the case when we were dealing solely with functional dependencies, we are interested also in decompositions that are lossless-join decompositions and that preserve dependencies. The following fact about multivalued dependencies and lossless joins shows that the algorithm of Figure 6.13 generates only lossless-join decompositions:

- Let R be a relation scheme and D a set of functional and multivalued dependencies on R. Let R_1 and R_2 form a decomposition of R. This decomposition is a lossless-join decomposition of R if and only if at least one of the following multivalued dependencies is in D^+:

$$R_1 \cap R_2 \twoheadrightarrow R_1$$
$$R_1 \cap R_2 \twoheadrightarrow R_2$$

Recall that we stated earlier that if $R_1 \cap R_2 \rightarrow R_1$ or $R_1 \cap R_2 \rightarrow R_2$, then R_1 and R_2 are a lossless-join decomposition of R. The above fact regarding multivalued dependencies is a more general statement about lossless joins. It says that for *every* lossless-join decomposition of R into two schemes R_1 and R_2, one of the two dependencies $R_1 \cap R_2 \twoheadrightarrow R_1$ or $R_1 \cap R_2 \twoheadrightarrow R_2$ must hold.

The question of dependency preservation when we have multivalued dependencies is not as simple as for the case in which we have only functional dependencies. Let R be a relation scheme and let $R_1, R_2, \ldots, R_n$ be a decomposition of R. Recall that for a set F of functional dependencies, the restriction F_i of F to R_i is all functional dependencies in F^+ that include *only* attributes of R_i. Now consider a set D of both functional and multivalued dependencies. The *restriction* of D to R_i is the set D_i, consisting of:

- All functional dependencies in D^+ that include only attributes of R_i

- All multivalued dependencies of the form

$$\alpha \twoheadrightarrow \beta \cap R_i$$

  where $\alpha \subseteq R_i$ and $\alpha \twoheadrightarrow \beta$ is in D^+.

A decomposition of scheme R into schemes $R_1, R_2, \ldots, R_n$ is a *dependency-preserving decomposition* with respect to a set D of functional and multivalued dependencies if for every set of relations $r_1(R_1)$, $r_2(R_2), \ldots, r_n(R_n)$ such that for all i, r_i satisfies D_i, there exists a relation $r(R)$ that satisfies D and for which $r_i = \Pi_{R_i}(r)$ for all i.

Let us apply the 4NF decomposition algorithm of Figure 6.13 to our example of $R = (A, B, C, G, H, I)$ with $D = \{A \twoheadrightarrow B, B \twoheadrightarrow HI, CG \rightarrow H\}$.

r_1:

A	B
a_1	b_1
a_2	b_1

r_2:

C	G	H
c_1	g_1	h_1
c_2	g_2	h_2

r_3:

A	I
a_1	i_1
a_2	i_2

r_4:

A	C	G
a_1	c_1	g_1
a_2	c_2	g_2

Figure 6.14   Projection of relation r onto a 4NF decomposition of R.

We shall then test the resulting decomposition for dependency preservation.

R is not in 4NF. Observe that $A \twoheadrightarrow B$ is not trivial, yet A is not a superkey. Using $A \twoheadrightarrow B$ in the first iteration of the **while** loop, we replace R with two schemes, (A, B) and (A, C, G, H, I). It is easy to see that (A, B) is in 4NF since all multivalued dependencies that hold on (A, B) are trivial. However, the scheme (A, C, G, H, I) is not in 4NF. Applying the multivalued dependency $CG \twoheadrightarrow H$ (which follows from the given functional dependency $CG \to H$ by the replication rule), we replace (A, C, G, H, I) by the two schemes (C, G, H) and (A, C, G, I). Scheme (C, G, H) is in 4NF, but scheme (A, C, G, I) is not. To see that (A, C, G, I) is not in 4NF recall that we showed earlier that $A \twoheadrightarrow HI$ is in D^+. Therefore $A \twoheadrightarrow I$ is in the restriction of D to (A, C, G, I). Thus, in a third iteration of the **while** loop, we replace (A, C, G, I) by two schemes (A, I) and (A, C, G). The algorithm then terminates and the resulting 4NF decomposition is $\{(A, B), (C, G, H), (A, I), (A, C, G)\}$.

This 4NF decomposition is not dependency-preserving since it fails to preserve the multivalued dependency $B \twoheadrightarrow HI$. Consider the relations of Figure 6.14. Figure 6.14 shows the four relations that may result from the projection of a relation on (A, B, C, G, H, I) onto the four schemes of our decomposition. The restriction of D to (A, B) is $A \twoheadrightarrow B$ and some trivial dependencies. It is easy to see that r_1 satisfies $A \twoheadrightarrow B$ because there is no pair of tuples with the same A value. Observe that r_2 satisfies *all* functional and multivalued dependencies since no two tuples in r_2 have the same value on any attribute. A similar statement can be made for r_3 and r_4. Therefore, the decomposed version of our database satisfies all the dependencies in the restriction of D. However, there is no relation r on (A, B, C, G, H, I) that satisfies D and decomposes into r_1, r_2, r_3, and r_4. Figure 6.15 shows the relation $r = r_1 \bowtie r_2 \bowtie r_3 \bowtie r_4$. Relation r does not satisfy $B \twoheadrightarrow HI$. Any relation s containing r and satisfying $B \twoheadrightarrow HI$ must include the tuple $(a_2, b_1, c_2, g_2, h_1, i_1)$. However, $\Pi_{CGH}(s)$ includes a tuple (c_2, g_2, h_1) that is not in r_2. Thus, our decomposition fails to detect a violation of $B \twoheadrightarrow HI$.

We have seen that if we are given a set of multivalued and functional dependencies, it is advantageous to find a database design that meets the three criteria of:

- 4NF.

- Dependency preservation.

- Lossless join.

If all we have are functional dependencies, the first criterion is just BCNF.

We have seen also that it is not always possible to achieve all three of these criteria. We succeeded in finding such a decomposition for the bank example, but failed for the example of scheme $R = (A, B, C, G, H, I)$.

When we cannot achieve our three goals, we compromise on 4NF, and accept BCNF or even 3NF, if necessary to ensure dependency preservation.

6.4 Normalization Using Join Dependencies

We have seen that the lossless-join property is one of several properties of a good database design. Indeed, this property is essential since, without it, information is lost. When we restrict the set of legal relations to those satisfying a set of functional and multivalued dependencies, we are able to use these dependencies to show that certain decompositions are lossless-join decompositions.

A	B	C	G	H	I
a_1	b_1	c_1	g_1	h_1	i_1
a_2	b_1	c_2	g_2	h_2	i_2

Figure 6.15   A relation $r(R)$ that does not satisfy $B \twoheadrightarrow HI$.

Because of the importance of the concept of lossless join, it is useful to be able to constrain the set of legal relations over a scheme R to those relations for which a given decomposition is a lossless-join decomposition. In this section, we define such a constraint, called a *join dependency*. As has been the case for other types of dependency, join dependencies will lead to another normal form called *project-join normal form* (PJNF).

6.4.1 Join Dependencies

Let R be a relation scheme and $R_1, R_2, \ldots, R_n$ be a decomposition of R. The join dependency $*(R_1, R_2, \ldots, R_n)$ is used to restrict the set of legal relations to those for which $R_1, R_2, \ldots, R_n$ is a lossless-join decomposition of R. Formally, if $R = R_1 \cup R_2 \cup \cdots \cup R_n$, we say that a relation $r(R)$ satisfies the *join dependency* $*(R_1, R_2, \ldots, R_n)$ if:

$$r = \Pi_{R_1}(r) \bowtie \Pi_{R_2}(r) \bowtie \cdots \bowtie \Pi_{R_n}(r)$$

A join dependency is *trivial* if one of the R_i is R itself.

Consider the join dependency $*(R_1, R_2)$ on scheme R. This dependency requires that for all legal $r(R)$:

$$r = \Pi_{R_1}(r) \bowtie \Pi_{R_2}(r)$$

Let r contain the two tuples t_1 and t_2 defined as follows:

$$t_1[R_1 - R_2] = (a_1, a_2, \ldots, a_i) \quad t_2[R_1 - R_2] = (b_1, b_2, \ldots, b_i)$$
$$t_1[R_1 \cap R_2] = (a_{i+1}, \ldots, a_j) \quad t_2[R_1 \cap R_2] = (a_{i+1}, \ldots, a_j)$$
$$t_1[R_2 - R_1] = (a_{j+1}, \ldots, a_n) \quad t_2[R_2 - R_1] = (b_{j+1}, \ldots, b_n)$$

Thus, $t_1[R_1 \cap R_2] = t_2[R_1 \cap R_2]$, but t_1 and t_2 have different values on all other attributes. Let us compute $\Pi_{R_1}(r) \bowtie \Pi_{R_2}(r)$. Figure 6.16 shows

	$R_1 - R_2$		$R_1 \cap R_2$	
$\Pi_{R_1}(t_1)$	a_1	$\cdots \quad a_i$	a_{i+1}	$\cdots \quad a_j$
$\Pi_{R_1}(t_2)$	b_1	$\cdots \quad b_i$	a_{i+1}	$\cdots \quad a_j$

	$R_1 \cap R_2$		$R_2 - R_1$	
$\Pi_{R_2}(t_1)$	a_{i+1}	$\cdots \quad a_j$	a_{j+1}	$\cdots \quad a_n$
$\Pi_{R_2}(t_2)$	a_{i+1}	$\cdots \quad a_j$	b_{j+1}	$\cdots \quad b_n$

Figure 6.16 $\Pi_{R_1}(r)$ and $\Pi_{R_2}(r)$.

	$R_1 - R_2$		$R_1 \cap R_2$		$R_2 - R_1$	
t_1	a_1 $\cdots$	a_i	a_{i+1} $\cdots$	a_j	a_{j+1} $\cdots$	a_n
t_2	b_1 $\cdots$	b_i	a_{i+1} $\cdots$	a_j	b_{j+1} $\cdots$	b_n
t_3	a_1 $\cdots$	a_i	a_{i+1} $\cdots$	a_j	b_{j+1} $\cdots$	b_n
t_4	b_1 $\cdots$	b_i	a_{i+1} $\cdots$	a_j	a_{j+1} $\cdots$	a_n

Figure 6.17   Tabular representation of $*(R_1, R_2)$.

$\Pi_{R_1}(r)$ and $\Pi_{R_2}(r)$. When we compute the join, we get two additional tuples besides t_1 and t_2, as shown by t_3 and t_4 in Figure 6.17.

If $*(R_1, R_2)$ holds, whenever we have tuples t_1 and t_2 we must also have t_3 and t_4. Thus, Figure 6.17 shows a tabular representation of the join dependency $*(R_1, R_2)$. Compare Figure 6.17 with Figure 6.10, in which we gave a tabular representation of $\alpha \twoheadrightarrow \beta$. If we let $\alpha = R_1 \cap R_2$ and $\beta = R_1$, then we can see that the two tabular representations in these figures are the same. Indeed, $*(R_1, R_2)$ is just another way of stating $R_1 \cap R_2 \twoheadrightarrow R_1$. Using the complementation and augmentation rules for multivalued dependencies, we can show that $R_1 \cap R_2 \twoheadrightarrow R_1$ implies $R_1 \cap R_2 \twoheadrightarrow R_2$. Thus, $*(R_1, R_2)$ is equivalent to $R_1 \cap R_2 \twoheadrightarrow R_2$. This observation is not surprising in light of the fact we noted earlier that R_1 and R_2 form a lossless-join decomposition of R if and only if $R_1 \cap R_2 \twoheadrightarrow R_2$ or $R_1 \cap R_2 \twoheadrightarrow R_1$.

Every join dependency of the form $*(R_1, R_2)$ is therefore equivalent to a multivalued dependency. However, there are join dependencies that are not equivalent to any multivalued dependency. The simplest example of such a dependency is on scheme $R = (A, B, C)$. The join dependency $*((A, B), (B, C), (A, C))$ is not equivalent to any collection of multivalued dependencies. Figure 6.18 shows a tabular representation of this join dependency. To see that no set of multivalued dependencies logically implies $*((A, B), (B, C), (A, C))$ consider Figure 6.18 as a relation

A	B	C
a_1	b_1	c_2
a_2	b_1	c_1
a_1	b_2	c_1
a_1	b_1	c_1

Figure 6.18   Tabular representation of $*((A, B), (B, C), (A, C))$.

$r\,(A, B, C)$ as shown in Figure 6.19. Relation r satisfies the join dependency $*((A, B), (B, C), (A, C))$, as can be verified by computing

$$\Pi_{AB}\,(r) \bowtie \Pi_{BC}\,(r) \bowtie \Pi_{AC}\,(r)$$

and showing that the result is exactly r. However, r does not satisfy any nontrivial multivalued dependency. To see this, verify that r fails to satisfy any of $A \twoheadrightarrow B$, $A \twoheadrightarrow C$, $B \twoheadrightarrow A$, $B \twoheadrightarrow C$, $C \twoheadrightarrow A$, or $C \twoheadrightarrow B$.

Just as a multivalued dependency is a way of stating the independence of a pair of relationships, a join dependency is a way of stating that a *set* of relationships are all independent. This notion of independence of relationships is a natural consequence of the way we generally define a relation. Consider

Borrow-scheme = (*branch-name, loan-number, customer-name, amount*)

from our banking example. We can define a relation *borrow* (*Borrow-scheme*) as the set of all tuples on *Borrow-scheme* such that:

- The loan represented by *loan-number* is made by the branch named *branch-name*.

- The loan represented by *loan-number* is made to the customer named *customer-name*.

- The loan represented by *loan-number* is in the amount given by *amount*.

The above definition of the *borrow* relation is a conjunction of three predicates: one on *loan-number* and *branch-name*, one on *loan-number* and *customer-name*, and one on *loan-number* and *amount*. Surprisingly, it can be shown that the above intuitive definition of *borrow* logically implies the join dependency $*((\text{loan-number, branch-name}), (\text{loan-number, customer-name}), (\text{loan-number, amount}))$.

Thus, join dependencies have an intuitive appeal and correspond to one of our three criteria for a good database design.

A	B	C
a_1	b_1	c_2
a_2	b_1	c_1
a_1	b_2	c_1
a_1	b_1	c_1

Figure 6.19   Relation $r\,(A, B, C)$.

For functional and multivalued dependencies, we were able to give a system of inference rules that are sound and complete. Unfortunately, no such set of rules is known for join dependencies. It appears to be necessary to consider more general classes of dependencies than join dependencies to construct a sound and complete set of inference rules. The bibliographic notes contain references to research in this area.

6.4.2 Project-Join Normal Form

Project-join normal form is defined in a manner similar to BCNF and 4NF, except that join dependencies are used. A relation scheme R is in *project-join normal form* (PJNF) with respect to a set D of functional, multivalued, and join dependencies if for all join dependencies in D^+ of the form $*(R_1, R_2, \ldots, R_n)$ where each $R_i \subseteq R$ and $R = R_1 \cup R_2 \cup \cdots \cup R_n$, at least one of the following holds:

- $*(R_1, R_2, \ldots, R_n)$ is a trivial join dependency.

- Every R_i is a superkey for R.

A database design is in PJNF if each member of the set of relation schemes comprising the design is in PJNF. PJNF is called *fifth normal form* (5NF) in some of the literature on database normalization.

Let us return to our banking example. Given the join dependency $*((loan\text{-}number,\ branch\text{-}name),\ (loan\text{-}number,\ customer\text{-}name),\ (loan\text{-}number,\ amount))$, *Borrow-scheme* is not in PJNF. To put *Borrow-scheme* into PJNF, we must decompose it into the three schemes specified by the join dependency: *(loan-number, branch-name)*, *(loan-number, customer-name)*, and *(loan-number, amount)*.

Because every multivalued dependency is also a join dependency, it is easy to see that every PJNF scheme is also in 4NF. Thus, in general, we may not be able to find a dependency-preserving decomposition for a given scheme into PJNF.

6.5 Domain-Key Normal Form

The approach we have taken toward normalization is to define a form of constraint (functional, multivalued, or join dependency) and then use that form of constraint to define a normal form. Domain-key normal form is based on three notions.

- **Domain declaration**. Let A be an attribute, and let **dom** be a set of values. The domain declaration $A \subseteq$ **dom** requires that the A value of all tuples be values in **dom**.

- **Key declaration**. Let R be a relation scheme with $K \subseteq R$. The key declaration **key** (K) requires that K be a superkey for scheme R — that is, $K \to R$. Note that all key declarations are functional dependencies but not all functional dependencies are key declarations.

- **General constraint**. A general constraint is a predicate on the set of all relations on a given scheme. The dependencies we have studied in this chapter are examples of a general constraint. In general, a general constraint is a predicate expressed in some agreed-upon form, such as first-order logic.

We now give an example of a general constraint that is not a functional, multivalued, or join dependency. Suppose that all accounts whose *account-number* begins with the digit 9 are special high-interest accounts with a minimum balance of \$2500. Then we would include as a general constraint "If the first digit of $t[account\text{-}number]$ is 9, then $t[balance]$ ≥ 2500."

Domain declarations and key declarations are easy to test in a practical database system. General constraints, however, may be extremely costly (in time and space) to test. The purpose of a domain-key normal form database design is to allow the general constraints to be tested using only domain and key constraints.

Formally, let **D** be a set of domain constraints and let **K** be a set of key constraints for a relation scheme R. Let **G** denote the general constraints for R. Scheme R is in *domain-key normal form* (DKNF) if **D** $\cup$ **K** logically imply **G**.

Let us return to the general constraint we gave above on accounts. The constraint implies that our database design is not in DKNF. To create a DKNF design, we need two schemes in place of *Account-info-scheme*:

> *Regular-acct-scheme* = (*branch-name, account-number, balance*)
> *Special-acct-scheme* = (*branch-name, account-number, balance*)

We retain all the dependencies we had on *Account-info-scheme* as general constraints. The domain constraints for *Special-acct-scheme* require that for each account:

- The account number begins with 9.
- The balance is greater than 2500.

The domain constraints for *Regular-acct-scheme* require that the account number not begin with 9. The resulting design is in DKNF although the proof of this fact is beyond the scope of this text.

Let us compare DKNF to the other normal forms we have studied. Under the other normal forms, we did not take into consideration domain constraints. We assumed (implicitly) that the domain of each attribute was some infinite domain such as the set of all integers or the set of all character strings. We allowed key constraints (indeed, we allowed functional dependencies). For each normal form, we allowed a restricted form of general constraint (a set of functional, multivalued, or join dependencies). Thus, we can rewrite the definitions of PJNF, 4NF, BCNF, and 3NF in a manner which shows them to be special cases of DKNF.

The following is a DKNF-inspired rephrasing of our definition of PJNF. Let $R = (A_1, A_2, \ldots , A_n)$ be a relation scheme. Let $dom(A_i)$ denote the domain of attribute A_i, and let all these domains be infinite. Then all domain constraints $\mathbf{D}$ are of the form $A_i \subseteq dom(A_i)$. Let the general constraints be a set $\mathbf{G}$ of functional, multivalued, or join dependencies. If F is the set of functional dependencies in $\mathbf{G}$, let the set $\mathbf{K}$ of key constraints be those nontrivial functional dependencies in F^+ of the form $\alpha \rightarrow R$. Scheme R is in PJNF if and only if it is in DKNF with respect to $\mathbf{D}$, $\mathbf{K}$, and $\mathbf{G}$.

A consequence of DKNF is that all insertion and deletion anomalies are eliminated.

DKNF represents an "ultimate" normal form because it allows arbitrary constraints rather than dependencies, yet it allows efficient testing of these constraints. Of course, if a scheme is not in DKNF we may be able to achieve DKNF via decomposition, but such decompositions, as we have seen, are not always dependency-preserving decompositions. Thus, while DKNF is a goal of a database designer, it may have to be sacrificed in a practical design.

6.6 Alternative Approaches to Database Design

In this section, we reexamine normalization of relation schemes with an emphasis on the impact of normalization on the design of practical database systems.

We have taken the approach of starting with a single relation scheme and decomposing it. One of our goals in choosing a decomposition was that the decomposition be a lossless-join decomposition. In order to consider losslessness, we assumed that it is valid to talk about the join of all the relations of the decomposed database.

Consider the database of Figure 6.20, showing a *borrow* relation decomposed in PJNF. In Figure 6.20, we represent a situation in which we have not yet determined the amount of loan 58, but wish to record the remainder of the data on the loan. If we compute the natural join of these relations we discover that all tuples referring to loan 58 disappear. In other words, there is no *borrow* relation corresponding to the relations of Figure 6.20. We refer to the tuples that "disappear" in computing the join as

branch-name	loan-number
Round Hill	58

loan-number	amount

loan-number	customer-name
58	Johnson

Figure 6.20   Decomposition in PJNF.

dangling tuples. Formally, let $r_1(R_1)$, $r_2(R_2)$, . . . , $r_n(R_n)$ be a set of relations. A tuple t of relation r_i is a *dangling tuple* if t is not in the relation:

$$\Pi_{R_i} (r_1 \bowtie r_2 \bowtie \cdots \bowtie r_n)$$

Dangling tuples may occur in practical database applications. They represent incomplete information, as in our example where we wish to store data about a loan still in the process of being negotiated. The relation $r_1 \bowtie r_2 \bowtie \cdots \bowtie r_n$ is called a *universal relation* since it involves all the attributes in the "universe" defined by $R_1 \cup R_2 \cup \cdots \cup R_n$.

The only way we can write a universal relation for the example of Figure 6.20 is to include *null values* in the universal relation. We saw in Chapter 3 that null values present serious difficulties. Research regarding null values and universal relations is discussed in the bibliographic notes. Because of the difficulty of managing null values, it may be desirable to view the relations of the "decomposed" design as representing "the" database, rather than the universal relation whose scheme we decomposed during the normalization process.

Note that not all incomplete information can be entered into the database of Figure 6.20 without resorting to the use of null values. For example, we cannot enter a loan number unless we know at least one of the following:

- The customer name.
- The branch name.
- The amount of the loan.

Thus, a particular decomposition defines a restricted form of incomplete information that is acceptable in our database.

The normal forms that we have defined generate good database designs from the point of view of representation of incomplete information. Returning again to the example of Figure 6.20, we would not want to allow the storage of the following fact: "There is a loan (whose number is unknown) to Jones in the amount of $100." Since *loan-number* → *customer-name amount*, the only way we can relate *customer-name* and *amount* is through *loan-number*. If we do not know the loan number, we cannot distinguish this loan from other loans with unknown numbers.

In other words, we do not want to store data for which the key attributes are unknown. Observe that the normal forms we have defined do not allow us to store that type of information unless we use null values. Thus, our normal forms allow representation of acceptable incomplete information via dangling tuples while prohibiting the storage of undesirable incomplete information.

If we allow dangling tuples in our database, we may prefer to take an alternative view of the database design process. Instead of decomposing a universal relation, we may *synthesize* a collection of normal form schemes from a given set of attributes. We are interested in the same normal forms regardless of whether we use decomposition or synthesis. The decomposition approach is better understood and more widely used. The bibliographic notes provide references to research into the synthesis approach.

Another consequence of our approach to database design is that attribute names must be unique in the universal relation. We cannot use *name* to refer to both *customer-name* and to *branch-name*. It is generally preferable to use unique names, as we have done. Nevertheless, if we defined our relation schemes directly rather than in terms of a universal relation, we could obtain relations on schemes such as the following for our banking example:

> *branch-loan (name, number)*
> *loan-customer (number, name)*
> *loan (number, amount)*

Observe that with the above relations, such expressions as *branch-loan* ⋈ *loan-customer* are meaningless. Indeed, the expression *branch-loan* ⋈ *loan-customer* finds loans made by branches to customers with the same name as the name of the branch.

However, in a language like SQL, there is no natural join operation, so in a query involving *branch-loan* and *loan-customer*, references to *name* must be disambiguated by prefixing the relation name. In such environments, the multiple roles for *name* (as branch name and as customer name) are less troublesome and may be simpler for some users.

We feel that the *unique role assumption*, that each attribute name has a unique meaning in the database, is generally preferable to the reuse of the same name in multiple roles. When the unique role assumption is not made, the database designer must be especially careful when constructing a normalized relational database design.

6.7 Summary

In this chapter we have presented criteria for a good database design:

- Lossless join.
- Dependency preservation.
- PJNF, BCNF, 4NF, or 3NF.

We have shown how to achieve these goals and how to find a good compromise when not all the criteria can be achieved.

In order to represent these criteria, we defined several types of data dependencies:

- Functional dependencies (defined in Chapter 5).
- Multivalued dependencies.
- Join dependencies.

We studied the properties of these dependencies with emphasis on what dependencies are logically implied by a set of dependencies.

DKNF is an idealized normal form that may be difficult to achieve in practice. Yet DKNF has desirable properties that should be included to the extent possible in a good database design.

Conspicuous by their absence from our discussion of 3NF, 4NF, and so on, are first and second normal forms. The reason for not discussing second normal form is because this form is of historical interest only. We, therefore, do not discuss it formally in this chapter. Rather, we define it and let the reader experiment with it in Exercise 6.14. Although we have not mentioned first normal form, we have assumed it since we introduced the relational model in Chapter 3. We say that a relation scheme R is in *first normal form* (1NF) if the domains of all attributes of R are atomic. A domain is *atomic* if elements of the domain are considered to be indivisible units. We discuss this further in Chapter 14.

In reviewing the issues we have discussed in this chapter, it is worthwhile to observe that the reason we could define rigorous approaches to relational database design is that the relational data model rests on a firm mathematical foundation. This is one of the primary advantages of the relational model as compared with the other data models we have studied.

Exercises

6.1 Explain what is meant by:

- repetition of information.

- inability to represent information.

- loss of information.

Explain why any one of these properties may indicate a bad relational database design.

6.2 Suppose we decompose the scheme $R = (A, B, C, D, E)$ into:

$$(A, B, C)$$
$$(A, D, E).$$

Show that this is a lossless-join decomposition if the following set F of functional dependencies hold.

$$A \rightarrow BC$$
$$CD \rightarrow E$$
$$B \rightarrow D$$
$$E \rightarrow A$$

6.3 Show that the following decomposition of the scheme R of Exercise 6.2 is not a lossless-join decomposition.

$$(A, B, C)$$
$$(C, D, E)$$

Hint: Give an example of a relation r on scheme R such that

$$\Pi_{A, B, C} (r) \bowtie \Pi_{C, D, E} (r) \neq r$$

6.4 Let $R_1, R_2, \ldots, R_n$ be a decomposition of scheme U. Let $u(U)$ be a relation and let $r_i = \Pi_{R_i} (u)$. Show that

$$u \subseteq r_1 \bowtie r_2 \bowtie \cdots \bowtie r_n$$

6.5 Show that the decomposition in Exercise 6.2 is not a dependency-preserving decomposition.

6.6 List the three design goals for relational databases and explain why they are desirable.

6.7 List all the multivalued dependencies satisfied by the relation of Figure 6.21.

6.8 Give a lossless-join decomposition of the scheme R of Exercise 6.2 into BCNF.

A	B	C
a_1	b_1	c_1
a_1	b_1	c_2
a_2	b_1	c_1
a_2	b_1	c_3

Figure 6.21   Relation of Exercise 6.7.

6.9 Give an example of a relation scheme R' and set F' of functional dependencies such that there are at least two distinct lossless-join decompositions of R' into BCNF.

6.10 In designing a relational database, why might we choose a non-BCNF design?

6.11 Give a lossless-join, dependency-preserving decomposition of the scheme R of Exercise 6.2 into 3NF.

6.12 Show that if a relation scheme is in BCNF then it is also in 3NF.

6.13 Show that the coalescence rule is sound. (Hint: Apply the definition of $\alpha \twoheadrightarrow \beta$ to a pair of tuples t_1 and t_2 such that $t_1[\alpha] = t_2[\alpha]$. Observe that since $\delta \cap \beta = \varnothing$, then if two tuples have the same value on $R - \beta$ then they have the same value on δ.)

6.14 A functional dependency $\alpha \to \beta$ is called a *partial* dependency if there is a proper superset γ of α such that $\gamma \to \beta$. We say that β is *partially dependent* on γ. A relation scheme R is in *second normal form* (2NF) if each attribute A in R either:

● appears in a candidate key

● is not partially dependent on a candidate key.

Show that every 3NF scheme is in 2NF. (Hint: show that every partial dependency is a transitive dependency.)

6.15 Given the three goals of relational database design, is there any reason to design a database scheme that is in 2NF but in no higher normal form? (See Exercise 6.14 for the definition of 2NF.)

6.16 Let a *prime* attribute be one that appears in at least one candidate key. Let α and β be sets of attributes such that $\alpha \to \beta$ holds, but $\beta \to \alpha$ does not hold. Let A be an attribute that is not in α and not in β and for which $\beta \to A$ holds. We say that A is *transitively dependent* on α. We can restate our definition of 3NF as follows.

- A relation scheme R is in 3NF with respect to a set F of functional dependencies if there are no nonprime attributes A in R for which A is transitively dependent on a key for R.

Show that this new definition is equivalent to the original one.

6.17 Use the definition of multivalued dependency to argue that the following axioms are sound:

- the complementation rule.

- the multivalued augmentation rule.

- the multivalued transitivity rule.

6.18 Use the definitions of functional and multivalued dependencies to show the soundness of the replication rule.

6.19 Use the axioms for functional and multivalued dependencies to show that the following rules are sound:

- the multivalued union rule.

- the intersection rule.

- the difference rule.

6.20 Let $R = (A, B, C, D, E)$ and let M be the following set of multivalued dependencies

$$A \twoheadrightarrow BC$$
$$B \twoheadrightarrow CD$$
$$E \twoheadrightarrow AD$$

List the nontrivial dependencies in M^+.

6.21 Give a lossless-join decomposition of scheme R in Exercise 6.20 into 4NF.

6.22 Give an example of a relation scheme R and a set of dependencies such that R is in BCNF but not in 4NF.

6.23 Explain why 4NF is a more desirable normal form than BCNF.

6.24 Give an example of relation scheme R and a set of dependencies such that R is in 4NF but not in PJNF.

6.25 Explain why PJNF is a more desirable normal form than 4NF.

6.26 Rewrite the definitions of 4NF and BCNF using the notions of domain constraints and general constraints.

6.27 Explain why DKNF is a highly desirable normal form, yet one that is difficult to achieve in practice.

6.28 Explain how dangling tuples may arise and what problems they may cause.

Bibliographic Notes

The first discussion of relational database design theory appeared in an early paper by Codd [1970]. In that paper, Codd also introduced first, second, and third normal forms.

BCNF was introduced in Codd [1972a]. The desirability of BCNF is discussed in Bernstein and Goodman [1980b]. A polynomial time algorithm for BCNF decomposition appears in Tsou and Fischer [1982]. Biskup et al. [1979] give the algorithm we used to find a lossless-join dependency-preserving decomposition into 3NF. Fundamental results on the lossless-join property appear in Aho et al. [1979b].

Multivalued dependencies are discussed by Zaniolo [1976]. Beeri et al. [1977] give a set of axioms for multivalued dependencies and prove that their axioms are sound and complete. Our axiomatization is based on theirs.

The notions of 4NF, PJNF, and DKNF are from Fagin [1977], Fagin [1979], and Fagin [1981], respectively. The synthesis approach to database design is discussed in Bernstein [1976].

Join dependencies were introduced by Rissanen [1979]. Sciore [1982] gives a set of axioms for a class of dependencies that properly includes the join dependencies. In addition to their use in PJNF, join dependencies are central to the definition of universal relation databases. Fagin et al. [1982] introduces the relationship between join dependencies and the definition of a relation as a conjunction of predicates (see Section 6.4.1). This use of join dependencies has led to a large amount of research into *acyclic* database schemes. Intuitively, a scheme is acyclic if every pair of attributes is related in a unique way. Formal treatment of acyclic schemes appears in Fagin [1983] and Beeri et al. [1983].

Additional dependencies are discussed in detail in Maier [1983]. Inclusion dependencies are discussed by Casanova et al. [1984] and Cosmadakis et al. [1990]. Template dependencies are covered by Sadri and Ullman [1982]. Mutual dependencies are discussed by Furtado [1978] and Mendelzon and Maier [1979].

Maier [1983] presents the design theory of relational databases in detail. Ullman [1988] presents a more theoretic coverage of many of the dependencies and normal forms presented here.

File and System Structure

In preceding chapters, we have emphasized the higher-level models of a database. At the *conceptual* or *logical* level, the database, in the relational model, was viewed as a collection of tables. The logical model of the database is the correct level for database *users* to focus on. The goal of a database system is to simplify and facilitate access to data. Users of the system should not be burdened unnecessarily with the physical details of the implementation of the system.

Nevertheless, a major factor in a user's satisfaction or lack thereof with a database system is its performance. If the response time for a request is too long, the value of the system is diminished. The performance of a system depends on the efficiency of the data structures used to represent the data in the database and on how efficiently the system is able to operate on these data structures. As is the case elsewhere in computer systems, a tradeoff must be made not only between space and time, but also between the efficiency of one kind of operation versus that of another.

In this chapter as well as in Chapter 8 we describe various methods for implementing the data model and languages presented in preceding chapters. We shall define various data structures that will allow fast access to data. We shall consider several alternative structures, each best suited to a different kind of access to data. The final choice of data structure needs to be made on the basis of the expected use of the system and the physical characteristics of the specific machine.

7.1 Overall System Structure

In this section, we divide a database system into modules that deal with each of the responsibilities of the overall system. Some of the functions of the database system may be provided by the computer's operating system. In most cases, the operating system provides only the most basic services and the database system must build on that base. Thus, our discussion of the design of a database system will include consideration of the interface between the database system and the operating system.

A database system consists of a number of functional components, including:

- The **file manager**, which manages the allocation of space on disk storage and the data structures used to represent information stored on disk.

- The **buffer manager**, which is responsible for the transfer of information between disk storage and main memory.

- The **query parser**, which translates statements in a query language into a lower-level language.

- The **strategy selector**, which attempts to transform a user's request into an equivalent but more efficient form, thus finding a good strategy for executing the query.

- The **authorization and integrity manager**, which tests for the satisfaction of integrity constraints (such as key constraints) and checks the authority of users to access data.

- The **recovery manager**, which ensures that the database remains in a consistent (correct) state despite system failures.

- The **concurrency controller**, which ensures that concurrent interactions with the database proceed without conflicting with one another.

In addition, several data structures are required as part of the physical system implementation, including:

- **Data files**, which store the database itself.

- **Data dictionary**, which stores information about the structure of the database, and authorization information, such as key constraints.

- **Indices**, which provide for fast access to data items holding particular values.

- **Statistical data**, which store information about the data in the database. This information is used by the strategy selector.

Figure 7.1 shows these components and the connections among them.

In this chapter, we shall discuss how the file manager, buffer manager, data files, and the data dictionary can be implemented. In Chapter 8, we show how indices can be implemented. In Chapter 9, we study how the query parser, the strategy selector, and statistical data are implemented. Chapter 10 describe the recovery manager, while Chapters 11 and 12 discuss concurrency control and transaction management. Chapter 16 describes authorization and integrity management.

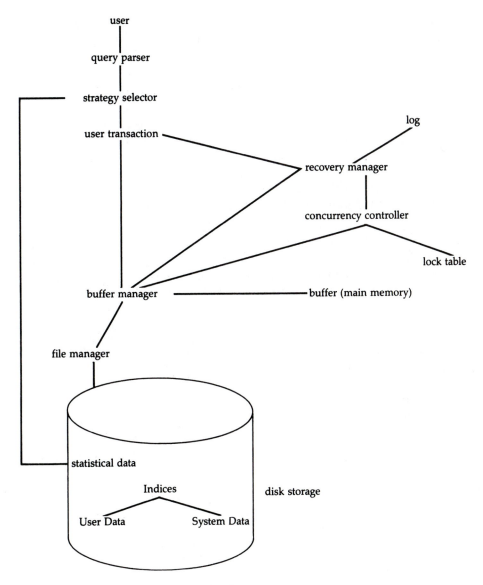

Figure 7.1   System structure.

7.2 Physical Storage Media

Several types of data storage exist in most computer systems. These storage media are classified by the speed with which data can be accessed, by the cost per unit of data to buy the memory, and by how "reliable" they are. Among the media typically available are:

- **Cache**. This is the fastest and most costly form of storage. The size of cache memory is very small and the use of cache is managed by the operating system. We shall not need to be concerned about managing cache storage in the database system.

- **Main memory**. This is the storage media used for data that is available to be operated on. The general-purpose machine instructions operate on main memory. Although main memory may contain several megabytes of data, main memory is generally too small to store the entire database. Main memory is sometimes referred to as *core* memory, a reference to a technology used in the 1960s and early 1970s to implement main memory. The contents of main memory are usually lost if a power failure or system crash occurs.

- **Disk storage**. This is the primary medium for the long-term storage of data. Typically, the entire database is stored on disk. Data must be moved from disk to main memory in order for the data to be operated on. After operations are performed, the data must be returned to disk. Disk storage is referred to as *direct-access* storage because it is possible to read data on disk in any order (unlike sequential-access storage). Disk storage usually survives power failures and system crashes. Disk storage devices themselves may fail and destroy data, but such failures are significantly less frequent than system crashes.

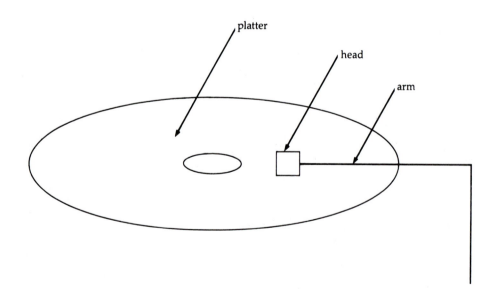

Figure 7.2   A single platter disk.

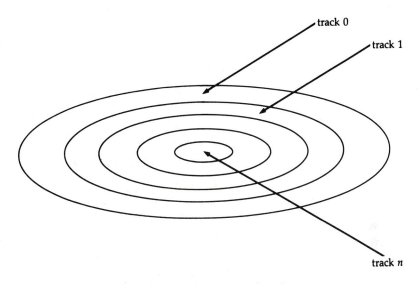

Figure 7.3   Structure of a platter.

- **Tape storage**. This is storage used primarily for backup and archival data. Although tape is much cheaper than disk, access to data is much slower, since the tape must be read sequentially from the beginning. For this reason, tape storage is referred to as *sequential-access* storage and is used primarily for recovery from disk failures (see Chapter 10). Tape devices are less complex than disks; thus, they are more reliable.

Since disk storage is of central importance in database implementation, we shall examine the characteristics of disks in more detail. Figure 7.2 shows a simple disk. The head is a device which stays close to the surface of the platter and reads or writes information encoded magnetically on the platter. The platter is organized into concentric tracks of data as shown in Figure 7.3. The *arm* can be positioned over any one of the tracks. The platter is spun at a high speed. To read or write information, the arm is positioned over the correct track; and, when the data to be accessed passes under the head, the **read** or **write** operation is performed.

Since the platter rotates at a high speed, it does not take very long for the contents of an entire track to pass under the head. This amount of time is referred to as the *disk latency time*. Relative to the latency time, it takes a long time to reposition the arm. The time for repositioning the arm, the *seek time*, grows as the distance that the arm must move increases. It is useful to store related information on the same track or on physically close tracks whenever possible in order to minimize the seek time.

The disk shown in Figures 7.2 and 7.3 is a very simple one. It is typical of disks in early computer systems and in personal computers. Medium-

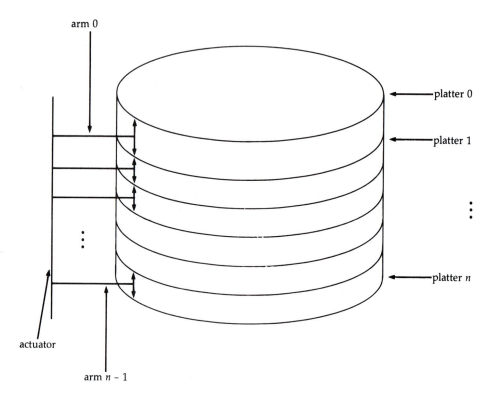

Figure 7.4   A disk pack.

and large-scale computers have high-capacity disks with multiple platters. Such a device is pictured in Figure 7.4. Multiple-platter disks are called disk packs when we wish to distinguish them from single-platter disks. Henceforth, when we use the term *disk*, we shall be referring to multiple-platter disks.

All the disk arms are moved as a unit by the *actuator*. Each arm has two heads: one to read and write the top surface of the platter below it, and one to read and write the bottom surface of the platter above it. At any moment, the set of tracks over which the heads are located form a *cylinder*. This cylinder holds the data that is accessible without any movement of the actuator. That is, all data within this cylinder is accessible within the disk latency time. Just as it is efficient to store related data in a single track or a collection of close tracks, so it is efficient to store related data in the same cylinder, or, if this is not possible, in cylinders that are close to one another.

Data is transferred between disk and main memory in units called *blocks*. A block is a contiguous sequence of bytes from a single track of one platter. Block sizes range from 512 bytes to several thousand bytes. If several blocks from a cylinder need to be transferred from disk to main memory, we may be able to save access time by requesting the blocks in the order in which they will pass under the heads. If the desired blocks are on different cylinders, it is advantageous to request the blocks in an order that minimizes actuator movement. The simplest way to optimize block access time is to organize the blocks on disk in a way that corresponds closely to the manner in which we expect data to be accessed. However, it may be costly to maintain such an organization as data is inserted into and deleted from the database. In other cases, it is impossible to organize data in a way that corresponds closely to the manner in which it is accessed. Such situations arise if an optional organization for one application is especially bad for another application sharing the same data. We shall examine these issues in the next section as we study the storage of data in disk files provided by the underlying operating system.

7.3 File Organization

A *file* is organized logically as a sequence of records. These records are mapped onto disk blocks. Files are provided as a basic construct in operating systems, so we shall assume the existence of an underlying *file system*. We need to consider ways of representing logical data models in terms of files.

Although blocks are of a fixed size determined by the physical properties of the disk and by the operating system, record sizes vary. In a relational database, tuples of distinct relations are generally of different sizes.

One approach to mapping the database to files is to use several files and store records of only one fixed length in any given file. An alternative is to structure our files in such a way that we can accommodate multiple lengths for records. Files of fixed-length records are easier to implement than files of variable-length records. Many of the techniques used for them can be applied to the variable-length case. Thus, we begin by considering a file of fixed-length records.

7.3.1 Fixed-Length Records

As an example, let us consider a file of *deposit* records for our bank database. Each record of this file is defined as follows:

> **type** *deposit* = **record**
>   *branch-name* : char (20);
>   *account-number* : integer;
>   *customer-name* : char (20);
>   *balance* : real;
> **end**

record 0	Perryridge	102	Hayes	400
record 1	Round Hill	305	Turner	350
record 2	Mianus	215	Smith	700
record 3	Downtown	101	Johnson	500
record 4	Redwood	222	Lindsay	700
record 5	Perryridge	201	Williams	900
record 6	Brighton	217	Green	750
record 7	Downtown	110	Peterson	600
record 8	Perryridge	218	Lyle	700

Figure 7.5   File containing *deposit* records.

If we assume that each character occupies a byte, an integer occupies 4 bytes, and a real 8 bytes, our *deposit* record is 52 bytes long. A simple approach is to use the first 52 bytes for the first record, the next 52 bytes for the second record, and so on (Figure 7.5). However, there are two problems with this simple approach:

- It is difficult to delete a record from this structure. The space occupied by the record to be deleted must be filled with some other record of the file, or we must have a way of marking deleted records so that they can be ignored.

- Unless the block size happens to be a multiple of 52 (which is unlikely), some records will cross block boundaries. That is, part of the record will be stored in one block and part in another. It would thus require two block accesses to read or write such a record.

record 0	Perryridge	102	Hayes	400
record 1	Round Hill	305	Turner	350
record 3	Downtown	101	Johnson	500
record 4	Redwood	222	Lindsay	700
record 5	Perryridge	201	Williams	900
record 6	Brighton	217	Green	750
record 7	Downtown	110	Peterson	600
record 8	Perryridge	218	Lyle	700

Figure 7.6   File of Figure 7.5 with record 2 deleted.

When a record is deleted, we could move the record that came after it into the space formerly occupied by the deleted record, and so on, until every record following the deleted record has been moved ahead (Figure 7.6). Such an approach requires moving a large number of records. It might be better simply to move the last record of the file into the space occupied by the deleted record, as shown in Figure 7.7.

It is undesirable to move records in order to occupy the space freed by a deleted record, since this requires additional block accesses. Since insertions tend to be more frequent than deletions, it is acceptable to leave the space occupied by the deleted record open, and wait for a subsequent insertion before reusing the space. A simple marker on a deleted record is not sufficient, since it is hard to find this available space when an insertion is being done. Thus, we need to introduce additional structure.

At the beginning of the file, we allocate a certain number of bytes as a *file header*. The header will contain a variety of information about the file. For now, all we need to store there is the address of the first record whose contents are deleted. We use this first record to store the address of the second available record, and so on. Intuitively, we may think of these stored addresses as *pointers* since they "point" to the location of a record. Figure 7.8 shows the file of Figure 7.5 after records 1, 4, and 6 have been deleted.

Upon insertion of a new record, we use the record pointed to by the header. We change the header pointer to point to the next available record. If no space is available, we add the record to the end of the file.

The use of pointers requires careful programming. If we move or delete a record to which another record contains a pointer, that pointer becomes incorrect in the sense that it no longer points to the desired record. Such pointers are called *dangling pointers* and, in effect, point to garbage. In order to avoid the dangling-pointer problem, we must avoid moving or deleting records that are pointed to by other records. We say that such records are *pinned*.

record 0	Perryridge	102	Hayes	400
record 1	Round Hill	305	Turner	350
record 8	Perryridge	218	Lyle	700
record 3	Downtown	101	Johnson	500
record 4	Redwood	222	Lindsay	700
record 5	Perryridge	201	Williams	900
record 6	Brighton	217	Green	750
record 7	Downtown	110	Peterson	600

Figure 7.7   File of Figure 7.5 with record 2 deleted.

header					
record 0		Perryridge	102	Hayes	400
record 1					
record 2		Mianus	215	Smith	700
record 3		Downtown	101	Johnson	500
record 4					
record 5		Perryridge	201	Williams	900
record 6					
record 7		Downtown	110	Peterson	600
record 8		Perryridge	218	Lyle	700

Figure 7.8   File of Figure 7.5 after deletion of records 1, 4, and 6.

Insertion and deletion for files of fixed-length records are quite simple to implement because the space made available by a deleted record is exactly the space needed to insert a record. If we allow records of variable length in a file, this is no longer the case. An inserted record may not fit in the space left free by a deleted record or it may fill only part of that space.

7.3.2 Variable-Length Records

Variable-length records arise in database systems in several ways:

- Storage of multiple record types in a file.
- Record types that allow variable lengths for one or more fields.
- Record types that allow repeating fields.

A number of different techniques for implementing variable-length records exist. For purposes of illustration, we shall use one example to demonstrate the various implementation techniques. We consider a different representation of the *deposit* information stored in the file of Figure 7.5, in which we use one variable-length record for each branch name and all of the account information for that branch. The format of the record is:

```
type deposit-list = record
                branch-name : char (20);
                account-info : array [1 .. ∞] of
                            record;
                            account-number : integer;
                            customer-name : char (20);
                            balance : real;
                        end
        end
```

0	Perryridge	102	Hayes	400	201	Williams	900	218	Lyle	700	⊥
1	Round Hill	305	Turner	350	⊥						
2	Mianus	215	Smith	700	⊥						
3	Downtown	101	Johnson	500	110	Peterson	600	⊥			
4	Redwood	222	Lindsay	700	⊥						
5	Brighton	217	Green	750	⊥						

Figure 7.9   Byte string representation of variable-length records.

We define *account-info* as an array with an arbitrary number of elements so that there is no limit to how large a record can be (up to, of course, the size of the disk!).

Byte String Representation

A simple method for implementing variable-length records is to attach a special *end-of-record* (⊥) symbol to the end of each record. We can then store each record as a string of consecutive bytes. Figure 7.9 shows such an organization to represent the file of fixed-length records of Figure 7.5 using variable-length records.

The byte string representation has several disadvantages. The most serious of these are:

- It is not easy to reuse space occupied formerly by a deleted record. Although techniques exist to manage insertion and deletion, they lead to a large number of small fragments of disk storage that are wasted.

- There is no space, in general, for records to grow longer. If a variable-length record becomes longer, it must be moved, and movement is costly if the record is pinned.

Thus, the byte string representation is not usually used for implementing variable-length records.

Fixed-Length Representation

In order to implement variable-length records efficiently in a file system, we use one or more fixed-length records to represent one variable-length record.

There are two techniques for implementing files of variable-length records using fixed-length records.

- **Reserved space.** If there is a maximum record length that is never exceeded, we may use fixed-length records of that length. Unused

0	Perryridge	102	Hayes	400	201	Williams	900	218	Lyle	700
1	Round Hill	305	Turner	350	$\perp$	$\perp$	$\perp$	$\perp$	$\perp$	$\perp$
2	Mianus	215	Smith	700	$\perp$	$\perp$	$\perp$	$\perp$	$\perp$	$\perp$
3	Downtown	101	Johnson	500	110	Peterson	600	$\perp$	$\perp$	$\perp$
4	Redwood	222	Lindsay	700	$\perp$	$\perp$	$\perp$	$\perp$	$\perp$	$\perp$
5	Brighton	217	Green	750	$\perp$	$\perp$	$\perp$	$\perp$	$\perp$	$\perp$

Figure 7.10 File of Figure 7.5 using the reserved-space method.

space (for records shorter than the maximum space) is filled with a special null, or "end-of-record" symbol.

- **Pointers**. The variable-length record is represented by a list of fixed-length records, chained together via pointers.

If we choose to apply the reserved-space method to our account example, we need to select a maximum record length. Figure 7.10 shows how the file of Figure 7.5 would be represented if we allow a maximum of three accounts per branch. A record in this file is of the *account-list* type, but with the array containing exactly three elements. Those branches with fewer than three accounts (for example, Round Hill) have records with null fields. We use the symbol $\perp$ to represent this in Figure 7.10. In practice, a particular value that can never represent real data is used (for example, a negative "account number" or a "name" beginning with an "*").

The reserved-space method is useful when most records are of length close to the maximum. Otherwise, a significant amount of space may be wasted. In our bank example, it may be the case that some branches have

0		Perryridge	102	Hayes	400
1		Round Hill	305	Turner	350
2		Mianus	215	Smith	700
3		Downtown	101	Johnson	500
4		Redwood	222	Lindsay	700
5			201	Williams	900
6		Brighton	217	Green	750
7			110	Peterson	600
8			218	Lyle	700

Figure 7.11 File of Figure 7.5 using the pointer method.

many more accounts than others. This leads us to consider use of the pointer method. To represent the file using the pointer method, we add a pointer field as we did in Figure 7.8. The resulting structure is shown in Figure 7.11.

In effect, the file structures of Figures 7.8 and 7.11 are the same except that, in Figure 7.8, we used pointers only to chain deleted records together, while in Figure 7.11, we chain together all records pertaining to the same branch.

A disadvantage to the structure of Figure 7.11 is that we waste space in all records except the first in a chain. The first record needs to have the *branch-name* value, but subsequent records do not. Nevertheless, we need to include a field for *branch-name* in all records, lest the records not be of fixed length. This wasted space is significant since we expect, in practice, that each branch has a large number of accounts. To deal with this problem, we allow two kinds of blocks in our file:

- **Anchor block**, which contains the first record of a chain.

- **Overflow block**, which contains records other than those that are the first record of a chain.

Thus, all records *within a block* have the same length, even though not all records in the file have the same length. Figure 7.12 shows this file structure.

7.4 Organization of Records into Blocks

A file may be viewed as a collection of records. However, since data is transferred between disk storage and main memory in units of a block, it is worthwhile to assign records to blocks in such a way that a single block

Figure 7.12 Anchor block and overflow block organization.

contains related records. If we assign records to blocks randomly, it will usually be the case that a different block must be accessed for each record accessed. On the other hand, if we can access several of the records desired using only one block access, we have saved some disk accesses. Since disk accesses are usually the bottleneck in the performance of a database system, careful assignment of records to blocks can pay significant performance dividends.

Earlier, we described a file structure in which all account information for a branch appeared in one (variable-length) record. Our fixed-length record representations of this file structure used several records to represent a variable-length record. If we can store several of these records together in a block, we reduce the number of block accesses required to read a variable-length record. It is easy to group records together this way if the database never changes. Suppose, however, that a new account is opened at the Perryridge branch. If we are using the structure shown in Figure 7.12, we would like to add the record for this account to the same block as the other Perryridge branch accounts. It is likely to be the case, however, that the block is filled with account records for other branches. Either we must move one of those records or we must abandon our goal of grouping together records representing a single variable-length record. Neither option is desirable.

As an alternative, let us consider a structure which uses slightly more space than the structure of Figure 7.12, but allows for improved efficiency in accessing data. We assign one chain of blocks to each *branch-name* value. The chain of blocks holds the entire variable-length record for the corresponding *branch-name* value. A chain consists of as many blocks as necessary to represent the data, but two different chains never share blocks. Figure 7.13 shows the appropriate structure for the *deposit* file. The chains are structured slightly differently from the previous fixed-length record structures we have used in that:

- The first record in each chain holds the *branch-name* value for the chain.

- Subsequent records hold the repeating fields. There is no need to repeat the *branch-name* since it is the same for all records in the chain. For the same reason, there is no need to chain records together since they represent only one variable-length record. (We may still use pointer chains to facilitate space recovery after deletion.)

Observe that there are two different record lengths in each chain. The first record holds a *branch-name* value. All other records hold three fields: *account-number*, *customer-name*, and *balance*. Since every chain must have *exactly* one record holding the *branch-name* value, there is no problem managing insertion and deletion of records from the chain using any of the techniques we described for fixed-length records.

Block 0	Perryridge		
	102	Hayes	400
	201	Williams	900
	218	Lyle	700

Block 1	Round Hill		
	305	Turner	350

Block 2	Mianus		
	215	Smith	700

Block 3	Downtown		
	101	Johnson	500
	110	Peterson	600

Block 4	Redwood		
	222	Lindsay	700

Block 5	Brighton		
	217	Green	750

Figure 7.13   A chain of blocks file structure.

In the example of Figure 7.13, each chain occupies exactly one block. If we expand our example to a more realistic one in which a branch has thousands of accounts, a chain may require several blocks. We chain blocks together using methods similar to those we used earlier to chain records together. We allocate a fixed amount of space at the beginning of each block as a *block header* and use it to store the chain pointers. Figure 7.14 shows part of a file structure for an expanded bank database. We have omitted the internal structure of each block except for the block header.

As a chain grows owing to insertion of records, new blocks may need to be added to it. As records are deleted, a block may become empty. As we did for deleted records, we can maintain a chain of available blocks and reuse them for other chains that expand beyond their current set of blocks.

The reuse of blocks appears to be a good idea from the standpoint of space efficiency. However, this strategy is not the best from the standpoint of time efficiency. When a chain is searched, each block must be read. In order to minimize the time that this search takes, we need to minimize the time it takes to transfer these blocks into main memory. Thus, we would like the blocks for a bucket to be stored on the same cylinder of the disk, or on adjacent cylinders. A bucket is a collection of one or more blocks

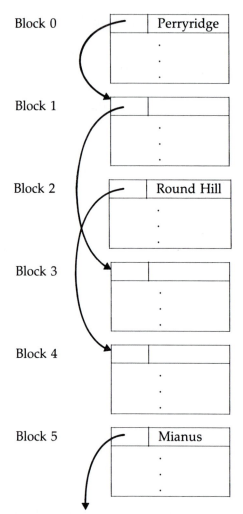

Figure 7.14   Expanded bank database.

chained together. If a block becomes empty, we would prefer that it be reused by the chain that formerly contained it, rather than have it reused by another chain. Such a policy could result in a large number of empty blocks, but this occurs only if deletion is more frequent than insertion. Since almost all database applications have at least as many insertions as deletions, the amount of wasted space is likely to be low.

In practice, it is not possible to maintain a perfect placement of blocks on disk without leaving an excessive amount of space empty. Eventually, chains will overflow their cylinder or cylinders and no room may be available on nearby cylinders. In such cases, any available space may be used. If the chain becomes sufficiently fragmented that performance begins to suffer, the database can be reorganized. The database is copied to tape and reloaded with the blocks relocated so that chains are no longer fragmented and reasonable room for chain growth exists. It is usually necessary to forbid user access to the database during such reorganizations.

7.5 Sequential Files

A *sequential file* is designed for efficient processing of records in sorted order based on some *search key*. To permit fast retrieval of records in search-key order, records are chained together by pointers. The pointer in each record points to the next record in search-key order. Furthermore, in order to minimize the number of block accesses in sequential file processing, records are stored physically in search-key order, or as close to search-key order as possible.

Figure 7.15 shows a sequential file of *deposit* records taken from our banking example. In the example of Figure 7.15, the records are stored in search-key order, using *branch-name* as the search key. It is difficult to maintain physical sequential order as records are inserted and deleted, since it is costly to move many records as a result of a single insertion or deletion. Deletion can be managed using pointer chains, as we saw previously. For insertion, we apply the following rules:

1. Locate the record in the file that comes before the record to be inserted in search-key order.

2. If there is a free record (that is, space left after a deletion) within the same block as this record, insert the new record there. Otherwise, insert the new record in an *overflow block*. In either case, adjust the pointers so as to chain the records together in search-key order.

Brighton	217	Green	750
Downtown	101	Johnson	500
Downtown	110	Peterson	600
Mianus	215	Smith	700
Perryridge	102	Hayes	400
Perryridge	201	Williams	900
Perryridge	218	Lyle	700
Redwood	222	Lindsay	700
Round Hill	305	Turner	350

Figure 7.15 Sequential file for *deposit* records.

Figure 7.16 shows the file of Figure 7.15 after the insertion of the record (North Town, 888, Adams, 800). The structure in Figure 7.16 allows for fast insertion of new records, but it forces sequential file-processing applications to process records in an order that does not match the physical order of the records.

If relatively few records need to be stored in overflow blocks, this approach works well. Eventually, however, the correspondence between search-key order and physical order may be totally lost, and sequential processing becomes significantly less efficient. At this point, the file should be *reorganized* so that it is once again physically in sequential order. Such reorganizations are costly and are done during times when the system load is low. The frequency with which reorganizations are needed depends on the frequency of insertion of new records. In the extreme case in which insertions rarely occur, it is possible always to keep the file in physically sorted order. In such a case, the pointer field shown in Figure 7.15 is not needed.

7.6 Mapping Relational Data to Files

Many relational database systems store each relation in a separate file. This allows the database system to take full advantage of the file system provided as part of the operating system. It is usually the case that tuples of a relation can be represented as fixed-length records. Thus, relations can be mapped to a simple file structure. This simple implementation of a relational database system is well suited to database systems designed for personal computers. In such systems, the size of the database is small, so less is gained from a sophisticated file structure. Furthermore, in some personal computers, small overall size of the object code for the database

Brighton	217	Green	750
Downtown	101	Johnson	500
Downtown	110	Peterson	600
Mianus	215	Smith	700
Perryridge	102	Hayes	400
Perryridge	201	Williams	900
Perryridge	218	Lyle	700
Redwood	222	Lindsay	700
Round Hill	305	Turner	350
North Town	888	Adams	800

Figure 7.16   Sequential file after an insertion.

system is essential. A simple file structure reduces the amount of code needed to implement the system.

This simple approach to relational database implementation becomes less satisfactory as the size of the database increases. We have seen that there are performance advantages to be gained from careful assignment of records to blocks and from careful organization of the blocks themselves. Thus, it is apparent that a more complicated file structure may be beneficial, even if we retain the strategy of storing each relation in a separate file.

However, many large-scale database systems do not rely directly on the underlying operating system for file management. Instead, one large operating system file is allocated to the database system. All relations are stored in this one file, and the management of this file is left to the database system. To see the advantage of storing many relations in one file, consider the following SQL query for the bank database:

> **select** *account-number, customer-name, street, customer-city*
> **from** *deposit, customer*
> **where** *deposit.customer-name = customer.customer-name*

The above query computes a join of the *deposit* and *customer* relations. Thus, for each tuple of *deposit*, the system must locate the *customer* tuples with the same value for *customer-name*. Ideally, these records will be located with the help of *indices*, which we shall discuss in Chapter 8. Regardless of how these records are located, however, they need to be transferred from disk into main memory. In the worst case, each record will reside on a different block, forcing us to do one block read for each record required by the query.

As a concrete example, consider the *deposit* and *customer* relations of Figures 7.17 and 7.18, respectively. In Figure 7.19, we show a file structure designed for efficient execution of queries involving *deposit* ⋈ *customer*. The *deposit* tuples for each *customer-name* are stored near the *customer* tuple for the corresponding *customer-name*. This structure mixes tuples of two relations together, but allows for efficient processing of the join. When a tuple of the *customer* relation is read, the entire block containing that tuple

branch-name	account-number	customer-name	balance
Perryridge	102	Hayes	400
Mianus	220	Hayes	600
Round Hill	503	Hayes	700
Round Hill	305	Turner	350

Figure 7.17 The *deposit* relation.

customer-name	street	customer-city
Hayes	Main	Harrison
Turner	Putnam	Stamford

Figure 7.18   The *customer* relation.

is copied from disk into main memory. Since the corresponding *deposit* tuples are stored on the disk near the *customer* tuple, the block containing the *customer* tuple contains tuples of the *deposit* relation needed to process the query. If a customer has so many accounts that the *deposit* records do not fit in one block, the remaining records appear on nearby blocks. This file structure, called *clustering*, allows us to read many of the required records using one block read. Thus, we are able to process this particular query more efficiently.

Our use of clustering has enhanced processing of a particular join, *deposit* ⋈ *customer*, but it results in slowing processing of other types of query. For example:

select *

from *customer*

requires more block accesses than in the scheme under which we stored each relation in a separate file. Instead of several *customer* records appearing in a block, each record is located in a distinct block. Indeed, simply finding all of the *customer* records is not possible without some additional structure. In order to locate all tuples of the *customer* relation in the structure of Figure 7.19, we need to chain all the records of that relation together using pointers, as shown in Figure 7.20.

The determination of when clustering is to be used depends upon the types of query that the database designer believes to be most frequent. Careful use of clustering can produce significant performance gains in query processing.

Hayes	Main	Harrison	
Perryridge	102	Hayes	400
Mianus	220	Hayes	600
Round Hill	503	Hayes	700
Turner	Putnam	Stamford	
Round Hill	305	Turner	350

Figure 7.19   Clustering file structure.

7.7 Data Dictionary Storage

So far, we have considered only the representation of the relations themselves. A relational database system needs to maintain data *about* the relations. This information is called the *data dictionary*, or *system catalog*. Among the types of information the system must store are:

- Names of the relations.
- Names of the attributes of each relation.
- Domains of attributes.
- Names of views defined on the database, and the definition of those views.
- Integrity constraints for each relation (for example, key constraints).

In addition to the above items, many systems keep the following data on users of the system:

- Names of authorized users.
- Accounting information about users.

In systems that use highly sophisticated structures to store relations, statistical and descriptive data about relations may be kept on the:

- Number of tuples in each relation.
- Method of storage used for each relation (for example, clustered or nonclustered).

In the next chapter, in which we study indices, we shall see a need to store information about each index on each of these relations:

Hayes	Main	Harrison	
Perryridge	102	Hayes	400
Mianus	220	Hayes	600
Round Hill	503	Hayes	700
Turner	Putnam	Stamford	
Round Hill	305	Turner	350

Figure 7.20　Clustering file structure with pointer chains.

- Name of the index.

- Name of the relation being indexed.

- Attributes that the index is on.

- Type of index.

All this information is, in effect, a miniature database. Some database systems store this information using special-purpose data structures and code. It is generally preferable to store the data about the database in the database itself. By using the database to store system data, we simplify the overall structure of the system and allow the full power of the database to be used to permit fast access to system data.

The exact choice of how to represent system data using relations must be made by the system designer. One possible representation is:

System-catalog-scheme = (*relation-name, number-of-attributes*)
Attribute-scheme = (*attribute-name, relation-name, domain-type, position*)
User-scheme = (*user-name, encrypted-password, group*)
Index-scheme = (*index-name, relation-name, index-type, index-attributes*)
View-scheme = (*view-name, definition*)

7.8 Buffer Management

We have already discussed the need to use disk storage for the database, and the need to transfer blocks of data between main memory and disk. A major goal of the file structures presented above is to minimize the number of blocks that must be accessed. Another way to reduce the number of disk accesses is to keep as many blocks as possible in main memory. The goal is to maximize the chance that when a block is accessed, it is already in main memory and, thus, no disk access is required.

Since it is not possible to keep all blocks in main memory, we need to manage the allocation of the space available in main memory for the storage of blocks. The *buffer* is that part of main memory available for storage of copies of disk blocks. There is always a copy kept on disk of every block, but the copy on disk may be an older version of the block than the version in the buffer. The subsystem responsible for the allocation of buffer space is called the *buffer manager*.

The buffer manager intercepts all requests made by the rest of the system for blocks of the database. If the block is already in the buffer, the requester is passed the address of the block in main memory. If the block is not in the buffer, the buffer manager reads the block in from disk into the buffer, and passes the address of the block in main memory to the requester. Thus, the buffer manager is transparent to those system programs that issue disk block requests. Readers familiar with operating system concepts will note that the buffer manager appears to be nothing more than a virtual memory manager as found in most operating systems. However, in order to serve the database system well, the buffer manager must use more sophisticated techniques than typical virtual memory management schemes:

- **Replacement strategy**. When there is no room left in the buffer, a block must be removed from the buffer before a new one can be read in. Typical operating systems use a least recently used (LRU) scheme, in which the block that was referenced least recently is written back to disk and removed from the buffer. This simple approach can be improved upon for database application.

- **Pinned blocks**. In order for the database system to be able to recover from crashes (Chapter 10), it is necessary to restrict those times when a block may be written back to disk. A block that is not allowed to be written back to disk is said to be *pinned*. Although many operating systems do not provide support for pinned blocks, such a feature is essential for the implementation of a database system that is resilient to crashes.

- **Forced output of blocks**. There are situations in which it is necessary to write the block back to disk even though the buffer space it occupies is not needed. This is called the *forced output* of a block. We shall see the reason for requiring forced output in Chapter 10. The requirement is due to the fact that main memory contents and thus buffer contents are lost in a crash while data on disk usually survives a crash.

We now discuss these issues in more detail.

The goal of a replacement strategy for blocks in the buffer is the minimization of accesses to the disk. For general-purpose programs, it is not possible to predict accurately which blocks will be referenced. Therefore, operating systems use the past pattern of block references as a predictor of future references. The assumption that is generally made is that blocks that have been referenced recently are likely to be referenced again. Therefore, if a block must be replaced, the least recently referenced block is replaced. This is called the LRU block replacement scheme.

LRU is an acceptable replacement scheme in operating systems. However, a database system is able to predict the pattern of future references more accurately than an operating system. A user request to the database system involves several steps. The database system is often able to determine in advance which blocks will be needed by each of the steps required to perform the user-requested operation. Thus, unlike operating systems, which must rely on the past to predict the future, database systems may have information regarding at least the short-term future.

To illustrate how information about future block access allows for improvement over the LRU strategy, consider the processing of the relational algebra expression

$$borrow \bowtie customer$$

Assume that the strategy chosen to process this request is given by the following pseudocode program:

```
for each tuple b of borrow do
    for each tuple c of customer do
        if b[customer-name] = c[customer-name]
        then begin
                let x be a tuple defined as follows:
                x[branch-name] := b[branch-name]
                x[loan-number] := b[loan-number]
                x[customer-name] := b[customer-name]
                x[amount] := b[amount]
                x[street] := c[street]
                x[customer-city] := c[customer-city]
                include tuple x as part of result of borrow ⋈ customer
            end
    end
end
```

Assume that the two relations of this example are stored in separate files. In this example, we can see that once a tuple of *borrow* has been processed, it is not needed again. Therefore, once processing of an entire block of *borrow* tuples is completed, that block is no longer needed in main memory, despite the fact that it has been used very recently. The buffer manager should be instructed to free the space occupied by a *borrow* block as soon as the last tuple has been processed. This buffer management strategy is called the *toss-immediate* strategy.

Now consider blocks containing *customer* tuples. We need to examine every block of *customer* tuples once for each tuple of the *borrow* relation. When processing of a *customer* block is completed, we know that it will not be accessed again until all other *customer* blocks have been processed. Thus, the most recently used *customer* block will be the last block to be re-referenced, and the least recently used *customer* block is the block that will be referenced next. This is the exact opposite of the assumptions that form the basis for the LRU strategy. Indeed, the optimal strategy for block replacement is the most recently used (MRU) strategy. If a *customer* block must be removed from the buffer, the MRU strategy chooses the most recently used block.

In order for the MRU strategy to work correctly for our example, the system must pin the *customer* block currently being processed. After the last *customer* tuple has been processed, the block is unpinned and it becomes the most recently used block.

In addition to using knowledge that the system may have about the request being processed, the buffer manager can use statistical information regarding the probability that a request will reference a particular relation. The data dictionary is one of the most frequently accessed parts of the database. Thus, the buffer manager should try not to remove data dictionary blocks from main memory unless other factors dictate otherwise. In the next chapter, we discuss indices for files. Since an index for a file may be accessed more frequently than the file itself, the buffer manager should, in general, not remove index blocks from main memory if alternatives are available.

The ideal database block replacement strategy needs knowledge of the database operations being performed. No single strategy is known that handles all of the possible scenarios well. Indeed, a surprisingly large number of database systems use LRU despite its faults. The exercises explore some alternative strategies.

The strategy used by the buffer manager for block replacement is influenced by other factors besides the time at which the block will be referenced again. If the system is processing requests by several users concurrently, the concurrency control subsystem (Chapter 11) may need to delay certain requests in order to ensure the preservation of database consistency. If the buffer manager is provided with information by the concurrency control subsystem as to which requests are being delayed, the buffer manager can use this information to alter its block replacement strategy. Specifically, blocks needed by active (nondelayed) requests can be retained in the buffer at the expense of blocks needed by the delayed requests.

The crash recovery subsystem (Chapter 10) imposes very stringent constraints on block replacement. If a block has been modified, the buffer manager is not allowed to write the new version of the block in the buffer back to disk since this would destroy the old version. Instead, the block manager must seek permission from the crash recovery subsystem before writing out a block. The crash recovery subsystem may demand that certain other blocks be force-output before it will grant permission to the buffer manager to output the block it requested. In Chapter 10, we define precisely the interaction between the buffer manager and the crash recovery subsystem.

7.9 Summary

A major factor in a user's satisfaction or lack thereof with a database system is its performance. If the response time for a request is too long, the value of the system is diminished. The performance of a system depends on the efficiency of the data structures used to represent the data in the database and on how efficiently the system is able to operate on these data structures. As is the case elsewhere in computer systems, a tradeoff must be made not only between space and time, but also between the efficiency of one kind of operation versus that of another.

Several types of data storage exist in most computer systems. These storage media are classified by the speed with which data can be accessed, by the cost per unit of data to buy the memory, and by how "reliable" they are. Among the media typically available are: cache, main memory, direct-access storage (disk storage), and sequential-access storage (tape storage).

A *file* is organized logically as a sequence of records which are mapped onto disk blocks. One approach to mapping the database to files is to use several files and store records of only one fixed length in any given file. An alternative is to structure files in such a way that they can accommodate multiple lengths for records. There are a number of different techniques for implementing variable-length records, including the pointer method and the reserved-space method.

Since data is transferred between disk storage and main memory in units of a block, it is worthwhile to assign file records to blocks in such a way that a single block contains related records. If we can access several of the records desired using only one block access, we have saved some disk accesses. Since disk accesses are usually the bottleneck in the performance of a database system, careful assignment of records to blocks can pay significant performance dividends.

One way to reduce the number of disk accesses is to keep as many blocks as possible in main memory. Since it is not possible to keep all blocks in main memory, we need to manage the allocation of the space available in main memory for the storage of blocks. The *buffer* is that part of main memory available for storage of copies of disk blocks. The subsystem responsible for the allocation of buffer space is called the *buffer manager*.

A database system consists of a number of functional components, including the file manager, the buffer manager, the query parser, the strategy selector, the recovery manager, and the concurrency controller. In addition, several data structures are required as part of the physical system implementation, including data files, system data files, indices, and statistical data.

Exercises

7.1 List the physical storage media available on your local computer and the speed with which data can be accessed on each medium.

7.2 Define the term *dangling pointer*.

7.3 Define the term *pinned record*.

7.4 Consider the deletion of record 5 from the file of Figure 7.7. Compare the relative merits of the following techniques for implementing the deletion:

- Move record 6 to the space occupied by record 5 and move record 7 to the space occupied by record 6.

- Move record 7 to the space occupied by record 5.

- Mark record 5 as deleted and move no records.

7.5 Show the structure of the file of Figure 7.8 after each step of the following series of steps:

- insert (Brighton, 323, Silver, 1600)

- delete record 2

- insert (Brighton, 626, Gray, 2000)

7.6 Give an example of a database application in which the reserved-space method of representing variable-length records is preferable to the pointer method.

7.7 Give an example of a database application in which the pointer method of representing variable length records is preferable to the reserved-space method.

7.8 Show the structure of the file of Figure 7.10 after each step of the following series of steps:

- insert (Mianus, 101, Thompson, 2800)

- insert (Brighton, 323, Silver, 1600)

- delete (Perryridge, 102, Hayes, 400)

7.9 What happens if we attempt to insert the record

(Perryridge, 929, Glenn, 3000)

into the file of Figure 7.10?

7.10 Show the structure of the file of Figure 7.11 after each step of the following series of steps:

- insert (Mianus, 101, Thompson, 2800)

- insert (Brighton, 323, Silver, 1600)

- delete (Perryridge, 102, Hayes, 400)

7.11 Explain why the allocation of records to blocks is an important issue in database system performance.

7.12 If a block becomes empty as a result of deletions, for what purposes should the block be reused? Why? If possible, determine the buffer management strategy used by the operating system running on your local computer system. Discuss how useful this strategy would be for the implementation of database systems.

7.13 In the sequential file organization, why is an overflow *block* used even if there is, at the moment, only one overflow record?

7.14 Give an example of a relational algebra expression and a query processing strategy such that:

- MRU is preferable to LRU
- LRU is preferable to MRU

7.15 List some advantages and disadvantages of each of the following strategies for storing a relational database:

- store each relation in one file
- store the entire database in one file

7.16 Consider a relational database with two relations:

course (*course-name, room, instructor*)
enrollment (*course-name, student-name, grade*)

Define instances of these relations for three courses, each having five students. Give a file structure of these relations that uses clustering.

7.17 Is it possible in general to have two clustering indices on the same relation for different search keys? Explain.

Bibliographic Notes

There are several papers describing the overall system structure of specific database systems. Astrahan et al. [1976] discuss System R. Chamberlin et al. [1981] review System R in retrospect. Stonebraker et al. [1976] describe the implementation of Ingres. Specific references to functional components of a database system (recovery, concurrency, etc.) appear in the bibliographic notes of subsequent chapters.

Wiederhold [1983], Bohl [1981], Trivedi et al. [1980] and ElMasri and Navathe [1989] discuss the physical properties of disks. Basic data structures are discussed in Knuth [1973], Aho et al. [1983], and Horowitz and Sahni [1976]. Textbook discussions of file organization and access methods for database systems include Teorey and Fry [1982], Smith and Barnes [1987], and Ullman [1988].

Buffer management is discussed in most operating system texts, including Silberschatz et al. [1991]. Stonebraker [1981] discusses the relationship between database system buffer managers and operating system buffer managers.

Alternative disk organizations for a high degree of fault tolerance include Gray et al. [1990], Patterson et al. [1988], and Bitton and Gray [1988]. *Disk striping*, a file organization that uses multiple disks to achieve high performance data access is described by Salem and Garcia-Molina [1986]. An example of an application of optical storage is Christodoulakis and Faloutsos [1986]. A software tool for the physical design of relational database is described by Finkelstein et al. [1988].

8

Indexing and Hashing

Many queries reference only a small proportion of the records in a file. For example, the query "Find all accounts at the Perryridge branch" references only a fraction of the account records. It is inefficient for the system to have to read every record and check the *branch-name* field for the name "Perryridge." Ideally, the system should be able to locate these records directly. In order to allow these forms of access, we design additional structures that we associate with files. We shall consider two general approaches to this problem: the construction of indices and the construction of hash functions.

8.1 Basic Concepts

An index for a file works in much the same way as a catalog in a library. If we are looking for a book by a particular author, we look in the author catalog and a card in the catalog tells us where to find the book. To assist us in searching the catalog, the cards are kept in alphabetic order, so we do not have to check every card to find the one we want.

In real-world databases, indices of the type described above may be too large to be handled efficiently. Instead, more sophisticated indexing techniques may be used. We shall discuss some of these techniques subsequently. As an alternative to indexing, techniques using *hash functions* may be used. We shall consider several techniques for both hashing and indexing. No one technique is the best. Rather, each technique is best suited to particular database applications. Each technique must be evaluated on the basis of:

- **Access time**. The time it takes to find a particular data item, using the technique in question.

- **Insertion time**. The time it takes to insert a new data item. This includes the time it takes to find the correct place to insert the new data item as well as the time it takes to update the index structure.

- **Deletion time**. The time it takes to delete a data item. This includes the time it takes to find the item to be deleted as well as the time it takes to update the index structure.

- **Space overhead**. The additional space occupied by an index structure. Provided that the amount of additional space is moderate, it is usually worthwhile to sacrifice the space to achieve improved performance.

It is often the case that we desire to have more than one index or hash function for a file. Returning to the library example, we note that most libraries maintain several card catalogs: for author, for subject, and for title. The attribute or set of attributes used to look up records in a file is called a *search key*. Note that this definition of *key* differs from that of primary key, candidate key, and superkey. This duplicate meaning for key is (unfortunately) well established in practice. Using the above notion of a search key, we see that if there are several indices on a file there are several search keys.

8.2 Indexing

In order to allow fast random access to records in a file, an index structure is used. Each index structure is associated with a particular search key. If the file is sequentially ordered, and if we choose to include several indices on different search keys, the index whose search key specifies the sequential order of the file is the *primary index*. The other indices are called *secondary indices*. The search key of a primary index is usually the primary key.

In this section we assume that all files are sequentially ordered and thus have a primary search key. Such files, together with a primary index are called *index-sequential files*. They are one of the oldest index schemes used in database systems. They are designed for applications that require

Brighton	217	Green	750
Downtown	101	Johnson	500
Downtown	110	Peterson	600
Mianus	215	Smith	700
Perryridge	102	Hayes	400
Perryridge	201	Williams	900
Perryridge	218	Lyle	700
Redwood	222	Lindsay	700
Round Hill	305	Turner	350

Figure 8.1   Sequential file for *deposit* records.

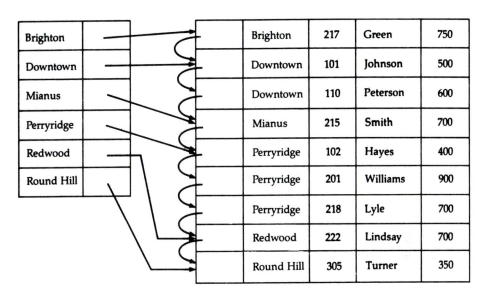

Brighton	217	Green	750
Downtown	101	Johnson	500
Downtown	110	Peterson	600
Mianus	215	Smith	700
Perryridge	102	Hayes	400
Perryridge	201	Williams	900
Perryridge	218	Lyle	700
Redwood	222	Lindsay	700
Round Hill	305	Turner	350

Figure 8.2   Dense index.

both sequential processing of the entire file and random access to individual records.

There are two types of indices that may be used:

- **Dense index**. An index record appears for every search-key value in the file. The record contains the search-key value and a pointer to the record.

- **Sparse index**. Index records are created for only some of the records. To locate a record, we find the index record with the largest search-key value that is less than or equal to the search-key value for which we are looking. We start at the record pointed to by that index record and follow the pointers in the file until we find the desired record.

8.2.1 Primary Index

Figure 8.1 shows a sequential file of *deposit* records taken from our banking example. In the example of Figure 8.1, the records are stored in search-key order, using *branch-name* as the search key.

Figures 8.2 and 8.3 show dense and sparse indices, respectively, for the *deposit* file. Suppose we are looking up records for the Perryridge branch. Using the dense index of Figure 8.2, we follow the pointer directly to the first Perryridge record. We process this record, and follow the pointer in that record to locate the next record in search-key (*branch-name*) order. We continue processing records until we encounter a record for a

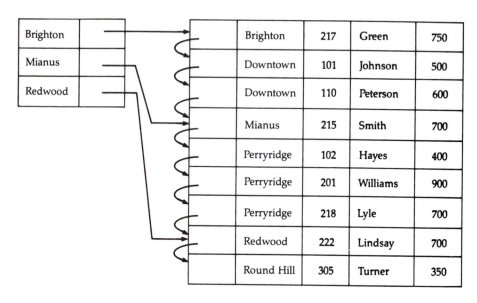

Brighton				Brighton	217	Green	750
Mianus				Downtown	101	Johnson	500
Redwood				Downtown	110	Peterson	600
				Mianus	215	Smith	700
				Perryridge	102	Hayes	400
				Perryridge	201	Williams	900
				Perryridge	218	Lyle	700
				Redwood	222	Lindsay	700
				Round Hill	305	Turner	350

Figure 8.3   Sparse index.

branch other than Perryridge. If we are using the sparse index (Figure 8.3), we do not find an index entry for "Perryridge." Since the last entry (in alphabetic order) before "Perryridge" is "Mianus," we follow that pointer. We then read the *deposit* file in sequential order until we find the first Perryridge record, and begin processing at that point.

As we have seen, it is generally faster to locate a record if we have a dense index rather than a sparse index. However, sparse indices have an advantage over dense indices in that they require less space and they impose less maintenance overhead for insertions and deletions.

There is a trade-off that the system designer must make between access time and space overhead. Although the decision regarding this trade-off is dependent on the specific application, a good compromise is to have a sparse index with one index entry per block. The reason this design is a good trade-off is that the dominant cost in processing a database request is the time it takes to bring a block from disk into main memory. Once we have brought the block in, the time to scan the entire block is negligible. Using this sparse index, we locate the block containing the record we are seeking. Thus, unless the record is on an overflow block (see Section 7.5), we minimize block accesses while keeping the size of the index (and thus, our space overhead) as small as possible.

For the above technique to be fully general, we must consider the case where records for one search-key value occupy several blocks. It is easy to modify our scheme to handle this.

Even if we use a sparse index, the index itself may become too large for efficient processing. It is not unreasonable, in practice, to have a file with 100,000 records, with 10 records stored in each block. If we have one index record per block, the index has 10,000 records. Index records are smaller than data records, so let us assume 100 index records fit on a block. Thus, our index occupies 100 blocks.

If an index is sufficiently small to be kept in main memory, search time is low. However, if the index is so large that it must be kept on disk, a search results in several disk block reads. If the index occupies b blocks, and binary search is used, we may read as many as $1 + \log_2(b)$ blocks. For our 100-block index, this means 7 block reads. Note that if overflow blocks have been used, binary search will not be possible. In that case, a sequential search is typically used which requires b block reads. Thus, the process of searching the index may be costly.

To deal with this problem, we treat the index just as we would treat any other sequential file, and we construct a sparse index on the primary index, as shown in Figure 8.4. To locate a record, we first use binary search on the outer index to find the record for the largest search-key value less than or equal to the one we desire. The pointer points to a block of the inner index. We scan this block until we find the record which has the largest search-key value less than or equal to the one we desire. The pointer in this record points to the block of the file that contains the record for which we are looking.

Using the two levels of indexing, we have read only one index block rather than 7, if we assume that the outer index is already in main memory. If our file is extremely large, even the outer index may grow too large to fit in main memory. In such a case, we can create yet another level of index. Indeed, we can repeat this process as many times as necessary. In practice, however, it is generally the case that two levels are sufficient, and situations requiring more than three levels are extremely rare. Frequently, each level of index corresponds to a unit of physical storage. Thus, we may have indices at the track, cylinder, and disk levels.

Regardless of what form of index is used, every index must be updated whenever a record is either inserted into or deleted from the file. We describe algorithms for updating single-level indices below.

- **Deletion**. In order to delete a record, it is necessary to look up the record to be deleted. If the deleted record was the last record with its particular search-key value, then we delete the search-key value from the index. For dense indices, we delete a search-key value similarly to deleting in a file. For sparse indices, we delete a key value by replacing its entry in the index (if one exists) with the next search-key value (in search-key order). If the next search-key value already has an index entry, we delete the entry.

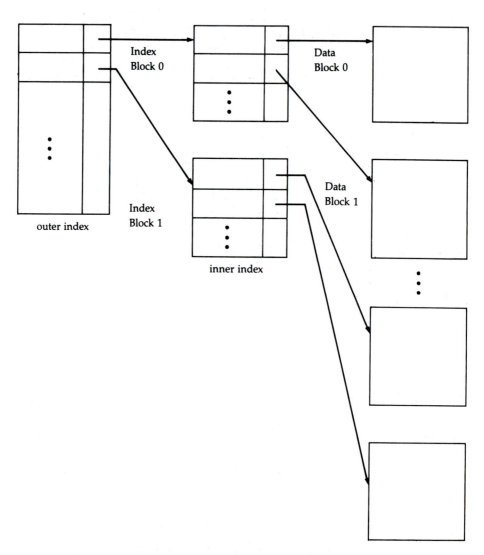

Figure 8.4   Two-level sparse index.

- **Insertion**. Perform a lookup using the search-key value appearing in the record to be inserted. If the index is dense, and the search-key value does not appear in the index, insert it. If the index is sparse, no change needs to be made to the index unless a new block is created. In this case, the first search-key value (in search-key order) appearing in the new block is inserted into the database.

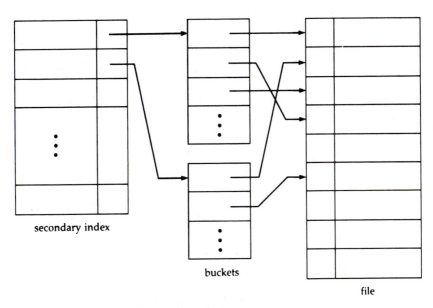

Figure 8.5   Secondary index.

8.2.2 Secondary Indices

Secondary indices may be structured differently from primary indices. Figure 8.5 shows the structure of a secondary index using an extra level of indirection. The pointers in the secondary index do not point directly to the file. Instead, each of these pointers points to a bucket which contains pointers to the file.

This approach allows all the pointers for one secondary search-key value to be stored together. Such an approach is useful in certain types of queries for which we may do considerable processing using only the pointers. For primary keys, we can obtain all the pointers for one primary search-key value using a sequential scan.

A *sequential scan* in primary-key order is efficient because records are stored physically in an order that approximates primary-key order. However, we cannot (except in rare special cases) store a file physically ordered both by the primary key and a secondary key. Because secondary-key order and physical-key order differ, if we attempt to scan the file sequentially in secondary-key order, the reading of each record is likely to require the reading of a new block from disk.

By storing pointers in a bucket as shown in Figure 8.5, we eliminate the need for extra pointers in the records themselves and eliminate the need for sequential scans in secondary-key order.

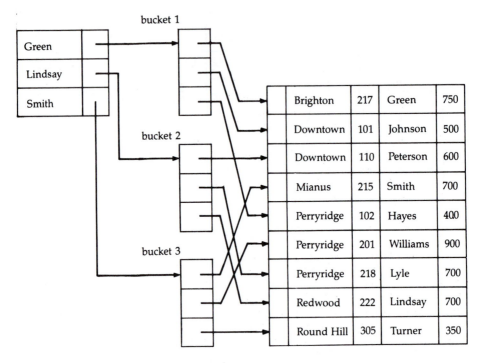

Figure 8.6   Sparse secondary index on *customer-name*.

The secondary index may be either dense or sparse. If it is dense, then the pointer in each individual bucket points to records with the appropriate search-key value. If the secondary index is sparse, then the pointer in each individual bucket points to records with search-key values in the appropriate range. In this case each bucket entry is either a single pointer or a record consisting of two fields: a search-key value and a pointer to some file record.

To illustrate these concepts, consider the sparse secondary index of Figure 8.6 on the search-key *customer-name*. If the buckets contain only pointers, then if we are performing a lookup on "Peterson," we must read all three records pointed to by entries in bucket 2. Only one entry points to a record for which the *customer-name* value is "Peterson," yet three records needed to be read. Since the file is not ordered physically by *customer-name*, we expect this lookup to require three disk block reads. Contrast this example with our earlier example of the sparse primary index of Figure 8.3. Since the file is stored physically in *branch-name* order, we expect only one block read for a lookup.

By associating a search-key value with each pointer in the bucket, we eliminate the need to read records with a secondary-search-key value other than the one on which we are performing a lookup.

The bucket structure can be eliminated if the secondary index is dense and the search-key values form a primary key.

The procedure described earlier for deletion and insertion can be applied to a file with multiple indices. Whenever the file is modified, *every* index must be updated.

Secondary indices improve the performance of queries that use keys other than the primary one. However, they impose a serious overhead on modification of the database. The designer of a database decides which secondary indices are desirable on the basis of an estimate of the relative frequency of queries and modifications.

8.3 B$^+$-Tree Index Files

The primary disadvantage of the index-sequential file organization is that performance degrades as the file grows. Although this degradation can be remedied by reorganization of the file, it is undesirable to perform such reorganizations frequently. The B$^+$-*tree file structure* is the most widely used of several file structures that maintain their efficiency despite insertion and deletion of data. A B$^+$-tree index takes the form of a *balanced* tree in which every path from the root of the tree to a leaf of the tree is of the same length. Each node in the tree has between $\lceil n/2 \rceil$ and n children, where n is fixed for a particular tree ($\lceil x \rceil$ denotes the smallest integer not less than x; that is, we round upward).

We shall see that the B$^+$-tree structure imposes some overhead on insertion and deletion as well as some added space overhead. Nevertheless, this overhead is acceptable for files with a high frequency of modification since the cost of file reorganization is avoided.

A B$^+$-tree index is a multilevel index, but it has a structure that differs from that of the multilevel index-sequential file. A typical node of a B$^+$-tree is shown in Figure 8.7. It contains up to $n - 1$ search-key values $K_1, K_2, \ldots, K_{n-1}$ and n pointers $P_1, P_2, \ldots, P_n$. The search-key values within a node are kept in sorted order; thus, if $i < j$, then $K_i < K_j$.

We consider first the structure of the leaf nodes. For $1 \le i < n$, P_i points to either a file record with search-key value K_i or to a bucket of pointers each of which points to a file record with search-key value K_i. The

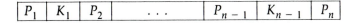

Figure 8.7   Typical node of a B$^+$-tree.

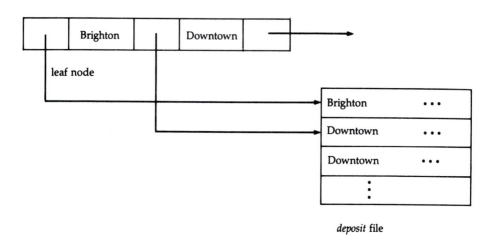

Figure 8.8   A leaf node for *deposit* B$^+$-tree index ($n = 3$).

bucket structure is used only if the search key does not form a primary key, and the file is not sorted in the search-key value order. Pointer P_n has a special purpose which we shall discuss shortly.

Figure 8.8 shows one leaf node of a B$^+$-tree for the *deposit* file, in which we have chosen n to be 3, and the search key is *branch-name*. Note that since the deposit file is ordered by *branch-name*, the pointers in the leaf node point directly to the file.

Now that we have seen the structure of a leaf node, let us consider how search-key values are assigned to particular nodes. Each leaf can hold up to $n - 1$ values. We allow leaf nodes to contain as few as $\lceil (n - 1)/2 \rceil$ values. The ranges of values in each leaf do not overlap. Thus, if L_i and L_j are leaf nodes and $i < j$, then every search-key value in L_i is less than every search-key value in L_j. The set of leaf nodes in a B$^+$-tree must form a dense index so that every search-key value appears in some leaf node.

Now we can explain the use of the pointer P_n. Since there is a linear order on the leaves based upon the search-key values they contain, we use P_n to chain the leaf nodes together in search-key order. This allows for efficient sequential processing of the file.

The nonleaf nodes of the B$^+$-tree form a multilevel (sparse) index on the leaf nodes. The structure of nonleaf nodes is the same as for leaf nodes except that all pointers are pointers to tree nodes. A node may hold up to n pointers, but must hold at least $\lceil n/2 \rceil$ pointers. Let us consider a node containing m pointers. If $1 < i < m$, pointer P_i points to the subtree containing search-key values less than K_i and greater than or equal to K_{i-1}. Pointer P_m points to the part of the subtree containing those key values greater than or equal to K_{m-1}, and pointer P_1 points to the part of the subtree containing those search-key values less than K_1.

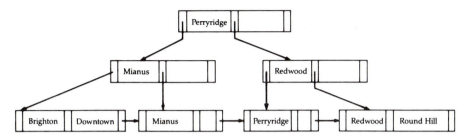

Figure 8.9   B⁺-tree for *deposit* file with $n = 3$.

The requirement that each node hold at least $\lceil n/2 \rceil$ pointers is imposed at all levels of the tree except for the root. Figure 8.9 shows a complete B⁺-tree for the *deposit* file (with $n = 3$). For simplicity, we have omitted both the pointers to the file itself and the null pointers. As an example of a B⁺-tree for which the root must have less than $\lceil n/2 \rceil$ values, we show a B⁺-tree for the *deposit* file in Figure 8.10 with $n = 5$. It is always possible to construct a B⁺-tree, for any n, in which all nonroot nodes contain at least $\lceil n/2 \rceil$ pointers.

The examples we have given of B⁺-trees have all been balanced. That is, the length of every path from the root to a leaf node is the same. This property is a requirement for a B⁺-tree. Indeed, the "B" in B⁺-tree stands for "balanced." It is the balance property of B⁺-trees that ensures good performance for lookup, insertion, and deletion.

Let us consider how queries are processed using a B⁺-tree. Suppose we wish to find all records with a search-key value of k. First, we examine the root node and look for the smallest search-key value greater than k. Assume this search-key value is K_i. We follow pointer P_i to another node. If $K < K_1$, then we follow P_1 to another node. If we have m pointers in the node, and $K \geq K_{m-1}$, then we follow P_m to another node. Once again, we look for the smallest search-key value greater than k and follow the corresponding pointer. Eventually, we reach a leaf node, at which point the pointer directs us to the desired record or bucket.

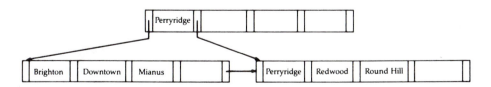

Figure 8.10   B⁺-tree for *deposit* file with $n = 5$.

Thus, in processing a query, a path is traversed in the tree from the root to some leaf node. If there are K search-key values in the file, the path is no longer than $\log_{\lceil n/2 \rceil}(K)$. In practice, this means that only a few nodes need to be accessed even if the file is extremely large. Typically, a node is made to be the same size as a disk block. Thus, it is reasonable for n to be between 10 and 100 (or even larger). Even if we have one million search-key values in the file, a lookup requires that only between 3 and 9 nodes be accessed.

Insertion and deletion are more complicated than lookup since it may be necessary to *split* a node that becomes too large as the result of an insertion or to *combine* nodes if a node becomes too small (fewer than $\lceil n/2 \rceil$ pointers). Furthermore, when a node is split or a pair of nodes is combined, we must ensure that balance is preserved. To introduce the idea behind insertion and deletion in a B$^+$-tree, let us assume temporarily that nodes never become too large or too small. Under this assumption, insertion and deletion are as defined below.

- **Insertion**. Using the same technique as for lookup, we find the leaf node in which the search-key value would appear. If the search-key value already appears in the leaf node, we add the new record to the file and, if necessary, a pointer to the bucket. If the search-key value does not appear, we insert the value in the leaf node, and position it so that the search keys are still in order. We then insert the new record in the file and, if necessary, create a new bucket with the appropriate pointer.

- **Deletion**. Using the same technique as for lookup, we find the record to be deleted, and remove it from the file. The search-key value is removed from the leaf node if there is no bucket associated with that search-key value or if the bucket becomes empty as a result of the deletion.

We now consider an example in which a node must be split. Assume that we wish to insert a record with a *branch-name* value of "Clearview" into the B$^+$-tree of Figure 8.9. Using the algorithm for lookup, we find that "Clearview" should appear in the node containing "Brighton" and "Downtown." There is no room to insert the search-key value "Clearview." Therefore, the node is *split* into two nodes. Figure 8.11 shows the two leaf nodes that result from inserting "Clearview" and splitting the node containing "Brighton" and "Downtown." In general, we take the n search-key values (the $n - 1$ values in the leaf node plus the value being inserted) and put the first $\lceil n/2 \rceil$ in the existing node and the remaining values in a new node.

Having split a leaf node, we must insert the new leaf node into the B$^+$-tree structure. In our example, the new node has "Downtown" as its

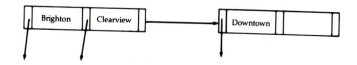

Figure 8.11   Split of leaf node on insertion of "Clearview."

smallest search-key value. We need to insert this search-key value into the parent of the leaf node that was split. The B$^+$-tree of Figure 8.12 shows the result of the insertion. The search-key value "Downtown" was inserted into the parent. It was possible to perform this insertion because there was room for an added search-key value. If this were not the case, the parent would have had to be split. In the worst case, all nodes along the path to the root must be split. If the root itself is split, the entire tree becomes deeper.

The general technique for insertion into a B$^+$-tree is to determine the leaf node l into which insertion must occur. If a split results, insert the new node into the parent of node l. If this insertion causes a split, proceed recursively until either an insertion does not cause a split or a new root is created.

We now consider deletions that cause tree nodes to contain too few pointers. First, let us delete "Downtown" from the B$^+$-tree of Figure 8.12. We locate the entry for "Downtown" using our lookup algorithm. When we delete the entry for "Downtown" from its leaf node, the leaf becomes empty. Since, in our example $n = 3$ and $0 < \lceil (n-1)/2 \rceil$, this node must be eliminated from the B$^+$-tree. To delete a leaf node, we must delete the pointer to it from its parent. In our example, this leaves the parent node, which formerly contained three pointers, with only two pointers. Since $2 \geq \lceil n/2 \rceil$, the node is still sufficiently large and the deletion operation is complete. The resulting B$^+$-tree is shown in Figure 8.13.

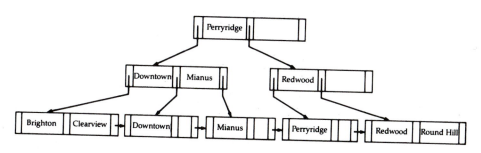

Figure 8.12   Insertion of "Clearview" into the B$^+$-tree of Figure 8.9.

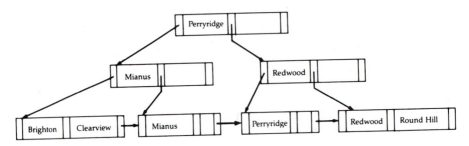

Figure 8.13   Deletion of "Downtown" from the B$^+$-tree of Figure 8.12.

When a deletion is made to a parent of a leaf node, the parent node itself may become too small. This is exactly what happens if we delete "Perryridge" from the B$^+$-tree of Figure 8.13. Deletion of the Perryridge entry causes a leaf node to become empty. When we delete the pointer to this node in its parent, the parent is left with only one pointer. Since $n = 3$, $\lceil n/2 \rceil = 2$, and thus only one pointer is too few. However, since the node contains useful information, we cannot simply delete it. Instead, we look at the sibling node (containing the one search key, Mianus). This sibling node has room to accommodate the information contained in our now-too-small node, so we coalesce these nodes, so that the sibling node now contains the keys "Mianus" and "Redwood." The other node (the node containing only the search key "Redwood") now contains redundant information and can be deleted from its parent (which happens to be the root in our example). Figure 8.14 shows the result. Notice that the root became empty after the deletion, so the depth of the B$^+$-tree has been decreased by 1.

It is not always possible to coalesce nodes. To illustrate this, let us delete "Perryridge" from the B$^+$-tree of Figure 8.12. In this example, the "Downtown" entry is still part of the tree. Once again, the leaf node containing "Perryridge" becomes empty. The parent of the leaf node becomes too small (only one pointer). However, in this example, the sibling node already contains the maximum number of pointers, three.

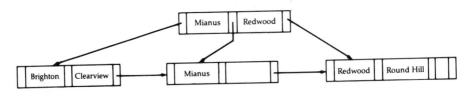

Figure 8.14   Deletion of "Perryridge" from the B$^+$-tree of Figure 8.13.

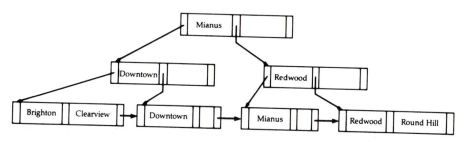

Figure 8.15   Deletion of "Perryridge" from the B$^+$-tree of Figure 8.12.

Thus, it cannot accommodate an additional pointer. The solution in this case is to *redistribute* the pointers so that each sibling has two pointers. The result is shown in Figure 8.15. Note that the redistribution of values necessitates a change of a search-key value in the parent of the two siblings. In general, to delete a value in a B$^+$-tree, we perform a lookup on the value and delete it. If the node is too small, we delete it from its parent. This results in recursive application of the deletion algorithm until the root is reached, a parent remains adequately full after deletion, or coalescence is applied.

Although insertion and deletion operations on B$^+$-trees are complicated, they require relatively few operations. It can be shown that the number of operations needed for a worst-case insertion or deletion is proportional to the logarithm of the number of search keys. It is the speed of operation on B$^+$-trees that makes them a frequently used index structure in database implementations.

8.4 B-Tree Index Files

B-tree indices are similar to B$^+$-tree indices. The primary distinction between the two approaches is that a B-tree eliminates the redundant storage of search-key values. In the B$^+$-tree of Figure 8.12, the search keys "Downtown," "Mianus," "Redwood," and "Perryridge" appear twice. Every search-key value appears in some leaf node.

A B-tree allows search-key values to appear only once. Figure 8.16 shows a B-tree that represents the same search keys as the B$^+$-tree of Figure 8.12. Since search keys are not repeated in the B-tree, we are able to store the index using fewer tree nodes than in the corresponding B$^+$-tree index. However, since search keys that appear in nonleaf nodes appear nowhere else in the B-tree, we are forced to include an additional pointer field for each search key in a nonleaf node. These additional pointers point to either file records or buckets for the associated search key.

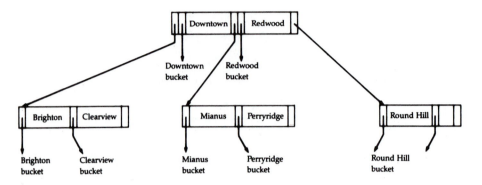

Figure 8.16   B-tree equivalent of B$^+$-tree in Figure 8.12.

A generalized B-tree leaf node appears in Figure 8.17a and a nonleaf node appears in Figure 8.17b. The pointers P_i are the tree pointers that we used also for B$^+$-trees. The pointers B_i in the nonleaf nodes are the bucket or file record pointers.

B-trees offer an additional advantage over B$^+$-trees besides the lack of redundant storage of search keys. In a lookup on a B$^+$-tree, it is always necessary to traverse a path from the root of the tree to some leaf node. However, in a B-tree, it is sometimes possible to find the desired value before reaching a leaf node. Thus, lookup is slightly faster in a B-tree, though, in general, lookup time is still proportional to the logarithm of the number of search keys.

These advantages of B-tree over B$^+$-trees are offset by several disadvantages.

- Leaf and nonleaf nodes are of the same size in a B$^+$-tree. In a B-tree, the nonleaf nodes are larger. This complicates storage management for the index.

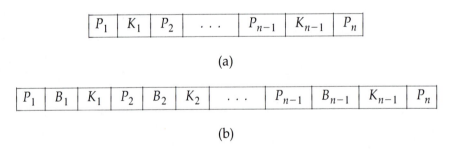

Figure 8.17   Typical nodes of a B-tree: (a) leaf node and (b) nonleaf node.

- Deletion in a B-tree is more complicated. In a B^+-tree, the deleted entry always appears in a leaf. In a B-tree the deleted entry may appear in a nonleaf node. The proper value must be selected as a replacement from the subtree of the node containing the deleted entry. Specifically, if search key K_i is deleted, the smallest search key appearing in the subtree of pointer P_{i+1} must be moved to the field formerly occupied by K_i.

The advantages of B-trees are marginal for large indices. Thus, the structural simplicity of a B^+-tree is preferred by many database system implementors. Details of the insertion and deletion algorithms for B-trees are explored in the exercises.

8.5 Static Hash Functions

One disadvantage of index schemes is that we must access an index structure in order to locate data. The technique of *hashing* allows us to avoid accessing an index structure. We assume that the dense index is partitioned among a number of different buckets. The address of the bucket containing a pointer to the desired data item is obtained directly by computing a function on the search-key value of the desired record. Formally, let K denote the set of all search-key values, and B the set of all bucket addresses. A *hash function h* is a function from K to B.

The principle behind hashing is that, although the set K of all possible search-key values is large (perhaps infinite), the set $\{K_1, K_2, \ldots, K_n\}$ of search-key values actually stored in the database is much smaller than K. We do not know at design time which search-key values will be stored in the database, but we know that there are too many possible values to justify allocating one bucket for every possible value. We *do* know, however, at design time approximately how many search-key values will be stored in the database. We choose the number of buckets to correspond to the number of search-key values we expect to have stored in the database. It is the hash function that defines the assignment of search-key values to particular buckets.

Hash functions require careful design. A bad hash function may result in lookup taking time proportional to the number of search keys in the file. A well-designed function gives an average-case lookup time that is a (small) constant, independent of the number of search keys in the file. This is accomplished by ensuring that, on average, records are distributed uniformly among the buckets.

Let h denote a hash function. To perform a lookup on a search-key value K_i, we simply compute $h(K_i)$ and search the bucket with that address. Suppose that two search keys, K_5 and K_7 have the same hash value, that is, $h(K_5) = h(K_7)$. If we perform a lookup on K_5, the bucket

$h(K_5)$ contains records with search-key values K_5 and records with search-key values K_7. Thus, we have to check the search-key value of every record in the bucket to verify that the record is one that we want.

The worst possible hash function maps all search-key values to the same bucket. This is undesirable because the entire dense index is kept in the same bucket, and thus lookup requires scanning the entire index. An ideal hash function maps every search-key value to a distinct bucket. Such a function is ideal because every record in the bucket searched as a result of a lookup has the desired search-key value.

Since we do not know at design time precisely which search-key values will be stored in the file, we want to choose a hash function that assigns search-key values to buckets such that:

- The distribution is uniform. That is, each bucket is assigned the same number of search-key values from the set of all possible search-key values.

- The distribution is random. That is, in the average case, each bucket will have nearly the same number of values assigned to it.

To illustrate these principles, let us attempt to choose a hash function for the *deposit* file using the search key *branch-name*. The hash function we choose must have desirable properties not only on the example *deposit* file we have been using, but also on a *deposit* file of realistic size for a large bank with many branches.

Assume that we decide to have 26 buckets and define a hash function that maps names beginning with the ith letter of the alphabet to the ith bucket. This hash function has the virtue of simplicity, but it fails to provide a uniform distribution since we expect more branch names to begin with such letters as "*B*" and "*R*" than "*Q*" and "*X*," for example.

Typical hash functions perform some computation on the internal binary machine representation of characters in the search key. A simple hash function of this type is to compute the sum, modulo the number of buckets allocated of the binary representations of characters of a key. Figure 8.18 shows the application of such a scheme, using 10 buckets, to the *deposit* file, under the assumption that the ith letter in the alphabet is represented by the integer i.

Insertion is almost as simple as lookup. If the search-key value of the record to be inserted is K_i, we compute $h(K_i)$ to locate the bucket for that record.

Deletion is equally straightforward. If the search-key value of the record to be deleted is K_i, we compute $h(K_i)$ and search the corresponding bucket for that record.

The form of hash structure we have described above is sometimes referred to as *open hashing*. Under an alternative approach, called *closed*

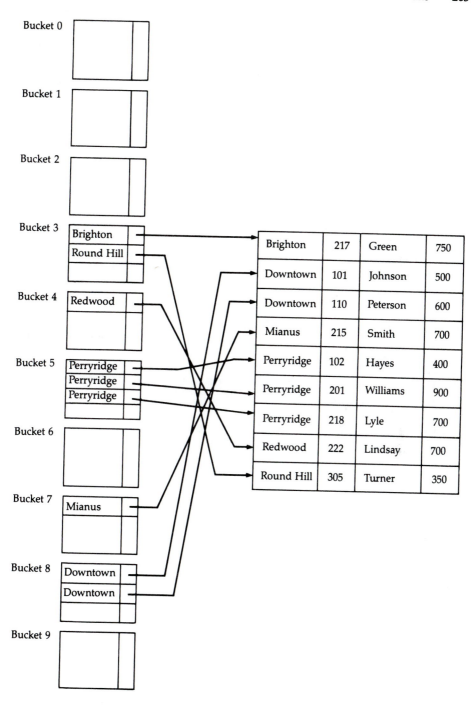

Figure 8.18 Hash table for *deposit* file using *branch-name* as the key.

hashing, all records are stored in one bucket and the hash function computes addresses within the bucket. Closed hashing is used frequently in the construction of symbol tables for compilers and assemblers, but open hashing is preferred for database systems. The reason is that deletion under closed hashing is troublesome. Typically, compilers and assemblers perform only lookup and insertion operations on their symbol tables. However, in a database system, it is important to be able to handle deletion as well as insertion. Thus, closed hashing is of only minor importance in database implementation.

An important drawback to the form of hashing we have described above is that the hash function must be chosen when we implement the system and cannot be changed easily thereafter. Since the function h maps search-key values to a fixed set B of bucket addresses, we waste space if B is excessively large. If B is too small, our buckets contain records of many different search-key values, and performance suffers. Typically, choosing the size of B to be twice the number of search-key values in the file gives a good space/performance trade-off.

8.6 Dynamic Hash Functions

As we have seen, the need to fix the set B of bucket addresses is a serious problem with the static hashing technique of the previous section. Most databases grow larger over time. If we are to use static hashing for such a database, we face three classes of options:

- Choose a hash function based on the current file size. This will result in performance degradation as the database grows.

- Choose a hash function based on the anticipated size of the file at some point in the future. Although performance degradation is avoided, a significant amount of space is wasted initially.

- Periodically reorganize the hash structure in response to file growth. Such a reorganization involves choosing a new hash function, recomputing the hash function on every record in the file, and generating new bucket assignments. This is a massive time-consuming reorganization. Furthermore, it is necessary to forbid access to the file during reorganization.

Several hashing techniques allow the hash function to be modified dynamically in order to accommodate the growth or shrinkage of the database. These techniques are called *dynamic hash functions*. Below, we describe one form of dynamic hashing called *extendable hashing*. The bibliographic notes provide references to other forms of dynamic hashing.

Extendable hashing copes with changes in database size by splitting and coalescing buckets as the database grows and shrinks. As a result, space efficiency is retained. Moreover, since the reorganization is performed on only one bucket at a time, the resulting performance overhead is acceptably low.

With extendable hashing, we choose a hash function h with the desirable properties of uniformity and randomness. However, this hash function generates values over a relatively large range, namely b-bit binary integers. A typical value for b is 32.

We do not create a bucket for each hash value. Indeed, 2^{32} is over 4 billion, and that many buckets is unreasonable for all but the largest databases. Instead, we create buckets on demand, as records are inserted into the file. We do not use the entire b bits of the hash initially. At any point, we use i bits, where $0 \leq i \leq b$. These i bits are used as an offset into an additional table of bucket addresses. The value of i grows and shrinks with the size of the database.

Figure 8.19 shows a general extendable hash structure. The i appearing above the bucket address table in the figure indicates that i bits of the hash $h(K)$ are required to determine the correct bucket for K. This number will, of course, change as the file grows. Although i bits are required to find the correct entry in the bucket address table, several consecutive table entries may point to the same bucket. All such entries will have a common hash prefix, but the length of this prefix may be less than i. Therefore, we associate with each bucket an integer giving the length of the common hash prefix. In Figure 8.19 the integer associated

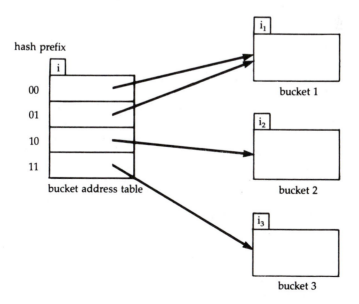

Figure 8.19   General extendable hash structure.

with bucket j is shown as i_j. The number of bucket address table entries that point to bucket j is

$$2^{(i - i_j)}$$

To locate the bucket containing search-key value K_l, we take the first i high-order bits of $h(K_l)$, look at the corresponding table entry for this bit string, and follow the bucket pointer in the table entry.

To insert a record with search-key value K_l, we follow the same procedure for lookup as above, ending up in some bucket, say, j. If there is room in the bucket, we insert the appropriate information and then insert the record in the file itself. If, on the other hand, the bucket is full, we must split the bucket and redistribute the current records, plus the new one. In order to split the bucket, we must first determine whether we need to increase the number of bits we use from the hash.

- If $i = i_j$, then only one entry in the bucket address table points to bucket j. Therefore, we need to increase the size of the bucket address table so that we can include pointers to the two buckets that result from splitting bucket j. We do this by considering an additional bit of the hash. We increment the value of i by 1, thus doubling the size of the bucket address table. Each entry is replaced by two entries, both of which contain the same pointer as the original entry. Now two entries in the bucket address table point to bucket j. We allocate a new bucket (bucket z) and set the second entry to point to the new bucket. We set i_j and i_z to i. Next, each record in bucket j is rehashed and, depending on the first i bits (remember we have added 1 to i), is either kept in bucket j or allocated to the newly created bucket. We now reattempt the insertion of the new record. Usually, the attempt will succeed. However, if all of the records in bucket j as well as the new record have the same hash value prefix, it will be necessary to split a bucket again, since all of the records in bucket j and the new record are assigned to the same bucket. If the hash function is carefully chosen, it is unlikely that a single insertion will require that a bucket be split more than once.

- If $i > i_j$, then more than one entry in the bucket address table points to bucket j. Thus, we can split bucket j without increasing the size of the bucket address table. Observe that all of the entries that point to bucket j correspond to hash prefixes that have the same value on the leftmost i_j bits. We allocate a new bucket (bucket z) and set i_j and i_z to the value resulting from adding 1 to the original i_j value. Next, we need to adjust the entries in the bucket address table that previously pointed to bucket j. (Note that all of the entries no longer correspond to hash prefixes that have the same value on the leftmost i_j bits.) We

Brighton	217	Green	750
Downtown	101	Johnson	500
Mianus	215	Smith	700
Perryridge	102	Hayes	400
Redwood	222	Lindsay	700
Round Hill	305	Turner	350
Clearview	117	Throggs	295

Figure 8.20   Sample *deposit* file.

leave the first half of the entries as they were (pointing to bucket j) and set all of the remaining entries to point to the newly created bucket (bucket z). Next, as in the case we saw above, each record in bucket j is rehashed and allocated to either bucket j or to the newly created bucket z. The insert is reattempted. In the unlikely case that it again fails, we apply one of the two cases, $i = i_j$ or $i > i_j$, as appropriate.

Note that in both cases we need to recompute the hash function on only the records in bucket j.

To delete a record with search-key value K_l, we follow the same procedure for lookup as above, ending up in some bucket, say, j. We remove both the search-key from the bucket and the record from the file. The bucket too is removed if it becomes empty. Note that at this point in time, several buckets may be coalesced, and that the size of the bucket address table may be cut in two. The procedure for deciding on when and how the coalescence of buckets can be accomplished is left as an exercise.

We illustrate the operation of insertion using our example *deposit* file (Figure 8.20). The 32-bit hash values on *branch-name* are shown in Figure 8.21. We assume that initially the file is empty, as shown in Figure 8.22. We insert the records one by one. In order to illustrate all the features of

branch-name	h(*branch-name*)
Brighton	0010 1101 1111 1011 0010 1100 0011 0000
Clearview	1101 0101 1101 1110 0100 0110 1001 0011
Downtown	1010 0011 1010 0000 1100 0110 1001 1111
Mianus	1000 0111 1110 1101 1011 1111 0011 1010
Perryridge	1111 0001 0010 0100 1001 0011 0110 1101
Redwood	1011 0101 1010 0110 1100 1001 1110 1011
Round Hill	0101 1000 0011 1111 1001 1100 0000 0001

Figure 8.21   Hash function for *branch-name*.

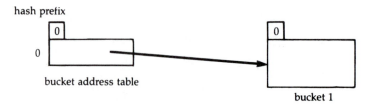

Figure 8.22   Initial extendable hash structure.

extendable hashing using a small structure, we shall make the unrealistic assumption that a bucket can hold only two records.

Let us insert the record (Perryridge, 102, Hayes, 400). The bucket address table contains a pointer to the one bucket and the record is inserted. Next, let us insert the record (Round Hill, 305, Turner, 350). This record is also placed in the one bucket of our structure.

When we attempt to insert the next record (Downtown, 101, Johnson, 500), we find that the bucket is full. Since $i = i_0$, we need to increase the number of bits we use from the hash. We now use one bit, allowing us $2^1 = 2$ buckets. This necessitates doubling the size of the bucket address table to two entries. We split the bucket, placing those records whose search key has a hash beginning with 1 in a new bucket, and leaving the other records in the original bucket. Figure 8.23 shows the state of our structure after the split.

Next, we insert (Redwood, 222, Lindsay, 700). Since the first bit of h(Redwood) is 1, we must insert this record into the bucket pointed to by the "1" entry in the bucket address table. Once again, we find the bucket full and $i = i_1$. We increase the number of bits we use from the hash to 2.

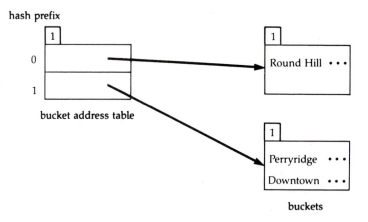

Figure 8.23   Hash structure after three insertions.

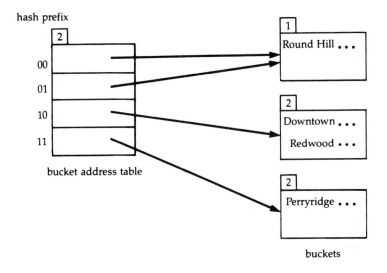

Figure 8.24   Hash structure after four insertions.

This necessitates doubling the size of the bucket address table to four entries, as shown in Figure 8.24. Since the bucket of Figure 8.23 for hash prefix 0 was not split, the two entries of the bucket address table of 00 and 01 both point to this bucket.

For each record in the bucket of Figure 8.23 for hash prefix 1 (the bucket being split), we examine the first 2 bits of the hash to determine which bucket of the new structure should hold it.

We continue in this manner until we have inserted all of the *deposit* records of Figure 8.20. The resulting structure is shown in Figure 8.25.

Let us now examine the advantages and disadvantages of extendable hashing as compared with the other schemes we have discussed. The main advantage of extendable hashing is that performance does not degrade as the file grows. Furthermore, there is minimal space overhead. Although the bucket address table is additional overhead, it contains one pointer for each hash value for the current prefix length. This table is thus small. The main space saving of extendable hashing over other forms of hashing is that no buckets need be reserved for future growth; rather, buckets can be allocated dynamically.

A disadvantage to extendable hashing is that lookup involves an additional level of indirection, since we must access the bucket address table before accessing the bucket itself. This extra reference has only a minor impact on performance. Although the hash structures we discussed earlier do not have this extra level of indirection, they lose their minor performance advantage as they become full.

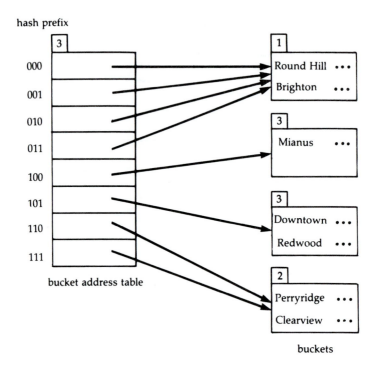

Figure 8.25   Extendable hash structure for the *deposit* file.

Thus, extendable hashing appears to be a highly attractive technique, provided we are willing to accept the added complexity involved in its implementation. More detailed descriptions of the implementation of extendable hashing are referenced in the bibliographic notes.

8.7 Comparison of Indexing and Hashing

We have seen several indexing schemes and several hashing schemes. Each scheme has advantages in certain situations. A database system implementor could provide many schemes and leave the final decision of which schemes to use to the database designer. However, such an approach requires the implementor to write more code, adding both to the cost of the system and to the space that the system occupies. Thus, most database systems use only a few or just one form of indexing or hashing.

In order to make a wise choice, the implementor or the database designer must consider the following issues:

- Is the cost of periodic reorganization of the index or hash structure acceptable?

- What is the relative frequency of insertion and deletion?

- Is it desirable to optimize average access time at the expense of increasing the worst-case access time?

- What types of queries are users likely to pose?

We have already examined the first three of the above issues in our review of the relative merits of specific indexing techniques and again in our discussion of hashing techniques. The fourth issue, the expected type of query, is critical to the choice of indexing or hashing.

If most queries are of the form

$$\textbf{select } A_1, A_2, \ldots, A_n$$
$$\textbf{from } r$$
$$\textbf{where } A_i = c$$

then, to process this query, the system will perform a lookup on an index or hash structure for attribute A_i, for value c. For queries of this form, a hashing scheme is preferable. An index lookup requires time proportional to the log of the number of values in r for A_i. In a hash structure, however, the average lookup time is a constant independent of the size of the database. The only advantage to an index over a hash structure for this form of query is that the worst-case lookup time is proportional to the log of the number of values in r for A_i. By contrast, if hashing is used, the worst-case lookup time is proportional to the number of values in r for A_i.

Index techniques are preferable to hashing in cases where a range of values is specified in the query. Such a query takes the following form:

$$\textbf{select } A_1, A_2, \ldots, A_n$$
$$\textbf{from } r$$
$$\textbf{where } A_i \leq c_2 \textbf{ and } A_i \geq c_1$$

In other words, the above query finds all records with A_i values between c_1 and c_2.

Let us consider how we would process this query using an index. First, we perform a lookup on value c_1. Once we have found the bucket for value c_1, we follow the pointer chain in the index to read the next bucket in alphabetic order and continue in this manner until we reach c_2.

If instead of an index we have a hash structure, we can perform a lookup on c_1 and locate the corresponding bucket — but it is not easy, in general, to determine the next bucket that must be examined. The difficulty arises from the fact that a good hash function assigns values randomly to buckets. Thus, there is no simple notion of "next bucket." The reason we cannot chain buckets together into alphabetic order is that each bucket is assigned many search-key values. Although, at any time, a bucket contains only a few values, the number of *possible* values is large. Since these values are randomly distributed, no chain of buckets can be guaranteed to represent search-key order.

If we want to support range queries using a hash structure, we must choose a hash function that *preserves order*. That is, if K_1 and K_2 are search-key values and $K_1 < K_2$, then $h(K_1) < h(K_2)$. Such a function ensures that the buckets are in key order. An order-preserving hash function that meets our requirements of uniformity and randomness is difficult to find in many cases. Our earlier example of a hash function on branch names that used the first letter of the name to identify one of 26 buckets preserved order but failed to provide uniformity. Consider a hash function on *balance* that maps a record to one of 100 buckets by computing *balance* / 1000 and dropping the values to the right of the decimal point. All records for which *balance* / 1000 > 100 are put in bucket 100. This hash function preserves order but fails to provide uniformity, since we believe that there are many more small accounts (under $10,000) than large accounts.

Because of the difficulty of finding good hash functions that preserve order, most systems use indexing instead — unless it is known in advance that range queries will be infrequent.

8.8 Index Definition in SQL

In Chapter 5, we saw how key declarations were expressed in the integrity enhancement feature of the SQL standard. The standard allows the SQL compiler the freedom to choose how to implement the enforcement of keys. Typical implementations enforce a key declaration by creating an index with the declared key as the search key of the index.

Some SQL implementations include specific data definition commands to create and drop indices. Among these are the original System R Sequel language and IBM SAA-SQL. Below, we present the IBM SAA-SQL index commands.

An index is created by the **create index** command, which takes the form:

create index <index-name> **on** <relation-name> (<attribute-list>)

The *attribute-list* is the list of attributes of the relations that form the search key for the index.

To define an index-name *b-index* on the *branch* relation with *branch-name* as the search key, we write:

create index *b-index* **on** *branch* (*branch-name*)

If we wish to declare that the search key is a candidate key, we add the attribute **unique** to the index definition. Thus, the command

create unique index *b-index* **on** *branch* (*branch-name*)

declares *branch-name* to be a candidate key for *branch*. If, at the time the **create unique index** command is entered, *branch-name* is not a candidate key, an error message will be displayed, and the attempt to create the index will fail. If the index creation attempt succeeds, any subsequent attempt to insert a tuple that violates the key declaration will fail.

Note that the **unique** feature of the SAA-SQL index is redundant if the key declaration of the integrity enhancement feature of the SQL standard is implemented.

The index-name specified for an index is required so that it is possible to drop indices. The **drop index** command takes the form:

drop index <index-name>

8.9 Multiple-Key Access

Until now, we have assumed implicitly that only one index (or hash table) is used to process a query on a relation. However, for certain types of queries it is advantageous to use multiple indices if they exist.

Assume the *deposit* file has two indices, one for *branch-name* and one for *customer-name*. Consider the following query: "Find the balance in all of Williams' accounts at the Perryridge branch." We write:

select *balance*
from *deposit*
where *branch-name* = "Perryridge" **and** *customer-name* = "Williams"

There are three strategies possible for processing this query:

- Use the index on *branch-name* to find all records pertaining to the Perryridge branch. Examine each such record to see if *customer-name* = "Williams."

- Use the index on *customer-name* to find all records pertaining to Williams. Examine each such record to see if *branch-name* = "Perryridge."

- Use the index on *branch-name* to find *pointers* to all records pertaining to the Perryridge branch. Also, use the index on *customer-name* to find pointers to all records pertaining to Williams. Take the intersection of these two sets of pointers. Those pointers that are in the intersection point to records pertaining to both Williams and Perryridge.

The third strategy is the only one of the three that takes advantage of the existence of multiple indices. However, even this strategy may be poor if all of the following hold:

- There are a large number of records pertaining to the Perryridge branch.

- There are a large number of records pertaining to Williams.

- There are only a small number of records pertaining to *both* Williams and to the Perryridge branch.

If these conditions hold, we must scan a large number of pointers to produce a small result.

To speed the processing of multiple search-key queries, several special structures can be maintained. We shall consider two such structures: the *grid structure* and *partitioned hash functions*.

8.9.1 Grid Structure

A grid structure for queries on two search keys is a two-dimensional array, indexed by the values for the search keys. Figure 8.26 shows part of a grid structure for the *deposit* file. To perform a lookup to answer our example query, we look for the entry in the "Williams" row and the "Perryridge" column. That entry contains pointers to all records with *customer-name* = "Williams" and *branch-name* = "Perryridge."

No special computations need be performed, and only the records needed to answer the query are accessed.

The grid structure is suitable also for queries involving one search key. Consider this query:

> **select** *
> **from** *deposit*
> **where** *branch-name* = "Perryridge"

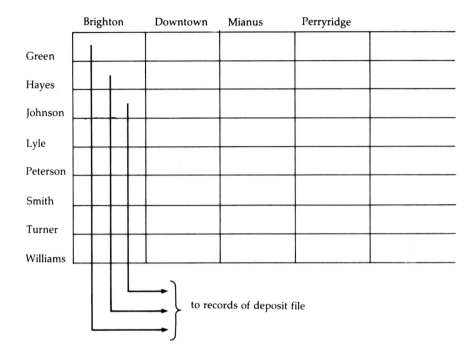

Figure 8.26   Grid structure for *deposit* file.

The pointers that appear in the Perryridge column point to all the records pertaining to Perryridge.

It is conceptually simple to extend the grid structure approach to any number of search keys. If we want our structure to be used for queries on *n* keys, we construct an *n*-dimensional array as our grid.

Grid structures provide significant improvement in the processing time for multiple-key queries. However, they impose a space overhead as well as a performance overhead on record insertion and deletion.

8.9.2 Partitioned Hash Function

An alternative approach to multiple-key queries is the use of a partitioned hash function. Suppose we wish to construct a structure suitable for queries on the *deposit* file involving *customer-name* and *branch-name*. We construct a hash structure for the key (*customer-name, branch-name*). The only difference between the structure we shall create and those we saw earlier is that we impose an additional constraint on the hash function *h*. Hash values are split into two parts. The first part depends only on the *customer-name* value and the second part depends only on the *branch-name*

search-key value	hash value
(Green, Brighton)	101 111
(Hayes, Perryridge)	110 101
(Johnson, Downtown)	111 001
(Lyle, Perryridge)	000 101
(Peterson, Downtown)	010 001
(Smith, Mianus)	011 111
(Turner, Round Hill)	011 000
(Williams, Perryridge)	001 101
(Hayes, Mianus)	110 111

Figure 8.27   Partitioned hash function for key (*customer-name, branch-name*).

value. The hash function is called *partitioned* because the hash values are split into segments that depend on each element of the key.

Figure 8.27 shows a sample hash function in which the first 3 bits depend on *customer-name* and the final 3 bits depend on *branch-name*. Thus, the hash values for (Hayes, Perryridge) and (Hayes, Mianus) agree on the first 3 bits, and the hash values for (Johnson, Downtown) and (Peterson, Downtown) agree on the last 3 bits.

The partitioned hash function of Figure 8.27 can be used to answer the query "Find the balance in all of Williams' accounts at the Perryridge branch." We simply compute h(Williams, Perryridge) and access the hash structure. The same hash structure is suitable for a query involving only one of the two search keys. To find all records pertaining to the Perryridge branch, we compute *part* of the partitioned hash. Since we have only the *branch-name* value, we are able to compute only the last 3 bits of the hash. For the value "Perryridge," these 3 bits are 101. We access the hash structure and scan those buckets for which the last 3 bits of the hash value are 101. In the example of Figure 8.27, we access the buckets for hash values 110 101, 000 101, and 001 101.

As was the case for the grid file, partitioned hashing extends to an arbitrary number of attributes. There are several improvements we can make in partitioned hashing if we know how frequently a user will specify each attribute in a query. The bibliographic notes reference these techniques.

Several other hybrid techniques for processing multiple-key queries exist. Such techniques may be useful in applications where the system implementor knows that most queries will be of a restricted form. Again, references to some of the more interesting techniques appear in the bibliographic notes.

8.10 Summary

Many queries reference only a small proportion of the records in a file. In order to reduce the overhead in searching for these records, we can construct *indices* for the files that store the database.

Index-sequential files are one of the oldest index schemes used in database systems. They are designed for applications that require both sequential processing of the entire file and random access to individual records. To permit fast retrieval of records in search-key order, records are chained together by pointers. In order to allow fast random access, an index structure is used. There are two types of indices that may be used; dense index and sparse index.

In a standard index-sequential file, only one index is maintained. If several indices on different search keys are used, the index whose search key specifies the sequential order of the file is the *primary index*. The other indices are called *secondary indices*. Secondary indices improve the performance of queries that use search keys other than the primary one. However, they impose a serious overhead on modification of the database.

The primary disadvantage of the index-sequential file organization is that performance degrades as the file grows. To overcome this deficiency, a B^+-*tree index* can be used. A B^+-tree index takes the form of a *balanced* tree in which every path from the root of the tree to a leaf of the tree is of the same length. Lookup in this scheme is quite straightforward and efficient. However, insertion and deletion are more complicated. Nevertheless, the number of operations required for insertion and deletion on B^+-trees is proportional to the logarithm of the size of the database.

B-tree indices are similar to B^+-tree indices. The primary advantage of a B-tree is that it eliminates the redundant storage of search-key values. The major disadvantage is that leaf and nonleaf nodes are not of the same size; thus, storage management for the index is complicated.

Index schemes require that we access an index structure to locate data. The technique of *hashing*, by contrast, allows us to find the address of a data item directly by computing a function on the search-key value of the desired record. Since we do not know at design time precisely which search-key values will be stored in the file, a good hash function to choose is one that assigns search-key values to buckets such that the distribution is both uniform and random.

A *static hash function* is one in which the set of bucket addresses is fixed. Such a function cannot easily accommodate databases that grow significantly larger over time. There are several hashing techniques that allow the hash function to be modified. These are called *dynamic hash functions*. One example is *extendable hashing*, which copes with changes in database size by splitting and coalescing buckets as the database grows and shrinks.

Exercises

8.1 When is it preferable to use a dense index rather than a sparse index?

8.2 Since indices speed query processing, why might they not be kept on several search keys? List as many reasons as possible.

8.3 What is the difference between a primary index and a secondary index?

8.4 Construct a B^+-tree for the following set of key values:

$$(2, 3, 5, 7, 11, 17, 19, 23, 29, 31)$$

assuming that the tree is initially empty, values are added in ascending order, and the number of pointers that will fit in one node is:

   a. 4

   b. 6

   c. 8

8.5 For each B^+-tree of Exercise 8.4, show the steps involved in the following queries:

- Find records with a search-key value of 11.

- Find records with a search-key value between 7 and 17, inclusive.

8.6 For each B^+-tree of Exercise 8.4, show the form of the tree after each of the following series of operations:

- Insert 9.

- Insert 10.

- Insert 8.

- Delete 23.

- Delete 19.

8.7 Repeat Exercise 8.4 for a B-tree.

8.8 Explain the distinction between closed and open hashing and discuss the relative merits of each technique in database applications.

8.9 If a hash structure is used on a search key for which range queries are likely, what property should the hash function have?

8.10 Suppose that we are using extendable hashing on a file containing records with the following search-key values:

$$2, 3, 5, 7, 11, 17, 19, 23, 29, 31.$$

Show the extendable hash structure for this file if the hash function is $h(x) = x \mod 8$ and buckets can hold three records.

8.11 Show how the extendable hash structure of Exercise 8.10 changes as the result of each of the following steps:

- Delete 11.
- Delete 31.
- Insert 1.
- Insert 15.

Bibliographic Notes

The basic data structures used in indexing and hashing are covered in several texts, including Aho et al. [1983], Horowitz and Sahni [1976], and Knuth [1973].

B-tree indices are discussed in Bayer [1972], Bayer and McCreight [1972], Nievergelt [1974], and Held and Stonebraker [1978]. B$^+$-trees are discussed in Comer [1979], Bayer and Unterauer [1977], and Knuth [1973]. Bayer and Schkolnick [1977] and Shasha and Goodman [1988] analyze the problem of managing a B-tree index for a file updated concurrently by several processes. Other discussions of concurrency control within B-trees and similar data structures include those of Lehman and Yao [1981], Kung and Lehman [1980], and Ford and Calhoun [1984]. An empirical study of insertion and deletion on trees appears in Eppinger [1983]. Several alternative tree and treelike search structures have been proposed. Tries are trees whose structure is based on the "digits" of keys (for example, a dictionary thumb index, which has one entry for each letter). Such trees may not be balanced in the sense of a B-tree. Tries are discussed by Ramesh et al. [1989], Orestein [1982], Litwin [1981], and Fredkin [1960]. Related work includes the digital B-trees of Lomet [1981].

Knuth [1973] analyzes a large number of different hashing techniques. Several dynamic hash function schemes exist. Extendable hashing was introduced by Fagin et al. [1979]. Linear hashing was introduced by Litwin [1978, 1980]. A performance analysis of this scheme was presented by Larson [1982]. Concurrency with this scheme is examined by Ellis [1987]. A variant of linear hashing is presented by Larson [1988]. Another scheme, called dynamic hashing, was proposed by Larson [1978]. Partitioned hash functions have been applied to several index structures.

The grid file structure appears in Nievergelt et al. [1984] and Hinrichs [1985]. Partial match retrieval uses a partitioned hash function to limit the number of buckets to be searched in processing a multiple-key query. See Rivest [1976], Burkhard [1976, 1979], and Ullman [1988]. King et al. [1983] use a combination of extendable hashing and partitioned hash functions in an index structure designed for multiple-key queries that include subset queries (as in keyword-based retrieval). Optimal choice of partitioning for a partitioned hash function is discussed in Bolour [1979] and Aho and Ullman [1979]. Other techniques for multiple-key queries include those of Lum [1974], Lum and Ling [1970], and Schneiderman [1976]. An alternative is given by Ramakrishna and Larson [1989] that allows retrieval in a single disk access at the price of a high overhead for a small fraction of database modifications.

Query Processing

In the preceding chapters, we have considered how to structure the data in the database — a decision that is made at the time the database is designed. Although it is possible to change the initial structure, it is relatively costly to do so. Thus, when a query is presented to the system, it is necessary to find the best method of finding the answer using the existing database structure. There are a large number of possible strategies for processing a query, especially if the query is complex. Nevertheless, it is usually worthwhile for the system to spend a substantial amount of time on the selection of a good strategy. The cost of processing a query is usually dominated by disk access. The difference between a good strategy and a bad strategy in terms of the number of disk accesses required is often substantial, and may be several orders of magnitude. Thus, the time spent in choosing a query-processing strategy is worthwhile even for a query that is executed only once.

9.1 Query Interpretation

Given a query, there are generally a variety of methods for computing the answer. For example, we saw that in SQL a query could be expressed in several different ways. Each way of expressing the query "suggests" a strategy for finding the answer. However, we do not expect users to write their queries in a way that suggests the most efficient strategy. Thus, it becomes the responsibility of the system to transform the query as entered by the user into an equivalent query which can be computed more efficiently. This "optimizing" or, more accurately, improving of the strategy for processing a query is called *query optimization*. There is a close analogy between code optimization by a compiler and query optimization by a database system. We shall study the issues involved in efficient query processing both in high-level languages and at the level of physical access to the data.

Query optimization is an important issue in any database system since the difference in execution time between a good strategy and a bad one may be huge. In the network model and the hierarchical model (discussed in Appendices A and B) query optimization is left, for the most part, to the application programmer. This is because the data manipulation language statements of these two models are usually embedded in a host programming language, and it is not easy to transform a network or hierarchical query into an equivalent one without knowledge of the entire application program.

Since a relational query can be expressed entirely in a relational query language without the use of a host language, it is possible to perform automatically a substantial amount of query optimization. In this chapter, we present the most useful techniques for efficient query processing.

Before query processing can begin, the system must translate the query into a usable form. A language such as SQL is suitable for human use, but ill-suited to be the system's internal representation of a query. A more useful internal representation is one based on the relational algebra. The only difference between the form of the relational algebra we shall use here and that used in Chapter 3 is the addition of redundant parentheses to indicate unambiguously the order of evaluating operations.

The first action the system must take on a query is to translate it into its internal form. This translation process is similar to the work performed by the parser of a compiler. In generating the internal form of the query, the parser checks the syntax of the user's query, verifies that the relation names appearing in the query are names of relations in the database, and so on. If the query was expressed in terms of a view, the parser replaces all references to the view name with the relational algebra expression in order to compute that view.

Parsing is covered in most compiler texts (see the bibliographic notes) and is beyond the scope of this book.

Once the query has been translated into an internal relational algebra form, the optimization process begins. The first phase of optimization is done at the relational algebra level. An attempt is made to find an expression that is equivalent to the given expression but that is more efficient to execute. The next phase involves the selection of a detailed strategy for processing the query. A choice must be made as to exactly how the query will be executed. The specific indices to use must be chosen. The order in which tuples are processed must be determined. The final choice of a strategy is based primarily on the number of disk accesses required.

9.2 Equivalence of Expressions

The relational algebra is a procedural language. Thus, each relational algebra expression represents a particular sequence of operations. We have already seen that there are several ways to express a given query in the relational algebra. The first step in selecting a query-processing strategy is to find a relational algebra expression that is equivalent to the given query and is more efficient to execute.

We use our bank example to illustrate the various optimization techniques. In particular, we shall use the relation schemes

Customer-scheme = (*customer-name, street, customer-city*)
Deposit-scheme = (*branch-name, account-number, customer-name, balance*)
Branch-scheme = (*branch-name, assets, branch-city*)

with instances *customer, deposit,* and *branch*, respectively.

9.2.1 Selection Operation

Let us consider the relational algebra expression for the query "Find the assets and name of all banks who have depositors living in Port Chester."

$$\Pi_{branch\text{-}name,\ assets}\ (\sigma_{customer\text{-}city\ =\ \text{"Port Chester"}}$$
$$(customer \bowtie deposit \bowtie branch))$$

This expression constructs a large relation, *customer* $\bowtie$ *deposit* $\bowtie$ *branch*. However, we are interested in only a few tuples of this relation (those pertaining to residents of Port Chester), and in only two of the eight attributes of this relation. The intermediate result

$$customer \bowtie deposit \bowtie branch$$

is probably too large to be kept in main memory and thus must be stored on disk. This means that in addition to accessing the disk to read the relations *customer, deposit,* and *branch*, the system will need to access the disk to read and write intermediate results. Clearly, we could process the query more efficiently if there were a way to reduce the size of the intermediate result.

Since we are concerned only with tuples in the *customer* relation that pertain to residents of Port Chester, we need not consider those tuples that do not have *customer-city* = "Port Chester." By reducing the number of tuples of the *customer* relation that we need to access, we reduce the size of the intermediate result. Our query is now represented by the relational algebra expression

$$\Pi_{branch\text{-}name,\ assets}\ (\ (\sigma_{customer\text{-}city\ =\ \text{"Port Chester"}}\ (customer))$$
$$\bowtie deposit \bowtie branch)$$

which is equivalent to our original algebra expression.

The above example suggests the following rule for transforming relational algebra queries:

- Perform selection operations as early as possible.

In our example, we recognized that the selection operator pertained only to the *customer* relation, and therefore we performed the selection on *customer* directly.

Suppose that we modify our original query to restrict attention to customers with a balance over \$1000. The new relational algebra query is:

$$\Pi_{branch\text{-}name,\ assets}\ (\sigma_{customer\text{-}city\ =\ \text{``Port Chester''}\ \wedge\ balance\ >\ 1000}$$
$$(customer\ \bowtie\ deposit\ \bowtie\ branch))$$

We cannot apply the selection

$$customer\text{-}city\ =\ \text{``Port Chester''}\ \wedge\ balance\ >\ 1000$$

directly to the *customer* relation, since the predicate involves attributes of both the *customer* and *deposit* relation. However, the *branch* relation does not involve either *customer-city* or *balance*. If we decide to process the join as

$$(customer\ \bowtie\ deposit)\ \bowtie\ branch$$

then we can rewrite our query as:

$$\Pi_{branch\text{-}name,\ assets}$$
$$((\sigma_{customer\text{-}city\ =\ \text{``Port Chester''}\ \wedge\ balance\ >\ 1000}\ (customer\ \bowtie\ deposit))$$
$$\bowtie\ branch)$$

Let us examine the subquery:

$$\sigma_{customer\text{-}city\ =\ \text{``Port Chester''}\ \wedge\ balance\ >\ 1000}\ (customer\ \bowtie\ deposit)$$

We can replace the above expression with the expression:

$$\sigma_{customer\text{-}city\ =\ \text{``Port Chester''}}\ (\sigma_{balance\ >\ 1000}\ (customer\ \bowtie\ deposit))$$

Both of the above expressions select tuples with *customer-city* = "Port Chester" and *balance* > 1000. However, the latter form of the expression provides a new opportunity to apply the "perform selections early" rule, resulting in:

$$\sigma_{customer\text{-}city\ =\ \text{``Port Chester''}}\ (customer)\ \bowtie\ \sigma_{balance\ >\ 1000}\ (deposit)$$

The above example suggests a second transformation rule:

- Replace expressions of the form

$$\sigma_{P_1 \wedge P_2} (e)$$

by

$$\sigma_{P_1} (\sigma_{P_2} (e))$$

where P_1 and P_2 are predicates and e is a relational algebra expression.

An easy way to remember this transformation is by noting the following equivalences among relational algebra expressions:

$$\sigma_{P_1} (\sigma_{P_2} (e)) = \sigma_{P_2} (\sigma_{P_1} (e)) = \sigma_{P_1 \wedge P_2} (e)$$

9.2.2 Projection Operation

We now consider another technique for reducing the size of temporary results. The projection operation, like the selection operation, reduces the size of relations. Thus, whenever we need to generate a temporary relation, it is advantageous to apply immediately any projections that are possible. This suggests a companion to the "perform selections early" rule we stated earlier:

- Perform projections early.

Consider the following form of our example query:

$$\Pi_{branch\text{-}name,\ assets} (((\sigma_{customer\text{-}city\ =\ \text{"Port Chester"}} (customer))$$
$$\bowtie\ deposit)\ \bowtie\ branch)$$

When we compute the subexpression

$$((\sigma_{customer\text{-}city\ =\ \text{"Port Chester"}} (customer))\ \bowtie\ deposit)$$

we obtain a relation whose scheme is:

(customer-name, street, customer-city, branch-name, account-number, balance)

We can eliminate several attributes from the scheme. The only attributes we must retain are those that either appear in the result of the query or are needed to process subsequent operations. By eliminating unneeded attributes, we reduce the number of columns of the intermediate result.

Thus, the size of the intermediate result is reduced. In our example, the only attribute we need is *branch-name*. Therefore, we modify the expression to:

$$\Pi_{branch\text{-}name,\ assets}\ ((\ \Pi_{branch\text{-}name}\ ((\sigma_{customer\text{-}city\ =\ \text{``Port Chester''}}\ (customer))\\ \Join\ deposit))\Join\ branch)$$

9.2.3 Natural Join Operation

Another way to reduce the size of temporary results is to choose an optimal ordering of the join operations. We mentioned in Chapter 3 that natural join is associative. Thus, for all relations r_1, r_2, and r_3:

$$(r_1 \Join r_2) \Join r_3 = r_1 \Join (r_2 \Join r_3)$$

Although these expressions are equivalent, the costs of computing them may differ. Consider again the expression:

$$\Pi_{branch\text{-}name,\ assets}\ ((\sigma_{customer\text{-}city\ =\ \text{``Port Chester''}}\ (customer))\\ \Join\ deposit \Join\ branch)$$

We could choose to compute *deposit* $\Join$ *branch* first and then join the result with:

$$\sigma_{customer\text{-}city\ =\ \text{``Port Chester''}}\ (customer)$$

However, *deposit* $\Join$ *branch* is likely to be a large relation since it contains one tuple for every account. By contrast,

$$\sigma_{customer\text{-}city\ =\ \text{``Port Chester''}}\ (customer)$$

is probably a small relation. To see this, note that since the bank has a large number of widely distributed branches, it is likely that only a small fraction of the bank's customers live in Port Chester. If we compute

$$(\sigma_{customer\text{-}city\ =\ \text{``Port Chester''}}\ (customer))\Join\ deposit$$

first, we obtain one tuple for each account held by a resident of Port Chester. Thus, the temporary relation we must store is smaller than if we compute *deposit* $\Join$ *branch* first.

There are other options to consider for evaluating our query. We do not care about the order in which attributes appear in a join, since it is easy to change the order before displaying the result. Thus, for all relations r_1 and r_2:

$$r_1 \bowtie r_2 = r_2 \bowtie r_1$$

That is, natural join is commutative.

Using this fact, we can consider rewriting our relational algebra expression as:

$$\Pi_{branch\text{-}name,\, assets} (((\sigma_{customer\text{-}city\, =\, \text{“Port Chester”}} (customer)) \bowtie branch) \bowtie deposit)$$

That is, we could join $\sigma_{customer\text{-}city\, =\, \text{“Port Chester”}} (customer)$ with branch as the first join operation performed. Note, however, that there are no attributes in common between Branch-scheme and Customer-scheme, so the join is really just a cartesian product. If there are c customers in Port Chester and b branches, this cartesian product generates bc tuples, one for every possible pair of customers and branches (without regard for whether the customer has an account at the branch). Thus, it appears that this cartesian product will produce a large temporary relation. As a result, we would reject this strategy. However, if the user had entered the above expression, we could use the associativity and commutativity of natural join to transform this expression to the more efficient expression we used earlier.

9.2.4 Other Operations

The example we have used involves a sequence of natural joins. We chose this example because natural joins arise frequently in practice and because natural joins are one of the more costly operations in query processing. However, we note that equivalences similar to those presented above hold for the union and set difference operations. We list some of these equivalences below:

$$\sigma_P(r_1 \cup r_2) = \sigma_P(r_1) \cup \sigma_P(r_2)$$
$$\sigma_P(r_1 - r_2) = \sigma_P(r_1) - r_2 = \sigma_P(r_1) - \sigma_P(r_2)$$
$$(r_1 \cup r_2) \cup r_3 = r_1 \cup (r_2 \cup r_3)$$
$$r_1 \cup r_2 = r_2 \cup r_1$$

We have seen several techniques for generating more efficient relational algebra expressions for a query. For queries whose structure is more complex than those of our example, there may be a large number of possible strategies that appear to be efficient. Some query processors simply choose from such a set of strategies on the basis of certain heuristics. Others retain all promising strategies and perform the latter phases of query optimization for each strategy. The final choice of strategy is made only after the details of each strategy have been worked out and an estimate has been made of the processing cost of each strategy.

9.3 Estimation of Query-Processing Cost

The strategy we choose for a query depends upon the size of each relation and the distribution of values within columns. In the example used in this chapter, the fraction of customers who live in Port Chester has a major impact on the usefulness of our techniques. In order to be able to choose a strategy on the basis of reliable information, database systems may store statistics for each relation r. These statistics include:

- n_r, the number of tuples in the relation r.

- s_r, the size of a record (tuple) of relation r in bytes.

- $V(A,r)$, the number of distinct values that appear in the relation r for attribute A.

The first two statistics allow us to estimate accurately the size of a cartesian product. The cartesian product $r \times s$ contains $n_r n_s$ tuples. Each tuple of $r \times s$ occupies $s_r + s_s$ bytes.

The third statistic is used to estimate how many tuples satisfy a selection predicate of the form:

$$<attribute\text{-}name> = <value>$$

However, in order to perform such an estimation, we need to know how often each value appears in a column. If we assume uniform distribution of values (that is, each value appears with equal probability), then the query $\sigma_{A\,=\,a}(r)$ is estimated to have

$$\frac{n_r}{V(A,r)}$$

tuples. However, it may not always be realistic to assume that each value appears with equal probability. The *branch-name* attribute in the *deposit* relation is an example of such a case. There is one tuple in the *deposit* relation for each amount. It is reasonable to expect that the large branches have more accounts than smaller branches. Therefore certain *branch-name* values appear with greater probability than others.

Despite the fact that our uniform distribution assumption is not always true, it is a good approximation of reality in many cases. Therefore, many query processors make such an assumption when choosing a strategy. For simplicity, we shall assume uniform distribution for the remainder of this chapter.

Estimation of the size of a natural join is somewhat more complicated than estimation of the size of a selection or a cartesian product. Let $r_1(R_1)$ and $r_2(R_2)$ be relations. If $R_1 \cap R_2 = \varnothing$, then $r_1 \bowtie r_2$ is the same as $r_1 \times r_2$, and we can use our estimation technique for cartesian products. If $R_1 \cap R_2$ is a key for R_1, then we know that a tuple of r_2 will join with exactly one tuple from r_1. Therefore, the number of tuples in $r_1 \bowtie r_2$ is no greater than the number of tuples in r_2.

The most difficult case to consider is when $R_1 \cap R_2$ is a key for neither R_1 nor R_2. In this case, we use the third statistic and assume, as before, that each value appears with equal probability. Consider a tuple t of r_1, and assume $R_1 \cap R_2 = \{A\}$. We estimate that tuple t produces

$$\frac{n_{r_2}}{V(A, r_2)}$$

tuples in $r_1 \bowtie r_2$, since this is the number of tuples in r_2 with an A value of $t[A]$. Considering all of the tuples in r_1, we estimate that there are

$$\frac{n_{r_1} n_{r_2}}{V(A, r_2)}$$

tuples in $r_1 \bowtie r_2$. Observe that if we reverse the roles of r_1 and r_2 in the above estimate, we obtain an estimate of

$$\frac{n_{r_1} n_{r_2}}{V(A, r_1)}$$

tuples in $r_1 \bowtie r_2$. These two estimates differ if $V(A, r_1) \neq V(A, r_2)$. If this situation occurs, there are likely to be some dangling tuples that do not participate in the join. Thus, the lower of the two estimates is probably the better one.

The above estimate of join size may be too high if the $V(A, r_1)$ values for attribute A in r_1 have few values in common with the $V(A, r_2)$ values for attribute A in r_2. However, it is unlikely that our estimate will be very far off in practice, since dangling tuples are likely to be only a small fraction of the tuples in a real-world relation. If dangling tuples appear frequently, then a correction factor could be applied to our estimates.

If we wish to maintain accurate statistics, then every time a relation is modified, we must also update the statistics. This is a substantial amount of overhead. Therefore, most systems do not update the statistics on every modification. Instead, this is done during periods of light system load. As a result, the statistics used for choosing a query-processing strategy may not be completely accurate. However, if the interval between the update of the statistics is not too long, the statistics will be sufficiently accurate to provide a good estimation of the size of the results of expressions.

Statistical information about relations is particularly useful when several indices are available to assist in the processing of a query, as we shall see in Section 9.4.

Statistics allow us to estimate the number of tuples in the result of a query. However, to measure the cost of a query, we need to estimate the number of disk accesses. The number of accesses required by a given strategy depends on the number of tuples in relations as well as on the physical organization of the database. In what follows, we shall use statistics to estimate numbers of tuples, but make worst-case assumptions regarding physical organization unless stated otherwise.

9.4 Estimation of Costs of Access Using Indices

The cost estimates we have considered for relational algebra expressions did not consider the effects of indices and hash functions on the cost of evaluating an expression. The presence of these structures, however, has a significant influence on the choice of a query-processing strategy.

- Indices and hash functions allow fast access to records containing a specific value on the index key.

- Indices (though not most hash functions) allow the records of a file to be read in sorted order. In Chapter 8, we pointed out that it is efficient to read the records of a file in an order corresponding closely to physical order. If an index allows the records of a file to be read in an order that corresponds to the physical order, that index is said to be a *clustering index*. Clustering indices allow us to take advantage of the physical clustering of records into blocks.

The detailed strategy for processing a query is called an *access plan* for the query. A plan includes not only the relational operations to be performed but also the indices to be used, the order in which tuples are to be accessed, and the order in which operations are to be performed.

Of course, the use of indices imposes the overhead of access to those blocks containing the index. We need to take these block accesses into account when we estimate the cost of a strategy that involves the use of indices.

In this section, we consider queries involving only one relation. We use the selection predicate to guide us in the choice of the best index to use in processing the query.

As an example of the estimation of the cost of a query using indices, assume that we are processing the query:

> **select** *account-number*
> **from** *deposit*
> **where** *branch-name* = "Perryridge" **and** *customer-name* = "Williams"
>   **and** *balance* > 1000

Assume also that we have the following statistical information about the *deposit* relation:

- 20 tuples of *deposit* fit in one block.
- $V(branch\text{-}name, deposit) = 50$.
- $V(customer\text{-}name, deposit) = 200$.
- $V(balance, deposit) = 5000$.
- The *deposit* relation has 10,000 tuples.

Let us assume as well that the following indices exist on *deposit*:

- A clustering, B^+-tree index for *branch-name*.
- A nonclustering, B^+-tree index for *customer-name*.

As before, we shall make the simplifying assumption that values are distributed uniformly.

Since $V(branch\text{-}name, deposit) = 50$, we expect that $10000/50 = 200$ tuples of the *deposit* relation pertain to the Perryridge branch. If we use the index on *branch-name*, we will need to read these 200 tuples and check each one for satisfaction of the **where** clause. Since the index is a clustering index, $200/20 = 10$ block reads are required to read the *deposit* tuples. In addition, several index blocks must be read. Assume the B^+-tree index stores 20 pointers per node. This means that the B^+-tree index must have between 3 and 5 leaf nodes. With this number of leaf nodes, the entire tree has a depth of 2, so 2 index blocks must be read. Thus, the above strategy requires 12 total block reads.

If we use the index for *customer-name*, we estimate the number of block accesses as follows. Since $V(customer\text{-}name, deposit) = 200$, we expect that $10000/200 = 50$ tuples of the *deposit* relation pertain to Williams. However, since the index for *customer-name* is nonclustering, we anticipate that one block read will be required for each tuple. Thus, 50 block reads are required, just to read the *deposit* tuples. Let us assume that 20 pointers fit into one node of the B^+-tree index for *customer-name*. Since there are 200 customer names, the tree has between 11 and 20 leaf nodes. So, as was the case for the other B^+-tree index, the index for *customer-name* has a depth of 2, and 2 block accesses are required to read the necessary index blocks. Therefore, this strategy requires a total of 52 block reads. We conclude that it is preferable to use the index for *branch-name*.

Observe that if both indices were nonclustering, we would prefer to use the index for *customer-name* since we expect only 50 tuples with *customer-name* = "Williams" versus 200 tuples with *branch-name* = "Perryridge." Without the clustering property, our first strategy could require as many as 200 block accesses to read the data since, in the worst case, each tuple is on a different block. We add this to the 2 index block accesses for a total of 202 block reads. However, because of the clustering property of the *branch-name* index, it is actually less expensive in this example to use the *branch-name* index.

Another way in which the indices could be used to process our example query is as follows. Use the index for *customer-name* to retrieve pointers to records with *customer-name* = "Williams" rather than the records themselves. Let P_1 denote this set of pointers. Similarly, use the index for *branch-name* to retrieve pointers to records with *branch-name* = "Perryridge". Let P_2 denote this set of pointers. Then $P_1 \cap P_2$ is a set of pointers to records with *branch-name* = "Perryridge" and *customer-name* = "Williams". These records must be retrieved and tested to see if *balance* > 1000.

Since this technique requires both indices to be accessed, a total of 4 index blocks are read. We estimate the number of blocks that must be read from the *deposit* file by estimating the number of pointers in $P_1 \cap P_2$.

Since V(*branch-name*, *deposit*) = 50 and V(*customer-name*, *deposit*) = 200, we estimate that one tuple in 50 × 200 or one in 10,000 has both *branch-name* = "Perryridge" and *customer-name* = "Williams". This estimate is based on an assumption of uniform distribution (which we made earlier) and an added assumption that the distribution of branch names and customer names are independent. Based on these assumptions, $P_1 \cap P_2$ is estimated to have only one pointer. Thus, only 1 block of *deposit* need be read. The total estimated cost of this strategy is 5 block reads.

We did not consider using the *balance* attribute and the predicate *balance* > 1000 as a starting point for a query-processing strategy for two reasons:

- There is no index for *balance*.

- The selection predicate on *balance* involves a "greater than" comparison. In general, equality predicates are more selective than "greater than" predicates. Since we have an equality predicate available to us (indeed, we have two), we prefer to start by using such a predicate since it is likely to select fewer tuples.

Estimation of the cost of access using indices allows us to estimate the complete cost, in terms of block accesses, of a strategy. For a given relational algebra expression, it may be possible to formulate several strategies. The *access plan selection* phase of a query optimizer chooses the best strategy for a given expression.

We have seen that different plans may have significant differences in cost. It is possible that a relational algebra expression for which a good plan exists may be preferable to an apparently more efficient algebra expression for which only inferior plans exist.

9.5 Join Strategies

In this section, we apply our techniques for estimating the cost of processing a query to the problem of estimating the *cost* of processing a join. We shall see that several factors influence the selection of an optimal strategy:

- The physical order of tuples in a relation.

- The presence of indices and the type of index (clustering or nonclustering).

- The cost of computing a temporary index for the sole purpose of processing one query.

Let us begin by considering the expression

$$deposit \bowtie customer$$

and assume that

- $n_{deposit} = 10,000.$
- $n_{customer} = 200.$

We shall consider several methods for computing this join and analyze their respective cost.

The number of disk accesses required to compute the join obviously depends on the buffer size and page replacement algorithm. We shall compute this number for:

- **Worst case scenario.** The buffer consists of 2 blocks, one to hold a block of the *deposit* relation and one to hold a block of the *customer* relation.

- **Best case scenario.** The buffer is large enough to accommodate both the *deposit* relation and the *customer* relation.

We shall derive these numbers assuming several different procedures (described below) for computing the join.

9.5.1 Simple Iteration

Let us assume for now that we have no indices whatsoever. If we are not willing to create an index, we must examine every possible pair of tuples t_d in *deposit* and t_c in *customer*. Thus, we must examine $10000 * 200 = 2000000$ pairs of tuples.

Suppose that we use the procedure of Figure 9.1 for computing the join. We read each tuple of *deposit* once. This may require as many as 10,000 block accesses if each *deposit* tuple resides on a different block. Each tuple of *customer* must be referenced once for each tuple of *deposit*. This means that we reference each tuple of *customer* 10,000 times. In the worst case scenario, each such reference requires a disk access. Since $n_{customer} = 200$, we could make as many as 2,000,000 accesses to read *customer* tuples. Putting it all together, in the worst case we could make as many as 2,010,000 block accesses to compute the join. In the best case scenario, however, we can read both relations only once and perform the computation. This requires at most 10,200 block accesses, a significant improvement over the worst case scenario.

If the tuples of *deposit* are stored together physically, fewer accesses are required. If we assume that 20 tuples of *deposit* fit in one block, then reading *deposit* requires 10000/20 = 500 block accesses. Similarly, if we assume that 20 *customer* tuples fit in one block, then at most 10 accesses are required to read the entire *customer* relation. Thus, only 10 accesses per tuple of *deposit* rather than 200 are required. This implies that in the worst case scenario at most 100,000 block accesses are required to read *customer* tuples. Thus, the cost of this simple approach is 500 accesses to *deposit* plus 100,000 accesses to *customer* for a total of 100,500 block accesses. In the best case scenario, however, we can read both relations only once, which requires at most 520 block accesses.

If the buffer is too small to hold entirely both relations in memory, then we can still have a major saving in block accesses if we process the relations on a per-block basis rather than on a per-tuple basis. Again, assuming that *deposit* tuples are stored together physically and that *customer* tuples are stored together physically, we can use the procedure of Figure 9.2 to compute *deposit* ⋈ *customer*. This procedure performs the join by considering an entire block of *deposit* tuples at once. We still must read the entire *deposit* relation at a cost of 500 accesses. However, instead of reading the *customer* relation once for each *tuple* of *deposit*, we read the *customer* relation once for each *block* of *deposit*. Thus, in the worst case scenario, since there are 500 blocks of *deposit* tuples and 10 blocks of

```
for each tuple d in deposit do
   begin
      for each tuple c in customer do
         begin
            test pair (d,c) to see if a tuple should be added to the result
         end
   end
```

Figure 9.1   Procedure for computing join.

```
for each block Bd of deposit do
  begin
    for each block Bc of customer do
      begin
        for each tuple d in Bd do
          begin
            for each tuple c in Bc do
              begin
                test pair (d,c) to see if a tuple
                should be added to the result
              end
          end
      end
  end
```

Figure 9.2   Procedure to compute *deposit* ⋈ *customer*.

customer tuples, reading *customer* once for every block of *deposit* tuples requires $10 \times 500 = 5000$ block accesses. Hence, the total cost in terms of block accesses is 5500 accesses (5000 accesses to *customer* blocks plus 500 accesses to *deposit* blocks). Clearly, this is a significant improvement over the number of accesses that were necessary for our initial strategy.

Our choice of *deposit* for the outer loop and *customer* for the inner loop was arbitrary. If we had used *customer* as the relation for the outer loop and *deposit* for the inner loop, the cost of our final strategy would have been slightly lower (5010 block accesses). See Exercise 9.10 for a derivation of these costs.

A major advantage to the use of the smaller relation (*customer*) in the inner loop is that it may be possible to store the entire relation in main memory temporarily. This speeds query processing significantly since it is necessary to read the inner loop relation only once. If *customer* is indeed small enough to fit in main memory, our strategy requires only 500 blocks to read *deposit* plus 10 blocks to read *customer* for a total of only 510 block accesses.

9.5.2 Merge-Join

In those cases in which neither relation fits in main memory, it is still possible to process the join efficiently if both relations happen to be stored in sorted order on the join attributes.

Suppose that both *customer* and *deposit* are sorted by *customer-name*. We can then perform a *merge-join* operation. We associate one pointer with each relation. These pointers point initially to the first tuple of the respective relations. As the algorithm proceeds, the pointers move through the relation. A group of tuples of one relation with the same value on the join attributes is read. Then the corresponding tuples (if any) of the other relation are read. Since the relations are in sorted order, tuples with the same value on the join attributes are in consecutive order. This allows us to read each tuple only once. In the case in which the tuples of the relations are stored together physically, this algorithm allows us to compute the join by reading each block exactly once.

Figure 9.3 shows how the merge-join scheme is applied to our example of *deposit* ⋈ *customer*. In this case, there is a total of 510 block accesses. This is as good as the earlier join method we presented for the special case in which the entire *customer* relation fit in main memory. The algorithm of Figure 9.3 does not require the entire relation to fit in main memory. Rather, it suffices to keep all tuples with the same value for the join attributes in main memory. This is usually feasible even if both relations are large.

A disadvantage of the merge-join method is that both relations must be sorted physically.

9.5.3 Use of an Index

The three strategies we have considered so far depend upon the physical techniques used for storing the relations. Merge-join requires sorted order. Block-oriented iteration requires that tuples of each relation be stored physically together. Only the third strategy, simple iteration, can be applied if no physical clustering of tuples exists. The cost of simple iteration for our example of *deposit* ⋈ *customer* is 2 million block accesses. When an index is used, but without any assumptions being made about physical storage, the join can be computed with significantly fewer block accesses.

Frequently, the join attributes form a search key for an index as one of the relations being joined. In such a case, we may consider a join strategy that uses such an index. The simple strategy of Figure 9.1 can be made more efficient if an index exists on *customer* for *customer-name*. Given a tuple d in *deposit*, it is no longer necessary to read the entire *customer* relation. Instead, the index is used to look up tuples in *customer* for which the *customer-name* value is d[*customer-name*].

We still need 10,000 accesses to read *deposit*. However, for each tuple of deposit only an index lookup is required. If we assume (as before) that $n_{customers} = 200$, and that 20 pointers fit in one block, then this lookup requires at most 2 index block accesses plus a block access to read the *customer* tuple itself. We access 3 blocks per tuple of *deposit* instead of 200. Adding this to the 10,000 accesses to read *deposit*, we find that the total cost of this strategy is 40,000 accesses.

Although a cost of 40,000 accesses appears high, we must remember that we achieved more efficient strategies only when we assumed that

pd := address of first tuple of *deposit*;
pc := address of first tuple of *customer*;
while ($pc \neq$ null) **do**
  begin
    t_c := tuple to which pc points;
    $s_c := \{t_c\}$;
    set pc to point to next tuple of *customer*;
    done := *false*;
    while (**not** *done* **and** $pc \neq$ null) **do**
      begin;
        t_c' := tuple to which pc points;
        if $t_c'[customer\text{-}name] = t_c[customer\text{-}name]$
          then begin
              $s_c := s_c \cup \{t_c'\}$;
              set pc to point to next tuple of customer;
            end
          else *done* := *true*;
      end
    t_d := tuple to which pd points;
    set pd to point to next tuple of *deposit*;
    while ($t_d[customer\text{-}name] < t_c[customer\text{-}name]$) **do**
      begin
        t_d := tuple to which pd points;
        set pd to point to next tuple of *deposit*;
      end
    while ($t_d[customer\text{-}name] = t_c[customer\text{-}name]$) **do**
      begin
        for each t **in** s_c **do**
          begin
            compute $t \bowtie t_d$ and add this to result;
          end
        set pd to point to next tuple of *deposit*;
        td := tuple to which pd points;
      end
  end.

Figure 9.3 Merge-join.

tuples were stored physically together. If this assumption does not hold for the relations being joined, then the strategy we just presented is highly desirable. Indeed the saving of 160,000 accesses is enough to justify creation of the index. Even if we create the index for the sole purpose of processing this one query and drop the index afterward, we may perform fewer accesses than if we use the strategy of Figure 9.1.

9.5.4 Hash Join

As we have just seen, it may be worthwhile to construct an index specifically for use in computing a join even if the index is not retained after the join is computed. Rather than constructing a B^+-tree index, it is often preferable to use hashing for a "use once" index constructed to assist in the computation of a single join.

A hash function h is used to hash tuples of both relations on the basis of join attributes. The resulting buckets, which contain pointers to tuples in the relations, are used to limit the number of pairs of tuples that must be compared. If d is a tuple in *deposit*, and c a tuple in *customer*, then d and c must be tested only if $h(c) = h(d)$. If $h(c) \neq h(d)$, then c and d must have different values for *customer-name*. However, if $h(c) = h(d)$ we must test c and d, since it is possible that c and d have different values for *customer-name* that hash to the same value.

Figure 9.4 shows the details of the hash-join algorithm as applied to our example of *deposit* $\bowtie$ *customer*. The hash function h should have the "goodness" properties of randomness and uniformity that we discussed in Chapter 8. We shall use those properties to estimate the cost of performing a hash-join. In Figure 9.4 we assume that:

- h is a hash function mapping *customer-name* values to $\{0, 1, \ldots, \text{max}\}$.

- $H_{c_0}, H_{c_1}, \ldots, H_{c_{max}}$ denote buckets of pointers to *customer* tuples, each initially empty.

- $H_{d_0}, H_{d_1}, \ldots, H_{d_{max}}$ denote buckets of pointers to *deposit* tuples, each initially empty.

We use those properties below to estimate the cost of performing a hash-join.

The assignment of pointers to hash buckets in the first two **for** loops of the algorithm calls for a complete reading of both relations. The cost of this operation requires 510 block accesses if *deposit* tuples are stored together physically and *customer* tuples are stored together physically. Since the buckets contain only pointers, we assume that they fit in main memory, so no disk accesses are required to access the buckets.

The final part of the algorithm iterates over the range of h. Let i be a value in the range of h. The final outer **for** loop computes

$$rd \bowtie rc$$

where rd is the set of *deposit* tuples that hash to bucket i and rc is the set of *customer* tuples that hash to bucket i. This join is computed using simple iteration, since we expect rd and rc to be sufficiently small for both to fit in main memory. Since a tuple hashes to exactly one bucket, each tuple is read only once by the final outer **for** loop. The order in which tuples are

```
for each tuple c in customer do
  begin
    i := h(c[customer-name]);
    H_{c_i} := H_{c_i} ∪ {pointer to c};
  end
for each tuple d in deposit do
  begin
    i := h(d[customer-name]);
    H_{d_i} := H_{d_i} ∪ {pointer to d};
  end
for i := 0 to max do
  begin
    rc := ∅ ;
    rd := ∅ ;
    for each pointer pc in H_{c_i} do
      begin
        c := tuple to which pc points;
        rc := rc ∪ {c};
      end
    for each pointer pd in H_{d_i} do
      begin
        d := tuple to which pd points;
        rd := rd ∪ {d};
      end
    for each tuple d in rd do
      begin
        for each tuple c in rc do
          begin
            test pair (d, c) to see if a tuple
            should be added to the result
          end
      end
  end
```

Figure 9.4   Hash-join.

read is determined by the hash function. So, despite the assumption that tuples of *deposit* are stored together physically, it requires 10,000 block accesses in the worst case to read all tuples of *deposit*. Likewise, 200 block accesses are required in the worst case to read all tuples of *customer*. Thus, the total estimated cost of a hash join is 10,710 accesses. If the query optimizer chooses to perform a hash-join, it is necessary to choose a hash function whose range is large enough to ensure that the buckets contain a sufficiently small number of pointers so that *rc* and *rd* fit in main memory.

The optimizer must not choose a hash function with a range that is so large that many buckets are empty. This would waste space and force the hash-join algorithm to incur the overhead of processing empty buckets.

9.5.5 Three-Way Join

Let us now consider a join involving three relations:

$$branch \bowtie deposit \bowtie customer$$

Assume that $n_{deposit} = 10{,}000$, $n_{customer} = 200$, and $n_{branch} = 50$. Not only do we have a choice of strategy for join processing; we also have a choice of which join to compute first. There are many possible strategies to consider. We shall analyze several of them below and leave others as exercises for the reader.

- **Strategy 1.** Compute the join *deposit* $\bowtie$ *customer* using one of the techniques we presented above. Since *customer-name* is a key for *customer*, we know that the result of this join has at most 10,000 tuples (the number of tuples in *deposit*). If we build an index on *branch* for *branch-name*, we can compute

  $$branch \bowtie (deposit \bowtie customer)$$

  by considering each tuple t of (*deposit* $\bowtie$ *customer*) and looking up the tuple in *branch* with a *branch-name* value of $t[branch\text{-}name]$. Since *branch-name* is a key for *branch*, we know that we must examine only one *branch* tuple for each of the 10,000 tuples in (*deposit* $\bowtie$ *customer*). The exact number of block accesses required by this strategy depends on the way we compute (*deposit* $\bowtie$ *customer*) and on the way in which *branch* is stored physically. Several exercises examine the costs of various possibilities.

- **Strategy 2.** Compute the three-way join without constructing any indices at all. This requires checking 50 * 10000 * 200 possibilities, or a total of 100,000,000.

- **Strategy 3.** Instead of performing two joins, we perform the pair of joins at once. The technique first involves building two indices:

  - On *branch* for *branch-name*.

  - On *customer* for *customer-name*.

  Next we consider each tuple t in *deposit*. For each t, we look up the corresponding tuples in *customer* and the corresponding tuples in *branch*. Thus, we examine each tuple of *deposit* exactly once.

Strategy 3 represents a form we have not considered before. It does not correspond directly to a relational algebra operation. Instead, it combines two operations into one special-purpose operation. With strategy 3, it is often possible to perform a join of three relations more efficiently than by using two joins of two relations. The relative costs depend on the way in which the relations are stored, the distribution of values within columns, and the presence of indices. The exercises provide an opportunity to compute these costs in several examples.

9.6 Join Strategies for Parallel Processors

The join strategies we have considered thus far assume that a single processor is available to compute the join. In this section, we consider the case where several processors are available for the parallel computation of the join. We assume a multiprocess environment where the processors are part of one computer system all sharing a single main memory. In Chapter 15, we discuss the case where the processors are separate computer systems linked by a network.

Numerous architectures have been proposed for parallel processors for database applications. Many of these *database machines* are discussed in references that appear in the bibliographic notes. We shall consider a simple architecture with the following features:

- All processors have access to all disks.

- All processors share main memory.

The techniques presented below for parallel join processing can be adapted to other architectures in which each processor has its own private memory.

9.6.1 Parallel-Join

In the techniques we have discussed for processing joins on a single processor, efficiency is achieved by reducing the number of pairs of tuples that need to be tested. The goal of a parallel-join algorithm is to split the pairs to be tested over several processors. Each processor then computes part of the join. In a final step, the results from each processor are collected to produce the final result.

Ideally, the overall work of computing the join is partitioned evenly over all processors. If such a split is achieved without any overhead, a parallel join using N processors will take $1/N$ times as long as the same join would take on a single processor. In practice, the speedup is less dramatic for several reasons:

- Overhead is incurred in partitioning the work among the processors.

- Overhead is incurred in collecting the results computed by each processor to produce the final result.

- The effort made to split work evenly is only an approximation, so some processors may have more work than others. The final result cannot be obtained until the last processor to finish has, in fact, finished.

- The processors may compete for shared system resources. This results in delays as processors wait for other processors to free resources.

Let us consider again our examples of *deposit* $\bowtie$ *customer*, assuming we have N processors $P_1, P_2, \ldots, P_N$. We partition *deposit* into N partitions of equal size; $deposit_1, deposit_2, \ldots, deposit_N$. (For simplicity, we assume that the size of the relation *deposit* is a multiple of N.) Then each processor P_i computes $deposit_i \bowtie customer$ in parallel. In the final step, we compute the union of the partial results computed by each processor.

The cost of this strategy depends on several factors:

- The choice of join algorithm used by each processor.

- The cost of assembling the final result.

- The delays imposed by contention for resources. Although each processor uses its own partition of *deposit*, all processors access *customer*. If main memory is not sufficiently large to hold the entire *customer* relation, the processors need to synchronize their access to *customer* so as to reduce the number of times that each block of *customer* must be read in from disk.

The potential contention for main memory to store *customer* tuples suggests that we use some care in partitioning the work among processors so as to reduce contention. There are several ways to accomplish this. A simple technique is to use a parallel version of the hash-join algorithm.

We choose a hash function whose range is $\{1, 2, \ldots, N\}$. This allows us to assign each of the N processors to exactly one hash bucket. Since the final outer **for** loop of the hash-join algorithm (Figure 9.4) iterates over buckets, each processor can process the iteration that corresponds to its assigned bucket. No tuple is assigned to more than one bucket, so there is no contention for *customer* tuples. Since each processor considers one pair of tuples at a time, the total main memory requirements of the parallel hash-join algorithm are sufficiently low that contention for space in main memory is unlikely.

9.6.2 Pipelined Multiway Join

In this section, we explore the possibility of computing several joins in parallel. This is an important issue since many real-world queries, particularly those posed through views, involve several relations.

Let us consider a join of four relations:

$$r_1 \bowtie r_2 \bowtie r_3 \bowtie r_4$$

Clearly, we can compute $t_1 \leftarrow r_1 \bowtie r_2$ in parallel with $t_2 \leftarrow r_3 \bowtie r_4$. When these two computations complete, we compute:

$$t_1 \bowtie t_2$$

Still greater parallelism can be achieved by setting up a "pipeline" that allows the three joins to be computed in parallel. Let processor P_1 be assigned the computation of $r_1 \bowtie r_2$ and let P_2 be assigned $r_3 \bowtie r_4$. As P_1 computes tuples in $r_1 \bowtie r_2$, it makes these tuples available to processor P_3. Likewise, as P_2 computes tuples in $r_3 \bowtie r_4$, it makes these tuples available to P_3. Thus, P_3 has available to it some of the tuples in $r_1 \bowtie r_2$ and $r_3 \bowtie r_4$ before P_1 and P_2 have finished their computation. P_3 can use those tuples available to it to begin computation of $(r_1 \bowtie r_2) \bowtie (r_3 \bowtie r_4)$ even before $r_1 \bowtie r_2$ and $r_3 \bowtie r_4$ have been fully computed.

This pipeline join is illustrated schematically in Figure 9.5, which shows a "flow" of tuples from P_1 to P_3 and from P_2 to P_3. In our assumed parallel machine, tuples are passed via the shared main memory. This technique is applicable to other parallel architectures as well.

Figure 9.6 shows the algorithm used by processor P_3 to compute the join. Tuples made available by P_1 and P_2 are queued for processing by P_3. The detailed description of the implementation of the queueing mechanism is left as an exercise. Processors P_1 and P_2 are free to use any of the join algorithms we have considered earlier. The only modification is that when a tuple t is added to the result, t must be made available to P_3 by entering

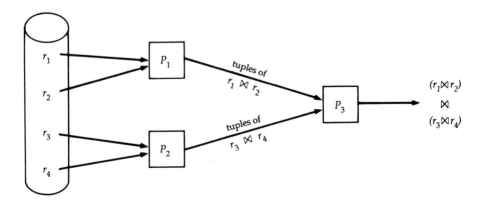

Figure 9.5   Pipeline join.

t into the queue. In addition, a special queue entry consisting of ENDP1 and ENDP2, respectively, is made upon completion of the computation.

The concept illustrated by a pipeline computation of the 4-way join $r_1 \bowtie r_2 \bowtie r_3 \bowtie r_4$ can be extended to handle n-way joins.

9.6.3 Physical Organization

The techniques we have considered for parallel join computation increase the rate at which accesses to disk occur. For the parallel 2-way join of Section 9.6.1, we saw that by choosing carefully the way in which the relation is partitioned, we could reduce contention for the disk. However, for that technique, as well as for the pipeline-join technique of the previous section, the disk is likely to be the bottleneck.

In order to reduce contention for disk access, the database can be partitioned over several disks. This allows several disk accesses to be serviced in parallel. However, in order to exploit the potential for parallel disk access, we must choose a good distribution of data among the disks.

The parallel 2-way join algorithm requires several processors to access relations in parallel. In order to reduce contention, it is useful to distribute

```
done1 := false;
done2 := false;
from1 := ∅ ;
from2 := ∅ ;
result := ∅ ;
while not done1 or not done2 do
    begin
        if queue is empty then wait until queue is not empty;
        t := top entry in queue;
        if t = ENDP1 then done1 := true
            else if t = ENDP2 then done2 := true
                else if t is from P1 then
                    begin
                        from1 := from1 ∪ {t};
                        result := result ∪ ({t} ⋈ from2);
                    end
                else /* t is from P2 */
                    begin
                        from2 := from2 ∪ {t};
                        result := result ∪ (from1 ⋈ {t});
                    end
    end
```

Figure 9.6   Algorithm run by processor P_3 for pipeline join.

tuples of individual relations among several disks. This technique is called *disk striping*. Let us consider one example of disk striping particularly well suited to the parallel version of the hash-join that we presented in Section 9.6.1. We use the hash function of the hash-join algorithm to assign tuples to disks. All groups of tuples that share a bucket are assigned to the same disk. Each group is assigned a separate disk if possible. Otherwise, the groups are distributed uniformly among the available disks. This form of striping allows the parallel 2-way hash-join to exploit parallel disk access. In the case where each group is assigned a separate disk, there is no contention for disk access at all!

The disk-striping technique is less helpful for the pipeline-join of Section 9.6.2. For the pipeline-join, it is desirable that each relation be kept on one disk, and that distinct relations be assigned to separate disks to the degree possible. In the scheme for Figure 9.5 for computing $(r_1 \bowtie r_2) \bowtie (r_3 \bowtie r_4)$, if each relation is on a different disk, contention is eliminated between processors P_1 and P_2.

Of course, the optimal physical organization differs for different queries. The database administrator must choose a physical organization that is believed to be good for the expected mix of database queries. The query optimizer of the database system must choose from the various parallel and sequential techniques we have considered by estimating the cost of each technique on the given physical organization.

9.7 Structure of the Query Optimizer

We have discussed only some of the many query-processing strategies used in various commercial database systems. Because most systems implement only a few strategies, the number of strategies to be considered by the query optimizer is limited. Other systems consider a large number of strategies. For each strategy a cost estimate is computed.

Some systems reduce the number of strategies that need to be fully considered by making a heuristic guess of a good strategy. Following this, the optimizer considers every possible strategy, but terminates as soon as it determines that the cost is greater than the best previously considered strategy. If the optimizer starts with a strategy that is likely to be of low cost, only a few competing strategies will require a full analysis of cost. This can reduce the overhead of query optimization.

In order to simplify the strategy selection task, a query may be split into several subqueries. This not only simplifies strategy selection but also allows the query optimizer to recognize cases where a particular subquery appears several times in the same query. If such subqueries are computed only once, time is saved both in the query-optimizing phase and in the execution of the query itself. Recognition of common subqueries is analogous to the recognition of *common subexpressions* in many optimizing compilers for programming languages.

Clearly, examination of the query for common subqueries and the estimation of the cost of a large number of strategies impose a substantial overhead on query processing. However, the added cost of query optimization is usually more than offset by the saving at query execution time. The achieved saving is magnified in those applications that run on a regular basis and reexecute the same queries on each run. Therefore, most commercial systems include relatively sophisticated optimizers. The bibliographic notes give references to descriptions of query optimizers of actual database systems.

9.8 Summary

There are a large number of possible strategies for processing a query, especially if the query is complex. Strategy selection can be done using information available in main memory, with few or no disk accesses. The actual execution of the query will involve many accesses to disk. Since the transfer of data from disk is slow relative to the speed of main memory and the central processor of the computer system, it is advantageous to spend a considerable amount of processing to save disk accesses.

Given a query, there are generally a variety of methods for computing the answer. It is the responsibility of the system to transform the query as entered by the user into an equivalent query which can be computed more efficiently. This "optimizing" or, more accurately, improving of the strategy for processing a query is called *query optimization*.

The first action the system must take on a query is to translate the query into its internal form which (for relational database systems) is usually based on the relational algebra. In the process of generating the internal form of the query, the parser checks the syntax of the user's query, verifies that the relation names appearing in the query are names of relations in the database, and so on. If the query was expressed in terms of a view, the parser replaces all references to the view name with the relational algebra expression to compute the view.

Each relational algebra expression represents a particular sequence of operations. The first step in selecting a query-processing strategy is to find a relational algebra expression that is equivalent to the given expression and is more efficient to execute. There are a number of different rules for transforming relational algebra queries, including:

- Perform selection operations as early as possible.

- Perform projections early.

The strategy we choose for a query depends upon the size of each relation and the distribution of values within columns. In order to be able to choose a strategy based on reliable information, database systems may store statistics for each relation r. These statistics include:

- The number of tuples in the relation r.

- The size of a record (tuple) of relation r in bytes.

- The number of distinct values that appear in the relation r for a particular attribute.

The first two statistics allow us to estimate accurately the size of a cartesian product. The third statistic allows us to estimate the number of tuples that satisfy a simple selection predicate.

Statistical information about relations is particularly useful when several indices are available to assist in the processing of a query. The presence of these structures has a significant influence on the choice of a query-processing strategy.

Queries involving a natural join may be processed in several ways, depending on the availability of indices and the form of physical storage used for the relations. If tuples of a relation are stored together physically, a *block-oriented* join strategy may be advantageous. If the relations are sorted, a *merge-join* may be desirable. It may be more efficient to sort a relation prior to join computation (so as to allow use of the merge-join strategy). It may also be advantageous to compute a temporary index for the sole purpose of allowing a more efficient join strategy to be used.

In a multiprocessor system, joins may be computed efficiently by partitioning the task among several processors. On a shared-memory machine it is possible to achieve parallelism by partitioning one of the two relations to be joined and processing each partition in parallel. A join of three or more relations can be processed in parallel by constructing a "pipeline" in which each join may be computed by a distinct processor.

Exercises

9.1 At what point during query processing does optimization occur?

9.2 Why is it not desirable to force users to make an explicit choice of a query-processing strategy? Are there cases in which it *is* desirable for users to be aware of the costs of competing query-processing strategies?

9.3 Consider the following SQL query for our bank database:

> **select** *T.branch-name*
> **from** *branch T, branch S*
> **where** *T.assets > S.assets* **and**
>   *S.branch-city* = "Brooklyn"

Write an efficient relational algebra expression that is equivalent to this query. Justify your choice.

9.4 Consider the following SQL query for our bank database:

> **select** *customer-name*
> **from** *deposit S*
> **where** (**select** *branch-name*
>   **from** *deposit T*
>   **where** *S.customer-name = T.customer-name*)
>   **contains**
>   (**select** *branch-name*
>   **from** *branch*
>   **where** *branch-city = "Brooklyn"*)

Write an efficient relational algebra expression that is equivalent to this query and propose an access strategy for evaluating the expression. Justify your choice. (Hint: Use the division operation in the algebra.) Propose a good access strategy for executing division.

9.5 Show that the following equivalences hold, and explain how they can be applied to improve the efficiency of certain queries:

a. $\sigma_P(r_1 \cup r_2) = \sigma_P(r_1) \cup \sigma_P(r_2)$

b. $\sigma_P(r_1 - r_2) = \sigma_P(r_1) - r_2 = \sigma_P(r_1) - \sigma_P(r_2)$

c. $(r_1 \cup r_2) \cup r_3 = r_1 \cup (r_2 \cup r_3)$

d. $r_1 \cup r_2 = r_2 \cup r_1$

9.6 Consider the relations $r_1(A,B,C)$, $r_2(C,D,E)$, and $r_3(E,F)$, with primary keys A, C, and E respectively. Assume that r_1 has 1000 tuples, r_2 has 1500 tuples, and r_3 has 750 tuples. Estimate the size of $r_1 \bowtie r_2 \bowtie r_3$, and give an efficient strategy for computing the join.

9.7 Consider the relations $r_1(A,B,C)$, $r_2(C,D,E)$, and $r_3(E,F)$ of Exercise 9.6 again, but now assume there are no primary keys except the entire scheme. Let $V(C,r_1)$ be 900, $V(C,r_2)$ be 1100, $V(E,r_2)$ be 50, and $V(E,r_3)$ be 100. Assume that r_1 has 1000 tuples, r_2 has 1500 tuples, and r_3 has 750 tuples. Estimate the size of $r_1 \bowtie r_2 \bowtie r_3$, and give an efficient strategy for computing the join.

9.8 Clustering indices may allow faster access to data than a nonclustering index. When must we create a nonclustering index despite the advantages of a clustering index?

9.9 What are the advantages and disadvantages of hash functions relative to B^+-tree indices? How might the type of index available influence the choice of a query-processing strategy?

9.10 Recompute the cost of the strategy of Section 9.5.2 using *deposit* as the relation of the inner loop and *customer* as the relation of the outer loop (thereby reversing the roles they played in the example of Section 9.5.2).

9.11 Let relations $r_1(A,B,C)$ and $r_2(C,D,E)$ have the following properties:

- r_1 has 20,000 tuples.
- r_2 has 45,000 tuples.
- 25 tuples of r_1 fit on one block.
- 30 tuples of r_2 fit on one block.

Estimate the number of block accesses required, using each of the following join strategies for $r_1 \bowtie r_2$:

- Simple iteration.
- Block-oriented iteration.
- Merge-join.
- Hash-join.

9.12 Design a variant of the merge-join algorithm for relations that are *not* physically sorted. (Hint: To compute $r_1 \bowtie r_2$, construct appropriate indices on the two relations. Use these indices to process the relations logically in sorted order independent of their physical organization.)

9.13 Estimate the number of block accesses required by your solution to Exercise 9.12 for $r_1 \bowtie r_2$, where r_1 and r_2 are as in Exercise 9.11.

9.14 Consider relations r_1 and r_2 of Exercise 9.11 along with a relation $r_3(E,F)$. Assume that r_3 has 30,000 tuples and that 40 tuples of r_3 fit on one block. Estimate the costs of the 3 strategies of Section 9.5.6 for computing $r_1 \bowtie r_2 \bowtie r_3$.

9.15 Give a schematic illustration similar to that of Figure 9.5 to show how 7 processors could compute

$$r_1 \bowtie r_2 \bowtie r_3 \bowtie r_4 \bowtie r_5 \bowtie r_6 \bowtie r_7 \bowtie r_8$$

in parallel using a pipeline join.

Bibliographic Notes

Some of the ideas used in query optimization are derived from solutions to similar problems in code optimization as performed by compilers of standard programming languages. There are several texts that present optimization from a programming languages point of view, including Aho et al. [1986] and Tremblay and Sorenson [1985]. Smith and Chang [1975] present an optimization algorithm for relational algebra.

Selinger et al. [1979] describe access path selection in System R. Kim [1982, 1984] describe join strategies and the optimal use of available main memory. These papers discuss many of the strategies that we presented in this chapter.

Wong and Youssefi [1976] introduce a technique called *decomposition*, which is used in the Ingres database system. The Ingres decomposition strategy motivated the third strategy we presented for three-way joins. In Ingres, an extension of this technique is used to choose a strategy for general queries. Ingres and System R are discussed in more detail in Chapter 17.

If an entire group of queries is considered, it is possible to discover *common subexpressions* that can be evaluated once for the entire group. Finkelstein [1982] and Hall [1976] consider optimization of a group of queries and the use of common subexpressions. When queries are generated through views, it is often the case that more relations are joined than is necessary to compute the query. A collection of techniques for join minimization has been grouped under the name *tableau optimization*. The notion of a tableau was introduced by Aho et al. [1979a, 1979c], and further extended by Sagiv and Yannakakis [1981]. Ullman [1988] and Maier [1983] provide a textbook coverage of tableaux.

Theoretical results on the complexity of the computation of relational algebra operations appear in Gotlieb [1975], Pecherer [1975], and Blasgen and Eswaren [1976]. A comparison of various query evaluation algorithms is given by Yao [1979b]. Additional discussions are presented in Kim et al. [1985]. A survey of query-processing techniques appears in Jarke and Koch [1984].

Klug [1982] discusses optimization of relational algebra expressions with aggregate functions. Query optimization in main memory database is covered by DeWitt et al. [1984], Shapiro [1986], and Whang and Krishnamurthy [1990].

Semantic query optimization in relational databases are covered by King [1981]. Malley and Zdonick [1986] present a knowledge-based approach to query optimization. Chakravarthy et al. [1990] use integrity constraints to assist in query optimization.

An actual query processor must translate statements in the query language into an internal form suitable for the analysis we have discussed in this chapter. Parsing of query languages differs little from parsing of traditional programming languages. Most compiler texts, including Aho et al. [1986] and Tremblay and Sorenson [1985] cover the main parsing techniques. A more theoretical presentation of parsing and language translation is given by Aho and Ullman [1972, 1973].

A parallel join algorithm in a pipeline query processing environment is presented by Mikkilineni and Su [1988]. Sellis [1988] considers the problem of optimizing the execution of several queries as a group. Disk striping is discussed by Salem and Garcia-Molina [1986].

Query processing for distributed database systems uses some concepts from this chapter. Techniques specific to distributed systems appear in Chapter 15 and the bibliographic notes to that chapter.

10
Recovery and Atomicity

A computer system, like any other mechanical or electrical device, is subject to failure. There are a variety of causes of such failure, including disk crash, power failure, software errors, a fire in the machine room, sabotage, and even a "black hole" passing through the building in which the computer system is residing. In each of these cases, information concerning the database system is lost. An integral part of a database system is a recovery scheme which is responsible for the detection of failures and the restoration of the database to a consistent state that existed prior to the occurrence of the failure.

Often, several operations on the database form a single logical unit of work. An example is funds transfer, in which one account is debited and another is credited. Clearly, it is essential to database consistency that either both the credit and debit occur, or that neither occur. That is, the funds transfer must happen in its entirety or not at all. This "all or none" requirement is called *atomicity*.

A transaction is a collection of operations that performs a single logical function in a database application. Each transaction is a unit of atomicity. We shall see that a major issue in processing database transactions is the preservation of atomicity despite the possibility of failures within the computer system.

10.1 Failure Classification

There are various types of failure that may occur in a system, each of which needs to be dealt with in a different manner. The simplest type of failure to deal with is one which does not result in the loss of information in the system. The failures that are more difficult to deal with are those that do result in loss of information. In order to determine how the system should recover from failures, we need to identify the failure modes of those devices used for storing data. Next, we must consider how these failure modes affect the contents of the database. We can then propose algorithms to ensure database consistency and transaction atomicity despite failures. These algorithms have two parts:

- Actions taken during normal transaction processing to ensure that enough information exists to allow for recovery from failures.

- Actions taken following a failure to ensure database consistency and transaction atomicity.

10.1.1 Storage Types

There are various types of storage media which are distinguished by their relative speed, capacity, and resilience to failure.

- **Volatile storage**. Information residing in volatile storage does not usually survive system crashes. Examples of such storage are main and cache memory. Access to volatile storage is very fast, both because of the speed of the memory access itself and because it is possible to access any data item in volatile storage directly.

- **Nonvolatile storage**. Information residing in nonvolatile storage usually survives system crashes. Examples of such storage are disk and magnetic tapes. Disk is used for online storage, while tapes are used for archival storage. Disks are more reliable than main memory but less reliable than magnetic tapes. Both, however, are subject to failure (for example, head crash) which may result in loss of information. At the current state of technology, nonvolatile storage is slower than volatile storage by several orders of magnitude. This distinction is the result of disk and tape devices being electromechanical rather than based entirely on chips as is volatile storage. In database systems, disks are used for most nonvolatile storage. Other nonvolatile media are normally used only for backup data.

- **Stable storage**. Information residing in stable storage is *never* lost (*never* should be taken with a grain of salt, since theoretically it cannot be guaranteed). To implement an approximation of such storage, we need to replicate information in several nonvolatile storage media (usually disk) with independent failure modes, and update the information in a controlled manner, as will be discussed in Section 10.9.

10.1.2 Failure Types

A recovery scheme must be invoked as a result of various types of failures. In this chapter we will consider only the following four types of failure.

- **Logical errors**. The transaction can no longer continue with its normal execution owing to some internal condition such as bad input, data not found, overflow, or resource limit exceeded.

- **System errors**. The system has entered an undesirable state (for example, deadlock), as a result of which the transaction cannot continue with its normal execution. The transaction, however, can be reexecuted at a later time.

- **System crash**. The hardware malfunctions, causing the loss of the content of volatile storage. The content of nonvolatile storage remains intact.

- **Disk failure**. A disk block loses its content as a result of either head crash or failure during a data transfer operation.

In Sections 10.4 through 10.7, we deal only with recovery from the first three types of failure. In Section 10.8, we consider what can be done in the case of the fourth type of failure.

The distinction among the various storage types is often less clear in practice than in our presentation. Certain systems provide battery backup so that some main memory can survive system crashes and power failures. Alternative forms of nonvolatile storage, such as optical media, provide an even higher degree of reliability than disks.

10.2 The Storage Hierarchy

The database system resides in nonvolatile storage (usually a disk). The database is partitioned into fixed-length storage units called *blocks* which are the units of both storage allocation and data transfer. Transactions input information from the disk to main memory and then output the information back onto the disk. The input and output operations are done in block units. The blocks residing on the disk are referred to as *physical blocks*, while the blocks residing temporarily in main memory are referred to as *buffer blocks*.

A block may contain several data items. The exact set of data items that a block contains is determined by the form of physical data organization being used (see Chapter 7). We shall assume that no data item spans two or more blocks. This assumption is realistic for most data-processing applications, such as our banking example. We consider situations where this assumption does not hold in Chapters 12–14.

Block movements between disk and main memory are initiated through the following two operations:

- **input**(X), which transfers the physical block in which data item X resides to main memory.

- **output**(X), which transfers the buffer block on which X resides to the disk and replaces the appropriate physical block there.

This scheme is illustrated in Figure 10.1.

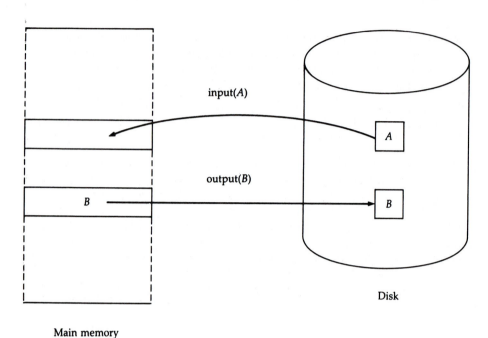

Figure 10.1   Block storage operations.

Transactions interact with the database system by transferring data from program variables to the database and from the database to program variables. This transfer of data is achieved using the following two operations:

- **read**(X,x_i), which assigns the value of data item X to the local variable x_i. This operation is executed as follows:

  1. If the block on which X resides is not in main memory, then issue **input**(X).

  2. Assign to x_i the value of X from the buffer block.

- **write**(X,x_i), which assigns the value of local variable x_i to data item X in the buffer block. This operation is executed as follows:

  1. If the block on which X resides is not in main memory, then issue **input**(X).

  2. Assign the value of x_i to X in the buffer block for X.

Note that both operations may require the transfer of a block from disk to main memory. They do not, however, specifically require the transfer of a block from main memory to disk.

A buffer block is eventually written out to the disk either because the buffer manager needs the memory space for other purposes or because the database system wishes to reflect the change to X on the disk. We shall say that the database system *force-outputs* the buffer block of X if it issues an **output**(X).

When a transaction needs to access a data item X for the first time, it must execute **read**(X,x_i). All updates to X are then performed on x_i. After the transaction accesses X for the last time, it must execute **write**(X,x_i) in order to reflect the change to X in the database itself.

The **output**(X) operation need not take effect immediately after the **write**(X,x_i) is executed, since the block on which X resides may contain other data items that are still being accessed. Thus, the actual output takes place later. Notice that if the system crashes after the **write**(X,x_i) operation was executed but before **output**(X) was executed, the new value of X is never written to disk and, thus, is lost.

10.3 Transaction Model

A transaction is a program unit that accesses and possibly updates various data items. Each one of these items is read precisely once by the transaction and is written at most once by the transaction if it updates that data item. We require that transactions do not violate any database consistency constraints. That is, if the database was consistent when a transaction started, the database must be consistent when the transaction successfully terminates. However, during the execution of a transaction, it may be necessary temporarily to allow inconsistency. This temporary inconsistency, though necessary, may lead to difficulty if a failure occurs.

10.3.1 Banking Example

Consider a somewhat simplified banking system consisting of several accounts and a set of transactions that access and update those accounts. Let T be a transaction that transfers $50 from account A to account B. This transaction may be defined as:

$$
\begin{aligned}
T:\ &\textbf{read}(A,a_1)\\
&a_1 := a_1 - 50\\
&\textbf{write}(A,a_1)\\
&\textbf{read}(B,b_1)\\
&b_1 := b_1 + 50\\
&\textbf{write}(B,b_1)
\end{aligned}
$$

The consistency constraint is that the sum of A and B is unchanged by the execution of the transaction.

Suppose that just prior to the execution of transaction T, the values of accounts A and B are \$1000 and \$2000, respectively. Further suppose that the main memory contains the buffer block of A, but not that of B (see Figure 10.2). When **read**(A,a_1) is executed, the action that takes place is to assign the value \$1000 to a_1. When **read**(B,b_1) is executed, however, the system must first bring the physical block of B to main memory by executing the operation **input**(B) (see Figure 10.3). After the completion of the **input** operation, b_1 is assigned the value \$2000.

During the execution of T, the values of a_1 and b_1 are changed to \$950 and \$2050, respectively. Thus, after the **write** operations are executed, the state of the system is as depicted in Figure 10.4. Note that at this point (in this example), the **output**(A) and **output**(B) operations have not yet been executed. Therefore, the values of A and B on the buffer and physical blocks differ.

Suppose that during the execution of transaction T a failure has occurred that prevented T from completing its execution successfully. Further, suppose that this happened after the **output**(A) operation was executed but before the **output**(B) operation was executed. In this case, the

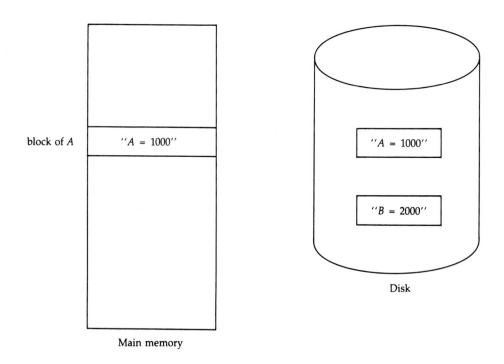

block of A "A = 1000"

Main memory

"A = 1000"

"B = 2000"

Disk

Figure 10.2   Memory and disk layout prior to execution of T.

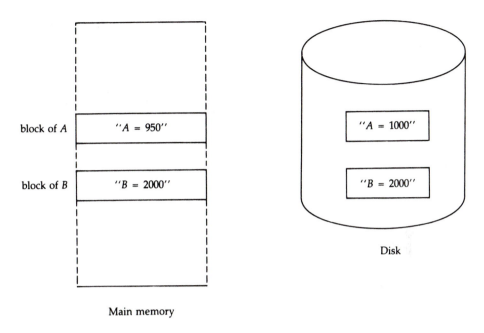

block of *A* | "*A* = 950"

block of *B* | "*B* = 2000"

Main memory

"*A* = 1000"

"*B* = 2000"

Disk

Figure 10.3   Memory and disk layout during the execution of *T*.

value of accounts *A* and *B* reflected in the database on the disk are $950 and $2000. We have destroyed $50 as a result of this failure. In particular, we note that the sum *A* + *B* is no longer preserved.

Thus, as the result of the failure, the state of the system no longer reflects a real state of the world that the database is supposed to capture. We term such a state an *inconsistent* state. Obviously, we must ensure that such inconsistencies are not visible in a database system. Note, however, that the system must at some point be in an inconsistent state. Even if transaction *T* is executed to completion, there exists a point at which the value of account *A* is $950 and the value of account *B* is $2000, which is clearly an inconsistent state. This state, however, is eventually replaced by the consistent state where the value of account *A* is $950, and the value of account *B* is $2050.

Note that it is the responsibility of the programmer to define properly the various transactions so that each preserves the consistency of the database. For example, the transaction to transfer funds from account *A* to account *B* could be defined to be composed of two separate programs, one which debits account *A*, and the other which credits account *B*. The execution of these two programs one after the other will indeed preserve consistency. However, each program by itself does not transform the database from a consistent state to a new consistent state. Thus, those programs are not transactions.

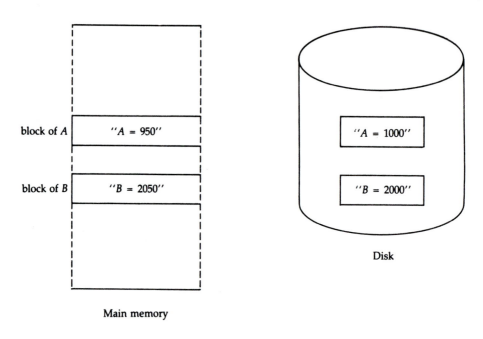

Figure 10.4   Memory and disk layout after execution of T.

10.3.2 Correctness and Atomicity

The above example illustrates the two requirements that we place on transactions:

- **Correctness**. Each transaction must be a program that preserves database consistency.

- **Atomicity**. All of the operations associated with a transaction must be executed to completion, or none at all.

Ensuring correctness is the responsibility of the application programmer who codes a transaction. This task may be facilitated by automatic testing of integrity constraints, as we discussed in Chapter 5. Ensuring atomicity is the responsibility of the database system itself — specifically, the transaction management component. In the absence of failures, all transactions complete successfully, and atomicity is achieved easily. However, as we saw earlier, a transaction may not always complete its execution successfully. Such a transaction is termed *aborted*. In order to ensure the atomicity property, an aborted transaction must have no effect on the state of the database. Thus, the state of the database must be restored to the state it was in just before the transaction in question started executing. We say that such a transaction has been *rolled back*. It is part of the responsibility of the recovery scheme to manage transaction aborts.

A transaction which successfully completes its execution is termed *committed*. A committed transaction that performs updates transforms the database into a new consistent state.

The effect of a committed transaction cannot be undone by aborting the transaction. It can be undone only by writing and executing a *compensating* transaction. The introduction of such a transaction is usually the responsibility of the user, not the database system itself. Chapter 12 includes a discussion of compensating transactions.

10.3.3 Transaction States

We need to be more precise about what is meant by "successful completion" of a transaction. To do so, we establish a simple abstract transaction model. A transaction must be in one of the following states:

- **Active**, the initial state.

- **Partially committed**, after the last statement has been executed.

- **Failed**, after the discovery that normal execution can no longer proceed.

- **Aborted**, after the transaction has been rolled back and the database restored to its state prior to the start of the transaction.

- **Committed**, after "successful" completion.

The state diagram corresponding to a transaction is shown in Figure 10.5.

We say that a transaction has committed only if it has entered the committed state. Similarly, we say that a transaction has aborted only if it has entered the aborted state. Furthermore, such a transaction will be said to have *terminated*. Once a transaction has terminated, a new transaction can be processed. (We shall defer to Chapter 11 consideration of cases where several transactions are being processed concurrently.)

A transaction starts in the active state. When it reaches its last statement it enters the partially committed state. At this point, the transaction has completed its execution, but it is still possible that it may have to be aborted since the actual output may not have been written to disk yet, and thus a hardware failure may preclude its successful completion. We, therefore, must be cautious when dealing with *observable external writes* — that is, writes that cannot be "erased" (such as those to a terminal or printer). Most systems allow such writes to take place only after the transaction has entered the committed state. One way to implement such a scheme is to store any value associated with such external writes temporarily in a nonvolatile storage, and to perform the actual writes only at commit time. A committed transaction will then

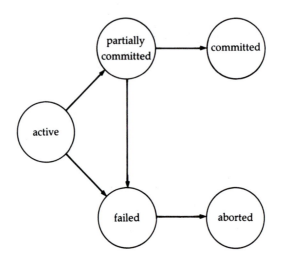

Figure 10.5   State diagram of a transaction.

always be able to complete its external writes except in case of disk failure. In order to ensure that even a disk crash will not prevent an observable external write, an approximation of stable storage may be used.

For certain applications, it may be desirable to allow active transactions to display data to users. This is true particularly for long-duration transactions that run for minutes or hours. Unfortunately, such output of observable data cannot be allowed unless we are willing to compromise transaction atomicity. Most current transaction systems ensure atomicity and, therefore, forbid this form of interaction with users. In Chapter 12, we discuss alternative transaction models that support long-duration, interactive transactions.

A transaction enters the failed state after it is determined that the transaction can no longer proceed with its normal execution (for example, because of hardware or logical errors). Such a transaction must be rolled back. Once this is accomplished, the transaction enters the aborted state. At this point in time the system has two options:

- **Restart the transaction.** This can take place only if the transaction was aborted as a result of some hardware or software error which was not created through the internal logic of the transaction. A restarted transaction is considered to be a new transaction.

- **Kill the transaction.** This usually takes place because of some internal logical error which can be corrected only by rewriting the application program, or because of bad input, or because the desired data was not found in the database.

A transaction enters the committed state if it has partially committed and it is guaranteed that it will never be aborted. In the following, we describe various schemes for ensuring this property.

10.4 Log-Based Recovery

Consider again our simplified banking system and transaction T that transfers $50 from account A to account B with initial values of A and B being $1000 and $2000, respectively. Suppose that a system crash has occurred during the execution of T after **output**(A) has taken place, but before **output**(B) was executed. Since the memory contents were lost, we do not know the fate of the transaction and, thus, could invoke one of two possible recovery procedures.

- **Reexecute** T. This will result in the value of A becoming $900 rather than $950. Thus, the system enters an inconsistent state.

- **Do not reexecute** T. The current system state is values of $950 and $2000 for A and B, respectively. Thus, the system enters an inconsistent state.

In either case, the database is left in an inconsistent state and thus this simple recovery scheme does not work. The reason for this difficulty is that we have modified the database without having assurance that the transaction will indeed commit. Our goal is either to perform all database modifications made by T or none at all. However, if T performed multiple database modifications, several output operations may be required and a failure may occur after some of these modifications have been made but before all of them are made.

In order to achieve our goal of atomicity, we must first output information describing the modifications to stable storage without modifying the database itself. As we shall see, this will allow us to output all the modifications made by committed transaction despite failures.

10.4.1 The Database Log

The most widely used structure for recording database modifications is the *log*. Each log record describes a single database write, and has the following fields:

- **Transaction name**. The unique name of the transaction that performed the **write** operation.

- **Data item name**. The unique name of the data item written.

- **Old value**. The value of the data item prior to the write.

- **New value**. The value that the data item will have after the write.

Other special log records exist to record significant events during transaction processing such as the start of a transaction and the commit or abort of a transaction. We denote the various types of log records as follows:

- $<T_i$ **start**>. Transaction T_i has started.

- $<T_i, X_j, V_1, V_2>$. Transaction T_i has performed a write on data item X_j. X_j had value V_1 before the write and will have value V_2 after the write.

- $<T_i$ **commit**>. Transaction T_i has committed.

Whenever a transaction performs a write, it is essential that the log record for that write be created before the database is modified. Once a log record exists we can output the modification to the database if this is desirable. Also, we have the ability to *undo* a modification that has already been output to the database. This is accomplished by using the old-value field in log records.

In order for log records to be useful for recovery from system and disk failures, the log must reside in stable storage. For now, we assume that every log record is written to stable storage as soon as it is created. In Section 10.5 we shall see when it is safe to relax this requirement so as to reduce the overhead imposed by logging. In the next two sections, we shall introduce two techniques for using the log to ensure transaction atomicity despite failures. Observe that the log contains a complete record of all database activity. As a result, the volume of data stored in the log may become unreasonably large. In Section 10.6, we shall show when it is safe to erase log information.

10.4.2 Deferred Database Modification

The deferred-modification technique ensures transaction atomicity by recording all database modifications in the log, but deferring the execution of all **write** operations of a transaction until the transaction partially commits.

When a transaction partially commits, the information on the log associated with the transaction is used in executing the deferred writes. If the system crashes before the transaction completes its execution, or if the transaction aborts, then the information on the log is simply ignored.

The execution of transaction T_i proceeds as follows. Before T_i starts its execution, a record $<T_i$ **start**> is written to the log. A **write**(X,x_j) operation by T_i results in the writing of a new record to the log. Finally, when T_i partially commits, a record $<T_i$ **commit**> is written to the log.

When transaction T_i partially commits, the records associated with it in the log are used in executing the deferred writes. Since a failure may occur while this updating is taking place, we must ensure that, prior to the start of these updates, all the log records are written out to stable storage. Once this has been accomplished, the actual updating can take place and the transaction enters the committed state.

Observe that only the new value of the data item is required by the deferred-modification technique. Thus, we may simplify the general log structure we saw in the previous section by omitting the old-value field.

To illustrate, let us reconsider our simplified banking system. Let T_0 be a transaction that transfers \$50 from account A to account B. This transaction may be defined as follows:

$$T_0: \textbf{read}(A, a_1)$$
$$a_1 := a_1 - 50$$
$$\textbf{write}(A, a_1)$$
$$\textbf{read}(B, b_1)$$
$$b_1 := b_1 + 50$$
$$\textbf{write}(B, b_1)$$

Let T_1 be a transaction that withdraws \$100 from account C. This transaction can be defined as:

$$T_1: \textbf{read}(C, c_1)$$
$$c_1 := c_1 - 100$$
$$\textbf{write}(C, c_1)$$

Suppose that these transactions are executed one after the other in the order T_0 followed by T_1, and that the values of accounts A, B, and C before the execution took place were \$1000, \$2000, and \$700, respectively. The portion of the log containing the relevant information on these two transactions is presented in Figure 10.6.

There are various orders in which the actual outputs can take place to both the database system and the log as a result of the execution of T_0 and T_1. One such order is presented in Figure 10.7. Note that the value of A is changed in the database only after the record $<T_0, A, 950>$ has been placed in the log.

$<T_0$ **starts**$>$
$<T_0, A, 950>$
$<T_0, B, 2050>$
$<T_0$ **commits**$>$
$<T_1$ **starts**$>$
$<T_1, C, 600>$
$<T_1$ **commits**$>$

Figure 10.6   Portion of the database log corresponding to T_0 and T_1.

Log   **Database**
$<T_0$ **starts**$>$
$<T_0, A, 950>$
$<T_0, B, 2050>$
$<T_0$ **commits**$>$
                $A = 950$
                $B = 2050$
$<T_1$ **starts**$>$
$<T_1, C, 600>$
$<T_1$ **commits**$>$
                $C = 600$

Figure 10.7   State of the log and database corresponding to T_0 and T_1.

Using the log, the system can handle any failure which results in the loss of information on volatile storage. The recovery scheme uses the following recovery procedure:

- **redo**(T_i), which sets the value of all data items updated by transaction T_i to the new values.

The set of data items updated by T_i and their respective new values can be found in the log.

The **redo** operation must be *idempotent*; that is, executing it several times must be equivalent to executing it once. This is required in order to guarantee correct behavior even if a failure occurs during the recovery process.

After a failure has occurred, the recovery subsystem consults the log to determine which transactions need to be redone. Transaction T_i needs to be redone if and only if the log contains both the record $<T_i$ **starts**$>$ and the record $<T_i$ **commits**$>$. Thus, if the system crashes after the transaction completes its execution, the information in the log is used in restoring the system to a previous consistent state.

To illustrate, let us return to our banking example with transactions T_0 and T_1 executed one after the other in the order T_0 followed by T_1. Figure 10.6 shows the log that results from the complete execution of T_0 and T_1. Let us suppose that the system crashes before the completion of the transactions and see how the recovery technique restores the database to a consistent state. Assume that the crash occurs just after the log record for the step

write(B,b_1)

of transaction T_0 has been written to stable storage. The log at the time of the crash is as shown in Figure 10.8a. When the system comes back up, no

$<T_0$ starts>	$<T_0$ starts>	$<T_0$ starts>
$<T_0, A, 950>$	$<T_0, A, 950>$	$<T_0, A, 950>$
$<T_0, B, 2050>$	$<T_0, B, 2050>$	$<T_0, B, 2050>$
	$<T_0$ commits>	$<T_0$ commits>
	$<T_1$ starts>	$<T_1$ starts>
	$<T_1, C, 600>$	$<T_1, C, 600>$
		$<T_1$ commits>
(a)	(b)	(c)

Figure 10.8   The same log, shown at three different times.

recovery action need be taken, since no commit record appears in the log. The values of accounts A and B remain $1000 and $2000, respectively.

Now, let us assume the crash comes just after the log record for the step

$$\text{write}(C, c_1)$$

of transaction T_1 has been written to stable storage. The log at the time of the crash is as shown in Figure 10.8b. When the system comes back up, the operation **redo**(T_0) is performed since the record

$$<T_0 \text{ commits}>$$

appears in the log on the disk. After this operation is executed, the values of accounts A and B are $950 and $2050, respectively. The value of account C remains $700.

Assume a crash occurs just after the log record

$$<T_1 \text{ commits}>$$

is written to stable storage. The log at the time of the crash is as shown in Figure 10.8c. When the system comes back up, two commit records are in the log: one for T_0 and one for T_1. Therefore, the operations **redo**(T_0) and **redo**(T_1) must be performed. After these operations are executed, the values of accounts A, B, and C are $950, $2050, and $600, respectively.

Finally, let us consider a case in which a second system crash occurs during recovery from the first crash. Some changes may have been made to the database as a result of the **redo** operations, but it may be the case that not all changes have been made. When the system comes up after the second crash, recovery proceeds exactly as in the above examples. For each commit record

$$<T_i \text{ commits}>$$

found in the log, the operation **redo**(T_i) is performed. In other words, the recovery actions are restarted from the beginning. Since **redo** writes values to the database independent of the values currently in the database, the result of a successful second attempt at **redo** is the same as if **redo** had succeeded the first time.

10.4.3 Immediate Database Modification

The immediate-update technique allows database modifications to be output to the database while the transaction is still in the active state. Data modifications written by active transactions are called *uncommitted modifications*. In the event of a crash or a transaction failure, the old-value field of the log records described in Section 10.4.1 must be used to restore the modified data items to the value they had prior to the start of the transaction. This is accomplished through the **undo** operation described below.

Before a transaction T_i starts its execution, the record $<T_i$ **starts**> is written to the log. During its execution, any **write**(X,x_i) operation by T_i is *preceded* by the writing of the appropriate new record to the log. When T_i partially commits, the record $<T_i$ **commits**> is written to the log.

Since the information in the log is used in reconstructing the state of the database, we cannot allow the actual update to the database to take place before the corresponding log record is written out to stable storage. We therefore require that prior to executing an **output**(X) operation, the log records corresponding to X be written onto stable storage. We shall return to this issue in Section 10.5.

To illustrate, let us reconsider our simplified banking system with transactions T_0 and T_1 executed one after the other in the order T_0 followed by T_1. The portion of the log containing the relevant information concerning these two transactions is presented in Figure 10.9.

One possible order in which the actual outputs took place to both the database system and the log as a result of the execution of T_0 and T_1 is described in Figure 10.10. Notice that this order could not be obtained in the deferred-modification scheme of Section 10.4.2.

$<T_0$ **starts**>
$<T_0, A, 1000, 950>$
$<T_0, B, 2000, 2050>$
$<T_0$ **commits**>
$<T_1$ **starts**>
$<T_1, C, 700, 600>$
$<T_1$ **commits**>

Figure 10.9   Portion of the system log corresponding to T_0 and T_1.

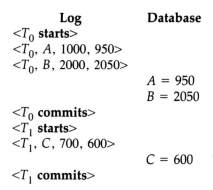

Log	**Database**
$<T_0$ **starts**$>$	
$<T_0, A, 1000, 950>$	
$<T_0, B, 2000, 2050>$	
	$A = 950$
	$B = 2050$
$<T_0$ **commits**$>$	
$<T_1$ **starts**$>$	
$<T_1, C, 700, 600>$	
	$C = 600$
$<T_1$ **commits**$>$	

Figure 10.10   State of system log and database corresponding to T_0 and T_1.

Using the log, the system can handle any failure which does not result in the loss of information on nonvolatile storage. The recovery scheme utilizes two recovery procedures:

- **undo**(T_i), which restores the value of all data items updated by transaction T_i to the old values.

- **redo**(T_i), which sets the value of all data items updated by transaction T_i to the new values.

The set of data items updated by T_i and their respective old and new values can be found in the log.

The **undo** and **redo** operations must be idempotent in order to guarantee correct behavior even if a failure occurs during the recovery process.

After a failure has occurred, the recovery scheme consults the log to determine which transactions need to be redone and which need to be undone. This classification of transactions is accomplished as follows:

- Transaction T_i needs to be undone if the log contains the record $<T_i$ **starts**$>$ but does not contain the record $<T_i$ **commits**$>$.

- Transaction T_i needs to be redone if the log contains both the record $<T_i$ **starts**$>$ and the record $<T_i$ **commits**$>$.

To illustrate this, let us return to our banking example with transaction T_0 and T_1 executed one after the other in the order T_0 followed by T_1. Let us suppose that the system crashes before the completion of the transactions. We shall consider three cases. The state of the logs for each of these cases is shown in Figures 10.11a to c.

$<T_0$ **starts**$>$	$<T_0$ **starts**$>$	$<T_0$ **starts**$>$
$<T_0, A, 1000, 950>$	$<T_0, A, 1000, 950>$	$<T_0, A, 1000, 950>$
$<T_0, B, 2000, 2050>$	$<T_0, B, 2000, 2050>$	$<T_0, B, 2000, 2050>$
	$<T_0$ **commits**$>$	$<T_0$ **commits**$>$
	$<T_1$ **starts**$>$	$<T_1$ **starts**$>$
	$<T_1, C, 700, 600>$	$<T_1, C, 700, 600>$
		$<T_1$ **commits**$>$
(a)	(b)	(c)

Figure 10.11   The same log, shown at three different times.

First, let us assume that the crash occurs just after the log record for the step

$$\textbf{write}(B, b_1)$$

of transaction T_0 has been written to stable storage (Figure 10.11a). When the system comes back up, it finds the record $<T_0$ **starts**$>$ in the log, but no corresponding $<T_0$ **commits**$>$ record. This means that transaction T_0 must be undone, so an **undo**(T_0) is performed. As a result, the values in accounts A and B (on the disk) are restored to $\$1000$ and $\$2000$, respectively.

Next, let us assume that the crash comes just after the log record for the step

$$\textbf{write}(C, c_1)$$

of transaction T_1 has been written to stable storage (Figure 10.11b). When the system comes back up, two recovery actions need to be taken. The operation **undo**(T_1) must be performed, since the record $<T_1$ **starts**$>$ appears in the log, but there is no record $<T_1$ **commits**$>$. The operation **redo**(T_0) must be performed since the log contains both the record $<T_0$ **starts**$>$ and the record $<T_0$ **commits**$>$. At the end of the entire recovery procedure, the values of accounts A, B, and C are $\$950$, $\$2050$, and $\$700$, respectively. Note that the **undo**(T_1) operation is performed before the **redo**(T_0). In this example, the same outcome would result if the order were reversed. However, we shall see in Chapter 12 that, in general, it is necessary to perform **undo** operations before **redo** operations.

Finally, let us assume that the crash occurs just after the log record

$$<T_1 \textbf{ commits}>$$

has been written to stable storage (Figure 10.11c). When the system comes back up, both T_0 and T_1 need to be redone, since the records $<T_0$ **starts**$>$ and $<T_0$ **commits**$>$ appear in the log as do the records $<T_1$ **starts**$>$ and

$<T_1$ **commits**$>$. After the recovery procedures **redo**(T_0) and **redo**(T_1) are performed, the values in accounts A, B, and C are \$950, \$2050, and \$600, respectively.

10.5 Buffer Management

In this section, we consider several subtle details that are essential to the implementation of a crash recovery scheme that ensures data consistency and imposes a minimal amount of overhead on interactions with the database.

10.5.1 Log Record Buffering

Earlier, we assumed that every log record is output to stable storage at the time it is created. This imposes a high overhead on system execution for the following reasons. Typically, output to stable storage is in units of blocks. In most cases, a log record is much smaller than a block. Thus, the output of each log record translates to a much larger output at the physical level. Furthermore, as we shall see in Section 10.9, the output of a block to stable storage may involve several output operations at the physical level.

The cost of performing the output of a block to stable storage is sufficiently high that it is desirable to output multiple log records at once. This means that a log record may reside only in main memory (volatile storage) for a considerable period of time before it is output to stable storage. Since such log records are lost if the system crashes, we must impose additional requirements on the recovery techniques to ensure transaction atomicity.

- Transaction T_i enters the commit state after the $<T_i$ **commit**$>$ log record has been output to stable storage.

- Before the $<T_i$ **commit**$>$ log record may be output to stable storage, all log records pertaining to transaction T_i must have been output to stable storage.

- Before a block of data in main memory is output to the database (in nonvolatile memory), all log records pertaining to data in that block must have been output to stable storage.

The above rules state situations in which certain log records *must* have been output to stable storage. There is no problem resulting from the output of log records earlier than necessary. Thus, when the system finds it necessary to output a log record to stable storage, it outputs an entire block of log records if there are enough log records in main memory to fill a block. If there are insufficient log records to fill the block, all log records in main memory are combined into a partially full block.

10.5.2 Database Buffering

In Section 10.2, we described the use of a two-level storage hierarchy. The database is stored in nonvolatile storage (disk), and blocks of data are brought into main memory as needed. Since main memory is typically much smaller than the size of the entire database, it may be necessary to overwrite a block B_1 in main memory when another block B_2 needs to be brought into memory. If B_1 has been modified, B_1 must be output prior to the input of B_2. This is the standard operating system concept of *virtual memory*, which we presented in Chapter 7.

The rules for the output of log records limit the freedom of the system to output blocks of data. If the input of block B_2 causes block B_1 to be chosen for output, all log records pertaining to data in B_1 must be output to stable storage before B_1 is output. Thus, the sequence of actions by the system would be:

- Output to stable storage all log records pertaining to block B_1.

- Output block B_1 to disk.

- Input block B_2 from disk to main memory.

To illustrate the need for this requirement, consider our banking example with transactions T_0 and T_1. Suppose that the state of the log is

$$<T_0 \text{ starts}>$$
$$<T_0, A, 1000, 950>$$

and that transaction T_0 issues a **read**(B,b_1). Assume that the block on which B resides is not in main memory, and that main memory is full. Suppose that the block on which A resides is chosen to be output to disk. If the system outputs this block to disk and then a crash occurs, the values in the database for accounts A, B, and C are \$950, \$2000, and \$700, respectively. This is an inconsistent database state. As we noted earlier, the log record

$$<T_0, A, 1000, 950>$$

must be output to stable storage prior to the output of the block on which A resides.

10.5.3 Operating System Issues

Most operating systems do not provide the capability to enforce the output of log records prior to the output of database blocks. This makes it difficult for database system implementations to utilize the virtual memory features provided by the operating system. There are two possible alternatives:

- The database system reserves part of main memory to serve as a buffer which it, not the operating system, manages. The database system manages data block transfer in accordance with the requirements we discussed above. This is the model we presented in Section 10.2.

- The database system implements its buffer within the virtual memory of the operating system. The database itself is stored in the operating system's file system. Transfers between the database files and the buffer in virtual memory are managed by the database system, which enforces the requirements discussed above.

The first approach has the drawback of limiting the amount of main memory available to the database buffer. Those parts of main memory that are reserved for other uses may be wasted when the database system is running. Likewise, nondatabase applications may not use that part of main memory reserved for the database buffer.

The second approach may result in extra output of data to disk. If a block B is output by the operating system, that block is not output to the database. Instead, it is output to the swap space for the operating system's virtual memory. When the database system needs to output B, the operating system may need first to input B from its swap space. Thus, instead of a single output of B, we require two outputs of B (one by the operating system and one by the database system) and one extra input of B.

Although both approaches suffer from some drawbacks, one must be chosen unless the operating system is designed to support the requirements of database logging. Unfortunately, few current operating systems support these requirements.

10.6 Checkpoints

When a system failure occurs, it is necessary to consult the log in order to determine those transactions that need to be redone and those that need to be undone. In principle, the entire log needs to be searched in order to determine this. There are two major difficulties with this approach:

- The searching process is time-consuming.

- Most of the transactions that according to our algorithm need to be redone have already actually written their updates into the database. Although redoing them will cause no harm, it will nevertheless cause recovery to take longer.

In order to reduce these types of overhead, we introduce the concept of *checkpoints*. During execution, the system maintains the log using one of the two techniques described in Sections 10.4.2 and 10.4.3. In addition, the system periodically performs checkpoints, which require the following sequence of actions to take place:

1. Output all log records currently residing in main memory onto stable storage.

2. Output all modified buffer blocks to the disk.

3. Output a log record <**checkpoint**> onto stable storage.

The presence of a <**checkpoint**> record in the log allows the system to streamline its recovery procedure. Consider a transaction T_i that committed prior to the checkpoint. For such a transaction, the <T_i **commits**> record appears in the log before the <**checkpoint**> record. Any database modifications made by T_i must have been written to the database either prior to the checkpoint or as part of the checkpoint itself. Thus, at recovery time, there is no need to perform a **redo** operation on T_i.

This observation allows us to refine our previous recovery schemes. After a failure has occurred, the recovery scheme examines the log to determine the last transaction T_i that started executing before the last checkpoint took place. Such a transaction can be found by searching the log backward to find the first <**checkpoint**> record, and then finding the subsequent <T_i **start**> record.

Once transaction T_i has been identified, the **redo** and **undo** operations need to be applied only to transaction T_i and all transactions T_j that started executing after transaction T_i. Let us denote these transactions by the set T. The remainder of the log can thus be ignored. The exact recovery operations to be performed depend on whether the immediate-modification technique or the deferred-modification technique is being used. The recovery operations that are required if the immediate-modification technique is employed are as follows:

- For all transactions T_k in T such that the record <T_k **commits**> appears in the log, execute **redo**(T_k).

- For all transactions T_k in T that have no <T_k **commits**> record in the log, execute **undo**(T_k).

Obviously, the **undo** operation need not be applied when the deferred-modification technique is being employed.

To illustrate, consider the set of transactions $\{T_0, T_1, \ldots, T_{100}\}$ executed in the order of the subscripts. Suppose that the last checkpoint took place during the execution of transaction T_{67}. Thus, only transactions

$T_{67}, T_{68}, \ldots, T_{100}$ need to be considered during the recovery scheme. Each of these needs to be redone if it has committed; otherwise it needs to be undone.

In Chapter 12, we consider an extension of the checkpoint technique for concurrent transaction processing.

10.7 Shadow Paging

An alternative to log-based crash recovery techniques is *shadow paging*. Under certain circumstances, shadow paging may require fewer disk accesses than the log-based methods discussed above. There are, however, disadvantages to the shadow-block approach, as we shall see.

As before, the database is partitioned into some number of fixed-length blocks which are referred to as *pages*. The term *page* is borrowed from operating systems since we are using a paging scheme for memory management. Let us assume there are n pages, numbered 1 through n. (In practice n may be in the hundreds of thousands.) These pages need not be stored in any particular order on disk (there are many reasons for this, as we saw in Chapter 7). However, there must be a way to find the ith page of the database for any given i. This is accomplished using a *page table*, as shown in Figure 10.12. The page table has n entries, one for each database page. Each entry contains a pointer to a page on disk. The first entry contains a pointer to the first page of the database, the second entry points to the second page, and so on. The example in Figure 10.12 shows that the logical order of database pages need not correspond to the physical order in which the pages are placed on disk.

The key idea behind the shadow-paging technique is to maintain *two* page tables during the life of a transaction, the *current* page table and the *shadow* page table. When the transaction starts, both page tables are identical. The shadow page table is never changed over the duration of the transaction. The current page table may be changed when a transaction performs a **write** operation. All **input** and **output** operations use the current page table to locate database pages on disk.

Suppose the transaction performs a **write**(X, x_j) operation and that X resides on the ith page. The **write** operation is executed as follows:

1. If the ith page (that is, the page on which X resides) is not already in main memory, then issue **input**(X).

2. If this is the first write performed on the ith page by this transaction, then modify the current page table as follows:

   a. Find an unused page on disk. Typically, the database system has access to a list of unused (free) pages, as we saw in Chapter 7.

   b. Delete the page found in step 2a from the list of free page frames.

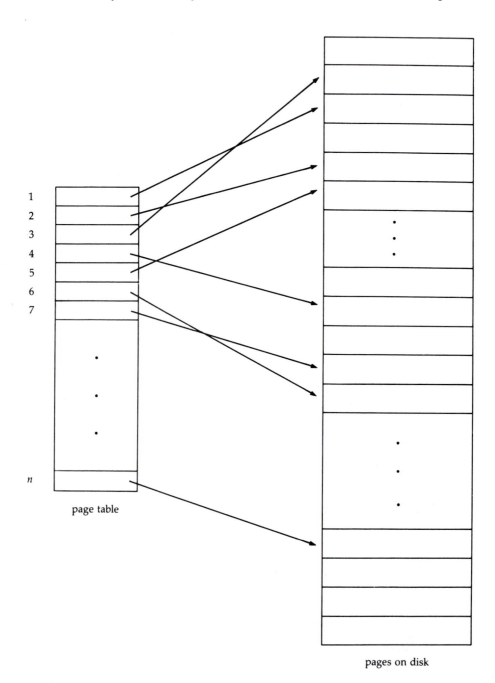

Figure 10.12   Sample page table.

    c. Modify the current page table so that the ith entry points to the page found in step 2a.

3. Assign the value of x_j to X in the buffer page.

Let us compare the above action for a **write** operation with that described in Section 10.2. The only difference is that we have added a new step. Steps 1 and 3 above correspond to steps 1 and 2 in Section 10.2. The added step, step 2 above, manipulates the current page table. Figure 10.13 shows the shadow and current page tables for a transaction performing a write to the fourth page of a database consisting of 10 pages.

Intuitively, the shadow page approach to recovery is to store the shadow page table in nonvolatile storage so that the state of the database prior to the execution of the transaction may be recovered in the event of a crash, or transaction abort. When the transaction commits, the current page table is written to nonvolatile storage. The current page table then becomes the new shadow page table and the next transaction is allowed to begin execution. It is important that the shadow page table be stored in nonvolatile storage since it provides the only means of locating database pages. The current page table may be kept in main memory (volatile storage). We do not care if the current page table is lost in a crash, since the system recovers using the shadow page table.

Successful recovery requires that we find the shadow page table on disk after a crash. A simple way of doing this is to choose one fixed location in stable storage that contains the disk address of the shadow page table. When the system comes back up after a crash, we copy the shadow page table into main memory and use it for subsequent transaction processing. Because of our definition of the **write** operation, we are guaranteed that the shadow page table points to the database pages corresponding to the state of the database prior to any transaction that was active at the time of the crash. Thus, aborts are automatic. Unlike our log-based schemes, no **undo** operations need be invoked.

In order to commit a transaction, we must do the following:

1. Ensure that all buffer pages in main memory that have been changed by the transaction are output to disk. (Note that these output operations will not change database pages pointed to by some entry in the shadow page table.)

2. Output the current page table to disk. Note that we must not overwrite the shadow page table since we may need it for recovery from a crash.

3. Output the disk address of the current page to the fixed location in stable storage containing the address of the shadow page table. This

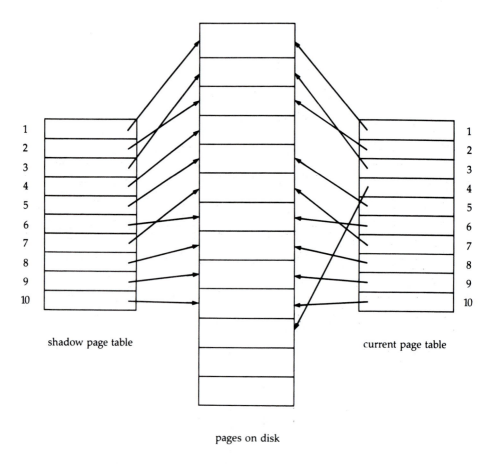

pages on disk

Figure 10.13   Shadow and current page tables.

overwrites the address of the old shadow page table. Therefore, the current page table has become the shadow page table and the transaction is committed.

If a crash occurs prior to the completion of step 3, we revert to the state just prior to the execution of the transaction. If the crash occurs after the completion of step 3, the effects of the transaction will be preserved. No **redo** operations need be invoked.

Shadow paging offers several advantages over log-based techniques. The overhead of log-record output is eliminated, and recovery from crashes is significantly faster (since no **undo** or **redo** operations are needed). However, there are drawbacks to the shadow page technique:

- **Data fragmentation**. In Chapter 7, we considered strategies to keep related database pages close physically on the disk. This locality allows for faster data transfer. Shadow paging causes database pages to change location when they are updated. As a result, either we lose the locality property of the pages or we must resort to more complex, higher-overhead schemes for physical storage management. (See the bibliographic notes for references.)

- **Garbage collection**. Each time a transaction commits, the database pages containing the old version of data changed by the transaction become inaccessible. In Figure 10.13, the page pointed to by the fourth entry of the shadow page table will become inaccessible once the transaction of that example commits. Such pages are considered *garbage*, since they are not part of free space and do not contain usable information. Garbage may be created also as a side effect of crashes. Periodically, it is necessary to find all the garbage pages and add them to the list of free pages. This process, called *garbage collection*, imposes additional overhead and complexity on the system. There are several standard algorithms for garbage collection. (See the bibliographic notes for references.)

In addition to the drawbacks of shadow paging we have just mentioned, shadow paging is more difficult than logging to adapt to systems that allow several transactions to execute concurrently. In such systems, some logging is typically required even if shadow paging is used. System R, for example, uses a combination of shadow paging and a logging scheme similar to that presented in Section 10.4.3. It is possible to use the log-based schemes of this chapter with minor changes in a concurrent database system without the use of shadow paging, as will be discussed in Chapter 11.

10.8 Failure with Loss of Nonvolatile Storage

Until now, we have considered only the case where a failure results in the loss of information residing in volatile storage while the content of the nonvolatile storage remains intact. Although failures in which the content of nonvolatile storage is lost are rare, we nevertheless need to be prepared to deal with this type of failure. In this section, we discuss only disk-type storage. Our discussions apply as well to other nonvolatile storage types.

The basic scheme is to *dump* the entire content of the database to stable storage periodically, say once a day. For example, we may dump the database to one or more magnetic tapes. If a failure occurs that results in the loss of physical database blocks, the most recent dump is used in restoring the database to a previous consistent state. Once this has been accomplished, the log is used to bring the database system to the most recent consistent state.

More precisely, no transaction may be active during the dump procedure and a procedure similar to checkpointing must take place:

1. Output all log records currently residing in main memory onto stable storage.

2. Output all buffer blocks onto the disk.

3. Copy the contents of the database to stable storage.

4. Output a log record <**dump**> onto the stable storage.

Steps 1, 2, and 4 correspond to the three steps used for checkpoints in Section 10.6.

To recover from the loss of nonvolatile storage, the database is restored to disk using the most recent dump. Then the log is consulted and all the transactions that have committed since the last dump occurred are redone. Notice that no **undo** operations need to be executed.

The simple dump procedure described above is costly for the following two reasons. First, the entire database must be be copied to stable storage, resulting in considerable data transfer. Second, since transaction processing is halted during the dump procedure, CPU cycles are wasted. Less costly forms of dumping exist, some of which are discussed in Chapter 12.

10.9 Stable Storage Implementation

As pointed out in Section 10.1.1, information residing in stable storage is *never* lost. To implement such a storage, we need to replicate the needed information in several nonvolatile storage media (usually disk) with independent failure modes, and update the information in a controlled manner to ensure that failure during data transfer does not damage the needed information. For the remainder of this section, we will discuss the issue of how the storage media can be protected from failure during data transfer.

Block transfer between memory and disk storage can result in:

- **Successful completion**. The transferred information arrived safely at its destination.

- **Partial failure**. A failure occurred in the midst of transfer and the destination block has incorrect information.

- **Total failure**. The failure occurred sufficiently early during the transfer so that the destination block remains intact.

We require that if a data-transfer failure occurs, the system detects it and invokes a recovery procedure to restore the block to a consistent state. To do so, the system must maintain two physical blocks for each logical database block. An output operation is executed as follows:

1. Write the information onto the first physical block.

2. When the first write successfully completes, write the same information onto the second physical block.

3. The output is completed only after the second write successfully completes.

During recovery, each pair of physical blocks is examined. If both are the same and no detectable error exists, then no further actions are necessary. If one block contains a detectable error, then replace its content with the value of the second block. If both blocks contain no detectable error, but they differ in content, then replace the content of the first block with the value of the second. This recovery procedure ensures that a write to stable storage either succeeds completely or results in no change. The attempt to write to stable storage succeeds only if all copies are written.

This procedure can be extended easily to allow the use of an arbitrarily large number of copies of each block of stable storage. Although a large number of copies reduces the probability of a failure to even lower than two copies, it is usually reasonable to simulate stable storage with only two copies.

10.10 Summary

A computer system, like any other mechanical or electrical device, is subject to failure. There are a variety of causes of such failure, including disk crash, power failure, and software errors. In each of these cases, information concerning the database system is lost. An integral part of a database system is a recovery scheme which is responsible for the detection of failures and the restoration of the database to a state that existed prior to the occurrence of the failure.

The various types of failure that may occur in a system must be dealt with in a different manner. The simplest type of failure to deal with is one which does not result in the loss of information in the system. The ones that are more difficult to deal with are those that do result in loss of information.

In case of failure, the state of the database system may no longer be consistent; that is, it may not reflect a state of the world that the database is supposed to capture. To preserve consistency, we require that each transaction be atomic; that is, either all the instructions associated with it are executed to completion, or none are performed. It is the responsibility of the recovery scheme to ensure the atomicity property.

There are three different schemes for ensuring atomicity.

- **Log with deferred modifications**. During the execution of a transaction all the **write** operations are deferred until the transaction partially commits. All updates are recorded on the log, which must be kept in stable storage. When a transaction partially commits, the information on the log associated with the transaction is used in executing the deferred writes. If the system crashes before the transaction completes its execution, or, if the transaction aborts, then the information on the log is simply ignored. Using the log, the system can handle any failure which does not result in the loss of information on nonvolatile storage. In particular, after a failure has occurred the recovery scheme consults the log and each committed transaction is redone using the **redo** operation. In order to reduce the overhead of searching the log and redoing transactions, the *checkpointing* technique can be used.

- **Log with immediate modifications**. All updates are applied directly to the database and a log of all the changes to the system state is kept in stable storage. If a crash occurs, the information in the log is used in restoring the state of the system to a previous consistent state. This is accomplished by using the **undo** and **redo** operations. As before, the log can be used to handle any failure which does not result in the loss of information on nonvolatile storage, and the checkpointing technique can be used to reduce the overhead of searching the log and performing **undo** and **redo** operations.

- **Shadow paging**. Two page tables are maintained during the life of a transaction: the *current* page table and the *shadow* page table. When the transaction starts, both page tables are identical. The shadow page table is never changed during the duration of the transaction. The current page table may be changed when a transaction performs a **write** operation. All **input** and **output** operations use the current page table to locate database pages on disk. When the transaction partially commits, the shadow page table is discarded and the current table becomes the new page table. If the transaction aborts, the current page table is simply discarded.

Efficient implementation of a recovery scheme requires that the number of writes to the database and to stable storage be minimized. Log records may be kept in volatile storage initially, but must be written to stable storage when one of the following conditions occurs:

- Before the $<T_i$ **commit**$>$ log record may be output to stable storage, all log records pertaining to transaction T_i must have been output to stable storage.

- Before a block of data in main memory is output to the database (in nonvolatile memory), all log records pertaining to data in that block must have been output to stable storage.

In order to recover from failures that result in the loss of nonvolatile storage, the entire contents of the database need to be dumped onto stable storage periodically, say once a day. If a failure occurs that results in the loss of physical database blocks, the most recent dump is used in restoring the database to a previous consistent state. Once this has been accomplished, the log is used to bring the database system to the most recent consistent state.

Exercises

10.1 Explain the difference between the three storage types — volatile, nonvolatile, and stable in terms of cost.

10.2 Compare the two log-based recovery schemes in terms of ease of implementation and overhead cost.

10.3 Suppose that you have been hired to implement a recovery scheme on a new database system. Which of the three recovery schemes discussed in this chapter (Sections 10.4.2, 10.4.3, and 10.7) would you choose? How might your choice depend on the particular application?

10.4 If immediate modification is used in a system, show by an example how an inconsistent database state could result if log records for a transaction are not output to stable storage prior to committing that transaction.

10.5 Explain how the buffer manager may cause the database to become inconsistent if some log records pertaining to a block are not output to stable storage before the block is output to disk.

10.6 Explain the purpose of the checkpoint mechanism. How often should a database management system do a checkpoint?

10.7 Explain the recovery procedure that needs to take place after a disk crash.

10.8 How often should checkpoints be performed? How does the frequency of checkpoints affect:

- system performance when no failure occurs?
- the time it takes to recover from a system crash?
- the time it takes to recover from a disk crash?

10.9 Compare the shadow paging recovery scheme with the log-based recovery schemes in terms of ease of implementation and overhead cost.

10.10 Consider a database consisting of 10 consecutive disk blocks (block 1, block 2, . . . , block 10). Show a possible physical ordering of the blocks after the following updates, assuming that shadow paging is used, and the buffer in main memory can hold only 3 blocks, and a LRU (least recently used) strategy is used for buffer management.

> **read** block 3
> **read** block 7
> **read** block 5
> **read** block 3
> **read** block 1
> **modify** block 1
> **read** block 10
> **modify** block 5

10.11 Stable storage cannot really be implemented.

  a. Explain why.

  b. How do database systems deal with this problem?

10.12 Explain the reasons why recovery of interactive transactions is more difficult to deal with than recovery of batch transactions. Is there a simple way to deal with this difficulty? (Hint: consider an automatic teller machine transaction in which cash is withdrawn.)

Bibliographic Notes

Two early papers presenting some initial theoretical work in the area of recovery are Davies [1973] and Bjork [1973].

Most of the recovery mechanisms introduced in this chapter are based on those used in System R. An overview of the recovery scheme of that system is presented by Gray, et al. [1981a]. The shadow paging mechanism of System R is described by Lorie [1977].

Operating system issues for database management are discussed in Stonebraker [1981], Traiger [1982, 1983], and Haskin, et al. [1988].

Discussions concerning analytic models for rollback and recovery strategies in database systems are offered by Chandy, et al. [1975]. A fast transaction-oriented logging scheme is presented by Reuter [1980]. Lilien and Bhargava [1985] introduce the integrity block construct to improve the efficiency of recovery.

Two tutorial and survey papers covering various recovery techniques for database systems are presented by Gray [1978] and Verhofstadt [1978].

A comprehensive presentation of the principles of recovery is offered by Haerder and Reuter [1983]. Basic textbook discussions are offered by Date [1983], Bernstein, et al. [1987], and Ullman [1988]. The ARIES transaction processing system is discussed in Mohan, et al. [1991] and Mohan [1990].

Gray [1981] and Korth and Speegle [1988, 1990] discuss long-duration transactions and alternatives to the transaction model presented in this chapter. Recovery issues for long duration are considered by Weikum, et al. [1984, 1990] and Korth et al. [1990a].

11
Concurrency Control

One of the most important concepts in modern systems is undoubtedly *multiprogramming*. By having several transactions executing at the same time, the processor may be shared among them. The benefits of multiprogramming are increased processor utilization and higher total transaction *throughput* — that is, the amount of work which is accomplished in a given time interval. In addition, in the case of interactive transactions where the user waits for the result, the *response* time should be as short as possible.

Thus, in a multiprogramming environment several transactions may be executed concurrently. As we shall see in this chapter, it is necessary for the system to control the interaction among the concurrent transactions in order to prevent them from destroying the consistency of the database. This control is achieved through a variety of mechanisms which we will refer to as *concurrency control* schemes.

In this chapter, we consider the management of concurrently executing transactions and ignore failures. We have already seen how the system can recover from failures in the absence of concurrency (Chapter 10). In Chapter 12, we shall examine how to implement both concurrency control and recovery management in a database system. For now, we focus on the concepts of correct concurrent executions.

11.1 Schedules

When several transactions run concurrently, database consistency can be destroyed despite the correctness of each individual transaction. In this section, we present the concept of serializability to help identify those executions that are guaranteed to ensure consistency.

To simplify notation, we shall deviate from our transaction definition syntax of Chapter 10 and drop the temporary local variable of the **read** and **write** operations. We shall assume that the temporary local variable has the same name as that of the datum being accessed. Thus, for the remainder of this book, we shall use **read**(Q) and **write**(Q) for **read**(Q,q) and **write**(Q,q).

T_0	T_1
read(A)	
$A := A - 50$	
write(A)	
read(B)	
$B := B + 50$	
write(B)	
	read(A)
	$temp := A * 0.1$
	$A := A - temp$
	write(A)
	read(B)
	$B := B + temp$
	write(B)

Figure 11.1   Schedule 1, a serial schedule in which T_0 is followed by T_1.

11.1.1 Serial and Nonserial Schedules

Consider the simplified banking system of Chapter 10, with several accounts and a set of transactions that access and update those accounts. Let T_0 and T_1 be two transactions that transfer funds from one account to another. Transaction T_0 transfers \$50 from account A to account B and is defined as:

$$T_0: \textbf{read}(A);$$
$$A := A - 50;$$
$$\textbf{write}(A);$$
$$\textbf{read}(B);$$
$$B := B + 50;$$
$$\textbf{write}(B).$$

Transaction T_1 transfers 10 percent of the balance from account A to account B and is defined as:

$$T_1: \textbf{read}(A);$$
$$temp := A * 0.1;$$
$$A := A - temp;$$
$$\textbf{write}(A);$$
$$\textbf{read}(B);$$
$$B := B + temp;$$
$$\textbf{write}(B).$$

Let the current values of accounts A and B be \$1000 and \$2000, respectively. Suppose that the two transactions are executed one at a time in the order T_0 followed by T_1. This execution sequence is represented in Figure 11.1. In the figure, the sequence of instruction steps is in chronological order from top to bottom, with instructions of T_0 appearing in the left column and instructions of T_1 appearing in the right column. The final values of accounts A and B after the execution in Figure 11.1 takes place are \$855 and \$2145, respectively. Thus, the total amount of money in accounts A and B, that is, the sum $A + B$, is preserved after the execution of both transactions.

Similarly, if the transactions are executed one at a time in the order T_1 followed by T_0, then the corresponding execution sequence is that of Figure 11.2. Again, as expected, the sum $A + B$ is preserved, and the final values of accounts A and B are \$850 and \$2150, respectively.

The execution sequences described above are called *schedules*. They represent the chronological order in which instructions are executed in the system. Clearly, a schedule for a set of transactions must consist of all instructions of those transactions, and must preserve the order in which the instructions appear in each individual transaction. For example, in transaction T_0, the instruction **write**(A) must appear before the instruction **read**(B), in any valid schedule. In the following discussion, we shall refer to the first execution sequence (T_0 followed by T_1) as schedule 1, and the second execution sequence (T_1 followed by T_0) as schedule 2.

The schedules described above are called *serial schedules*. Each serial schedule consists of a sequence of instructions from various transactions where the instructions belonging to one single transaction appear together

T_0	T_1
	read(A)
	$temp := A * 0.1$
	$A := A - temp$
	write(A)
	read(B)
	$B := B + temp$
	write(B)
read(A)	
$A := A - 50$	
write(A)	
read(B)	
$B := B + 50$	
write(B)	

Figure 11.2   Schedule 2, a serial schedule in which T_1 is followed by T_0.

in that schedule. Thus, for a set of n transactions there exist $n!$ different valid serial schedules.

When several transactions are executed concurrently, the corresponding schedule need no longer be serial. Thus, the number of possible schedules for a set of n transactions is much larger than $n!$. Returning to our previous example, suppose that the two transactions are executed concurrently. Several execution sequences are possible since the various instructions from both transactions may now be interleaved. One such schedule is shown in Figure 11.3. After this execution takes place, we arrive at the same state as the one in which the transactions are executed serially in the order T_0 followed by T_1. The sum $A + B$ is indeed preserved.

Not all concurrent executions result in a correct state. To illustrate, consider the nonserial schedule of Figure 11.4. After the execution of this schedule, we arrive at a state where the final values of accounts A and B are \$950 and \$2100, respectively. This final state is an *inconsistent state*, since we have gained \$50 in the process of the concurrent execution. Indeed, the sum $A + B$ is not preserved by the execution of the two transactions.

We require that a transaction be a program that preserves consistency. That is, each transaction, when executed alone, transfers the system from one consistent state into a new consistent state. During the execution of a transaction, however, the system may temporarily enter an inconsistent state, as we saw in Chapter 10. It is this temporary inconsistency that creates the potential for inconsistency in nonserial schedules.

T_0	T_1
read(A)	
$A := A - 50$	
write(A)	
	read(A)
	$temp := A * 0.1$
	$A := A - temp$
	write(A)
read(B)	
$B := B + 50$	
write(B)	
	read(B)
	$B := B + temp$
	write(B)

Figure 11.3   Schedule 3, a concurrent, serializable schedule.

T_0	T_1
read(A) $A := A - 50$	
	read(A) $temp := A * 0.1$ $A := A - temp$ **write**(A) **read**(B)
write(A) **read**(B) $B := B + 50$ **write**(B)	
	$B := B + temp$ **write**(B)

Figure 11.4   Schedule 4, a nonserializable schedule.

Clearly, a schedule, after execution, must leave the database in a consistent state. Furthermore, the effect of a schedule should be one that could have occurred with no concurrent execution. That is, the schedule should, in some sense, be equivalent to a serial schedule. To make this concept precise, we need to define equivalence of schedules.

Since transactions are programs, it is computationally difficult to determine the exact operations that a transaction performs and how operations of various transactions interact. For this reason, we shall not interpret the type of operations that a transaction can perform on a data item. Instead, we consider only two operations, **read** and **write**. We thus assume that between a **read**(Q) instruction and a **write**(Q) instruction on a data item Q, a transaction may perform an arbitrary sequence of operations on the value of Q. Thus, the only significant operations of a transaction, from a scheduling point of view, are its **read** and **write** instructions. Because of this, we shall usually show only **read** and **write** instructions in schedules, as in the representation of schedule 3 that is shown in Figure 11.5.

11.1.2 Conflict Serializable Schedules

Let us consider a schedule S in which there are two consecutive instructions I_i and I_j of transactions T_i and T_j respectively. If I_i and I_j refer to different data items, then we can swap I_i and I_j without affecting the results of any instruction in the schedule. However, if I_i and I_j refer to the same data item Q, then the order of the two steps may matter. Since we

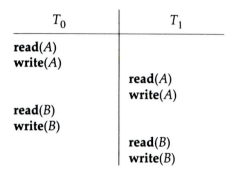

T_0	T_1
read(A)	
write(A)	
	read(A)
	write(A)
read(B)	
write(B)	
	read(B)
	write(B)

Figure 11.5   Schedule 3, showing only the **read** and **write** instructions.

are dealing only with **read** and **write** instructions, there are four cases that need to be considered:

- $I_i = $ **read**(Q), $I_j = $ **read**(Q). The order of I_i and I_j does not matter since the same value of Q is read by T_i and T_j regardless of the order.

- $I_i = $ **read**(Q), $I_j = $ **write**(Q). If I_i comes before I_j, then T_i does not read the value of Q that is written by T_j in instruction I_j. If I_j comes before I_i, then T_i reads the value of Q that is written by T_j. Thus, the order of I_i and I_j matters.

- $I_i = $ **write**(Q), $I_j = $ **read**(Q). The order of I_i and I_j matters for reasons similar to those of the previous case.

- $I_i = $ **write**(Q), $I_j = $ **write**(Q). Since both instructions are **write** operations, the order of these instructions does not affect either T_i or T_j. However, the value obtained by the next **read**(Q) instruction of S is affected, since only the result of the latter of the two **write** instructions is preserved in the database. If there is no other **write**(Q) instruction after I_i and I_j in S, then the order of I_i and I_j directly affects the final value of Q in the database state that results from schedule S.

Thus, only in the case where both I_i and I_j are **read** instructions does the relative order of their execution not matter.

We say that I_i and I_j *conflict* if they are operations by different transactions on the same data item, and at least one of these instructions is a **write** operation.

To illustrate the concept of conflicting instructions, consider schedule 3 as shown in Figure 11.5. The **write**(A) instruction of T_0 conflicts with the **read**(A) instruction of T_1. However, the **write**(A) instruction of T_1 does not conflict with the **read**(B) instruction of T_0 because the two instructions access different data items.

T_0	T_1
read(A)	
write(A)	
	read(A)
read(B)	
	write(A)
write(B)	
	read(B)
	write(B)

Figure 11.6   Schedule 5, schedule 3 after swapping a pair of instructions.

Let I_i and I_j be consecutive instructions of a schedule S. If I_i and I_j are instructions of different transactions and I_i and I_j do not conflict, then we can swap the order of I_i and I_j to produce a new schedule S'. We expect S to be equivalent to S' since all instructions appear in the same order in both schedules except for I_i and I_j, whose order does not matter.

Since the **write**(A) instruction of T_1 in schedule 3 of Figure 11.5 does not conflict with the **read**(B) instruction of T_0, we may swap these instructions to generate an equivalent schedule, schedule 5, as shown in Figure 11.6. Regardless of the initial system state, schedules 3 and 5 both produce the same final system state.

Let us continue to swap nonconflicting instructions as follows:

- Swap the **read**(B) instruction of T_0 with the **read**(A) instruction of T_1.

- Swap the **write**(B) instruction of T_0 with the **write**(A) instruction of T_1.

- Swap the **write**(B) instruction of T_0 with the **read**(A) instruction of T_1.

The final result of these swaps, as shown in schedule 6 of Figure 11.7, is a serial schedule. Thus, we have shown that schedule 3 is equivalent to a serial schedule. This implies that regardless of the initial system state, schedule 3 will produce the same final state as some serial schedule.

If a schedule S can be transformed into a schedule S' by a series of swaps of nonconflicting instructions, we say that S and S' are *conflict equivalent*.

Returning to our previous examples, we note that schedule 1 is not conflict equivalent to schedule 2. However, schedule 1 is conflict equivalent to schedule 3 because the **read**(B) and **write**(B) instruction of T_0 can be swapped with the **read**(A) and **write**(A) instruction of T_1.

The concept of conflict equivalence leads to the concept of conflict serializability. We say that a schedule S is *conflict serializable* if it is conflict

T_0	T_1
read(A)	
write(A)	
read(B)	
write(B)	
	read(A)
	write(A)
	read(B)
	write(B)

Figure 11.7   Schedule 6, a serial schedule equivalent to schedule 3.

equivalent to a serial schedule. Thus, schedule 3 is conflict serializable, since it is conflict equivalent to the serial schedule 1.

Finally, consider schedule 7 of Figure 11.8 consisting of only the significant operations (that is, the **read** and **write**) of transactions T_2 and T_3. This schedule is not conflict serializable, since it is not equivalent to either the serial schedule $<T_2,T_3>$ or the serial schedule $<T_3,T_2>$.

It is possible to have two schedules that produce the same outcome that are not conflict equivalent. For example, consider transaction T_4 that transfers \$10 from account B to account A. Let schedule 8 be as defined in Figure 11.9. We claim that schedule 8 is not conflict equivalent to the serial schedule $<T_0,T_4>$, since in schedule 8, the **write**(B) instruction of T_4 conflicts with the **read**(B) instruction of T_0. Thus, we cannot move all the instructions of T_0 before those of T_4 by swapping consecutive nonconflicting instructions. However, the final values of accounts A and B after the execution of either schedule 8 or the serial schedule $<T_0,T_4>$ are the same — namely, \$960 and \$2040, respectively.

We can see from this example that there are less stringent definitions of schedule equivalence than conflict equivalence. However, we shall see in Section 11.2 that testing for conflict equivalence can be done efficiently. In order for the system to determine that schedule 8 produces the same outcome as the serial schedule $<T_0,T_4>$, it would be necessary to analyze the actual computation performed by T_0 and T_4 rather than just the **read**

T_2	T_3
read(Q)	
	write(Q)
write(Q)	

Figure 11.8   Schedule 7.

T_0	T_4
read(A) $A := A - 50$ **write**(A)	
	read(B) $B := B - 10$ **write**(B)
read(B) $B := B + 50$ **write**(B)	
	read(A) $A := A + 10$ **write**(A)

Figure 11.9   Schedule 8.

and **write** operations.   In general, such analysis is computationally expensive.

11.1.3 View Serializability

In this section, we consider a form of equivalence that is less stringent than conflict equivalence but, like conflict equivalence, is based only on the **read** and **write** operations of transactions.

Consider two schedules S and S' where the same set of transactions participate in both schedules.   The schedules S and S' are said to be *view equivalent* if the following three conditions are met:

1. For each data item Q, if transaction T_i reads the initial value of Q in schedule S, then transaction T_i must, in schedule S', also read the initial value of Q.

2. For each data item Q, if transaction T_i executes **read**(Q) in schedule S, and that value was produced by transaction T_j (if any), then transaction T_i must in schedule S' also read the value of Q that was produced by transaction T_j.

3. For each data item Q, the transaction (if any) that performs the final **write**(Q) operation in schedule S must perform the final **write**(Q) operation in schedule S'.

Conditions 1 and 2 ensure that each transaction reads the same values in both schedules and, therefore, performs the same computation. Condition 3, coupled with conditions 1 and 2, ensures that both schedules result in the same final system state.

Returning to our previous examples, we note that schedule 1 is not view equivalent to schedule 2, since in schedule 1 the value of account A read by transaction T_1 was produced by T_0, while this is not the case in schedule 2. However, schedule 1 is view equivalent to schedule 3 because the values of account A and B read by transaction T_1 were produced by T_0 in both schedules.

The concept of view equivalence leads to the concept of view serializability. We say that a schedule S is *view serializable* if it is view equivalent to a serial schedule.

To illustrate, suppose that we augment schedule 7 with transaction T_5 and obtain schedule 9 depicted in Figure 11.10. Schedule 9 is view serializable. Indeed, it is view equivalent to the serial schedule $<T_2,T_3,T_5>$, since the one **read**(Q) instruction reads the initial value of Q in both schedules and T_5 performs the final write of Q in both schedules.

Every conflict serializable schedule is view serializable, but there are view serializable schedules that are not conflict serializable. Indeed, schedule 9 is not conflict serializable since every pair of consecutive instructions conflicts and, thus, no swapping of instructions is possible.

Observe that in schedule 9, transactions T_3 and T_5 perform **write**(Q) operations without having performed a **read**(Q) operation. Writes of this sort are called *blind writes*. Blind writes appear in any view serializable schedule that is not conflict serializable.

11.2 Testing for Serializability

Suppose that we are given a particular schedule S, and we wish to determine whether this schedule is serializable. In this section, we shall present methods for determining conflict and view serializability.

11.2.1 Testing for Conflict Serializability

In this section, we show that there exists a simple and efficient algorithm to determine conflict serializability.

Let S be a schedule. We construct a directed graph, called a *precedence graph* from S. This graph consists of a pair $G = (V,E)$ where V is a set of

T_2	T_3	T_5
read(Q)		
	write(Q)	
write(Q)		
		write(Q)

Figure 11.10   Schedule 9, a view serializable schedule.

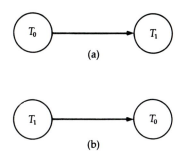

Figure 11.11   Precedence graph for (a) schedule 1 and (b) schedule 2.

vertices and E is a set of edges. The set of vertices consists of all the transactions participating in the schedule. The set of edges consists of all edges $T_i \rightarrow T_j$ for which one of the following three conditions hold

- T_i executes **write**(Q) before T_j executes **read**(Q).
- T_i executes **read**(Q) before T_j executes **write**(Q).
- T_i executes **write**(Q) before T_j executes **write**(Q).

If an edge $T_i \rightarrow T_j$ exists in the precedence graph, this implies that in any serial schedule S' equivalent to S, T_i must appear before T_j.

For example, the precedence graph for schedule 1 is shown in Figure 11.11a. It contains the single edge $T_0 \rightarrow T_1$, since all the instructions of T_0 are executed before the first instruction of T_1 is executed. Similarly, Figure 11.11b shows the precedence graph for schedule 2 with the single edge $T_1 \rightarrow T_0$, since all the instructions of T_1 are executed before the first instruction of T_0 is executed.

The precedence graph for schedule 4 is depicted in Figure 11.12. It contains the edge $T_0 \rightarrow T_1$ because T_0 executes **read**(A) before T_1 executes **write**(A). It also contains the edge $T_1 \rightarrow T_0$ because T_1 executes **read**(B) before T_0 executes **write**(B).

If the precedence graph for S has a cycle, then the schedule S is not conflict serializable. If the graph contains no cycles, then the schedule S is conflict serializable. The serializability order can be obtained through

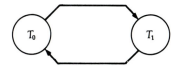

Figure 11.12   Precedence graph for schedule 4.

topological sorting, which determines a linear order consistent with the partial order of the precedence graph. There are, in general, several possible linear orders which can be obtained through a topological sorting. For example, the graph of Figure 11.13a has two acceptable linear orderings, as illustrated in Figure 11.13b and Figure 11.13c.

Thus, in order to test for conflict serializability, we need to construct the precedence graph and invoke a cycle detection algorithm. Since finding a cycle in a graph requires on the order of n^2 operations, where n is the number of vertices in the graph (that is, the number of transactions), we have a practical scheme for determining conflict serializability.

Returning to our previous examples, note that the precedence graphs for schedules 1 and 2 (Figure 11.11) indeed do not contain cycles. The precedence graph for schedule 4 (Figure 11.12), on the other hand, contains a cycle, indicating that this schedule is not conflict serializable.

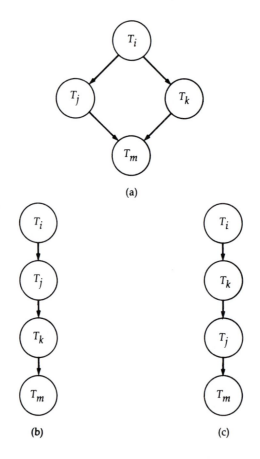

Figure 11.13   Illustration of topological sorting.

11.2.2 Testing for View Serializability

We shall show that there is no efficient algorithm for determining view serializability. We begin by showing how the precedence graph test for conflict serializability must be modified to apply to a test for view serializability.

In the case of testing for conflict serializability, we know that if two transactions, T_i and T_j, access a data item Q, and at least one of these transactions writes Q, then either the edge $T_i \rightarrow T_j$ or the edge $T_j \rightarrow T_i$ is inserted in the precedence graph. This, however, is no longer the case when testing for view serializability. As we shall see shortly, this is the cause of our inability to come up with an efficient algorithm for such a test.

Consider schedule 9, which we saw earlier in Figure 11.10. If we follow the rule in the conflict serializability test for forming the precedence graph, we get the graph of Figure 11.14. This graph contains a cycle, indicating that schedule 9 is not conflict serializable. However, as we saw earlier, schedule 9 is view serializable, since it is view equivalent to the serial schedule $<T_2,T_3,T_5>$. The edge $T_3 \rightarrow T_2$ should *not* have been inserted in the graph, since the values of item Q produced by T_2 and T_3 were never used by any other transaction, and T_5 produced a new final value of Q. The **write**(Q) instructions of T_2 and T_3 are called *useless writes*.

What we have pointed out above is that we cannot simply use the precedence graph scheme of Section 11.2.1 to test for view serializability, We need to develop a scheme for deciding whether an edge needs to be inserted in a precedence graph.

Let S be a schedule. Suppose that transaction T_j reads the value of data item Q written by T_i. Clearly, if S is view serializable, then in any serial schedule S' that is equivalent to S, T_i must precede T_j. Suppose now that in schedule S transaction T_k executed a **write**(Q). Then in schedule S', T_k must either precede T_i or follow T_j. It cannot appear between T_i and T_j, since otherwise T_j would not read the value of Q written by T_i and thus S would not be view equivalent to S'.

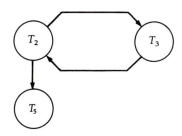

Figure 11.14   Precedence graph for schedule 9.

The above constraints cannot be expressed in terms of the simple precedence graph model previously discussed. The difficulty stems from the fact that we know that in the above example one of the pair of edges $T_k \rightarrow T_i$, $T_j \rightarrow T_k$ must be inserted in the graph, but we have not yet formed the rule for determining the appropriate choice.

To do so, we need to extend the precedence graph to include labeled edges. We term such a graph a *labeled precedence graph*. As before, the nodes of the graph are the transactions participating in the schedule. The rules for inserting labeled edges are described below.

Let S be a schedule consisting of transactions $\{T_0, T_1, \ldots, T_n\}$. Let T_b and T_f be two dummy transactions such that T_b issues **write**(Q) for each Q accessed in S, and T_f issues **read**(Q) for each Q accessed in S. We construct a new schedule S' from S by inserting T_b at the beginning of S and appending T_f to the end of S. We construct the labeled precedence graph for schedule S' as follows:

1. Add an edge $T_i \overset{0}{\rightarrow} T_j$, if transaction T_j reads the value of data item Q written by transaction T_i.

2. Remove all the edges incident on useless transactions. A transaction T_i is *useless* if there exists no path, in the precedence graph, from T_i to transaction T_f .

3. For each data item Q such that

   - T_j reads the value of Q written by T_i
   - T_k executes **write**(Q) and $T_k \neq T_b$

   do the following:

   a. If $T_i = T_b$ and $T_j \neq T_f$, then insert the edge $T_j \overset{0}{\rightarrow} T_k$ in the labeled precedence graph.

   b. If $T_i \neq T_b$ and $T_j = T_f$, then insert the edge $T_k \overset{0}{\rightarrow} T_i$ in the labeled precedence graph.

   c. If $T_i \neq T_b$ and $T_j \neq T_f$, then insert the pair of edges $T_k \overset{p}{\rightarrow} T_i$, and $T_j \overset{p}{\rightarrow} T_k$ in the labeled precedence graph where p is a unique integer larger than 0 not used before for labeling edges.

Rule (c) reflects the fact that if T_i writes a data item that T_j reads, then a transaction T_k that writes the same data item must come before T_i or after T_j. Rules (a) and (b) are special cases that result from the fact that T_b and T_f are necessarily the first and last transactions, respectively. When we apply rule (c), we are *not* requiring T_k to be *both* before T_i *and* after T_j. Rather, we have a choice of where T_k may appear in an equivalent serial ordering.

To illustrate, consider again schedule 7 (Figure 11.8). The graph constructed in steps 1 and 2 is depicted in Figure 11.15a. It contains the edge $T_b \overset{0}{\rightarrow} T_2$, since T_2 reads the value of Q written by T_b. It contains the edge $T_2 \overset{0}{\rightarrow} T_f$, since T_2 was the last transaction that wrote Q and, thus, T_f read that value. The final graph corresponding to schedule 7 is depicted in Figure 11.15b. It contains the edge $T_2 \overset{0}{\rightarrow} T_3$ as a result of step 3a. It contains the edge $T_3 \overset{0}{\rightarrow} T_2$ as a result of step 3b.

Consider now schedule 9 (Figure 11.10). The graph constructed in steps 1 and 2 is depicted in Figure 11.16a. The final graph is shown in Figure 11.16b. It contains the edges $T_2 \overset{0}{\rightarrow} T_3$ and $T_2 \overset{0}{\rightarrow} T_5$ as a result of step 3a. It contains the edges $T_2 \overset{0}{\rightarrow} T_5$ (already in the graph) and $T_3 \overset{0}{\rightarrow} T_5$ as a result of step 3b.

Finally, consider schedule 10 of Figure 11.17. Schedule 10 is view serializable since it is view equivalent to the serial schedule $<T_2,T_3,T_6>$.

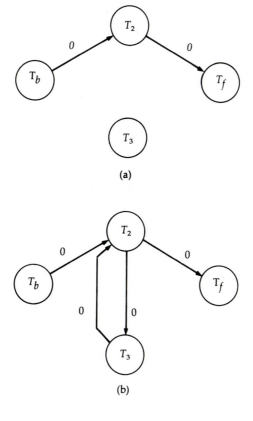

(a)

(b)

Figure 11.15   Labeled precedence graph of schedule 7.

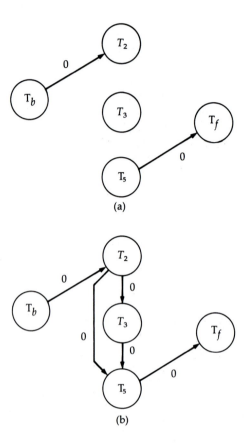

Figure 11.16   Labeled precedence graph of schedule 9.

The corresponding labeled precedence graph, constructed in steps 1 and 2, is depicted in Figure 11.18a. The final graph is depicted in Figure 11.18b. The edges $T_2 \xrightarrow{0} T_3$ and $T_2 \xrightarrow{0} T_6$ were inserted as a result of rule 3a. The pair of edges $T_2 \xrightarrow{1} T_3$ and $T_6 \xrightarrow{1} T_2$ were inserted as the result of a *single* application of rule 3c.

T_2	T_3	T_6
read(Q)		
	write(Q)	
		read(Q)
write(Q)		
		write(Q)

Figure 11.17   Schedule 10.

The graphs depicted in Figures 11.15b and 11.18b contain the following two minimal cycles, respectively:

- $T_2 \xrightarrow{0} T_3 \xrightarrow{0} T_2$
- $T_2 \xrightarrow{0} T_6 \xrightarrow{1} T_2$

The graph in Figure 11.16b, on the other hand, contains no cycles.

If the graph contains no cycle, the corresponding schedule is view serializable. Indeed, the graph of Figure 11.16b contains no cycle and its corresponding schedule 9 is view serializable. However, if the graph contains a cycle, this does *not* necessarily imply that the corresponding schedule is not view serializable. Indeed, the graph of Figure 11.15b contains a cycle and its corresponding schedule 7 is not view serializable. The graph of Figure 11.18b, on the other hand, contains a cycle, but its corresponding schedule 10 is view serializable.

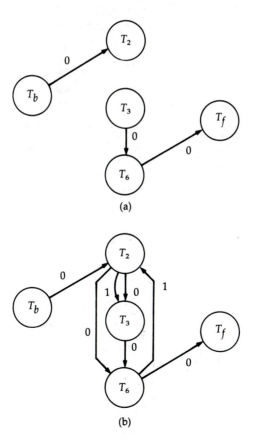

(a)

(b)

Figure 11.18   Labeled precedence graph of schedule 10.

How, then, do we determine whether a schedule is view serializable or not? The answer simply lies in an appropriate interpretation of the precedence graph. Suppose that there are n distinct edge pairs. That is, we applied rule 3c n times in the construction of the precedence graph. Then there exist 2^n different graphs, where each graph contains only one edge from each pair. If any one of these graphs is acyclic, then the corresponding schedule is view serializable. The serializability order is determined by the removal of the dummy transactions T_b and T_f, and the topological sorting of the remaining acyclic graph.

Returning to the graph of Figure 11.18b, since there is exactly one distinct pair, there are two different graphs that need to be considered. The two graphs are depicted in Figure 11.19. Since the graph of Figure 11.19a is acyclic, we know that the corresponding schedule 10 is view serializable.

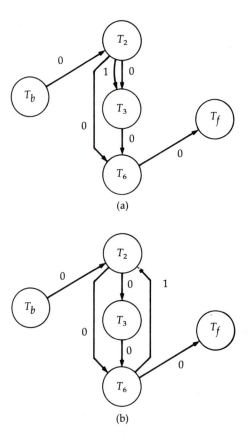

(a)

(b)

Figure 11.19   Two distinct precedence graphs.

The algorithm described above requires exhaustive testing of all possible distinct graphs. It has been shown that the problem of testing for an acyclic graph in this set falls in the class of NP-complete problems (see the bibliographic notes for references to discussion of the theory of NP-complete problems). An algorithm for an NP-complete problem will almost certainly run in exponential time as a function of the size of the problem.

11.3 Lock-Based Protocols

One way to ensure serializability is to require that access to data items be done in a mutually exclusive manner; that is, while one transaction accesses a data item, no other transaction can modify that data item. The most common method used to implement this is to allow a transaction to access a data item only if it is currently holding a lock on that item.

11.3.1 Locks

There are various modes in which a data item may be locked. In this section, we restrict our attention to two modes:

- **Shared**. If a transaction T_i has obtained a shared-mode lock (denoted by S) on item Q, then T_i can read this item but it cannot write Q.

- **Exclusive**. If a transaction T_i has obtained an exclusive-mode lock (denoted by X) on item Q, then T_i can both read and write Q.

We require that every transaction request a lock in an appropriate mode on data item Q depending on the type of operations it will perform on Q.

Given a set of lock modes, we can define a *compatibility function* on them as follows. Let A and B represent arbitrary lock modes. Suppose that a transaction T_i requests a lock of mode A on item Q on which transaction T_j ($T_i \neq T_j$) currently holds a lock of mode B. If transaction T_i can be granted a lock on Q immediately, in spite of the presence of the mode B lock, then we say mode A is *compatible* with mode B. Such a function can be represented conveniently by a matrix. The compatibility relation between the two modes of locking used in this section is given by the

	S	X
S	true	false
X	false	false

Figure 11.20 Lock compatibility matrix **comp**.

matrix **comp** of Figure 11.20. An element **comp**(A,B) of the matrix has the value *true* if and only if mode A is compatible with mode B.

Note that shared mode is compatible with shared mode, but not with exclusive mode. At any time, several shared-mode locks can be held simultaneously (by different transactions) on a particular data item. A subsequent exclusive-mode lock request has to wait until the currently held shared mode locks are released.

A transaction requests a shared lock on data item Q by executing the **lock-S**(Q) instruction. Similarly, an exclusive lock is requested through the **lock-X**(Q) instruction. A data item Q may be unlocked via the **unlock**(Q) instruction.

In order to access a data item, transaction T_i must first lock it. If the data item is already locked by another transaction in an incompatible mode, then T_i must *wait* until all incompatible locks held by other transactions have been released. Transaction T_i may unlock a data item which it had locked at some earlier point.

It should be noted that a transaction must hold a lock on a data item as long as it accesses it. Moreover, it is not always desirable for a transaction to unlock a data item immediately after its last access of that data item, since serializability may not be ensured.

To illustrate, consider again our simplified banking system. Let A and B be two accounts that are accessed by transactions T_7 and T_8. Transaction T_7 transfers \$50 from account B to account A, and is defined as:

$$T_7: \textbf{lock-X}(B);$$
$$\textbf{read}(B);$$
$$B := B - 50;$$
$$\textbf{write}(B);$$
$$\textbf{unlock}(B);$$
$$\textbf{lock-X}(A);$$
$$\textbf{read}(A);$$
$$A := A + 50;$$
$$\textbf{write}(A);$$
$$\textbf{unlock}(A).$$

Transaction T_8 displays the total amount of money in accounts A and B, that is, the sum $A + B$, and is defined as:

$$T_8: \textbf{lock-S}(A);$$
$$\textbf{read}(A);$$
$$\textbf{unlock}(A);$$
$$\textbf{lock-S}(B);$$
$$\textbf{read}(B);$$
$$\textbf{unlock}(B);$$
$$\textbf{display}(A + B).$$

T_7	T_8
lock-X(B)	
read(B)	
$B := B - 50$	
write(B)	
unlock(B)	
	lock-S(A)
	read(A)
	unlock(A)
	lock-S(B)
	read(B)
	unlock(B)
	display($A + B$)
lock-X(A)	
read(A)	
$A := A + 50$	
write(A)	
unlock(A)	

Figure 11.21   Schedule 11.

Suppose that the values of accounts A and B are $100 and $200, respectively. If these two transactions are executed serially, either in the order T_7, T_8 or the order T_8, T_7, then transaction T_8 will display the value $300. If, however, these transactions are executed concurrently, then schedule 11, as shown in Figure 11.21, is possible. In this case, transaction T_8 displays $250, which is incorrect. The reason for this is that the transaction T_7 has unlocked data item B too early as a result of which T_8 saw an inconsistent state.

Suppose now that unlocking is delayed to the end of the transaction. Transaction T_9, below, corresponds to T_7 with unlocking delayed and is defined as:

$$T_9: \quad \textbf{lock-X}(B);$$
$$\textbf{read}(B);$$
$$B := B - 50;$$
$$\textbf{write}(B);$$
$$\textbf{lock-X}(A);$$
$$\textbf{read}(A);$$
$$A := A + 50;$$
$$\textbf{write}(A);$$
$$\textbf{unlock}(B);$$
$$\textbf{unlock}(A).$$

Transaction T_{10} below, corresponds to T_8 with unlocking delayed and is defined as:

$$T_{10}: \quad \textbf{lock-S}(A);$$
$$\textbf{read}(A);$$
$$\textbf{lock-S}(B);$$
$$\textbf{read}(B);$$
$$\textbf{display}(A + B);$$
$$\textbf{unlock}(A);$$
$$\textbf{unlock}(B).$$

Consider the partial schedule of Figure 11.22 for T_9 and T_{10}. Since T_9 is holding an exclusive-mode lock on B and T_{10} is requesting a shared-mode lock on B, T_{10} is waiting for T_9 to unlock B. Similarly, since T_{10} is holding a shared-mode lock on A and T_9 is requesting an exclusive-mode lock on A, T_9 is waiting for T_{10} to unlock A. Thus, we have arrived at a state where neither of these transactions can ever proceed with its normal execution. This situation is called *deadlock*. When deadlock occurs, the system must roll back one of the two transactions. Once a transaction has been rolled back, the data items that were locked by that transaction are unlocked. These data items are then available to the other transaction, which can continue with its execution. We shall return to the issue of deadlock handling in Chapter 12.

What we have pointed out here is that locking should be used cautiously. If we try to maximize concurrency by unlocking data items as soon as possible, we may get inconsistent states. If we do not unlock a data item before requesting a lock on another data item, deadlocks may occur.

T_9	T_{10}
lock-X(B)	
read(B)	
$B := B - 50$	
write(B)	
	lock-S(A)
	read(A)
	lock-S(B)
lock-X(A)	

Figure 11.22   Schedule 12.

We shall require that each transaction in the system follow a set of rules, called a *locking protocol*, indicating when a transaction may lock and unlock each of the data items. Locking protocols restrict the number of possible schedules. The set of all such schedules is a proper subset of all possible serializable schedules. We shall present several locking protocols that allow only conflict serializable schedules. Before doing so, we need a few definitions.

Let $\{T_0, T_1, \ldots, T_n\}$ be a set of transactions participating in a schedule S. We say that T_i *precedes* T_j in S, written $T_i \rightarrow T_j$, if there exists a data item Q such that T_i has held lock mode A on Q and T_j has held lock mode B on Q later, and **comp**(A,B) = false. If $T_i \rightarrow T_j$, then this implies that in any equivalent serial schedule, T_i must appear before T_j. Observe that this graph is similar to the precedence graph we used in Section 11.2.1 to test for conflict serializability. Conflicts between instructions correspond to noncompatibility of lock modes.

We say that a schedule S is *legal* under a given locking protocol if S is a possible schedule for a set of transactions following the rules of the locking protocol. We say that a locking protocol *ensures conflict serializability* if and only if for all legal schedules, the associated $\rightarrow$ relation is acyclic.

11.3.2 The Two-Phase Locking Protocol

One protocol that ensures serializability is the *two-phase locking protocol*. This protocol requires that each transaction issue lock and unlock requests in two phases:

- **Growing phase**. A transaction may obtain locks but may not release any lock.

- **Shrinking phase**. A transaction may release locks but may not obtain any new locks.

Initially, a transaction is in the growing phase. The transaction acquires locks as needed. Once the transaction releases a lock, it enters the shrinking phase and no more lock requests may be issued.

For example, transactions T_9 and T_{10} are two-phase. On the other hand, transactions T_7 and T_8 are not two-phase.

The two-phase locking protocol ensures conflict serializability (see Exercise 11.7). It does not, however, ensure freedom from deadlock. To demonstrate this, observe that transactions T_9 and T_{10} are two-phase, but in schedule 12 (Figure 11.22) they are deadlocked.

If T_i is a non-two-phase transaction, it is always possible to find another transaction T_j that is two-phase such that there is a schedule possible for T_i and T_j that is not conflict serializable.

Consider the following two transactions for which we have shown only some of the significant **read** and **write** operations. Transaction T_{11} is defined as:

$$T_{11}: \textbf{read}(a_1);$$
$$\textbf{read}(a_2);$$
$$\cdots$$
$$\textbf{read}(a_n);$$
$$\textbf{write}(a_1).$$

while transaction T_{12} is defined as:

$$T_{12}: \textbf{read}(a_1);$$
$$\textbf{read}(a_2);$$
$$\textbf{display}(a_1 + a_2).$$

If we employ the two-phase locking protocol, then T_{11} must lock a_1 in exclusive mode. Therefore, any concurrent execution of both transactions amounts to a serial execution. Notice, however, that T_{11} needs an exclusive lock on a_1 only at the end of its execution, when it writes a_1. Thus, if T_{11} could initially lock a_1 in shared mode, and then later change the lock to exclusive mode, we could get more concurrency, since T_{11} and T_{12} could access a_1 and a_2 simultaneously.

This observation leads us to a refinement of the basic two-phase locking protocol, in which lock *conversions* are allowed. We shall provide a mechanism for upgrading a shared lock to an exclusive lock, and downgrading an exclusive lock to a shared lock. We denote conversion from shared to exclusive modes by **upgrade**, and from exclusive to shared by **downgrade**. Lock conversion cannot be allowed to occur arbitrarily. Rather, upgrading can take place only in the growing phase, while downgrading can take place only in the shrinking phase.

Returning to our example, transactions T_{11} and T_{12} can run concurrently under the refined two-phase locking protocol as shown in the incomplete schedule of Figure 11.23, where only some of the locking instructions are shown.

Note that a transaction attempting to upgrade a lock on an item Q may be forced to wait. This occurs if Q is currently locked by *another* transaction in shared mode.

We now describe a simple scheme that can be used to generate the appropriate lock instructions for a transaction. When a transaction T_i issues a **read**(Q) operation the system issues a **lock-S**(Q) instruction followed by the **read**(Q) instruction. When T_i issues a **write**(Q) operation, the system checks to see whether T_i already holds a shared lock on Q. If this is the case, then the system issues an **upgrade**(Q) instruction followed by the

T_{11}	T_{12}
lock-S(a_1)	
	lock-S(a_1)
lock-S(a_2)	
	lock-S(a_2)
lock-S(a_3)	
lock-S(a_4)	
	unlock(a_1)
	unlock(a_2)
lock-S(a_n)	
upgrade(a_1)	

Figure 11.23   Incomplete schedule with a lock conversion.

write(Q) instruction. Otherwise, the system issues a lock-X(Q) instruction followed by the write(Q) instruction.

It is possible that, for a set of transactions, there are conflict serializable schedules that cannot be obtained through the two-phase locking protocol. However, in order to do better than two-phase locking, we need either to have additional information about the transactions or to impose some structure or ordering upon the set of data items in the database.

11.3.3 Graph-Based Protocols

As was pointed out above, in the absence of information concerning the manner in which data items are accessed, the two-phase locking protocol is both necessary and sufficient for ensuring serializability. Thus, if we wish to develop protocols that are not two-phase, we need to have some additional information on how each transaction will access the database. There are various models that differ in the amount of such information provided. The simplest model requires that we have prior knowledge as to the order in which the database items will be accessed. Given such information, it is possible to construct locking protocols that are not two-phase but, nevertheless, ensure conflict serializability.

To acquire such prior knowledge, we impose a partial ordering $\rightarrow$ on the set $D = \{d_1, d_2, \ldots, d_h\}$ of all data items. If $d_i \rightarrow d_j$, then any transaction accessing both d_i and d_j must access d_i before accessing d_j. This partial ordering may be the result of either the logical or physical organization of the data, or it may be imposed solely for the purpose of concurrency control.

The partial ordering implies that the set D may now be viewed as a directed acyclic graph, called a *database graph*. In this section, for the sake of simplicity, we will restrict our attention only to graphs that are rooted trees. We will present a simple protocol, called the *tree protocol*, which is restricted to employ only *exclusive* locks. References to other, more complex graph-based locking protocols are provided in the bibliographic notes.

In the tree protocol, the only lock instruction allowed is **lock-X**. Each transaction T_i can lock a data item at most once and must observe the following rules:

1. The first lock by T_i may be on any data item.

2. Subsequently, a data item Q can be locked by T_i only if the parent of Q is currently locked by T_i.

3. Data items may be unlocked at any time.

4. A data item that has been locked and unlocked by T_i cannot subsequently be relocked by T_i.

As we stated earlier, all schedules that are legal under the tree protocol are conflict serializable.

To illustrate this protocol, consider the database graph of Figure 11.24. The following four transactions follow the tree protocol on this graph. We have shown only the lock and unlock instructions:

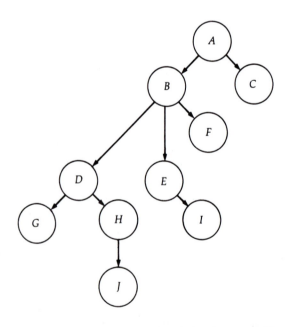

Figure 11.24   Tree structured database graph.

T_{13} : **lock-X**(B); **lock-X**(E); **unlock**(E); **lock-X**(D); **unlock**(B); **lock-X**(G);
unlock(D); **unlock**(G).
T_{14} : **lock-X**(D); **lock-X**(H); **unlock**(D); **lock-X**(J); **unlock**(J); **unlock**(H).
T_{15} : **lock-X**(B); **lock-X**(E); **unlock**(E); **unlock**(B).
T_{16} : **lock-X**(D); **lock-X**(H); **unlock**(D); **unlock**(H).

One possible schedule in which these four transactions participated is
depicted in Figure 11.25. Note that during its execution, transaction T_{13}
holds locks on two *disjoint* subtrees.

Observe that the schedule of Figure 11.25 is conflict serializable. It can
be shown not only that the tree protocol ensures conflict serializability, but
also that it ensures freedom from deadlock.

The tree-locking protocol has the advantage over the two-phase locking
protocol in that unlocking may occur earlier. This may lead to less waiting
time, and an increase in concurrency. In addition, since it is deadlock-free,
no rollbacks are required. However, the protocol has the disadvantage that
in some cases it is necessary for a transaction to lock data items that it does
not access. For example, a transaction that needs to access data items A
and J in the database graph of Figure 11.24 must lock not only A and J but

T_{13}	T_{14}	T_{15}	T_{16}
lock-X(B)			
	lock-X(D)		
	lock-X(H)		
	unlock(D)		
lock-X(E)			
unlock(E)			
lock-X(D)			
unlock(B)			
		lock-X(B)	
		lock-X(E)	
	unlock(H)		
lock-X(G)			
unlock(D)			
			lock-X(D)
			lock-X(H)
			unlock(D)
			unlock(H)
		unlock(E)	
		unlock(B)	
unlock(G)			

Figure 11.25   Serializable schedule.

also data items B, D, and H. This results in increased locking overhead, the possibility of additional waiting time, and a potential decrease in concurrency.

It is possible that, for a set of transactions, there are conflict serializable schedules that cannot be obtained through the tree protocol. Indeed, there are schedules possible under the two-phase locking protocol that are not possible under the tree protocol and vice versa. Examples of such schedules are explored in the exercises.

11.4 Timestamp-Based Protocols

In the locking protocols described above, the order between every pair of conflicting transactions is determined at execution time by the first lock they both request that involves incompatible modes. Another method for determining the serializability order is to select an ordering among transactions in advance. The most common method for doing so is to use a *timestamp-ordering* scheme.

11.4.1 Timestamps

With each transaction T_i in the system, we associate a unique fixed timestamp, denoted by $TS(T_i)$. This timestamp is assigned by the database system before the transaction T_i starts execution. If a transaction T_i has been assigned timestamp $TS(T_i)$, and a new transaction T_j enters the system, then $TS(T_i) < TS(T_j)$. There are two simple methods for implementing this scheme:

- Use the value of the system clock as the timestamp; that is, a transaction's timestamp equals the value of the clock when the transaction enters the system.

- Use a logical counter that is incremented after a new timestamp has been assigned; that is, a transaction's timestamp equals the value of the counter when the transaction enters the system.

The timestamps of the transactions determine the serializability order. Thus, if $TS(T_i) < TS(T_j)$, then the system must ensure that the produced schedule is equivalent to a serial schedule in which transaction T_i appears before transaction T_j.

To implement this scheme, we associate with each data item Q two timestamp values:

- **W-timestamp**(Q), which denotes the largest timestamp of any transaction that successfully executed **write**(Q).

- **R-timestamp**(Q), which denotes the largest timestamp of any transaction that successfully executed **read**(Q).

These timestamps are updated whenever a new **read**(Q) or **write**(Q) instruction is executed.

11.4.2 The Timestamp-Ordering Protocol

The timestamp-ordering protocol ensures that any conflicting **read** and **write** operations are executed in timestamp order. This protocol operates as follows:

- Suppose that transaction T_i issues **read**(Q).

  ○ If $TS(T_i)$ < W-timestamp(Q), then this implies that T_i needs to read a value of Q which was already overwritten. Hence, the **read** operation is rejected and T_i is rolled back.

  ○ If $TS(T_i) \geq$ W-timestamp(Q), then the **read** operation is executed, and R-timestamp(Q) is set to the maximum of R-timestamp(Q) and $TS(T_i)$.

- Suppose that transaction T_i issues **write**(Q).

  ○ If $TS(T_i)$ < R-timestamp(Q), then this implies that the value of Q that T_i is producing was previously needed and it was assumed that it would never be produced. Hence, the **write** operation is rejected and T_i is rolled back.

  ○ If $TS(T_i)$ < W-timestamp(Q), then this implies that T_i is attempting to write an obsolete value of Q. Hence, this **write** operation is rejected and T_i is rolled back.

  ○ Otherwise, the **write** operation is executed.

A transaction T_i, which is rolled back by the concurrency control scheme as result of issuing either a **read** or **write** operation, is assigned a new timestamp and is restarted.

To illustrate this protocol, consider the transactions T_{17} and T_{18} defined below. Transaction T_{17} displays the contents of accounts A and B, and is defined as:

$$T_{17}: \textbf{read}(B);$$
$$\textbf{read}(A);$$
$$\textbf{display}(A + B).$$

Transaction T_{18} transfers \$50 from account A to account B and then displays the contents of both.

$$T_{18}: \quad \textbf{read}(B);$$
$$B := B - 50;$$
$$\textbf{write}(B);$$
$$\textbf{read}(A);$$
$$A := A + 50;$$
$$\textbf{write}(A);$$
$$\textbf{display}(A + B).$$

In presenting schedules under the timestamp protocol, we shall assume that a transaction is assigned a timestamp immediately before its first instruction. Thus, in schedule 13 of Figure 11.26, $TS(T_{17}) < TS(T_{18})$, and the schedule is possible under the timestamp protocol.

We note that the above execution can also be produced by the two-phase locking protocol. There are, however, schedules that are possible under the two-phase locking protocol but are not possible under the timestamp protocol, and vice versa (see Exercise 11.17).

The timestamp-ordering protocol ensures conflict serializability. This follows from the fact that conflicting operations are processed in timestamp order. The protocol ensures freedom from deadlock, since no transaction ever waits.

11.4.3 Thomas' Write Rule

We now present a modification to the timestamp-ordering protocol that allows greater potential concurrency than the protocol of Section 11.4.2. Let us consider again schedule 7 of Figure 11.8, and apply the timestamp-ordering protocol. Since T_2 starts before T_3, we shall assume that $TS(T_2) < TS(T_3)$. The **read**(Q) operation of T_2 succeeds, as does the **write**(Q) operation of T_3. When T_2 attempts its **write**(Q) operation, we find that $TS(T_2) < W$-timestamp(Q), since W-timestamp(Q) = $TS(T_3)$. Thus,

T_{17}	T_{18}
read(B)	
	read(B)
	$B := B - 50$
	write(B)
read(A)	
	read(A)
display(A + B)	
	$A := A + 50$
	write(A)
	display(A + B)

Figure 11.26   Schedule 13.

the **write**(Q) by T_2 would be rejected and transaction T_2 must be rolled back.

Although the rollback of T_2 is required by the timestamp-ordering protocol, it is unnecessary. Since T_3 has already written Q, the value that T_2 is attempting to write is one that will never need to be read. Any transaction T_i with $TS(T_i) < TS(T_3)$ that attempts a **read**(Q) will be rolled back since $TS(T_i) < $ W-timestamp(Q). Any transaction T_j with $TS(T_j) > TS(T_3)$ must read the value of Q written by T_3, not the value written by T_2.

This observation leads to a modified version of the timestamp-ordering protocol in which obsolete **write** operations may be ignored under certain circumstances. The protocol rules for **read** operations remain unchanged. The protocol rules for **write** operations, however, are slightly different from the timestamp-ordering protocol of Section 11.4.2.

Suppose that transaction T_i issues **write**(Q).

- If $TS(T_i) < $ R-timestamp(Q), then this implies that the value of Q that T_i is producing was previously needed and it was assumed that the value would never be produced. Hence, the **write** operation is rejected and T_i is rolled back.

- If $TS(T_i) < $ W-timestamp(Q), then this implies that T_i is attempting to write an obsolete value of Q. Hence, this **write** operation can be ignored.

- Otherwise, the write is executed.

The difference between the above rules and those of Section 11.4.2 is in the second rule. The timestamp-ordering protocol requires that T_i be rolled back if T_i issues **write**(Q) and $TS(T_i) < $ W-timestamp(Q). However, here, in those cases where $TS(T_i) \geq $ R-timestamp(Q), we ignore the obsolete **write**. This modification to the timestamp-ordering protocol is called *Thomas' Write Rule*.

Thomas' Write Rule works by, in effect, deleting obsolete **write** operations from the transactions that issue them. This modification of transactions makes it possible to generate serializable schedules that would not be possible under the other protocols presented in this chapter. For example, schedule 7 of Figure 11.8 is not conflict serializable and, thus, is not possible under any of two-phase locking, the tree protocol, or the timestamp-ordering protocol. Under Thomas' Write Rule, the **write**(Q) operation of T_2 would be ignored. The result is an execution that is equivalent to the serial schedule $<T_2,T_3>$.

11.5 Validation Techniques

In cases where the majority of transactions are read-only transactions, the rate of conflicts among transactions may be very low. Thus, many of these transactions, if executed without the supervision of a concurrency control scheme, would nevertheless leave the system in a consistent state. A concurrency control scheme imposes some overhead of code execution and possible delay of transactions. It may be desirable to use an alternative scheme that imposes less overhead. A difficulty in reducing the overhead is that we do not know in advance which transactions will be involved in a conflict. To do so, we need to provide a scheme for *monitoring* the system.

We assume that each transaction T_i executes in two or three different phases in its lifetime, depending on whether it is a read-only or an update transaction.

1. **Read phase**. During this phase, the execution of transaction T_i takes place. The values of the various data items are read and stored in variables local to T_i. All **write** operations are performed on temporary local variables, without updating the actual database.

2. **Validation phase**. Transaction T_i performs a validation test to determine whether it can copy to the database the temporary local variables that hold the results of **write** operations without causing a violation of serializability.

3. **Write phase**. If transaction T_i succeeds in validation (step 2), then the actual updates are applied to the database. Otherwise, T_i is rolled back.

All three phases of concurrently executing transactions can be interleaved.

The read and write phases are self-explanatory. The only phase that needs further discussion is the validation phase. In order to perform the validation test, we need to know when the various phases of transactions T_i took place. We shall, therefore, associate three different timestamps with transaction T_i:

- **Start**(T_i), the time when T_i started its execution.

- **Validation**(T_i), the time when T_i finished its read phase and started its validation phase.

- **Finish**(T_i), the time when T_i finished its write phase.

The serializability order is determined by the timestamp-ordering technique using the value of the timestamp Validation(T_i). Thus, the value $TS(T_i) = $ Validation(T_i) and, if $TS(T_j) < TS(T_k)$, then any produced schedule must be equivalent to a serial schedule in which transaction T_j appears before transaction T_k. The reason we have chosen Validation(T_i) rather than Start(T_i) as the timestamp of transaction T_i is because we can expect better response time provided that conflict rates among transactions are indeed low.

The validation test for transaction T_j requires that for all transactions T_i with $TS(T_i) < TS(T_j)$ one of the following two conditions must hold:

1. $Finish(T_i) < Start(T_j)$. Since T_i completes its execution before T_j started, the serializability order is indeed maintained.

2. The set of data items written by T_i does not intersect with the set of data items read by T_j, and T_i completes its write phase before T_j starts its validation phase ($Start(T_j) < Finish(T_i) < Validation(T_j)$). This condition ensures that the writes of T_i and T_j do not overlap. Since the writes of T_i do not affect the read of T_j, and since T_j cannot affect the read of T_i, the serializability order is indeed maintained.

To illustrate, consider again transactions T_{17} and T_{18}. Suppose that $TS(T_{17}) < TS(T_{18})$. Then the validation phase succeeds in producing schedule 14, which is depicted in Figure 11.27. Observe that this schedule is serializable, but it cannot be produced either by the two-phase locking protocol or by the timestamp-ordering scheme.

The validation scheme automatically guards against cascading rollbacks since the actual writes take place only after the transaction issuing the write has committed.

11.6 Multiple Granularity

In the concurrency control schemes described thus far, we have used each individual data item as the unit on which synchronization is performed.

There are circumstances, however, where it would be advantageous to group several data items and treat them as one individual synchronization unit. For example, if a transaction T_i needs to access the entire database,

T_{17}	T_{18}
read(B)	
	read(B)
	$B := B - 50$
	write(B)
	read(A)
	$A := A + 50$
	write(A)
read(A)	
display($A + B$)	
	display($A + B$)

Figure 11.27   Schedule 14, a schedule produced using validation.

and a locking protocol is used, then T_i must lock each item in the database. Clearly, this is time-consuming. It would be better if T_i could issue a *single* lock request to lock the entire database. On the other hand, if transaction T_j needs to access only a few data items, it should not be required to lock the entire database, since otherwise concurrency is lost.

What is needed is a mechanism to allow the system to define multiple levels of *granularity*. This can be accomplished by allowing data items to be of various sizes and define a hierarchy of data granularities, where the small granularities are nested within larger ones. Such a hierarchy can be represented graphically as a tree. Note that the tree we describe here is significantly different from that used by the tree protocol (Section 11.3.3). A nonleaf node of the multiple granularity tree represents the data associated with its descendants. In the tree protocol, each node is an independent data item.

To illustrate, consider the tree of Figure 11.28 consisting of four levels of nodes. The highest level represents the entire database. Below it are nodes of type *area*. Each area in turn has nodes of type *file* as its descendants. Finally, each file has nodes of type *record*.

Each node in the tree can be locked individually. As in the two-phase locking protocol, we shall use *shared* and *exclusive* lock modes. When a transaction locks a node, in either *shared* or *exclusive* mode, this implies that the transaction also has locked all the descendants of that node in the same lock mode. For example, if transaction T_i explicitly locks file F_c of Figure 11.28, in exclusive mode, then it has locked *implicitly* in exclusive

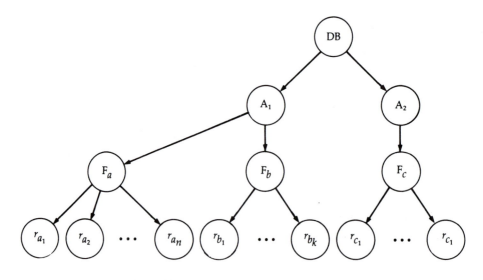

Figure 11.28   Granularity hierarchy.

mode all the records belonging to that file. It need not lock the individual records of F_c *explicitly*.

Suppose that transaction T_j wishes to lock record r_{b_6} of file F_b. Since T_i has locked F_b explicitly, it follows that r_{b_6} is also locked (implicitly). But, when T_j issues a lock request for r_{b_6}, r_{b_6} is not explicitly locked! How does the system determine whether T_j can lock r_{b_6} or not? To do so, T_j must traverse the tree from the root to record r_{b_6}. If any node in that path is locked in an incompatible mode, then T_j must be delayed.

Suppose now that transaction T_k wishes to lock the entire database. To do so, it simply must lock the root of the hierarchy. Note, however, that T_k should not succeed in locking the root node, since T_i is currently holding a lock on part of the tree (specifically, file F_b). But how does the system determine this? One possibility is to search the entire tree. This, however, defeats the whole purpose of the multiple granularity locking scheme. A more efficient way to achieve this is to introduce a new class of lock modes, called *intention* lock modes. If a node is locked in an intention mode, it implies that explicit locking is being done at a lower level of the tree (that is, at a finer granularity). Intention locks are put on all the ancestors of a node before that node is locked explicitly. Thus, a transaction need not not search the entire tree to determine whether it can lock a node successfully or not. To accomplish this, a transaction wishing to lock a node, say Q, must traverse a path in the tree from the root to Q. While traversing the tree, the transaction locks the various nodes in an intention mode.

There is an intention mode associated with *shared* mode and one with *exclusive* mode. If a node is locked in *intention-shared* mode (denoted by IS), this implies that explicit locking is being done at a lower level of the tree but only with shared-mode locks. Similarly, if a node is locked in *intention-exclusive* mode (denoted by IX), then explicit locking is being done at a lower level with exclusive-mode or shared-mode locks. Finally, if a node is locked in *shared and intention-exclusive* mode (denoted by SIX), this implies that the subtree rooted by that node is locked explicitly in shared mode and that explicit locking is being done at a lower level with exclusive-mode locks. The compatibility function for these lock modes is presented in Figure 11.29.

The multiple granularity locking protocol presented below ensures serializability. Each transaction T_i can lock a node Q, using the following rules:

1. The lock compatibility function of Figure 11.29 must be observed.

2. The root of the tree must be locked first, and may be locked in any mode.

3. A node Q can be locked by T_i in S or IS mode only if the parent of Q is currently locked by T_i in either IX or IS mode.

	IS	IX	S	SIX	X
IS	true	true	true	true	false
IX	true	true	false	false	false
S	true	false	true	false	false
SIX	true	false	false	false	false
X	false	false	false	false	false

Figure 11.29   Compatibility matrix.

4. A node Q can be locked by T_i in X, SIX, or IX mode only if the parent of Q is currently locked by T_i in either IX or SIX mode.

5. T_i can lock a node only if it has not previously unlocked any node (that is, T_i is two-phase).

6. T_i can unlock a node Q only if none of the children of Q are currently locked by T_i.

Observe that the multiple granularity protocol requires that locks be acquired in top-down (root-to-leaf) order, while locks are released in bottom-up (leaf-to-root) order.

To illustrate the protocol, consider the tree of Figure 11.28 and the following transactions:

- Let transaction T_{19} read record r_{a_2} in file F_a. T_{19} needs to lock the database, area A_1, and F_a in IS mode (and in that order), and then lock r_{a_2} in S mode.

- Let transaction T_{20} modify record r_{a_9} in file F_a. T_{20} needs to lock the database, area A_1, and file F_a in IX mode, and then lock r_{a_9} in X mode.

- Let transaction T_{21} read all the records in file F_a. T_{21} needs to lock the database and area A_1 in IS mode and then lock F_a in S mode.

- Let transaction T_{22} read the entire database. T_{22} can do so by locking the database in S mode.

We note that transactions T_{19}, T_{21}, and T_{22} can access the database concurrently. Transaction T_{20} can execute concurrently with T_{19} but not with either T_{21} or T_{22}.

This protocol enhances concurrency and reduces lock overhead. This is particularly useful in applications that include a mix of:

- Short transactions that access only a few data items.

- Long transactions that produce reports from an entire file or set of files.

There is a similar locking protocol which is applicable to database systems in which data granularities are organized in the form of a directed acyclic graph. We refer the interested reader to the bibliographic notes for additional references. Deadlock is possible in the protocol presented above, as was the case for the two-phase locking protocol. There are techniques to reduce deadlock frequency in the multiple granularity protocol and to eliminate deadlock entirely. These techniques are referenced in the bibliographic notes.

11.7 Multiversion Schemes

The concurrency control schemes discussed thus far ensure serializability by either delaying an operation or aborting the transaction that issued the operation. For example, a **read** operation may be delayed because the appropriate value has not been written yet; or it may be rejected (that is, the issuing transaction must be aborted) because the value it was supposed to read has already been overwritten. These difficulties could be avoided if old copies of each data item are kept in a system.

In *multiversion* database systems, each **write**(Q) operation creates a new version of Q. When a **read**(Q) operation is issued, the system selects one of the versions of Q to be read. The concurrency control scheme must ensure that the selection of the version to be read is done in a manner that ensures serializability. It is also crucial, for performance reasons, that a transaction can determine easily and quickly which version of the data item should be read.

The most common technique used among multiversion schemes is timestamping. With each transaction T_i in the system, we associate a unique static timestamp, denoted by $TS(T_i)$. This timestamp is assigned in the same manner as described in Section 11.4.

With each data item Q, a sequence of versions $<Q_1, Q_2, \ldots, Q_m>$ is associated. Each version Q_k contains three data fields:

- **Content**, the value of version Q_k.

- **W-timestamp**(Q_k), which denotes the timestamp of the transaction that created version Q_k.

- **R-timestamp**(Q_k), which denotes the largest timestamp of any transaction that successfully read version Q_k.

A transaction, say T_i, creates a new version Q_k of data item Q by issuing a **write**(Q) operation. The content field of the version holds the value written by T_i. The W-timestamp and R-timestamp are initialized to $TS(T_i)$. The R-timestamp value is updated whenever a transaction T_j reads the content of Q_k, and R-timestamp(Q_k) < $TS(T_j)$.

The multiversion timestamp scheme presented below ensures serializability. The scheme operates as follows. Suppose that transaction T_i issues a **read**(Q) or **write**(Q) operation. Let Q_k denote the version of Q whose write timestamp is the largest write timestamp less than $TS(T_i)$.

1. If transaction T_i issues a **read**(Q), then the value returned is that of the content of version Q_k.

2. If transaction T_i issues a **write**(Q), and if $TS(T_i) < $ R-timestamp(Q_k), then transaction T_i is rolled back; otherwise a new version Q is created.

The justification for rule 1 is clear. A transaction reads the most recent version that comes before it in time. The second rule forces a transaction to abort if it is "too late" in doing a write. More precisely, if T_i attempts to write a version that some other transaction would have read, then we cannot allow that write to succeed.

The scheme has the desirable property that a read request never fails and is never made to wait. In typical database systems, where reading is a more frequent operation than writing, this advantage may be of major practical significance.

The scheme, however, suffers from two undesirable properties. First, the reading of a data item also requires the updating of the R-timestamp field, resulting in two potential disk accesses rather than one. Second, the conflicts between transactions are resolved through rollbacks rather than waits. This may be quite expensive. An algorithm to alleviate this problem is referenced in the bibliographic notes.

11.8 Insert and Delete Operations

Until now, we have restricted our attention to **read** and **write** operations. This restriction limits transactions to data items already in the database. Some transactions require not only access to existing data items, but also the ability to create new data items. Others require the ability to delete data items. In order to examine how such transactions affect concurrency control, we introduce the following additional operations:

- **delete**(Q), which deletes data item Q from the database.

- **insert**(Q), which inserts a new data item Q into the database and assigns Q an initial value.

An attempt by a transaction T_i to perform a **read**(Q) operation after Q has been deleted results in a logical error in T_i. Likewise, an attempt by a transaction T_i to perform a **read**(Q) operation before Q has been inserted results in a logical error in T_i. It is also a logical error to attempt to delete a nonexistent data item.

11.8.1 Deletion

In order to understand how the presence of **delete** instructions affects concurrency control, we must decide when a **delete** instruction conflicts with another instruction. Let I_i and I_j be instructions of T_i and T_j, respectively, that appear in schedule S in consecutive order. Let $I_i =$ **delete**(Q). We consider several instructions I_j below:

- $I_j =$ **read**(Q). I_i and I_j conflict. If I_i comes before I_j, T_j will have a logical error. If I_j comes before I_i, T_j can execute the **read** operation successfully.

- $I_j =$ **write**(Q). I_i and I_j conflict. If I_i comes before I_j, T_j will have a logical error. If I_j comes before I_i, T_j can execute the **write** operation successfully.

- $I_j =$ **delete**(Q). I_i and I_j conflict. If I_i comes before I_j, T_j will have a logical error. If I_j comes before I_i, T_i will have a logical error.

- $I_j =$ **insert**(Q). I_i and I_j conflict. Suppose that data item Q did not exist prior to the execution of I_i and I_j. Then, if I_i comes before I_j, a logical error results for T_i. If I_j comes before I_i, then no logical error results. Likewise, if Q existed prior to the execution of I_i and I_j, then a logical error results if I_j comes before I_i, but not otherwise.

We can conclude from this that, if two-phase locking is used, an exclusive lock is required on a data item before it can be deleted. Under the timestamp-ordering protocol, a test similar to that for a **write** must be performed. Suppose that transaction T_i issues **delete**(Q).

- If $TS(T_i) <$ R-timestamp(Q), then this implies that the value of Q that T_i was to delete has already been read by a transaction T_j with $TS(T_j) > TS(T_i)$. Hence, the **delete** operation is rejected and T_i is rolled back.

- If $TS(T_i) <$ W-timestamp(Q), then this implies that a transaction T_j with $TS(T_j) > TS(T_i)$ has written Q. Hence, this **delete** operation is rejected and T_i is rolled back.

- Otherwise, the **delete** is executed.

11.8.2 Insertion

We have already seen that an **insert**(Q) operation conflicts with a **delete**(Q) operation. Similarly, **insert**(Q) conflicts with a **read**(Q) operation or a **write**(Q) operation. No **read** or **write** can be performed on a data item before it exists.

Since an **insert**(Q) assigns a value to data item Q, an **insert** is treated similarly to a **write** for concurrency control purposes:

- Under the two-phase locking protocol, if T_i performs an **insert**(Q) operation, T_i is given an exclusive lock on the newly created data item Q.

- Under the timestamp-ordering protocol, if T_i performs an **insert**(Q) operation, the values R-timestamp(Q) and W-timestamp(Q) are set to TS(T_i).

11.8.3 The Phantom Phenomenon

Consider a transaction T_{23}, which executes the following SQL query on the bank database:

> **select sum**(*balance*)
> **from** *deposit*
> **where** *branch-name* = "Perryridge"

Transaction T_{23} requires access to all tuples of the *deposit* relation pertaining to the Perryridge branch.

Let T_{24} be a transaction which executes the following SQL insertion:

> **insert into** *deposit*
> **values** ("Perryridge", 9732, "Smith", 1200)

Let S be a schedule involving T_{23} and T_{24}. We expect there to be potential for a conflict for the following reasons:

- If T_{23} uses the tuple newly inserted by T_{24} in computing **sum**(*balance*), then T_{23} read a value written by T_{24}. Thus, in a serial schedule equivalent to S, T_{24} must come before T_{23}.

- If T_{23} does not use the tuple newly inserted by T_{24} in computing **sum**(*balance*), then in a serial schedule equivalent to S, T_{23} must come before T_{24}.

The second of these two cases is curious. T_{23} and T_{24} do not access any tuple in common, yet they conflict with each other! In effect, T_{23} and T_{24} conflict on a "phantom" tuple. Thus, the phenomenon we have just described is called the *phantom phenomenon*. If concurrency control is performed at the tuple granularity, this conflict would go undetected. In order to prevent the phantom phenomenon, it is necessary to allow T_{23} to prevent other transactions from creating new tuples in the *deposit* relation with *branch-name* = "Perryridge." We shall consider two approaches to the problem: use of a coarser granularity, and index locking.

We could require that the granularity of data for concurrency control be relations rather than tuples. T_{23} would then have to lock the *deposit* relation in shared mode, while T_{24} would have to lock it in exclusive mode. Thus, T_{23} and T_{24} would conflict on a "real" data item rather than on a phantom. There is a major disadvantage to this approach, however. A significant amount of concurrency is lost by switching to a coarser granularity.

A better solution to the phantom phenomenon is the *index-locking* technique. Any transaction that inserts a tuple into a relation must insert information into every index maintained on the relation. We eliminate the phantom phenomenon by imposing a locking protocol for indices.

As we saw in Chapter 8, every search-key value is associated with either an index record or a bucket. A query will usually use one or more indices to access a relation. An insert must insert the new tuple in all indices on the relation. In our example, assume there is an index on *deposit* for *branch-name*. Then T_{24} must modify the Perryridge bucket. If T_{23} read the Perryridge bucket to locate all tuples pertaining to the Perryridge branch, then T_{23} and T_{24} conflict on that bucket.

The index-locking protocol takes advantage of the availability of indices on a relation by turning instances of the phantom phenomenon into conflicts on locks on index buckets. The protocol operates as follows:

- Every relation must have at least one index.

- A transaction T_i may lock a tuple t_i of a relation in S-mode only if it holds an S-mode lock on an index bucket that contains a pointer to t_i.

- A transaction T_i may lock a tuple t_i of a relation in X-mode only if it holds an X-mode lock on an index bucket that contains a pointer to t_i.

- A transaction T_i may not insert a tuple t_i into a relation r without updating all indices to r. T_i must obtain locks in X-mode on all index buckets it modifies.

- The rules of the two-phase locking protocol must be observed.

Variants of the index-locking technique exist for eliminating the phantom phenomenon under the other concurrency control protocols presented in this chapter.

11.9 Summary

When several transactions execute concurrently in the database, the consistency of data may no longer be preserved. It is necessary for the system to control the interaction among the concurrent transactions, and this control is achieved through one of a variety of mechanisms which are commonly referred to as *concurrency control* schemes.

A transaction is a unit that preserves consistency. We therefore require that any schedule produced by processing a set of transactions concurrently will be computationally equivalent to a schedule produced by running these transactions serially in some order. A system that guarantees this property is said to ensure *serializability*. There are a number of different forms of equivalence leading to the notions of *conflict serializability* and *view serializability*.

In order to determine whether serializability is maintained, we must construct a *precedence graph*. In the case where a transaction must read a data item before it can write into it, testing can be done by searching for a cycle in the graph which can be done in order n^2 time. In the case where a transaction writes onto a data item without first reading that item, testing can be done in order 2^n time by constructing a *labeled precedence graph* and searching for all possible distinct labeled graphs for a cycle.

In order to ensure serializability, a number of different concurrency control schemes can be used. All these do so by either delaying an operation or aborting the transaction that issued the operation. The most common ones are *locking protocols*, *timestamp-ordering* schemes, *validation* techniques, and *multiversion* schemes.

A locking protocol is a set of rules which state when a transaction may lock and unlock each of the data items in the database. The *two-phase* locking protocol allows a transaction to lock a new data item only if it has not yet unlocked any data item. The protocol ensures serializability but not deadlock freedom. In the absence of information concerning the manner in which data items are accessed, the two-phase locking protocol is both necessary and sufficient for ensuring serializability.

A timestamp-ordering scheme ensures serializability by selecting an ordering in advance between every pair of transactions. A unique fixed timestamp is associated with each transaction in the system. The timestamps of the transactions determine the serializability order. Thus, if the timestamp of transaction T_i is smaller than the timestamp of transaction T_j, then the scheme ensures that the produced schedule is equivalent to a serial schedule in which transaction T_i appears before transaction T_j. This is done by rolling back a transaction whenever such an order is violated.

A validation scheme is an appropriate concurrency control method in cases where the majority of transactions are read-only transactions, and thus the rate of conflicts among these transactions may be very low. A unique fixed timestamp is associated with each transaction in the system. The serializability order is determined by the timestamp of the transaction. A transaction in this scheme is never delayed. It must, however, pass a validation test, in order to complete. If it does not pass the validation test, it is rolled back to its initial state.

A multiversion concurrency control scheme assumes that each **write**(Q) operation creates a new version of Q. When a **read**(Q) operation is issued, the system selects one of the versions of Q to be read. The concurrency control scheme ensures that the selection of the version to be read is done in a manner that ensures serializability. This is accomplished through the use of timestamps. A read operation always succeeds, while a write operation may result in the rollback of the transaction.

There are circumstances where it would be advantageous to group several data items and treat them as one aggregate data item for purposes of working, resulting in multiple levels of *granularity*. This can be accomplished by allowing data items of various sizes and defining a hierarchy of data items, where the small items are nested within larger ones. Such a hierarchy can be represented graphically as a tree. Locks are acquired in root-to-leaf order, while locks are released in leaf-to-root order. The protocol ensures serializability but not freedom from deadlock.

A **delete** operation may be performed only if the transaction deleting the tuple has an exclusive lock on the tuple to be deleted. A transaction that inserts a new tuple into the database is given an X-mode lock on the tuple. Insertions can lead to the *phantom phenomenon*, in which an insertion conflicts with a query even though the two transactions may access no tuple in common. The index-locking technique solves this problem by requiring locks on certain index buckets. These locks ensure that all conflicting transactions conflict on a "real" data item rather than on a phantom.

Exercises

11.1 Explain the concept of transaction atomicity.

11.2 Consider the following two transactions:

$$
\begin{aligned}
T_0: \quad &\textbf{read}(A); \\
&\textbf{read}(B); \\
&\textbf{if } A = 0 \textbf{ then } B := B + 1; \\
&\textbf{write}(B). \\
T_1: \quad &\textbf{read } (B); \\
&\textbf{read } (A); \\
&\textbf{if } B = 0 \textbf{ then } A := A + 1; \\
&\textbf{write}(A).
\end{aligned}
$$

Let the consistency requirement be $A = 0 \lor B = 0$, with $A = B = 0$ the initial values.

    a. Show that every serial execution involving these two transactions preserves the consistency of the database.

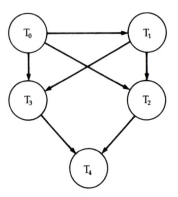

Figure 11.30   Precedence graph.

   b. Show a concurrent execution of T_0 and T_1 which produces a
   nonserializable schedule.

   c. Is there a concurrent execution of T_0 and T_1 which produces a
   serializable schedule?

11.3 Since every conflict serializable schedule is view serializable, why
do we emphasize conflict serializability rather than view
serializability?

11.4 Consider the precedence graph of Figure 11.30. Is the
corresponding schedule conflict serializable? Explain your answer.

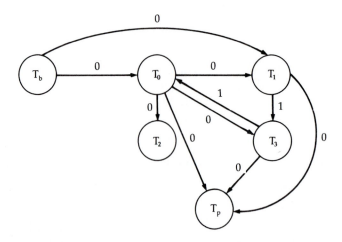

Figure 11.31   Labeled precedence graph.

11.5 Consider the labeled precedence graph of Figure 11.31. Is the corresponding history view serializable? Explain your answer.

11.6 Testing for conflict serializability is not a practical method for dealing with the serializability issue. Nevertheless, it is covered in great detail in this chapter. Can you guess why?

11.7 Show that the two-phase locking protocol ensures conflict serializability.

11.8 Add lock and unlock instructions to transactions T_0 and T_1 of Exercise 11.2 so that they observe the two-phase locking protocol. Can the execution of these transactions result in a deadlock? Show how two-phase locking avoids the nonserializable schedule of Exercise 11.2b.

11.9 Consider the following extension to the tree-locking protocol which allows both shared and exclusive locks:

- A transaction can be either a read-only transaction in which case it can request only shared locks, or an update transaction in which case it can request only exclusive locks.

- Each transaction must follow the rules of the tree protocol. Read-only transactions may lock any data item first, while update transactions must lock the root first.

Show that the protocol ensures serializability and deadlock freedom.

11.10 Consider a database organized in the form of a rooted tree. Suppose that we insert a dummy vertex between each pair of vertices. Show that if we follow the tree protocol on the new tree, we get more concurrency than if we follow the tree protocol on the original tree.

11.11 Consider the following graph-based locking protocol which allows only exclusive lock modes and which operates on data graphs which are in the form of a rooted directed acyclic graph.

- A transaction can lock any vertex first.

- To lock any other vertex, the transaction must be holding a lock on the majority of the parents of the vertex.

Show that the protocol ensures serializability and deadlock freedom.

11.12 Show that there are schedules possible under the tree protocol that are not possible under the two-phase locking protocol, and vice versa.

11.13 Consider the following graph-based locking protocol which allows only exclusive lock modes and which operates on data graphs which are in the form of a rooted directed acyclic graph.

- A transaction can lock any vertex first.

- To lock any other vertex, the transaction must have visited all the parents of that vertex and must be holding a lock on one of the parents of the vertex.

Show that the protocol ensures serializability and deadlock freedom.

11.14 Consider a variant of the tree protocol called the *forest* protocol. The database is organized as a forest of rooted trees. Each transaction T_i must follow the following rules:

- The first lock in each tree may be on any data item.

- The second, and all subsequent locks in a tree may be requested only if the parent of the requested mode is currently locked.

- Data items may be unlocked at any time.

- A data item may not be relocked by T_i after it has been unlocked by T_i.

Show that the forest protocol does not ensure serializability.

11.15 Consider a database system which includes an atomic **increment** operation in addition to the **read** and **write** operations. Let V be the value of data item X. The operation

$$\textbf{increment}(X) \text{ by } C$$

sets the value of X to $V + C$ in an atomic step. The value of X is not available to the transaction unless it executes a **read**(X). Figure 11.32 shows a lock compatibility matrix for three lock modes: share mode, exclusive mode, and incrementation mode.

a. Show that if all transactions lock data they access in the corresponding mode that two-phase locking ensures serializability.

b. Show that the inclusion of **increment** mode locks allows for increased concurrency. (Hint: Consider check-clearing transactions in our bank example.)

11.16 Consider the validation concurrency control scheme of Section 11.5. Show that by choosing Validation(T_i) rather than Start(T_i) as the timestamp of transaction T_i we can expect better response time provided that conflict rates among transactions are indeed low.

	S	X	I
S	true	false	false
X	false	false	false
I	false	false	true

Figure 11.32 Lock compatibility matrix.

11.17 Show that there are schedules that are possible under the two-phase locking protocol but are not possible under the timestamp protocol, and vice versa.

11.18 For each of the following protocols, describe aspects of practical applications that would lead you to suggest use of the protocol, and aspects that would suggest not using the protocol:

- two-phase locking

- two-phase locking with multiple granularity locking

- the tree protocol

- timestamp ordering

- validation

- multiversion timestamp ordering

11.19 Most implementations of database systems use two-phase locking. Suggest reasons for the popularity of this protocol.

11.20 Explain the phantom phenomenon. Why may this phenomenon lead to an incorrect concurrent execution despite the use of a protocol that ensures serializability?

11.21 Devise a timestamp-based protocol that avoids the phantom phenomenon.

Bibliographic Notes

The concept of serializability was formulated by Eswaran, et al. [1976] in connection to their work on concurrency control for System R. The results concerning serializability testing are from Papadimitriou et al. [1977], and Papadimitriou [1979]. Additional results are presented by Soisalon-Soininen and Wood [1982].

The two-phase locking protocol was introduced by Eswaran, et al. [1976]. The tree-locking protocol is from Silberschatz and Kedem [1980]. Other non-two-phase locking protocols that operate on more general graphs were developed by Yannakakis, et al. [1979], Kedem and Silberschatz [1983], and Buckley and Silberschatz [1985]. General discussions concerning locking protocols are offered by Lien and Weinberger [1978], Yannakakis, et al. [1979], Yannakakis [1981], and Papadimitriou [1982]. Korth [1983] explores various lock modes which can be obtained from the basic shared and exclusive lock modes. Various algorithms for concurrent access to dynamic search trees were developed by Bayer and Schkolnick [1977], Ellis [1980a, 1980b], Lehman and Yao [1981], and Manber and Ladner [1984]. Exercise 11.9 is from Kedem and Silberschatz [1983]. Exercise 11.10 is from Buckley and Silberschatz [1984]. Exercise 11.11 is from Kedem and Silberschatz [1979]. Exercise 11.12 is from Yannakakis, et al. [1979]. Exercise 11.13 is from Korth [1983].

The timestamp-based concurrency control scheme is from Reed [1983]. An exposition of various timestamp-based concurrency control algorithms is presented by Bernstein and Goodman [1980a]. A timestamp algorithm that does not require any rollback to ensure serializability is presented by Buckley and Silberschatz [1983]. The validation concurrency control scheme is from Kung and Robinson [1981]. A single site and distributed validation concurrency control scheme is presented by Bassiouni [1988].

The locking protocol for multiple granularity data items is from Gray, et al. [1975]. A detailed description is presented by Gray, et al. [1976]. The effects of locking granularity is discussed by Ries and Stonebraker [1977]. Korth [1983] formalizes multiple granularity locking for an arbitrary collection of lock modes (allowing for more semantics than simply read and write). This approach includes a class of lock modes called *update* modes to deal with lock conversion. Carey [1983] extends the multiple granularity idea to timestamp-based concurrency control. An extension of the protocol to ensure deadlock freedom is presented by Korth [1982].

Discussions concerning multiversion concurrency control are offered by Bernstein et al. [1983]. A multiversion tree locking algorithm appears in Silberschatz [1982]. Multiversion timestamp order was introduced in Reed [1978, 1983]. Lai and Wilkinson [1984] describes a multiversion two-phase locking certifier.

Several NP-completeness results exist for concurrency control. Papadimitriou [1979] shows that testing for serializability is NP-complete. Korth [1981] shows that minimizing the number of locks taken by transactions under multiple granularity locking is NP-complete. The theory of NP-completeness is presented in Aho, et al. [1974], and Garey and Johnson [1979].

A comprehensive survey paper is presented by Gray [1978]. Textbook discussions are offered by Bernstein et al. [1987] and Papadimitriou [1986].

12

Transaction Processing

In Chapter 10, we addressed issues of recovery and atomicity without considering concurrent transaction processing. In Chapter 11, we addressed concurrency control with only a brief consideration of recovery from failures. In this chapter, we address the construction of the transaction-processing component of the database manager. Thus, we consider issues of concurrency control and recovery together. We also discuss issues concerning interactive long-duration transactions.

12.1 Storage Model

As we discussed in Section 10.5, when a transaction executes a **write** instruction, the update is not necessarily written to disk. The **write** affects only a copy of the data item in the database buffer in main memory. The database itself is modified by a subsequent **output** operation performed by the system on a page of data. Likewise, log records are kept in main memory when they are created. Records are output to stable storage by the system according to the rules we presented in Section 10.5.1.

Regardless of the number of concurrent transactions, there is a single, shared database buffer and a single, shared log buffer. Each transaction has its own workspace in which it stores its copy of the data items it accessed. Typically, the transaction workspaces are stored in the virtual memory of the operating system. Figure 12.1 shows a typical storage model. The main memory holds three buffers:

- **System buffer**. This buffer holds pages of system object code and the local workspaces of active transactions. Data in the system buffer is under the control of the operating system's virtual memory manager.

- **Log buffer**. This buffer holds pages of log records until they are output to stable storage (see Section 10.5.1).

- **Database buffer**. This buffer, which holds pages of the database, is managed either by the database system or by the operating system (see Section 10.5.3). During a database dump, pages are output to archival stable storage.

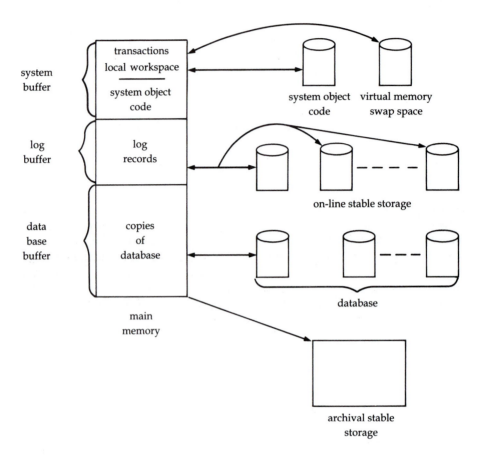

Figure 12.1   Storage Model

Secondary storage is partitioned into several categories:

- **System object code**, the code for the system itself.

- **Virtual memory swap space**, the disk space used to store those pages of local transactions' workspace that is not kept in main memory.

- **Online stable storage**, an approximation of stable storage that holds those log records required for recovery from failure of volatile storage.

- **Archival stable storage**, an offline approximation of stable storage holding data needed only for recovery from failure of nonvolatile storage.

This storage model is similar to the one we have used in Chapters 10 and 11. We emphasize that all transactions share the log buffer and the database buffer, but each transaction has its own local workspace. Online stable storage allows immediate recovery from system crashes and transaction failures. Since the loss of nonvolatile storage is less frequent, that part of the stable storage required only for recovery from such failures is kept offline.

Several alternatives to the model of Figure 12.1 are used in practice. Some or all of the buffers may be combined under the control of one buffer manager. In some applications, fast recovery from failure of nonvolatile storage is required. This is accomplished using *mirrored disks*, in which all database pages are stored twice on separate disks. Instead of storing the database on an array of disks, it is stored on an array of disk pairs. One such pair is shown in Figure 12.2. A **read** operation may be directed to either disk (based on load). A **write** operation must write both disks in the pair. The **write** operation is not considered complete until both physical disk writes have completed. In the event that one disk in a pair fails, a new disk is allocated and data is copied to it as soon as possible to create a new second member of the pair.

To obtain greater resilience to failure, not only the disk but also the disk controller may be duplicated. In multiprocessor systems, at least two processors may be given physical access to each controller to provide resilience to processor failure. Figure 12.3 illustrates mirrored disks with pairs of controllers and processors.

12.2 Recovery from Transaction Failure

If a transaction T fails, for whatever reason, we may use the techniques of Chapter 10 to undo the changes made to the database by T. In a system

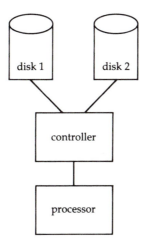

Figure 12.2   Mirrored disks with single controller and processor.

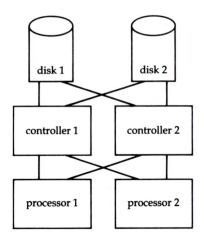

Figure 12.3   Mirrored disks with pairs of controllers and processors.

that allows concurrent execution, it is necessary also to ensure that any concurrent transaction T' that is dependent on T (that is, T' reads data written by T) is also aborted. In this section, we will see how this can be ensured.

12.2.1 Cascading Rollback

In order to recover correctly from the failure of a transaction T, it may be necessary to roll back several transactions. Such situations occur if transactions have read data written by T.

To illustrate this, consider the partial schedule of Figure 12.4. Transaction T_1, writes a value of A that is read by transaction T_2. Transaction T_2 writes a value of A that is read by transaction T_3. Suppose that, at this point, T_1 fails. T_1 must be rolled back. Since T_2 is dependent on T_1, T_2 must be rolled back. Since T_3 is dependent on T_2, T_3 must be

T_1	T_2	T_3
read(A)		
read(B)		
write(A)		
	read(A)	
	write(A)	
		read(A)

Figure 12.4   Partial schedule.

rolled back. This phenomenon, in which a single transaction failure leads to a series of transaction rollbacks, is called *cascading rollback*.

Cascading rollback may occur under two-phase locking. Figure 12.5 shows the partial schedule of Figure 12.4 with lock steps inserted. Notice that each transaction observes the two-phase locking protocol, but the failure of T_1 after the **read**(A) step of T_3 leads to cascading rollback of T_2 and T_3.

The timestamp-based protocol may result in cascading rollback. To illustrate, consider again the partial schedule of Figure 12.4. If the timestamps of transactions T_1, T_2, and T_3 are such that $TS(T_1) < TS(T_2) < TS(T_3)$, then this partial schedule is possible under the timestamp protocol. However, the validation protocol automatically guards against cascading rollbacks since the actual write of a data value by a transaction takes place only after the transaction issuing the write has committed.

Cascading rollback is undesirable since it leads to the undoing of a significant amount of work. It is useful to design protocols for transaction processing that do not have the potential of cascading rollback.

12.2.2 Recoverable Schedules

Consider the schedule of Figure 12.6 in which T_5 is a transaction that performs only one instruction, **read**(A). Suppose that the system allows T_5 to commit immediately after executing the **read**(A) instruction. Thus T_5 commits before T_4. Now suppose that T_4 fails before it commits. Since T_5 has read the value of data item A written by T_4, it is necessary to abort T_5 to ensure transaction atomicity. However, T_5 has already committed and

T_1	T_2	T_3
lock-X(A)		
read(A)		
lock-S(B)		
read(B)		
write(B)		
unlock(A)		
	lock-X(A)	
	read(A)	
	write(A)	
	unlock(A)	
		lock-S(A)
		read(A)

Figure 12.5   Partial schedule under two-phase locking.

T_4	T_5
read(A)	
write(A)	
	read(A)
read(B)	

Figure 12.6   Sample schedule.

cannot be aborted. Thus, we have a situation where it is impossible to recover correctly from the failure of T_4. Clearly, transaction-processing systems must ensure that it is possible to recover from the failure of any active transaction. Thus, nonrecoverable scenarios, such as the one described above, must be avoided.

The validation protocol ensures recoverability and avoids cascading rollbacks by ensuring that uncommitted writes cannot be read.

The timestamp protocol can be modified to prevent nonrecoverable executions and to avoid cascading rollbacks as follows: Associate a *commit bit* b_i with each transaction T_i. Initially b_i is *false*. When T_i commits, b_i is set to *true*. A transaction T_j that attempts to read a data item Q must satisfy the requirements of the timestamp protocol. If it does, then the commit bit of the transaction that was the last to write Q is checked. If this bit is *true*, the read by T_j is allowed. Otherwise, T_j must wait until the bit is set to true.

This modification to the timestamp protocol introduces waiting, but deadlock is not possible. To see this, observe that a transaction may wait only for a transaction with an earlier (smaller) timestamp. Thus, a cycle of waits is not possible.

Under two-phase locking, cascading rollback can be avoided by imposing an additional requirement that all exclusive locks taken by a transaction T must be held until T commits. This ensures that any data written by an uncommitted transaction is locked in exclusive mode, preventing any other transaction from reading the data.

This requirement is more stringent than the commit-bit scheme we used for the timestamp protocol since it restricts **write** instructions as well as **read** instructions.

12.2.3 Log Scanning

In Chapter 10, we used checkpoints to reduce the number of log records that must be scanned when the system recovers from a crash. Since we assumed no concurrency, it was necessary to consider only the following transactions during recovery:

- Those transactions that started after the last checkpoint

- The one transaction, if any, that was active at the time of the last checkpoint

The situation is more complex when transactions may execute concurrently since several transactions may have been active at the time of the last checkpoint.

In a concurrent transaction-processing system, we require that the checkpoint log record be of the form <**checkpoint** L>, where L is a list of transactions active at the time of the checkpoint. When the system recovers from a crash it constructs two lists: The *undo-list* consists of transactions to be undone and the *redo-list* consists of transactions to be redone.

These two lists are constructed on recovery as follows. Initially they are both empty. We scan the log backward, examining each record, until the first <**checkpoint**> record is found:

- For each record found of the form <T_i **commits**>, we add T_i to *redo-list*.

- For each record found of the form <T_i **starts**>, if T_i is not in *redo-list* then we add T_i to *undo-list*.

When all the appropriate log records have been examined, we check the list L. For each transaction T_i in L, if T_i is not in *redo-list* then we add T_i to the *undo-list*.

Once the redo-list and undo-list have have been constructed, the recovery proceeds as follows:

1. Re-scan the log from the most recent record backward and perform an **undo** for each log record that belongs transaction T_i on the *undo-list*.

2. Locate the last <**checkpoint** L> record on the log. Notice that this may involve scanning the log forward, in the case that the checkpoint record was passed in step 1.

3. Scan the log forward and perform **redo** for each log record that belongs to transaction T_i on the *redo-list*.

It is important in step 1 to process the log backward to ensure that the resulting state of the database is correct. To illustrate, consider the pair of log records

$$<T_i, A, 10, 20>$$
$$<T_j, A, 20, 30>$$

which represent a modification of data item A by T_i followed by a modification of A by T_j. If T_i and T_j are both on the *undo-list*, then A

should be restored to the value 10. This can be achieved if the log is processed backward since A is set first to 20 and then to 10. If the log were processed in the forward direction the result would be incorrect.

After all transactions on the *undo-list* have been undone, those transactions on the *redo-list* are redone. It is important in this case to process the log forward. When the recovery process has completed, transaction processing resumes.

12.3 Deadlock Handling

A system is in a deadlock state if there exists a set of transactions such that every transaction in the set is waiting for another transaction in the set. More precisely, there exists a set of waiting transactions $\{T_0, T_1, \ldots, T_n\}$ such that T_0 is waiting for a data item which is held by T_1, and T_1 is waiting for a data item which is held by T_2, and $\cdots$ and T_{n-1} is waiting for a data item which is held by T_n, and T_n is waiting for a data item which is held by T_0. The only remedy to this undesirable situation is for the system to invoke some drastic action, such as rolling back some of the transactions involved in the deadlock.

There are two principal methods for dealing with the deadlock problem. We can use a *deadlock prevention* protocol to ensure that the system will *never* enter a deadlock state. Alternatively, we can allow the system to enter a deadlock state and then try to recover using a *deadlock detection and recovery* scheme. As we shall see, both methods may result in transaction rollback. Prevention is commonly used if the probability that the system would enter a deadlock state is relatively high; otherwise, detection and recovery should be used.

We note that a detection and recovery scheme requires overhead that includes not only the run time cost of maintaining the necessary information and executing the detection algorithm, but also the potential losses inherent in recovery from a deadlock.

12.3.1 Deadlock Prevention

There are a number of different schemes that can be used for deadlock prevention. The simplest scheme requires that each transaction locks all its data items before it begins execution. Moreover, either all are locked in one step or none are locked. There are two main disadvantages to these protocols. First, *data item utilization* may be very low, since many of the data items may be locked but unused for a long period of time. Second, *starvation* is possible. A transaction that needs several popular data items may have to wait indefinitely while at least one of the data items that it needs is always allocated to some other transaction.

Another method for preventing deadlocks is to impose a partial ordering of all data items and require that a transaction can lock a data item only in the order specified by the partial order. We have seen one such scheme in the tree protocol.

Another approach for preventing deadlocks is to use preemption and transaction rollbacks. To control the preemption, we assign a unique timestamp to each transaction. These timestamps are used to decide whether a transaction should wait or roll back. If a transaction is rolled back, it retains its *old* timestamp when restarted. Two different deadlock prevention schemes using timestamps have been proposed:

- The **wait-die** scheme is based on a nonpreemptive technique. When transaction T_i requests a data item currently held by T_j, T_i is allowed to wait only if it has a smaller timestamp than that of T_j (that is, T_i is older than T_j). Otherwise, T_i is rolled back (dies). For example, suppose that transactions T_6, T_7, and T_8 have timestamps 5, 10, and 15 respectively. If T_6 requests a data item held by T_7, T_6 will wait. If T_8 requests a data item held by T_7, T_8 will be rolled back.

- The **wound-wait** scheme is based on a preemptive technique and is a counterpart to the *wait-die* scheme. When transaction T_i requests a data item currently held by T_j, then T_i is allowed to wait only if it has a larger timestamp than T_j (that is, T_i is younger than T_j). Otherwise, T_j is rolled back (T_j is *wounded* by T_i). Returning to our previous example, with transactions T_6, T_7, and T_8, if T_6 requests a data item held by T_7, then the data item will be preempted from T_7 and T_7 will be rolled back. If T_8 requests a data item held by T_7, then T_8 will wait.

Both schemes avoid starvation. This follows from the fact that at any time, there is a transaction with the smallest timestamp. This transaction *cannot* be required to roll back in either scheme. Since timestamps always increase, and since transactions are *not* assigned new timestamps when they are rolled back, a transaction which is rolled back will eventually have the smallest timestamp. Thus, it will not be rolled back again.

There are, however, significant differences in the way the two schemes operate.

- In the *wait-die* scheme, an older transaction must wait for a younger one to release its data item. Thus, the older the transaction gets, the more it tends to wait. By contrast, in the *wound-wait* scheme, an older transaction never waits for a younger transaction.

- In the *wait-die* scheme, if a transaction T_i dies and is rolled back because it requested a data item held by transaction T_j, then T_i may reissue the same sequence of requests when it is restarted. If the data item is still held by T_j, then T_i will die again. Thus, T_i may die several times before acquiring the needed data item. Contrast this series of events with what happens in the *wound wait* scheme. Transaction T_i is wounded and rolled back because T_j requested a data item it holds. When T_i is restarted and requests the data item now being held by T_j, T_i waits. Thus, there may be fewer rollbacks in the *wound-wait* scheme.

The major problem with all these schemes is that some unnecessary rollbacks may occur.

12.3.2 Deadlock Detection and Recovery

If a system does not employ some protocol that ensures deadlock freedom, then a detection and recovery scheme must be used. An algorithm that examines the state of the system is invoked periodically to determine whether a deadlock has occurred. If it has, then the system must attempt to recover from the deadlock. In order to do so the system must:

- Maintain information about the current allocation of data items to transactions, as well as any outstanding data item requests.

- Provide an algorithm that uses this information to determine whether the system has entered a deadlock state.

- Recover from the deadlock when the detection algorithm determines that a deadlock exists.

In this section, we elaborate on the above issues.

Deadlock Detection

Deadlocks can be described precisely in terms of a directed graph called a *wait-for graph*. This graph consists of a pair $G = (V, E)$ where V is a set of vertices and E is a set of edges. The set of vertices consists of all the transactions in the system. Each element in the set E of edges is an

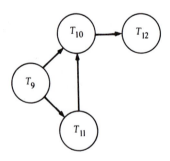

Figure 12.7   Wait-for graph with no cycle.

ordered pair $T_i \rightarrow T_j$. If $T_i \rightarrow T_j$ is in E, then there is a directed edge from transaction T_i to T_j, implying that transaction T_i is waiting for transaction T_j to release a data item that it needs.

When transaction T_i requests a data item currently being held by transaction T_j, then the edge $T_i \rightarrow T_j$ is inserted in the wait-for graph. This edge is removed only when transaction T_j is no longer holding a data item needed by transaction T_i.

A deadlock exists in the system if and only if the wait-for graph contains a cycle. Each transaction involved in the cycle is said to be deadlocked. In order to detect deadlocks, the system needs to maintain the wait-for graph and periodically invoke an algorithm that searches for a cycle in the graph.

To illustrate these concepts, consider the wait-for graph in Figure 12.7, which depicts the following situation:

- Transaction T_9 is waiting for transactions T_{10} and T_{11}.

- Transaction T_{11} is waiting for transaction T_{10}.

- Transaction T_{10} is waiting for transaction T_{12}.

Since the graph has no cycle, the system is not in a deadlock state.

Suppose now that transaction T_{12} is requesting an item held by T_{11}. The edge $T_{12} \rightarrow T_{11}$ is added to the wait-for graph, resulting in a new system state as depicted in Figure 12.8. This time, the graph contains the cycle:

$$T_{10} \rightarrow T_{12} \rightarrow T_{11} \rightarrow T_{10}$$

implying that transactions T_{10}, T_{11}, and T_{12} are all deadlocked.

Consequently, the question arises: When should we invoke the detection algorithm? The answer depends on two factors:

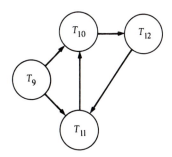

Figure 12.8 Wait-for graph with a cycle.

- How often does a deadlock occur?

- How many transactions will be affected by the deadlock?

If deadlocks occur frequently, then the detection algorithm should be invoked more frequently. Data items allocated to deadlocked transactions will be unavailable to other transactions until the deadlock can be broken. In addition, the number of cycles in the graph may also grow. In the worst case, we would invoke the detection algorithm every time a request for allocation cannot be granted immediately.

Recovery from Deadlock

When a detection algorithm determines that a deadlock exists, the system must *recover* from the deadlock. The most common solution is to roll back one or more transactions in order to break the deadlock. To do so, three issues need to be addressed:

- **Selecting a victim**. Given a set of deadlocked transactions, we must determine which transaction (or transactions) to roll back in order to break the deadlock. We should roll back those transactions that will incur the minimum cost. Unfortunately, the term "minimum cost" is not a precise one. Many factors may determine the cost of a rollback, including:

  1. How long the transaction has computed, and how much longer the transaction will compute before completing its designated task.

  2. How many data items the transaction has used.

  3. How many more data items the transaction needs in order to complete.

  4. How many transactions will be involved in the rollback.

- **Rollback**. Once we have decided that a particular transaction must be rolled back, we must determine how far this transaction should be rolled back. The simplest solution is a total rollback: Abort the transaction and then restart it. However, it is more effective to roll back the transaction only as far as necessary to break the deadlock. But this method requires the system to keep additional information about the state of all the running transactions. We refer the interested reader to the bibliographic notes section for relevant references.

- **Starvation**. In a system where the selecting of victims is based primarily on cost factors, it may happen that the same transaction is always picked as a victim. As a result, this transaction never completes its designated task. This situation is called *starvation*, and needs to be dealt with in any practical system. Clearly, we must ensure that transaction can be picked as a victim only a (small) finite number of times. The most common solution is to include the number of rollbacks in the cost factor.

12.4 Weak Levels of Consistency

In Chapter 11, the concept of serializability was presented and protocols were defined to ensure that only serializable schedules are possible. Serializability is a useful concept because it allows programmers to ignore issues related to concurrency when they code transactions. If every transaction has the property that it maintains database consistency if executed alone, then serializability ensures that concurrent executions maintain consistency. However, the protocols required to ensure serializability may allow too little concurrency for certain applications. In these cases, weaker levels of consistency are used. The use of weaker levels of consistency places additional burdens on programmers for ensuring database correctness.

12.4.1 Degree-Two Consistency

The purpose of degree-two consistency is to avoid cascading aborts without necessarily ensuring serializability. The locking protocol for degree-two consistency uses the same two lock modes as we used for the two-phase locking protocol: shared (S) and exclusive (X). A transaction must hold the appropriate lock mode when it accesses a data item.

In contrast to two-phase locking, S-locks may be released at any time and locks may be acquired at any time. Exclusive locks cannot be released until the transaction either commits or aborts. Serializability is not ensured by this protocol. Indeed, a transaction may read the same data item twice and obtain different results. In Figure 12.9, T_{13} reads the value of Q before and after it is written by T_{14}.

The potential for inconsistency under degree-two consistency makes it undesirable for many applications.

12.4.2 Cursor Stability

Cursor stability is a form of degree-two consistency designed for programs written in general-purpose, record-oriented languages such as Pascal, C, Cobol, PL/I, or Fortran. Such programs often iterate over the tuples of a relation. Rather than locking the entire relation, cursor stability ensures that:

- The tuple that is currently being processed by the iteration is locked in shared mode.

- Any modified tuples are locked in exclusive mode until the transaction commits.

T_{13}	T_{14}
lock-S(Q) read(Q) unlock(Q)	
	lock-X(Q) read(Q) write(Q) unlock(Q)
lock-S(Q) read(Q) unlock(Q)	

Figure 12.9   Nonserializable schedule with degree-two consistency.

These rules ensure that degree-two consistency is obtained. Two-phase locking is not required. Serializability is not guaranteed. Cursor stability is used in practice on heavily-accessed relations as a means of increasing concurrency and improving system performance. Applications that use cursor stability must be coded in a way that ensures database consistency despite the possibility of nonserializable schedules. Thus, the use of cursor stability is limited to specialized situations with very simple consistency constraints.

12.5 High-Performance Transaction Systems

In order to allow a high rate of transaction processing (hundreds or thousands of transactions per second), it is necessary to use high-performance hardware and exploit parallelism. This alone, however, is insufficient to obtain high performance in transaction processing for the following reasons:

- Many context switch operations (between the various transactions) are required within the operating system.

- Log records must be written to stable storage before buffer pages can be output to disk and before a transaction can commit. This results in a large number of writes to the disks used to simulate stable storage. These writes may delay transactions commitment and slow down buffer management.

In this section, we discuss some of the techniques used to allow the algorithms we have studied for transaction processing to execute correctly without imposing severe limitations on transaction performance.

12.5.1 Main Memory Databases

Usually, performance of database systems is limited by the speed at which data is read from and written to disk. The degree to which a database system is disk-bound can be reduced by increasing the size of the database buffer. Recent advances in main-memory technology have made it possible to construct large main memories at relatively low cost. Main memories as large as one gigabyte are now available. Such memories may be large enough to hold the entire database for some applications. For large databases (often a terabyte or more), main memory will not hold the entire database but it will hold a substantial amount of data.

Large main memories allow faster processing of transactions. However, there are some limitations:

- If the database buffer is large, the rate at which blocks are output to disk can be reduced significantly. As a result, a large number of blocks will be marked modified at the time a checkpoint is taken. Thus, the taking of a checkpoint becomes an extremely long process requiring the output of a large number of blocks to disk.

- If the system crashes, all of main memory is lost. Upon recovery, the system has an empty database buffer, and data items must be input from disk when they are accessed. Therefore, even after recovery is complete, it will take some time before we again have most of the database in main memory and high-speed processing of transactions can resume.

- Log records must be written to stable storage before a transaction is committed. The improved performance made possible by a large main memory may result in the logging process becoming a bottleneck. This can be alleviated by creating stable main memory using battery backup. The overhead imposed by logging can be reduced by the *group commit* technique discussed below.

12.5.2 Group Commit

The process of committing a transaction T requires at least two separate output operations to stable storage.

1. All log records associated with T must be output to main memory. This requires at least one, and possibly more, output operations.

2. The <T **commits**> log record must be output to stable storage.

These output operations frequently require the output of blocks that are only partially filled. In order to ensure that nearly full blocks are output, the *group commit* technique is used. Instead of attempting to commit T when T completes, the system waits until several transactions have completed. It then commits this group of transactions together. Blocks written to stable storage may contain records of several transactions. By careful choice of group size, the system can ensure that blocks are full when they are written to stable storage. This results, on average, in fewer output operations per committed transaction.

Although group commit reduces the overhead imposed by logging, this results in transactions being delayed in committing until a sufficiently large group of transactions are ready to commit. The delay is acceptable in high-performance transaction systems since it does not take much time for a group of transactions to be ready to commit.

12.5.3 Transaction Monitors

In order to reduce the overhead imposed on transaction processing by the operating system, a *transaction monitor* may be used. The transaction monitor provides scheduling of concurrent transactions, data transfer between the processor and users' terminals, and other transaction management activities within a single operating system process. This reduces the need for task switching the operating system and allows database and log buffers to be shared by concurrently executing transactions.

12.6 Concurrency in Index Structures

It is possible to treat access to index structures like any other database structure and apply transaction management techniques discussed in Chapters 10 and 11. However, there are special features of index structures that allow alternative approaches to be used:

- An index contains no unique data. That is, an index can be reconstructed from the database itself if a failure occurs.

- It is acceptable to have nonserializable concurrent access to an index as long as the accuracy of the index is maintained.

Below, we show a technique for managing concurrent access to B^+-trees. The bibliographic notes reference other techniques for B^+-trees as well as techniques for other index structures.

The technique we present for B^+-trees is based on locking, but neither two-phase locking nor the tree protocol will be employed. The algorithms for lookup, insertion, and deletion are those used in Chapter 8, with only minor modifications. We require that every node (not just the leaves) maintains a pointer to its right sibling. This pointer is required because a lookup that occurs while a node is being split may have to search not only that node but also its right sibling (if one exists). We shall illustrate this with an example after the modified procedures have been presented.

- **Lookup**. Each node of the B^+-tree must be locked in shared mode before it is accessed. This lock is released before any lock on any other node in the B^+-tree is requested. If a split (see below) occurs concurrently with a lookup, the desired search key value may no longer appear within the range of values represented by a node accessed during lookup. In such a case, the search-key value is represented by a sibling node, located by following the pointer to the right sibling.

- **Insertion and deletion**. The rules for lookup are followed to locate the node into which the insertion or deletion is to be made. The shared-mode lock on this node is upgraded to exclusive mode and the insertion or deletion is performed.

- **Split**. If a node is split, a new node is created according to the algorithm of Section 8.3. The right sibling pointers of both the original node and the new node are set. Following this, the exclusive lock on the original node is released and an exclusive lock is requested on the parent so that a pointer to the new node can be inserted.

- **Coalescence**. If a node has too few search-key values after a deletion, the node with which it will be coalesced must be locked in exclusive mode. Once these two nodes have been coalesced, an exclusive lock is requested on the parent so that the deleted node can be removed. At this point, the lock on the coalesced node is released. Unless the parent node must be coalesced also, its lock is released.

It is important to observe that an insertion or deletion may lock a node, unlock it, and subsequently relock it. Furthermore, a lookup that runs concurrently with a split or coalescence operation may find that the desired search key has been moved to the right sibling node by the split or coalescence operation.

To illustrate, consider the B^+-tree in Figure 12.10. Assume that there are two concurrent operations on this B^+-tree:

- Insert "Clearview"

- Lookup "Downtown"

Let us assume that the insertion operation begins first. It does a lookup on "Clearview," and finds that the node into which "Clearview" should be inserted is full. It therefore converts its shared lock on the node to exclusive mode and creates a new node. The original node now contains the search-key values "Brighton" and "Clearview." The new node contains the search-key value "Downtown."

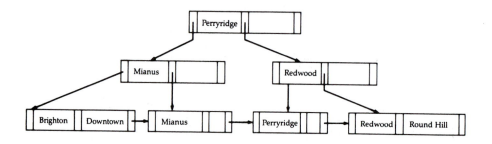

Figure 12.10   B$^+$-tree for *deposit* file with $n = 3$.

Now assume that a context switch occurs which results in control passing to the lookup operation. This lookup operation accesses the root and follows the pointer to the left child of the root. It then accesses that node and obtains a pointer to the left child. This left child node originally contained the search key values "Brighton" and "Downtown." Since this node is currently locked by the insertion operation in exclusive mode, the lookup operation must wait. Note that at this point, the lookup operation holds no locks at all!

The insertion operation now unlocks the leaf node and relocks its parent, this time in exclusive mode. It completes the insertion, leaving the B$^+$-tree as shown in Figure 12.11. The lookup operation proceeds. However, it is holding a pointer to the wrong leaf node. It therefore follows the right sibling pointer to locate the correct node. It can be shown that if a lookup holds a pointer to an incorrect node, then its right sibling must be the correct node.

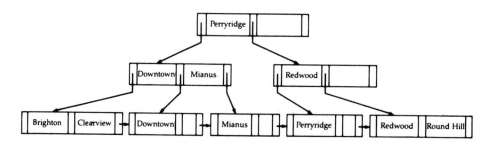

Figure 12.11   Insertion of "Clearview" into the B$^+$-tree of Figure 12.10.

Lookup and insertion operations cannot lead to deadlock. Deletion can lead to deadlock if a lookup has locked the parent of nodes being coalesced. The simplest way to avoid such deadlocks is to leave nodes uncoalesced. This results in nodes that contain too few search-key values and violate some properties of B^+-trees. However, since in most databases, insertions are more frequent than deletions, it is likely that nodes that have too few search-key values will gain additional values relatively quickly.

12.7 Transaction Definition in SQL

A data manipulation language must include a construct for specializing the set of actions that comprise a transaction. The SQL standard specifies that a transaction begins implicitly. Transactions end implicitly at the end of a "unit of work," or by one of the following SQL statements:

- **Commit work**, which commits the current transaction and begins a new one.

- **Rollback work**, which causes the current transaction to abort.

The standard also specifies that the system must ensure both serializability and freedom from cascading rollback. The definition of serializability used by the standard is that a schedule must have the "same effect" as a serial schedule. Thus, conflict and view serializability are both acceptable.

12.8 Long-duration Transactions

The transaction concept was developed initially in the context of data-processing applications in which most transactions are noninteractive and of short duration. Although the techniques presented here and earlier in Chapters 10 and 11 work well in those applications, serious problems arise when this concept is applied to database systems that involve human interaction. Such transactions have the following key properties:

- **Long duration**. Once there is any human interaction with an active transaction, that transaction becomes a long-duration transaction from the perspective of the computer, since human response time is slow relative to computer speed. Furthermore, in design applications, the human activity being modeled may involve hours, days, or an even longer period. Thus, transactions may be of long duration in human terms as well as machine terms.

- **Exposure of uncommitted data**. Data generated and displayed to a user by a long-duration transaction is uncommitted, since the transaction may abort. Thus, users, and as a result other transactions, may be forced to read uncommitted data. If several users are cooperating on a design, user transactions may need to exchange data prior to transaction commit.

- **Subtasks**. An interactive transaction may consist of a set of subtasks initiated by the user. The user may wish to abort a subtask without necessarily causing the entire transaction to abort.

- **Recoverability**. It is unacceptable to abort a long-duration interactive transaction because of a system crash. The active transaction must be recovered to a state that existed shortly before the crash so that relatively little human work is lost.

- **Performance**. Good performance in an interactive transaction system is defined as fast response time. This is in contrast to noninteractive systems, in which high throughput (number of transactions per second) is the goal. Systems with high throughput make efficient use of system resources. However, in the case of interactive transactions, the most costly "resource" is the user. To optimize the efficiency and satisfaction of the user, response time should be fast (from a human perspective). In those cases where a task takes a long time, response time should be predictable (that is, the variance in response times should be low) so that users can manage their time well.

In this section, we shall see why these five properties are incompatible with the techniques presented thus far, and discuss how those techniques can be modified to accommodate long-duration interactive transactions.

12.8.1 Nonserializable Executions

The properties discussed above make it impractical to enforce the requirement used in earlier chapters that only serializable schedules be permitted. Each of the concurrency control protocols of Chapter 11 have adverse effects on long-duration transactions:

- **Two-phase locking**. When a lock cannot be granted, the transaction requesting the lock is forced to wait for the data item in question to be unlocked. The duration of this wait is proportional to the duration of the transaction holding the lock. If the data item is locked by a short-duration transaction, we expect that the waiting time will be short (except in case of deadlock or extraordinary system load). However, if the data item is locked by a long-duration transaction, the wait will be of long duration. Long waiting times lead to both longer response time and an increased chance of deadlock.

- **Graph-based protocols**. Graph-based protocols allow for locks to be released earlier than under the two-phase locking protocols, and they prevent deadlock. However, they impose an ordering on the data items. Transactions must lock data items in a manner consistent with this ordering. As a result, a transaction may have to lock more data than it needs. Furthermore, a transaction must hold a lock until there is no chance that the lock will be needed again. Thus, long-duration lock waits are likely.

- **Timestamp-based protocols**. Timestamp protocols never require a transaction to wait. However, they do require transactions to abort under certain circumstances. If a long-duration transaction is aborted, a substantial amount of work is lost. For noninteractive transactions, this lost work is a performance issue. For interactive transactions, the issue is also one of user satisfaction. It is highly undesirable for a user to find that several hours' work has been undone.

- **Validation**. Like timestamp-based protocols, validation protocols enforce serializability by means of transaction abort.

Thus, it appears that the enforcement of serializability results in either long-duration waits, abort of long-duration transactions, or both. There are theoretical results cited in the bibliographic notes that substantiate this conclusion.

Further difficulties with the enforcement of serializability arise when we consider recovery issues. We previously discussed the problem of cascading rollback, in which the abort of a transaction may lead to the abort of other transactions. This phenomenon is undesirable, particularly for long-duration transactions. If locking is used, exclusive locks must be held until the end of the transaction if cascading rollback is to be avoided. This, however, increases the length of transaction waiting time.

Thus, it appears that the enforcement of transaction atomicity must either lead to an increased probability of long-duration waits or create a possibility of cascading rollback.

These considerations motivate the alternative concepts of correctness of concurrent executions and transaction recovery that we consider in the remainder of this section.

12.8.2 Concurrency Control

The fundamental goal of database concurrency control is to ensure that concurrent execution of transactions does not result in a loss of database consistency. The concept of serializability achieves this goal, since all serializable schedules preserve consistency of the database. However, not all schedules that preserve consistency of the database are serializable. Let us illustrate this by considering again a bank database consisting of two accounts A and B, with the consistency requirement that the sum $A + B$ be preserved. For example, although the schedule of Figure 12.12 is not conflict serializable, it nevertheless preserves the sum of $A + B$. It also illustrates two important points about the concept of correctness without serializability.

- Correctness depends on the specific consistency constraints for the database.

- Correctness depends on the properties of operations performed by each transaction.

It is of prohibitive computational cost to perform an automatic analysis of low-level operations by transactions and their potential effect on a fully specified database consistency constraint. However, there are simpler, less costly techniques. One is to use the database consistency constraints as the basis for a split of the database into subdatabases on which concurrency can be managed separately. Another is to treat some operations besides **read** and **write** as fundamental low-level operations and extend concurrency control to deal with them.

The bibliographic notes reference other techniques for ensuring consistency without requiring serializability. Many of these techniques exploit variants of multiversion concurrency control (see Section 11.7). For older data-processing applications that need only one version, multiversion protocols impose a high space overhead to store the extra versions. Since many of the new database applications require the maintenance of versions of data, concurrency control techniques that exploit multiple versions are practical.

T_{15}	T_{16}
read(A)	
$A := A - 50$	
write(A)	
	read(B)
	$B := B - 10$
	write(B)
read(B)	
$B := B + 50$	
write(B)	
	read(A)
	$A := A + 10$
	write(A)

Figure 12.12   A non-conflict-serializable schedule.

12.8.3 Nested Transactions

A long-duration transaction may be viewed as a collection of related subtasks or subtransactions. By structuring a transaction as a set of subtransactions, we are able to enhance parallelism, since it may be possible to run several subtransactions in parallel. Furthermore, it is possible to deal with failure of a subtransaction (due to abort, system crash, and so on) without having to roll back the entire long-duration transaction.

A nested transaction T is represented by a set $T' = \{t_1, t_2, \ldots, t_n\}$ of subtransactions and a partial order P on T. A subtransaction t_i in T may abort without forcing T to abort. Instead, T may either restart t_i or simply choose not to run t_i. If t_i commits, this does not make t_i permanent (unlike the situation in Chapter 10). Instead, t_i *commits to* T, and may still abort if T aborts. An execution of T must not violate the partial order P. That is, if an edge $t_i \rightarrow t_j$ appears in the precedence graph, then $t_j \rightarrow t_i$ must not be in the transitive closure of P.

Nesting may be several levels deep, representing a subdivision of a transaction into subtasks, sub-subtasks, and so on. At the lowest level of nesting, we have the standard database operations **read** and **write** that we have used previously.

Although the main practical value of nested transactions arises in complex, long-duration transactions, we shall use the simple example of Figure 12.12 to show how nesting can create higher-level operations that may enhance concurrency. We rewrite transaction T_{15} using subtransactions t_a and t_b that perform increment or decrement operations:

- T_{15} consists of:

  - t_a subtracts 50 from A

  - t_b adds 50 to B

Similarly, we rewrite transaction T_{16} using subtransactions t_c and t_d that perform increment or decrement operations:

- T_{16} consists of:

  - t_c subtracts 10 from B

  - t_d adds 10 to A

No ordering is specified on t_a, t_b, t_c, and t_d. Any execution of these subtransactions will generate a correct result. The schedule of Figure 12.12 corresponds to the schedule $<t_a, t_c, t_b, t_d>$.

12.8.4 Compensating Transactions

In Chapter 10, we used the **undo** operation in order to eliminate changes to the database made by an aborted transaction. The ensures the atomicity of transactions.

Adherence to this approach has adverse effects on long-duration transactions, as we saw in Section 12.8.1. In order to reduce the frequency of long-duration waiting, it is desirable for uncommitted updates to be exposed to other concurrently executing transactions. However, the exposure of uncommitted data creates the potential for cascading rollbacks.

The concept of *compensating transactions* deals with this problem by providing an alternative to the **undo** operation for recovery from transaction failure. Instead of strict undoing of all changes made by the failed transaction, special action is taken to "compensate" for the failure. We give several examples of compensation below.

- Consider the schedule of Figure 12.12, which we have shown to be correct, though not conflict serializable. Suppose T_{16} fails just prior to termination. Following the rules for **undo**, T_{16} and T_{15} would have to be undone. Instead, we can run a compensating transaction that subtracts 10 from A and adds 10 to B.

- Consider a database insert by transaction T_i that, as a side effect, causes a B^+-tree index to be updated. The insert operation may have modified several nodes of the B^+-tree index. Other transactions may have read these nodes in accessing data other than the record inserted by T_i. All of these transactions would be undone if the undo rule is followed. Instead, we can run a compensating transaction for T_i that deletes the record inserted by T_i. The result is a correct consistent B^+-tree, but not necessarily one with exactly the same structure as before T_i started.

- Consider a long-duration transaction T representing a travel reservation. Transaction T has three subtransactions: t_1, which makes airline reservations, t_2 which reserves rental cars, and t_3 which reserves a hotel room. Suppose the hotel cancels the reservation. Instead of undoing all of T, the failure of t_3 is compensated for by deleting the old reservation and making a new one.

Compensation for the failure of a transaction requires use of semantics of the failed transaction. For certain operations, like incrementation or insertion into a B^+-tree, the corresponding compensation is easily defined. For more complex transactions, the application programmers may have to define the correct form of compensation at the time the transaction is coded. For complex interactive transactions, it may be necessary for the system to interact with the user to determine the proper form of compensation.

12.8.5 Implementation Issues

The transaction concepts discussed in this section create serious difficulties for implementation. We present a few of them here and discuss how the problems may be addressed.

Long-duration transactions must survive system crashes. This can be achieved by performing a **redo** on committed subtransactions and performing either an **undo** or compensation for any short-duration subtransactions that were active at the time of the crash. However, this is only part of the problem. In typical database systems, such internal system data as lock tables and transactions timestamps are kept in volatile storage. For a long-duration transaction to be resumed after a crash, this data must be restored. Therefore, it is necessary to log not only changes to the database but also changes to internal system data pertaining to long-duration transactions.

Logging of updates is made more complex by the types of data items that may exist in the database. A data item may be a CAD design, text of a document, or another form of composite design. Such data items are physically large. Thus, storing both the old and new values of the data item in a log record is undesirable.

There are two approaches to reducing the overhead of ensuring the recoverability of large data items:

- **Operation logging**. Only the operation performed on the data item and the data item name are stored in the log. For each operation, an inverse operation must exist. **Undo** is performed using the inverse operation and **redo** is performed using the operation itself. Recovery through operation logging is more difficult, since **redo** and **undo** are not idempotent.

- **Logging and shadow paging**. Logging is used for modifications to small data items, but large data items are made recoverable using a shadow page technique (see Section 10.7). By using shadowing, only those pages that are actually modified need to be stored in duplicate.

Regardless of the technique used, the complexities introduced by long-duration transactions and large data items complicate the recovery process. Thus, it is desirable to allow certain noncritical data to be exempt from logging and to rely instead on offline backups and human intervention.

12.8.6 Temporal Constraints

The constraints we have considered until now pertain to the values stored in the database. In certain applications, the constraints include *deadlines* by which a task must be completed. Examples of such applications include plant management, traffic control, and scheduling. When deadlines are included, correctness of an execution is no longer solely an issue of database consistency. Rather, we are concerned with how many deadlines are missed and by how much time they are missed. Deadlines are characterized as:

- **Hard**. The task has zero value if it is completed after the deadline.

- **Soft**. The task has diminishing value if it is completed after the deadline, with the value approaching zero as the degree of lateness increases.

Systems with deadlines are called *real-time* systems.

Transaction management in real-time systems must take deadlines into account. If the concurrency control protocol determines that a transaction T must wait, it may cause T to miss its deadline. In such cases, it may be preferable to preempt the transaction holding the lock and allow T to proceed. Preemption must be used with care, however, because the time lost by the preempted transaction (due to rollback and restart) may cause it to miss its deadline.

Unfortunately, it is difficult to determine whether rollback or waiting is preferable in a given situation. The difficulty arises from the variance in transaction execution time. In the best case, all data accesses reference data in the database buffer. In the worst case, each access causes a buffer page to be written to disk (preceded by the requisite log records) followed by the reading from disk of the page containing the data to be accessed. Because the two or more disk accesses required in the worst case take several orders of magnitude more time than the main memory references required in the best case, transaction execution time can be estimated only very poorly.

The problems of real-time databases are not yet well understood. The bibliographic notes reference some initial research in this area.

12.9 Summary

Transaction processing is based upon a storage model in which main memory holds a log buffer, a database buffer, and a system buffer. The system buffer holds pages of system object code and local workspaces of transactions. Secondary storage includes the complete object code for the system, swap space for virtual memory, and the database itself. Stable storage that must be accessible online is simulated using mirrored disks which provide redundant data storage. Offline, or archival, stable storage may consist of multiple tape copies of data stored in a physically secure location.

Transaction failure may lead to cascading rollback of transactions that have read data written by a failed transaction. If cascading rollback results in the abort of an already committed transaction, then the schedule is said to be nonrecoverable. Recoverable schedules can be ensured, and cascading rollback avoided, under two-phase locking by requiring that locks be held by a transaction until it either commits or aborts.

Various locking protocols, including the multiple granularity locking scheme, do not guard against deadlocks. One way to prevent deadlock is to use preemption and transaction rollbacks. To control the preemption, we assign a unique timestamp to each transaction. These timestamps are used to decide whether a transaction should wait or roll back. If a transaction is rolled back, it retains its *old* timestamp when restarted. The *wait-die* and *wound-wait* schemes are two preemptive schemes. Another method for dealing with deadlock is to use a deadlock detection and recovery scheme. To do so, a *wait-for* graph is constructed. A system is in a deadlock state if and only if the wait-for graph contains a cycle. When a detection algorithm determines that a deadlock exists, the system must *recover* from the deadlock. This is accomplished by rolling back one or more transactions in order to break the deadlock.

Alternative notions of consistency that do not ensure serializability are sometimes used as a means to improve performance. Cursor stability and degree-two consistency ensure that no transaction may read data written by an uncommitted transaction. However, nonserializable executions are possible.

Large main memories are exploited in some systems to achieve high system throughput. In such systems, logging is a bottleneck. Under the group-commit concept, the number of outputs to stable storage can be reduced, thus releasing this bottleneck.

Special concurrency control techniques can be developed for special data structures. Often, special techniques are applied in B^+-trees to allow greater concurrency. These techniques allow nonserializable access to the B^+-tree but they ensure that the B^+-tree structure is correct, and may ensure that accesses to the database itself are serializable.

The efficient management of long-duration interactive transactions is more complex because of the long-duration waits, and the possibility of aborts. Since the concurrency control techniques used in Chapter 11 use either waits, aborts, or both, alternative techniques must be considered. These techniques must ensure correctness without requiring serializability. A long-duration transaction is represented as a nested transaction with atomic database operations at the lowest level. If a transaction fails, only active short-duration transactions abort. Active long-duration transactions resume once any short duration transactions have recovered. Recovery may be accomplished using the **undo** mechanism discussed in Chapter 10. However, it is often possible to use a compensating transaction instead of an **undo**. A compensating transaction corrects, or compensates for, the failure of a transaction without causing cascading rollback.

In systems with time constraints, correctness of execution involves not only database consistency but also the satisfaction of deadlines. The wide variance of execution times for **read** and **write** operations complicates the transaction management problem for time-constrained systems.

Exercises

12.1 Explain why a nonrecoverable schedule results in a loss of transaction atomicity.

12.2 Explain why cascading rollback is potentially costly.

12.3 Under the modified version of the timestamp protocol, we required that a commit bit be tested to see if a **read** request must wait. Why is this not necessary for **write** requests?

12.4 When the system recovers from a crash, in what order must transactions be undone and redone? Why is this order important?

12.5 Suppose that the system crashes during the time it is recovering from a prior crash. When the system again recovers, what action must be taken?

12.6 Under what conditions is it better to avoid deadlock than to allow deadlocks to occur and detect them?

12.7 If deadlock is avoided, is starvation still possible? Explain.

12.8 Explain the motivation for the use of degree-two consistency. What disadvantages are there?

12.9 Let T_1 and T_2 be transactions that each modify two data items. Assume 100 log records fit on one block. How many block writes are required if T_1 and T_2 are committed separately? How many are required if T_1 and T_2 are committed as a group?

12.10 Suppose we use the tree protocol of Section 11.3.3 to manage concurrent access to a B^+-tree. Since a split may occur on insert that affects the root, it appears that an insert operation cannot release any locks until it has completed the entire operation. Under what circumstances is it possible to release a lock earlier?

12.11 What is the purpose of compensating transactions? Present two examples of their use.

12.12 Suppose that we allow transactions to be nested within other transactions. Discuss the modifications that need to be made in each of the recovery schemes covered in this chapter.

Bibliographic Notes

Textbook presentations of transaction processing include Date [1983] and Bernstein et al. [1987]. Transaction processing issues are discussed in Garza and Kim [1988], Korth et al. [1988], Lynch et al. [1988], Kaiser [1990], and Weihl and Liskov [1990].

Dijkstra [1965] was one of the first and most influential contributors in the deadlock area. Holt [1971, 1972] was the first to formalize the notion of deadlocks in terms of a graph model similar to the one presented in this chapter. The timestamp deadlock detection algorithm is from Rosenkrantz et al. [1978]. An analysis of the probability of waiting and deadlock is presented by Gray et al. [1981b]. Theoretical results concerning deadlocks and serializability are presented by Fussell et al. [1981] and Yannakakis [1981].

Degree-two consistency was introduced in Gray et al [1975]. Concurrency in B^+-trees was studied partially by Bayer and Schkolnick [1977]. The technique presented in Section 12.4 is based on Kung and Lehman [1980] and Lehman and Yao [1981]. Related work includes Kwong and Wood [1982], Manber and Ladner [1984], and Ford and Calhoun [1984]. Shasha and Goodman [1988] present a good characterization of concurrency protocols for index structures. Ellis [1987] presents a concurrency control technique for linear hashing. Concurrent algorithms for other index structures appear in Ellis [1980a, 1980b].

Nested transactions are presented by Lynch [1983], Moss [1982, 1985], Lynch [1986], Lynch and Merritt [1986], Fekete et al. [1987, 1990], Korth and Speegle [1988], and Pu et al. [1988]. Performance issues are considered in Badrinath and Ramamritham [1990]. Relaxation of serializability is discussed in Garcia-Molina [1983] and Sha et al. [1988]. Recovery issues in nested transaction systems are discussed by Moss [1987], and Haerder and Rothermel [1987]. Gray [1981], Skarra and Zdonik [1989], and Korth and Speegle [1988, 1990] discuss long-duration transactions. Recovery issues for long duration are considered by Weikum and Schek [1984], Haerder and Rothermel [1987], Weikum et al. [1990], and Korth et al. [1990a].

Transaction processing issues in real-time databases are discussed by Abbot and Garcia-Molina [1988] and Dayal et al. [1990]. Complexity and correctness issues are addressed by Korth et al. [1990b].

13

Object-Oriented Model

The object-oriented model is based on the object-oriented programming paradigm. This approach to programming was first introduced by the language Simula 67, which was designed for programming simulations. More recently, the languages C++ and Smalltalk have become the most widely known object-oriented programming languages. We shall introduce the concepts of object-oriented programming and then consider the use of these concepts in the definition of a data model.

13.1 New Database Applications

The purpose of database systems is the management of large bodies of information. Early databases developed from file management systems. These systems evolved first into either network or hierarchical databases and, later, into relational databases. Among the common features of these "old" applications are:

- **Uniformity**. There are large numbers of similarly structured data items, all of which have the same size (in bytes).

- **Record orientation**. The basic data items consist of fixed-length records.

- **Small data items**. Each record is short. Often records are 80 bytes or less, reflecting the size of punched cards, as used in the 1960s. At most, records are a few hundred bytes long.

- **Atomic fields**. Fields within a record are short and of fixed length. There is no structure within fields. In other words, first normal form holds (see Chapter 6).

- **Short transactions**. Transactions are programs with an execution time measured in fractions of a second. There is no human interaction with a transaction during its execution. Instead, the user prepares a transaction, submits it for execution, and awaits the response.

- **Static conceptual schemes**. The database scheme is changed only infrequently. When it is changed, the types of change allowed are simple. In a relational system, the only scheme modifications typically allowed are create relation, remove relation, add attributes to a relation scheme, and remove attributes from a relation scheme.

In recent years, however, database technology has been applied to applications outside the realm of data processing that, in general, fail to have at least one of the above features. These new applications include:

- **Computer-aided design** (CAD). A CAD database stores data pertaining to an engineering design, including the components of the item being designed, the interrelationship of components, and old versions of designs.

- **Computer-aided software engineering** (CASE). A CASE database stores data required to assist software developers. These data include source code, dependencies among software modules, definitions and uses of variables, and the development history of the software system.

- **Multimedia databases**. A multimedia database contains spatial data, audio data, video data, and the like. Databases of this sort arise from geophysical data, voice mail systems, and graphics applications.

- **Office information systems** (OIS). Office automation includes workstation-based tools for document creation and document retrieval, tools for maintaining appointment calendars, and so on. An OIS database must allow queries pertaining to schedules, documents, and contents of documents.

- **Expert database systems**. An expert database system includes not only data but also explicit rules representing integrity constraints, triggers, and other knowledge about the enterprise modeled by the database.

These new applications of databases were not considered in the 1970s, when most current commercial database systems were initially designed. They are now practical owing to the increase in available main memory size, the speedup of central processing units, the lower cost of hardware, and the improved understanding of database management that has developed in recent years.

These new applications require new data models, new query languages, and new transaction models. Among the requirements of these new applications are:

- **Complex objects**. A complex object is an item that is viewed as a single object in the real world, but that contains other objects. These objects may have an arbitrarily complex internal structure. Often objects are structured hierarchically, representing the containment relationship. The modeling of complex objects has led to the development of *object-oriented databases*, which are based on the concepts of object-oriented programming languages, and *nested relational databases*, in which relations may be stored within other relations (see Chapter 14).

- **Behavioral data**. Distinct objects may need to respond in different ways to the same command. For example, deletion of certain tuples may require the deletion of other tuples, as is the case for weak entities. In CAD and CASE applications the behavior of distinct objects in response to a given command may be widely different. This behavioral information can be captured by storing executable code with objects in the database. This capability is provided by the *methods* of object-oriented database systems and by the rule base of knowledge base systems.

- **Meta knowledge**. Often the most important data about applications are general rules about the application rather than specific tuples. In our banking example, such a rule might be "All checking accounts pay 5 percent interest if the balance is over $1000; otherwise, they pay no interest." Facts of this sort cannot easily be represented in traditional database systems. However, they can be represented easily by rules in *logic databases*. Rules form an important part of expert database systems.

- **Long-duration transactions**. CAD and CASE applications involve human interaction with the data. Some of these interactions may be "what if" modifications that the user may wish to undo. Concurrent design efforts involving several designers may lead to conflicts among transactions. Because these transactions involve human interaction with the system, the consequences of transaction aborts, waits for locks, and so on, are much more serious than in the short, noninteractive transactions commonly used in business-type applications. We have already discussed a new transaction model to support these applications in Section 12.8. Among the concepts we have introduced are *nested transactions* and *correct, nonserializable executions*.

In this chapter, as well as Chapter 14 and Section 12.8, we consider several concepts that have been developed to meet the needs of these applications. We shall not discuss the features of all of the above applications in detail. Rather, we shall use some of the above applications as examples for those concepts not well illustrated by our banking example. Here, we consider these concepts as they relate to the object-oriented paradigm.

13.2 Object Structure

The object-oriented paradigm is based on encapsulating code and data into a single unit, called an *object*. The interface between an object and the rest of the system is defined by a set of *messages*.

The motivation for this approach can be illustrated by considering a document database in which documents are prepared using one of several text-formatting software packages. To print a document, the correct formatter must be run on the document. Under an object-oriented approach, each document is an object containing the text of a document and the code to operate on the object. All document objects respond to the *print* message but do so in different ways. Each document responds by executing the formatting code appropriate to itself. By encapsulating within the document object itself the information about how to print the document, we can have all documents present the same external interface to users.

In general, an object has associated with it:

- A set of *variables* that contain the data for the object. The value of each variable is itself an object.

- A set of *messages* to which the object responds.

- A *method*, which is a body of code to implement each message. A method returns a value as the *response* to the message.

The term *message* in an object-oriented context does not imply the use of a physical message in a computer network. Rather, it refers to the passing of requests among objects without regard to specific implementation details.

Since the only external interface presented by an object is the set of messages to which it responds, it is possible to modify the definition of methods and variables without affecting other objects. It is also possible to replace a variable with a method that computes a value. For example, a document object could contain either a *size* variable containing the number of bytes of text in the document or a *size* method that computes the size of the document by reading the document and counting the number of bytes.

The ability to modify the definition of an object without affecting the rest of the system is considered to be one of the major advantages of the object-oriented programming paradigm.

13.3 Class Hierarchy

Usually, there are many similar objects in a database. By similar, we mean that they respond to the same messages, use the same methods, and have variables of the same name and type. It would be wasteful to define each such object separately. Therefore, we group similar objects to form a *class*.

Each such object is called an *instance* of its class. All objects in a class share a common definition, though they differ in the values assigned to the variables. Example of classes in our bank database are customers, accounts, and loans.

The concept of classes is similar to the concept of abstract data types. However, there are several additional aspects to the class concept beyond those of abstract data types. To represent these additional properties, we treat each class as itself being an object. A class object includes:

- A set-valued variable whose value is the set of all objects that are instances of the class.

- Implementation of a method for the message *new*, which creates a new instance of the class.

An object-oriented database scheme typically requires a large number of classes. However, it is often the case that several classes are similar. For example, assume that we have an object-oriented database for our banking application. We would expect the class of bank customers to be similar to the class of bank employees in that both define variables for name, address, telephone-number, and so on. However, there are variables specific to employees (*salary*, for example) and variables specific to customers (*credit-rating*, for example). It would be desirable to define a representation for the common variables in one place. This can be done only if employees and customers are combined into one class.

In order to allow the direct representation of similarities among classes, we need to place classes in a specialization hierarchy like that defined in Chapter 2 for the entity-relationship model. Employees and customers may be represented by classes that are specializations of a *Person* class. Variables and methods specific to employees are associated with the *Employee* class. Variables and methods specific to customers are associated with the *Customer* class. Variables and methods that apply both to employees and to customers are associated with the *Person* class. Figure 13.1 shows a class hierarchy that represents people involved in the operation of our bank example. The variables associated with each class in our example are as follows:

- *Person: social-security-number, name, address, home-telephone-number, date-of-birth*

- *Customer: credit-rating, tax-withholding-status, work-phone-number*

- *Employee: date-of-hire, salary, number-of-dependents*

- *Officer: job-title, office-number, expense-account-number*

- *Teller: hours-per-week, station-number*

- *Secretary: hours-per-week, supervisor*

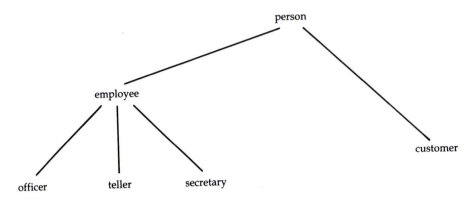

Figure 13.1   Class hierarchy for the banking example.

For brevity, we do not present the methods associated with these classes, although they would be included in a full definition of the bank database.

An object representing an officer contains all the variables of classes *Officer*, *Employee*, and *Person*. This is referred to as the *inheritance* of properties from a more general class. Methods are inherited in a manner identical to inheritance of variables. The specializations of a class are called *subclasses*. Thus, for example, *Employee* is a subclass of *Person*; *Teller* is a subclass of *Employee*. Conversely, *Employee* is a *superclass* of *Teller*, and *Person* is a superclass of *Employee*.

Earlier we noted that each class is itself an object and that that object includes a variable containing the set of all instances of the class. It is easy to determine which objects are associated with classes at the leaves of the hierarchy. For example, we associate with the *Customer* class the set of all customers of the bank. For nonleaf classes, however, the issue is more complex. In the hierarchy of Figure 13.1, there are two plausible ways of associating objects with classes:

- We could associate with the *Employee* class all employee objects including those that are instances of *Officer*, *Teller*, and *Secretary*.

- We could associate with the *Employee* class only those employee objects that are instances of neither *Officer* nor *Teller* nor *Secretary*.

Typically, the latter choice is made in object-oriented systems. It is possible to determine the set of all employee objects in this case by taking the union of those objects associated with all classes in the subtree rooted at *Employee*.

As we noted earlier, the class/subclass hierarchy is similar to the concept of specialization (the "ISA" relationship) in the entity-relationship model. We say that *Teller* is a specialization of *Employee* because the set of all tellers is a subset of the set of all employees. That is, every teller is an employee.

Specialization allows for the possibility that an employee may be neither a teller, nor a secretary, nor an officer. An alternative form of the "ISA" relationship is the concept of *generalization*. In the entity-relationship model, generalization is the result of taking the union of two or more (lower-level) entity sets to produce a higher-level entity set. If we apply the concept of generalization to the object-oriented model, then every object must be an instance of a leaf class in the hierarchy. This would require us to define a subclass of *Employee* called *Other-employee* to represent employees who are neither tellers, nor secretaries, nor officers.

In most object-oriented systems, specialization rather than generalization is the default. Thus, in what follows, we shall assume that the class/subclass hierarchy is based on specialization.

13.4 Multiple Inheritance

In most cases, a hierarchical organization of classes is adequate to describe applications. In such cases, all superclasses of a class are ancestors or descendants of one another in the hierarchy. However, there are situations that cannot be represented well in a class hierarchy.

Suppose that we wish to distinguish between full-time and part-time tellers and secretaries in our example of Figure 13.1. Further assume that we require different variables and methods to represent these two types of employees. We could create subclasses: *Part-time-teller*, *Full-time-teller*, *Part-time-secretary* and *Full-time-secretary*. The resulting hierarchy shown in Figure 13.2 does not provide a good model of the bank enterprise for several reasons:

- As we noted above, there are certain variables and methods specific to full-time employment and others specific to part-time employment. In Figure 13.2, the variables and methods for full-time employees must be defined twice, once for *Full-time-secretary* and once for *Full-time-teller*. A similar redundancy exists for part-time employees. Redundancy of this form is undesirable since any change to the properties of full− or part-time employees must be made in two places, leading to potential inconsistency.

- The hierarchy has no means of representing employees who are neither tellers nor secretaries unless we expand the hierarchy further to include the classes *Full-time-employee* and *Part-time-employee*.

If we had several job classifications instead of the two in our simple example, the limitations of the model would become even more apparent.

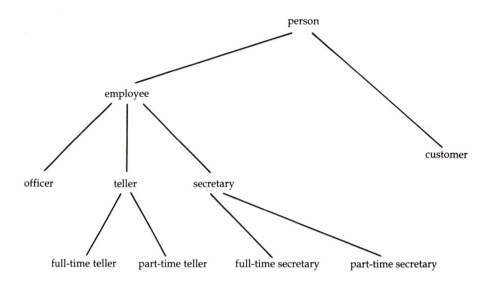

Figure 13.2   Class hierarchy for full− and part-time employees.

The difficulties we have just observed are dealt with in the object-oriented model by the concept of *multiple inheritance*, which refers to the ability of class to inherit variables and methods from multiple superclasses. The class/subclass relationship is represented by a rooted directed acyclic graph (DAG) in which a class may have more than one superclass. Let us return to our banking example. Using a DAG, we can define properties of full− and part-time employment in one place. As shown in Figure 13.3, we define a class *Part-time*, which defines those variables and methods specific to part-time employment, and a class *Full-time*, which defines those variables and methods specific to full-time employment. The class *Part-time-teller* is a subclass of both *Teller* and *Part-time*. It inherits from *Teller* those variables and methods pertaining to tellers and from *Part-time* those variables and methods pertaining to part-time employment. The redundancy of the hierarchy of Figure 13.2 is eliminated.

Using the DAG of Figure 13.3, we can represent full− and part-time employees who are neither tellers nor secretaries as instances of classes *Full-time* and *Part-time*, respectively.

When multiple inheritance is used, there is potential ambiguity if the same variable or method can be inherited from more than one superclass. In our banking example, assume that instead of defining *salary* for class *Employee*, we define a variable *pay* for each of *Full-time*, *Part-time*, *Teller*, and *Secretary* as follows:

- *Full-time*: *pay* is an integer from 0 to 100,000 containing annual salary.

- *Part-time*: *pay* is an integer from 0 to 20, containing an hourly rate of pay.

- *Teller*: *pay* is an integer from 0 to 20,000 containing the annual salary.

- *Secretary*: *pay* is an integer from 0 to 25,000 containing the annual salary.

Consider the class *Part-time-secretary*. It could inherit the definition of *pay* from either *Part-time* or *Secretary*. The result is different depending on the choice made. Among the options chosen by various implementations of the object-oriented model are the following:

- Include both variables, renaming them to *Part-time.pay* and *Secretary.pay*.

- Choose one or the other based on the order in which the classes *Part-time* and *Secretary* were created.

- Force the user to make a choice at the time the class *Part-time-secretary* is defined.

No single solution has been accepted as best.

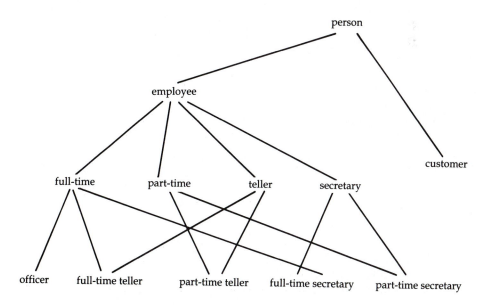

Figure 13.3   Class DAG for the banking example.

Not all cases of multiple inheritance lead to ambiguity. If, instead of defining *pay*, we retain the definition of variable *salary* in class *Employee*, and define it nowhere else, then classes *Part-time*, *Full-time*, *Secretary*, and *Teller* all inherit *salary* from *Employee*. Since all four of these classes share the same definition of *salary*, no ambiguity results in the inheritance of *salary* by *Part-time-secretary*, *Full-time-secretary*, and so on.

13.5 Object Identity

Objects in an object-oriented database usually correspond to an entity in the enterprise being modeled by the database. An entity retains its identity even if some of its properties change over time. Likewise, an object retains its identity even if some or all of the values of variables or definitions of methods change over time. This concept of identity does not apply to tuples of a relational database. In relational systems, the tuples of a relation are distinguished only by the values they contain.

Object identity is a stronger notion of identity than that typically found in programming languages or data models not based on object orientation. We illustrate several forms of identity below.

- **Value**. A data value is used for identity. This is the form of identity used in relational systems.

- **Name**. A user-supplied name is used for identity. This is the form of identity typically used for variables in procedures. Each variable is given a name that uniquely identifies the variable regardless of the value it contains.

- **Built-in**. A notion of identity is built into the data model or programming language, and no user-supplied identifier is required. This is the form of identity used in object-oriented systems.

An issue related to identity type is the permanence of identity. A simple way to achieve built-in identity is through pointers to physical locations in storage. However, the association of an object with a physical location in storage may change over time. Below, we list several degrees of permanence of identity.

- **Intraprogram**. Identity persists only during the execution of a single program or query. Examples of intraprogram identity are variable names in programming languages and tuple identifiers in SQL.

- **Interprogram**. Identity persists from one program execution to another. Examples of interprogram identity are relation names in a relational query language such as SQL.

- **Persistent**. Identity persists not only among program executions but also among structural reorganizations of the data. Relations in SQL do not have persistent identity, since a database reorganization may result in a new database scheme with relations with new names. It is the persistent form of identity that is required for object-oriented systems.

The above forms of identity serve to distinguish between *identity* in object-oriented systems and *pointers* in physical data organization. Main memory or virtual memory pointers offer only intraprogram identity. Pointers to file system data on disk offer only interprogram identity. Thus, identity of objects — that is, persistent identity — is a stronger notion than that provided by pointers.

13.6 Object Containment

We noted earlier that the value of a variable of an object is itself an object. This creates a *containment hierarchy* among objects. An object O_2 is the child of an object O_1 if O_1 *contains* O_2; that is, O_2 is the value of a variable of O_1. Objects that contain other objects are called *complex* or *composite* objects.

To illustrate containment, consider the simplified computer system design database of Figure 13.4. The database holds information on several computer systems. Each computer system contains a set of boards, a set of buses, a set of devices, and a set of machine-level instructions. Boards contain a set of chips, and buses provide a set of interfaces.

The hierarchy of Figure 13.4 shows the containment relationship among objects in a schematic way by listing class names rather than individual objects. Consider the class *Computer-system*. It may include variables *computer-name*, *project-id*, *manager*, and *completion-date*, which contain descriptive data about an instance of the class. Although the values of these variables are considered objects, they are instances of standard data types (such as character string) that are implemented directly

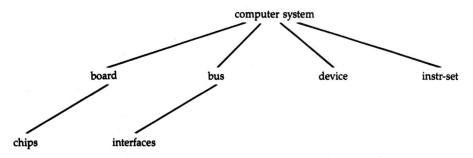

Figure 13.4 Containment hierarchy for computer system design database.

at a low level for performance reasons. Class *Computer-system* also includes variables *board*, *bus*, *device*, and *instr-set*. These variables take on as values sets of objects from the classes *Board*, *Bus*, *Device*, and *Instr-set*, respectively.

In certain applications, an object may be contained in several objects. In such cases, the containment relationship is represented by a DAG rather than a hierarchy.

Containment is an important concept in object-oriented systems because it allows data to be viewed at different granularities by different users. A chip designer can focus on instances of class *Chip* without much, if any, concern about the objects of class *Board* or *Computer-system* that contain the instances. A marketing staff person, attempting to price an entire computer system, can reference all data pertaining to the system by referencing the appropriate instance of class *Computer-system*.

13.7 Physical Organization

The structure of object-oriented databases lacks the uniformity of relational databases. In order to construct an easily maintained physical structure, objects are typically represented as follows:

- Certain classes are treated as basic building-block classes that are implemented directly by the computer system. Typically, the basic classes correspond to the standard programming language data types such as integer, float, character, and string.

- Instances of classes that are not basic are represented as follows:

  ○ Variables are represented by fields of a record type. Each field contains either the object value itself, for instances of the basic classes, or the object identifier for instances of nonbasic classes.

  ○ Set-valued variables are represented by a linked list of the objects that are members of the set.

This physical structuring makes it possible to use fixed-length records to implement an object-oriented database, though scheme modification (see Section 13.9) may complicate this.

When the containment relationship is hierarchical, the database scheme for an object-oriented database can be represented using the nested relational model, which we discuss in Chapter 14.

Not all variables fit conveniently into the structure we have described above. Several of the applications cited at the beginning of this chapter include highly specialized data types that are physically large and that, for practical reasons, are usually manipulated using application programs that are not part of the set of methods with classes:

- **Text data**. Text is usually treated as a byte string manipulated by editors and formatters.

- **Audio data**. Audio data is typically a digitized, compressed representation of speech that is handled by separate application software.

- **Video and graphical data**. Video data may be represented as a bit map or as a set of lines, boxes, and other geometric objects. Although some graphical data is often managed within the database system itself, special application software is used for many cases. An example of the latter is a VLSI design.

Variables containing data of the above types are often called *long fields* because a relational implementation of objects containing such variables requires records containing fields whose length may be several megabytes. A long field is stored in a special file (or collection of files) reserved for long-field storage.

The most widely used method for accessing long fields is the *checkout/checkin* method. A user *checks out* a copy of a long-field object, operates on this copy using special-purpose application programs, and then *checks in* the modified copy. The notions of *checkout* and *checkin* correspond roughly to a read and a write. However, the result of a checkin operation is usually not a write in the sense of Chapter 10, but rather the creation of a new version (see Chapter 12).

13.8 Object-Oriented Queries

Object-oriented programming languages require that all interaction with objects be through the sending of messages. This presents serious limitations to database applications. Consider our computer system design example and the query "Find all computer systems using chips sold by the Oldblock Corporation." If we follow strictly the object-oriented programming paradigm, a message must be sent to each instance of the class *Chip* to test its *vendor* value. If we view this request instead as a database problem, we would expect an index to exist for the class *Chip* that allows us to perform a lookup on "Oldblock Corporation" and obtain directly the identifiers of those instances of *Chip* for which the vendor field is "Oldblock Corporation."

The latter view of how a query is to be processed corresponds to a relational view of the object database as we saw in Section 13.7. Indeed, we could pose queries that involve joins of sets of objects. However, the relation view of objects is limited to variables, and much of the attractiveness of the object-oriented approach arises from the use of methods.

Thus, a query language for an object-oriented database system must include both the object-at-a-time message-passing model as well as the set-at-a-time message-passing model. The mix of object-at-a-time and set-at-a-time processing leads to serious language design complications often referred to as an "impedance mismatch." Several proposed languages exist. As there are currently no clear standards emerging, we do not present specific languages here but instead provide references in the bibliographic notes.

13.9 Scheme Modification

In the introduction to this chapter, we noted that the types of modification that can be made to a relational database scheme are fairly simple:

- Create or drop a relation.

- Add or delete attributes from a relation scheme.

This simplicity does not hold for object-oriented database schemes. The complication arises from two sources:

- **Complex changes**. The types of modification that can be made to an object-oriented scheme are more complex than those that can be made to a relational database scheme.

- **Frequent changes**. The applications that motivate the use of the object-oriented model require frequent scheme changes. Design applications often involve the alteration of the structure of the item being designed, whereas in our banking example, the descriptive data required for loans, accounts, and so on changes relatively rarely.

To illustrate the complexity of object-oriented schema modification, we list several types of modification below:

- **Addition of a new class**. The addition of a new class in an object-oriented database involves more than the addition of a relation scheme involved in a relational database. The new class must be placed in the class/subclass hierarchy or DAG, and inheritance issues must be resolved. If the new class is not a leaf node in the hierarchy or DAG, subclasses of the new class may need to inherit variables or methods from the new class. The same applies to sub-subclasses, and so on.

- **Deletion of a class**. The deletion of a class in an object-oriented database requires several operations. Inheritance of variables and methods by subclasses of the deleted class must be reexamined. Any changes to a subclass may need to be propagated to sub-subclasses, and so on. Instances of the deleted class must be made instances of another class, typically a parent of the deleted class.

- **Modification of a class definition**. A new variable or method may be defined or a variable or method definition may be deleted. As for the above cases, the definition of subclasses may be affected.

- **Repositioning of classes in the hierarchy or** DAG. Any restructuring of the class hierarchy or DAG has consequences on inheritance by old and new subclasses of the repositioned class.

Further complicating object-oriented scheme modification is the fact that instances of modified classes must be modified to conform to the new definition. For a large database, the amount of processing required to effect this change is substantial. Among the techniques used to reduce the overhead of scheme modification are:

- **Modification on access**. When an object is accessed, its structure is compared with the current definition of its class. Any necessary changes are made before the object is made available. As a result, the overhead of scheme modification is spread over the accesses to objects.

- **Versions of schemes**. Rather than requiring that an object be modified to conform to the current definition of its class, old versions of the class definition are retained for access to old objects. The maintenance of multiple versions imposes space overhead. It also complicates the coding of methods because of the need to handle multiple versions of the class definition.

Issues in the management of scheme modification are a subject of current research. Some initial proposals and descriptions of implementations are referenced in the bibliographic notes.

13.10 Summary

Database applications in such areas as computer-aided design, software engineering, and document processing do not fit the set of assumptions made for older, data-processing-style applications. The object-oriented data model has been proposed to deal with some of these new type of applications.

The object-oriented data model is an adaptation of the object-oriented programming paradigm to database systems. It is based on the concept of encapsulating data, and code that operates on that data, in an object. Structured objects are grouped into classes. The set of classes is structured into sub− and superclasses based on an extension of the ISA concept of the entity-relationship model. Since the value of a data item in an object is also an object, it is possible to represent object containment, resulting in a composite object.

Exercises

13.1 For each of the following application areas, explain why a 1970-era database system would be inadequate. List specific system components that would need to be modified.

    a. computer-aided design

    b. computer-aided software engineering

    c. multimedia databases

    d. office information systems

13.2 How does the concept of an object in the object-oriented model differ from the concept of an entity in the entity-relationship model?

13.3 Design an object-oriented database scheme for a vehicle database that describes the types of vehicles manufactured by a major company. Show the classes and subclasses. For each class, list variables and methods. For inherited variables and methods, indicate the class from which they are inherited.

13.4 Explain how the concept of object identity in the object oriented-model differs from the concept of tuple equality in the relational model.

13.5 Consider a system that provides persistent objects. Is such a system necessarily a database system? Why or why not?

13.6 Let O_1 and O_2 be composite objects that contain the same set of objects. Must O_1 be identical to O_2? Explain.

13.7 Suppose a new class C' is created as a subclass of a class C. What changes may have to be made to the database objects?

Bibliographic Notes

Applications of database concepts to CAD are discussed in Haskin and Lorie [1982], Lorie and Plouffe [1983], Katz and Weiss [1984], Kim, et al. [1984], Lorie, et al. [1985], Ranft, et al. [1990], and Bancilhon, et al. [1985a, 1985b].

    Object-oriented programming is discussed in Goldberg and Robson [1983], Cox [1986], Stefik and Bobrow [1986], Peterson [1987], and Stroustrup [1988]. There are several implemented object-oriented database systems including Orion (Banerjee, et al. [1987a, 1987b, 1988] and Kim [1989, 1990a], Kim et al. [1988b]), O_2 (Lecluse, et al. [1988]), Cactis (Hudson and King [1989]) Gemstone (Maier, et al. [1986]), and Iris (Fishman, et al. [1990]). POSTGRES (Stonebraker and Rowe [1986], Stonebraker [1986a, 1987], and Stonebraker et al. [1987a, 1987b]) and several other systems are not object-oriented, but include certain features of such systems.

Applications to software development are discussed by Hudson and King [1987].

An approach to the development of database systems for design applications is *extensible* systems that can be adapted to specific applications. Such systems include Genesis (Batory et al. [1986, 1988]), Exodus (Carey et al. [1986, 1988, 1990]), and Starburst (Haas et al. [1989]).

Object identity is characterized in detail by Khoshafian and Copeland [1990]. Further discussion of object identity appears in Abiteboul and Kanellakis [1989] and Zaniolo [1989]. Scheme modification is discussed in Banerjee, et al. [1987b] as it pertains to Orion and in Penny and Stein [1987] as it pertains to Gemstone. Other discussions of scheme modification and semantics appears in Skarra and Zdonik [1986]. Query processing for object-oriented databases is discussed in Maier and Stein [1986], Beech [1988], Bertino and Kim [1989], Cluet, et al. [1989], Kim [1989], and Kim, et al. [1989].

Overviews of object-oriented database research include Kim and Lochovsky [1989], Kim [1990b, 1990c, 1990d], and Zdonik and Maier [1990]. Recent advances in object-oriented databases are discussed in Dittrich [1988].

Extended Relational Systems

In Chapter 13, we noted that several new application areas for database systems are limited by restrictions imposed by the relational data model. Among these limitations are uniformity, record orientation, and atomicity of fields. We also noted that certain of these applications require languages with greater expressive power than SQL or the relational algebra.

The object-oriented model presented in Chapter 13 is one way of overcoming the limitations of relational systems. That model, however, sacrifices many of the advantages of the relational model, especially in query processing. In this chapter, we present extensions to the relational model that broaden the applicability of the model without sacrificing the relational foundation. First we present Datalog, a Prolog-like logic-based language that allows recursive queries. Next we present the nested relational model, which allows relations that are not in first normal form. Nested relations allow direct representation of hierarchical structures similar to the complex objects discussed in Chapter 13. Finally, we discuss expert database systems in which logic-based rules are combined with triggers.

14.1 Logic-Based Data Model

Datalog is a nonprocedural query language that is based on first-order logic. A user describes the information desired without giving a specific procedure for obtaining that information. We shall show how the various fundamental operations in the relational algebra can be implemented in Datalog. As in relational algebra, all these operations produce a new relation as their result.

14.1.1 Basic Structure

A Datalog database consists of two types of relations:

- **Base relations**, which are stored in the database and are the same as those used previously. They are sometimes referred to as *extensional databases* (EDB).

- **Derived relations**, which are not necessarily stored in the database. They are usually temporary relations that hold intermediate results computed during the execution of a query. They are sometimes referred to as *intensional databases* (IDB).

Each relation has a unique name and a fixed arity.

In contrast to the relational algebra, the attributes of a relation in Datalog are not explicitly named. Rather, the position of an attribute determines its value.

Datalog programs are a finite set of rules, involving both base and derived relations. Before presenting a formal definition of a rule, let us present an example using our banking enterprise. Consider the rule:

$$ca \ (Y, X) :- \ deposit \ (\text{“Perryridge”}, X, Y, Z), Z > 1200$$

This rule consists of the base relation *deposit,* and the one derived relation *ca.* This rule derives the set of all pairs *<customer-name, account>* of all customers having an account at the Perryridge branch with a balance greater than \$1200.

The above rule is equivalent to the domain relational calculus expression

$$\{<y, x > | \ \exists \ w, z \ (\ <w, x, y, z > \ \epsilon \ deposit \ \wedge \ w = \ \text{“Perryridge”} \ \wedge \ z > 1200)\}$$

with the result inserted into the new derived relation *ca.*

Now that we have informally explained what a rule and its meaning are, let us formally define these concepts. Rules are built out of *literals* that have the form

$$p \ (A_1, A_2, \ldots , A_n)$$

where:

- p is the name of either a base or derived relation.

- Each A_i is either a constant or a variable name.

We use the same convention as in the relational algebra model in denoting relation names, constants, and variable names.

A *rule* in Datalog is of the form

$$p \ (x_1, \ldots , x_n) :- \ q_1 \ (x_{11}, \ldots , x_{1m_1}), q_2 \ (x_{21}, \ldots , x_{2m_2}), \ldots ,$$
$$q_r \ (x_{r1}, \ldots , x_{rm_r}), e$$

where:

- p is the name of a derived relation.

- Each q_i is the name of either a base or derived relation.

- e is an arithmetic predicate expression over the variables appearing in p and all q_is.

- Each variable appearing in p also appears in one of q_is.

The literal $p\ (x_1, \ldots , x_n)$ is called the *head* of the rule, while the rest of the rule is called the *body* of the rule.

Let us return to our previous rule to compute the set of all pairs <customer-name, account> of all customers having an account at the Perryridge branch with a balance greater than $1200. The rule consists of two literals: the base relation *deposit* and one derived relation *ca*. There are three variable names, X, Y and Z, and one constant, "Perryridge." There is one arithmetic predicate expression $Z > 1200$. The head of the rule consists of the literal *ca* (Y, X), while the rest of the rule is its body.

In order to understand precisely how a rule in Datalog is interpreted, we must define the notion of *rule substitution* and *rule instantiation*. A substitution applied to the rule is the replacement of each variable in the rule by either a variable or a constant. If a variable appears several times in a rule, then the same variable name or constant must be used in the substitution.

For example, in the rule above, the following is a valid substitution:

ca ("Smith", 217) :$-$ *deposit* ("Perryridge", 217, "Smith", W), $W > 1200$

We have replaced variable X by the constant 217, variable Y by the constant "Smith," and variable Z by the variable name W.

In contrast, the following is not a valid substitution:

ca ("Smith", 217) :$-$ *deposit* ("Perryridge", 300, "Smith", 1500), $1500 > 1200$

Here we have replaced variable X by two different constants: 217 and 300.

An instantiation of a rule is a valid substitution such that each of the variables is replaced by some constant. For example, in the rule above, an instantiation is:

ca ("Smith", 217) :$-$ *deposit* ("Perryridge", 217, "Smith", 1500), $1500 > 1200$

Notice that for a particular rule there exist many possible valid instantiations.

Now let us see how a Datalog rule is interpreted. Consider the instantiated rule:

$$p\,(c_1, \ldots, c_n) :- q_1\,(c_{11}, \ldots, c_{1m_1}),\, q_2\,(c_{21}, \ldots, c_{2m_2}), \ldots,$$
$$q_r\,(c_{r1}, \ldots, c_{rm_r}),\, e$$

We say that p is true if the expression

$$q_1\,(c_{11}, \ldots, c_{1m_1}) \wedge q_2\,(c_{21}, \ldots, c_{2m_2}) \wedge \cdots \wedge q_r\,(c_{r1}, \ldots, c_{rm_r}) \wedge e$$

evaluates to the value true. A literal $q_i\,(c_{i1}, c_{i2}, \ldots, c_{im_i})$ is true if the tuple $(c_{i1}, c_{i2}, \ldots, c_{im_i})$ appears in relation q_i.
Returning to our rule:

$$ca\,(Y, X) :- deposit\,(\text{``Perryridge''}, X, Y, Z),\, Z > 1200$$

We have ca ("Smith", 217) being true if there exists a constant c_1 such that the following two conditions are met:

- $c_1 > 1200$.

- tuple ("Perryridge", 217, "Smith", c_1) appears in relation *deposit*.

A rule is thus evaluated in a manner similar to the evaluation of a query in relational calculus. In essence, we derive the set of all possible constants that make the head of the rule true, and assign these values to the new relation named in the head of the rule. The main difference between the two is that a rule may include both base and derived relations, whereas in relational calculus only base relations are included. We shall return to the issue of general query evaluation later.

A Datalog program is a finite set of rules. The execution of the program is carried out by evaluating all the rules of the program as described above. Since the rules of the program may depend on one another, more needs to be said about the various evaluation strategies of a collection of rules. This will be done in the next few sections.

Let us illustrate by considering the program:

$$b\,(X) :- deposit\,(X, Y, \text{``Jones''}, Z)$$
$$query\,(C) :- deposit\,(A, B, C, D),\, b\,(A)$$

This program computes the set of all customers who have an account at some bank at which Jones has an account. This program is executed by first evaluating the rule:

$$b\,(X) :- deposit\,(X, Y, \text{``Jones''}, Z)$$

Once this is accomplished, the second rule is evaluated giving us the desired results.

We are finally in a position to explain how queries are defined. A query is composed of:

- A Datalog program which is a finite (possible empty) set of rules.

- A single literal of the form

$$p\,(x_1, x_2, \ldots, x_n)\ ?$$

where each x_i is either a constant or a variable name.

The execution of a query proceeds by first computing the Datalog program (if it exists). Next, $p\,(x_1, x_2, \ldots, x_n)$? is evaluated. This procedure is essentially the same as a simple selection on the relation p, with the appropriate constraints.

To illustrate, consider the query "Find all tuples of the *borrow* relation where the branch is Perryridge."

$$borrow\,(\text{``Perryridge''},\ X,\ Y,\ Z)\ ?$$

Note that in this query there was no Datalog program involved.

As another example, consider the query to compute the set of all customers of the Perryridge branch who have accounts with a balance greater than \$1200.

$$c\,(Y) :- deposit\,(\text{``Perryridge''},\ X,\ Y,\ Z),\ Z > 1200$$
$$c\,(Y)\ ?$$

The Datalog program above consists of one single rule.

Note that in the above example, the statement "$c\,(Y)$?" is almost superfluous; it is included only to specify which derived relation needs to be displayed. This pattern is repeated in many other circumstances. To eliminate superfluousness, whenever no confusion may arise, we shall use the following shorthand notation. We dispose of the statement $p\,(x_1, x_2, \ldots, x_n)$? and require that the Datalog program include one single distinguished rule

$$query\,(x_1, x_2, \ldots, x_n) :- \cdots$$

where each x_i is a variable name. The understanding is that we implicitly include the statement

$$query\,(x_1, \ldots, x_n)\ ?$$

as part of the query. Thus, the query

$$query\ (Y) :- deposit\ (\text{``Perryridge''},\ X,\ Y,\ Z),\ Z > 1200$$

is equivalent to the one above.

14.1.2 General Evaluational Strategies

Let us reconsider the query to compute the set of all customers of the Perryridge branch who have accounts with a balance greater than \$1200. In the previous section we have formed it as:

$$query\ (Y) :- deposit\ (\text{``Perryridge''},\ X,\ Y,\ Z),\ Z > 1200$$

Note that we could have obtained the same result by writing the query differently, as:

$$ca\ (Y,\ W) :- deposit\ (W,\ X,\ Y,\ Z),\ Z > 1200$$
$$query\ (Y) :- ca\ (Y,\ \text{``Perryridge''})$$

The main difference between the two forms of the query is that in the first one we compute only the set of all customers of the Perryridge branch who have an account with a balance greater than \$1200. In the second one, we initially compute all customers of the bank who have an account with a balance greater than \$1200, and then select those tuples in which *branch-name* is Perryridge. Clearly, naively computed, the first query form will be executed much faster.

We should point out here that there are two complementary general evaluation methods: *bottom-up* and *top-down*. The bottom-up strategy orders the various rules of the Datalog program and then evaluates the rules using that order. This method was used earlier in the evaluation of the query to find the set of all customers who have an account at some bank at which Jones has an account. The top-down strategy, on the other hand, starts with the single literal *p*? and works backward to the base relations using our substitution and insertion rules. Thus, in the last query, we start with the rule:

$$query\ (Y) :- ca\ (Y,\ \text{``Perryridge''})$$

Since the relation *ca* is not yet computed, we work backward to the first rule. By the time we reach this rule we know that we are interested in only the customer of the Perryridge branch. We then evaluate the rule restricting the variable *w* to "Perryridge."

The top-down strategy is used in the evaluation of queries in the language Prolog (Datalog is a proper subset of Prolog). The bottom-up method is used in the evaluation of queries in the language LDL (a new database query language). In this text we confine our discussion to only bottom-up strategies.

The order in which rules are specified in a query is of no importance. It is the responsibility of the compiler to generate the appropriate strategy for evaluating the query. Thus, Datalog is a nonprocedural language, as is relational calculus.

Although it appears at the surface that queries specified in Datalog are quite similar in structure to those specified in relational calculus, this is not the case. No restrictions are placed on the type of literals that may appear in the body of the rules. This turns out to increase the power of the language, as we shall discuss in Section 14.1.6.

14.1.3 Query Structure

In the previous section we have informally described how queries can be evaluated in Datalog. We have simplified our discussion by restricting our attention to cases where only base relations appear in the body of the rule. With this restriction, our evaluation algorithm turns out to be quite similar to the way we evaluate queries in one of the relational languages described in Chapter 3.

In general, however, the removal of the stated restriction results in much more complicated evaluation schemes. In order to describe these schemes, it is convenient to define the notion of a *rule graph* for a query q. A rule graph is a directed graph such that:

- The nodes of the graph correspond to the set of all literal symbols appearing in the rules of q.

- The edges of the graph correspond to a precedence relation that exists between the literal appearing in the body of the rule and the literal appearing in the head of the rule. Thus, the graph contains the edge

$$a_i \leftarrow a_j$$

if the rule is contained in the query q:

$$a_i :- \cdots a_j \cdots$$

Note that our construction does not take into account the set of variables and constants appearing in the various rules of the query. The only information we use is the set of literal symbols and their relation in the various rules.

To illustrate, consider the query:

$$p_1 (X, Y, Z) :- q_1 (X, Y), q_2 (X, Z), q_3 (Y, Z)$$
$$p_2 (A, B) :- p_1 (A, B), q_4 (B, A)$$
$$query (B) :- p_2 (A, B), p_3 (B, A)$$

The rule graph corresponding to the query is shown in Figure 14.1. Note that this graph is acyclic. Queries whose corresponding rule graph is acyclic are commonly referred to as *nonrecursive* queries.

As another example, consider the query:

$$p_1 (A, B, C) :- q_1 (A, B), p_2 (B, C)$$
$$p_2 (X, Y) :- q_2 (X), p_1 (X, Y, Z)$$
$$query (A, B) :- p_1 (A, B, C), p_2 (B, C)$$

The rule graph corresponding to the query is shown in Figure 14.2. Note that this graph contains a cycle. Queries whose corresponding rule graph contains a cycle are commonly referred to as *recursive* queries.

As we shall see in Section 14.1.6, there is a significant difference between recursive and nonrecursive queries in terms of the type of questions that can be posed to the database. It is also the case that the evaluation of recursive queries is more complicated than that for nonrecursive queries.

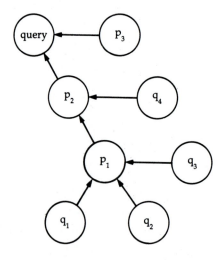

Figure 14.1   Rule graph for a nonrecursive query.

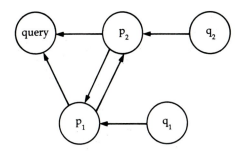

Figure 14.2   Rule graph for a recursive query.

14.1.4 Negation

The rules we have considered thus far include only *positive* literals. Unfortunately, this does not provide sufficient power to express all desired queries. We also need to allow the inclusion of *negative* literals, which have the form:

$$\neg\, p\, (A_1, A_2, \ldots, A_n)$$

A negative literal is interpreted as follows. Let $\neg p$ be a negative literal appearing in rule r. We say that $\neg p$ is true if there exists no valid instantiation of the rule r with $\neg p\, (c_1, c_2, \ldots, c_n)$ such that tuple $(c_1, c_2, \ldots, c_n)$ appears in relation p. For this interpretation to be effective, we shall require that at the time when we evaluate the rule in which that negative literal $\neg p\, (A_1, A_2, \ldots, A_n)$ appears, the relation p contains all the possible valid tuples that should be used in the evaluation of the rule. We shall discuss this issue in a moment.

To illustrate, consider the rule which computes the set of all customers who have a deposit but no loan at the Perryridge branch.

$c\, (Y) :- deposit$ ("Perryridge", X, Y, Z), $\neg borrow$ ("Perryridge", A, Y, B)

Note that since *borrow* is a base relation, our requirement that this relation be computed by the time we evaluate the rule is met trivially.

Let us now return to the issue of ensuring that when a rule is evaluated in which a negative literal p appears, the relation p must already be computed. In order to ensure this properly, we shall require that if we have a query that includes the rule

$$p :- \cdots \neg\, q \cdots$$

then there is no path from p to q in the corresponding rule graph. Queries satisfying this restriction are referred to as being *stratified*. The proof that stratification ensures our above stated desired property is left as an exercise for the reader.

Now consider the query:

$$p_1 (X, Y) :- q_1 (X, Y), \neg q_2 (Y, Z)$$
$$q_2 (A, B) :- q_3 (A, C), q_4 (C, B)$$
$$query (X, Y) :- p_1 (X, Y), q_2 (Y, Y)$$

This query is stratified, since in the corresponding rule graph (Figure 14.3) these is no path from p_1 to q_2. On the other hand, the query:

$$p_1 (X, Y) :- q_1 (X, Y), \neg q_2 (Y, Z)$$
$$q_2 (A, B) :- q_3 (A, C), \neg p_1 (C, B)$$
$$query (X, Y) :- p_1 (X, Y), q_2 (Y, Y)$$

is not stratified, since in the corresponding rule graph (Figure 14.4) there is a path from p_1 to q_2.

14.1.5 Nonrecursive Queries

Datalog with positive and negative literals, restricted to nonrecursive queries, is equivalent in expressive power to relational algebra. We shall not formally prove this here. Rather, we will show through examples how the various relational algebra operations can be simulated in Datalog.

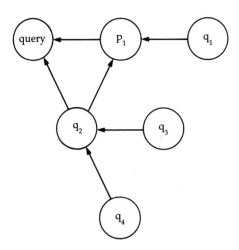

Figure 14.3   Rule graph for a stratified query.

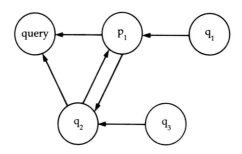

Figure 14.4   Rule graph for a nonstratified query.

The simplest form of selection of tuples from relation r can be obtained by writing the query

$$r\ (x_1, x_2, \ldots, x_n)\ ?$$

where each x_i is a variable name, or a constant. Thus, to select those tuples of the *branch* relation whose city is Brooklyn, we write:

$$branch\ (X,\ Y,\ \text{``Brooklyn''})\ ?$$

In the case that the selection includes an arithmetic expression, we must form a rule with the right-hand side consisting of a single literal with symbol r, and the appropriate arithmetic expression. The literal r consists of variable and constants representing the selection criteria. Thus, to find the name of all customers who have a loan of more than \$1200 we write:

$$query\ (Y) :- borrow\ (\text{``Perryridge''},\ X,\ Y,\ Z),\ Z > 1200$$

Cartesian product of two relations r_1 and r_2 can be obtained in Datalog as follows

$$query\ (X_1, \ldots, X_n, Y_1, \ldots, Y_m) :- r_1\ (X_1, \ldots, X_n),\ r_2\ (Y_1, \ldots, Y_m)$$

where the X_is and Y_js are all distinct variable names.
The union of two relations r_1 and r_2 is formed as follows:

$$query\ (X_1, X_2, \ldots, X_n) :- r_1\ (X_1, X_2, \ldots, X_n)$$
$$query\ (Y_1, Y_2, \ldots, Y_n) :- r_2\ (Y_1, Y_2, \ldots, Y_n)$$

Note that we need two separate rules to represent the union operation.

To find the name of all customers of the Perryridge branch, we write:

$$query \ (Y) :- \ borrow \ (\text{"Perryridge"}, X, Y, Z)$$
$$query \ (B) :- \ deposit \ (\text{"Perryridge"}, A, B, C)$$

Finally, set difference of two relations r_1 and r_2 is formed as follows:

$$query \ (X_1, X_2, \ldots, X_n) :- \ r_1 \ (X_1, X_2, \ldots, X_n), \neg \ r_2 \ (X_1, X_2, \ldots, X_n)$$

The set of variables appearing in r_1 and r_2 must be the same. However, the set of variables appearing in *query* may be a subset of those appearing in r_1 and r_2, if we wish to do a projection on the result.

To find all customers of the Perryridge branch who have an account but do not have a loan, we write:

$$query \ (Y) :- \ deposit \ (\text{"Perryridge"}, X, Y, Z), \ \neg \ borrow \ (\text{"Perryridge"}, A, Y, B)$$

It is possible to show that any nonrecursive Datalog query can be simulated using the relational algebra operators. We leave this as an exercise for the reader. We have thus established the equivalence of relational algebra and Datalog restricted to nonrecursive queries.

Let us present several more complicated query examples in Datalog.

- Find all customers having a loan at the Perryridge branch and their cities.

$$query \ (Z, B) :- \ borrow \ (\text{"Perryridge"}, Y, Z, W), \ customer \ (Z, A, B)$$

- Find the assets and names of all branches which have depositors (that is, customers with an account) living in Port Chester.

$$query \ (A, P) :- \ customer \ (X, Y, \text{"Port Chester"}), \ deposit \ (A, B, X, C),$$
$$branch \ (A, P, Q)$$

- Find all customers who have an account at some branch at which Jones has an account.

$$query \ (Z) :- \ deposit \ (X, Y, Z, W), \ deposit \ (X, B, \text{"Jones"}, D)$$

A final issue that needs to be discussed in regard to nonrecursive queries is query evaluation strategies. It turns out that for this restricted class of queries there exists a simple bottom-up evaluation strategy that is both efficient and straightforward.

Let q be a nonrecursive query. Obviously, the rule graph corresponding to query q is acyclic. This in turn implies that we can obtain a total order of the various rules such that if $r_i < r_j$ then it follows that rule r_j can be evaluated independently of rule r_i. To execute the query, we simply evaluate the rules in the inverse order of the total order.

To illustrate, consider again the nonrecursive, stratified query:

$$p_1 (X, Y) :- q_1 (X, Y), \neg q_2 (Y, Z)$$
$$q_2 (A, B) :- q_3 (B, C), q_4 (C, D)$$
$$query (X, Y) :- p_1 (X, Y), q_2 (Y, Y)$$

The corresponding rule graph is shown in Figure 14.3. The order in which we should evaluate the three rules is to first obtain q_2, then p_1, and finally *query*.

In the case that either p_1 or q_2 (in the query above) contains some constants, we simply push these constants down to the base relations appearing in the various rules, to reduce the amount of computation that needs to be done in evaluating the query.

Consider the query:

$$ca (Y, W) :- deposit (W, X, Y, Z)$$
$$query (Y) :- ca (Y, \text{“Perryridge”})$$

Since *ca* contains the constant "Perryridge," we push that constant down to the first rule obtaining the new rule:

$$ca (Y, \text{“Perryridge”}) :- deposit (\text{“Perryridge”}, X, Y, Z)$$

This rule can be evaluated more efficiently than the original rule. The result of the query, however, is obviously the same.

14.1.6 Recursion

Datalog with recursive queries has more expressive power than any of the formal relational languages we have described in Chapter 3. This means that we can pose some questions to the database that can be answered in Datalog but not in relational algebra. Here is a simple example.

Suppose that we have a relation scheme

$$Manager\text{-}scheme = (employee\text{-}name, manager\text{-}name)$$

which depicts an *employee-manager* relationship. Let *manager* be a relation on the above scheme (see Figure 14.5).

employee-name	manager-name
Jones	King
Smith	King
Reyna	Smith
Lew	Smith
Davin	Jones
Bandu	Jones
Duke	Jones
Cherry	Lew
Bank	Reyna
Levy	Davin
Higgins	Davin
Cumby	Bandu
Prince	Duke
Garner	Duke

Figure 14.5   The *manager* relation.

To get the names of all employees working directly under Jones (first-level employees of Jones) we write:

$$query\ (X) :- manager\ (X, \text{``Jones''})$$

To get the names of all employees whose direct manager works under Jones (second-level employees of Jones), we write:

$$query\ (X) :- manager\ (X, Y), manager\ (Y, \text{``Jones''})$$

It is easy to see how this pattern can be extended to deal with the query "Get the names of all n^{th} (where n is fixed) level employees of Jones." This could also be done in relational algebra. However, the query to get the names of all employees working (directly or indirectly) under Jones, cannot be formed in relational algebra (or Datalog restricted to nonrecursive rules). The reason is that we do not know what the level of management of Jones is. We can, however, form such a query in Datalog as follows:

$$e\ (X) :- manager\ (X, \text{``Jones''})$$
$$e\ (X) :- manager\ (X, Y), e\ (Y)$$
$$query\ (X) :- e\ (X)$$

Note that the above is a recursive query.

In order to see that the above query indeed computes the desired result, we must explain the general ideas governing the evaluation of recursive queries.

It is possible to convert any recursive query to one with no recursion but with finite iteration. We shall represent the iteration using the **repeat** construct of Pascal. The termination condition of the **until** statement will consist of set testing (for example, equality, containment, emptiness), where the derived relations are treated as sets. Thus, the above recursive query can be evaluated as:

$$e' (X) :- manager (X, \text{“Jones”})$$
repeat
$$\quad e (X) :- e' (X)$$
$$\quad e' (X) :- manager (X, Y), e (Y)$$
until $e = e'$

The first rule computes all first-level (direct) employees of Jones. Once this is accomplished, the rules enclosed in the **repeat** statement are evaluated. At each successive iteration, the next level of employee is computed and added to the set e. This procedure is terminated when the sets e and e' are equal — that is, when no new elements can be added to the set e. Such a termination point must be reached since the set of managers is finite.

Let us illustrate by tracing the execution of the query:

1. $e' = \{\text{Davin, Bandu, Duke}\}$

2. $e = \{\text{Davin, Bandu, Duke}\}$

3. $e' = \{\text{Davin, Bandu, Duke, Levy, Higgins, Cumby, Prince, Garner}\}$

4. $e = \{\text{Davin, Bandu, Duke, Levy, Higgins, Cumby, Prince, Garner}\}$

The reader is encouraged to verify (using Figure 14.5) that after the query is executed, set e indeed includes all the employees working under Jones.

We could obtain the same result by writing the query differently, as:

$$m (X, Y) :- manager (X, Y)$$
$$m (X, Y) :- manager (X, Z), m(Z, Y)$$
$$query(X) :- m (X, \text{“Jones”})$$

The main difference between the two forms of the query is that in the first one, we compute only all the employees of Jones, while in the second one we initially compute all possible *employee-manager* relations, and then select those pairs in which “Jones” is the manager. Clearly, naively computed, the first query form will be executed much faster.

In contrast to nonrecursive queries, there are many possible evaluation strategies. We shall not cover all of them in this text. Rather, we shall concentrate on one simple but general bottom-up evaluation method which can be further refined to obtain more efficient execution. The bibliographic notes include references to these.

The bottom-up strategy we used above in evaluating the recursive query e is called *naive evaluation*. It is the simplest but least efficient of the bottom-up strategies. The inefficiency is due to the fact that whenever we computed the recursive rule, the entire previous set e was used in the computation. To avoid this inefficiency, a *semi-naive* evaluation can be used. Here, only the new elements added in the previous iteration are used in evaluating the rule.

$$i := 0;$$
$$e_i (X) :- manager (X, \text{``Jones''})$$
repeat
$$e (X) :- e_i (X)$$
$$e_{i + 1} (X) :- manager (X, Y), e_i (Y)$$
$$i := i + 1$$
until $e_i \subseteq e$

Let us use the semi-naive evaluation strategy on our second query, the one that computes all possible *employee-manager* relations, and then selects those pairs in which Jones is the manager:

$$i := 0;$$
$$m_i (X, Y) :- manager (X, Y)$$
repeat
$$m (X, Y) :- m_i (X, Y)$$
$$m_{i + 1} (X, Y) :- manager (X, Z), m_i (Z, Y)$$
$$i := i + 1$$
until $m_i \subseteq m$
$$query (X) :- m (X, \text{``Jones''})$$

Note that although we are using semi-naive evaluation, which is more efficient than naive evaluation, we still are not doing as well in terms of efficiency as in our previous query (which computes the same result). There are a variety of optimization techniques to remedy the deficiency of semi-naive evaluation. We shall not cover these in the text. References to them appear in the bibliographic notes.

14.2 The Nested Relational Model

In Chapter 6, we defined *first normal form* (1NF), which requires that all attributes have *atomic domains*. A domain is *atomic* if elements of the domain are considered to be indivisible units.

For example, the set of integers is an atomic domain, but the set of all sets of integers is a nonatomic domain. The distinction is that we do not normally consider integers to have subparts, but we consider set of integers to have subparts — namely, the integers comprising the set. If we were to consider each integer to be an ordered list of digits, then the domain of all integers would be considered nonatomic. Thus, the important issue in 1NF is not the domain itself, but the way we use domain elements in the database.

We have not drawn attention to the 1NF assumption until now because the assumption of 1NF is a natural one in the examples we have considered. However, the examples that have motivated new database applications are not always compatible with the 1NF assumption. Rather than viewing the database as a set of records, users of new applications view the database as a set of objects. These objects may require several records for their representation. We shall see that a simple, easy-to-use interface requires a one-to-one correspondence between the user's intuitive notion of an object and the database system's notion of a data item.

The nested relational model is an extension of the relational model in which domains may be either atomic or relation-valued. Thus, the value of a tuple on an attribute may be a relation and relations may be stored within relations. This allows a complex object to be represented by a single tuple of a nested relation. If we view a tuple of a nested relation as a data item, we have a one-to-one correspondence between data items and objects in the user's view of the database.

14.2.1 Document Retrieval Example

We illustrate the nested relational model by an example drawn from office information systems. Consider a document retrieval system in which we store for each document the following information:

- Document title.
- Author list.
- Date.
- Keyword list.

We can see that if we define a relation for the above information, several domains will be nonatomic.

- **Authors**. A document may have a set of authors. Nevertheless, we may want to find all documents of which Jones was one of the authors. Thus, we are interested in a subpart of the domain element "set of authors."

- **Keywords**. If we store a set of keywords for a document, we expect to be able to retrieve all documents whose keywords include one or more keywords. Thus, we view the domain of *keyword-list* as nonatomic.

title	author-list	date	keyword-list
		day month year	
salesplan	{Smith, Jones}	1 April 79	{profit, strategy}
status report	{Jones, Frick}	17 June 85	{profit, personnel}

Figure 14.6   Non-1NF document relation, *doc*.

- **Date**. Unlike *keywords* and *authors*, *date* does not have a set-valued domain. However, we may view *date* as consisting of the subfields *day*, *month*, and *year*. This makes the domain of *date* nonatomic.

Figure 14.6 shows an example document relation, *doc*. The *doc* relation can be represented in 1NF, as shown in Figure 14.7. Since we must have atomic domains in 1NF, yet want access to individual authors and to individual keywords, we need one tuple for each (keyword, author) pair. The *date* attribute is replaced in the 1NF version by three attributes: one for each subfield of *date*.

Much of the awkwardness of the *doc'* relation in Figure 14.7 is removed if we assume that the following multivalue dependencies hold:

- *title* →→ *author*
- *title* →→ *keyword*
- *title* → *day month year*

Then, we can decompose the relation into 4NF using the schemes:

- (*title, author*)
- (*title, keyword*)
- (*title, day, month, year*)

Figure 14.8 shows the projection of the relation *doc'* of Figure 14.7 onto the above decomposition.

Although 1NF can represent our example document database adequately, the non-1NF representation may be an easier-to-understand model, since the typical user of a document retrieval system thinks of the database in terms of our non-1NF design. The 4NF design would require users to include joins in their queries, thereby complicating interaction with the system. We could define a view that eliminates the need for users to write joins in their query. However, in such a view, we lose the one-to-one correspondence between tuples and documents.

title	author	day	month	year	keyword
salesplan	Smith	1	April	79	profit
salesplan	Jones	1	April	79	profit
salesplan	Smith	1	April	79	strategy
salesplan	Jones	1	April	79	strategy
status report	Jones	17	June	85	profit
status report	Frick	17	June	85	profit
status report	Jones	17	June	85	personnel
status report	Frick	17	June	85	personnel

Figure 14.7　*doc′*, a 1NF version of non-1NF relation *doc*.

14.2.2 Definition of a Nested Relation Scheme

In the relational model, we define a database scheme by listing the relation schemes for relations in the database. Similarly, in the nested relational model, we define a list of nested relation schemes. This definition is more complex than that of a nonnested relation scheme since we must define the schemes for each level of nesting.

title	author
salesplan	Smith
salesplan	Jones
status report	Jones
status report	Frick

title	keyword
salesplan	profit
salesplan	strategy
status report	profit
status report	personnel

title	day	month	year
salesplan	1	April	79
status report	17	June	85

Figure 14.8　4NF version of the relation *doc′* of Figure 14.7.

For example, we define the scheme *Doc-scheme* for the *doc* relation as follows:

$$Doc\text{-}scheme = (title, author\text{-}list, date, keyword\text{-}list)$$
$$author\text{-}list = (author)$$
$$date = (day, month, year)$$
$$keyword\text{-}list = (keyword)$$

This definition states that the scheme *Doc-scheme* has four attributes: *title*, *author-list*, *date*, and *keyword-list*. The *title* attribute has an atomic domain. Since the other three attributes have relation-valued domains, a scheme must be defined for them as well. A relational on scheme *author-list* is simply a set of authors. That is, it is a relation on one attribute, *author*. Similarly, a relation on scheme *keyword-list* is a relation on one attribute, *keyword*. The scheme *date* is on three attributes: *day*, *month*, and *year*. Note that by defining the scheme *date* in this way, we allow a set of tuples over (*day*, *month*, *year*) even though our example has only one date for each document.

In general, a nested relational database scheme is defined by a set of *rules*, where each rule is of the form:

$$R_i = (R_{i_1}, R_{i_2}, \ldots, R_{i_n})$$

In the above rule, R_i is referred to as the *left side* of the rule. In a database scheme, no two rules may have the same left side. The Rs are called *names*, since they may refer either to schemes or to attributes. A name that does not appear on the left side of a rule is an *attribute*. A name that does not appear on the right side is a rule is called an *external name* or *external scheme*. External names are the schemes for the top level of a nesting hierarchy. All other names are *internal schemes*.

In the above rule, the names *accessible* from R_i are all names that either are one of the R_i or are accessible from one of the R_{i_j}. If R_i is accessible from itself, the database scheme is *recursive*. Many nested relational database systems require that the database scheme be nonrecursive.

14.2.3 Nested Relational Query Languages

The relational algebra operations we saw in Chapter 3 apply also to nested relations. To these operators we add two others that restructure nested relations:

- **Nest**. The nest operator, denoted by (ν), partitions the tuples of a relation into groups. Each group's members are aggregated into a single tuple.

- **Unnest**. The unnest operator, denoted by (μ), "unravels" a nested subrelation. A separate tuple is generated for each tuple of the nested subrelation.

We illustrate the use of these operations below.

Suppose we wish to generate the 1NF relation doc' (Figure 14.7) from the non-1NF relation doc (Figure 14.6). There are three nested subrelations to be unnested, and this can be done in any order. If we start with the $author\text{-}list$ subrelation, we write

$$\mu_{author\text{-}list\ =\ (author)}\ (doc)$$

and obtain the relation doc_1 shown in Figure 14.9. Note that in the relation doc, the first tuple contains an $author\text{-}list$ consisting of 2 tuples: (Smith) and (Jones). In doc_1, however, we have one tuple for each author. The values for the other attributes are repeated. Thus, to generate the relation doc' we must unnest further:

$$\mu_{date\ =\ (day,\ month,\ year)}\ (\mu_{keyword\text{-}list\ =\ (keyword)}\ (doc_1))$$

Suppose we wish to generate the non-1NF relation doc (Figure 14.6) from the 1NF relation doc' (Figure 14.7). This can be done by means of several nest operations. Consider the relation doc' of Figure 14.7. The expression

$$\nu_{author\text{-}list\ =\ (author)}\ (doc')$$

takes doc' and groups tuples together that have the same value on all attributes except $author$. For example, the tuples (salesplan, Smith, 1, April, 79, profit) and (salesplan, Jones, 1, April, 79, profit) are grouped together. For each group, a single tuple is created in which the authors for the group are placed in a set-valued attribute. The result is the relation

title	author	date	keywords
		month year	
salesplan	Smith	1 April 79	{profit, strategy}
salesplan	Jones	1 April 79	{profit, strategy}
status report	Jones	17 June 85	{profit, personnel}
status report	Frick	17 June 85	{profit, personnel}

Figure 14.9   Relation doc_1, the unnesting of doc on $author\text{-}list = (author)$.

title	author-list	day	month	year	keyword
	author				
salesplan	{Smith, Jones}	1	April	79	profit
salesplan	{Smith, Jones}	1	April	79	strategy
status report	{Jones, Frick}	17	June	85	profit
status report	{Jones, Frick}	17	June	85	personnel

Figure 14.10   Nesting the relation of Figure 14.7 on *author-list* = (*author*).

shown in Figure 14.10. We can generate *doc* by nesting further:

$$\nu_{date = (day,\ month,\ year)}\ (\nu_{keyword\text{-}list = (keyword)}\ (\nu_{author\text{-}list = (author)}\ (doc')))$$

These examples of the nest and unnest operators can help us understand their exact definition. Let r be a relation (possibly nested) with a scheme $R = (A_1, A_2, \ldots, A_n)$ and consider

$$\nu_{B = (B_1, B_2, \ldots, B_m)}\ (r)$$

where each B_i is a distinct A_j for some j. Let $C_1, C_2, \ldots, C_{n-m}$ be those A_j that are not equal to any B_i. Then the result of the above expression is a relation r' on scheme R'.

- The rule $B = (B_1, B_2, \ldots, B_n)$ is added to the database scheme.
- The rule $R' = (C_1, C_2, \ldots, C_{n-m}, B)$ is added to the database scheme.
- The relation r' is the result of the following steps:

   o Split r into groups of tuples that agree on $C_1, C_2, \ldots, C_{n-m}$. Let $G_1, G_2, \ldots, G_p$ denote these groups.
   o Include in r' one tuple t_i for each group G_i where t_i takes its values on $C_1, C_2, \ldots, C_{n-m}$ from the common value held by all tuples in G_i, and $t_i [B]$ is the set of $(B_1, B_2, \ldots, B_n)$ values held by tuples in G_i.

We can express r' in a tuple relational calculus-like form as

$$\{t \mid \exists\, u \in r\ (t[C_1, C_2, \ldots, C_{n-m}] = u[C_1, C_2, \ldots, C_{n-m}]$$
$$\wedge\ t[B] = \{v[B_1, B_2, \ldots, B_m] \mid \exists\, w \in r$$
$$(w[B_1, B_2, \ldots, B_m] = v[B_1, B_2, \ldots, B_m]\ \wedge$$
$$w[C_1, C_2, \ldots, C_{n-m}] = t[C_1, C_2, \ldots, C_{n-m}])\}\})\}$$

Let us now examine the unnest operator. Let r be a relation with scheme $R = (A_1, A_2, \ldots, A_i, B, A_{i+1}, A_{i+2}, \ldots, A_n)$ and let the rule $B = (B_1, B_2, \ldots, B_m)$ be part of the database scheme. Consider:

$$\mu_{B = (B_1, B_2, \ldots, B_m)} (r)$$

The result of this expression is a relation r' on scheme R' where:

- The rule

$$R' = (A_1, A_2, \ldots, A_i, B_1, B_2, \ldots, B_m, A_{i+1}, A_{i+2}, \ldots, A_n)$$

  is added to the database scheme.

- The relation r' is obtained as the result of the following steps:

> **for each** u **in** r **do**
>   **for each** v **in** $t[B]$ **do**
>   include a tuple t in r' with
> $t[A_1, A_2, \ldots, A_n] = u[A_1, A_2, \ldots, A_n]$
> $t[B_1, B_2, \ldots, B_m] = v[B_1, B_2, \ldots, B_m]$

We can express r' in a tuple relational calculus-like form as:

$$\{t \mid \exists\, u \in r\, (t[A_1, A_2, \ldots, A_n] = u[A_1, A_2, \ldots, A_n] \wedge$$
$$t[B_1, B_2, \ldots, B_m] \in u[B])\}$$

Although nest and unnest are necessary for the restructuring of nested relations, it is usually more convenient to operate on nested relations directly. We shall illustrate the application of nested relations by considering the language SQL/NF, which is a version of SQL extended to incorporate nested relational operations.

As we saw in Chapter 4, a SQL query takes the form

> **select** $A_1, A_2, \ldots, A_n$
> **from** $r_1, r_2, \ldots, r_m$
> **where** P

In SQL, the A_is represent attribute names and the r_is represent relation names. In SQL/NF there is no distinction between attribute names and relation names. Thus, a relation name may appear in SQL/NF anywhere an attribute name may appear in SQL. Furthermore, while SQL restricts the **from** clause to be a list of relation names (or view names), SQL/NF allows an expression evaluating to a relation to appear anywhere a relation name may appear.

The ability to use subexpressions freely in SQL/NF makes it possible to take advantage of the structure of a nested relation. Consider the relation *doc* of Figure 14.6 and the query "Find the title of documents written by Jones pertaining to profit." In SQL/NF this can be written as:

> **select** *title*
> **from** *doc*
> **where** "Jones" **in** *author-list*
>   **and** "profit" **in** *keyword-list*

Note that we have used relation-valued attributes in positions where SQL would have required a **select-from-where** subexpression. In particular, note the use of **in** to test for membership in the *keyword-list* subrelation of *doc*.

Let us now consider a modification of the above query, "Find the title and year of publication of documents written by Jones pertaining to profit." Note that we are asking only for the *year*, not the full date (day, month, year).

> **select** *title*, (**select** *year* **from** *date*)
> **from** *doc*
> **where** "Jones" **in** *author-list*
>   **and** "profit" **in** *keyword-list*

In the above example, *date* is an attribute of relation *doc*. Since *date* is relation-valued, we can apply a selection to it. For each tuple *t* of *doc* satisfying the **where** clause, the query provides the title and the result of the nested selection on the *date* relation of *t*.

SQL/NF includes **nest** and **unnest** operators that allow the restructuring of relations as part of a query. For example, to unnest *doc* fully, we write:

> **unnest** *doc* **on** *author-list, keyword-list*

The nesting of a relation requires the specification of the rules being used. The expression

> **nest** *doc'* **on** *author* **as** *author-list*

results in the relation of Figure 14.10.

To generate the relation of Figure 14.6, we write:

> **nest** (**nest** *doc'* **on** *author* **as** *author-list*) **on** *keyword* **as** *keyword-list*

The **nest** operation is useful in expressing queries involving aggregate operations. The **group by** clause of SQL produces what, in effect, is a temporary nested relation on which a value is computed by an aggregate function. We shall see that nested relations allow aggregate queries to be simplified considerably.

Aggregate functions (**avg, min, max, sum, count**) take a set as an argument and return a value as their result. SQL/NF allows aggregate functions to be applied to any relation-valued expression.

Let us consider first a simple query: "Find the title and number of authors for each document," which can be written as:

> **select** *title*, **count**(*author-list*)
> **from** *doc*

Since *author-list* is a relation-valued attribute containing one tuple for each author, a count of this nested subrelation provides the number of authors.

If the set on which we wish to perform an aggregate function does not exist, we may use the nest operator to create it. To illustrate, we consider the query previously used in our banking scheme of Chapter 4: "Find the name and average account balance of all branches." In SQL/NF, we first construct a relation on (*branch-name*, *balance*). Next, we construct a nested relation whose tuples are pairs of the form (branch name, set of all balances of accounts at that branch). Finally we apply the **avg** aggregate function. The resulting query is:

> **select** *branch-name*, **avg**(*account-balances*)
> **from nest select** *branch-name*, *balance*
>   **from** *deposit*
>   **on** *balance*
>   **as** *account-balances*

The explicit definition of the nested relation allows predicates on the nested relation to appear in a **where** clause. This eliminates the need for SQL's **group by** and **having** constructs. Consider the query above, but with attention restricted to branches where the average account balance is more than $1200. We write:

> **select** *branch-name*, **avg**(*account-balances*)
> **from nest select** *branch-name*, *balance*
>   **from** *deposit*
>   **on** *balance*
>   **as** *account-balances*
>   **where avg**(*account-balances*) > 1200

SQL/NF allows the use of **group by** and **having** for purposes of upward compatibility with standard SQL.

14.3 Expert Database Systems

In Section 14.1 we discussed the incorporation of logic-based rules into a relational database. Roughly speaking, such rules stated that if a certain set of tuples are in the database, so must be a certain other tuple. Expert database systems take this concept a step further by allowing arbitrary actions to be taken. An expert database system includes *rules* of the form "If a certain set of tuples are in the database, then a specific procedure is executed." This procedure may modify the database. As a result of these modifications, the **if** clause of other rules may become true. This process continues indefinitely. As a result, systems of this form are also referred to as *active databases*.

The structure of an expert database system is similar to that of an artificial intelligence expert system. The primary distinction between these two is the use of a database rather than just main (or virtual) memory.

In its simplest form, an expert database system consists of a standard database system and a standard expert system. The expert system submits queries in a database language such as SQL and awaits an answer from the database system. Although this is relatively easy to implement, it is not an optimal design since the rules in the knowledge base are not available for use in processing a database query. Furthermore, in the likely case that the expert system poses a series of queries, the database system cannot take advantage of the similarity of the queries and must process each one individually.

Because of the inefficiencies of this form of expert system interaction with a database system, several alternatives are being considered, including:

- Loading into the expert system that part of the database that is needed for processing rules. The database itself is stored and maintained separately from the expert system. Periodically, the expert system's copy of the data is updated.

- Implementing a database system within the expert system.

- Translating into the relational algebra certain logical queries posed to the expert system. The resulting algebra expression is passed to the database system for optimization and execution.

The integration of database management and expert systems is a rapidly growing area of research and development. Reference to current work is provided in the bibliographic notes.

14.4 Summary

The logic database model used in Datalog allows the specification of relations derived from base relations using **if-then** rules. These rules may be recursive. Evaluation of a nonrecursive Datalog query can be performed by constructing a rule graph. This graph shows for each derived relation the set of base and derived relations on which it depends. A topological sort of this graph computes the result in a bottom-up manner from the base relations. If the Datalog query is recursive, then the rule graph must contain a cycle. We saw two interactive techniques for evaluating recursive queries: naive evaluation and semi-naive evaluation.

The nested relational model extends the relational model to allow nonatomic domains (relations not in first normal form). These nonatomic domains are relation-valued. Thus, a hierarchy of nested relations is formed. The algebra operations *nest* and *unnest* are added to incorporated restructuring of nested relations into the relational algebra. SQL/NF, a modification of SQL for nested relations, was used to illustrate queries on nested relations.

Expert database systems consist of **if-then** rules. Unlike Datalog, the **then** clause may be an arbitrary transaction in the database. An expert database system continually tests for the satisfaction of the **if** conditions of the rules. When this occurs, one or more rules are chosen and the corresponding **then** clause is executed. Such systems are similar to expert systems with the additional feature of close interaction with a database.

Exercises

14.1 Consider the relational database scheme:

> *lives* (*person-name, street, city*)
> *works* (*person-name, company-name, salary*)
> *located-in* (*company-name, city*)
> *manages* (*person-name, manager-name*)

Write a Datalog query for:

   a. Find the name and city of all employees who work for First Bank Corporation.

   b. Find the name, street, and city of all employees who work for First Bank Corporation and earn more than $10,000.

   c. Find all employees who live in the same city as the company for which they work.

   d. Find all employees who live in the same city and on the same street as their manager.

e. Find all employees who do not work for First Bank Corporation.

f. Find all employees who earn more than every employee of Small Bank Corporation.

g. Find all employees working (directly or indirectly) under "Jones."

14.2 Let the following relation schemes be given:

$$R = (A,B,C)$$
$$S = (D,E,F)$$

Let relations $r(R)$ and $s(S)$ be given. Write Datalog queries equivalent the following relational algebra expressions:

a. $\Pi_A(r)$

b. $\sigma_{B = 17}(r)$

c. $r \times s$

d. $\Pi_{A,F}(\sigma_{C = D}(r \times s))$

14.3 Let $R = (A,B)$ and $S = (A,C)$, and let $r(R)$ and $s(S)$ be relations. Write Datalog queries equivalent to the following domain relational calculus expressions.

a. $\{<a > | \; \exists \, b \, (<a,b > \in r \wedge b = 17)\}$

b. $\{<a,b,c > | \; <a,b > \in r \wedge <a,c > \in s)\}$

c. $\{<b > | \; \forall \, a \, (\neg \, (<a,47> \in s) \vee <a,b > \in r)\}$

d. $\{<a > | \; \exists \, c \, (<a,c > \in s \wedge \exists \, b_1,b_2 \, (<a,b_1> \in r \wedge <c, b_2> \in r \wedge b_1 > b_2))\}$

14.4 Consider the nested relational database scheme:

$$Emp = (ename, \; Children, \; Skills)$$
$$Children = (name, \; Birthday)$$
$$Birthday = (day, \; month, \; year)$$
$$Skills = (type, \; Exams)$$
$$Exams = (year, \; city)$$

Write the following queries in the nested relational algebra for a relation *emp (Emp)*.

a. Find the names of all employees who have a child with a birthday in March.

b. Find those employees who took an exam for the skill-type "typing" in the city "Dayton."

c. List all skill-types in the relation *emp*.

14.5 Repeat Exercise 14.1 for the nested relational calculus.

14.6 Repeat Exercise 14.1 for SQL/NF.

14.7 Redesign the database of Exercise 14.4 into first normal form and fourth normal form. List any functional or multivalued dependencies you assumed.

Bibliographic Notes

The nested relational model was introduced in Makinouchi [1977] and Jaeschke and Schek [1982]. Various algebraic query languages are presented in Fischer and Thomas [1983], Zaniolo [1983], Abiteboul and Bidoit [1984], Bidoit [1987], Deshpande and Larson [1987], Ozsoyoglu, et al. [1987], Van Gucht [1987], and Roth, et al. [1988]. Query optimization for the nested relation algebra is discussed in Scholl [1986], Deshpande and Van Gucht [1987], Colby [1989], and Korth and Peltier [1990]. The management of null values in nested relations is discussed in Roth, et al. [1989]. Design and normalization issues are discussed in Ozsoyoglu and Yuan [1987] and Roth and Korth [1987].

Implementations of nested relational database systems include the Advanced Information Management Prototype at the IBM Heidleberg Scientific Center (Dadam, et al. [1986] and Pistor and Dadam [1989]), the DASDB project at the Technical University of Darmstadt (Schek and Scholl [1989]), the VERSO database machine (Scholl, et al. [1989]), and the ANDA project at Indiana University (Deshpande and Van Gucht [1988, 1989]). SQL-like languages for nested relational queries are presented in Bradley [1983], Pistor and Anderson [1986], Pistor and Traunmueller [1986], Roth, et al. [1987], and Korth and Roth [1989].

The use of the relational and nested relational models to describe text databases, user interfaces, and operating system interfaces is discussed in Henderson, et al. [1983], Sciore, et al. [1983], Bernstein, et al. [1984], Kim et al. [1988a], Korth and Silberschatz [1985], and Korth [1986]. A collection of recent papers on nested relations appears in Abiteboul, et al. [1989].

General discussions concerning logic databases are offered by Gallaire and Minker [1978] and Gallaire et al. [1984]. A good collections of selected papers on this subject can be found in Minker [1988]. Chandra and Harel [1982] discuss issues concerning semantics of logic databases. The bottom-up semi-naive evaluation technique has been proposed independently by a number of different researchers including Bancilhon [1985], Bayer [1985], and Balbin and Ramamohanarao [1986]. A good survey on optimization of logic queries is presented by Bancilhon and Ramakrishnan [1986]. Detailed discussions are given by Ullman [1988]. Stratified logic is discussed by Chandra and Harel [1982] and Apt and Pugin [1987]. Techniques for parallelizing sequential logic programs are discussed by Wolfson and Silberschatz [1988], Valduriez and Khoshafian [1989], Ganguly et al. [1990], and Wolfson and Ozeri [1990]. Two logic-based database system prototypes are NAIL! described by Morris et al. [1986], and LDL described by Tsur and Zaniolo [1986].

Vassiliou et al. [1985] presents a survey of knowledge bases and their relation to databases. Wiederhold et al. [1983a, 1983b] describes the KBMS project, in which artificial intelligence techniques are applied to database management. Trends in expert database systems are discussed in Stonebraker and Hearst [1988].

15

Distributed Databases

In a distributed database system, the database is stored on several computers. The computers in a distributed system communicate with one another through various communication media, such as high-speed buses or telephone lines. They do not share main memory, nor do they share a clock.

The processors in a distributed system may vary in size and function. They may include small microcomputers, work stations, minicomputers, and large general-purpose computer systems. These processors are referred to by a number of different names, such as *sites*, *nodes*, and *computers*, depending on the context in which they are mentioned. We mainly use the term *site*, in order to emphasize the physical distribution of these systems.

A distributed database system consists of a collection of sites, each of which may participate in the execution of transactions which access data at one site, or several sites. The main difference between centralized and distributed database systems is that, in the former, the data resides in one single location, while in the latter, the data resides in several locations. This distribution of data is the cause of many difficulties that will be addressed in this chapter.

15.1 Structure of Distributed Databases

A distributed database system consists of a collection of sites, each of which maintains a local database system. Each site is able to process *local transactions*, those transactions that access data only in that single site. In addition, a site may participate in the execution of *global transactions*, those transactions that access data in several sites. The execution of global transactions requires communication among the sites.

The sites in the system can be connected physically in a variety of ways. The various topologies are represented as graphs whose nodes correspond to sites. An edge from node A to node B corresponds to a direct connection between the two sites. Some of the most common configurations are depicted in Figure 15.1. The major differences among these configurations involve:

- **Installation cost**. The cost of physically linking the sites in the system.

- **Communication cost**. The cost in time and money to send a message from site A to site B.

- **Reliability**. The frequency with which a link or site fails.

- **Availability**. The degree to which data can be accessed despite the failure of some links or sites.

As we shall see, these differences play an important role in choosing the appropriate mechanism for handling the distribution of data.

The sites of a distributed database system may be distributed physically either over a large geographical area (such as the United States) or over a small geographical area (such as a single building or a number of adjacent buildings). The former type of network is referred to as a *long-haul* network; the latter is referred to as a *local-area* network.

Since the sites in long-haul networks are distributed physically over a large geographical area, the communication links are likely to be relatively slow and less reliable as compared with local-area networks. Typical long-haul links are telephone lines, microwave links, and satellite channels. In contrast, since all the sites in local-area networks are close to one another, the communication links are of higher speed and lower error rate than their counterparts in long-haul networks. The most common links are twisted pair, baseband coaxial, broadband coaxial, and fiber optics.

Let us illustrate these concepts by considering a banking system consisting of four branches located in four different cities. Each branch has its own computer with a database consisting of all the accounts maintained at that branch. Each such installation is thus a site. There also exists one single site which maintains information about all the branches of the bank. Each branch maintains (among others) a relation *deposit(Deposit-scheme)* where:

Deposit-scheme = (*branch-name, account-number, customer-name, balance*)

The site containing information about the four branches maintains the relation *branch(Branch-scheme)*, where:

Branch-scheme = (*branch-name, assets, branch-city*)

There are other relations maintained at the various sites which are ignored for the purpose of our example.

A local transaction is one that accesses accounts in the *single* site at which the transaction was initiated. A global transaction, on the other hand, is one which either accesses accounts in a site different from the one

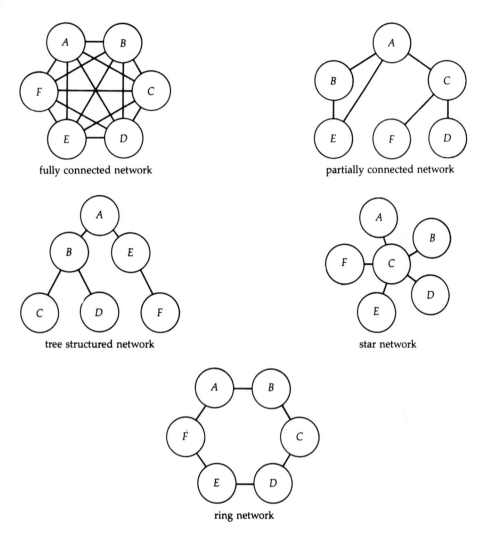

fully connected network

partially connected network

tree structured network

star network

ring network

Figure 15.1   Network topology.

at which the transaction was initiated or accesses accounts in several different sites. To illustrate the difference, consider the transaction to add $50 to account number 177 located at the Valleyview branch. If the transaction was initiated at the Valleyview branch, then it is considered local; otherwise, it is considered global. A transaction to transfer $50 from account 177 to account 305, which is located at the Hillside branch, is a global transaction, since accounts in two different sites are accessed as a result of its execution.

What makes the above configuration a distributed database system are the facts that:

- The various sites are aware of one another.

- Each site provides an environment for executing both local and global transactions.

We shall assume that each site is running the same distributed database management software. If this assumption does not hold, it is very difficult to manage global transactions, and we defer consideration of this issue to Section 15.11.

15.2 Trade-offs in Distributing the Database

There are several reasons for building distributed database systems, including sharing of data, reliability and availability, and speedup of query processing. However, along with these advantages come several disadvantages, including software development cost, greater potential for bugs, and increased processing overhead. In this section, we elaborate briefly on each of these.

15.2.1 Advantages of Data Distribution

The primary advantage of distributed database systems is the ability to share and access data in a reliable and efficient manner.

Data Sharing and Distributed Control

If a number of different sites are connected, then a user at one site may be able to access data available at another site. For example, in the distributed banking system described in Section 15.1, it is possible for a user in one branch to access data in another branch. Without this capability, a user wishing to transfer funds from one branch to another would have to resort to some external mechanism that would, in effect, be a single centralized database.

The primary advantage of sharing data by means of data distribution is that each site is able to retain a degree of control over data stored locally. In a centralized system, the database administrator of the central site controls the database. In a distributed system, there is a global database administrator responsible for the entire system. A part of these responsibilities is delegated to the local database administrator for each site. Depending upon the design of the distributed database system, each administrator may have a different degree of *local autonomy*. The possibility of local autonomy is often a major advantage of distributed databases.

Reliability and Availability

If one site fails in a distributed system, the remaining sites may be able to continue operating. In particular, if data items are replicated in several sites, a transaction needing a particular data item may find it in any of several sites. Thus, the failure of a site does not necessarily imply the shutdown of the system.

The failure of one site must be detected by the system, and appropriate action may be needed to recover from the failure. The system must no longer use the services of the failed site. Finally, when the failed site recovers or is repaired, mechanisms must be available to integrate it smoothly back into the system.

Although recovery from failure is more complex in distributed systems than in centralized systems, the ability of most of the system to continue to operate despite the failure of one site results in increased availability. Availability is crucial for database systems used for real-time applications. Loss of access to data by, for example, an airline may result in the loss of potential ticket buyers to competitors.

Speedup of Query Processing

If a query involves data at several sites, it may be possible to split the query into subqueries that can be executed in parallel. We may use some of the parallel-join computation strategies of Section 9.6. However, in a distributed system, there is no sharing of main memory, so not all of the join strategies for parallel processors can be applied directly to distributed systems. In those cases in which data is replicated, queries may be directed by the system to the least heavily loaded sites. We examine distributed query-processing issues in Section 15.5.

15.2.2 Disadvantages of Data Distribution

The primary disadvantage of distributed database systems is the added complexity required to ensure proper coordination among the sites. This increased complexity takes the form of:

- **Software development cost**. It is more difficult to implement a distributed database system and, thus, more costly.

- **Greater potential for bugs**. Since the sites that comprise the distributed system operate in parallel, it is harder to ensure the correctness of algorithms. The potential exists for extremely subtle bugs.

- **Increased processing overhead**. The exchange of messages and the additional computation required to achieve intersite coordination are a form of overhead that does not arise in centralized systems.

In choosing the design for a database system, the designer must balance the advantages against the disadvantages of distribution of data. We shall see that there are several approaches to distributed database design, ranging from fully distributed designs to ones that include a large degree of centralization.

15.3 Design of Distributed Databases

The principles of database design discussed earlier apply to distributed databases as well. In this section, we focus on those design issues that are specific to distributed databases.

Consider a relation r that is to be stored in the database. There are several issues involved in storing this relation in the distributed database, including:

- **Replication**. The system maintains several identical replicas (copies) of the relation. Each replica is stored in a different site, resulting in data replication. The alternative to replication is to store only one copy of relation r.

- **Fragmentation**. The relation is partitioned into several fragments. Each fragment is stored in a different site.

- **Replication and Fragmentation**. This is a combination of the above two notions. The relation is partitioned into several fragments. The system maintains several identical replicas of each such fragment.

In the following subsections, we elaborate on each of these.

15.3.1 Data Replication

If relation r is replicated, a copy of relation r is stored in two or more sites. In the most extreme case, we have *full replication*, in which a copy is stored in every site in the system.

There are a number of advantages and disadvantages to replication.

- **Availability**. If one of the sites containing relation r fails, then the relation r may be found in another site. Thus, the system may continue to process queries involving r despite the failure of one site.

- **Increased parallelism**. In the case where the majority of access to the relation r results in only the reading of the relation, then several sites can process queries involving r in parallel. The more replicas of r there are, the greater the chance that the needed data is found in the site where the transaction is executing. Hence, data replication minimizes movement of data between sites.

- **Increased overhead on update**. The system must ensure that all replicas of a relation r are consistent; otherwise erroneous computations may result. Thus, whenever r is updated, the update must be propagated to all sites containing replicas. The result is increased overhead. For example, in a banking system, where account information is replicated in various sites, it is necessary to ensure that the balance in a particular account agrees in all sites.

In general, replication enhances the performance of **read** operations and increases the availability of data to **read** transactions. However, update transactions incur greater overhead. The problem of controlling concurrent updates by several transactions to replicated data is more complex than the centralized approach to concurrency control that we saw in Chapter 11. We may simplify the management of replicas of relation r by choosing one of them as the *primary copy of r*. For example, in a banking system, an account may be associated with the site in which the account has been opened. Similarly, in an airline reservation system, a flight may be associated with the site at which the flight originates. We shall examine the options for distributed concurrency control in Section 15.8.

15.3.2 Data Fragmentation

If the relation r is fragmented, r is divided into a number of *fragments* r_1, $r_2, \ldots, r_n$. These fragments contain sufficient information to reconstruct the original relation r. As we shall see, this reconstruction can take place through the application of either the union operation or a special type of join operation on the various fragments. There are two different schemes for fragmenting a relation: *horizontal* fragmentation and *vertical* fragmentation. Horizontal fragmentation splits the relation by assigning each tuple of r to one or more fragments. Vertical fragmentation splits the relation by decomposing the scheme R of relation r in a special way that we shall discuss. These two schemes can be applied successively to the same relation, resulting in a number of different fragments. Note that some information may appear in several fragments.

Below we discuss the various ways for fragmenting a relation. We shall illustrate these by fragmenting the relation *deposit*, with scheme:

    Deposit-scheme = (*branch-name, account-number, customer-name, balance*)

The relation *deposit* (*Deposit-scheme*) is shown in Figure 15.2.

Horizontal Fragmentation

The relation r is partitioned into a number of subsets, $r_1, r_2, \ldots, r_n$. Each tuple of relation r must belong to one of the fragments, so that the original relation can be reconstructed, if needed.

branch-name	account-number	customer-name	balance
Hillside	305	Lowman	500
Hillside	226	Camp	336
Valleyview	177	Camp	205
Valleyview	402	Kahn	10000
Hillside	155	Kahn	62
Valleyview	408	Kahn	1123
Valleyview	639	Green	750

Figure 15.2   Sample *deposit* relation.

A fragment may be defined as a *selection* on the global relation r. That is, a predicate P_i is used to construct fragment r_i as follows:

$$r_i = \sigma_{P_i} (r)$$

The reconstruction of the relation r can be obtained by taking the union of all fragments, that is:

$$r = r_1 \cup r_2 \cup \cdots \cup r_n$$

To illustrate, suppose that the relation r is the *deposit* relation of Figure 15.2. This relation can be divided into n different fragments, each of which consists of tuples of accounts belonging to a particular branch. If the banking system has only two branches, Hillside and Valleyview, then there are two different fragments:

$$deposit_1 = \sigma_{branch\text{-}name \,=\, \text{"Hillside"}} (deposit)$$
$$deposit_2 = \sigma_{branch\text{-}name \,=\, \text{"Valleyview"}} (deposit)$$

These two fragments are shown in Figure 15.3. Fragment $deposit_1$ is stored in the Hillside site. Fragment $deposit_2$ is stored in the Valleyview site.

In our example, the fragments are disjoint. By changing the selection predicates used to construct the fragments, we may have a particular tuple of r appear in more than one of the r_i. This form of data replication is discussed further at the end of this section.

Vertical Fragmentation

In its simplest form, vertical fragmentation is the same as decomposition (see Chapter 6). Vertical fragmentation of $r(R)$ involves the definition of several subsets $R_1, R_2, \ldots, R_n$ of R such that:

$$R = R_1 \cup R_2 \cup \cdots \cup R_n$$

branch-name	account-number	customer-name	balance
Hillside	305	Lowman	500
Hillside	226	Camp	336
Hillside	155	Kahn	62

$deposit_1$

branch-name	account-number	customer-name	balance
Valleyview	177	Camp	205
Valleyview	402	Kahn	10000
Valleyview	408	Kahn	1123
Valleyview	639	Green	750

$deposit_2$

Figure 15.3   Horizontal fragmentation of relation *deposit*.

Each fragment r_i of r is defined by:

$$r_i = \Pi_{R_i}(r)$$

Relation r can be reconstructed from the fragments by taking the natural join:

$$r = r_1 \bowtie r_2 \bowtie r_3 \bowtie \cdots \bowtie r_n$$

More generally, vertical fragmentation is accomplished by adding a special attribute called a *tuple-id* to the scheme R. A tuple-id is a physical or logical address for a tuple. Since each tuple in r must have a unique address, the *tuple-id* attribute is a key for the augmented scheme.

branch-name	account-number	customer-name	balance	tuple-id
Hillside	305	Lowman	500	1
Hillside	226	Camp	336	2
Valleyview	177	Camp	205	3
Valleyview	402	Kahn	10000	4
Hillside	155	Kahn	62	5
Valleyview	408	Kahn	1123	6
Valleyview	639	Green	750	7

Figure 15.4   The *deposit* relation of Figure 15.2 with tuple-ids.

In Figure 15.4, we show the relation *deposit'*, the *deposit* relation of Figure 15.2 with tuple-ids added. Figure 15.5 shows a vertical decomposition of the scheme *Deposit-scheme* ∪ *{tuple-id}* into:

$$Deposit\text{-}scheme\text{-}3 = (branch\text{-}name,\ customer\text{-}name,\ tuple\text{-}id)$$
$$Deposit\text{-}scheme\text{-}4 = (account\text{-}number,\ balance,\ tuple\text{-}id)$$

The two relations shown in Figure 15.5 result from computing:

$$deposit_3 = \Pi_{Deposit\text{-}scheme\text{-}3}\ (deposit')$$
$$deposit_4 = \Pi_{Deposit\text{-}scheme\text{-}4}\ (deposit')$$

To reconstruct the original *deposit* relation from the fragments, we compute:

$$\Pi_{Deposit\text{-}scheme}\ (deposit_3 \bowtie deposit_4)$$

branch-name	customer-name	tuple-id
Hillside	Lowman	1
Hillside	Camp	2
Valleyview	Camp	3
Valleyview	Kahn	4
Hillside	Kahn	5
Valleyview	Kahn	6
Valleyview	Green	7

$$deposit_3$$

account-number	balance	tuple-id
305	500	1
226	336	2
177	205	3
402	10000	4
155	62	5
408	1123	6
639	750	7

$$deposit_4$$

Figure 15.5   Vertical fragmentation of relation *deposit*.

Note that the expression

$$deposit_3 \bowtie deposit_4$$

is a special form of natural join. The join attribute is *tuple-id*. Since the *tuple-id* value represents an address, it is possible to pair a tuple of $deposit_3$ with the corresponding tuple of $deposit_4$ by using the address given by the *tuple-id* value. This address allows direct retrieval of the tuple without the need for an index. Thus, this natural join may be computed much more efficiently than typical natural joins.

Although the *tuple-id* attribute facilitates the implementation of vertical partitioning, it is important that this attribute not be visible to users. If users are given access to tuple-ids, it becomes impossible for the system to change tuple addresses. Furthermore, the accessibility of internal addresses violates the notion of data independence, one of the main virtues of the relational model.

Mixed Fragmentation

The relation r is divided into a number of fragment relations $r_1, r_2, \ldots, r_n$. Each fragment is obtained as the result of applying either the horizontal fragmentation or vertical fragmentation scheme on relation r, or a fragment of r which was obtained previously.

To illustrate, suppose that the relation r is the *deposit* relation of Figure 15.2. This relation is divided initially into the fragments $deposit_3$ and $deposit_4$ as defined above. We can now further divide fragment $deposit_3$ using the horizontal fragmentation scheme into the following two fragments:

$$deposit_{3a} = \sigma_{branch\text{-}name\ =\ \text{"Hillside"}}(deposit_3)$$
$$deposit_{3b} = \sigma_{branch\text{-}name\ =\ \text{"Valleyview"}}(deposit_3)$$

Thus relation r is divided into three fragments: $deposit_{3a}$, $deposit_{3b}$, and $deposit_4$. Each of these may reside in a different site.

15.3.3 Data Replication and Fragmentation

The techniques described above for data replication and data fragmentation can be applied successively to the same relation. That is, a fragment can be replicated; replicas of fragments can be fragmented further; and so on. For example, consider a distributed system consisting of sites $S_1, S_2, \ldots, S_{10}$. We can fragment *deposit* into $deposit_{3a}$, $deposit_{3b}$, and $deposit_4$, and, for example, store a copy of $deposit_{3a}$ at sites S_1, S_3, and S_7, a copy of $deposit_{3b}$ at sites S_7 and S_{10}, and a copy of $deposit_4$ at sites S_2, S_8, and S_9.

15.4 Transparency and Autonomy

In the previous section, we saw that a relation r may be stored in a variety of ways in a distributed database system. It is essential that the system minimize the degree to which a user needs to be aware of how a relation is stored. As we shall see, a system can hide the details of the distribution of data in the network. We call this *network transparency*.

Network transparency is related, in some sense, to local autonomy. Network transparency is the degree to which system users may remain unaware of the details of the design of the distributed system. Local autonomy is the degree to which a designer or administrator of one site may be independent of the remainder of the distributed system.

We shall consider the issues of transparency and autonomy from the points of view of:

- Naming of data items.

- Replication of data items.

- Fragmentation of data items.

- Location of fragments and replicas.

15.4.1 Naming and Local Autonomy

Every data item in the database must have a unique name. This property is easy to ensure in a nondistributed database. However, in a distributed database, care must be taken to ensure that two sites do not use the same name for distinct data items.

One solution to this problem is to require all names to be registered in a central *name server*. This approach, however, suffers from several disadvantages:

- The name server may become a bottleneck.

- If the name server crashes, it may not be possible for any site in the distributed system to continue to run.

- There is little local autonomy since naming is controlled centrally.

An alternative approach that results in increased local autonomy is to require that each site prefix its own site identifier to any name it generates. This ensures that no two sites generate the same name (since each site has a unique identifier). Furthermore, no central control is required.

The above solution achieves local autonomy but fails to achieve network transparency, since site identifiers are attached to names. Thus, the *deposit* relation might be referred to as *site17.deposit* rather than simply *deposit*. We shall soon see how to overcome this problem.

Each replica of a data item and each fragment of a data item must have a unique name. It is important that the system be able to determine those replicas that are replicas of the same data item and those fragments that are fragments of the same data item. We adopt the convention of postfixing ".*f1*", ".*f2*", . . . , ".*fn*" to fragments of a data item and ".*r1*", ".*r2*", . . . , ".*rn*" to replicas. Thus

$$site17.deposit.f3.r2$$

refers to replica 2 of fragment 3 of *deposit*, and this item was generated by site 17.

15.4.2 Replication and Fragmentation Transparency

It is undesirable to expect users to refer to a specific replica of a data item. Instead, the system should determine which replica to reference on a **read** request, and update all replicas on a **write** request.

When a data item is requested, the specific replica need not be named. Instead, a catalog table is used by the system to determine all replicas for the data item.

Similarly, a user should not be required to know how a data item is fragmented. As we observed earlier, vertical fragments may contain *tuple-ids*, which represent addresses of tuples. Horizontal fragments may involve complicated selection predicates. Therefore, a distributed database system should allow requests to be stated in terms of the unfragmented data items. This presents no major difficulty, since it is always possible to reconstruct the original data item from its fragments. However, it may be inefficient to reconstruct data from fragments. Returning to our horizontal fragmentation of *deposit*, consider the query:

$$\sigma_{branch\text{-}name = \text{``Hillside''}} (deposit)$$

This query could be answered using only the $deposit_1$ fragment. However, fragmentation transparency requires that the user not be aware of the existence of fragments $deposit_1$ and $deposit_2$. If we reconstruct *deposit* prior to processing the above query, we obtain the expression:

$$\sigma_{branch\text{-}name = \text{``Hillside''}} (deposit_1 \cup deposit_2)$$

The optimization of this expression is left to the query optimizer (see Section 15.5).

15.4.3 Location Transparency

If replication and fragmentation transparency are provided by the system, a large part of the design of the distributed database is hidden from the user. However, the site-identifier component of names forces the user to be aware of the fact that the system is distributed.

Location transparency is achieved by creating a set of alternative names or *aliases* for each user. A user may thus refer to data items by simple names that are translated by the system to complete names.

With aliases, the user can be unaware of the physical location of a data item. Furthermore, the user is unaffected if the database administrator should decide to move a data item from one site to another.

15.4.4 Complete Naming Scheme

We have seen that a name provided by the user is translated in several steps before it refers to a specific replica of a specific fragment at a specific site. Figure 15.6 shows the complete translation scheme. To illustrate the operation of the scheme, consider a user located in the Hillside branch (site S_1). This user uses the alias *local-deposit* for the local fragment *deposit.f1* of the *deposit* relation. When this user references *local-deposit*, the query-processing subsystem looks up *local-deposit* in the alias table and replaces it with S_1.*deposit.f1*. It is possible that S_1.*deposit.f1* is replicated. If so, the replica table must be consulted in order to choose a replica. This replica could itself be fragmented, requiring examination of the fragmentation table. In most cases, only one or two tables must be consulted. However, the name translation scheme of Figure 15.6 is sufficiently general to deal with any combination of successive replication and fragmentation of relations.

```
if name appears in the alias table
    then expression := map (name)
    else expression := name;
function map (n)
if n appears in the replica table
    then result := name of replica of n;
if n appears in the fragment table
    then begin
            result := expression to construct fragment;
            for each n' in result do begin
                replace n' in result with map (n');
            end
        end
return result;
```

Figure 15.6   Name translation algorithm.

15.4.5 Transparency and Updates

Providing transparency for users that update the database is somewhat more difficult than providing transparency for readers. The main problem is ensuring that all replicas of a data item are updated and that all affected fragments are updated.

In its full generality, the update problem for replicated and fragmented data is related to the view update problem that we discussed earlier. Consider our example of the *deposit* relation and the insertion of the tuple:

$$(\text{``Valleyview''}, 733, \text{``Jones''}, 600)$$

If *deposit* is fragmented horizontally, there is a predicate P_i associated with the ith fragment. We apply P_i to the tuple ("Valleyview", 733, "Jones", 600) to test whether that tuple must be inserted in the ith fragment. Using our example of *deposit* being fragmented into

$$deposit_1 = \sigma_{branch\text{-}name\ =\ \text{``Hillside''}}\ (deposit)$$

$$deposit_2 = \sigma_{branch\text{-}name\ =\ \text{``Valleyview''}}\ (deposit)$$

the tuple would be inserted into $deposit_2$.

Now consider a vertical fragmentation of deposit into $deposit_3$ and $deposit_4$. The tuple ("Valleyview", 733, "Jones", 600) must be split into two fragments: one to be inserted into $deposit_3$ and one to be inserted into $deposit_4$.

If the *deposit* relation is replicated, the tuple ("Valleyview", 733, "Jones", 600) must be inserted in all replicas. This presents a problem if there is concurrent access to the *deposit* relation, since it is possible that one replica will be updated earlier than another. We consider this problem in Section 15.8.

15.5 Distributed Query Processing

In Chapter 9, we saw that there are a variety of methods for computing the answer to a query. We saw several techniques for choosing a strategy for processing a query that minimize the amount of time it takes to compute the answer. For centralized systems, the primary criterion for measuring the cost of a particular strategy is the number of disk accesses. In a distributed system, we must take into account several other issues, including:

- The cost of data transmission over the network.

- The potential gain in performance from having several sites process parts of the query in parallel.

The relative cost of data transfer over the network and data transfer to and from disk varies widely depending on the type of network and speed of the disks. Thus, in general, we cannot focus solely on disk costs or on network costs. Rather, we must find a good trade-off between the two.

15.5.1 Replication and Fragmentation

Let us consider an extremely simple query, "Find all the tuples in the *deposit* relation." Although the query is simple, indeed trivial, processing of this query is not trivial, since the *deposit* relation may be fragmented, replicated, or both, as we saw in Section 15.3. If the *deposit* relation is replicated, we have a choice of replica to make. If no replicas are fragmented, we choose the replica for which the transmission cost is lowest. However, if a replica is fragmented, the choice is not as easy to make, since several joins or unions need to be computed to reconstruct the *deposit* relation. In this case, the number of strategies for our simple example may be large. Indeed, choosing a strategy may be as complex a task as making an arbitrary query.

Fragmentation transparency implies that a user may write a query such as:

$$\sigma_{branch\text{-}name\ =\ \text{``Hillside''}} (deposit)$$

Since *deposit* is defined as

$$deposit_1 \cup deposit_2$$

the expression that results from the name translation scheme is:

$$\sigma_{branch\text{-}name\ =\ \text{``Hillside''}} (deposit_1 \cup deposit_2)$$

Using the query optimization techniques of Chapter 9, we can simplify the above expression automatically. This results in the expression

$$\sigma_{branch\text{-}name\ =\ \text{``Hillside''}} (deposit_1) \cup \sigma_{branch\text{-}name\ =\ \text{``Hillside''}} (deposit_2)$$

which includes two subexpressions. The first involves only $deposit_1$ and thus can be evaluated at the Hillside site. The second involves only $deposit_2$ and thus can be evaluated at the Valleyview site.

There is a further optimization that can be made in evaluating

$$\sigma_{branch\text{-}name\ =\ \text{``Hillside''}} (deposit_1)$$

Since $deposit_1$ has only tuples pertaining to the Hillside branch, we can eliminate the selection operation. In evaluating

$$\sigma_{branch\text{-}name\ =\ \text{``Hillside''}}\ (deposit_2)$$

we can apply the definition of the $deposit_2$ fragment to obtain

$$\sigma_{branch\text{-}name\ =\ \text{``Hillside''}}\ (\sigma_{branch\text{-}name\ =\ \text{``Valleyview''}}\ (deposit))$$

This expression is the empty set regardless of the contents of the *deposit* relation.

Thus, our final strategy is for the Hillside site to return $deposit_1$ as the result of the query.

15.5.2 Simple Join Processing

As we saw in Chapter 9, a major aspect of the selection of a query-processing strategy is choosing a join strategy. Consider the relational algebra expression:

$$customer \bowtie deposit \bowtie branch$$

Assume that the three relations are neither replicated nor fragmented and that *customer* is stored at site S_c, *deposit* at S_d, and *branch* at S_b. Let S_I denote the site at which the query was issued. The system needs to produce the result at site S_I. Among the possible strategies for processing this query are the following:

- Ship copies of all three relations to site S_I. Using the techniques of Chapter 9, choose a strategy for processing the entire query locally at site S_I.

- Ship a copy of the *customer* relation to site S_d and compute *customer* $\bowtie$ *deposit* at S_d. Ship *customer* $\bowtie$ *deposit* from S_d to S_b, where (*customer* $\bowtie$ *deposit*) $\bowtie$ *branch* is computed. The result of this computation is shipped to S_I.

- Strategies similar to the one above may be devised with the roles of S_c, S_d, S_b exchanged.

No one strategy is always the best one. Among the factors that must be considered are the amount of data being shipped, the cost of transmitting a block of data between a pair of sites, and the relative speed of processing at each site. Consider the first two strategies listed above. If we ship all three relations to S_I, and indices exist on these relations, we may need to re-create these indices at S_I. This entails extra processing overhead and extra disk accesses. However, the second strategy has the disadvantage that a potentially large relation (*customer* $\bowtie$ *deposit*) must be shipped from S_d to S_b. This relation repeats the address data for a customer once for each account the customer has. Thus, the second strategy may result in extra network transmission as compared with the first strategy.

15.5.3 Join Strategies That Exploit Parallelism

Let us consider a join of four relations

$$r_1 \bowtie r_2 \bowtie r_3 \bowtie r_4$$

where relation r_i is stored at site S_i. Assume that the result must be presented at site S_1. There are, of course, many strategies to be considered. One attractive approach is to use the pipelined-join strategy of Section 9.6.2. For example, r_1 can be shipped to S_2 and $r_1 \bowtie r_2$ computed at S_2. At the same time, r_3 can be shipped to S_4 and $r_3 \bowtie r_4$ computed at S_4.

Site S_2 can ship tuples of $(r_1 \bowtie r_2)$ to S_1 as they are produced rather than waiting for the entire join to be computed. Similarly, S_4 can ship tuples of $(r_3 \bowtie r_4)$ to S_1. Once tuples of $(r_1 \bowtie r_2)$ and $(r_3 \bowtie r_4)$ arrive at S_1, the computation of $(r_1 \bowtie r_2) \bowtie (r_3 \bowtie r_4)$ can begin in parallel with the computation of $(r_1 \bowtie r_2)$ at S_2 and the computation of $(r_3 \bowtie r_4)$ at S_4.

15.5.4 Semijoin Strategy

Suppose that we wish to evaluate the expression $r_1 \bowtie r_2$, where r_1 and r_2 are stored at sites S_1 and S_2, respectively. Let the schemes of r_1 and r_2 be R_1 and R_2. Suppose we wish to obtain the result at S_1. If there are many tuples of r_2 that do not join with any tuple of r_1, then shipping r_2 to S_1 entails the shipment of tuples that fail to contribute to the result. It is desirable to remove such tuples before shipping data to S_1, particularly if network costs are high.

A strategy for doing this is as follows:

1. Compute $temp1 \leftarrow \Pi_{R_1 \cap R_2}(r_1)$ at S_1.

2. Ship $temp1$ from S_1 to S_2.

3. Compute $temp2 \leftarrow r_2 \bowtie temp1$ at S_2.

4. Ship $temp2$ from S_2 to S_1.

5. Compute $r_1 \bowtie temp2$ at S_1. This is the result of $r_1 \bowtie r_2$.

Before considering the efficiency of this strategy, let us verify that it computes the correct answer. In step 3, $temp2$ has the result of $r_2 \bowtie \Pi_{R_1 \cap R_2}(r_1)$. In step 5, we compute:

$$r_1 \bowtie r_2 \bowtie \Pi_{R_1 \cap R_2}(r_1)$$

Since join is associative and commutative, we may rewrite this as:

$$(r_1 \bowtie \Pi_{R_1 \cap R_2} (r_1)) \bowtie r_2$$

Since $r_1 \bowtie \Pi_{(R_1 \cap R_2)} (r_1) = r_1$, the above expression is, indeed, equal to $r_1 \bowtie r_2$.

The above strategy is particularly advantageous when relatively few tuples of r_2 contribute to the join. This situation is likely to occur if r_1 is the result of a relational algebra expression involving selection. In such a case, *temp2* may have significantly fewer tuples than r_2. The cost saving of the strategy results from having to ship only *temp2*, rather than all of r_2, to S_1. Additional cost is incurred in shipping *temp1* to S_2. If a sufficiently small fraction of tuples in r_2 contribute to the join, the overhead of shipping *temp1* will be dominated by the saving of shipping only a fraction of the tuples in r_2.

This strategy is called a *semijoin strategy*, after the semijoin operator of the relational algebra, denoted $\ltimes$. The semijoin of r_1 with r_2, denoted $r_1 \ltimes r_2$, is:

$$\Pi_{R_1} (r_1 \bowtie r_2)$$

Thus, $r_1 \ltimes r_2$ selects those tuples of r_1 that contributed to $r_1 \bowtie r_2$. In step 3 above, *temp2* $= r_2 \ltimes r_1$.

For joins of several relations, the above strategy can be extended to a series of semijoin steps. A substantial body of theory bas been developed regarding the use of semijoins for query optimization. Some of this theory is referenced in the bibliographic notes.

15.6 Recovery in Distributed Systems

We have defined a transaction to be a program unit whose execution preserves the consistency of the database. A transaction must be executed *atomically*. That is, either all the instructions associated with it are executed to completion or none are performed. In addition, in the case of concurrent execution, the effect of executing a transaction must be the same as if the transaction had completed alone in the system.

15.6.1 System Structure

The atomicity property is ensured by the various recovery and concurrency control schemes we introduced in Chapters 10, 11, and 12. When we are dealing with a distributed database system, however, it becomes much more complicated to ensure the atomicity property of a transaction, since several sites may be participating in its execution. The failure of one of these sites, or the failure of a communication link connecting these sites, may result in erroneous computations.

It is the function of the *transaction manager* of a distributed database system to ensure that the execution of the various transactions in the distributed system preserves atomicity. Each site has its own local transaction manager. The various transaction managers cooperate to execute global transactions. To understand how such a manager can be implemented, let us define an abstract model of a transaction system. Each site of the system contains two subsystems:

- **Transaction manager,** whose function is to manage the execution of those transactions (or subtransactions) that access data stored in a local site. Note that each such transaction may be either a local transaction (that is, a transaction that only executes at that site) or part of a global transaction (that is, a transaction that executes at several sites).

- **Transaction coordinator,** whose function is to coordinate the execution of the various transactions (both local and global) initiated at that site.

The overall system architecture is depicted in Figure 15.7.

The structure of a transaction manager is similar in many respects to the structure used in the centralized system case. Each transaction manager is responsible for:

- Maintaining a log for recovery purposes.

- Participating in an appropriate concurrency control scheme to coordinate the concurrent execution of the transactions executing at that site.

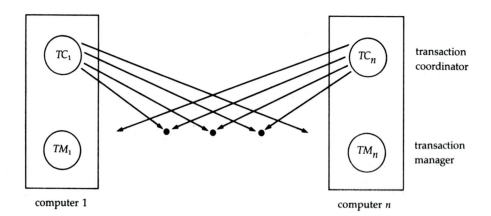

Figure 15.7   System architecture.

As we shall see, both the recovery and concurrency schemes need to be modified in order to accommodate the distribution of transactions.

The transaction coordinator subsystem is not needed in the centralized environment, since a transaction accesses data only at one single site. A transaction coordinator, as its name implies, is responsible for coordinating the execution of all the transactions initiated at that site. For each such transaction, the coordinator is responsible for:

- Starting the execution of the transaction.

- Breaking the transaction into a number of subtransactions, and distributing these subtransactions to the appropriate sites for execution.

- Coordinating the termination of the transaction, which may result in the transaction being committed at all sites or aborted at all sites.

15.6.2 Robustness

A distributed system may suffer from the same types of failure that a centralized system does (for example, memory failure, disk crash). There are, however, additional failures that need to be dealt with in a distributed environment, including:

- The failure of a site.

- The failure of a link.

- Loss of messages.

- Network partition.

In order for the system to be robust, it must therefore *detect* any of these failures, *reconfigure* the system so that computation may continue, and *recover* when a processor or a link is repaired.

It is generally not possible to differentiate among link failure, site failure, message loss, and network partition. The system can usually detect that a failure has occurred, but it may not be able to identify what kind of failure it is. For example, suppose that site S_1 is not able to communicate with S_2. If could be that S_2 has failed. However, another possibility is that the link between S_1 and S_2 has failed.

Suppose that site S_1 has discovered that a failure has occurred. It must then initiate a procedure that will allow the system to reconfigure and continue with its normal mode of operation.

- If replicated data is stored at the failed site, the catalog should be updated so that queries do not reference the copy at the failed site.

- If transactions were active at the failed site at the time of the failure, these transactions should be aborted. It is desirable to abort such transactions promptly since they may hold locks on data at sites that are still active.

- If the failed site is a central server for some subsystem, an "election" must be held to determine the new server (see Section 15.10.2). Examples of central servers include a name server, a concurrency coordinator, or a global deadlock detector.

Since it is, in general, not possible to distinguish between network link failures and site failures, any reconfiguration scheme must be designed to work correctly in case of a partitioning of the network. In particular, the following situations must be avoided:

- Two or more central servers are elected in distinct partitions.

- More than one partition updates a replicated data item.

Reintegration of a repaired site or link into the system also requires some care. When a failed site recovers, it must initiate a procedure to update its system tables to reflect changes made while it was down. If the site had replicas of any data items, it must obtain the current values of these data items and ensure that it receives all future updates. This is more complicated than it seems to be at first glance, since there may be updates to the data items processed during the time the site is recovering.

An easy solution is temporarily to halt the entire system while the failed site rejoins it. In most applications, this temporary halt is unacceptably disruptive. A preferable solution is to represent the recovery tasks as a series of transactions. The concurrent control subsystem and transaction management subsystem may then be relied upon for proper reintegration of the site.

If a failed link recovers, two or more partitions may be rejoined. Since a partitioning of the network limits the allowable operations by some or all sites, it is desirable to broadcast a message promptly informing all sites of the recovery of the link. In networks in which broadcast is not feasible, alternative schemes may be used (see the bibliographic notes).

15.7 Commit Protocols

In order to ensure atomicity, all the sites in which a transaction T executed must agree on the final outcome of the execution. T must either commit at all sites or it must abort at all sites. In order to ensure this property, the transaction coordinator of T must execute a *commit protocol*.

Among the simplest and most widely used commit protocols is the *two-phase commit*. An alternative is the *three-phase commit* protocol, which avoids certain disadvantages of the two-phase commit but adds to complexity and overhead.

15.7.1 Two-Phase Commit

Let T be a transaction initiated at site S_i, and let the transaction coordinator at S_i be C_i.

The Commit Protocol

When T completes its execution — that is, when all the sites at which T has executed inform C_i that T has completed — then C_i starts the two-phase commit protocol.

- **Phase 1**. C_i adds the record <**prepare** T> to the log and forces it onto stable storage. It then sends a **prepare** T message to all sites at which T executed. Upon receiving such a message, the transaction manager at that site determines whether it is willing to commit its portion of T or not. If the answer is no, it adds a record <**no** T> to the log and then it responds by sending an **abort** T message to C_i. If the answer is yes, it adds a record <**ready** T> to the log and forces all the log records corresponding to T onto stable storage. The transaction manager then replies with a **ready** T message to C_i.

- **Phase 2**. When C_i receives responses to the **prepare** T message from all the sites, or when a prespecified interval of time has elapsed since the **prepare** T message was sent out, C_i can determine whether the transaction T can be committed or aborted. Transaction T can be committed if C_i received a **ready** T message from all the participating sites. Otherwise, transaction T must be aborted. Depending on the verdict, either a record <**commit** T> or a record <**abort** T> is added to the log and forced onto stable storage. At this point, the fate of the transaction has been sealed. Following this, the coordinator sends either a **commit** T or an **abort** T message to all participating sites. When a site receives that message, it records it in the log.

A site at which T executed can unconditionally abort T at any time prior to its sending the message **ready** T to the coordinator. The **ready** T message is, in effect, a promise by a site to follow the coordinator's order to commit T or abort T. The only means by which a site can make such a promise is if the needed information is stored in stable storage. Otherwise, if the site crashes after sending **ready** T, it may be unable to make good on its promise.

Since unanimity is required to commit a transaction, the fate of T is sealed as soon as at least one site responds **abort** T. Since the coordinator site S_i is one of the sites at which T executed, the coordinator can decide unilaterally to abort T. The final verdict regarding T is determined at the time the coordinator writes that verdict (commit or abort) to the log and forces it to stable storage. In some implementations of the two-phase commit protocol, a site sends an **acknowledge** T message to the coordinator at the end of the second phase of the protocol. When the coordinator receives the **acknowledge** T message from all the sites, it adds the record <**complete** T> to the log.

Handling of Failures

We now examine in detail how two-phase commit responds to various types of failures.

- **Failure of a participating site**. When a participating site S_k recovers from a failure, it must examine its log to determine the fate of those transactions that were in the midst of execution when the failure occurred. Let T be one such transaction. We consider each of the possible cases below.

  - The log contains a <**commit** T> record. In this case, the site executes **redo**(T).

  - The log contains an <**abort** T> record. In this case, the site executes **undo**(T).

  - The log contains a <**ready** T> record. In this case, the site must consult C_i to determine the fate of T. If C_i is up, it notifies S_k as to whether T committed or aborted. In the former case, it executes **redo**(T); in the latter case, it executes **undo**(T). If C_i is down, S_k must try to find the fate of T from other sites. It does so by sending a **query-status** T message to all the sites in the system. Upon receiving such a message, a site must consult its log to determine whether T has executed there, and if so, whether T committed or aborted. It then notifies S_k about this outcome. If no site has the appropriate information (that is, whether T committed or aborted), then S_k can neither abort nor commit T. The decision concerning T is postponed until S_k can obtain the needed information. Thus, S_k must periodically resend the **query-status** message to the other sites. This is continued until the point when a site recovers that contains the needed information. Note that the site at which C_i resides always has the needed information.

  - The log contains no control records (**abort, commit, ready**) concerning T. This implies that S_k failed before responding to the **prepare** T message from C_i. Since the failure of S_k precludes the sending of such a response, by our algorithm C_i must abort T. Hence, S_k must execute **undo**(T).

- **Failure of the coordinator**. If the coordinator fails in the midst of the execution of the commit protocol for transaction T, then the participating sites must decide on the fate of T. We shall see that in certain cases the participating sites cannot decide on whether to commit or abort T, and therefore it is necessary for these sites to wait for the recovery of the failed coordinator.

    ○ If an active site contains a <**commit** T> record in its log, then T must be committed.

    ○ If an active site contains an <**abort** T> record in its log, then T must be aborted.

    ○ If some active site does *not* contain a <**ready** T> record in its log, then the failed coordinator C_i cannot have decided to commit T. This is because a site that does not have a <**ready** T> record in its log cannot have sent a **ready** T message to C_i. However, the coordinator may have decided to abort T, but not to commit T. Rather than wait for C_i to recover, it is preferable to abort T.

    ○ If none of the above cases holds, then all active sites must have a <**ready** T> record in their logs, but no additional control records (such as <**abort** T> or <**commit** T>). Since the coordinator has failed, it is impossible to determine whether a decision has been made, and if so, what that decision is, until the coordinator recovers. Thus, the active sites must wait for C_i to recover. Since the fate of T remains in doubt, T may continue to hold system resources. For example, if locking is used, T may hold locks on data at active sites. Such a situation is undesirable because it may take hours or days before C_i is again active. During this time other transactions may be forced to wait for T. As as result, data items are unavailable not only on the failed site (C_i) but on active sites as well. The number of unavailable data items increases as the downtime of C_i grows. This situation is called the *blocking* problem because T is blocked pending the recovery of site C_i.

- **Failure of a link**. When a link fails, all the messages that are in the process of being routed through the link do not arrive at their destination intact. From the viewpoint of the sites connected throughout that link, it appears that the other sites have failed. Thus, our previous schemes apply here as well.

- **Network partition**. When a network partitions, two possibilities exist.

    ○ The coordinator and all of its participants remain in one partition. In this case, the failure has no effect on the commit protocol.

○ The coordinator and its participants belong to several partitions. In this case, messages between the participant and the coordinator are lost, reducing the case to a link failure discussed above.

Thus, one major disadvantage of the two-phase commit protocol is that coordinator failure may result in blocking, where a decision either to commit or to abort T may have to be postponed until C_i recovers.

15.7.2 Three-Phase Commit

The three-phase commit protocol is designed to avoid the possibility of blocking in a restricted case of possible failures. The protocol requires that:

- No network partition can occur.

- At any point, at least one site must be up.

- At any point, at most K participating sites can fail simultaneously (K being a parameter indicating the resiliency of the protocol to site failures).

The protocol achieves this nonblocking property by adding an extra phase in which a preliminary decision is reached regarding the fate of T. The information made available to the participating sites as a result of this preliminary decision allows a decision to be made despite the failure of the coordinator.

The Commit Protocol

As above, let T be a transaction initiated at site S_i and let the transaction coordinator at S_i be C_i.

- **Phase 1.** This phase is identical to phase 1 of the two-phase commit protocol.

- **Phase 2.** If C_i receives an **abort** T message from a participating site, or if C_i receives no response within a prespecified interval from a participating site, then C_i decides to abort T. The abort decision is implemented in the same way as the two-phase commit protocol. If C_i receives a **ready** T message from every participating site, C_i makes the preliminary decision to "precommit" T. Precommit differs from commit in that T may still be aborted eventually. The precommit decision allows the coordinator to inform each participating site that all participating sites are "ready." C_i adds a record <**precommit** T> to the log and forces it onto stable storage. Following this, C_i sends a **precommit** T message to all participating sites. When a site receives a message from the coordinator (either **abort** T or **precommit** T) it records it in its log, forces this information to stable storage, and sends a message **acknowledge** T to the coordinator.

- **Phase 3**. This phase is executed only if the decision in phase 2 was to precommit. After the **precommit** T messages are sent to all participating sites, the coordinator must wait until it receives at least K **acknowledge** T messages. Following this, the coordinator reaches a commit decision. It adds a <**commit** T> record to its log and forces it to stable storage. Following this, C_i sends a **commit** T message to all participating sites. When a site receives that message, it records it in its log.

Just as in the two-phase commit protocol, a site at which T executed can unconditionally abort T at any time prior to it sending the message **ready** T to the coordinator. The **ready** T message is, in effect, a promise by a site to follow the coordinator's order to commit T or abort T. In contrast to the two-phase commit protocol, in which the coordinator can unconditionally abort T at any time prior to its sending the message **commit** T, the **precommit** T message in the three-phase commit protocol is a promise by the coordinator to follow the participant's order to commit T.

Since phase 3 always leads to a commit decision, it may seem to be of little use. The role of the third phase becomes apparent in the manner by which the three-phase commit protocol handles failures.

In some implementations of the three-phase commit protocol, a site sends a message **ack** T to the coordinator upon receipt of the **commit** T message. (Note the use of **ack** to distinguish this from the **acknowledge** messages that were used in phase 2.) When the coordinator receives the **ack** T message from all sites, it adds the record <**complete** T> to the log.

Handling of Failures

We now examine in detail how three-phase commit protocol responds to various types of failures.

- **Failure of a participating site**. When a participating site S_k recovers from a failure, it must examine its log to determine the fate of those transactions that were in the midst of execution when the failure occurred. Let T be one such transaction. We consider each of the possible cases below.

  - The log contains a <**commit** T> record. In this case, the site executes **redo**(T).

  - The log contains an <**abort** T> record. In this case, the site executes **undo**(T).

○ The log contains a <**ready** *T*> record, but no <**abort** *T*> or <**precommit** *T*> record. In this case, the site attempts to consult C_i to determine the fate of *T*. If C_i responds with a message that *T* aborted, the site executes **undo**(*T*). If C_i responds with a message **precommit** *T*, the site (as in phase 2) records this in its log and resumes the protocol by sending an **acknowledge** *T* message to the coordinator. If C_i responds with a message that *T* committed, the site executes **redo**(*T*). In the event that C_i fails to respond within a prespecified interval, the site executes a coordinator failure protocol (see below).

○ The log contains a <**precommit** *T*> record, but no <**abort** *T*> or <**commit** *T*> record. As in the case above, the site consults C_i. If C_i responds that *T* aborted or committed, the site executes **undo**(*T*) or **redo**(*T*), respectively. If C_i responds that *T* is still in the precommit state, the site resumes the protocol at this point. If C_i fails to respond within a prescribed interval, the site executes the coordinator failure protocol.

● **Failure of the coordinator.** When a participating site fails to receive a response from the coordinator, for whatever reason, it executes the coordinator failure protocol. This protocol results in the selection of a new coordinator. When the failed coordinator recovers, it does so in the role of a participating site. It no longer acts as coordinator. Rather, it must determine the decision that has been reached by the new coordinator.

Coordinator Failure Protocol

The coordinator failure protocol is triggered by a participating site that fails to receive a response from the coordinator within a prespecified interval. Since we assume no network partition, the only possible cause for this situation is the failure of the coordinator.

1. The active participating sites select a new coordinator using an election protocol (see Section 15.10).

2. The new coordinator, C_{new}, sends a message to each participating site requesting the local status of *T*.

3. Each participating site, including C_{new}, determines the local status of *T*:

   ○ **committed.** The log contains a <**commit** *T*> record.

   ○ **aborted.** The log contains an <**abort** *T*> record.

- **ready**. The log contains a <**ready** T> record but no <**abort** T> or <**precommit** T> record.

- **precommitted**. The log contains a <**precommit** T> record but no <**abort** T> or <**commit** T> record.

- **not-ready**. The log contains neither a <**ready** T> nor an <**abort** T> record.

Each participating site sends its local status to C_{new}.

4. Depending upon the responses received, C_{new} decides either to commit or abort T, or to restart the three-phase commit protocol:

- If at least one site has local status = **committed**, then commit T.

- If at least one site has local status = **aborted**, then abort T. (Note that it is not possible for some site to have local status = **committed** while another has local status = **aborted**.)

- If no site has local status = **aborted** and no site has local status = **committed** but at least one site has local status = **precommitted**, then C_{new} resumes the three-phase commit protocol by sending new **precommit** messages.

- Otherwise, abort T.

The coordinator failure protocol allows the new coordinator to obtain knowledge about the state of the failed coordinator, C_i.

If any site has a <**commit** T> in its log, then C_i must have decided to commit T. If a site has <**precommit** T> in its log, then C_i must have reached a preliminary decision to precommit T, which means that all sites, including any that may have failed, have reached **ready** states. It is therefore safe to commit T. C_{new} does not commit T, however, since this would create the same blocking problem, if C_{new} fails, as in two-phase commit. It is for this reason that phase 3 is resumed by C_{new}.

If no site has received a precommit message from C_i, it is possible that C_i decided to abort T prior to C_i failing. Rather than cause blocking, the protocol aborts T.

Our assumption of no network partitions is crucial to the above discussion. Network partitioning could lead to the election of two new coordinators whose decisions may not agree.

The assumption that not all sites fail at once is crucial also. If all sites fail, it is only the last site to fail that can make a decision. This leads to the blocking problem, since other sites must wait for the recovery of this last site. Determining the last site to fail after a failure of all sites is also difficult.

Finally, the choice of the parameter K is crucial, since if fewer than K participants are active, blocking may result.

15.7.3 Comparison of Protocols

The two-phase commit protocol is widely used despite the potential for blocking. The probability of blocking occurring in practice is usually sufficiently low that the extra cost of the three-phase commit is not justified. The vulnerability of the three-phase commit to link failures is another practical issue. This disadvantage can be overcome by network-level protocols, but doing so adds to overhead.

Both protocols can be streamlined to reduce the number of messages sent and to reduce the number of times records must be forced to stable storage. The bibliographic notes contain references to some of these techniques.

15.8 Concurrency Control

In this section, we show how some of the concurrency control schemes discussed earlier can be modified so that they can be used in a distributed environment.

15.8.1 Locking Protocols

The various locking protocols described in Chapter 11 can be used in a distributed environment. The only change that needs to be incorporated is in the way the lock manager is implemented. Below, we present several possible schemes, the first of which deals with the case where no data replication is allowed. The other schemes are applicable to the more general case where data can be replicated in several sites. As in Chapter 11, we shall assume the existence of the *shared* and *exclusive* lock modes.

Nonreplicated Scheme

If no data is replicated in the system, then the locking schemes described in Section 11.4 can be applied as follows. Each site maintains a local lock manager whose function is to administer the lock and unlock requests for those data items that are stored in that site. When a transaction wishes to lock data item Q at site S_i, it simply sends a message to the lock manager at site S_i requesting a lock (in a particular lock mode). If data item Q is locked in an incompatible mode, then the request is delayed until it can be granted. Once it has been determined that the lock request can be granted, the lock manager sends a message back to the initiator indicating that the lock request has been granted.

The scheme has the advantage of simple implementation. It requires two message transfers for handling lock requests, and one message transfer for handling unlock requests. However, deadlock handling is more complex. Since the lock and unlock requests are no longer made at a single site, the various deadlock-handling algorithms discussed in Chapter 12 must be modified, as will be discussed in Section 15.9.

Single-Coordinator Approach

Under the single-coordinator approach, the system maintains a *single* lock manager that resides in a *single* chosen site, say S_i. All lock and unlock requests are made at site S_i. When a transaction needs to lock a data item, it sends a lock request to S_i. The lock manager determines whether the lock can be granted immediately. If so, it sends a message to that effect to the site at which the lock request was initiated. Otherwise, the request is delayed until it can be granted, at which time a message is sent to the site at which the lock request was initiated. The transaction can read the data item from *any* one of the sites at which a replica of the data item resides. In the case of a write, all the sites where a replica of the data item resides must be involved in the writing.

The scheme has the following advantages:

- **Simple implementation**. This scheme requires two messages for handling lock requests, and one message for handling unlock requests.

- **Simple deadlock handling**. Since all lock and unlock requests are made at one site, the deadlock-handling algorithms discussed in Chapter 12 can be applied directly to this environment.

The disadvantages of the scheme include the following:

- **Bottleneck**. The site S_i becomes a bottleneck, since all requests must be processed there.

- **Vulnerability**. If the site S_i fails, the concurrency controller is lost. Either processing must stop or a recovery scheme must be used (see Section 15.10).

A compromise between the advantages and disadvantages noted above can be achieved through a *multiple-coordinator approach*, in which the lock manager function is distributed over several sites.

Each lock manager administers the lock and unlock requests for a subset of the data items. Each lock manager resides in a different site. This reduces the degree to which the coordinator is a bottleneck, but it complicates deadlock handling, since the lock and unlock requests are not made at one single site.

Majority Protocol

The majority protocol is a modification of the nonreplicated data scheme that we presented earlier. The system maintains a lock manager at each site. Each manager manages the locks for all the data items or replicas of data items stored at that site. When a transaction wishes to lock a data item Q, which is replicated in n different sites, it must send a lock request to more than half of the n sites in which Q is stored. Each lock manager determines whether the lock can be granted immediately (as far as it is concerned). As before, the response is delayed until the request can be granted. The transaction does not operate on Q until it has successfully obtained a lock on a majority of the replicas of Q.

This scheme deals with replicated data in a decentralized manner, thus avoiding the drawbacks of central control. However, it suffers from its own disadvantages:

- **Implementation**. The majority protocol is more complicated to implement than the previous schemes. It requires $2(n/2 + 1)$ messages for handling lock requests, and $(n/2 + 1)$ messages for handling unlock requests.

- **Deadlock handling**. Since the lock and unlock requests are not made at one site, the deadlock-handling algorithms must be modified (see below). In addition, it is possible for a deadlock to occur even if only one data item is being locked. To illustrate, consider a system with four sites and full replication. Suppose that transactions T_1 and T_2 wish to lock data item Q in exclusive mode. Transaction T_1 may succeed in locking Q at sites S_1 and S_3, while transaction T_2 may succeed in locking Q at sites S_2 and S_4. Each then must wait to acquire the third lock, and hence a deadlock has occurred.

Biased Protocol

The biased protocol is based on a model similar to that of the majority protocol. The difference is that requests for shared locks are given more favorable treatment than requests for exclusive locks. The system maintains a lock manager at each site. Each manager manages the locks for all the data items stored at that site. *Shared* and *exclusive* locks are handled differently.

- **Shared locks**. When a transaction needs to lock data item Q, it simply requests a lock on Q from the lock manager at one site containing a replica of Q.

- **Exclusive locks**. When a transaction needs to lock data item Q, it requests a lock on Q from the lock manager at all sites containing a replica of Q.

As before, the response to the request is delayed until it can be granted.

The scheme has the advantage of imposing less overhead on **read** operations than does the majority protocol. This is especially significant in common cases in which the frequency of **read** is much greater than the frequency of **write**. However, the additional overhead on writes is a disadvantage. Furthermore, the biased protocol shares the majority protocol's disadvantage of complexity in handling deadlock.

Primary Copy

In the case of data replication, we may choose one of the replicas as the primary copy. Thus, for each data item Q, the primary copy of Q must reside in precisely one site, which we call the *primary site of Q*.

When a transaction needs to lock a data item Q, it requests a lock at the primary site of Q. As before, the response to the request is delayed until it can be granted.

Thus, the primary copy enables concurrency control for replicated data to be handled in a manner similar to that for unreplicated data. This allows for a simple implementation. However, if the primary site of Q fails, Q is inaccessible even though other sites containing a replica may be accessible.

15.8.2 Timestamping

The principal idea behind the timestamping scheme discussed in Section 11.4 is that each transaction is given a *unique* timestamp that is used in deciding the serialization order. Our first task, then, in generalizing the centralized scheme to a distributed scheme is to develop a scheme for generating unique timestamps. Once this has been accomplished, our previous protocols can be directly applied to the nonreplicated environment.

Generating Unique Timestamps

There are two primary methods for generating unique timestamps, one centralized and one distributed. In the centralized scheme, a single site is chosen for distributing the timestamps. The site can use a logical counter or its own local clock for this purpose.

In the distributed scheme, each site generates a unique local timestamp using either a logical counter or the local clock. The global unique timestamp is obtained by concatenating the unique local timestamp with the site identifier, which must be unique (Figure 15.8). The order of concatenation is important! We use the site identifier in the least significant

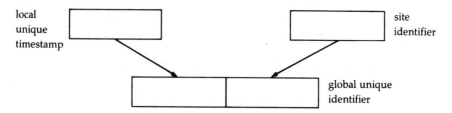

Figure 15.8   Generating unique timestamps.

position in order to ensure that the global timestamps generated in one site are not always greater than those generated in another site. Compare this technique for generating unique timestamps with the one we presented earlier for generating unique names.

We may still have a problem if one site generates local timestamps at a faster rate than other sites. In such a case, the fast site's logical counter will be larger than that of other sites. Therefore, all timestamps generated by the fast site will be larger than those generated by other sites. What is needed is a mechanism to ensure that local timestamps are generated fairly across the system. To accomplish this, we define within each site S_i a *logical clock* (LC_i), which generates the unique local timestamp. The logical clock can be implemented as a counter that is incremented after a new local timestamp is generated. To ensure that the various logical clocks are synchronized, we require that a site S_i advance its logical clock whenever a transaction T_i with timestamp $<x,y>$ visits that site and x is greater than the current value of LC_i. In this case, site S_i advances its logical clock to the value $x + 1$.

If the system clock is used to generate timestamps, then timestamps are assigned fairly provided that no site has a system clock that runs fast or slow. Since clocks may not be perfectly accurate, a technique similar to that used for logical clocks must be used to ensure that no clock gets very far ahead or behind another clock.

Concurrency Control Schemes

The basic timestamp scheme introduced in Section 11.4 can be extended in a straightforward manner to a distributed system. As in the centralized case, cascading rollbacks may result if no mechanism is used to prevent a transaction from reading a data item value which is not yet committed. To eliminate cascading rollbacks, we can combine the basic timestamp scheme of Section 11.4 with the two-phase commit protocol of Section 15.7 to obtain a protocol that ensures serializability with no cascading rollbacks. We leave the development of such an algorithm as an exercise for the reader.

The basic timestamp scheme described above suffers from the undesirable property that conflicts between transactions are resolved through rollbacks rather than waits. To alleviate this problem, we can buffer the various **read** and **write** operations (that is, *delay* them) until a time when we are assured that these operations can take place without causing aborts. A **read**(x) operation by T_i must be delayed if there exists a transaction T_j that will perform a **write**(x) operation but has not yet done so, and $TS(T_j) < TS(T_i)$. Similarly, a **write**(x) operation by T_i must be delayed if there exists a transaction T_j that will perform either **read**(x) or **write**(x) operation and $TS(T_j) < TS(T_i)$. There are various methods for ensuring this property. One such method, called the *conservative timestamp-ordering scheme*, requires each site to maintain a **read** and **write** queue consisting of all the **read** and **write** requests, respectively, that are to be executed at the site and that must be delayed in order to preserve the above property. We shall not present the scheme here. Rather, we leave the development of the algorithm as an exercise for the reader.

15.9 Deadlock Handling

The deadlock prevention and detection algorithms presented in Chapter 12 can be used in a distributed system, provided that some modifications are made. For example, the tree protocol can be used by defining a *global* tree among the system data items. Similarly, the timestamp-ordering approach could be directly applied to a distributed environment, as we saw in Section 15.8.2.

Deadlock prevention may result in some unnecessary waiting and rollback. Furthermore, some of the deadlock prevention techniques may require more sites to be involved in the execution of a transaction than would otherwise be the case.

If we allow deadlocks to occur and rely on deadlock detection, the main problem in a distributed system is deciding how to maintain the wait-for graph. Common techniques for dealing with this issue require that each site keep a *local* wait-for graph. The nodes of the graph correspond to all the transactions (local as well as nonlocal) that are currently either holding or requesting any of the items local to that site. For example, Figure 15.9 depicts a system consisting of two sites, each maintaining its local wait-for graph. Note that transactions T_2 and T_3 appear in both graphs, indicating that the transactions have requested items at both sites.

These local wait-for graphs are constructed in the usual manner for local transactions and data items. When a transaction T_i on site S_1 needs a resource held by transaction T_j in site S_2, a request message is sent by T_i to site S_2. The edge $T_i \rightarrow T_j$ is then inserted in the local wait-for graph of site S_1.

Clearly, if any local wait-for graph has a cycle, deadlock has occurred. On the other hand, the fact that there are no cycles in any of the local

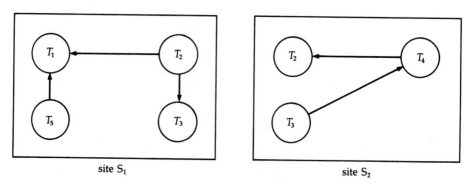

Figure 15.9   Local wait-for graphs.

wait-for graphs does not mean that there are no deadlocks. To illustrate this problem, consider the local wait-for graphs of Figure 15.9. Each wait-for graph is acyclic; nevertheless, a deadlock exists in the system because the *union* of the local wait-for graphs contains a cycle. This graph is shown in Figure 15.10.

Several common schemes for organizing the wait-for graph in a distributed system are described below.

15.9.1 Centralized Approach

In the centralized approach, a global wait-for graph (union of all the local graphs) is constructed and maintained in a *single* site, the deadlock detection coordinator. Since there is communication delay in the system, we must distinguish between two types of wait-for graphs. The *real* graph describes the real but unknown state of the system at any instance in time, as would be seen by an omniscient observer. The *constructed* graph is an approximation generated by the controller during the execution of its

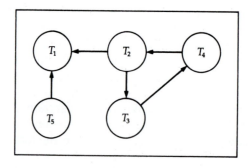

Figure 15.10   Global wait-for graph for Figure 15.9.

algorithm. Obviously, the constructed graph must be generated in such a way that whenever the detection algorithm is invoked, the reported results are correct in the sense that, if a deadlock exists it is reported promptly, and if the system reports a deadlock, it is indeed in a deadlock state.

The global wait-for graph may be constructed:

- Whenever a new edge is inserted or removed in one of the local wait-for graphs.

- Periodically, when a number of changes have occurred in a local wait-for graph.

- Whenever the coordinator needs to invoke the cycle detection algorithm.

When the deadlock detection algorithm is invoked, the coordinator searches its global graph. If a cycle is found, a victim is selected to be rolled back. The coordinator must notify all the sites that a particular transaction has been selected as victim. The sites, in turn, roll back the victim transaction.

We note that this scheme may produce unnecessary rollbacks, as a result of one of the following:

- *False cycles* may exist in the global wait-for graph. To illustrate, consider a snapshot of the system represented by the local wait-for graphs of Figure 15.11. Suppose that T_2 releases the resource it is holding in site S_1, resulting in the deletion of the edge $T_1 \rightarrow T_2$ in S_1. Transaction T_2 then requests a resource held by T_3 at site S_2, resulting in the addition of the edge $T_2 \rightarrow T_3$ in S_2. If the **insert** $T_2 \rightarrow T_3$ message from S_2 arrives before the **remove** $T_1 \rightarrow T_2$ message from S_1, the coordinator may discover the false cycle $T_1 \rightarrow T_2 \rightarrow T_3$ after the **insert** (but before the **remove**). Deadlock recovery may be initiated, although no deadlock has occurred.

- Unnecessary rollbacks may also result when a *deadlock* has indeed occurred and a victim has been picked, while at the same time one of the transactions was aborted for reasons unrelated to the deadlock. For example, suppose that site S_1 in Figure 15.9 decides to abort T_2. At the same time, the coordinator has discovered a cycle and picked T_3 as a victim. Both T_2 and T_3 are now rolled back, although only T_2 needed to be rolled back.

15.9.2 Fully Distributed Approach

In the *fully distributed* deadlock detection algorithm, all controllers share the responsibility for detecting deadlock equally. In this scheme, every site

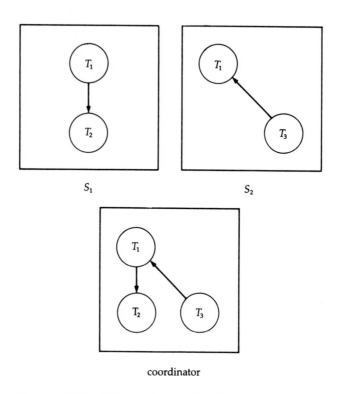

coordinator

Figure 15.11   False cycles in the global wait-1or graph.

constructs a wait-for graph which represents a part of the total graph, depending on the dynamic behavior of the system. The idea is that if a deadlock exists, a cycle will appear in (at least) one of the partial graphs. Below we present one such algorithm which involves construction of partial graphs in every site.

Each site maintains its own local wait-for graph. A local wait-for graph differs from the one described above in that we add one additional node T_{ex} to the graph. An arc $T_i \rightarrow T_{ex}$ exists in the graph if T_i is waiting for a data item in another site being held by *any* transaction. Similarly, an arc $T_{ex} \rightarrow T_j$ exists in the graph if a transaction at another site is waiting to acquire a resource currently being held by T_j in this local site.

To illustrate, consider the two local wait-for graphs of Figure 15.9. The addition of the node T_{ex} in both graphs results in the local wait-for graphs shown in Figure 15.12.

If a local wait-for graph contains a cycle which does not involve node T_{ex}, then the system is in a deadlock state. However, the existence of a cycle involving T_{ex} implies that there is a *possibility* of a deadlock. In order to ascertain this, a distributed deadlock detection algorithm must be invoked.

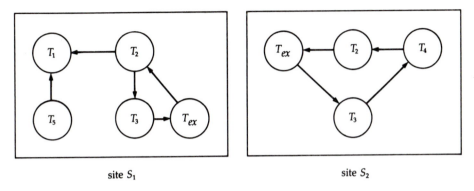

site S_1 site S_2

Figure 15.12   Local wait-for graphs.

Suppose that site S_i contains a cycle in its local wait-for graph involving node T_{ex}. This cycle must be of the form

$$T_{ex} \to T_{k_1} \to T_{k_2} \to \cdots \to T_{k_n} \to T_{ex}$$

which indicates that transaction T_{k_n} in S_i is waiting to acquire a data item in some other site, say S_j. Upon discovering this cycle, site S_i sends to site S_j a deadlock detection message containing information about that cycle.

When site S_j receives this deadlock detection message, it updates its local wait-for graph with the new information it has obtained. Next, it searches the newly constructed wait-for graph for a cycle not involving T_{ex}. If one exists, a deadlock is found and an appropriate recovery scheme is invoked. If a cycle involving T_{ex} is discovered, then S_j transmits a deadlock detection message to the appropriate site, say S_k. Site S_k, in return, repeats the above procedure. Thus, after a finite number of rounds, either a deadlock is discovered, if one exists, or the deadlock detection computation halts, if none exists.

To illustrate, consider the local wait-for graphs of Figure 15.12. Suppose that site S_1 discovers the cycle:

$$T_{ex} \to T_2 \to T_3 \to T_{ex}$$

Since T_3 is waiting to acquire a data item in site S_2, a deadlock detection message describing that cycle is transmitted from site S_1 to site S_2. When site S_2 receives this message, it updates its local wait-for graph, obtaining the wait-for graph of Figure 15.13. This graph contains the cycle

$$T_2 \to T_3 \to T_4 \to T_2$$

which does not include node T_{ex}. Therefore, the system is in a deadlock state and an appropriate recovery scheme must be invoked.

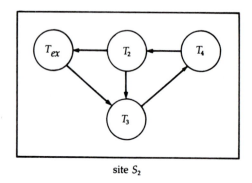

site S_2

Figure 15.13   Local wait-for graph.

Note that the outcome would be the same if site S_2 discovered the cycle first in its local wait-for graph and sent the deadlock detection message to site S_1. In the worst case, both sites discover the cycle at about the same time, and two deadlock detection messages are sent, one by S_1 to S_2 and another by S_2 to S_1. This unnecessary message transfer adds to overhead in updating the two local wait-for graphs and searching for cycles in both graphs.

To reduce message traffic, we assign to each transaction T_i a unique identifier, which we denote by $ID(T_i)$. When site S_k discovers that its local wait-for graph contains a cycle involving node T_{ex} of the form

$$T_{ex} \to T_{K_1} \to T_{K_2} \to \cdots \to T_{K_n} \to T_{ex}$$

it will send a deadlock detection message to another site only if:

$$ID(T_{K_n}) < ID(T_{K_1})$$

Otherwise, site S_k continues with its normal execution, leaving the burden of initiating the deadlock detection algorithm to some other site.

Consider again the wait-for graphs maintained at sites S_1 and S_2 in Figure 15.12. Suppose that:

$$ID(T_1) < ID(T_2) < ID(T_3) < ID(T_4)$$

Let both sites discover these local cycles at about the same time. The cycle in site S_1 is of the form:

$$T_{ex} \to T_2 \to T_3 \to T_{ex}$$

Since $ID(T_3) > ID(T_2)$, site S_1 does not send a deadlock detection message to site S_2.

The cycle in site S_2 is of the form:.

$$T_{ex} \rightarrow T_3 \rightarrow T_4 \rightarrow T_2 \rightarrow T_{ex}$$

Since $ID\ (T_2) < ID\ (T_3)$, site S_2 does send a deadlock detection message to site S_1. Upon receiving the message, S_1 updates its local wait-for graph, searches for a cycle in the graph, and discovers that the system is in a deadlock state.

15.10 Coordinator Selection

Some of the algorithms we have presented above require the use of a coordinator. If the coordinator fails because of some failure of the site at which it resides, the system can continue execution only by restarting a new coordinator on some other site. This can be accomplished by maintaining a backup to the coordinator that is ready to assume responsibility if the coordinator fails. Another approach is to choose the new coordinator after the coordinator has failed. The algorithms that determine where a new copy of the coordinator should be restarted are called *election* algorithms.

15.10.1 Backup Coordinators

A *backup coordinator* is a site which, in addition to other tasks, maintains enough information locally to allow it to assume the role of coordinator with minimal disruption to the distributed system. All messages directed to the coordinator are received by both the coordinator and its backup. The backup coordinator executes the same algorithms and maintains the same internal state information (such as, for a concurrency coordinator, the lock table) as the actual coordinator. The only difference in function between the coordinator and its backup is that the backup does not take any action that affects other sites. Such actions are left to the actual coordinator.

In the event that the backup coordinator detects the failure of the actual coordinator, it assumes the role of coordinator. Since the backup has all of the information available to it that the failed coordinator had, processing can continue without interruption.

The prime advantage to the backup approach is the ability to continue processing immediately. If a backup were not ready to assume the coordinator's responsibility, a newly appointed coordinator would have to seek information from all sites in the system so that it could execute the coordination tasks. Frequently, the only source of some of the requisite information is the failed coordinator. In this case, it may be necessary to abort several (or all) active transactions and restart them under the aegis of the new coordinator.

Thus, the backup coordinator approach avoids a substantial amount of delay while the distributed system recovers from a coordinator failure. The disadvantage is the overhead of duplicate execution of the coordinator's tasks. Furthermore, a coordinator and its backup need to communicate regularly to ensure that their activities are synchronized.

In short, the backup coordinator approach involves overhead during normal processing in order to allow fast recovery from a coordinator failure. In the next section, we consider a lower-overhead recovery scheme that requires somewhat more effort in order to recover from a failure.

15.10.2 Election Algorithms

Election algorithms require that a unique identification number be associated with each active site in the system. For ease of notation, we shall assume that the identification number of site S_i is i. Also, to simplify our discussion, we assume that the coordinator always resides at the site with the largest identification number. The goal of an election algorithm is to choose a site for the new coordinator. Hence, when a coordinator fails, the algorithm must elect that active site with the largest identification number. This number must be sent to each active site in the system. Additionally, the algorithm must provide a mechanism by which a site recovering from a crash may identify the current coordinator.

The various election algorithms usually differ in terms of the network configuration. In this section, we present one of these algorithms, the *bully* algorithm.

Suppose that site S_i sends a request that is not answered by the coordinator within a prespecified time interval T. In this situation, it is assumed that the coordinator has failed, and S_i tries to elect itself as the site for the new coordinator.

Site S_i sends an election message to every site with a higher identification number. Site S_i then waits for a time interval T for an answer from any one of these sites. If no response is received within time T, it is assumed that all sites with numbers greater than i have failed, and S_i elects itself as the site for the new coordinator and sends a message to inform all active sites with identification numbers lower than i that S_i is the site at which the new coordinator resides.

However, if an answer is received, S_i begins a time interval T, waiting to receive a message informing it that a site with a higher identification number has been elected. (Some other site is electing itself coordinator, and should report the results within time T'.) If no message is sent within T', then the site with a higher number is assumed to have failed, and site S_i restarts the algorithm.

After a failed site recovers, it immediately begins execution of the same algorithm. If there are no active sites with higher numbers, the recovered site forces all sites with lower numbers to let it become the coordinator site, even if there is a currently active coordinator with a lower number. It is for this reason that the algorithm is termed the *bully* algorithm.

15.11 Multidatabase Systems

In recent years new database applications have developed that often require data from a variety of preexisting databases located in various heterogeneous hardware and software environments. Manipulation of information located in a heterogeneous database requires an additional software layer on top of existing database systems. This software layer is called a *multidatabase* (MDBS) system. The local database systems may employ different logical models and data definition and data manipulation languages, and may differ in their concurrency control and transaction management mechanisms. A multidatabase system creates the illusion of logical database integration without requiring physical database integration.

A multidatabase system offers many advantages. It significantly extends user capabilities, enabling users to access and share data without the added burden of learning the intricacies of different database management systems. Preexisting programs and procedures remain operational in the integrated multidatabase environment.

15.11.1 Unified View of Data

Each local DBMS may be using a different data model. That is, some may employ the relational model, while others may employ the network model (see Appendix A) or the hierarchical model (see Appendix B).

Since the MDBS is suppose to provide the illusion of a single-layout, integrated database system, a common data model must be used. The natural choice is obviously the relational model, with SQL as the common query language. Indeed, there are several prototype systems available today to allow SQL queries to a nonrelational database management system.

Another difficulty that must be overcome is the provision of a common conceptual scheme. Each local DBMS provides its own conceptual scheme. The MDBS must integrate these separate schemes into one common scheme. Scheme integration is a very complicated task, owing mainly to the semantic heterogeneity.

15.11.2 Transaction Management

A multidatabase system supports two types of transactions:

- **Local transactions**. These transactions are executed by each local DBMS, outside of the MDBS system control.

- **Global transactions**. These transactions are executed under the MDBS system control.

The MDBS is aware of the fact that local transactions may run at the local sites, but it is not aware of any specifics of the transactions and what data they may access.

Ensuring the local autonomy of each DBMS requires that no changes can be made to the local DBMS software. This implies that a DBMS at one site is not able to communicate directly with a DBMS at any other sites to synchronize the execution of a global transaction active at several sites.

The correctness criterion for concurrent execution is serializability. Since the MDBS has no control over the execution of local transactions, each local DBMS must use some concurrency control scheme to ensure that its schedule is serializable (for example, two-phase locking or timestamping). In addition, in case of locking, the local DBMS must be able to guard against the possibility of local deadlocks.

The guarantee of local serializability is not sufficient to ensure global serializability. To illustrate, consider two global transactions T_1 and T_2 each of which accesses and updates two data items A and B, located at sites S_1 and S_2, respectively. Suppose that the local schedules are serializable. It is still possible to have a situation where at site S_1, T_2 follows T_1, while at S_2, T_1 follows T_2, resulting in a nonserializable global schedule. One way to avoid this difficulty is to prohibit global transactions from updating local data items. That is, global transactions are restricted to read-only access. Local transactions, however, can both read and write local data items. This restriction limits the access capabilities of the MDBS.

The situation becomes much more complicated when global transactions are allowed to both read and write local data items.

A sufficient condition for global serializability is that in *all* local schedules the serializability order of the global transaction is the same. That is, let T_i and T_j be two global transactions that execute at site S_k. Suppose that the local schedule at site S_k is equivalent to a serial schedule in which T_i appears before T_j. Then, for all other sites in which T_i and T_j execute, the same must also hold.

One way to ensure the same serial schedules, is to require that the local DBMS provide the MDBS with its local schedule information. The MDBS can use this information to guarantee global serializability. This, however, requires design changes in the local DBMS resulting in the violation of local autonomy.

There are several schemes for ensuring global serializability without sacrificing local autonomy. If each local DBMS uses the strict two-phase locking protocol, and for each global transaction locks are released only after the transaction finishes its execution, then correctness is ensured.

If the local DBMS uses a different type of transaction management scheme, then the MDBS must use some form of a concurrency control scheme to ensure global serializability. One simple scheme is the *transaction-graph* scheme. A transaction graph is a bipartite *undirected* graph with a set of nodes consisting of global transaction names and local sites names. An undirected edge between global transaction T_i and local site S_k exists in the graph if T_i accesses some data at site S_k. Global serializability is ensured if the transaction graph contains no undirected cycles.

15.12 Summary

A distributed database system consists of a collection of sites, each of which maintains a local database system. Each site is able to process *local transactions*, those transactions that access data only in that single site. In addition, a site may participate in the execution of *global transactions*, those transactions that access data in several sites. The execution of global transactions requires communication among the sites.

There are several reasons for building distributed database systems, including sharing of data, reliability and availability, and speedup of query processing. However, along with these advantages come several disadvantages, including software development cost, greater potential for bugs, and increased processing overhead. The primary disadvantage of distributed database systems is the added complexity required to ensure proper coordination among the sites.

There are several issues involved in storing a relation in the distributed database, including replication and fragmentation. It is essential that the system minimize the degree to which a user needs to be aware of how a relation is stored.

A distributed system may suffer from the same types of failure that a centralized system does. There are, however, additional failures that need to be dealt with in a distributed environment, including the failure of a site, the failure of a link, loss of messages, and network partition. Each of these needs to be considered in the design of a distributed recovery scheme. In order for the system to be robust, therefore, it must *detect* any of these failures, *reconfigure* the system so that computation may continue, and *recover* when a processor or a link is repaired.

In order to ensure atomicity, all the sites in which a transaction T executed must agree on the final outcome of the execution. T either commits at all sites or aborts at all sites. In order to ensure this property, the transaction coordinator of T must execute a *commit protocol*. The most widely used commit protocol is the *two-phase commit* protocol.

Two-phase commit may lead to *blocking*, a situation in which the fate of a transaction cannot be determined until a failed site (the coordinator) recovers. To avoid blocking, we may use the *three-phase commit* protocol.

The various concurrency control schemes which can be used in a centralized system can be modified for use in a distributed environment. In the case of locking protocols, the only change that needs to be incorporated is in the way the lock manager is implemented. There are a variety of different approaches here. One or more central coordinators may be used. If, instead, a distributed approach is taken, replicated data must be treated specially. Protocols for doing this include the majority, biased, and primary-copy protocols. In the case of timestamping and validation schemes, the only needed change is to develop a mechanism for generating unique *global* timestamps. This can be done by either concatenating a local timestamp with the site identification or by advancing local clocks whenever a message arrives with a larger timestamp.

The primary method for dealing with deadlocks in a distributed environment is deadlock detection. The main problem is in deciding how to maintain the wait-for graph. Different methods for organizing the wait-for graph include a centralized approach, a hierarchical approach, and a fully distributed approach.

Some of the distributed algorithms require the use of a coordinator. If the coordinator fails owing to the failure of the site at which it resides, the system can continue execution only by restarting a new copy of the coordinator on some other site. This can be accomplished by maintaining a backup to the coordinator that is ready to assume responsibility if the coordinator fails. Another approach is to choose the new coordinator after the coordinator has failed. The algorithms that determine where a new copy of the coordinator should be restarted are called *election* algorithms.

A *multidatabase* (MDBS) system provides an environment in which new database applications can access data from a variety of preexisting databases located in various heterogeneous hardware and software environments. The local database systems may employ different logical models and data definition and data manipulation languages, and may differ in their concurrency control and transaction management mechanisms. A multidatabase system creates the illusion of logical database integration without requiring physical database integration.

Exercises

15.1 Discuss the relative advantages of centralized and distributed databases.

15.2 Explain the difference between:

    a. Fragmentation transparency.

    b. Replication transparency.

    c. Location transparency.

15.3 How might a distributed database designed for a local-area network differ from one designed for a long-haul network?

15.4 When is it useful to have replication or fragmentation of data? Explain.

15.5 Explain the notions of transparency and autonomy. Why are they desirable from a human factors standpoint?

15.6 Consider a relation that is fragmented horizontally by *plant-number*:

employee (name, address, salary, plant-number)

Assume each fragment has two replicas: one stored at the New York site and one stored locally at the plant site. Describe a good processing strategy for the following queries entered at the San Jose site.

a. Find all employees at the Boca plant.

b. Find the average salary of all employees.

c. Find the highest-paid employee at each of the following sites: Toronto, Edmonton, Vancouver, Montreal.

d. Find the lowest-paid employee in the entire company.

15.7 Consider the relations:

employee (name, address, salary, plant-number)
machine (machine-number, type, plant-number)

Assume the *employee* relation is fragmented horizontally by *plant-number* and each fragment is stored locally at its corresponding plant site. Assume the *machine* relation is stored in its entirety at the Armonk site. Describe a good strategy for processing each of the following queries.

a. Find all employees at the plant containing machine number 1130.

b. Find all employees at plants containing machines whose type is "milling machine."

c. Find all machines at the Almaden plant.

d. Find employee ⋈ machine.

15.8 For each of the strategies of Exercise 15.7, state how your choice of a strategy depends upon:

● The site at which the query was entered.

● The site at which the result is desired.

15.9 Compute $r \bowtie s$ for the following relations:

r	A	B	C
	1	2	3
	4	5	6
	1	2	4
	5	3	2
	8	9	7

s	C	D	E
	3	4	5
	3	6	8
	2	3	2
	1	4	1
	1	2	3

15.10 Does $r_i \bowtie r_j$ necessarily equal $r_j \bowtie r_i$? Under what conditions does $r_i \bowtie r_j = r_j \bowtie r_i$ hold?

15.11 In order to build a robust distributed system, it is important to know what kinds of failures can occur.

   a. List possible types of failure in a distributed system.

   b. Which items in your list are applicable also to a centralized system?

15.12 Consider a failure that occurs during two-phase commit for a transaction. For each possible failure listed in Exercise 15.11a, explain how two-phase commit ensures transaction atomicity despite the failure.

15.13 Repeat exercise 15.12 for three-phase commit.

15.14 List those types of failure which three-phase commit cannot handle. Describe how failures of these types could be handled by lower-level protocols.

15.15 Consider a distributed deadlock detection algorithm in which the sites are organized in a hierarchy. Each site checks for deadlocks local to the site and for global deadlocks that involve descendant sites in the hierarchy. Complete a detailed description of this algorithm and argue that it detects all deadlocks. Compare the relative merits of this hierarchical scheme with those of the centralized scheme and the fully distributed scheme.

15.16 Consider a distributed system with two sites, A and B. Can site A distinguish among the following?

   a. B goes down.

   b. The link between A and B goes down.

c. *B* is extremely overloaded and response time is 100 times longer than normal.

What implications does your answer have for recovery in distributed systems?

15.17 If we apply a distributed version of the multiple-granularity protocol of Chapter 11 to a distributed database, the site responsible for the root of the DAG may become a bottleneck. Show that the following modifications to that protocol alleviate this problem without allowing any nonserializable schedules.

● Only intention mode locks are allowed on the root.

● All transactions are given all possible intention mode locks on the root automatically.

15.18 Discuss the advantages and disadvantages of the two methods we presented for generating globally unique timestamps.

15.19 Consider the following *hierarchical* deadlock detection algorithm, in which the global wait-for graph is distributed over a number of different *controllers*, which are organized in a tree. Each nonleaf controller maintains a wait-for graph which contains relevant information from the graphs of the controllers in the subtree below it. In particular, let S_A, S_B, and S_C be controllers such that S_C is the lowest common ancestor of S_A and S_B (S_C must be unique, since we are dealing with a tree). Suppose that node T_i appears in the local wait-for graph of controllers S_A and S_B. Then T_i must also appear in the local wait-for graph of:

● Controller S_C.

● Every controller in the path from S_C to S_A.

● Every controller in the path from S_C to S_B.

In addition, if T_i and T_j appear in the wait-for graph of controller S_D and there exists a path from T_i to T_j in the wait-for graph of one of the children of D, then an edge $T_i \rightarrow T_j$ must be in the wait-for graph of S_D.

Show that if a cycle exists in any of the wait-for graphs, then the system is deadlocked.

15.20 Consider the following deadlock detection algorithm. When transaction T_i, at site S_A, requests a resource from T_j, at site S_B, a request message with timestamp n is sent. The edge (T_i, T_j, n) is inserted in the local wait-for of S_A. The edge (T_i, T_j, n) is inserted in the local wait-for graph of S_B only if T_j has received the request message and cannot immediately grant the requested resource. A request from T_i to T_j in the same site is handled in the usual manner; no timestamps are associated with the edge (T_i,T_j). The detection algorithm is invoked by a central coordinator by sending an initiating message to each site in the system:

1. Upon receiving this message, a site sends its local wait-for graph to the coordinator. Note that such a graph contains all of the local information the site has about the state of the real graph. The wait-for graph reflects an instantaneous state of the site, but it is not synchronized with respect to any other site.

2. When the controller has received a reply from each site, it constructs a graph as follows:

   a. The graph contains a vertex for every transaction in the system.

   b. The graph has an edge (T_i,T_j) if and only if:

      i. There is an edge (T_i,T_j) in one of the wait-for graphs.

      ii. An edge (T_i,T_j,n) (for some n) appears in more than one wait-for graph.

Show that if there is a cycle in the constructed graph, then the system is in a deadlock state, and that if there is no cycle in the constructed graph, then the system was not in a deadlock state when the execution of the algorithm began.

15.21 Show that global serializability of an MDBS is ensured if the transaction graph (Section 15.11.2) contains no undirected cycles.

15.22 Show that global serializability of an MDBS is ensured if each local DBMS uses the strict two-phase locking protocol, and for each global transaction locks are released only after the transaction finishes its execution.

Bibliographic Notes

A survey paper discussing some of the major issues concerning distributed database systems has been written by Rothnie and Goodman [1977]. Conference proceedings devoted to distributed databases are in Delobel and Litwin [1980], Schneider [1982], and the annual ACM SIGACT-SIGOPS Symposium on the Principles of Distributed Computing. Textbook discussions are offered by Bray [1982], Date [1983], Ceri and Pelagatti [1984], and Ullman [1988]. Comprehensive discussions concerning computer networks are offered by Davies, et al. [1979] and Tanenbaum [1981].

Issues in the design of distributed databases are presented by Chen and Akoka [1980] and Ceri, et al. [1983]. A paper dealing with horizontal and vertical fragmentation of relations is presented by Chang and Cheng [1980].

Discussions concerning the file and resource allocation in problems are offered by Chu [1969], Casey [1972], Eswaran [1974], Mahmoud and Riordan [1976], Morgan and Levin [1977], Fisher and Hochbaum [1980], Trivedi, et al. [1980], and Dowdy and Foster [1982].

Distributed query processing is discussed in Wong [1977], Epstein, et al. [1978], Hevner and Yao [1979], Epstein and Stonebraker [1980], Adiba [1981], King [1981], Cheung [1982], Chu and Hurley [1982], Kerschberg, et al. [1982], Apers, et al. [1983], Ceri and Pelagatti [1983], and Wong [1983].

Selinger and Adiba [1980] and Daniels, et al. [1982]. discuss the approach to distributed query processing taken by the R* system (a distributed version of System R). Theoretical results concerning semijoins are presented by Bernstein and Chiu [1981] Chiu and Ho [1980], Bernstein and Goodman [1981b], and Kambayashi et al. [1982].

Papers dealing with the problems of implementing the transaction concept in a distributed database are presented by Gray [1981], Traiger, et al. [1982], and Spector and Schwarz [1983]. Papers covering distributed concurrency control are offered by Rosenkrantz, et al. [1978], Bernstein, et al. [1978, 1980a], Menasce, et al. [1980], Bernstein and Goodman [1980a, 1981a, 1982], Minoura and Wiederhold [1982], Kohler [1981], and Garcia-Molina and Wiederhold [1982]. The transaction manager of R* is described in Mohan et al. [1986].

Concurrency control for replicated data that is based on the concept of voting is presented by Gifford [1979], Thomas [1979], Paris [1986], and Jajodia and Mutchler [1987, 1990]. The group paradigm for concurrency control is presented by ElAbbadi and Toueg [1988].

Validation techniques for distributed concurrency control schemes are described by Schlageter [1981], Ceri and Owicki [1983], and Bassiouni [1988]. Discussions concerning semantic-based transaction management techniques are offered by Garcia-Molina [1983] and Kumar and Stonebraker [1988].

Attar, et al. [1984] discuss the use of transaction in distributed recovery in database systems with replicated data. Hailpern and Korth [1983] describe an experimental database system for a network of personal workstations. A survey of techniques for recovery in distributed database systems is presented by Kohler [1981]. Bhargava [1987] presents a collection of papers on concurrency and reliability in database systems.

The two-phase commit protocol is due to Lampson and Sturgis [1976] and Gray [1978]. The three-phase commit protocol is from Skeen [1981]. Mohan and Lindsay [1983] discuss two modified versions of two-phase commit, called presume-commit and presume-abort, that reduce the overhead of two-phase commit by defining default assumption regarding the fate of transactions.

Performance analyses of various concurrency control schemes are presented by Gelembe and Sevcik [1978], Garcia-Molina [1978], Ries [1979], and Badal [1980, 1981].

Distributed deadlock detections are presented by Gray [1978], Rosenkrantz, et al. [1978], Menasce and Muntz [1979], Gligor and Shattuck [1980], Chandy and Misra [1982], and Chandy, et al. [1983]. Knapp [1987] surveys the distributed deadlock detection literature. The algorithm presented in section 15.9.2 comes from Obermark [1982]. Exercise 15.17 is from Menasce and Muntz [1979]. Exercise 15.18 is from Stuart, et al. [1984]. The bully algorithm presented in Section 15.10.2 is from Garcia-Molina [1982]. Distributed clock synchronization is discussed in Lamport [1978].

Multidatabase issues are discussed by Ferrier and Stangret [1984], Motro [1987], Breitbart and Silberschatz [1988], Du and Elmagarmid [1984], Breitbart et al. [1990], Pu [1987], and Litwin and Abdellatif [1986]. Breitbart [1990] provides a review of recent literature on multidatabases.

16

Security and Integrity

The data stored in the database needs to be protected from unauthorized access, malicious destruction or alteration, and accidental introduction of inconsistency. In Chapter 5, we saw how integrity constraints could be specified. In Chapter 6, we saw how databases could be designed to facilitate checking of integrity constraints. In Chapters 10, 11, and 12, we saw how to preserve integrity despite failures, crashes, and potential anomalies from concurrent processing. In Chapter 15, we saw how to preserve integrity in distributed systems. Until now, we have considered only how to prevent the accidental loss of data integrity. In this chapter, we examine the ways in which data may be misused or intentionally made inconsistent. We then present mechanisms to guard against this occurrence.

16.1 Security and Integrity Violations

Misuse of the database can be categorized as being either intentional (malicious) or accidental. Accidental loss of data consistency may result from:

- Crashes during transaction processing.

- Anomalies caused by concurrent access to the database.

- Anomalies caused by the distribution of data over several computers.

- A logical error that violates the assumption that transactions preserve the database consistency constraints.

It is easier to protect against accidental loss of data consistency than to protect against malicious access to the database. Among the forms of malicious access are the following:

- Unauthorized reading of data (theft of information).

- Unauthorized modification of data.

- Unauthorized destruction of data.

Absolute protection of the database from malicious abuse is not possible, but the cost to the perpetrator can be made sufficiently high to deter most if not all attempts to access the database without proper authority. Database *security* usually refers to security from malicious access, while *integrity* refers to the avoidance of accidental loss of consistency. In practice, the dividing line between security and integrity is not always clear. We shall use the term *security* to refer to both *security* and *integrity* in cases where the distinction between these concepts is not essential.

In order to protect the database, security measures must be taken at several levels:

- **Physical**. The site or sites containing the computer systems must be physically secured against armed or surreptitious entry by intruders.

- **Human**. Users must be authorized carefully to reduce the chance of any such user giving access to an intruder in exchange for a bribe or other favors.

- **Operating system**. No matter how secure the database system is, weakness in operating system security may serve as a means of unauthorized access to the database. Since almost all database systems allow remote access through terminals or networks, software-level security within the operating system is as important as physical security.

- **Database system**. Some database system users may be authorized to access only a limited portion of the database. Other users may be allowed to issue queries, but may be forbidden to modify the data. It is the responsibility of the database system to ensure that these restrictions are not violated.

Security at all of the above levels must be maintained in order to ensure database security. A weakness at a low level of security (physical or human) allows circumvention of strict high-level (database) security measures.

It is worthwhile in many applications to devote a considerable effort to preserving the integrity and security of the database. Large databases containing payroll or other financial data are inviting targets to thieves. Databases that contain data pertaining to corporate operations may be of interest to unscrupulous competitors. Furthermore, loss of such data, whether via accident or fraud, can seriously impair the ability of the corporation to function.

In the remainder of this chapter, we shall address security at the database system level. Security at the physical and human levels, though important, is far beyond the scope of this text. Security within the operating system is implemented at several levels, ranging from passwords for access to the system to the isolation of concurrent processes running within the system. The file system also provides some degree of protection. The bibliographic notes reference coverage of these topics in operating system texts. We shall present our discussion of security in terms of the relational data model, although the concepts of this chapter are equally applicable to all data models.

16.2 Authorization and Views

In Chapter 3, we introduced the concept of *views* as a means of providing a user with a "personalized" model of the database. A view can hide data that a user does not need to see. The ability of views to hide data serves both to simplify usage of the system and to enhance security. System usage is simplified because the user is allowed to restrict attention to the data of interest. Security is provided if there is a mechanism to restrict the user to a personal view or views. Relational database systems typically provide security at two levels:

- **Relation**. A user may be permitted or denied direct access to a relation.

- **View**. A user may be permitted or denied access to data appearing in a view.

Although a user may be denied direct access to a relation, the user may be able to access part of that relation through a view. Thus, a combination of relational-level security and view-level security can be used to limit a user's access to precisely the data that user needs.

In our banking example, consider a clerk who needs to know the names of the customers of each branch. This clerk is not authorized to see information regarding specific loans and accounts that the customer may have. Thus, the clerk must be denied direct access to the *borrow* and *deposit* relations. But, in order to have access to the information needed, the clerk must be granted access to the view *all-customer*, which consists only of the names of customers and the branches at which they do business. We defined this view using SQL in Chapter 4 as follows:

> **create view** *all-customer* **as**
>   (**select** *branch-name, customer-name*
>   **from** *deposit*)
>   **union**
>   (**select** *branch-name, customer-name*
>   **from** *borrow*)

Suppose the clerk issues the SQL query:

> **select** *
> **from** *all-customer*

Clearly, the clerk is authorized to see the result of this query. However, when the query is translated by the query processor into a query on the actual relations in the database, we obtain a query on *borrow* and *deposit*. Thus, authorization must be checked on the clerk's query before query processing begins.

A user may have several forms of authorization on parts of the database. Among these are the following:

- **Read authorization**, which allows reading, but not modification of data.

- **Insert authorization**, which allows insertion of new data, but not modification of existing data.

- **Update authorization**, which allows modification, but not deletion of data.

- **Delete authorization**, which allows deletion of data.

A user may be assigned all, none, or a combination of the above types of authorization. In addition to the above forms of authorization for access to data, a user may be granted authorization to modify the database scheme:

- **Index authorization**, which allows the creation and deletion of indices.

- **Resource authorization**, which allows the creation of new relations.

- **Alteration authorization**, which allows the addition or deletion of attributes in a relation.

- **Drop authorization**, which allows the deletion of relations.

The **drop** and **delete** authorization differ in that **delete** authorization allows deletion of tuples only. If a user deletes all tuples of a relation, the relation still exists, but it is empty. If a relation is dropped, it no longer exists.

The ability to create new relations is regulated through **resource** authorization so that the use of storage space can be controlled. A user with **resource** authorization who creates a new relation is given all privileges on that relation automatically.

Creation of a view does not require **resource** authorization. A user who creates a view does not necessarily receive all privileges on that view. Such a user receives only those privileges that provide no additional authorization beyond what the user already had. For example, a user cannot be given **update** authorization on a view without having **update** authorization on the relations used to define the view. If a user creates a view on which authorization cannot be granted, the view creation request is denied. In our example using *all-customer* view, the creator of the view must have **read** authorization on both the *borrow* and *deposit* relations.

Index authorization may appear unnecessary, since the creation or deletion of an index does not alter data in relations. Rather, indices are a structure for performance enhancements. However, indices also consume space and all database modifications are required to update indices.

If **index** authorization were granted to all users, those who performed updates would be tempted to delete indices, while those who issued queries would be tempted to create numerous indices. In order to allow the database administrator (DBA) to regulate the use of system resources, it is necessary to treat index creation as a privilege.

The ultimate form of authority is that given to the database administrator. The database administrator may authorize new users, restructure the database, and so on. This form of authorization is analogous to that provided to a "superuser" or operator for an operating system.

A user who has been granted some form of authority may be allowed to pass this authority on to other users. However, care must be taken about how authorization may be passed among users in order to ensure that such authorization can be revoked at some future time.

Consider, as an example, the granting of update authorization on the *deposit* relation of the bank database. Assume that, initially, the database administrator grants update authorization on *deposit* to users U_1, U_2, and U_3, who may in turn pass this authorization on to other users. The passage of authorization from one user to another may be represented by an *authorization graph*. The nodes of this graph are the users. An edge (U_i, U_j) is included in the graph if user U_i grants update authorization on *deposit* to U_j. A sample graph appears in Figure 16.1. Observe that user U_5

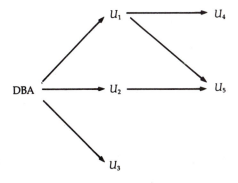

Figure 16.1   An authorization-grant graph.

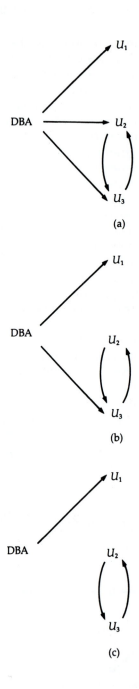

Figure 16.2   Attempt to defeat authorization revocation.

is granted authorization by both U_1 and U_2, while U_4 is granted authorization only by U_1.

Suppose that the database administrator decides to revoke the authorization of user U_1. Since U_4 has authorization granted from U_1, that authorization should be revoked as well. However, U_5 was granted authorization by both U_1 and U_2. Since the database administrator did not revoke update authorization on *deposit* from U_2, U_5 retains update authorization on *deposit*. If U_2 eventually revokes authorization from U_5, then U_5 loses the authorization.

A pair of devious users might attempt to defeat the above rules for revocation of authorization by granting authorization to each other, as shown in Figure 16.2a. If the database administrator revokes authorization from U_2, U_2 retains authorization through U_3, as shown in Figure 16.2b. If authorization is revoked subsequently from U_3, U_3 retains authorization through U_2, as shown in Figure 16.2c.

To avoid problems like that above, we require that all edges in an authorization graph be part of some path originating with the database administrator. Under this rule, the authorization graph of Figure 16.2b would still be the result of revocation of authorization from U_2. However, when the database administrator subsequently revokes authorization from U_3, the edges from U_3 to U_2 and from U_2 to U_3 are no longer part of a path starting with the database administrator. Therefore, those edges are deleted and the resulting authorization graph is as shown in Figure 16.3.

16.3 Security Specification in SQL

The SQL data definition language includes commands to grant and revoke privileges. The exact set of privileges available depends on the version of SQL we consider. The original language included a set of privileges on

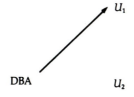

Figure 16.3   Authorization graph.

relations and views similar to those of Section 16.2. IBM SAA SQL includes a modified list of privileges: **alter**, **delete**, **index**, **insert**, **select**, and **update**. The **select** privilege corresponds to the **read** privilege. The SQL standard includes **delete**, **insert**, **select**, and **update** privileges. It also includes a **references** privilege that restricts a user's ability to create relations. If the relation to be created includes a foreign key that references attributes of another relation, the user must have been granted **references** privilege on those attributes. The **grant** statement is used to confer authorization. The basic form of this statement is as follows:

> **grant** <privilege list> **on** <relation name or view name> **to** <user list>

The *privilege list* allows the granting of several privileges in one command. The following **grant** statement grants users U_1, U_2, and U_3 **select** authorization on the *branch* relation:

> **grant select on** *branch* **to** U_1, U_2, U_3

In both IBM SAA and ANSI standard SQL, **update** authorization applies to an entire relation. In the original version of SQL, **update** authorization may be given on all attributes of the relation or only some. If **update** authorization is included in a **grant** statement, the list of attributes on which update authorization is to be granted appears in parentheses. The following **grant** statement gives users U_1, U_2, and U_3 update authorization on the *balance* attribute of the *deposit* relation:

> **grant update** (*balance*) **on** *deposit* **to** U_1, U_2, U_3

The ANSI standard SQL **references** privilege is granted on specific attributes in a manner similar to that shown above for the **update** privilege. The following **grant** statement allows user U_1 to create relations that reference the foreign key *branch-name* on the *branch* relation:

> **grant references** (*branch-name*) **on** *branch* **to** U_1

By default, a user who is granted a privilege in SQL is not authorized to grant that privilege to another user. In order to grant a privilege and allow the recipient to pass the privilege on to other users, the **with grant option** clause is appended to the appropriate **grant** command. For example, if we wish to allow U_1 the **select** privilege on *branch* and allow U_1 to grant this privilege to others, we write:

> **grant select on** *branch* **to** U_1 **with grant option**

To revoke authorization, the **revoke** statement is used. It takes a form almost identical to that of **grant**:

> **revoke** <privilege list>
> **on** <relation name or view name> **from** <user list>

Thus, to revoke the privileges we granted above, we write:

> **revoke select on** *branch* **from** U_1, U_2, U_3
> **revoke update** (*balance*) **on** *deposit* **from** U_1, U_2, U_3
> **revoke references** (*branch-name*) **on** *branch* **from** U_1

As we saw in the previous section, the revocation of a privilege from a user may cause other users also to lose that privilege.

16.4 Encryption

The various provisions a database system may make for authorization may not be sufficient protection for highly sensitive data. In such cases, data may be *encrypted*. It is not possible for encrypted data to be read unless the reader knows how to decipher (*decrypt*) such data.

There are a vast number of techniques for the encryption of data. Simple encryption techniques may not provide adequate security, since it may be easy for an unauthorized user to break the code. As an example of a bad encryption technique, consider the substitution of each character with the next character in the alphabet. Thus:

Perryridge

becomes:

Qfsszsjehf

If an unauthorized user sees only "Qfsszsjehf," there is probably insufficient information to break the code. However, if the intruder sees a large number of encrypted branch names, the intruder could use statistical data regarding the relative frequency of characters (for example, *e* is more common than *x*) to guess what substitution is being made.

A good encryption technique has the following properties:

- It is relatively simple for authorized users to encrypt and decrypt data.

- The encryption scheme depends not on the secrecy of the algorithm but on a parameter of the algorithm called the *encryption key*.

- It is extremely difficult for an intruder to determine the encryption key.

One approach, the *Data Encryption Standard*, does both a substitution of characters and a rearrangement of their order on the basis of an encryption key. In order for this scheme to work, the authorized users must be provided with the encryption key via a secure mechanism. This is a major weakness, since the scheme is no more secure than the secureness of the mechanism by which the encryption key is transmitted.

An alternative scheme that avoids some of the problems with the Data Encryption Standard is called *public-key encryption*. It is based on two keys, a *public key* and a *private key*. Each user U_i has a public key E_i and private key D_i. All public keys are published. Each user's private key is known only to the one user to whom the key belongs. If user U_1 wants to store encrypted data, U_1 encrypts it using public key E_1. Decryption requires the private key D_1.

Because the encryption key for each user is public, it is possible to exchange information securely using this scheme. If user U_1 wants to share data with U_2, U_1 encrypts the data using E_2, the public key of U_2. Since only user U_2 knows how to decrypt the data, information is transferred securely.

For public key encryption to work, there must be a scheme for encryption that can be made public without making it easy to figure out the scheme for decryption. Such a scheme does exist and is based on the following:

- There is an efficient algorithm for testing whether or not a number is prime.

- No efficient algorithm is known for finding the prime factors of a number.

For purposes of this scheme, data is treated as a collection of integers. A public key is created by computing the product of two large prime numbers, P_1 and P_2. The private key consists of the pair (P_1, P_2), and the decryption algorithm cannot be used successfully if only the product P_1P_2 is known. Since all that is published is the product P_1P_2, an unauthorized user would need to be able to factor P_1P_2 in order to steal data. By choosing P_1 and P_2 to be sufficiently large (over 100 digits), we can make the cost of factoring P_1P_2 prohibitively high (on the order of years of computation time even on the fastest computers).

The details of public key encryption and the mathematical justification of its properties are referenced in the bibliographic notes.

16.5 Statistical Databases

Suppose that in our banking example the bank grants an outsider access to its database under the condition that only statistical studies (averages, medians, and so on) are made on the data and that information about individual customers is not divulged. In this section, we examine the difficulty of ensuring the privacy of individuals while allowing use of data for statistical purposes.

One weakness in a statistical database is unusual cases. For example, suppose that a user asks for the total bank account balances for all customers living in Smalltown. If only one customer happens to live in Smalltown, the system has divulged information about an individual. Of course, a security breach has occurred only if the user knows that only one customer lives in Smalltown. However, that information is easily determined by the statistical query "Find the number of customers living in Smalltown."

A simple way to deal with potential security breaches like that described above is for the system to reject any query that involves fewer than some predetermined number of individuals. Suppose this predetermined number is n. A malicious user who has an account with the bank can find an individual's balance in two queries. Suppose the user wants to find how much money Rollo has on deposit. The user chooses n customers and issues two queries to compute:

- x, the total balances for the malicious user and the n customers.

- y, the total balances for Rollo and the n customers.

Rollo's total balance is:

$$y - x + \text{the malicious user's balance}$$

The critical flaw that was exploited in the above example is that the two queries referred to many of the same data items. The number of data items the two queries have in common is called their *intersection*.

Thus, in addition to requiring that a query reference data pertaining to at least n individuals, we may require that no two queries have an intersection larger than m. By adjusting n and m, we can increase the difficulty of a user determining data about an individual, but we cannot eliminate it entirely.

These two restrictions do not preclude the possibility of some extremely clever query that divulges individual data. However, if all queries are restricted to computing sums, counts, or averages, and if a malicious user knows only the data value for himself, it can be shown that it will take at least $1 + (n - 2)/m$ queries for the malicious user to determine data about another individual. The proof of this is beyond the scope of this text and is referenced in the bibliographic notes. This fact is, nonetheless, only partially reassuring. We can limit a user to fewer than $1 + (n - 2)/m$ queries, but a conspiracy of two malicious users can result in data being divulged.

Another approach to security is *data pollution*, or the random falsification of data provided in response to a query. This falsification must be done in such a way that the statistical significance of the response is not destroyed. A similar technique involves random modification of the query itself. For both of these techniques, the goals involve a trade-off between accuracy and security.

Regardless of the approach taken to security of statistical data, it is possible for a malicious user to determine individual data values. However, good techniques can make the expense in terms of cost and time sufficiently high to be a deterrent.

16.6 Summary

The data stored in the database needs to be protected from unauthorized access, malicious destruction or alteration, and accidental introduction of inconsistency. It is easier to protect against accidental loss of data consistency than to protect against malicious access to the database. Absolute protection of the database from malicious abuse is not possible, but the cost to the perpetrator can be made sufficiently high to deter most if not all attempts to access the database without proper authority.

The concept of *views* provides a means for a user to design a "personalized" model of the database. A view can hide data that a user does not need to see. Security is provided if there is a mechanism to restrict the user to a personal view or views. A combination of relational-level security and view-level security can be used to limit a user's access to precisely the data that user needs.

A user may have several forms of authorization on parts of the database. Authorization is a means by which the database system can be protected against malicious or unauthorized access. A user who has been granted some form of authority may be allowed to pass this authority on to other users. However, care must be taken about how authorization may be passed among users in order to ensure that such authorization can be revoked at some future time.

The various authorization provisions in a database system may not be sufficient protection for highly sensitive data. In such cases, data may be *encrypted*. It is not possible for encrypted data to be read unless the reader knows how to decipher (*decrypt*) the encrypted data.

It is difficult to ensure the privacy of individuals while allowing use of data for statistical purposes. A simple way to deal with potential security breaches is for the system to reject any query that involves fewer than some predetermined number of individuals. Another approach to security is *data pollution*, or the random falsification of data provided in response to a query. A similar technique involves random modification of the query itself. For both of these techniques, the goals involve a trade-off between accuracy and security. Regardless of the approach taken to security of statistical data, it is possible for a malicious user to determine individual data values. However, good techniques can make the expense in terms of cost and time sufficiently high to be a deterrent.

Exercises

16.1 Make a list of security concerns for a bank. For each item on your list, state whether this concern relates to physical security, human security, operating system security, or database security.

16.2 Using the relations of our sample bank database, write an SQL expression to define the following views:

    a. A view containing the account numbers and customer names (but not the balances) for all accounts at the Deer Park branch.

    b. A view containing the names and addresses of all customers who have an account with the bank but do not have a loan.

    c. A view containing the name and average account balance of every customer of the Rock Ridge branch.

16.3 For each of the views you defined in Exercise 16.2, explain how updates would be performed (if they should be allowed at all). (Hint: See the discussion of views in Chapter 3.)

16.4 In Chapter 3, we described the use of views to simplify access to the database by those who need only part of the database. In this chapter, we described the use of views as a security mechanism. Do these two purposes for views ever conflict? Explain.

16.5 What is the purpose of having separate categories for index authorization and resource authorization?

16.6 Database systems that store each relation in a separate operating system file may use the operating system's security and authorization scheme rather than defining a special scheme within the database system. Discuss the advantages and disadvantages of such an approach.

16.7 What are the advantages of encrypting data stored in the database?

16.8 How does data encryption affect the index schemes of Chapter 8? In particular, how might it affect schemes that attempt to store data in sorted order?

16.9 Suppose that the bank of our running example maintains a statistical database containing the average balances of all

customers. The scheme for this relation is (*customer-name,
customer-city, avg-balance*). Assume that, for security reasons, the
following restrictions are imposed on queries against this data:

- Every query must involve at least 10 customers.

- The intersection of any pair of queries may be at most 5.

Construct a series of queries to find the average balance of a
customer. (Hint: This can be done in fewer than 7 queries.)

16.10 Perhaps the most important data items in any database system are
the passwords that control access to the database. Suggest a
scheme for the secure storage of passwords. Be sure that your
scheme allows the system to test passwords supplied by users
attempting to log into the system.

Bibliographic Notes

Security aspects of computer systems in general are discussed in Bell and
LaPadula [1976] and U.S. Dept. of Defense [1985].

The security subsystem of System R is described by Griffiths and Wade
[1976] and Fagin [1978], whose model provided the basis for our discussion
of authorization graphs. Zloof [1978] presents the approach taken to
security by the QBE database system. Stonebraker and Wong [1974] discuss
the Ingres approach to security, which involves the modification of users'
queries so as to ensure that they do not access data for which
authorization has not been granted.

Security aspects of ANSI standard SQL are discussed by Date [1989] and
in [ANSI 1986]. IBM SAA SQL is discussed in [IBM 1987]. Chin and
Ozsoyoglu [1981] discuss the design of statistical databases.

Several papers provide mathematical analyses of the number of queries
required to "break" a database under a variety of assumptions. Among
these are Kam and Ullman [1977], Chin [1978], DeMillo, et al. [1978],
Dobkin, et al. [1979], Yao [1979a], Denning [1980], and Leiss [1982b].

Another aspect of security that has been studied from a mathematical
standpoint is data encryption. Public-key encryption is discussed by
Rivest, et al. [1978]. The Data Encryption Standard is presented in [U.S.
Dept. of Commerce 1977]. Other discussions on cryptography include
Diffie and Hellman [1979], Lempel [1979], Simmons [1979], Davies [1980],
Fernandez, et al. [1981], Denning [1982], Leiss [1982a], and Akl [1983].

Security in relational databases is covered in Lunt et al. [1990],
Stachour and Thuraisingham [1990], Jajodia and Sandhu [1990], and Kogan
and Jajodia [1990]. Security in object-oriented databases is discussed by
Rabitti et al. [1988].

Denning and Denning [1979] survey database security. Textbook discussions of security and integrity include Leiss [1982a], Date [1983], Wiederhold [1983], and Ullman [1988]. Operating system security issues are discussed in most operating system texts, including Silberschatz, et al. [1991]. An issue not discussed in this chapter is the legal and social implications of database security. Martin and Norman [1970] and Martin [1973] provide a textbook discussion of some of these issues.

17

Case Studies

In this chapter, we discuss a few selected database systems that either are commercially available or are experimental systems with significant impact. We do not provide complete details for the selected systems. Rather, we draw attention to some of the more significant features of the systems.

Given the large number of commercial systems available and the large number of systems being released as of this writing, the following discussion of actual systems is far from a complete one. We have chosen particular systems in order to illustrate concepts presented in this book. Thus, our selection of a system for this chapter should not be interpreted as an endorsement of the product.

Examples of systems based on the network and hierarchical data models are presented in Appendices A and B, respectively. In this chapter, we emphasize relational systems.

17.1 System R

The System R research project began at the IBM San Jose Research Laboratory (now the IBM Almaden Research Center) in 1974. The goal of the project was to demonstrate the practicality of the then newly proposed relational data model. This involved both verifying the appropriateness of the relational model as a user interface and discovering ways of implementing a relational system for efficient query processing.

The success of this effort is clear from the fact that a substantial number of fundamental concepts as well as commercial products were derived from the System R research. By 1979, the System R project was completed. Shortly thereafter, IBM announced the database product *SQL/Data System* (SQL/DS). The IBM *Database 2* (DB2) system, announced in 1983, was heavily influenced by the System R research. Products introduced by vendors other than IBM were influenced by those System R publications that appeared in the academic literature (see the bibliographic notes).

Among the key contributions of the System R effort were:

- The SQL query language.

- Query compilation and optimization.

- Integration of a relational language with a conventional programming language.

- Serializability and two-phase locking.

- Multiple-granularity locking.

We have discussed SQL in detail in Chapter 4, presented query optimization in Chapter 9, and examined serializability and multiple-granularity locking in Chapter 11. We present a discussion of problems in the integration of a relational language (SQL) with general-purpose programming languages in Section 17.5.

17.1.1 Overall System Structure

The internal architecture of System R consists of two main components:

- The relational storage system (RSS), which is responsible for storage management (disk storage and main memory), crash recovery, and concurrency control.

- The relational data system (RDS), which is responsible for views, authorization, and integrity.

The RSS allows access on a record-by-record basis to relations in the logical model. Higher-level access is obtained by the RDS interface. This interface accepts SQL expressions.

An arbitrary number of interfaces to the shared System R database can be built on top of the RDS. The most popular of these is the user-friendly interface (UFI), a program that accepts SQL statements from the user, passes them to the RDS, and displays the results. Application programs can be written that use the RDS directly.

17.1.2 Query Compilation

Commercial users of database systems have a collection of queries that are run regularly to generate reports. In order to eliminate the need to choose a query-processing strategy each time such a query is run, System R allows for the *precompilation* of queries. Precompilation involves the parsing of the query and the selection of a complete strategy for processing the query. The result of precompilation is called a *plan*. Plans are stored in the System R database and accessed when the query is executed.

Since a plan includes such details as the choice of join strategies and the use of particular indices, it is possible for the plan to become invalid. For example, an index used by a plan might be deleted. In such a case, it is necessary to rerun the compilation step before the query can be executed.

17.1.3 Host Languages

Relational languages are limited in their expressive power. System R made it possible to use the relational model while retaining the full expressive power of general-purpose programming languages by means of *embedded* SQL, a slightly modified form of SQL that can be used within a host programming language. System R allows two host languages: PL/I and Cobol. In our discussion, we shall consider PL/I only.

The primary difficulties in merging the language concepts of SQL into PL/I arise from the fact that PL/I operates on records, while SQL operates on sets of records (relations). Therefore, a mechanism is needed to present the result of an SQL query (that is, a relation) to the PL/I program one tuple (record) at a time. A *cursor* is a pointer defined on relations to be processed by the PL/I program. Cursors are used to iterate over tuples of a relation. The normal method by which a PL/I program accesses the database is summarized as follows:

- A call is made to a procedure that causes the SQL query to be executed.

- A *cursor* is opened on the relation resulting from execution of the query. This cursor is used to process tuples of the result relation one at a time.

- A **fetch** call is made in order to retrieve the "next" tuple. A **fetch** retrieves the first tuple of a relation associated with a newly opened cursor. Subsequent **fetch** calls advance the cursor to the next tuple of the relation and then retrieve the tuple to which the cursor points. The tuple retrieved is placed in a PL/I record that can be manipulated by the PL/I program.

- **Fetch** calls are repeated until all tuples have been processed. A special code returned by the **fetch** call allows the program to determine when all tuples have been processed.

Access by a PL/I program with embedded SQL is somewhat more complicated because:

- A preprocessor must translate the SQL statements before the program is compiled by the PL/I compiler. Special commands to the preprocessor are needed.

- A method must be provided to transfer values from a tuple into PL/I variables.

- The size of tuples returned by a **fetch** may depend upon input to the program. This occurs, for example, if the user inputs an SQL query to the program as it is executing.

The embedded SQL language used by System R provided the basis for a similar language included in the ANSI standard SQL document.

17.1.4 Consistency and Concurrency

The concepts of two-phase locking and multiple-granularity locking originated from the System R project. By default, transactions in System R hold all locks until the end of transaction execution in order to ensure serializability and avoid cascading rollback. System R allows for alternative *degrees of consistency* that enable locks to be released early. An application programmer designing a transaction for System R might opt for a weaker degree of consistency, since early release of locks should reduce the chances of another transaction having to wait for a lock.

Multiple-granularity locking has worked well in System R. However, a slight modification to the scheme as presented in Chapter 11 was added to deal with the following problem. Often, a transaction accumulates a large number of record-granularity locks on a relation but fails to take a relation-granularity lock. As a result, the lock manager is forced to maintain a large lock table and lock overhead increases. To cope with such a situation, System R automatically performs *lock escalation*. The record-granularity locks are exchanged (if possible) for a lock at the relation or file granularity. This lock escalation procedure is transparent to the application programmer and to the user.

The System R recovery manager uses *both* shadow paging and logging. This combined strategy is a reflection of the evolution of System R from a single-user system (for which shadow paging works well) to a multiuser system. Shadow paging does not generalize well to the case of concurrent accesses to the database. The form of logging used is called *write-ahead logging* and is essentially the same as logging with immediate database modification, as discussed in Chapter 10.

17.1.5 Remarks

System R is well documented in the open literature, since it is a research project rather than a commercial product. Besides influencing several commercial products, System R has spawned several subsequent research projects within IBM, including the R* distributed database project, research into extending System R to support complex objects (see Chapter 14), and the Starburst extensible relational system. Furthermore, the concepts developed by the System R project have provided the foundation for a significant amount of academic research on relational database systems.

17.2 Academic Ingres

At approximately the same time that the IBM San Jose Research Laboratory was developing the System R prototype, a group at the University of California at Berkeley was developing an experimental database system called Ingres. Although both projects were based on the ideas of the relational data model, they differ substantially in their system design and user interface.

The Ingres research project led to the development of a commercial product with the same name, available through Ingres, Inc. (formerly Relational Technology, Inc.). In this section, we discuss the academic version of Ingres, though some of our remarks are applicable also to the commercial version.

Ingres was developed on a PDP-11 computer running the UNIX operating system. The UNIX operating system influenced the way in which Ingres was structured internally. Several processes are used, each of which is responsible for a specific task:

- Query formulation and user interaction.

- Lexical analysis and parsing and query optimization.

- Execution of queries.

- Index maintenance.

A user request is passed from process to process as necessary.

This multiprocess design allows for concurrency within Ingres itself since, for example, one query can be parsed while another is executing. However, the interprocess communication (via UNIX pipes) imposes some overhead. Historically, a major factor motivating the Ingres design was the PDP-11 limitation of 64 kilobyte address spaces for each individual process.

Ingres introduced the query language Quel and an embedding of Quel into the host language C called Equel. Quel was discussed in Chapter 4. The characters ## are used to indicate a Quel statement appearing within a C program. The ## characters mark those C declarations that pertain to variables referenced with a Quel statement.

Equel differs from embedded SQL in its analog to SQL's cursors. Recall that in embedded SQL, a cursor is *open*ed for a query and then individual tuples are retrieved by means of a **fetch** call. Equel uses a more structured approach in which a specific body of code is executed once per tuple in the result of a Quel query. Figure 17.1 shows a sample Equel program to print the name and city of customers with more than x dollars in an account.

```
## char a[20], b[20];
## float x;
main () {
```
·
·
·
```
## range of d is deposit
## range of c is customer
## retrieve a = c.customer-name, b = c.customer-city
## where d.balance > x
  #{ printf ("%5, %7.2f\n", a, b)
  #}
```
·
·
·

Figure 17.1   Sample Equel program.

The code delimited by #{ and #} is executed once for each tuple of the result. The values of the tuple on each of the attributes of the result relation are stored in the variables in the **retrieve** clause (a and b in Figure 17.1).

Ingres does not allow precompilation of Quel queries even in cases where the Quel query is embedded in a C (Equel) program. Query optimization is performed during query interpretation rather than being done at precompilation time. A particularly useful query optimization technique introduced by Ingres is called *decomposition*. A *query graph* is constructed whose nodes are relations and whose edges represent theta joins or natural joins. If an edge represents a join of a small relation with another relation, the expected result of this join is another small relation. Therefore, joins of this sort are processed first. When no such joins remain, decomposition is performed.

Let us illustrate decomposition by considering part of a query graph as shown in Figure 17.2. This graph illustrates a join of three relations, r_1, r_2,

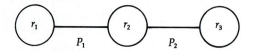

Figure 17.2   Part of an Ingres query graph.

and r_3. Let their schemes be R_1, R_2, and R_3 respectively. P_1 and P_2 are predicates on the joins $r_1 \bowtie r_2$ and $r_2 \bowtie r_3$, respectively. Relation r_2 is decomposed by:

- Building an index on r_1 for $R_1 \cap R_2$ (unless such an index already exists).

- Building an index on r_3 for $R_3 \cap R_2$ (unless such an index already exists).

- Decomposing r_2 into several relations. Each relation is on scheme R_2 and contains exactly one tuple of r_2. A new query graph is produced for each decomposed relation. In each such graph a decomposed relation takes the place of r_2.

- Processing each query graph and taking the union of the results.

Since all the query graphs generated by an application of decomposition have the same structure, it is easy to process them.

17.3 Commercial Systems

A vast number of relational database products are available on the market. These include, among others, IBM's DB2 and SQL/DS as well as Oracle, Unify, Progress, Informix, Ingres, and Sybase. We shall not describe each system in detail here. Rather, we shall focus briefly on two of IBM's database products.

The term *relational* has been applied to a large number of systems, including some that, though they use *tables*, do not capture the full spirit of the original definition of the relational data model. In order for a system to be relational, we require that it meet the following:

- Data is stored in tables.

- No pointers or links are visible to the user.

- The query language is relationally complete.

- Queries may be expressed without the use of iteration or recursion.

Systems that use tables as the basic data structure, but impose restrictions on allowable joins, are not considered relational. We use the term *tabular* for such systems.

17.3.1 SQL/Data System

SQL/Data System (SQL/DS) is an intermediate-size commercial database system available from IBM. Its scope is between that of mainframe database systems (for example, DB2 and IMS) and personal computer database systems (for example, dBase). SQL/DS runs under either of two IBM operating systems: DOS/VSE or VM/SP.

There are a large number of similarities between SQL/DS and System R, since the SQL/DS product was influenced strongly by the System R research effort. These similarities include:

- The SQL query language and embedded SQL.

- Precompilation.

- Concurrency control and transaction management.

Most of what was stated about these subjects for System R (Section 17.1) is applicable to SQL/DS as well.

An important area in which SQL/DS goes beyond System R is in its ability to extract data from IMS databases using the DL/I query language of IMS. The DL/I extract feature allows data from a (hierarchical) IMS database to be copied into part of a (relational) SQL/DS database. Once the data is stored in the SQL/DS system, it can be queried using SQL. It is not possible, however, to modify the IMS database using SQL.

The data definition language of SQL/DS includes the usual SQL statements: **create table**, **create index**, **create view**, and so on. In addition, SQL/DS has statements that allow the database administrator to control the physical database structure.

A *database space* (*dbspace* in SQL/DS terminology) is a section of physical disk into which relations and their indices are stored. The security mechanism of SQL/DS is used to control the authority to add new relations to a database space. For example, users may be assigned personal database spaces for their own relations and granted resource authority for them.

When a database space is created, it can be associated with a particular disk. The power to assign database spaces to specific disks in a multidisk computer system enables the database administrator to distribute the data accesses over several physical devices. This distribution of workload should lead to enhanced performance.

The user interface to SQL/DS includes both a precompiler and an interactive interface similar to System R's UFI. The precompiler syntax is different from that of System R, but the basic language constructs and concepts are the same.

The *interactive SQL* interface (ISQL) allows a user to enter SQL queries directly. In addition to SQL statements, ISQL includes statements to control the output format of answers to queries, commands to save and edit queries, and statements to facilitate the generation of reports.

17.3.2 Database 2

Database 2 (DB2) is a commercial database system available from IBM for use on large mainframes running the MVS operating system.

Although DB2 and SQL/DS are distinct systems, there is a high degree of similarity between them. Both use a nearly identical version of the SQL query language, and nearly identical syntax for embedded SQL. The two systems cannot share data directly, but it is possible to transfer data between SQL/DS and DB2.

The concepts underlying DB2 are similar to those of SQL/DS and, therefore, similar to System R. The primary significance of DB2 is that it has the size and sophistication to handle large databases. Therefore, unlike SQL/DS, DB2 is a competitor of IMS for the management of large databases. The introduction of DB2 in 1983 indicates the increasing importance of the relational data model in the commercial environment and the waning importance of the hierarchical model. The DXT features of DB2 allow data to be moved from IMS to DB2 (analogously to the DL/I extract feature of SQL/DS).

DB2 interacts with three different subsystems running under MVS, each of which provides a form of transaction management. These three subsystems — IMS, TSO (the MVS time-sharing option), and CICS (Customer Information Control System) — predate DB2. Thus, the interaction of DB2 with these subsystems was a practical necessity. Nevertheless, it creates an interesting application of the *distributed* database concepts of transaction commit. In Chapter 15, we assumed that a distributed system consists of computers connected by a network. Within DB2, the subsystems all coexist on the same machine. However, as is the case for distributed systems, the subsystems must reach agreement either to commit or abort transactions that use the services of more than one subsystem. This is accomplished in DB2 using the two-phase commit protocol discussed in Chapter 15.

The DB2 *query management facility* (QMF) is an interface to DB2 that allows interaction with the database using:

- SQL.

- QBE.

- A report writer facility.

As mentioned in Chapter 4, the most noteworthy feature of the QBE system is its query language. Since QBE and SQL are both relational query languages, it is feasible for a database system to offer its users both languages. Under QMF, DB2 users may share data even if some use SQL and others use QBE. The report writer facility is available both to SQL users and to QBE users. QMF automatically generates a format for the report. The user may alter this format if desired. The QMF facility is also available under SQL/DS.

17.4 Microcomputer Database Systems

The primary characteristic of microcomputer database systems is simplicity. The limited capability of personal computers imposes restrictions on both the size of the database and the degree of sophistication of the system. Although most database systems are designed with ease of use in mind, this is a critical concern in the personal computer market, since users cannot rely on a skilled database administrator for assistance. Each user of a microcomputer database system serves as database administrator.

Let us compare the typical features of microcomputer database systems with those of larger systems.

- **Data model**. Since microcomputer database systems are relatively new, almost all such systems are based on the relational model. Some systems are better described as *tabular*, since they are based on tables but still too primitive to be called relational.

- **Query language**. Even the higher-level languages we have discussed may be too complex for the casual user of a microcomputer database system. Many languages are based on a form interface in which the user interacts with the system by filling in a form.

- **Physical implementation**. The space occupied by the object code of a microcomputer database system is an important issue to system implementors. If the space requirements are reduced, the system can be run on machines with less main memory. This can have a major impact on the potential market. As a result, few systems employ sophisticated storage management and indexing techniques. Rather, a single type of index is chosen, and little or no query optimization is performed.

- **Recovery**. Many systems have no recovery subsystem. The user is expected to back up data regularly.

- **Concurrency**. Concurrency control is not needed for single-user personal computers.

The distinction between microcomputer database systems and larger systems is eroding. Early microcomputer database systems were little more than interfaces for accessing a single file of fixed-length records. As the power of personal computers has grown, so have the sophistication and complexity of microcomputer database systems. Indeed, versions of some large-scale database systems are beginning to appear on top-of-the-line personal computers.

17.5 Database Programming Languages

In Section 17.1.3, we saw how System R used SQL embedded in PL/I and Cobol as a means to provide both the full expressive power of a general-purpose programming language and relational operations. As noted, it is difficult to combine relational operations with typical commercially used programming languages because the former are set-oriented whereas the latter are record-oriented. This distinction has been called an "impedance mismatch" between programming languages and relational languages.

A further difficulty in providing full expressive power to database application programmers is the need to have a means for generating displays on a screen, special forms, and so on. Such user interface programming tasks are not expressible in relational languages and are cumbersome to express in standard programming languages.

In this section, we briefly discuss the techniques used to deal with these issues.

17.5.1 Embedded SQL

The most widely used form of database programming language is SQL embedded in a general-purpose programming language referred to as the host language. The basic form of these languages follows that of the System R embedding of SQL into PL/I, as discussed in Section 17.1.3. The ANSI SQL standard document includes a specification for embedded SQL in several widely used languages, as does IBM's SAA SQL document.

In embedded SQL, all query processing is performed by the database system. The result of the query is then made available to the program one tuple (record) at a time.

An embedded SQL program must be processed by a special preprocessor prior to compilation. Embedded SQL requests are replaced with host language declarations and procedure calls that allow run-time execution of the database accesses. Then, the resulting program is compiled by the host language compiler. In order to identify embedded SQL requests to the preprocessor, the EXEC SQL statement is used, which has the form:

EXEC SQL <embedded SQL statement > END EXEC

The statement SQL INCLUDE is placed in the program to identify the place where the preprocessor should insert the special variables used for communication between the program and the database system. Variables of the host language may be used within embedded SQL statements, but they must be preceded by a colon (:) to distinguish them from SQL variables.

Embedded SQL statements are of a form similar to the SQL statements we described in Chapter 4. There are, however, several important differences, as noted in what follows.

To write a relational query, the **declare cursor** statement is used. The result of the query is not yet computed. Rather, the program must use the **open** and **fetch** commands (discussed below) to obtain the result tuples.

Consider the banking scheme we used in Chapter 4. Assume that we have a host language variable *amount* and that we wish to find the name and city of customers with more than *amount* dollars in some account. This can be written as follows:

> EXEC SQL
> > **declare** *c* **cursor for**
> > **select** *customer-name, customer-city*
> > **from** *deposit, customer*
> > **where** *deposit.customer-name* = *customer.customer-name*
> > > **and** *deposit.balance* > *:amount*
> > END-EXEC

The variable *c* in the above expression is called a *cursor* for the query. This variable is used to identify the query in the **open** statement, which causes the query to be evaluated, and the **fetch** statement, which causes the values of one tuple to be placed in host language variables.

The **open** statement for our sample query is as follows:

> EXEC SQL **open** *c* END-EXEC

This causes the database system to execute the query and to save the results within a temporary relation. If the SQL query results in an error, the database system encodes an error diagnostic in the SQL communication area (SQLCA) whose declarations are inserted by the SQL INCLUDE statement.

A series of **fetch** statements are executed to make tuples of the result available to the program. The **fetch** statement requires one host language variable for each attribute of the result relation. For our example query, we need a variable to hold the *customer-name* value and another to hold the *customer-city* value. Suppose those variables are *cn* and *cc*, respectively. A tuple of the result relation is obtained by the statement:

> EXEC SQL **fetch** *c* **into** *:cn, :cc* END-EXEC

The program can then manipulate the variables *cn* and *cc* using the features of the host programming language.

A single **fetch** request returns only one tuple. To obtain all tuples of the result, the program must contain a loop to iterate over all tuples. Embedded SQL assists the programmer in managing this iteration. Although a relation is conceptually a set, the tuples of the result of a query are in some fixed physical order. When an **open** statement is executed, the cursor is set to point to the first tuple of the result. When a **fetch** statement is executed, the cursor is updated to point to the next tuple of the result. A variable in the SQLCA is set to indicate that no further tuples remain to be processed. Thus, a **while** loop (or the equivalent, depending on the host language) can be used to process each tuple of the result.

The **close** statement must be used to tell the database system to delete the temporary relation that held the result of the query. For our example, this statement takes the form:

EXEC SQL **close** c END-EXEC

Embedded SQL expressions for database modification (**update, insert, delete**) do not return a result. Thus, they are somewhat simpler to express. A database modification request takes the form:

EXEC SQL < any valid **update, insert,** or **delete**> END-EXEC

Host language variables, preceded by a colon, may appear in the SQL database modification expression. If an error condition arises in the execution of the statement, a diagnostic is set in the SQLCA.

17.5.2 Fourth-Generation Languages

Embedded SQL allows a host language program to access the database, but it provides no assistance in presenting results to the user or in generating reports. Most commercial database products include a special language to assist application programmers in creating templates on the screen for a user interface and in formatting data for report generation. These special languages are called *fourth-generation languages*.

Some fourth-generation languages also include high-level constructs to allow iteration over relations to be expressed directly, without forcing programmers to deal with the details of cursor management. However, unlike SQL and embedded SQL, no single accepted standard currently exists for fourth-generation languages. Rather, each product provides its own proprietary language.

17.5.3 Object-Oriented Languages

The cumbersome interface between general-purpose programming languages and relational languages arises from the "impedance mismatch" that we discussed earlier. Object-oriented database systems avoid this problem by including a general-purpose language within the model itself for use in coding methods. These languages are often limited to accessing local instance variables of the object and sending messages to other objects (see Chapter 13). Query capabilities are being added to object-oriented languages as part of several research efforts so that set-oriented operations similar to those of relational languages can be included within the object-oriented language used for writing methods. Several of these ongoing research projects are referenced in the bibliographic notes.

Bibliographic Notes

The distinction between relational and tabular database systems is based on [Codd 1982].

Various aspects of System R are presented in a large number of published papers. Astrahan et al. [1976], Astrahan et al. [1979], and Blasgen et al. [1981] present an overview of System R. Chamberlin et al. [1976] introduced the SQL language, An analysis of the human factors of SQL is given by Reisner et al. [1975], Reisner [1977], and Chamberlin [1980]. Concurrency control in System R is discussed by Gray et al. [1975, 1976], Eswaren et al. [1976], and Gray [1978]. Gray et al. [1981a] discuss the System R approach to crash recovery. Security and authorization in System R are discussed by Griffiths and Wade [1976], Chamberlin et al. [1978], and Fagin [1978]. Lorie and Wade [1979] and Selinger et al. [1979] explain how query compilation is done in System R. Chamberlin et al. [1981] give an overview of System R written after completion of the project.

An overview of R*, an experimental distributed version of System R, is presented in Williams et al. [1982]. A more detailed survey of the R* approach to distributed data management is given in Lindsay et al. [1980]. Recovery is discussed in Traiger et al. [1982]; distributed naming in Lindsay [1981]; distributed execution of data definition statements in Wilms et al. [1983]; the transaction model in Lindsay et al. [1984]; and distributed query compilation in Daniels et al. [1982].

SQL/DS is described in [IBM 1982]. Date and White [1988] give a detailed description of the Database 2 (DB2) product.

The most significant papers arising out of the Ingres research project have been collected in Stonebraker [1986b]. This collection includes a retrospective on Ingres in Stonebraker [1980], a history of the implementation of Ingres in Stonebraker et al. [1976], and a discussion of the relationship between database systems and operating systems in Stonebraker [1981]. The Stonebraker [1986b] collection discusses all aspects of the Ingres project, including the decision to produce a commercial version of Ingres. Malamud [1989] and Date [1987] describe the commercial version of Ingres. The decomposition approach to query optimization used by Ingres is discussed in Wong and Youssefi [1976].

A

Network Model

In the relational model, the data and the relationships among data are represented by a collection of tables. The network model differs from the relational model in that data is represented by collections of *records* and relationships among data are represented by *links*.

A.1 Basic Concepts

A network database consists of a collection of records which are connected to one another through links. A record is in many respects similar to an entity in the entity-relationship model. Each record is a collection of fields (attributes), each of which contains only one data value. A link is an association between precisely two records. Thus, a link can be viewed as a restricted (binary) form of relationship in the sense of the E-R model.

To illustrate, consider a database representing a *customer-account* relationship in a banking system. There are two record types, *customer* and *account*. As we saw earlier, the *customer* record type can be defined, using Pascal-like notation, as follows:

> **type** *customer* = **record**
> > *name*: string;
> > *street*: string;
> > *city*: string;
> **end**

The *account* record type can be defined as follows:

> **type** *account* = **record**
> > *number*: integer;
> > *balance*: integer;
> **end**

The sample database in Figure A.1 shows that Lowman has account 305, Camp has accounts 226 and 177, and Kahn has account 155.

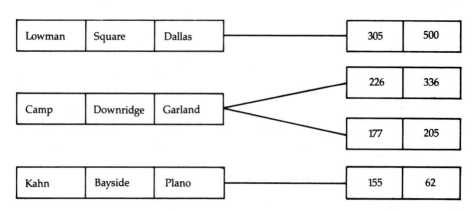

Figure A.1   Sample database.

A.2 Data-Structure Diagrams

A *data-structure diagram* is a scheme representing the design of a network database. Such a diagram consists of two basic components:

- **Boxes**, which correspond to record types.
- **Lines**, which correspond to links.

A data-structure diagram serves the same purpose as an entity-relationship diagram; namely, it specifies the overall logical structure of the database. To understand how such diagrams are structured, we shall show how to transform entity-relationship diagrams into their corresponding data-structure diagrams.

A.2.1 Binary Relationship

Consider the entity-relationship diagram of Figure A.2a, consisting of two entity sets, *customer* and *account*, related through a binary, many-to-many relationship *CustAcct*, with no descriptive attributes. This diagram specifies that a customer may have several accounts and that an account may belong to several different customers. The corresponding data-structure diagram is illustrated in Figure A.2b. The record type *customer* corresponds to the entity set *customer*. It includes three fields — *name*, *street*, and *city* — as defined in Section A.1. Similarly, *account* is the record type corresponding to the entity set *account*. It includes the two fields *number* and *balance*. Finally, the relationship *CustAcct* has been replaced with the link *CustAcct*.

The relationship *CustAcct* is many-to-many. If the relationship *CustAcct* were one-to-many from *customer* to *account*, then the link *CustAcct* would have an arrow pointing to *customer* record type (Figure A.3a). Similarly, if the relationship *CustAcct* were one-to-one, then the link *CustAcct* would

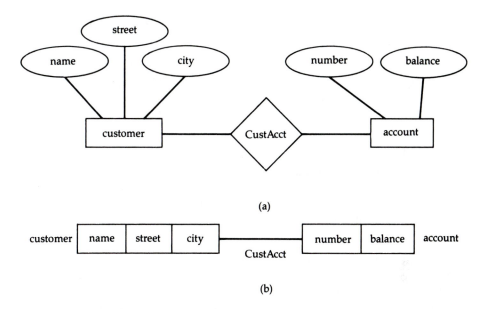

(a)

(b)

Figure A.2   E-R diagram and its corresponding data-structure diagram.

have two arrows, one pointing to *account* record type and one pointing to *customer* record type (Figure A.3b). Since, in the E-R diagram of Figure A.2a, the *CustAcct* relationship is many-to-many, we draw no arrows on the link *CustAcct* in Figure A.2b.

A database corresponding to the above-described scheme may thus contain a number of *customer* records linked to a number of *account* records, as depicted in Figure A.1.

A sample database corresponding to the data-structure diagram of Figure A.2 is shown in Figure A.4. Since the relationship is many-to-many, we show that Katz has accounts 256 and 347 and that account 347 is

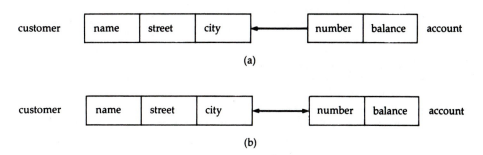

Figure A.3   Two data-structure diagrams.

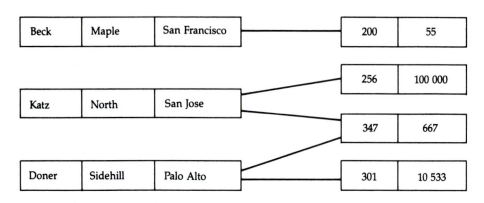

Figure A.4   Sample database corresponding to diagram of Figure A.2b.

owned by both Katz and Doner. A sample database corresponding to the data-structure diagram of Figure A.3a is depicted in Figure A.1. Since the relationship is one-to-many from *customer* to *account*, a customer may have more than one account, as is the case with Camp, who owns both 226 and 177. An *account*, however, cannot belong to more than one customer, as is indeed observed in the sample database. Finally, a sample database corresponding to the data-structure diagram of Figure A.3b is shown in Figure A.5. Since the relationship is one-to-one, an account can be owned by precisely one customer, and a customer can have only one account, as is indeed the case in the sample database.

If a relationship includes descriptive attributes, the transformation from an E-R diagram to a data-structure diagram is somewhat more complicated. This is due to the fact that a link cannot contain any data value. In this case, a new record type needs to be created and links need to be established as described below.

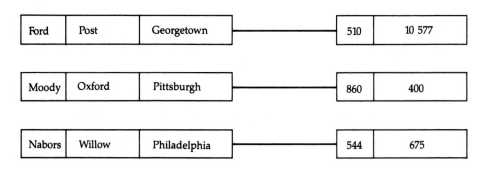

Figure A.5   Sample database corresponding to diagram of Figure A.3b.

Consider the E-R diagram of Figure A.2a. Suppose that we add the attribute *date* to the relationship *CustAcct*, to denote the last time the customer has accessed the account. This newly derived E-R diagram is depicted in Figure A.6a. To transform this diagram to a data-structure diagram we need to:

1. Replace entities *customer* and *account* with record types *customer* and *account*, respectively.

2. Create a new record type *date* with a single field to represent the date.

3. Create the following many-to-one links:

   - *CustDate* from the *date* record type to the *customer* record type.

   - *AcctDate* from the *date* record type to the *account* record type.

The resulting data-structure diagram is depicted in Figure A.6b.

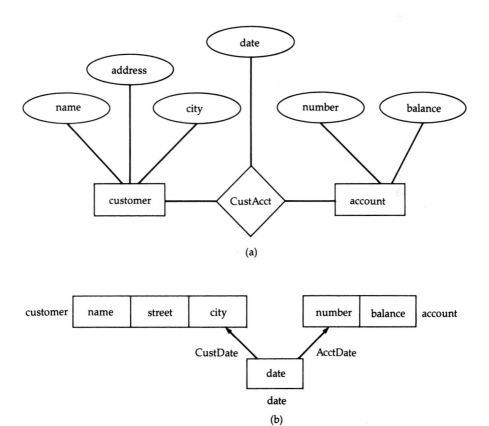

Figure A.6   E-R diagram and its corresponding network diagram.

An instance of a database corresponding to the above-described scheme appears in Figure A.7. It shows the following:

- Lowman has account 305, which was last accessed on 15 September 1980.

- Camp has two accounts: 226, which was last accessed on 1 October 1983, and 177, which was last accessed on 23 November 1984.

- Kahn has account 155, which was last accessed on 15 September 1980.

A.2.2 General Relationships

Consider the entity-relationship diagram of Figure A.8a, which consists of three entity sets — *account*, *customer*, and *branch* — related through the general relationship *CAB* with no descriptive attribute. This diagram specifies that a customer may have several accounts, each located in a specific bank branch, and that an account may belong to several different customers.

Since a link can connect precisely two different record types, we need to connect these three record types through a new record type that is linked to each of these three records directly, as described below.

To transform the E-R diagram of Figure A.8a to a network data-structure diagram we need to do the following:

1. Replace entity sets *account*, *customer*, and *branch* with record types *account*, *customer*, and *branch*, respectively.

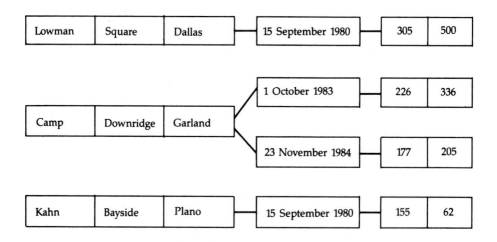

Figure A.7   Sample database corresponding to diagram of Figure A.6b.

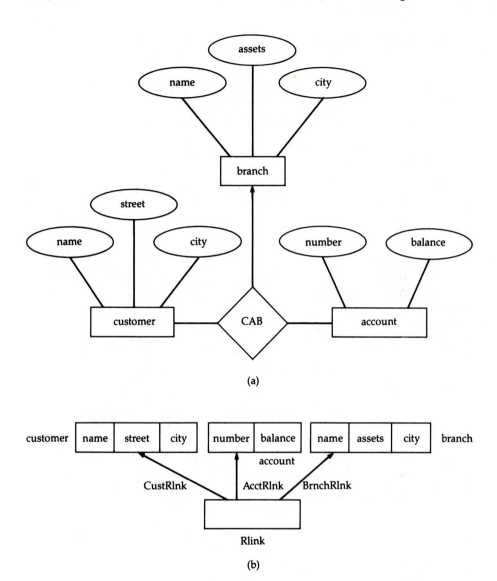

Figure A.8   E-R diagram and its corresponding data-structure diagram.

2. Create a new record type *Rlink* that may either have no fields or have a single field containing a unique identifier. This identifier is supplied by the system and is not used directly by the application program. This new type of record is sometimes referred to as a *dummy* (or *link* or *junction*) record type.

3. Create the following many-to-one links:

- *CustRlnk* from *Rlink* record type to *customer* record type.
- *AcctRlnk* from *Rlink* record type to *account* record type.
- *BrncRlnk* from *Rlink* record type to *branch* record type.

The resulting data-structure diagram is depicted in Figure A.8b.

A sample database corresponding to the above-described scheme appears in Figure A.9. It shows that Lowman has account 305 in the Hillside branch, Camp has accounts 226 and 177 in the Hillside and Valleyview branches, respectively, and Kahn has account 155 in the Valleyview branch.

This technique can be extended in a straightforward manner to deal with relationships that span more than three entity sets. We create a many-to-one link from the *Rlink* record to the record types corresponding to each entity set involved in the relationship. The technique can also be extended to deal with a general relationship that has some descriptive attributes. We need to add one field to the dummy record type for each descriptive attribute.

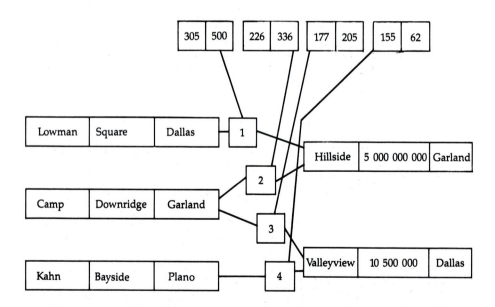

Figure A.9   Sample database corresponding to diagram of Figure A.8b.

A.3 The DBTG CODASYL Model

The first database standard specification, called the CODASYL DBTG 1971 report, was written in the late 1960s by the Database Task Group. Since then, a number of changes have been suggested to that report, the last official one in 1978. In 1981, a new draft proposal was published which has not yet been officially adopted. We have chosen this draft as the primary source for our discussion concerning the DBTG model.

A.3.1 Link Restriction

In the DBTG model, only many-to-one links can be used. Many-to-many links are disallowed in order to simplify the implementation. One-to-one links are represented using a many-to-one link. These restrictions imply that the various algorithms of Section A.2 for transforming an entity-relationship diagram to a data-structure diagram must be revised.

Consider a binary relationship that is either one-to-many or one-to-one. In this case, the transformation algorithm defined in Section A.2.1 can be applied directly. Thus, for our customer-account database, if the *CustAcct* relationship is one-to-many with no descriptive attributes, then the appropriate data-structure diagram is as shown in Figure A.10a. If the relationship has a descriptive attribute (for example, *date*), then the appropriate data-structure diagram is as shown in Figure A.10b.

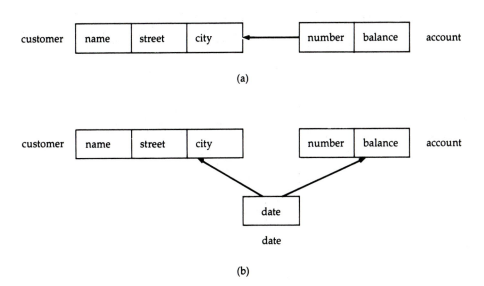

Figure A.10   Two data-structure diagrams.

If the *CustAcct* relationship, however, is many-to-many, then our transformation algorithm must be refined as follows. If the relationship has no descriptive attributes (Figure A.11a), then the following algorithm must be employed:

1. Replace the entity sets *customer* and *account* with record types *customer* and *account*, respectively.

2. Create a new dummy record type, *Rlink*, that may either have no fields or have a single field containing an externally defined unique identifier.

3. Create the following two many-to-one links:

   - *CustRlnk* from *Rlink* record type to *customer* record type.

   - *AcctRlnk* from *Rlink* record type to *account* record type.

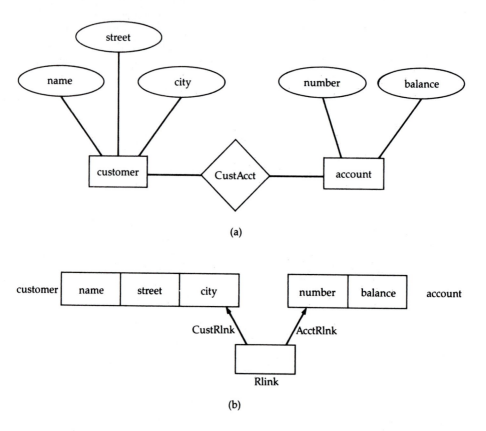

(a)

(b)

Figure A.11   E-R diagram and its corresponding data-structure diagram.

The corresponding data-structure diagram is as shown in Figure A.11b. An instance of a database corresponding to the above-described scheme is depicted in Figure A.12. We encourage the reader to compare this sample database with the one described in Figure A.4.

If the relationship *CustAcct* is many-to-many with a descriptive attribute (for example, *date*), then the transformation algorithm is similar to the one described above. The only difference is that the new record type *Rlink* now contains the field *date*.

In the case of general (that is, nonbinary) relationships, the transformation algorithm is the same as the one described in Section A.2.2. Thus, the E-R diagram of Figure A.8a is transformed into the data-structure diagram of Figure A.8b.

A.3.2 DBTG Sets

Given that only many-to-one links can be used in the DBTG model, a data-structure diagram consisting of two record types that are linked together has the general form of Figure A.13. This structure is referred to in the DBTG model as a *DBTG-set*. The name of the set is usually chosen to be the same as the name of the link connecting the two record types.

In each such DBTG-set, the record type *A* is designated as the *owner* (or *parent*) of the set, and the record type *B* is designated as the *member* (or *child*) of the set. Each DBTG-set can have any number of *set occurrences* — that is, actual instances of linked records. For example, in Figure A.14, we have three set occurrences corresponding to the DBTG-set of Figure A.13.

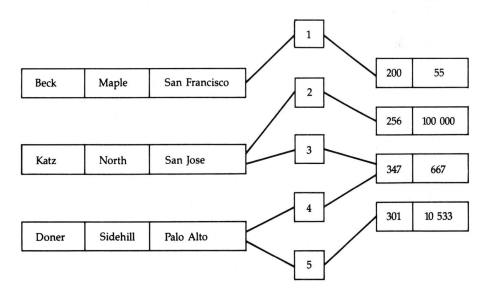

Figure A.12   Sample database corresponding to the diagram of Figure A.11.

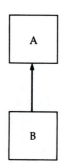

Figure A.13   DBTG-set.

Since many-to-many links are disallowed, each set occurrence has precisely one owner and zero or more member records. In addition, no member record of a set can participate in more than one occurrence of the set at any point. A member record, however, can participate simultaneously in several set occurrences of *different* DBTG-sets.

To illustrate, consider the data-structure diagram of Figure A.15. There are two DBTG-sets:

- *CustAcct*, having *customer* as the owner of the DBTG-set, and *account* as the member of the DBTG-set.

- *BrncAcct*, having *branch* as the owner of the DBTG-set, and *account* as the member of the DBTG-set.

The set *CustAcct* may be defined as follows:

set name is *CustAcct*
owner is *customer*
member is *account*

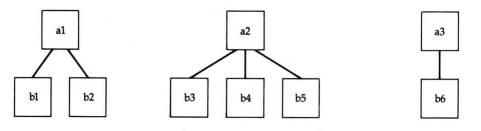

Figure A.14   Three set occurrences.

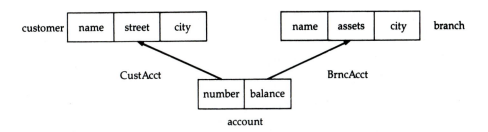

Figure A.15   Data-structure diagram.

The set *BrncAcct* may be defined similarly as:

> **set name is** *BrncAcct*
> **owner is** *branch*
> **member is** *account*

An instance of the database is depicted in Figure A.16. There are five set occurrences listed below: three of set *CustAcct* (sets 1, 2, and 3) and two of set *BrncAcct* (sets 4 and 5).

1. Owner is *customer* record Lowman with a single member *account* record 305.

2. Owner is *customer* record Camp with two member *account* records 177 and 226.

3. Owner is *customer* record Kahn with three member *account* records 155, 402, and 408.

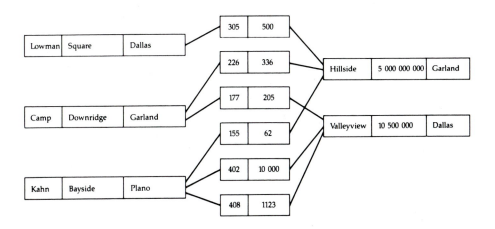

Figure A.16   Five set occurrences.

4. Owner is *branch* record Hillside with three member *account* records 305, 226, and 155.

5. Owner is *branch* record Valleyview with three member *account* records 177, 402, and 408.

Note that an *account* record (which is, in this case, a member of both DBTG-sets) cannot appear in more than one set occurrence of one individual set type. This is because an account can belong to exactly one customer, and can be associated with only one bank branch. An account, however, can appear in two set occurrences of different set types. For example, account 305 is a member of set occurrence 1 of type *CustAcct* and is also a member of set occurrence 4 of type *BrncAcct*.

The member records of a set occurrence may be ordered in a variety of ways. We shall discuss this issue in greater detail in Section A.6.6, after we describe the mechanism for inserting and deleting records into a set occurrence.

The DBTG model allows more complicated set structures in which one single owner type and several different member types exist. For example,

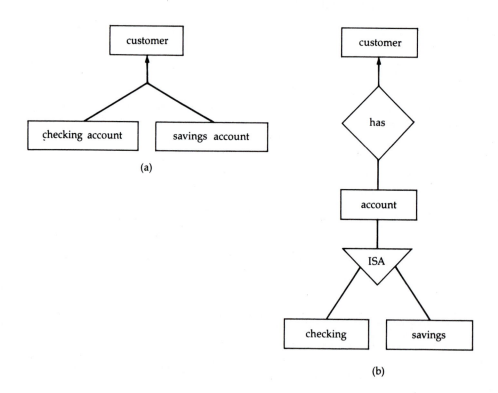

(a)

(b)

Figure A.17   Data-structure and E-R diagram.

suppose that we have two types of bank accounts: checking and saving. Then the data-structure diagram for the customer-account scheme is as depicted in Figure A.17a. Such a scheme is similar in nature to the E-R diagram of Figure A.17b.

The DBTG model also provides for the definition of a special set, referred to as a *singular set* (or *system set*). In such a set, the owner is a system-defined, unique record type, called *system*, with no fields. Such a set has a *single* set occurrence. This scheme is useful in searching records of one particular type, as will be discussed in Section A.4.4.

A.3.3 Repeating Groups

The DBTG model provides a mechanism for a field (or collection of fields) to have a set of values, rather than one single value. For example, suppose that a customer has several addresses. In this case, the *customer* record type will have the (*street, city*) pair of fields defined as a repeating group. Thus, the *customer* record for Kahn may be as shown in Figure A.18.

The repeating-groups construct is another way of representing the notion of weak entities in the E-R model. To illustrate, let us partition the entity set *customer* into two sets:

- *customer*, with descriptive attribute *name*.

- *address*, with descriptive attributes *street* and *city*.

The *address* entity set is a weak entity set, since it depends on the strong entity set *customer*.

The E-R diagram describing this scheme is depicted in Figure A.19a. If we do not use the repeating-group construct in the scheme, then the corresponding data-structure diagram is the one in Figure A.19b. If, on the other hand, the repeating-group construct is used, then the data structure diagram simply consists of one single record type *customer*.

A.4 DBTG Data Retrieval Facility

The data manipulation language of the DBTG proposal consists of a number of commands that are embedded in a host language. In this section, we

Kahn	Bayside	Plano
	Main	Garland

Figure A.18   A *customer* record.

shall present some of these commands and use Pascal as the host language. To illustrate the various concepts, we shall use the example of the customer-account-branch scheme discussed in Section A.3.2. In particular, the data-structure diagram corresponding to our scheme is the one depicted in Figure A.15, and the database sample is the one shown in Figure A.16.

A.4.1 Program Work-Area

Each application program executing in the system consists of a sequence of statements; some are Pascal statements while others are DBTG command statements. Each such program is called a *run unit*. These statements access and manipulate database items as well as locally declared variables. For each such application program, the system maintains a *program work-area* (referred to in the DBTG model as a *user work area*), a buffer storage area which contains the following variables:

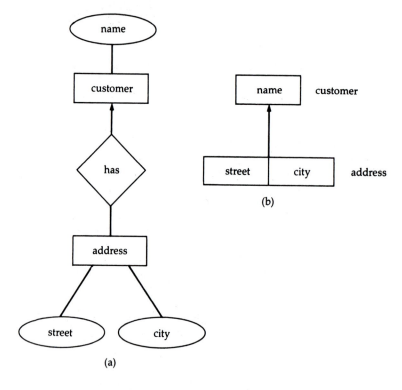

Figure A.19   E-R and data-structure diagram.

- **Record templates,** a record (in the Pascal sense) for each record type accessed by the application program.

- **Currency pointers,** a set of pointers to various database records most recently accessed by the application program. Currency pointers are of the following types:

  - **Current of record type,** one currency pointer for each record type T referenced by the application program. Each pointer contains the *address* (location on disk) of the most recently accessed record of type T.

  - **Current of set type,** one currency pointer for each set type S referenced by the application program. Each pointer contains the *address* of the most recently accessed record of that set type. Note that this pointer may point to a record of either the owner or member type, depending on whether an owner or a member was most recently accessed.

  - **Current of run unit,** one single currency pointer, containing the *address* of the record (regardless of type) most recently accessed by the application program.

- **Status flags,** a set of variables used by the system to communicate to the application program the outcome of the last operation applied to the database. The most frequently used one is:

  - **DB-status,** set to 0 if the most recent operation succeeded; otherwise, it is set to an error-code.

  The additional status variables, **DB-set-name**, **DB-record-name**, and **DB-data-name** are set when the last operation fails, in order to help identify the source of the difficulty encountered.

We emphasize again that a particular program work-area is associated with precisely one application program.

For our customer-account-branch database example, a particular program work-area contains the following:

- **Templates,** three record types:

  - *customer* record.

  - *account* record.

  - *branch* record.

- **Currency pointers**, six pointers:

  - Three currency pointers for record types, one to the most recently accessed *customer* record, one to the most recently accessed *account* record, and one to the most recently accessed *branch* record.

  - Two currency pointers for set types, one to the most recently accessed record in an occurrence of the set *CustAcct*, and one to the most recently accessed record in an occurrence of the set *BrncAcct*.

  - One current of run-unit pointer.

- **DB-status**, the four status variables we defined above.

A.4.2 The Find and Get Commands

The two most frequently used DBTG commands are:

- **find**, which locates a record in the database and sets the appropriate currency pointers.

- **get**, which copies the record to which the current of run-unit points from the database to the appropriate program work-area template.

Let us illustrate the general effect that the **find** and **get** statements have on the program work-area. Consider the sample database of Figure A.16. Suppose that the current state of the program work-area of a particular application program is as shown in Figure A.20. Further suppose that a **find** command is issued to locate the customer record belonging to Camp. This command causes the following changes to occur in the state of the program work-area:

- The current of record type *customer* now points to the record of Camp.

- The current of set type *CustAcct* now points to the set owned by Camp.

- The current of run unit now points to *customer* record Camp.

   If the **get** command is executed, the result is to load the information pertaining to Camp into the *customer* record template.

A.4.3 Access of Individual Records

The **find** command has a number of forms. We shall present only a few of these commands in this Appendix. There are two different **find**

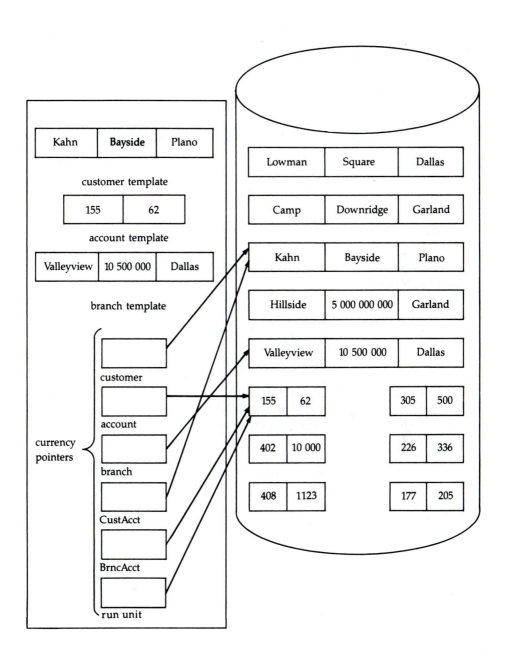

Figure A.20   Program work-area.

commands for locating individual records in the database. The simplest command has the form:

find any <record type> **using** <record-field>

This command locates a record of type <record type> whose <record-field> value is the same as the value of <record-field> in the <record type> template in the program work-area. Once such a record is found, the following currency pointers are set to point to that record:

- The current of run-unit pointer.

- The record-type currency pointer for <record type>.

- For each set in which that record belongs, the appropriate set currency pointer.

To illustrate, let us construct the DBTG query that prints the street address of Lowman.

> *customer.name* := "Lowman";
> **find any** *customer* **using** *name;*
> **get** *customer;*
> **print** (*customer.street*);

There may be several records with the specified value. The **find** command locates the first of these in some prespecified ordering (see Section A.6.6). To locate other database records which match the <record-field>, we use the command

find duplicate <record type> **using** <record-field>

which locates (according to a system-dependent ordering) the next record which matches the <record-field>. The currency pointers noted above are affected.

As an example, let us construct the DBTG query that prints the names of all the customers who live in Dallas:

> *customer.city* := "Dallas";
> **find any** *customer* **using** *city;*
> **while** *DB-status* = 0 **do**
>   **begin**
>   **get** *customer;*
>   **print** (*customer.name*);
>   **find duplicate** *customer* **using** *city;*
>   **end;**

We have enclosed part of the query in a **while** loop because we do not know in advance how many such customers exist. We exit from the loop when DB-status ≠ 0. This indicates that the last **find duplicate** operation failed, implying that we have exhausted all customers residing in Dallas.

A.4.4 Access of Records within a Set

The previous **find** commands located *any* database record of type <record type>. In this subsection, we concentrate on **find** commands that locate records in a particular DBTG-set. The set in question is the one that is pointed to by the <set-type> currency pointer. There are three different types of commands. The basic **find** command is

find first <record type> within <set-type>

which locates the first database record of type <record type> belonging to the current <set-type>. The various ways in which a set may be ordered are discussed in Section A.6.6.

To locate the other members of a set, we adopt the following format:

find next <record type> within <set-type>

This command finds the next element in the set <set-type>.

To illustrate how these commands execute, let us construct the DBTG query that prints the total balance of all accounts belonging to Lowman.

```
sum := 0;
customer.name := "Lowman";
find any customer using name;
find first account within CustAcct;
while DB-status = 0 do
    begin
        get account;
        sum := sum + account.balance;
        find next account within CustAcct;
    end
print (sum);
```

Note that we exit from the **while** loop and print out the value of *sum* only when the DB-status is set to a value not equal to zero. This occurs after the **find next** operation fails, indicating that we have exhausted all the members of a set occurrence of type *CustAcct*, whose owner is the record of customer Lowman.

The previous **find** commands locate records within a particular DBTG-set. There are many circumstances, however, where it may be necessary to locate the owner of a particular DBTG-set. This can be accomplished through the following command:

find owner within <set-type>

The set in question is <set-type>. Note that for each set occurrence, there exists precisely one single owner.

To illustrate, consider the DBTG query that prints all the customers of the Hillside branch:

> *branch.name* := "Hillside";
> **find any** *branch* **using** *name*;
> **find first** *account* **within** *BrncAcct*;
> **while** *DB-status* = 0 **do**
>   **begin**
>   **find owner within** *CustAcct*;
>   **get** *customer*;
>   **print** (*customer.name*);
>   **find next** *account* **within** *BrncAcct*;
>   **end**

Note that if a customer has several accounts in the Hillside branch, then his name will be printed several times.

As a final example, consider the DBTG query that prints the names of all the customers of the bank. Such a query cannot be formed easily with the mechanism we have described thus far, since no one single set has all the customer records as its members. The remedy is to define a singular set (Section A.3.2) consisting of members of type *customer*. This set is defined as follows:

> **set name is** *AllCust*
> **owner is** *system*
> **member is** *customer*

Once such a set has been defined, we can form our query as follows:

> **find first** *customer* **within** *AllCust*;
> **while** *DB-status* = 0 **do**
>   **begin**
>   **get** *customer*;
>   **print** (*customer.name*);
>   **find next** *customer* **within** *AllCust*;
>   **end**

A.4.5 Predicates

The **find** statements described above allow the value of a field in one of the record templates to be matched with the corresponding field in the appropriate database records. Although with this technique we can formulate a variety of DBTG queries in a convenient and concise way, there are many queries in which a field value must be matched with a specified range of values, not only one. To accomplish this, we need to **get** the appropriate records into memory and examine each one separately for a match in order to determine whether it is the target of our **find** statement.

To illustrate, consider the DBTG query to print the total number of accounts in the Hillside branch with a balance greater than $10,000:

```
count := 0;
branch.name := "Hillside";
find any branch using name;
find first account within BrncAcct;
while DB-status = 0 do
    begin
        get account;
        if account.balance > 10000 then count := count + 1;
        find next account within BrncAcct;
    end
print (count);
```

A.5 DBTG Update Facility

In Section A.4, we described the various DBTG commands for querying the database. In this section, we describe the mechanisms available for updating information in the database. These include the creation of new records and deletion of old records as well as the modification of the content of existing records.

A.5.1 Creating New Records

In order to create a new record of type <record type>, we insert the appropriate values in the corresponding <record type> template. We then add this new record to the database by executing:

store <record type>

Note that this technique allows us to create and add new records only one at a time.

To illustrate, consider the DBTG program for adding a new customer, Jackson, to the database:

> *customer.name* := "Jackson";
> *customer.street* := "Old Road";
> *customer.city* := "Richardson";
> **store** *customer;*

Note that if a new record is created that must belong to a particular DBTG set (for example, a new *account*), then in addition to the **store** operation we need a mechanism for inserting records into sets. This mechanism is described in Section A.6.

A.5.2 Modifying an Existing Record

In order to modify an existing record of type <record type>, we must find that record in the database, get that record into memory, and then change the desired fields in the template of <record type>. Once this is accomplished, we reflect the changes to the record to which the currency pointer of <record type> points by executing:

> **modify** <record type>

The DBTG model requires that the **find** command executed prior to modifying a record must have the additional clause **for update** so that the system is aware of the fact that a record is to be modified. We are not required to update a record that we "find for update." However, we cannot update a record unless it is found for update.

As an example, consider the DBTG program to change the street address of Kahn to North Loop.

> *customer.name* := "Kahn";
> **find for update any** *customer* **using** *name;*
> **get** *customer;*
> *customer.city* := "North Loop";
> **modify** *customer;*

A.5.3 Deleting a Record

In order to delete an existing record of type <record type>, the currency pointer of that type must point to the record in the database to be deleted. Following this, we can delete that record by executing:

> **erase** <record type>

Note that as in the case of record modification, the **find** command must have the attribute **for update** attached to it.

To illustrate, consider the DBTG program to delete account 402 belonging to Kahn:

> *finish* := false;
> *customer.name* := "Kahn";
> **find any** *customer* **using** *name*;
> **find for update first** *account* **within** *CustAcct*;
> **while** *DB-status* = 0 **and not** finish **do**
> > **begin**
> > > **get** *account*;
> > > **if** *account.number* = 402 **then**
> > > > **begin**
> > > > > **erase** *account*;
> > > > > *finish* := true;
> > > > **end**
> > > **else find for update next** *account* **within** *CustAcct*;
> > **end**

It is possible to delete an entire set occurrence by finding the owner of the set — say, a record of type <record type> — and executing:

erase all <record type>

This will delete the owner of the set as well as all of its members. If a member of the set is an owner of another set, the members of that set are also deleted. Thus the **erase all** operation is recursive.

Consider the DBTG program to delete customer "Camp" and all of her accounts:

> *customer.name* := "Camp";
> **find for update any** *customer* **using** *name*;
> **erase all** *customer*;

A natural question arises as to what needs to be done when we wish to delete a record which is an owner of a set, but we do not specify **all** in the erase statement. In this case several possibilities exist, including:

- Delete only that record.

- Delete the record and all its members.

- Do not delete any records.

It turns out that each of these options may be specified in the DBTG model. We discuss this in Section A.6.

A.6 DBTG Set-Processing Facility

We saw in Section A.5 that the **store** and **erase** statements are closely tied to the set-processing facility. In particular, a mechanism must be provided for inserting records into and removing records from a particular set occurrence. In the case of deletion, we have a number of different options to consider if the record to be deleted is the owner of a set.

A.6.1 The Connect Statement

In order to insert a new record of type <record type> into a particular occurrence of <set-type>, we must first insert the record into the database (if it is not already there). Then, we need to set the currency pointers of <record type> and <set-type> to point to the appropriate record and set occurrence. Once this is accomplished, the new record can be inserted into the set by executing:

connect <record type> **to** <set-type>

A new record can be inserted as follows:

1. Create a new record of type <record type> (see Section A.5.1). This sets the appropriate <record type> currency pointer.

2. Find the appropriate owner of the set <set-type>. This automatically sets the appropriate currency pointer of <set-type>.

3. Insert the new record into the set by executing the **connect** statement.

To illustrate, consider the DBTG query for creating new account 267 which belongs to Jackson:

account.number := 267;
account.balance := 0;
store account;
customer.name := "Jackson";
find any customer using name;
connect account to CustAcct;

A.6.2 The Disconnect Statement

In order to remove a record of type <record type> from a set occurrence of type <set-type>, we need to set the currency pointer of <record type> and <set-type> to point to the appropriate record and set occurrence. Once this is accomplished, the record can be removed from the set by executing:

disconnect <record type> **from** <set-type>

Note that this operation only removes a record from a set; it does not delete that record from the database. If deletion is desired, the record can be deleted by executing **erase** <record type>.

Assume we wish to close account 177. To do so, we need to delete the relationship between account 177 and its customer. However, we shall need to keep the record of account 177 in the database for the bank's internal archives. The program below shows how to do this within the DBTG model. This program will remove account 177 from the set occurrence of type *CustAcct*. The account will still be accessible in the database for recordkeeping purposes.

> *account.number* := 177;
> **find for update any** *account* **using** *number*;
> **get** *account*;
> **find** *owner* **within** *CustAcct*;
> **disconnect** *account* **from** *CustAcct*;

A.6.3 The Reconnect Statement

In order to move a record of type <record type> from one set occurrence to another set occurrence of type <set-type>, we need to find the appropriate record and the owner of the set occurrences to which that record is to be moved. Once this is done, we can move the record by executing:

> **reconnect** <record type> **to** <set-type>

Consider the DBTG program to move all accounts of Lowman that are currently at the Hillside branch to the Valleyview branch.

> *customer.name* := "Lowman";
> **find any** *customer* **using** *name*;
> **find first** *account* **within** *CustAcct*;
> **while** *DB-status* = 0 **do**
>   **begin**
>   **find** *owner* **within** *BrncAcct*;
>   **get** *branch*;
>   **if** *branch.name* = "Hillside" **then**
>   **begin**
>   *branch.name* := "Valleyview";
>   **find any** *branch* **using** *name*;
>   **reconnect** *account* **to** *BrncAcct*;
>   **end**
>   **find next** *account* **within** *CustAcct*;
>   **end**

A.6.4 Set Insertion and Retention

When a new set is defined, we must specify how member records are to be inserted. In addition, we must specify the conditions under which a record must be retained in the set occurrence in which it was initially inserted.

Set Insertion

A newly created member record of type <record type> of a set type <set-type> can be added to a set occurrence either explicitly (manually) or implicitly (automatically). This distinction is specified at set definition time via

insertion is <insert mode>

where <insert mode> can take one of two forms:

- **Manual**. The new record can be inserted into the set manually (explicitly) by executing:

connect <record type> **to** <set-type>

- **Automatic**. The new record is inserted into the set automatically (implicitly) when it is created, that is, when we execute:

store <record type>

In either case, just prior to insertion, the <set-type> currency pointer must point to the set occurrence into which the insertion is to be made.

To illustrate, consider the creation of account 535 that belongs to Lowman and is at the Valleyview branch. Suppose that set insertion is **manual** for set type *CustAcct* and is **automatic** for set type *BrncAcct*. The appropriate DBTG program is:

> *branch.name* := "Valleyview";
> **find any** *branch* **using** *name;*
> *account.number* := 535;
> *account.balance* := 0;
> **store** *account;*
> *customer.name* := "Lowman";
> **find any** *customer* **using** *name;*
> **connect** *account* **to** *CustAcct;*

Set Retention

There are various restrictions on how and when a member record can be removed from a set occurrence into which it has been inserted previously. These restrictions are specified at set definition time via

retention is <retention-mode>

where <retention-mode> can take one of the three forms:

- **Fixed.** Once a member record has been inserted into a particular set occurrence, it cannot be removed from that set. If retention is fixed, then to reconnect a record to another set, we must first erase that record, re-create it, and then insert it into the new set occurrence.

- **Mandatory.** Once a member record has been inserted into a particular set occurrence, it can be reconnected only to another set occurrence of type <set-type>. It can neither be disconnected nor be reconnected to a set of another type.

- **Optional.** No restrictions are placed on how and when a member record can be removed from a set occurrence. A member record can be reconnected, disconnected, and connected at will.

The decision as to which option to choose is dependent on the application. For example, in our banking database, the **optional** retention mode seems to be appropriate for the *CustAcct* set, while the **mandatory** retention mode seems to be appropriate for the *BrncAcct* set.

A.6.5 Deletion

When a record is deleted (erased) and that record is the owner of set occurrence of type <set-type>, the best way of handling this deletion depends on the specification of the set retention of <set-type>.

- If the retention status is **optional**, then the record will be deleted and every member of the set it owns will be disconnected. These records, however, are kept in the database.

- If the retention status is **fixed**, then the record and all of its owned members will be deleted. This follows from the fact that the fixed status indicates that a member record cannot be removed from the set occurrence without being deleted.

- If the retention status is **mandatory**, then the record cannot be erased. This is because the mandatory status indicates that a member record must belong to a set occurrence; it cannot be disconnected from that set.

A.6.6 Set Ordering

The members of a set occurrence of type <set-type> may be ordered in a variety of ways. These orders are specified by a programmer when the set is defined via

order is <order-mode>

where <order-mode> can be:

- **first**. When a new record is added to a set, it is inserted in the first position. Thus, the set is in reverse chronological ordering.

- **last**. When a new record is added to a set, it is inserted in the last position. Thus, the set is in chronological ordering.

- **next**. Suppose that the currency pointer of <set-type> points to record X. If X is a member type, then when a new record is added to the set, it is inserted in the next position following X. If X is an owner type, then when a new record is added, it is inserted in the first position.

- **prior**. Suppose that the currency pointer of <set-type> points to record X. If X is a member type, then when a new record is added to the set, it is inserted in the position just prior to X. If X is an owner type, then when a new record is added, it is inserted in the last position.

- **system default**. When a new record is added to a set, it is inserted in an arbitrary position determined by the system.

- **sorted**. When a new record is added to a set, it is inserted in a position that ensures that the set will remain sorted. The sorting order is specified by a particular key value when a programmer defines the set. The programmer must specify whether members are ordered in ascending or descending order relative to that key.

Consider again Figure A.16, where the set occurrence of type *CustAcct* with the owner record customer Kahn and member record accounts 155, 402, and 408 are ordered as indicated. Suppose that we add a new account 125 into that set. For each <order-mode> option, the new set ordering is as follows:

- first: {125,155,402,408}.
- last: {155,402,408,125}.

- next: Suppose that the currency pointer points to record "Kahn." Then the new set order is {125,155,402,408}.

- prior: Suppose that the currency pointer points to record 402. Then the new set order is {155,125,402,408}.

- system default: Any arbitrary order is acceptable. Thus, {155,402,125,408} is a valid set ordering.

- sorted: The set must be ordered in ascending order with account number being the key. Thus, the ordering must be {125,155,402,408}.

A.7 Mapping Networks to Files

A network database consists of records and links. Links are implemented by adding *pointer fields* to records that are associated via a link. Each record must have one pointer field for each link with which it is associated. To illustrate, let us return to the data-structure diagram of Figure A.2b and the sample database corresponding to it in Figure A.4. Figure A.21 shows the sample instance with pointer fields to represent the links. Each line in Figure A.4 is replaced in Figure A.21 by two pointers.

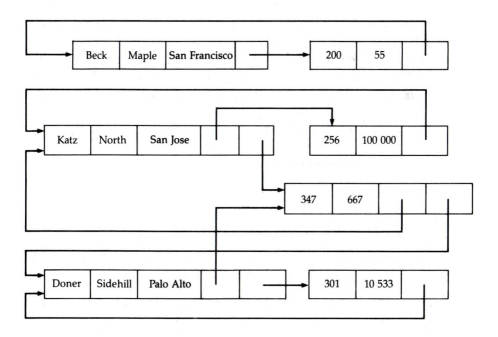

Figure A.21   Implementation of instance of Figure A.4.

Since the *CustAcct* link is many-to-many, each record may be associated with an arbitrary number of records. Thus, it is not possible to limit the number of pointer fields in a record. Therefore, even if a record itself is of fixed length, the actual record used in the physical implementation is a variable-length record.

These complications led the architects of the DBTG model to restrict links to be either one-to-one or one-to-many. We shall see that, under this restriction, the number of pointers needed is reduced and it is possible to retain fixed-length records. To illustrate the implementation of the DBTG model, let us assume that the *CustAcct* link is one-to-many and represented by the DBTG-set *CustAcct* as defined below:

> **set name is** *CustAcct*
> **owner is** *customer*
> **member is** *account*

A sample database corresponding to this scheme was shown in Figure A.1.

An *account* record may be associated with only one *customer* record. Thus, we need only one pointer in the *account* record to represent the *CustAcct* relationship. However, a *customer* record may be associated with many *account* records. Rather than using multiple pointers in the *customer* record, we can use a *ring structure* to represent the entire occurrence of the DBTG-set *CustAcct*. In a ring structure, the records of both the owner and member types for a set occurrence are organized into a circular list. There is one circular list for each set occurrence (that is, for each record of the owner type).

Figure A.22 shows the ring structure for the example of Figure A.1. Let us examine the DBTG-set occurrence owned by the "Camp" record. There are two member-type (*account*) records. Rather than containing one pointer to each member record, the owner (Camp) record contains a pointer to only the "first" member record (account 226). This member record contains a pointer to the next member record (account 177). Since the record for account 177 is the "last" member record, it contains a pointer to the owner record.

If we represent DBTG-sets using the ring structure, a record contains exactly one pointer for each DBTG-set it is involved in, regardless of whether it is of the owner type or member type. Thus, fixed-length records can be represented within a ring structure without the need to resort to variable-length records. This structural simplicity is offset by added complexity in accessing records within a set. To find a particular member record of a set occurrence, the pointer chain must be traversed to navigate from the owner record to the desired member record. Under the implementation scheme we presented earlier, there is a pointer from the owner to each member.

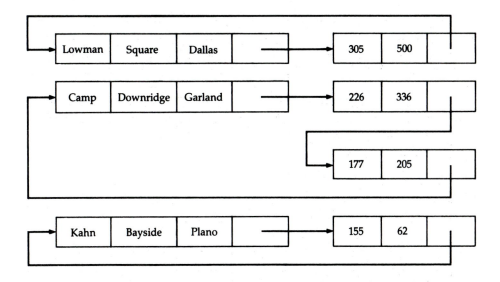

Figure A.22   Ring structure for instance of Figure A.1.

The ring structure implementation strategy for the DBTG model provided the motivation for the DBTG data retrieval facility. Recall the statements:

- **find first** <*record type*> **within** <*set type*>
- **find next** <*record type*> **within** <*set type*>

The terms **first** and **next** in these statements refer to the ordering of records given by the ring-structure pointers. Thus, once the owner has been found, it is easy to do a **find first**, since all the system must do is follow a pointer. Similarly, all the system must do in response to a **find next** is follow the ring-structure pointer.

The **find owner** statement of the DBTG query language is reflected in a modified form of the ring structure in which every member-type record contains a second pointer, which points to the owner record. This structure is illustrated in Figure A.23. Under this implementation strategy, a record has one pointer for each DBTG-set for which it is of the owner type and two pointers (a *next-member* pointer and an *owner* pointer) for each DBTG-set for which it is of the member type. This strategy allows for efficient execution of a **find owner** statement. Under our earlier strategy, it is necessary to traverse the ring structure until we find the owner.

The physical placement of records is important for an efficient implementation of a network database, as is the case for a relational database.

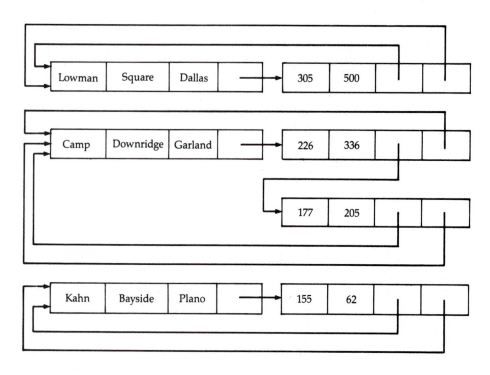

Figure A.23   Ring structure of Figure A.22 with owner pointers.

The statements **find first**, **find next**, and **find owner** are designed for processing a sequence of records within a particular DBTG-set occurrence. Since these are the most frequently used statements in a DBTG query, it is desirable to store records of a DBTG-set occurrence physically close to one another on disk. To specify the strategy that the system is to use to store a DBTG-set, a **placement** clause is added to the definition of the member record type.

Consider the DBTG-set *CustAcct* and the example shown in Figure A.1. If we add the clause

placement clustered via *CustAcct*

to the definition of record type *account* (the member record type *CustAcct* of the DBTG-set), the system will store members of each set occurrence close to one another physically on disk. To the extent possible, members of a set occurrence will be stored in the same block. Figure A.24 illustrates this storage strategy for the instance of Figure A.1.

The clustered placement strategy does not require the owner record of a DBTG-set to be stored near the set's members. Thus, each record type can be stored in a distinct file. If we are willing to store more than one record

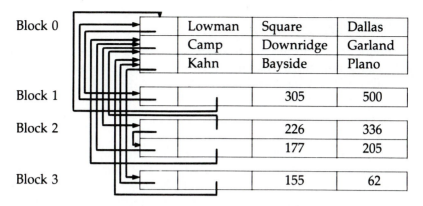

Figure A.24   Clustered record placement for instance of Figure A.1.

type in a file, we can specify that owner and member records are to be stored close to one another physically on disk. We do so by adding the clause **near owner** to the **placement** clause. For our example of the *CustAcct* set, we would add the clause

placement clustered via *CustAcct* **near owner**

to the definition of the record type *account*. Figure A.25 illustrates this storage strategy. By storing member records in the same block as the owner, we reduce the number of block accesses required to read an entire set occurrence. This form of storage is analogous to the clustering file structure we proposed earlier for the relational model. This similarity is not surprising, since queries that require traversal of DBTG-set occurrences under the network model require natural joins under the relational model.

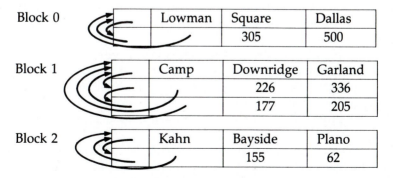

Figure A.25   Record placement using clustering with the **near owner** option.

A.8 Network Systems

The network model forms the foundation of most of the older database systems and some recent systems. In this section, we consider briefly two popular network systems: Total and IDMS.

A.8.1 Total

The Total database system dates from the late 1960s. It runs on a wide variety of machines, ranging from minicomputers to mainframes.

Although the Total system is based on the DBTG model, its query language differs from the one based on the DBTG standard as presented in Sections A.4 to A.6. Total's query language, though similar in function, uses a different syntax.

All statements in the Total data manipulation language must be embedded in a host language (Cobol, PL/I, Fortran, or RPG). A call is made to the *database* procedure with parameters that specify the DML statement. These statements are of a nature similar to the **find**, **find owner**, and **find next** commands we saw in Section A.4, although the terminology used by Total is motivated by some of the concepts of the IMS DL/I language. Owner types are called single-entry data sets and member types are called variable-entry data sets.

The internal physical implementation of Total and the access schemes used are unpublished.

A.8.2 IDMS

IDMS is a network database system developed by Cullinane Database Systems, Inc. IDMS adheres closely to the DBTG model as presented in Sections A.4 to A.6. It includes a detailed data manipulation language allowing the database designer a high degree of control over the physical organization of the database. The data manipulation language includes features identical (or nearly so) to those of the DBTG DML described in Sections A.4 to A.6. Additional features are included to allow increased programmer convenience and to enable knowledgeable programmers to write more efficient queries.

An example of a feature in IDMS not covered previously in this chapter is the **obtain** command, which combines the **find** and **get** commands into one request. An optional **where** clause may be attached to an **obtain** to find and get the next record satisfying the **where** predicate. This feature relieves the programmer of the need to write an explicit test of a record located via the **find** command.

The bibliographic notes reference documents describing in detail the internal file management and index techniques used by IDMS.

A.9 Summary

A network database consists of a collection of *records* which are connected to one another through *links*. A link is an association between precisely two records. Records are organized in the form of an arbitrary graph.

A *data-structure diagram* is a scheme for a network database. Such a diagram consists of two basic components: boxes, which correspond to record types, and lines, which correspond to links. A data-structure diagram serves the same purpose as an E-R diagram; namely, it specifies the overall logical structure of the database. For every E-R diagram, there is a corresponding data-structure diagram.

In the late 1960s, several commercial database systems based on the network model emerged. These systems were studied extensively by the Database Task Group (DBTG) within the CODASYL group. In the DBTG model, only many-to-one links can be used. Many-to-many links are disallowed in order to simplify the implementation. One-to-one links are represented as many-to-one links. A data-structure diagram consisting of two record types that are linked together is referred to in the DBTG model as a *DBTG-set*. Each DBTG-set has one record type designated as the *owner* of the set and the other record type designated as the *member* of the set. A DBTG-set can have any number of *set occurrences.*

The data manipulation language of the DBTG model consists of a number of commands that are embedded in a host language. These commands access and manipulate database variables as well as locally declared variables. For each such application program, the system maintains a *program work-area* which contains *record templates, currency pointers,* and *status flags.*

The two most frequently used DBTG commands are **find** and **get**. There are a number of different formats for the **find** command. The main distinction among them is whether individual records are to be located or whether records within a particular set occurrence are to be located.

There are various mechanisms available in the DBTG model for updating information in the database. These include the creation and deletion of new records (via the **store** and **erase** operations) as well as the modification (via the **modify** operation) of the content of existing records. The **connect**, **disconnect**, and **reconnect** operations provide for inserting records into and removing records from a particular set occurrence.

When a new set is defined, we must specify how member records are to be inserted and under what conditions they can be moved from one set occurrence to another. A newly created member record can be added to a set occurrence either explicitly or implicitly. This distinction is specified at set-definition time via the **insertion is** statement with the **manual** and **automatic** insert mode options.

There are various restrictions on how and when a member record can be removed from a set occurrence it has been previously inserted in. These restrictions are specified at set-definition time via the **retention is** statement with the **fixed, mandatory,** and **optional** retention mode options.

Implementation techniques for the DBTG model exploit the restrictions of the model to allow the physical representation of DBTG sets without the need for variable-length records. A DBTG set is represented by one ring structure for each occurrence.

Finally, we noted some features of two commercial DBTG database systems: Total and IDMS.

Exercises

A.1 Transform the E-R diagram of Figure A.26 to a data-structure diagram assuming that the data model is:

a. Network

b. DBTG.

A.2 Construct a sample database for the data-structure diagram of Exercise A.1, with ten students and three different classes.

A.3 Show the set of variables which exist in a program work-area for the data-structure diagram corresponding to the E-R diagram of Figure A.26.

A.4 Suppose that the attribute *grade* is added to the relationship *enrollment* of Figure A.26. Show the corresponding data-structure diagram assuming the network and DBTG model.

A.5 Transform the E-R diagram of Figure A.27 to a data-structure diagram.

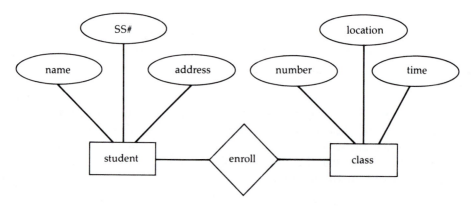

Figure A.26   Class enrollment E-R diagram.

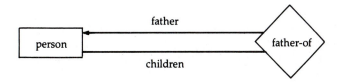

Figure A.27   Parent-child E-R diagram.

A.6 Define the following terms:

a. DBTG-set.

b. Owner of a set.

c. Member of a set.

d. Set occurrence.

A.7 Explain why a member record of a set occurrence cannot participate in more than one occurrence of the set at any point.

A.8 Suppose that the **find owner** statement is not provided as part of the DBTG query language. Would it be still possible to answer the set of queries as before?

A.9 The DBTG **find** statement does not allow specification of predicates.

a. Discuss the drawbacks of this limitation.

b. Can you suggest a modification to the language to overcome this difficulty?

A.10 Transform the E-R diagram of Figure A.28 to a data-structure diagram assuming the DBTG model.

A.11 For the data-structure diagram corresponding to the E-R diagram of Figure A.28, construct the following DBTG queries:

a. Find the total number of people whose car was involved in an accident in 1983.

b. Find the number of accidents in which the cars belonging to "John Smith" were involved.

c. Add a new customer to the database.

d. Delete the car "Mazda" belonging to "John Smith."

e. Add a new accident record for the Toyota belonging to "Jones."

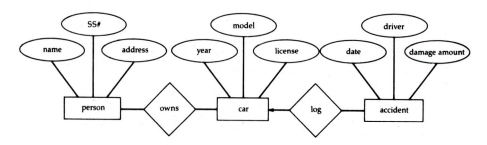

Figure A.28   Car insurance E-R diagram.

A.12 What is a *system set* and why was it introduced in the DBTG model?

A.13 Explain the concept of "repeating groups." Is it necessary to have this construct available in the network model?

A.14 Explain the difference between the **connect**, **disconnect**, and **reconnect** statements.

A.15 Explain the difference between the **manual** and **automatic** option in set insertion.

A.16 Explain the difference between the **fixed**, **mandatory**, and **optional** options in set retention.

A.17 What are the appropriate set insertion and set retention options for the data-structure diagram corresponding to Figure A.28?

A.18 Give a network data-structure diagram for the following relational database:

> *lives (person-name, street, city)*
> *works (person-name, company-name, salary)*
> *located-in (company-name, city)*
> *manages (person-name, manager-name)*

A.19 Construct the following DBTG queries for the data-structure diagram obtained as a solution to Exercise A.18.

   a. Find the name of all employees who work for First Bank Corporation.

   b. Find the name and city of all employees who work for First Bank Corporation.

   c. Find the name, street, and city of all employees who work for First Bank Corporation and earn more than $10,000.

   d. Find all employees who live in the same city as the company they work for.

e. Find all employees who live in the same city and on the same street as their manager.

f. Find all employees who do not work for First Bank Corporation.

g. Find all employees who earn more than every employee of Small Bank Corporation.

h. Assume the companies may be located in several cities. Find all companies located in every city in which Small Bank Corporation is located.

i. Find all employees who earn more than the average salary of employees working in their company.

j. Find the company employing the most people.

k. Find the company with the smallest payroll.

l. Find those companies that pay more, on average, than the average salary at First Bank Corporation.

m. Modify the database so that Jones now lives in Newtown.

n. Give all employees of First Bank Corporation a 10 percent raise.

o. Give all managers a 10 percent raise.

p. Give all managers a 10 percent raise unless the salary becomes greater than $100,000. In such cases, give only a 3 percent raise.

q. Delete all employees of Small Bank Corporation.

A.20 Give a network data-structure diagram for the following relational database:

course (course-name, room, instructor)
enrollment (course-name, student-name, grade)

Bibliographic Notes

In the late 1960s, several commercial database systems emerged that relied on the network model. The most influential of these were the Integrated Data Store (IDS) system, which was developed in General Electric under the guidance of Charles Bachman [Bachman and Williams 1964] and Associate PL/I (APL) [Dodd 1969]. These and other systems were studied extensively by the Database Task Group (DBTG) within the CODASYL (Conference on Data Systems Languages) group that earlier set the standard for COBOL. This study has resulted in the first database standard specification, called the CODASYL DBTG 1971 report [CODASYL 1971]. Since then, a number of changes have been suggested to that report, the last official one in 1978 [CODASYL 1978]. In 1981, a new draft proposal was published which has not yet been officially adopted.

The concept of data-structure diagrams was introduced by Bachman [1969]. The original presentation of data-structure diagrams used arrows to point from owner to member record types. This corresponds to the physical pointer implementation. We have used the arrows pointing from member to owner record types to be consistent with our presentation of the E-R model. The same convention is used by Ullman [1988].

Implementation and design issues concerning the DBTG model are discussed by Schenk [1974], Gerritsen [1975], Dahl and Bubenko [1982], and Whang, et al. [1982]. Discussions concerning the view level of DBTG (the external level) are offered by Zaniolo [1979a, 1979b] and Clemons [1978, 1979]. A high level query language for the network model is proposed by Bradley [1978]. Translation of network queries to relational queries is discussed by Katz and Wong [1982].

Many commercial database management systems are based on the network model. The DMS 1100 database system is described in [Sperry Univac 1973]. Total is described by Tsichritzis and Lochovsky [1977], by Cardenas [1985], and in [Cincom 1974, 1978]. IDMS is described by Tsichritzis and Lochovsky [1977], in [Cullinane 1975], and in [Cullinet 1983a, 1983b]. IDS II is described in [Honeywell 1975]. ADABAS is described by Tsichritzis and Lochovsky [1977] and in [Software AG 1978].

A survey paper on the DBTG model is presented by Taylor and Frank [1976]. Basic textbook discussions are offered by Tsichritzis and Lochovsky [1977], Olle [1978], Cardenas [1985], Date [1990a], Ullman [1988], Tsichritzis and Lochovsky [1982], and Kroenke and Dolan [1988].

B

Hierarchical Model

In the network model, the data is represented by collections of *records* and relationships among data are represented by *links*. This is true of the hierarchical model as well. The only difference is that in the hierarchical model, records are organized as collections of trees rather than as arbitrary graphs.

B.1 Basic Concepts

A hierarchical database consists of a collection of *records* which are connected to one another through *links*. A record is similar to a record in the network model. Each record is a collection of fields (attributes), each of which contains only one data value. A link is an association between precisely two records. Thus, a link is similar to the link concept in the network model.

Consider a database representing a *customer-account* relationship in a banking system. There are two record types, *customer* and *account*. The *customer* record type can be defined in the same manner as in Appendix A. It consists of three fields: *name*, *street*, and *city*. Similarly, the *account* record consists of two fields: *number* and *balance*.

A sample database appears in Figure B.1. It shows that customer Lowman has account 305, customer Camp has accounts 226 and 177, and customer Kahn has account 155.

Note that the set of all customer and account records is organized in the form of a rooted tree where the root of the tree is a dummy node. As we shall see, a hierarchical database is a collection of such rooted trees, and hence forms a forest. We shall refer to each such rooted tree as a *database tree*.

The content of a particular record may have to be replicated in several different locations. For example, in our customer-account banking system, an account may belong to several customers. The information pertaining to that account, or the information pertaining to the various customers to which it may belong, will have to be replicated. This replication may occur

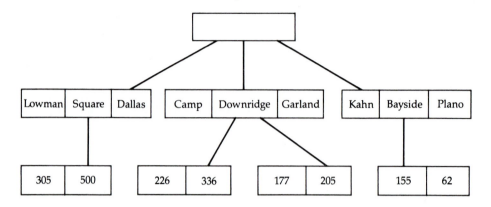

Figure B.1   Sample database.

either in the same database tree or in several different trees. Record replication has two major drawbacks:

- Data inconsistency may result when updating takes place.
- Waste of space is unavoidable.

We shall deal with this issue in Section B.5 by introducing the concept of a *virtual record*.

B.2 Tree-Structure Diagrams

A *tree-structure diagram* is the scheme for a hierarchical database. Such a diagram consists of two basic components:

- **Boxes**, which correspond to record types.
- **Lines**, which correspond to links.

A tree-structure diagram serves the same purpose as an entity-relationship diagram; namely, it specifies the overall logical structure of the database. A tree-structure diagram is similar to a data-structure diagram in the network model. The main difference is that, in the latter, record types are organized in the form of an arbitrary graph, while in the former, record types are organized in the form of a *rooted tree*.

We have to be more precise about what is meant by a rooted tree. First, there can be no cycles in the underlying graph. Second, the relationships formed in the graph must be such that only one-to-many or one-to-one relationships exist between a parent and a child. The general form of a tree-structure diagram is illustrated in Figure B.2. Note that the

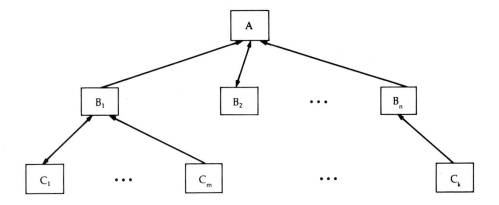

Figure B.2   General structure of a tree-structure diagram.

arrows are pointing from children to parents. A parent *may* have an arrow pointing to a child, but a child must have an arrow pointing to its parent.

The database scheme is represented as a collection of tree-structure diagrams. For each such diagram, there exists one *single* instance of a database tree. The root of this tree is a dummy node. The children of that node are instances of the appropriate record type. Each such child instance may, in turn, have several instances of various record types, as specified in the corresponding tree-structure diagram.

To understand how tree-structure diagrams are formed, we shall show how to transform entity-relationship diagrams to their corresponding tree-structure diagrams. We first show how such transformations can be applied to single relationships. We then address the issue of how to ensure that the resulting diagrams are in the form of rooted trees.

B.2.1 Single Relationships

Consider the entity-relationship diagram of Figure B.3a, consisting of the two entity sets *customer* and *account* related through a binary, one-to-many relationship *CustAcct*, with no descriptive attributes. This diagram specifies that a customer may have several accounts but an account may belong to only one customer. The corresponding tree-structure diagram is depicted in Figure B.3b. The record type *customer* corresponds to the entity set *customer*. It includes three fields: *name*, *street*, and *city*. Similarly, *account* is the record type corresponding to the entity set *account*. It includes two fields: *number* and *balance*. Finally, the relationship *CustAcct* has been replaced with the link *CustAcct*, with an arrow pointing to *customer* record type.

An instance of a database corresponding to the above-described scheme may thus contain a number of *customer* records linked to a number

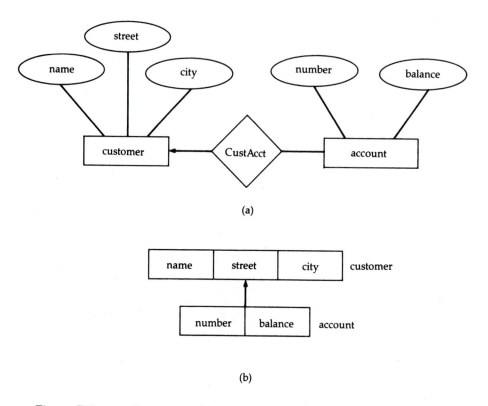

(a)

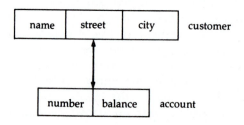

(b)

Figure B.3   E-R diagram and its corresponding tree-structure diagram.

of *account* records, as shown in Figure B.1. Since the relationship is one-to-many from *customer* to *account*, a customer may have more than one account, as is the case with Camp, who has both accounts 226 and 177. An account, however, cannot belong to more than one customer, as is indeed observed in the sample database.

Figure B.4   Tree-structure diagram with one-to-one relationship.

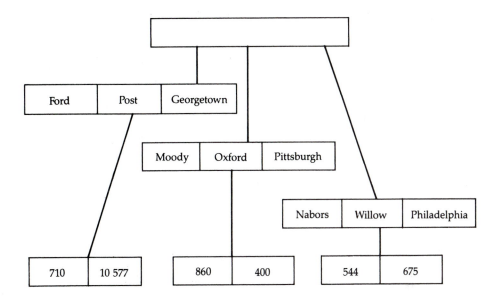

Figure B.5   Sample database corresponding to diagram of Figure B.4.

If the relationship *CustAcct* is one-to-one, then the link *CustAcct* has two arrows, one pointing to *account* record type, and one pointing to *customer* record type (Figure B.4). A sample database corresponding to this scheme appears in Figure B.5. Since the relationship is one-to-one, an account can be owned by precisely one customer, and a customer can have only one account, as is indeed the case in the sample database.

If the relationship *CustAcct* is many-to-many (see Figure B.6a), then the transformation from an E-R diagram to a tree-structure diagram is more complicated. This is due to the fact that only one-to-many and one-to-one relationships can be directly represented in the hierarchical model.

There are a number of different ways to transform this E-R diagram to a tree-structure diagram. All these diagrams, however, share the property that the underlying database tree (or trees) will have replicated records.

The decision as to which transformation should be used depends on many factors, including:

- The type of queries expected on the database.

- The degree to which the overall database scheme being modeled fits the given E-R diagram.

We shall present a transformation which is as general as possible. That is, all other possible transformations are a special case of this one transformation.

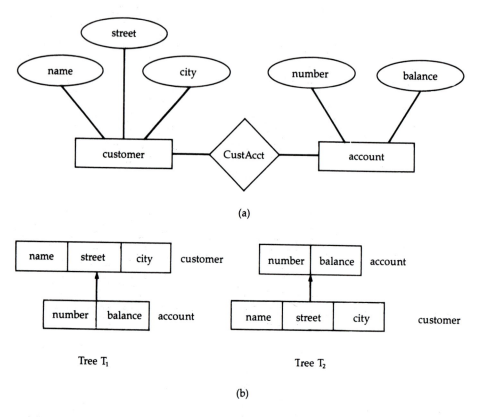

Figure B.6   E-R diagram and its corresponding tree-structure diagrams.

In order to transform the E-R diagram of Figure B.6a to a tree-structure diagram, we need to do the following:

1. Create two separate tree-structure diagrams, T_1 and T_2, each having the *customer* and *account* record types. In tree T_1, *customer* is the root, while in tree T_2, *account* is the root.

2. Create the following two links:

   - *CustAcct*, a many-to-one link from *account* record type to *customer* record type, in T_1.

   - *AcctCust*, a many-to-one link from *customer* record type to *account* record type, in T_2.

The resulting tree-structure diagram is depicted in Figure B.6b.

A sample database corresponding to the tree-structure diagram of Figure B.6b is shown in Figure B.7. There are two database trees. The first tree (Figure B.7a) corresponds to the tree-structure diagram T_1, while the second tree (Figure B.7b) corresponds to the tree-structure diagram T_2. As can be seen, all *customer* and *account* records are replicated in both database trees. In addition, *account* record 347 appears twice in the first tree, while *customer* records Katz and Doner appear twice in the second tree.

If a relationship also includes a descriptive attribute, the transformation from an E-R diagram to a tree-structure diagram is more complicated. This is due to the fact that a link cannot contain any data value. In this case, a new record type needs to be created and the appropriate links need to be established. The manner in which links are formed depends on the way the relationship *CustAcct* is defined.

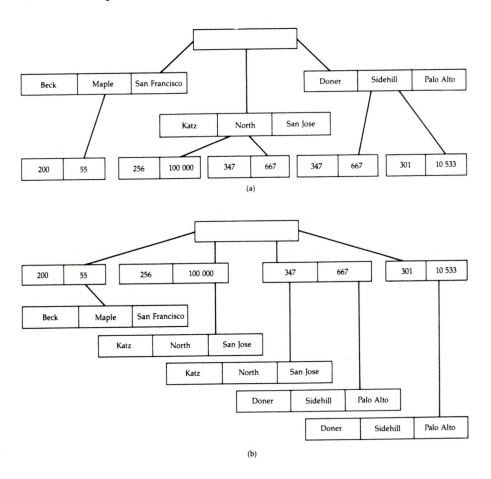

Figure B.7   Sample database corresponding to diagram of Figure B.6b.

Consider the E-R diagram of Figure B.3a. Suppose that we add the attribute *date* to the relationship *CustAcct*, to denote the last date on which a customer has accessed the account. This newly derived E-R diagram is depicted in Figure B.8a. To transform this diagram to a tree-structure diagram we need to:

1. Create a new record type *date* with a single field.
2. Create the following two links:

   • *CustDate*, a many-to-one link from *date* record type to *customer* record type.

   • *DateAcct*, a many-to-one link from *account* record type to *date* record type.

The resulting tree-structure diagram is illustrated in Figure B.8b.

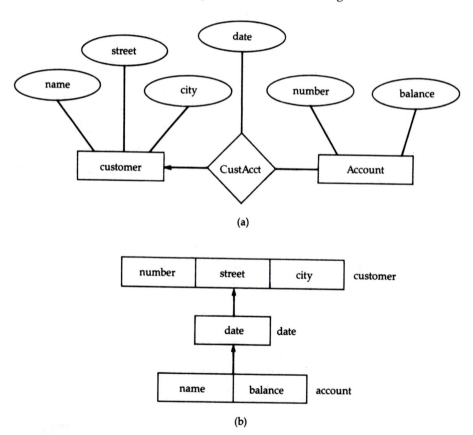

Figure B.8   E-R diagram and its corresponding tree-structure diagram.

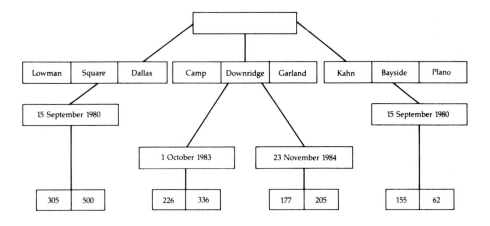

Figure B.9　Sample database corresponding to diagram of Figure B.8b.

An instance corresponding to the above-described scheme appears in Figure B.9. It shows the following:

- Lowman has account 305, which was last accessed on 15 September 1980.

- Camp has two accounts: 226 which was last accessed on 1 October 1983, and 177 which was last accessed on 23 November 1984.

- Kahn has account 155, which was last accessed on 15 September 1980.

Note that two different accounts can be opened on the same date, as is the case with accounts 155 and 305. Since these accounts belong to two different customers, the *date* record must be replicated to preserve the hierarchy.

If the relationship *CustAcct* were one-to-one with the attribute *date*, then the transformation algorithm would be similar to the one described above. The only difference is that the two links *CustDate* and *DateAcct* would be one-to-one links.

If the relationship *CustAcct* were many-to-many with the attribute *date*, then there are again a number of alternative transformations. We shall use the most general transformation, similar to the one applied to the case where the relationship *CustAcct* has no descriptive attribute. The record types *customer, account,* and *date* need to be replicated, and two separate tree-structure diagrams must be created, as depicted in Figure B.10. A sample database corresponding to this scheme is depicted in Figure B.11.

Until now, we have considered only binary relationships. We shift our attention here to general relationships. To transform E-R diagrams corresponding to general relationships into tree-structure diagrams is quite complicated. Rather than presenting a general transformation algorithm,

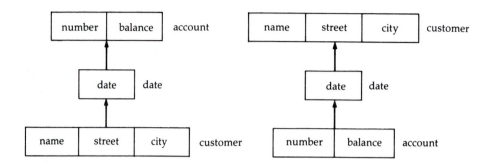

Figure B.10   Tree-structure diagram with many-to-many relationships.

we present a single example to illustrate the overall strategy that can be applied in dealing with such a transformation.

Consider the entity-relationship diagram of Figure B.12a, which consists of three entity sets *customer*, *account*, and *branch*, related through the general relationship set *CAB* with no descriptive attribute. This diagram specifies that a customer may have several accounts each located in a specific bank branch, and that an account may belong to several different customers.

There are a number of different ways to transform this E-R diagram to a tree-structure diagram. Again, all these share the property that the underlying database tree (or trees) will have replicated records. The most straightforward transformation is to create two tree-structure diagrams, as shown in Figure B.12b.

An instance of the database corresponding to the above-described scheme is illustrated in Figure B.13. It shows that Beck has account 200 in the Northcross branch, Katz has accounts 256 and 347 in the Northcross and Highland branches, respectively, and that Doner has accounts 347 and 301 in the Highland branch.

The above transformation algorithm can be extended in a straightforward manner to deal with relationships that span more than three entity sets. We simply replicate the various record types and generate as many tree-structure diagrams as necessary. This approach, in turn, can be extended to deal with a general relationship that has some descriptive attributes. All that is needed is to create a new record type with one field for each descriptive attribute, and then insert that record type in the appropriate location in the tree-structure diagram.

B.2.2 Several Relationships

The scheme described above to transform an E-R diagram to a tree-structure diagram ensures that for each single relationship, the transformation will

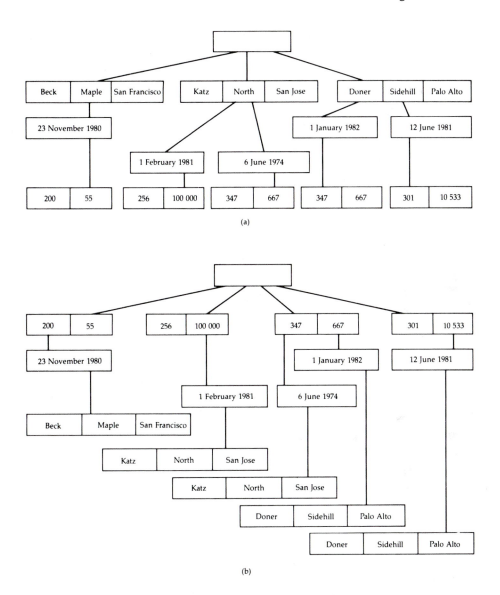

Figure B.11 Sample database corresponding to diagram of Figure B.10.

result in diagrams which are of the form of rooted trees. Unfortunately, applying such a transformation individually to each relationship in an E-R diagram does not necessarily result in diagrams that are rooted trees.

Below, we discuss means for resolving the problem. The technique is to split the diagrams in question into several diagrams each of which is a rooted tree. The large number of different possibilities makes it

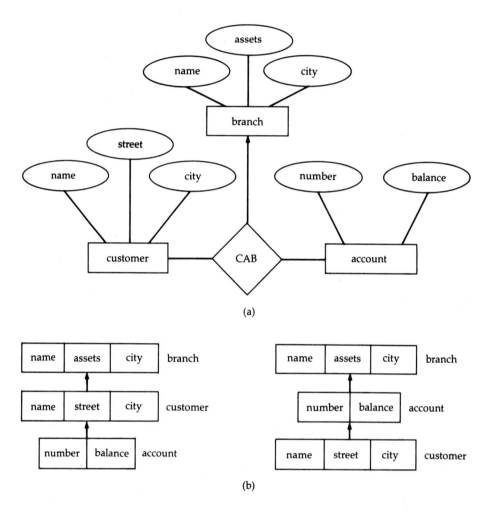

Figure B.12   E-R diagram and its corresponding tree-structure diagrams.

cumbersome to present a general transformation algorithm. Instead, we present two examples to illustrate the overall strategy that can be applied in dealing with such transformations.

Consider the E-R diagram of Figure B.14a. By applying the transformation algorithm described in Section B.2.1 separately to the relationships *BrncAcct* and *CustAcct*, we obtain the diagram of Figure B.14b. This diagram is not a rooted tree, since the only possible root can be the record type *account*, but this record type has many-to-one relationships with both its children, which violates our definition of a rooted tree (see Section B.2). To transform this diagram into one which is in the form of a rooted tree, we replicate the *account* record type, and create two separate

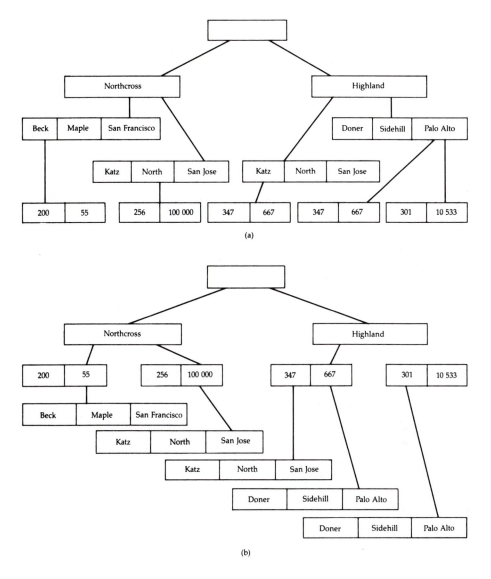

Figure B.13   Sample database corresponding to diagram of Figure B.12b.

trees, as shown in Figure B.15. Note that each such tree is indeed a rooted tree. Thus, in general, we can split such a diagram into several diagrams, each of which is a rooted tree.

Consider the E-R diagram of Figure B.16a. By applying the transformation algorithm described in Section B.2.1, we obtain the diagram depicted in Figure B.16b. This diagram is not in the form of a rooted tree, since it contains a cycle. To transform the diagram to a tree-structure

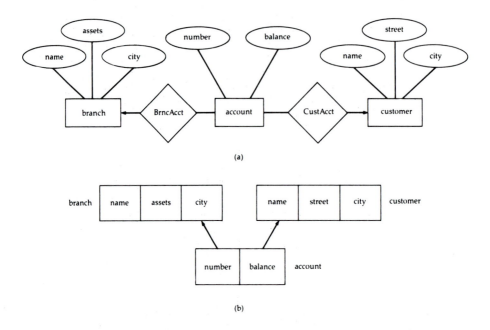

(a)

(b)

Figure B.14   E-R diagram and its corresponding tree-structure diagram.

diagram, we replicate all three record types and create two separate diagrams, as illustrated in Figure B.17. Note that each such diagram is indeed a rooted tree. Thus, in general, we can split such a diagram into several diagrams, each of which is a rooted tree.

B.3 Data Retrieval Facility

In this section, we present a query language for hierarchical databases which is derived from DL/I, the data manipulation language of IMS. In order to simplify the presentation, we shall deviate from the DL/I syntax and use a simplified notation. Our language consists of a number of commands

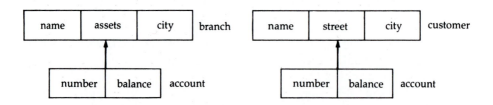

Figure B.15   Tree-structure diagram corresponding to Figure B.14a.

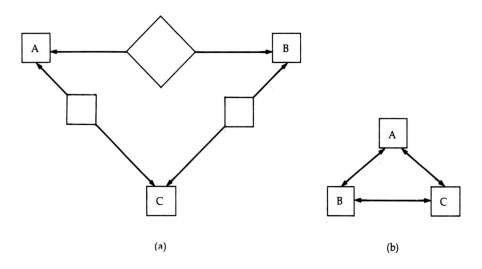

(a)   (b)

Figure B.16   E-R diagram and its corresponding tree-structure diagram.

that are embedded in a host language, Pascal. We shall use a simple example of a *customer-account-branch* scheme. The tree-structure diagram corresponding to this scheme appears in Figure B.18. It specifies that a branch may have several customers each of which may have several accounts. An account, however, may belong to only one customer, and a customer can belong to only one branch. An instance corresponding to this scheme is shown in Figure B.19.

B.3.1 Program Work-Area

Each application program executing in the system consists of a sequence of statements. Some of these are Pascal statements, while others are data

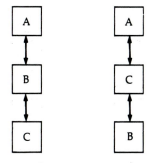

Figure B.17   Tree-structure diagram corresponding to Figure B.16a.

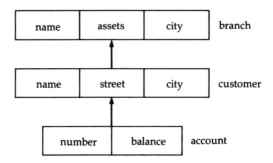

Figure B.18   Tree-structure diagram.

manipulation language command statements. These statements access and manipulate database items as well as locally declared variables. For each such application program, the system maintains a *program work-area*, a buffer storage area which contains the following variables:

- **Record templates**, a record (in the Pascal sense) for each record type accessed by the application program.

- **Currency pointers**, a set of pointers, one for each database tree, containing the *address* of the record in that particular tree (regardless of type) most recently accessed by the application program.

- **Status flag**, a variable set by the system to indicate to the application program the outcome of the last database operation. We call this flag *DB-status* and use the same convention as in the DBTG model to denote failure; namely, if *DB-status* = 0, then the last operation succeeded.

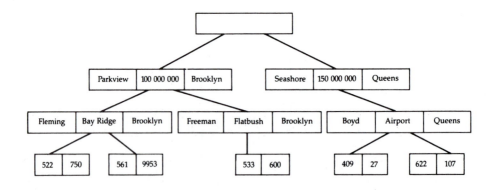

Figure B.19   Sample database corresponding to Figure B.18.

We emphasize again that a particular program work-area is associated with precisely one application program.

For our branch-customer-account example, a particular program work-area contains the following:

- **Templates**, one record for each of three record types:

    - *branch* record.

    - *customer* record.

    - *account* record.

- **Currency pointer**, a pointer to the last accessed record of *branch*, *customer*, or *account* type.

- **Status**, one status variable.

B.3.2 The Get Command

Data retrieval is accomplished through the **get** command. The actions taken in response to a **get** are as follows:

- Locate a record in the database and set the currency pointer to it.

- Copy that record from the database to the appropriate program area template.

The **get** command must specify which of the database trees is to be searched. For our example, we assume that the only database tree to be searched is the sample database of Figure B.19, and thus we omit this specification in our queries.

To illustrate the general effect that the **get** command has on the program work-area, consider the sample database of Figure B.19. Suppose that a **get** command was issued to locate the *customer* record belonging to Freeman. Once this command successfully executes, the changes that occur in the state of the program work-area are:

- The currency pointer points now to the record of Freeman.

- The information pertaining to Freeman is copied into the *customer* record work-area template.

- *DB-status* is set to the value 0.

To scan all records in a consistent manner, we must impose an ordering on the records. The one commonly used is *preorder*. A preorder search starts at the root and searches the subtrees of the root from left to right, recursively. Thus, we start at the root, visit the leftmost child, visit its leftmost child, and so on, until we reach a leaf (childless) node. We then move back to the parent of the leaf and visit the leftmost unvisited child. We proceed in this manner until the entire tree is visited. For example, the preordered listing of the records in the database tree of Figure B.19 is as follows:

> Parkview, Fleming, 522, 561, Freeman, 533,
> Seashore, Boyd, 409, 622

B.3.3 Access within a Database Tree

There are two different **get** commands for locating records in a database tree. The simplest command has the form:

> **get first** <record type>
> **where** <condition>

The **where** clause is optional. The attached <condition> is a predicate that may involve any record type which is either an ancestor of <record type> or the <record type> itself.

The **get** command locates the first record (in preorder) of type <record type> in the database that satisfies the <condition> of the **where** clause. If the **where** clause is omitted, then the first record of type <record-type> is located. Once such a record is found, the currency pointer is set to point to that record, and the content of the record is copied into the appropriate work-area template. If no such record exists in the database tree, then the search fails and the variable *DB-status* is set to an appropriate error message.

To illustrate, let us construct the database query that prints the address of customer Fleming.

> **get first** *customer*
>   **where** *customer.name* = "Fleming";
> **print** (*customer.address*);

As another example, consider the query that prints an account belonging to Fleming with balance greater than $10,000 (if one such exists).

> **get first** *account*
>   **where** *customer.name* = "Fleming" **and** *account.balance* > 10000;
>   **if** *DB-status* = 0 **then print** (*account.number*);

There may be several similar records in the database that we wish to retrieve. The **get first** command locates one of these. In order to locate the other database records, the following command can be used:

get next <record type>
where <condition>

This command locates the next record (in preorder) that satisfies <condition>. If the **where** clause is omitted, then the next record of type <record type> is located. Note that the currency pointer is used by the system to determine from where to resume the search. As before, the currency pointer, the work-area template of type <record-type>, and *DB-status* are affected.

To illustrate, let us construct the database query that prints the account number of all the accounts with a balance greater than $500.

```
get first account
    where account.balance > 500;
while DB-status = 0 do
    begin
        print (account.number);
        get next account
            where account.balance > 500;
    end
```

We have enclosed part of the query in a **while** loop, since we do not know in advance how many such accounts exist. We exit from the loop when *DB-status* ≠ 0. This indicates that the last **get next** operation failed, implying that we have exhausted all account records with *account.balance* > 500.

The two previous **get** commands locate a database record of type <record type> within a particular database tree. There are, however, many circumstances where we wish to locate such a record within a particular subtree. That is, we want to limit the search to one specific subtree rather than the entire database tree. The root of the subtree in question is the *last* record which was located with either the **get first** or **get next** command. The **get** command to locate a record within that subtree has the form:

get next within parent <record type>
where <condition>

which locates the next record (in preorder) which satisfies <condition> in the subtree whose root is the parent of current of <record type>. If the **where** clause is omitted, then the next record of type <record type> within the designated subtree is located. Note that the currency pointer is used by the system to determine from where to resume the search. As before, the currency pointer and the work-area template of type <record type> are affected. In this case, however, the *DB-status* is set to a nonzero value if no such record exists in the designated subtree, not in the entire tree.

To illustrate how this **get** command executes, let us construct the query that prints the total balance of all accounts belonging to Boyd:

> *sum* := 0;
> **get first** *customer*
>   **where** *customer.name* = "Boyd";
> **get next within parent** *account*;
> **while** *DB-status* = 0 **do**
>   **begin**
>   *sum* := *sum* + *account.balance*;
>   **get next within parent** *account*;
>   **end**
> **print** (*sum*);

Note that we exit from the **while** loop and print out the value of *sum* only when the *DB-status* is set to a value not equal to 0. This occurs after the **get next within parent** operation fails, indicating that we have exhausted all the accounts whose owner is customer Boyd.

B.4 Update Facility

In Section B.3, we described commands for querying the database. In this section, we describe the mechanisms available for updating information in the database. These include the insertion and deletion of records as well as the modification of the content of existing records.

B.4.1 Creating New Records

In order to insert a record of type <record type> into the database, we must first set the appropriate values in the corresponding <record type> work-area template. Once this is done, we add this new record to the database tree by executing:

> **insert** <record type>
>   **where** <condition>

If the **where** clause is included, the system searches the database tree (in preorder) for a record that satisfies the <condition> in the **where** clause. Once such a record, say *X*, is found, the newly created record is inserted in the tree as the leftmost child of *X*. If the **where** clause is omitted, the record is inserted in the first position (in preorder) in the database tree where a record type <record type> can be inserted in accordance with the scheme specified by the corresponding tree-structure diagram.

Consider the program for adding a new customer, Jackson, to the Seashore branch:

> *customer.name* := "Jackson";
> *customer.street* := "Old Road";
> *customer.city* := "Queens";
> **insert** *customer*
>   **where** *branch.name* = "Seashore";

The result of executing this program is the database tree of Figure B.20.

As another example, consider the program for creating a new account numbered 655 which belongs to customer "Jackson":

> *account.name* := 655;
> *account.balance* := 100;
> **insert** *account*
>   **where** *customer.name* = "Jackson";

The result of executing this program is the database tree of Figure B.21.

B.4.2 Modifying an Existing Record

In order to modify an existing record of type <record type>, we must get that record into the work-area template for <record type> and change the desired fields in that template. Once this is accomplished, we reflect the changes in the database by executing:

replace

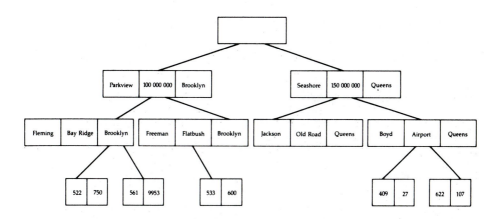

Figure B.20   New database tree.

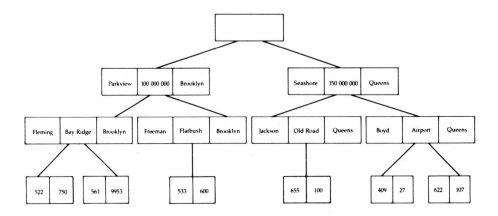

Figure B.21   New database tree.

Note that the **replace** command does not have <record type> as an argument. The record that is affected is the one to which the currency pointer points, which must be the desired record.

The DL/I language requires that prior to modifying a record, the **get** command must have the additional clause **hold** so that the system is aware of the fact that a record is to be modified.

As an example, consider the program to change the street address of Boyd to Northview:

> **get hold first** *customer*
> > **where** *customer.name* = "Boyd";
> *customer.street* := "Northview";
> **replace**;

Note that in our example, we have only one record containing the address of Boyd. If that were not the case, our program would have included a loop to search all Boyd records.

B.4.3 Deleting a Record

In order to delete a record of type <record type>, the currency pointer must be set to point to that record. Following this, we can delete that record by executing:

delete

Note that, as in the case of record modification, the **get** command must have the attribute **hold** attached to it.

To illustrate, consider the program to delete account 561:

> **get hold first** *account*
>   **where** *account.number* = 561;
> **delete**;

A delete operation deletes not only the record in question but the entire subtree rooted by that record. Thus, to delete customer Boyd and all of his accounts, we write:

> **get hold first** *customer*
>   **where** *customer.name* = "Boyd";
> **delete**;

B.5 Virtual Records

We have seen that in the case of many-to-many relationships, record replication is necessary to preserve the tree-structure organization of the database. Record replication has two major drawbacks:

- Data inconsistency may result when updating takes place.
- Waste of space is unavoidable.

In the following, we discuss ways to eliminate these drawbacks.

In order to eliminate record replication, we need to relax our requirement that the logical organization of data be constrained to a tree structure. This, however, needs to be done cautiously, since otherwise we will end up with the network model.

The solution is to introduce the concept of a *virtual record*. Such a record contains no data value; it does contain a logical pointer to a particular physical record. When a record is to be replicated in several database trees, we keep a single copy of that record in one of the trees and replace every other record with a virtual record containing a pointer to that physical record.

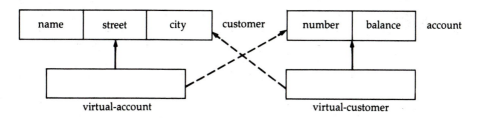

Figure B.22   Tree-structure diagram with virtual records.

To be more specific, let R be a record type that is replicated in several tree-structure diagrams, say $T_1, T_2, \ldots, T_n$. To eliminate replication, we create a new virtual record type *virtual-R*, and replace R in each of the $n - 1$ trees with a record of type *virtual-R*.

As an example, consider the E-R diagram of Figure B.6a and its corresponding tree-structure diagram, which consists of two separate trees, each consisting of both *customer* and *account* record types (Figure B.6b).

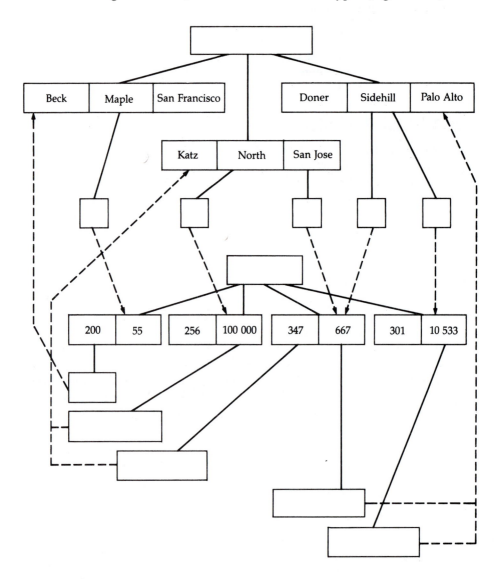

Figure B.23   Sample database corresponding to diagram of Figure B.22.

To eliminate data replication, we create two virtual record types: *virtual-customer* and *virtual-account*. We then replace record type *account* with record type *virtual-account* in the first tree, and replace record type *customer* with record type *virtual-customer* in the second tree. We also add a dashed line from *virtual-customer* record to *customer* record, and a dashed line from *virtual-account* record to *account* record, to specify the association between a virtual record and its corresponding physical record. The resulting tree-structure diagram is depicted in Figure B.22.

A sample database corresponding to the diagram of Figure B.22 is depicted in Figure B.23. Note that only a single copy of the information for each customer and each account exists. Contrast this with the same information depicted in Figure B.7, where replication is allowed.

The data manipulation language for this new configuration remains the same as in the case where record replication is allowed. Thus, a user need not be aware of these changes. Only the internal implementation is affected.

B.6 Mapping Hierarchies to Files

A straightforward technique for implementing the instance of a tree-structure diagram is to associate one pointer with a record for each child that the record has. Consider the database tree of Figure B.1. Figure B.24 shows an implementation of this database using parent-to-child pointers. Parent-child pointers, however, are not an ideal structure for the implementation of hierarchical databases, since a parent record may have an arbitrary number of children. Thus, fixed-length records become variable-length records once the parent-child pointers are added.

Instead of parent-child pointers, we may use *leftmost-child* and *next-sibling* pointers. A record has only two pointers. The leftmost-child pointer points to one child. The next-sibling pointer points to another child of the same parent. Figure B.25 shows this structure for the database tree of Figure B.1. Under this structure, every record has exactly two pointers.

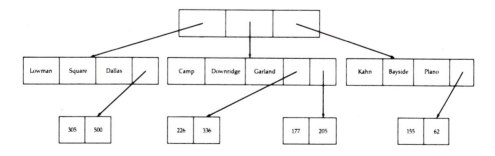

Figure B.24   Implementation with parent-child pointers.

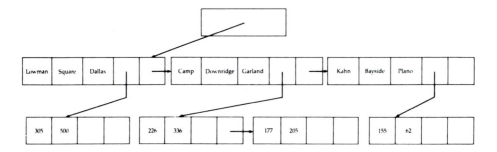

Figure B.25   Implementation with leftmost child and next-sibling pointers.

Thus, fixed-length records retain their fixed length when we add the necessary pointers.

Observe that several pointer fields are unused in Figure B.25. In general, the last child of a parent has no next sibling; thus, its next-sibling field is set to null. Rather than place nulls in such fields, it is useful to place pointers there to facilitate the preorder traversal required to process queries on hierarchical databases. We place a pointer in the next-sibling field of the rightmost siblings to the next record in preorder. Figure B.26 shows this modification to the structure of Figure B.25. These pointers make it possible to process a tree instance in preorder simply by following pointers. For this reason, the pointers are sometimes referred to as *preorder threads*.

A parent pointer is often added to records in an implementation of a hierarchical database. This pointer facilitates the processing of queries that give a value for a child record and request a value from the corresponding parent record. If we include parent pointers, a total of exactly three pointer fields is added to each record.

In order to see how best to locate records of a hierarchical database physically on disk, we draw an analogy between the parent-child

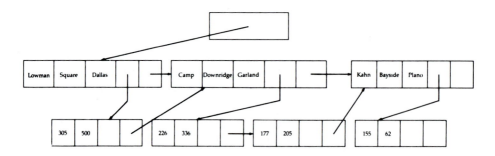

Figure B.26   Implementation using preorder threads.

relationship within a hierarchy and the owner-member relationship within a DBTG-set. In both cases, a one-to-many relationship is being represented. We desire to store the members and the owners of a set occurrence together. Similarly, we desire to store child records and their parent physically close on disk. This form of storage allows a sequence of **get first**, **get next**, and **get next within parent** statements to be executed with a minimal number of block accesses.

B.7 Hierarchical Systems

The hierarchical model is significant primarily because of the importance of IBM's IMS database system. In this section, we discuss both IMS and another widely used hierarchical system, System 2000.

B.7.1 IMS

The IBM Information Management System (IMS) is one of the oldest and most widely used database systems. It runs under the MVS operating system on large machines based on the IBM 370 architecture. Since IMS databases have historically been among the largest, the IMS developers were among the first to deal with such issues as concurrency, recovery, integrity, and efficient query processing. Through several releases, IMS acquired a large number of features and options. As a result, IMS is a highly complex system. We shall consider only a few features of IMS here.

Queries on IMS databases are issued through embedded calls in a host language. The embedded calls are part of the IMS database language DL/I. (The language used in this appendix is a simplified form of DL/I.)

Since performance is critically important in large databases, IMS allows the database designer a broad number of options in the data definition language. The database designer defines a physical hierarchy as the database scheme. Several subschemes (or views) may be defined by constructing a logical hierarchy from the record types comprising the scheme. The various options available in the data definition language (block sizes, special pointer fields, and so on) allow the database administrator to "tune" the system for improved performance.

Several record access schemes are available in IMS:

- HSAM (hierarchical sequential-access method) is used for physically sequential files (such as tape files). Records are stored physically in preorder.

- HISAM (hierarchical indexed-sequential-access method) is an index-sequential organization at the root level of the hierarchy.

- HIDAM (hierarchical indexed-direct-access method) is an index organization at the root level with pointers to child records.

- HDAM (hierarchical direct-access method) is similar to HIDAM but with hashed access at the root level.

The original version of IMS predated the development of concurrency control theory. Early versions of IMS had a simple form of concurrency control. Only one update application program could run at a time. However, any number of read-only applications could run concurrent with an update application. This feature permitted applications to read uncommitted updates and allowed nonserializable executions. Exclusive access to the database was the only option available to applications that demanded a greater degree of isolation from the anomalies of concurrent processing.

Later versions of IMS included a more sophisticated *program isolation feature* that allowed for both improved concurrency control and more sophisticated transaction recovery techniques (such as logging). These features became of increasing importance as more IMS users began to use online transactions as opposed to the batch transactions that were originally the norm.

The need for high-performance transaction processing led to the introduction of *IMS Fast Path*. Fast Path uses an alternative physical data organization designed to allow the most active parts of the database to reside in main memory. Instead of forcing updates to disk at the end of a transaction (as standard IMS does), update is deferred until a checkpoint or synchronization point. In the event of a crash, the recovery subsystem must redo all committed transactions whose updates were not forced to disk. These and other "tricks" allow for extremely high rates of transaction throughput. As main memory has become larger and less expensive, there has been a growing interest in developing "main-memory database systems." IMS Fast Path is a forerunner of much of this work.

IMS database may be queried, though not updated, using SQL. The DXT feature of DB2 and the DL/I extract feature of SQL/DS (see Chapter 16) allow IMS data to be stored in a relational database on which SQL queries may be issued.

The full details of IMS are beyond the scope of this brief survey. Although IMS is an old system and the hierarchical model is fading in significance, the history and evolution of IMS provide an interesting framework for the study of the development of database system concepts.

B.7.2 System 2000

System 2000 is a hierarchical database system originally developed by MRI Corporation and later acquired by Intel. System 2000 runs on IBM 370-like computers, Univac 1100 computers, and CDC 6000 and Cyber computers. Although the data model used is the same as IMS, the language features offered by System 2000 differ in several interesting ways from the IMS DL/I language.

The primary concept in the DL/I data definition language is the one-to-many parent-child relationship. In our bank example, assume there is a one-to-many relationship between *customer* and *account*. We would design our hierarchical bank database with *account* as a child of *customer*. An alternative manner of viewing this one-to-many relationship is to consider a record that may have repeating fields. Within the *customer* record of a particular customer, we may store the set of accounts belonging to that customer by creating a repeating *account* field. It is this repeating-field approach that motivates the System 2000 data definition language.

In our bank example, the *customer* record has the fields *customer-name*, *street*, and *customer-city* and the *account* record has the fields *account-number* and *balance*. Below we show the statements for this part of the bank database using System 2000 data definition language.

> 1* *customer-name* (name);
> 2* *street* (name);
> 3* *customer-city* (name);
> 4* *account* (repeating group);
> 5* *account-number* (integer);
> 6* *balance* (money);

Name, integer, and money are three of the built-in data types in System 2000. Each field can be specified as *key* or *nonkey*. A *key* field is one on which System 2000 builds an index.

Consider the query "Find the name and city of all customers holding an account with a balance greater than $10,000." Using the DL/I-like language introduced earlier, we must loop over all account records for each customer by writing our own **while** loop in a host language. The System 2000 query language, QUEST, allows us to write this query as a single statement:

> **list** *customer-name, customer-city*
> **while** *customer* **has** *balance* > 10000

It is possible also to embed System 2000 queries in a host language. A precompiler processes the program. Queries are parsed at the precompilation phase. Like most commercial systems, System 2000 includes facilities to assist in report generation.

B.8 Summary

A hierarchical database consists of a collection of *records* which are connected to one another through *links*. A record is a collection of fields, each of which contains only one data value. A link is an association between precisely two records. The hierarchical model is thus similar to the network model in the sense that data and relationships among data are also represented by records and links, respectively. The hierarchical model differs from the network model in that the records are organized as collections of trees rather than as arbitrary graphs.

A *tree-structure diagram* is a scheme for a hierarchical database. Such a diagram consists of two basic components: boxes, which correspond to record types, and lines, which correspond to links. A tree-structure diagram serves the same purpose as an entity-relationship diagram; namely, it specifies the overall logical structure of the database. A tree-structure diagram is similar to a data-structure diagram in the network model. The main difference is that in the former record types are organized in the form of an arbitrary graph, while in the latter record types are organized in the form of a *rooted tree*. For every entity-relationship diagram, there is a corresponding tree-structure diagram.

The database scheme is thus represented as a collection of tree-structure diagrams. For each such diagram, there exists a *single* instance of a database tree. The root of this tree is a dummy node. The children of that node are actual instances of the appropriate record type. Each such instance may, in turn, have several instances of various record types, as specified in the corresponding tree-structure diagram.

The data manipulation language discussed in this appendix consists of a number of commands that are embedded in a host language. These commands access and manipulate database items as well as locally declared variables. For each application program the system maintains a *program work-area* which contains *record templates, currency pointers*, and a *status flag*.

Data items are retrieved through the **get** command, which locates a record in the database and sets the currency pointer to point to it, and then copies that record from the database to the appropriate program work-area template. There are a number of different forms of the **get** command. The main distinction among them is whether a record is to be located in an entire database tree or within a subtree.

Various mechanisms are available for updating information in the database. These include the creation and deletion of records (via the **insert** and **delete** operations) and the modification (via the **replace** operation) of the content of existing records.

In the case of many-to-many relationships, record replication is necessary to preserve the tree-structure organization of the database. Record replication has two major drawbacks: Data inconsistency may result when updating takes place, and waste of space is unavoidable. The solution is to introduce the concept of a *virtual record*. Such a record contains no data value; it does contains a logical pointer to a particular physical record. When a record is to be replicated in several database trees, a single copy of that record is kept in one of the trees and all other records are replaced with a virtual record containing a pointer to that physical record. The data manipulation language for this new configuration remains the same as in the case where record replication is allowed. Thus, a user need not be aware of these changes. Only the internal implementation is affected.

Implementations of hierarchical databases do not use parent-to-child pointers, since these would require the use of variable-length records. Instead preorder threads are used. This technique allows each record to contain exactly two pointers. Optionally, a third child-to-parent pointer may be added.

Finally, we noted some features of two commercial hierarchical database systems, IMS and System 2000.

Exercises

B.1 Transform the E-R diagram of Figure B.27 to a tree-structure diagram.

B.2 Construct a sample database for the tree-structure diagram of Exercise B.1, with ten students and three different classes.

B.3 Show the preorder order of the sample database of Exercise B.2.

B.4 Show the set of variables which exist in a program work-area for the tree-structure diagram corresponding to the E-R diagram of Figure B.27.

B.5 Suppose that we add the attribute "grade" to the relationship *enrollment* of Figure B.27. Show the corresponding tree-structure diagram.

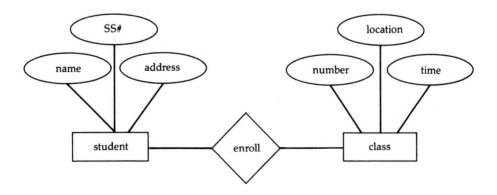

Figure B.27   Class enrollment E-R diagram.

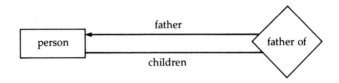

Figure B.28   Parent-child E-R diagram.

B.6 Transform the E-R diagram of Figure B.28 into a tree-structure diagram.

B.7 Compare the hierarchical model with the relational model in terms of ease of learning and ease of use.

B.8 Are certain applications easier to code in the hierarchical model than in the relational model? If so, give an example of one.

B.9 Transform the E-R diagram of Figure B.29 into a tree-structure diagram.

B.10 For the tree-structure diagram corresponding to the E-R diagram of Figure B.29, construct the following queries:

   a. Find the total number of people whose car was involved in an accident in 1983.

   b. Find the number of accidents in which the cars belonging to "John Smith" were involved.

   c. Add a new customer to the database.

   d. Delete the car "Mazda" belonging to "John Smith."

   e. Add a new accident record for the Toyota belonging to "Jones."

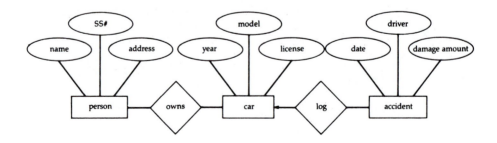

Figure B.29   Car insurance E-R diagram.

B.11 The addition of virtual records to the hierarchical model results in a structure which is no longer treelike. In effect, the underlying structure is quite similar to the network model. What are the differences between the hierarchical model with virtual records and the network model?

B.12 Give an appropriate tree-structure diagram for the following relational database:

> *lives (person-name, street, city)*
> *works (person-name, company-name, salary)*
> *located-in (company-name, city)*
> *manages (person-name, manager-name)*

B.13 Consider the database scheme corresponding to the tree-structure diagram obtained as a solution to Exercise B.12. For each of the queries below construct the appropriate program:

  a. Find the name of all employees who work for First Bank Corporation.

  b. Find the name and city of all employees who work for First Bank Corporation.

  c. Find the name, street, and city of all employees who work for First Bank Corporation and earn more than $10,000.

  d. Find all employees who live in the same city as the company they work for.

  e. Find all employees who live in the same city and on the same street as their manager.

  f. Find all employees who do not work for First Bank Corporation.

  g. Find all employees who earn more than every employee of Small Bank Corporation.

  h. Assume the companies may be located in several cities. Find all companies located in every city in which Small Bank Corporation is located.

  i. Find all employees who earn more than the average salary of employees working in their company.

  j. Find the company employing the most people.

  k. Find the company with the smallest payroll.

  l. Find those companies that pay more, on average, than the average salary at First Bank Corporation.

m. Modify the database so that Jones now lives in Newtown.

n. Give all employees of First Bank Corporation a 10 percent raise.

o. Give all managers a 10 percent raise.

p. Give all managers a 10 percent raise unless the salary becomes greater than $100,000. In such cases, give only a 3 percent raise.

q. Delete all employees of Small Bank Corporation.

B.14 Give a tree-structure diagram for the following relational database:

course (course-name, room, instructor)
enrollment (course-name, student-name, grade)

Bibliographic Notes

Two influential database systems relying on the hierarchical model are IBM's Information Management System (IMS) [IBM 1978a, McGee 1977], and MRI's system 2000 [MRI 1974, 1979]. The first IMS version was developed in the late 1960s by IBM and North American Aviation (Rockwell International) for the Apollo moon landing program. System 2000 is an outgrowth of TDMS, which was developed at System Development Corporation [Vorhaus and Mills 1967], and RFMS, which was developed at the University of Texas at Austin [Everett, et al. 1971].

A survey paper on the hierarchical data model is presented by Tsichritzis and Lochovsky [1976]. Textbook discussions covering IMS are offered by Tsichritzis and Lochovsky [1977, 1982], Cardenas [1985], Date [1990a], and Ullman [1988]. A description of DL/I, the query language of IMS, can be found in Kroenke and Dolan [1988]. The simplified version of DL/I used in this appendix is similar to the one presented by Ullman [1988]. Kapp and Leben [1978] present programming techniques for IMS. System 2000 is discussed in the textbooks by Tsichritzis and Lochovsky [1977] and Cardenas [1985].

Obermarck [1980] discusses the IMS program isolation feature and gives a brief history of the concurrency control component of IMS. Bjorner and Lovengren [1982] present a formal definition of IMS.

Bibliography

[Abbott and Garcia-Molina 1988] R. Abbott and H. Garcia-Molina, "Scheduling Real-Time Transactions: A Performance Evaluation," *Proceedings of the International Conference on Very Large Data Bases* (1988), pages 1−12.

[Abiteboul and Bidoit 1984] S. Abiteboul and N. Bidoit, "Non-first Normal Form Relations to Represent Hierarchically Organized Data," *Proceedings of the ACM SIGACT-SIGMOD Symposium on the Principles of Database Systems* (1984), pages 191−200.

[Abiteboul and Kanellakis 1989] S. Abiteboul and P. Kanellakis, "Object Identity as a Query Language Primitive," *Proceedings of the ACM SIGMOD International Conference on the Management of Data* (1989), pages 159−173.

[Abiteboul et al. 1989] S. Abiteboul, P. C. Fischer, and H. J. Schek (Editors), *Nested Relations and Complex Objects in Databases*, Lecture Notes in Computer Science 361, Springer-Verlag (1989).

[Abrial 1974] J. R. Abrial, "Data Semantics," in **[Klimbie and Koffeman 1974]**, pages 1−59.

[Adiba 1981] M. E. Adiba, "Derived Relations: A Unified Mechanism for Views, Snapshots and Distributed Data," *Proceedings of the International Conference on Very Large Data Bases* (1981), pages 293−305.

[Aho and Ullman 1972] A. V. Aho and J. D. Ullman, *The Theory of Parsing, Translation and Compiling, Volume I: Parsing*, Prentice-Hall, Englewood Cliffs, NJ (1972).

[Aho and Ullman 1973] A. V. Aho and J. D. Ullman, *The Theory of Parsing, Translation and Compiling, Volume II: Compiling*, Prentice-Hall, Englewood Cliffs, NJ (1973).

[Aho and Ullman 1979] A. V. Aho and J. D. Ullman, "Optimal Partial Match Retrieval When Fields Are Independently Specified," *ACM Transactions on Database Systems*, Volume 4, Number 2 (June 1979), pages 168−179.

[Aho et al. 1974] A. V. Aho, J. E. Hopcroft, and J. D. Ullman, *The Design and Analysis of Computer Algorithms*, Addison-Wesley, Reading, MA (1974).

[Aho et al. 1979a] A. V. Aho, Y. Sagiv, and J. D. Ullman, "Equivalences among Relational Expressions," *Siam Journal of Computing*, Volume 8, Number 2 (June 1979), pages 218−246.

[Aho et al. 1979b] A. V. Aho, C. Beeri, and J. D. Ullman, "The Theory of Joins in Relational Databases," *ACM Transactions on Database Systems*, Volume 4, Number 3 (September 1979), pages 297−314.

[Aho et al. 1979c] A. V. Aho, Y. Sagiv, and J. D. Ullman, "Efficient Optimization of a Class of Relational Expressions," *ACM Transactions on Database Systems*, Volume 4, Number 4 (December 1979), pages 435−454.

[Aho et al. 1983] A. V. Aho, J. E. Hopcroft, and J. D. Ullman, *Data Structures and Algorithms*, Addison-Wesley, Reading, MA (1983).

[Aho et al. 1986] A. V. Aho, R. Sethi, and J. D. Ullman, *Compilers: Principles, Techniques, and Tools*, Addison-Wesley, Reading, MA (1986).

[Akl 1983] S. Akl, "Digital Signatures, A Tutorial Survey," *IEEE Computer*, Volume 16, Number 2 (February 1983), pages 15−24.

[ANSI 1975] "Study Group on Data Base Management Systems: Interim Report," *FDT*, Volume 7, Number 2, ACM, New York, NY (1975).

[ANSI 1986] "American National Standard for Information Systems: Database Language SQL," *FDT*, ANSI X3,135−1986, American National Standards Institute, New York (1986).

[Apers et al. 1983] P. M. G. Apers, A. R. Hevner, and S. B. Yao, "Optimization Algorithms for Distributed Queries," *IEEE Transactions on Software Engineering*, Volume SE-9, Number 1 (January 1983), pages 57−68.

[Apt and Pugin 1987] K. R. Apt and J. -M. Pugin, "Maintenance of Stratified Database Viewed as a Belief Revision System," *Proceedings of the ACM SIGACT-SIGMOD Symposium on the Principles of Database Systems* (1987), pages 136−145.

[Armstrong 1974] W. W. Armstrong, "Dependency Structures of Data Base Relationships," *Proceedings of the 1974 IFIP Congress* (1974), pages 580−583.

[Astrahan et al. 1976] M. M. Astrahan, M. W. Blasgen, D. D. Chamberlin, K. P. Eswaran, J. N. Gray, P. P. Griffiths, W. F. King, R. A. Lorie, P. R. McJones, J. W. Mehl, G. R. Putzolu, I. L. Traiger, B. W. Wade, and V. Watson, "System R, A Relational Approach to Data Base Management," *ACM Transactions on Database Systems*, Volume 1, Number 2 (June 1976), pages 97−137.

[Astrahan et al. 1979] M. M. Astrahan, M. W. Blasgen, D. D. Chamberlin, J. N. Gray, W. F. King, B. G. Lindsay, R. A. Lorie, J. W. Mehl, T. G. Price, G. R. Putzolu, M. Schkolnick, P. G. Selinger, D. R. Slutz, H. R. Strong, P. Tiberio, I. L. Traiger, B. W. Wade, and R. A. Yost, "System R: A Relational

Database Management System," *Computer*, Volume 12, Number 5 (May 1979), pages 43−48.

[Attar et al. 1984] R. Attar, P. A. Bernstein, and N. Goodman, "Site Initialization, Recovery, and Backup in a Distributed Database System," *IEEE Transactions on Software Engineering*, Volume SE-10, Number 6 (November 1984), pages 645−650.

[Bachman 1969] C. W. Bachman, "Data Structure Diagrams," *Journal of ACM SIGBDP* Volume 1, Number 2 (March 1969), pages 4−10.

[Bachman and Daya 1977] C. W. Bachman and M. Daya, "The Role Concept in Data Models," *Proceedings of the International Conference on Very Large Data Bases* (1977), pages 464−476.

[Bachman and Williams 1964] C. W. Bachman and S. S. Williams, "A General Purpose Programming System for Random Access Memories," *Proceedings of the Fall Joint Computer Conference*, Volume 26, AFIPS Press (1964), pages 411−422.

[Badal 1980] D. S. Badal, "The Analysis of the Effects of Concurrency Control on Distributed Database System Performance," *Proceedings of the International Conference on Very Large Data Bases* (1980), pages 376−383.

[Badal 1981] D. S. Badal, "Concurrency Control Overhead or A Closer Look at Blocking vs. Nonblocking Concurrency Control Mechanism," *Proceedings of the Berkeley Workshop on Distributed Data Management and Computer Networks* (1981), pages 85−104.

[Badal and Popek 1979] D. S. Badal and G. Popek, "Cost and Performance Analysis of Semantic Integrity Validation Methods," *Proceedings of the ACM SIGMOD International Conference on Management of Data* (1979), pages 109−115.

[Badrinath and Ramamritham 1990] B. R. Badrinath and K. Ramamritham, "Performance Evaluation of Semantics-Based Multilevel Concurrency Control Protocols," *Proceedings of the ACM SIGMOD International Conference on the Management of Data* (1990), pages 163−172.

[Balbin and Ramamohanarao 1986] I. Balbin and K. Ramamohanarao, "A Different Approach to Query Optimization in Recursive Deductive Databases," Technical Report 86/7, Department of Computer Science, University of Melbourne, Melbourne, Australia (1986).

[Bancilhon 1985] F. Bancilhon, "A Note on the Performance of Rule Based Systems," Technical Report DB-022-85, MCC, Austin TX (1985).

[Bancilhon and Ramakrishnan 1986] F. Bancilhon and R. Ramakrishnan, "An amateur's Introduction to Recursive Query-Processing Strategies," *Proceedings of the ACM SIGMOD International Conference on Management of Data* (1986), pages 16−52.

[Bancilhon and Buneman 1990] F. Bancilhon and P. Buneman, *Advances in Database Programming Languages,* ACM Press, New York, NY (1990).

[Bancilhon and Spyratos 1981] F. Bancilhon and N. Spyratos "Update Semantics and Relational Views," *ACM Transactions on Database Systems,* Volume 6, Number 4 (December 1981), pages 557−575.

[Bancilhon et al. 1985a] F. Bancilhon, W. Kim, and H. F. Korth, "A Model of CAD Transactions," *Proceedings of the International Conference on Very Large Data Bases* (1985), pages 25−31.

[Bancilhon et al. 1985b] F. Bancilhon, W. Kim, and H. F. Korth, "Transactions and Concurrency Control in CAD Databases," *Proceedings of the IEEE International Conference on Computer Design: VLSI in Computers* (1985).

[Banerjee et al. 1987a] J. Banerjee, H. T. Chou, J. F. Garza, W. Kim, D. Woelk, N. Ballou, and H. J. Kim, "Data Model Issues for Object-Oriented Applications," *ACM Transactions on Office Information Systems* (January 1987).

[Banerjee et al. 1987b] J. Banerjee, W. Kim, H. J. Kim, and H. F. Korth, "Semantics and Implementation of Schema Evolution in Object-Oriented Databases," *Proceedings of the ACM SIGMOD International Conference on Management of Data* (1987), pages 311−322.

[Banerjee et al. 1988] J. Banerjee, W. Kim, and K. C. Kim, "Queries in Object-Oriented Databases," *Proceedings of the International Conference on Data Engineering* (February 1988).

[Bassiouni 1988] M. Bassiouni, "Single-site and Distributed Optimistic Protocols for Concurrency Control," *IEEE Transactions on Software Engineering,* Volume SE-14, Number 8 (August 1988), pages 1071−1080.

[Batory and Gotlieb 1982] D. S. Batory and C. C. Gotlieb, "A Unifying Model of Physical Databases," *ACM Transactions on Database Systems,* Volume 7, Number 4 (December 1982), pages 509−539.

[Batory et al. 1986] D. S. Batory, J. Barnett, J. Garza, K. Smith, K. Tsukuda, B. Twichell, and T. Wise, "GENESIS: An Extensible Database Management System," *IEEE Transactions on Software Engineering,* Volume SE-14, Number 11 (November 1988), pages 1711−1730.

[Batory et al. 1988] D. S. Batory, T. Y. Leung, and T. E. Wise, "Implementation Concepts for an Extensible Data Model and Data Language," *ACM Transactions on Database Systems,* Volume 13, Number 3 (September 1988), pages 231−262.

[Bayer 1972] R. Bayer, "Symmetric Binary B-trees: Data Structure and Maintenance Algorithms," *Acta Informatica,* Volume 1, Number 4 (1972), pages 290−306.

[Bayer 1985] R. Bayer, "Query Evaluation and Recursion in Deductive Database Systems," unpublished memorandum, Technical University of Munich, Munich, Germany (1985).

[Bayer and McCreight 1972] R. Bayer and E. M. McCreight, "Organization and Maintenance of Large Ordered Indices," *Acta Informatica*, Volume 1, Number 3 (1972), pages 173−189.

[Bayer and Schkolnick 1977] R. Bayer and M. Schkolnick, "Concurrency of Operating on B-trees," *Acta Informatica*, Volume 9, Number 1 (1977), pages 1−21.

[Bayer and Unterauer 1977] R. Bayer and K. Unterauer, "Prefix B-trees," *ACM Transactions on Database Systems*, Volume 2, Number 1 (March 1977) pages 11−26.

[Bayer et al. 1978] R. Bayer, R. M. Graham, and G. Seegmuller (Editors), *Operating Systems: An Advanced Course*, Springer-Verlag, Berlin, Germany (1978).

[Beech 1988] D. Beech, "OSQL: A Language for Migrating from SQL to Object Databases," *Proceedings of the International Conference on Extending Database Technology* (March 1988).

[Beeri et al. 1977] C. Beeri, R. Fagin, and J. H. Howard, "A Complete Axiomatization for Functional and Multivalued Dependencies," *Proceedings of the ACM SIGMOD International Conference on Management of Data* (1977), pages 47−61.

[Beeri et al. 1983] C. Beeri, R. Fagin, D. Maier, and M. Yannakakis, "On the Desirability of Acyclic Database Schemes," *Journal of the ACM*, Volume 30, Number 3 (July 1983), pages 479−513.

[Bell and LaPadula 1976] D. E. Bell and L. J. LaPadula, "Secure Computer Systems: Unified Exposition and Multics Interpretation," Mitre Corporation, Bedford, MA (1976).

[Benneworth et al. 1981] R. L. Benneworth, C. D. Bishop, C. J. M. Turnbull, W. D. Holman, and F. M. Monette, "The Implementation of GERM, an Entity-Relationship Data Base Management System," *Proceedings of the International Conference on Very Large Data Bases* (1981), pages 478−484.

[Bernstein 1976] P. A. Bernstein, "Synthesizing Third Normal Form Relations from Functional Dependencies," *ACM Transactions on Database Systems*, Volume 1, Number 4 (December 1976), pages 277−298.

[Bernstein and Chiu 1981] P. A. Bernstein and D. W. Chiu, "Using Semijoins to Solve Relational Queries," *Journal of the ACM*, Volume 28, Number 1 (January 1981), pages 25−40.

[Bernstein and Goodman 1980a] P. A. Bernstein and N. Goodman, "Timestamp-based Algorithms for Concurrency Control in Distributed Database Systems," *Proceedings of the International Conference on Very Large Data Bases* (1980), pages 285−300.

[Bernstein and Goodman 1980b] P. A. Bernstein and N. Goodman, "What Does Boyce-Codd Normal Form Do?," *Proceedings of the International Conference of Very Large Data Bases* (1980), pages 245−259.

[Bernstein and Goodman 1981a] P. A. Bernstein and N. Goodman, "Concurrency Control in Distributed Database Systems," *ACM Computing Surveys*, Volume 13, Number 2 (June 1981), pages 185−221.

[Bernstein and Goodman 1981b] P. A. Bernstein and N. Goodman, "The Power of Natural Semijoins," *Siam Journal of Computing*, Volume 10, Number 4 (December 1981), pages 751−771.

[Bernstein and Goodman 1982] P. A. Bernstein and N. Goodman, "A Sophisticate's Introduction to Distributed Database Concurrency Control," *Proceedings of the International Conference on Very Large Data Bases* (1982), pages 62−76.

[Bernstein et al. 1978] P. A. Bernstein, N. Goodman, J. B. Rothnie, Jr., and C. H. Papadimitriou, "Analysis of Serializability of SDD-1: A System of Distributed Databases (the Fully Redundant Case)," *IEEE Transactions on Software Engineering*, Volume SE-4, Number 3 (May 1978), pages 154−168.

[Bernstein et al. 1980a] P. A. Bernstein, D. W. Shipman, and J. B. Rothnie, Jr., "Concurrency Control in a System for Distributed Databases (SDD-1)," *ACM Transactions on Database Systems*, Volume 5, Number 1 (March 1980), pages 18−51.

[Bernstein et al. 1980b] P. A. Bernstein, B. Blaustein, and E. Clarke, "Fast Maintenance of Semantic Integrity Assertions Using Redundant Aggregate Data," *Proceedings of the International Conference on Very Large Data Bases* (1980).

[Bernstein et al. 1983] P. A. Berstein, N. Goodman, and M. Y. Lai, " Analyzing Concurrency Control when User and System Operations Differ," *IEEE Transactions on Software Engineering*, Volume SE-9 Number 3 (May 1983), pages 233−239.

[Bernstein et al. 1984] A. Bernstein, J. Heller, P. B. Henderson, Z. M. Kedem, E. Sciore, D. S. Warren, L. D. Wittie, and A. Zorat, "A Data Oriented Network System," Technical Report 84/091, Department of Computer Science, State University of New York at Stony Brook, Stony Brook, NY (1984).

[Bernstein et al. 1987] A. Bernstein, V. Hadzilacos, and N. Goodman, *Concurrency Control and Recovery in Database Systems*, Addison-Wesley, Reading, MA (1987).

[Bertino and Kim 1989] E. Bertino and W. Kim, "Indexing Techniques for Queries on Nested Objects," *IEEE Transactions on Knowledge and Data Engineering* (October 1989).

[Bhargava 1987] B. Bhargava (Editor), *Concurrency and Reliability in Distributed Systems*, Van Nostrand Reinhold, New York, NY (1987).

[Bidoit 1987] N. Bidoit, "The VERSO Algebra or How to Answer Queries with Fewer Joins," *Journal of Computer and System Sciences*, Volume 35, Number 3 (December 1987), pages 321−364.

[Biskup et al. 1979] J. Biskup, U. Dayal, and P. A. Bernstein, "Synthesizing Independent Database Schemas," *Proceedings of the ACM SIGMOD International Conference on Management of Data* (1979), pages 143−152.

[Bitton and Gray 1988] D. Bitton and J. N. Gray, "Disk Shadowing," *Proceedings of the International Conference on Very Large Data Bases* (1988), pages 331−338.

[Bjork 1973] L. A. Bjork, "Recovery Scenario for a DB/DC System," *Proceedings of the ACM Annual Conference* (1973), pages 142−146.

[Bjorner and Lovengren 1982] D. Bjorner and H. Lovengren, "Formalization of Database Systems and a Formal Definition of IMS," *Proceedings of the International Conference on Very Large Data Bases* (1982), pages 334−347.

[Blasgen and Eswaran 1976] M. W. Blasgen and K. P. Eswaran, "On the Evaluation of Queries in a Relational Database System," *IBM Systems Journal*, Volume 16 (1976), pages 363−377.

[Blasgen et al. 1981] M. W. Blasgen, D. D. Chamberlin, J. N. Gray, W. F. King, B. G. Lindsay, R. A. Lorie, J. W. Mehl, T. G. Price, G. R. Putzolu, M. Schkolnick, P. G. Selinger, D. R. Slutz, I. L. Traiger, B. W. Wade, and R. A. Yost, "System R: An Architectural Overview," *IBM Systems Journal*, Volume 20, Number 1 (January 1981), pages 41−62.

[Bobrow and Collins 1975] D. G. Bobrow and A. M Collins (Editors), *Representation and Understanding*, Academic Press, New York, NY (1975).

[Bohl 1981] M. Bohl, *Introduction to IBM Direct Access Storage Devices*, Science Research Associates, Chicago, IL (1981).

[Bolour 1979] A. Bolour, "Optimal Retrieval Algorithms for Small Region Queries," *Journal of the ACM*, Volume 26, Number 2 (April 1979), pages 721−741.

[Boyce et al. 1975] R. Boyce, D. D. Chamberlin, W. F. King, and M. Hammer, "Specifying Queries as Relational Expressions," *Communications of the ACM*, Volume 18, Number 11 (November 1975), pages 621−628.

[Bracchi and Nijssen 1979] G. Bracchi and G. M. Nijssen (Editors), *Data Base Architecture*, North Holland, Amsterdam, The Netherlands (1979).

[Bracchi et al. 1976] G. Bracchi, P. Paolini, and G. Pelagatti, "Binary Logical Associations in Data Modeling," in **[Nijssen 1976]**, pages 125−148.

[Brachman 1979] R. J. Brachman, "On the Epistemological Status of Semantic Networks," in **[Findler 1979]**, pages 3−50.

[Bradley 1978] J. Bradley, "An Extended Owner-Coupled Set Data Model and Predicate Calculus for Database Management," *ACM Transactions on Database Systems*, Volume 3, Number 4 (December 1978), pages 385−416.

[Bradley 1983] J. Bradley, "Application of SQL/N to the Attribute-Relation Associations Implicit in Functional Dependencies," *International Journal of Computer and Information Sciences*, Volume 12, Number 2 (1983), pages 65−86.

[Bray 1982] O. H. Bray, *Distributed Database Management Systems*, Lexington Books (1982).

[Breitbart 1990] Y. Breitbart, "Multidatabase Interoperability," *ACM SIGMOD Record,* Volume 19, Number 3 (1990).

[Breitbart and Silberschatz 1988] Y. Breitbart and A. Silberschatz, "Multidatabase Update Issues," *Proceedings of the ACM SIGMOD International Conference on the Management of Data* (1988), pages 135−142.

[Breitbart et al. 1990] Y. Breitbart, A. Silberschatz, and G. Thompson, "Reliable Transaction Management in a Multidatabase System," *Proceedings of the ACM SIGMOD International Conference on the Management of Data* (1990), pages 215−224.

[Buckley and Silberschatz 1983] G. Buckley and A. Silberschatz, "Obtaining Progressive Protocols for a Simple Multiversion Database Model," *Proceedings of the International Conference on Very Large Data Bases* (1983), pages 74−81.

[Buckley and Silberschatz 1984] G. Buckley and A. Silberschatz, "Concurrency Control in Graph Protocols by Using Edge Locks," *Proceedings of the ACM SIGACT-SIGMOD Symposium on the Principles of Database Systems* (1984), pages 45−50.

[Buckley and Silberschatz 1985] G. Buckley and A. Silberschatz, "Beyond Two-Phase Locking," *Journal of the ACM*, Volume 32, Number 2 (April 1985), pages 314−326.

[Buneman and Frankel 1979] P. Buneman and R. Frankel, "FQL: A Functional Query Language," *Proceedings of the ACM SIGMOD International Conference on the Management of Data* (1979), pages 52−58.

[Burkhard 1976] W. A. Burkhard, "Hashing and Trie Algorithms for Partial Match Retrieval," *ACM Transactions on Database Systems*, Volume 1, Number 2 (June 1976), pages 175–187.

[Burkhard 1979] W. A. Burkhard, "Partial-match Hash Coding: Benefits of Redundancy," *ACM Transactions on Database Systems*, Volume 4, Number 2 (June 1979), pages 228–239.

[Campbell et al. 1985] D. Campbell, D. Embley, and B. Czejdo, "A Relationally Complete Query Language for the Entity-Relationship Model," *Proceedings of the International Conference on Entity-Relationship Approach* (1985).

[Cardenas 1985] A. F. Cardenas, *Data Base Management Systems*, Second Edition, Allyn and Bacon, Boston, MA (1985).

[Carey 1983] M. J. Carey, "Granularity Hierarchies in Concurrency Control," *Proceedings of the ACM SIGACT-SIGMOD Symposium on the Principles of Database Systems* (1983), pages 156–165.

[Carey et al. 1986] M. J. Carey, D. DeWitt, J. Richardson, and E. Shekita, "Object and File Management in the EXODUS Extensible Database System," *Proceedings of the International Conference on Very Large Data Bases* (1986), pages 91–100.

[Carey et al. 1988] M. J. Carey, D. DeWitt, and S. Vandenberg, "A Data Model and Query Language for EXODUS," *Proceedings of the ACM SIGMOD International Conference on the Management of Data* (1988), pages 413–423.

[Carey et al. 1990] M. J. Carey, D. DeWitt, G. Graefe, D. Haight, J. Richardson, D. Schuh, E. Shekita, and S. Vandenberg, "The EXODUS Extensible DBMS Project: An Overview," in **[Zdonik and Maier 1990]**, pages 474–499.

[Casanova 1984] M. A. Casanova, "Mapping Uninterpreted Schemes in Entity-Relationship Diagrams: Two Applications to Conceptual Schema Design," *IBM Journal of Research and Development*, Volume 28, Number 1 (January 1984), pages 82–94.

[Casanova et al. 1984] M. A. Casanova, R. Fagin, and C. Papadimitriou, "Inclusion Dependencies and Their Interaction with Functional Dependencies," *Journal of Computer and System Sciences*, Volume 28, Number 1 (January 1984), pages 29–59.

[Casey 1972] R. G. Casey, "Allocation of Copies of a File in an Information Network," *Proceedings of the Spring Joint Computer Conference* (1972), pages 617–625.

[Ceri and Owicki 1983] S. Ceri and S. Owicki, "On the Use of Optimistic Methods for Concurrency Control in Distributed Databases," *Proceedings of the Sixth Berkeley Workshop on Distributed Data Management and Computer Networks* (1983).

[Ceri and Pelagatti 1983] S. Ceri and G. Pelagatti, "Correctness of Query Execution Strategies in Distributed Databases," *ACM Transactions on Database Systems*, Volume 8, Number 4 (December 1983), pages 577–607.

[Ceri and Pelagatti 1984] S. Ceri and G. Pelagatti, *Distributed Databases: Principles and Systems*, McGraw-Hill, NY (1984).

[Ceri et al. 1983] S. Ceri, B. Navathe, and G. Wiederhold, "Distribution Design of Logical Database Schemas," *IEEE Transactions on Software Engineering*, Volume SE-9, Number 4 (July 1983), pages 487–503.

[Chakravarthy et al. 1990] V. S. Chakravarthy, J. Grant, and J. Minker, "Logic-Based Approach to Semantic Query Optimization," *ACM Transactions on Database Systems*, Volume 15, Number 2 (June 1990), pages 162–207.

[Chamberlin 1980] D. D. Chamberlin, "A Summary of User Experience with the SQL Data Sublanguage," *Proceedings of the International Conference on Very Large Data Bases* (1980), pages 181–203.

[Chamberlin and Boyce 1974] D. D. Chamberlin and R. F. Boyce, "SEQUEL: A Structured English Query Language," *Proceedings of the ACM SIGMOD Workshop on Data Description, Access, and Control* (1974), pages 249–264.

[Chamberlin et al. 1976] D. D. Chamberlin, M. M. Astrahan, K. P. Eswaran, P. P. Griffiths, R. A. Lorie, J. W. Mehl, P. Reisner, and B. W. Wade, "SEQUEL 2: A Unified Approach to Data Definition, Manipulation, and Control," *IBM Journal of Research and Development*, Volume 20, Number 6 (November 1976), pages 560–575.

[Chamberlin et al. 1978] D. D. Chamberlin, J. N. Gray, P. P. Griffiths, M. Mresse, I. L. Traiger, and B. W. Wade, "Data Base System Authorization," in **[DeMillo et al. 1978]**.

[Chamberlin et al. 1981] D. D. Chamberlin, M. M. Astrahan, M. W. Blasgen, J. N. Gray, W. F. King, B. G. Lindsay, R. A. Lorie, J. W. Mehl, T. G. Price, P. G. Selinger, M. Schkolnick, D. R. Slutz, I. L. Traiger, B. W. Wade, and R. A. Yost, "A History and Evaluation of System R," *Communications of the ACM*, Volume 24, Number 10 (October 1981), pages 632–646.

[Chandra and Harel 1982] A. K. Chandra and D. Harel, "Structure and Complexity of Relational Queries," *Journal of Computer and System Sciences*, Volume 15, Number (January 1982), pages 99–128.

[Chandy and Misra 1982] K. M. Chandy and J. Misra, "A Distributed Algorithm for Detecting Resource Deadlocks in Distributed Systems," *Proceedings of the ACM SIGACT-SIGOPS Symposium on the Principles of Distributed Computing* (1982), pages 157–164.

[Chandy et al. 1975] K. M. Chandy, J. C. Browne, C. W. Dissley, and W. R. Uhrig, "Analytic Models for Rollback and Recovery Strategies in Database

Systems," *IEEE Transactions on Software Engineering*, Volume SE-1, Number 1 (March 1975), pages 100−110.

[Chandy et al. 1983] K. M. Chandy, L. M. Haas, and J. Misra, " Distributed Deadlock Detection," *ACM Transactions on Computer Systems*, Volume 1, Number 2 (May 1983), pages 144−156.

[Chang and Cheng 1980] S. K. Chang and W. H. Cheng, "A Methodology for Structured Database Decomposition," *IEEE Transactions on Software Engineering*, Volume SE-6, Number 2 (March 1980), pages 205−218.

[Chen 1976] P. P. Chen, "The Entity-Relationship Model: Toward a Unified View of Data," *ACM Transactions on Database Systems*, Volume 1, Number 1 (January 1976), pages 9−36.

[Chen 1977] P. P. Chen, *The Entity-Relationship Approach to Logical Data Base Design*, QED Information Sciences, Data Base Monograph Series, Number 6 (1977).

[Chen and Akoka 1980] P. P. Chen and J. Akoka, "Optimal Design of Distributed Information Systems," *IEEE Transactions on Computers*, Volume C-29, Number 12 (December 1980), pages 1068−1079.

[Cheung 1982] T. Y. Cheung, "A Method for Equijoin Queries in Distributed Relational Databases," *IEEE Transactions on Computers*, Volume C-31, Number 8 (August 1982), pages 746−751.

[Chin 1978] F. Y. Chin, "Security in Statistical Databases for Queries with Small Counts," *ACM Transactions on Database Systems*, Volume 3, Number 1 (January 1978), pages 92−104.

[Chin and Ozsoyoglu 1981] F. Y. Chin and G. Ozsoyoglu, "Statistical Database Design," *ACM Transactions on Database Design*, Volume 6, Number 1 (January 1981), pages 113−139.

[Chiu and Ho 1980] D. M. Chiu and Y. C. Ho, "A Methodology for Interpreting Tree Queries into Optimal Semi-join Expressions," *Proceedings of the ACM SIGMOD International Conference on the Management of Data* (1980), pages 169−178.

[Christodoulakis and Faloutsos 1986] S. Christodoulakis and C. Faloutsos, "Design and Performance Considerations for an Optical Disk-Based Multimedia Object Server," *IEEE Computer*, Volume 19, Number 12 (December 1986), pages 45−56.

[Chu 1969] W. W. Chu, "Optimal File Allocation in a Multiple Computer System," *IEEE Transactions on Computers*, Volume C-18, Number 10 (October 1969), pages 885−889.

[Chu and Hurley 1982] W. W. Chu and P. Hurley, "Optimal Query Processing for Distributed Database Systems," *IEEE Transactions on Computers*, Volume C-31, Number 9 (September 1982), pages 835–850.

[Cincom 1974] *Total/7* Publications: *Application Programming Reference Manual*, PO2–1321–2, *Data Base Administration Reference Manual*, PO2–1322–2, Cincom Systems, Inc., Cincinnati, OH (1974).

[Cincom 1978] *OS TOTAL Reference Manual*, Cincom Systems, Inc., Cincinnati, OH (1978).

[Clemons 1978] E. K. Clemons, "An External Schema Facility to Support Data Base Update," in **[Schneiderman 1978]**, pages 371–398.

[Clemons 1979] E. K. Clemons, "An External Schema Facility for CODASYL 1978," *Proceedings of the International Conference on Very Large Data Bases* (1979), pages 119–128.

[Clifford and Tansel 1985] J. Clifford and A. Tansel, "On an Algebra for Historical Relational Databases: Two Views," *Proceedings of the ACM SIGMOD International Conference on Management of Data* (1985), pages 247–267.

[Cluet et al. 1989] S. Cluet, C. Delobel, C. Lecluse, and P. Richard, "Reloop: An Algebra-Based Query Language for an Object-Oriented Database System," *Proceedings of the International Conference on Deductive and Object-Oriented Databases* (December 1989).

[CODASYL 1971] "CODASYL Data Base Task Group April 71 Report," ACM, New York, NY (1971).

[CODASYL 1978] *CODASYL Data Description Language Journal of Development*, Material Data Management Branch, Department of Supply and Services, Ottawa, Ontario (1978).

[Codd 1970] E. F. Codd, "A Relational Model for Large Shared Data Banks," *Communications of the ACM*, Volume 13, Number 6 (June 1970), pages 377–387.

[Codd 1972a] E. F. Codd, "Further Normalization of the Data Base Relational Model," in **[Rustin 1972]**, pages 33–64.

[Codd 1972b] E. F. Codd, "Relational Completeness of Data Base Sublanguages," in **[Rustin 1972]**, pages 65–98.

[Codd 1979] E. F. Codd, "Extending the Database Relational Model to Capture More Meaning," *ACM Transactions on Database Systems*, Volume 4, Number 4 (December 1979), pages 397–434.

[Codd 1982] E. F. Codd, "The 1981 ACM Turing Award Lecture: Relational Database: A Practical Foundation for Productivity," *Communications of the ACM*, Volume 25, Number 2 (February 1982), pages 109–117.

[Codd 1990] E. F. Codd, *The Relational Model for Database Management: Version 2*, Addison-Wesley, Reading, MA (1990).

[Colby 1989] L. Colby, "A Recursive Algebra and Query Optimization for Nested Relations," *Proceedings of the ACM SIGMOD International Conference on Management of Data* (1989), pages 273–283.

[Comer 1979] D. Comer, "The Ubiquitous B-tree," *ACM Computing Surveys*, Volume 11, Number 2 (June 1979), pages 121–137.

[Cosmadakis and Papadimitriou 1984] S. S. Cosmadakis and C. H. Papadimitriou, "Updates of Relational Views," *Journal of the ACM*, Volume 31, Number 4 (October 1984), pages 742–760.

[Cosmadakis et al. 1990] S. Cosmadakis, P. Kanellakis, and M. Vardi, "Polynomial-Time Implication Problems for Unary Inclusion Dependencies," *Journal of the ACM*, Volume 37, Number 1 (January 1990), pages 15–46.

[Cox 1986] B. J. Cox, *Object-Oriented Programming: An Evolutionary Approach*, Addison-Wesley, Reading, MA (1986).

[Cullinane 1975] Cullinane Corporation, *Integrated Database Management System (IDMS)*, Cullinane Corporation, Wellesley, MA (1975).

[Cullinet 1983a] Cullinet Software Inc., *IDMS Sequential Processing Facility*, Order Number TDDB-0801–57P0, Cullinet Software Inc., Westwood, MA (1983).

[Cullinet 1983b] Cullinet Software Inc., *IDMS Programmer's Reference Guide*, Order Number TDDB-0321–5710, Cullinet Software Inc., Westwood, MA (1983).

[Dadam et al. 1986] P. Dadam, R. Kuespert, F. Andersen, H. Blanken, R. Erbe, J. Guenauer, V. Lum, P. Pistor, and G. Walsh, "A DBMS Prototype to Support Extended NF2 Relations: An Integrated View on Flat Tables and Hierarchies," *Proceedings of the ACM SIGMOD International Conference on Management of Data* (1986), pages 356–366.

[Dahl and Bubenko 1982] R. Dahl and J. Bubenko, "IDBD: An Interactive Design Tool for CODASYL DBTG Type Databases," *Proceedings of the International Conference on Very Large Data Bases* (1982), pages 108–121.

[Daniels et al. 1982] D. Daniels, P. G. Selinger, L. M. Haas, B. G. Lindsay, C. Mohan, A. Walker, and P. F. Wilms, "An Introduction to Distributed Query Compilation in R*," in **[Schneider 1982]**.

[Date 1983] C. J. Date, *An Introduction to Database Systems*, Volume II, Addison-Wesley, Reading, MA (1983).

[Date 1984] C. J. Date, "A Critique of the SQL Database Language," *ACM SIGMOD Record*, Volume 14, Number 3 (November 1984), pages 8–54.

[Date 1986] C. J. Date, *Relational Databases: Selected Writings*, Addison-Wesley, Reading, MA (1986).

[Date 1987] C. J. Date, *A Guide to Ingres*, Addison-Wesley, Reading, MA (1987).

[Date 1989] C. J. Date, *A Guide to the SQL Standard*, Second Edition, Addison-Wesley, Reading, MA (1989).

[Date 1990a] C. J. Date, *An Introduction to Database Systems*, Volume I, Fifth Edition, Addison-Wesley, Reading, MA (1990).

[Date 1990b] C. J. Date, *Relational Database Writings, 1985-1989*, Addison-Wesley, Reading, MA (1990).

[Date and White 1988] C. J. Date and C. J. White, *A Guide to DB2*, Second Edition, Addison-Wesley, Reading, MA (1988).

[Date and White 1989] C. J. Date and C. J. White, *A Guide to SQL/DS*, Addison-Wesley, Reading, MA (1989).

[Davies 1973] C. T. Davies, Jr., "Recovery Semantics for a DB/DC System," *Proceedings of the ACM Annual Conference* (1973), pages 136−141.

[Davies 1980] D. W. Davies, "Protection," in *Distributed Systems: An Advanced Course*, Springer-Verlag, Berlin, Germany (1980), pages 211−245.

[Davies et al. 1979] D. W. Davies, D. L. A. Barber, W. L. Price, and C. M. Solomoides, *Computer Networks and Their Protocols*, John Wiley and Sons, New York, NY (1979).

[Davis et al. 1983] C. Davis, S. Jajodia, P. A. Ng, and R. Yeh (Editors), *Entity-Relationship Approach to Software Engineering*, North Holland, Amsterdam, The Netherlands (1983).

[Dayal and Bernstein 1978] U. Dayal and P. A. Bernstein, "The Updatability of Relational Views," *Proceedings of the International Conference on Very Large Data Bases* (1978), pages 368−377.

[Dayal and Bernstein 1982] U. Dayal and P. A. Bernstein, "On the Correct Translation of Update Operations on Relational Views," *ACM Transactions on Database Systems*, Volume 3, Number 3 (September 1982), pages 381−416.

[Dayal et al. 1990] U. Dayal, M. Hsu, and R. Ladin, "Organizing Long-Running Activities with Triggers and Transactions," *Proceedings of the ACM SIGMOD International Conference on the Management of Data* (1990), pages 204−215.

[Deheneffe et al. 1974] C. Deheneffe, H. Hennebert, and W. Paulus, "Relational Model for a Data Base," *Proceedings of the IFIP Conference* (1974), pages 1022−1025.

[Delobel and Litwin 1980] C. Delobel and W. Litwin, (Editors), "Distributed Data Bases," *Proceedings of the International Symposium on Distributed Databases*, North Holland, Amsterdam, The Netherlands (1980).

[DeMillo et al. 1978] R. A. DeMillo, D. P. Dobkin, A. K. Jones, and R. J. Lipton, *Foundations of Secure Computation*, Academic Press, New York, NY (1978).

[Denning 1980] D. E. Denning, "Secure Statistical Databases with Random Sample Queries," *ACM Transactions on Database Systems*, Volume 5, Number 3 (September 1980), pages 291−315.

[Denning 1982] P. J. Denning, *Cryptography and Data Security*, Addison-Wesley, Reading, MA (1982).

[Denning and Denning 1979] D. E. Denning and P. J. Denning, "Data Security," *ACM Computing Surveys*, Volume 11, Number 3 (September 1979), pages 227−250.

[Deshpande and Larson 1987] A. Deshpande and P. Larson, "An Algebra for Nested Relations," Research Report CS-87-65, Department of Computer Science, University of Waterloo, Ontario, Canada (1987).

[Deshpande and Van Gucht 1987] A. Deshpande and D. Van Gucht, "A Storage Structure for Unnormalized Relations," *Proceedings of the GI Conference on Database Systems for Office Automation, Engineering and Scientific Applications*, Darmstadt (1987), pages 481−486.

[Deshpande and Van Gucht 1988] A. Deshpande and D. Van Gucht, "An Implementation for Nested Relational Databases," *Proceedings of the International Conference on Very Large Data Bases* (1988).

[Deshpande and Van Gucht 1989] A. Deshpande and D. Van Gucht, "A Storage Structure for Nested Relational Databases," in **[Abiteboul et al. 1989]**, pages 69−84.

[DeWitt et al. 1984] D. DeWitt, R. Katz, F. Olken, L. Shapiro, M. Stonebraker, and D. Wood, "Implementation Techniques for Main Memory Databases," *Proceedings of the ACM SIGMOD International Conference on Management of Data* (1984), pages 1−8.

[Di Battista and Lenzerini 1989] G. Di Battista and M. Lenzerini "A Deductive Method for Entity-Relationship Modeling," *Proceedings of the International Conference on Very Large Data Bases* (1989), pages 13−22.

[Diffie and Hellman 1979] W. Diffie and M. E. Hellman, "Privacy and Authentication," *Proceedings of the IEEE*, Volume 67, Number 3 (March 1979), pages 397−427.

[Dijkstra 1965] E. W. Dijkstra, "Cooperating Sequential Processes," Technical Report EWD-123, Technological University, Eindhoven, The Netherlands (1965); *reprinted in* **[Genuys 1968]**, pages 43−112.

[Dittrich 1988] K. Dittrich (Editor), *Advances in Object-Oriented Database Systems*, Lecture Notes in Computer Science 334, Springer-Verlag (1988).

[Dobkin et al. 1979] D. Dobkin, A. K. Jones, and R. J. Lipton, "Secure Databases: Protection Against User Inference," *ACM Transactions on Database Systems*, Volume 4, Number 1 (March 1979), pages 97−106.

[Dodd 1969] G. G. Dodd, "APL-A Language for Associative Data Handling in PL/I," *Proceedings of the Fall Joint Computer Conference* (1969), pages 667−684.

[Dos Santos et al. 1979] C. Dos Santos, E. Neuhold, and A. Furtado, "A Data Type Approach to the Entity-Relationship Model," *Proceedings of the International Conference on Entity-Relationship Approach* (1979).

[Dowdy and Foster 1982] L. W. Dowdy and D. V. Foster, "Comparative Models of the File Assignment Problem," *ACM Computing Surveys*, Volume 14, Number 2 (June 1982), pages 287−314.

[Draffen and Poole 1980] I. W. Draffen and F. Poole (Editors), *Distributed Data Bases*, Cambridge University Press, Cambridge, England (1980).

[Du and Elmagarmid 1989] W. Du and A. Elmagarmid, "Quasi Serializability: A Correctness Criterion for Global Database Consistency in InterBase," *Proceedings of the International Conference on Very Large Data Bases* (1989), pages 347−356.

[ElAbbadi and Toueg 1988] A. ElAbbadi and S. Toueg, "The Group Paradigm for Concurrency Control," *Proceedings of the ACM SIGMOD International Conference on Management of Data* (1988), pages 126−134.

[ElMasri and Larson 1985] R. ElMasri and J. Larson, "A Graphical Query Facility for E-R Databases," *Proceedings of the International Conference on Entity-Relationship Approach* (1985).

[ElMasri and Wiederhold 1981] R. ElMasri and G. Wiederhold, "GORDAS: A Formal High-Level Query Language for the Entity-Relationship Model," *Proceedings of the International Conference on Entity-Relationship Approach* (1981).

[ElMasri and Navathe 1989] R. ElMasri and S. B. Navathe, *Fundamentals of Database Systems*, Benjamin Cummings, Redwood City, CA (1989).

[Ellis 1980a] C. S. Ellis, "Concurrent Search and Insertion in 2−3 Trees," *Acta Informatica*, Volume 14 (1980), pages 63−86.

[Ellis 1980b] C. S. Ellis, "Concurrent Search and Insertion in AVL Trees," *IEEE Transactions on Computers*, Volume C-29, Number 3 (September 1980), pages 811−817.

[Ellis 1987] C. S. Ellis, "Concurrency in Linear Hashing" *ACM Transactions on Database Systems*, Volume 12, Number 2 (June 1987), pages 195−217.

[Eppinger 1983] J. L. Eppinger, "An Empirical Study of Insertion and Deletion in Binary Search Trees," *Communications of the ACM*, Volume 26, Number 9 (September 1983), pages 663−669.

[Epstein and Stonebraker 1980] R. Epstein and M. R. Stonebraker, "Analysis of Distributed Database Processing Strategies," *Proceedings of the International Conference on Very Large Data Bases* (1980), pages 92−110.

[Epstein et al. 1978] R. Epstein, M. R. Stonebraker, and E. Wong, "Distributed Query Processing in a Relational Database System," *Proceedings of the ACM SIGMOD International Conference on Management of Data* (1978), pages 169−180.

[Eswaran 1974] K. P. Eswaran, "Placement of Records in a File and File Allocation in a Computer Network," *Proceedings of the IFIP Congress* (1974), pages 304−307.

[Eswaran and Chamberlin 1975] K. P. Eswaran and D. D. Chamberlin, "Functional Specifications of a Subsystem for Database Integrity," *Proceedings of the International Conference on Very Large Data Bases* (1975), pages 48−68.

[Eswaran et al. 1976] K. P. Eswaran, J. N. Gray, R. A. Lorie, and I. L. Traiger, "The Notions of Consistency and Predicate Locks in a Database System," *Communications of the ACM*, Volume 19, Number 11 (November 1976), pages 624−633.

[Everett et al. 1971] G. D. Everett, C. W. Dissly, and W. T. Hardgrave, *Remote File Management System (RFMS) Users Manual*, TRM-16, Computation Center, University of Texas at Austin, Austin, TX (1981).

[Fagin 1977] R. Fagin, "Multivalued Dependencies and a New Normal Form for Relational Databases," *ACM Transactions on Database Systems*, Volume 2, Number 3 (September 1977), pages 262−278.

[Fagin 1978] R. Fagin, "On an Authorization Mechanism," *ACM Transactions on Database Systems*, Volume 3, Number 3 (September 1978), pages 310−319.

[Fagin 1979] R. Fagin, "Normal Forms and Relational Database Operators," *Proceedings of the ACM SIGMOD International Conference on Management of Data* (1979), pages 153−160.

[Fagin 1981] R. Fagin, "A Normal Form for Relational Databases That Is Based on Domains and Keys," *ACM Transactions on Database Systems*, Volume 6, Number 3 (September 1981), pages 387−415.

[Fagin 1983] R. Fagin, "Types of Acyclicity of Hypergraphs and Relational Database Schemes," *Journal of the ACM*, Volume 30, Number 3 (July 1983), pages 514–550.

[Fagin et al. 1979] R. Fagin, J. Nievergelt, N. Pippenger, and H. R. Strong, "Extendible Hashing — A Fast Access Method for Dynamic Files," *ACM Transactions on Database Systems*, Volume 4, Number 3 (September 1979), pages 315–344.

[Fagin et al. 1982] R. Fagin, A. O. Mendelzon, and J. D. Ullman, "A Simplified Universal Relation Assumption and Its Properties," *ACM Transactions on Database Systems*, Volume 7, Number 3 (September 1982), pages 343–360.

[Fekete et al. 1987] A. Fekete, N. Lynch, M. Merritt, and W. Weihl, "Nested Transactions and Read/Write Locking," *Proceedings of the ACM SIGACT-SIGMOD Symposium on the Principles of Database Systems* (1987), pages 97–111.

[Fekete et al. 1990] A. Fekete, N. Lynch, and W. Weihl, "A Serialization Graph Construction for Nested Transactions," *Proceedings of the ACM SIGACT-SIGMOD-SIGART Symposium on the Principles of Database Systems* (1990), pages 94–108.

[Fernandez et al. 1981] E. Fernandez, R. Summers, and C. Wood, *Database Security and Integrity*, Addison-Wesley, Reading, MA (1981).

[Ferrier and Stangret 1982] A. Ferrier and C. Stangret, "Heterogeneity in the Distributed Database Management System SIRIUS-DELTA," *Proceedings of the International Conference on Very Large Data Bases* (1982), pages 45–53.

[Findler 1979] N. Findler (Editor), *Associative Networks*, Academic Press, New York, NY (1979).

[Finkelstein 1982] S. Finkelstein, "Common Expression Analysis in Database Applications," *Proceedings of the ACM SIGMOD International Conference on Management of Data* (1982), pages 235–245.

[Finkelstein et al. 1988] S. Finkelstein, M. Schkolnick, and P. Tiberio, "Physical Database Design for Relational Databases," *ACM Transactions on Database Systems*, Volume 13, Number 1 (March 1988), pages 53–90.

[Fischer and Thomas 1983] P. C. Fischer and S. Thomas, "Operators for Non-First-Normal-Form Relations," *Proceedings of the International Computer Software Applications Conference* (1983), pages 464–475.

[Fisher and Hochbaum 1980] M. L. Fisher and D. S. Hochbaum, "Database Location in Computer Networks," *Journal of the ACM*, Volume 27, Number 4 (October 1980), pages 718–735.

[Fishman et al. 1990] D. Fishman, D. Beech, H. Cate, E. Chow, T. Connors, J. Davis, N. Derrett, C. Hoch, W. Kent, P. Lyngbaek, B. Mahbod, M. Neimat,

T. Ryan, and M. Shan, "IRIS: An Object-Oriented Database Management System," in **[Zdonik and Maier 1990]**, pages 216−226.

[Ford and Calhoun 1984] R. Ford and J. Calhoun, "Concurrency Control Mechanism and the Serializability of Concurrent Tree Algorithms," *Proceedings of the ACM SIGACT-SIGMOD Symposium on the Principles of Database Systems* (1984), pages 51−60.

[Fredkin 1960] E. Fredkin, "Trie Memory," *Communications of the ACM*, Volume 4, Number 2 (September 1960), pages 490−499.

[Fry and Sibley 1976] J. Fry and E. Sibley, "Evolution of Data-Base Management Systems," *ACM Computing Surveys*, Volume 8, Number 1 (March 1976), pages 7−42.

[Furtado 1978] A. L. Furtado, "Formal Aspects of the Relational Model," *Information Systems*, Volume 3, Number 2 (1978), pages 131−140.

[Fussell et al. 1981] D. S. Fussell, Z. Kedem, and A. Silberschatz, "Deadlock Removal Using Partial Rollback in Database Systems," *Proceedings of the ACM SIGMOD International Conference on the Management of Data* (1981), pages 65−73.

[Gadia 1986] S. K. Gadia, "Weak Temporal Relations," *Proceedings of the ACM SIGACT-SIGMOD Symposium on the Principles of Database Systems* (1986), pages 70−77.

[Gadia 1988] S. K. Gadia, "A Homogeneous Relational Model and Query Language for Temporal Databases," *ACM Transactions on Database Systems*, Volume 13, Number 4 (December 1988), pages 418−448.

[Gallaire and Minker 1978] H. Gallaire and J. Minker (Editors), *Logic and Databases*, Plenum Press, New York, NY (1978).

[Gallaire et al. 1984] H. Gallaire, J. Minker, and J. M. Nicolas, "Logic and Databases: A Deductive Approach," *ACM Computing Surveys*, Volume 16, Number 2 (June 1984), pages 154−185.

[Ganguly et al. 1990] S. Ganguly, A. Silberschatz, and S. Tsur, "A Framework for the Parallel Processing of Datalog Queries," *Proceedings of the ACM SIGMOD International Conference on Management of Data* (1990), pages 143−152.

[Garcia-Molina 1978] H. Garcia-Molina, "Performance Comparison of Two Update Algorithms for Distributed Databases," *Proceedings of the Berkeley Workshop on Distributed Data Management and Computer Networks* (1978), pages 108−119.

[Garcia-Molina 1982] H. Garcia-Molina, "Elections in Distributed Computing Systems," *IEEE Transactions on Computers*, Volume C-31, Number 1 (January 1982), pages 48−59.

[Garcia-Molina 1983] H. Garcia-Molina, "Using Semantic Knowledge for Transaction Processing in a Distributed Database," *ACM Transactions on Database Systems*, Volume 8, Number 2 (June 1983), pages 186−213.

[Garcia-Molina and Wiederhold 1982] H. Garcia-Molina and G. Wiederhold, "Read-only Transactions in a Distributed Database," *ACM Transactions on Database Systems*, Volume 7, Number 2 (June 1982), pages 209−234.

[Gardarin and Valduriez 1989] G. Gardarin and P. Valduriez, *Relational Databases and Knowledge Bases*, Addison-Wesley, Reading, MA (1989).

[Garey and Johnson 1979] M. R. Garey and D. S. Johnson, *Computers and Intractability: A Guide to the Theory of NP-Completeness*, Freeman, New York, NY (1979).

[Garza and Kim 1988] J. Garza and W. Kim, "Transaction Management in an Object-Oriented Database System," *Proceedings of the ACM SIGMOD International Conference on the Management of Data* (1988), pages 37−45.

[Gelembe and Sevcik 1978] E. Gelembe and R. Sevcik, "Analysis of Update Synchronization for Multiple Copy Data Bases," *Proceedings of the Berkeley Workshop on Distributed Data Management and Computer Networks* (1978), pages 69−90.

[Genuys 1968] F. Genuys (Editor), *Programming Languages*, Academic Press, London, England (1968).

[Gerritsen 1975] R. Gerritsen, "A Preliminary System for the Design of DBTG Data Structures," *Communications of the ACM*, Volume 18, Number 10 (October 1975) pages 551−557.

[Gifford 1979] D. K. Gifford, "Weighted Voting for Replicated Data," *Proceedings of the ACM SIGOPS Symposium on Operating Systems Principles* (1979), pages 150−162.

[Gligor and Shattuck 1980] V. D. Gligor and S. H. Shattuck, "On Deadlock Detection in Distributed Systems," *IEEE Transactions on Software Engineering*, Volume SE-6, Number 5 (September 1980), pages 435−439.

[Goldberg and Robson 1983] A. Goldberg and D. Robson, *Smalltalk-80: The Language and Its Implementation*, Addison-Wesley, Reading, MA (1983).

[Gotlieb 1975] L. R. Gotlieb, "Computing Joins of Relations," *Proceedings of the ACM SIGMOD International Conference on the Management of Data* (1975), pages 55−63.

[Graham et al. 1986] M. H. Graham, A. O. Mendelzon, and M. Y. Vardi, "Notions of Dependency Satisfaction," *Journal of the ACM*, Volume 33, Number 1 (January 1986), pages 105−129.

[Gray 1978] J. N. Gray, "Notes on Data Base Operating System," in **[Bayer et al. 1978]**, pages 393−481.

[Gray 1981] J. N. Gray, "The Transaction Concept: Virtues and Limitations," *Proceedings of the International Conference on Very Large Data Bases* (1981), pages 144−154.

[Gray et al. 1975] J. N. Gray, R. A. Lorie, and G. R. Putzolu, "Granularity of Locks and Degrees of Consistency in a Shared Data Base," *Proceedings of the International Conference on Very Large Data Bases* (1975), pages 428−451.

[Gray et al. 1976] J. N. Gray, R. A. Lorie, G. R. Putzolu, and I. L. Traiger, "Granularity of Locks and Degrees of Consistency in a Shared Data Base," in **[Nijssen 1976]**, pages 365−395.

[Gray et al. 1981a] J. N. Gray, P. R. McJones, and M. Blasgen, "The Recovery Manager of the System R Database Manager," *ACM Computing Surveys*, Volume 13, Number 2 (June 1981), pages 223−242.

[Gray et al. 1981b] J. N. Gray, P. Homan, H. F. Korth, and R. Obermarck, "A Straw Man Analysis of the Probability of Waiting and Deadlock," Research Report RJ3066, IBM Research Laboratory, San Jose, CA (1981).

[Gray et al. 1990] J. N. Gray, B. Horst, and M. Walker, "Parity Striping of Disc Arrays: Low-Cost Reliable Storage with Acceptable Throughput," *Proceedings of the International Conference on Very Large Data Bases* (1990), pages 148−161.

[Griffiths and Wade 1976] P. P. Griffiths and B. W. Wade, "An Authorization Mechanism for a Relational Database System," *ACM Transactions on Database Systems*, Volume 1, Number 3 (September 1976), pages 242−255.

[Haas et al. 1989] L. M. Haas, J. C. Freytag, G. M. Lohman, and H. Pirahesh, "Extensible Query Processing in Starburst," *Proceedings of the ACM SIGMOD International Conference on Management of Data* (1989), pages 377−388.

[Haerder and Reuter 1983] T. Haerder and A. Reuter, "Principles of Transaction-Oriented Database Recovery," *ACM Computing Surveys*, Volume 15, Number 4 (December 1983), pages 287−318.

[Haerder and Rothermel 1987] T. Haerder and K. Rothermel, "Concepts for Transaction Recovery in Nested Transactions," *Proceedings of the ACM SIG-MOD International Conference on Management of Data* (1987), pages 239−248.

[Hailpern and Korth 1983] B. T. Hailpern and H. F. Korth, "An Experimental Distributed Database System," *Proceedings of the ACM SIGMOD-SIGBDB Database Week* (1983).

[Hainaut and Lecharlier 1974] J. L. Hainaut and B. Lecharlier, "An Extensible Semantic Model of Data Base and Its Data language," *Proceedings of the IFIP Conference* (1974), pages 1026–1030.

[Hall 1976] P. A. V. Hall, "Optimization of a Single Relational Expression in a Relational Database System," *IBM Journal of Research and Development*, Volume 20, Number 3 (1976), pages 244–257.

[Hammer and McLeod 1975] M. Hammer and D. McLeod, "Semantic Integrity in a Relational Data Base System," *Proceedings of the International Conference on Very Large Data Bases* (1975), pages 25–47.

[Hammer and McLeod 1981] M. Hammer and D. McLeod, "Database Description with SDM: A Semantic Data Model," *ACM Transactions on Database Systems*, Volume 6, Number 3 (September 1980), pages 351–386.

[Hammer and Sarin 1978] M. Hammer and S. Sarin, "Efficient Monitoring of Database Assertions," *Proceedings of the ACM SIGMOD International Conference on Management of Data* (1978).

[Haskin and Lorie 1982] R. Haskin and R. A. Lorie, "On Extending the Functions of a Relational Database System," *Proceedings of the ACM SIGMOD International Conference on the Management of Data* (1982), pages 207–212.

[Haskin et al. 1988] R. Haskin, Y. Malachi, W. Sawdon, and G. Chan, "Recovery Management in Quicksilver," *ACM Transactions on Computer Systems*, Volume 6, Number 1 (January 1988), pages 82–108.

[Hayes 1977] P. J. Hayes, "On Semantic Nets, Frames, and Associations," *Proceedings of the International Joint Conference on Artificial Intelligence* (1977), pages 99–107.

[Held and Stonebraker 1978] G. Held and M. Stonebraker, "B-trees Reexamined," *Communications of the ACM*, Volume 21, Number 2 (February 1978), pages 139–143.

[Henderson et al. 1983] P. B. Henderson, E. Sciore, and D. S. Warren, "A Relational Model of Operating System Environments," *Proceedings of the DEC Workshop* (1983).

[Hendrix 1977] G. G. Hendrix, "Some General Comments on Semantic Networks," *Proceedings of the International Joint Conference on Artificial Intelligence* (1977), pages 984–985.

[Hevner and Yao 1979] A. R. Hevner and S. B. Yao, "Query Processing in Distributed Database Systems," *IEEE Transactions on Software Engineering*, Volume SE-5, Number 3 (May 1979), pages 177–187.

[Hinrichs 1985] K. H. Hinrichs, "The Grid File System: Implementation and Case Studies of Applications," Ph.D. thesis, Swiss Federal Institute of Technology, Zurich, Switzerland (1985).

[Holt 1971] R. C. Holt, "Comments on Prevention of System Deadlocks," *Communications of the ACM*, Volume 14, Number 1 (January 1971), pages 36–38.

[Holt 1972] R. C. Holt, "Some Deadlock Properties of Computer Systems," *ACM Computing Surveys*, Volume 4, Number 3 (September 1972), pages 179–196.

[Honeywell 1975] "Integrated Data Store/II: Database Administrator's Guide," Honeywell Information Systems, Waltham, MA (1975).

[Horowitz and Sahni 1976] E. Horowitz and S. Sahni, *Fundamentals of Data Structures*, Computer Science Press, Rockville, MD (1976).

[Hsu and Imielinsky 1985] A. Hsu and T. Imielinsky, "Integrity Checking for Multiple Updates," *Proceedings of the ACM SIGMOD International Conference on Management of Data* (1985), pages 152–168.

[Hudson and King 1987] S. E. Hudson and R. King, "Object-Oriented Database Support for Software Environments," *Proceedings of the ACM SIGMOD International Conference on the Management of Data* (1987), pages 491–503.

[Hudson and King 1989] S. E. Hudson and R. King, "Cactis: A Self-Adaptive, Concurrent Implementation of an Object-Oriented Database Management System," *ACM Transactions on Database Systems*, Volume 14, Number 3 (September 1989), pages 291–321.

[Hull and King 1987] R. Hull and R. King, "Semantic Database Modeling: Survey, Applications and Research Issues," *ACM Computing Surveys*, Volume 19, Number 3 (September 1987), pages 201–260.

[IBM 1978a] IBM Corporation, *Information Management System/Virtual Storage General Information*, IBM Form Number GH20–1260, SH20–9025, SH20–9026, SH20–9027.

[IBM 1978b] IBM Corporation, *Query-by Example Terminal Users Guide*, IBM Form Number SH20–20780 (1978).

[IBM 1982] IBM Corporation, *SQL/Data System Terminal Users Guide*, IBM Form Number SH24–5017–1 (1982).

[IBM 1987] IBM Corporation, *Systems Application Architecture: Common Programming Interface, Database Reference*, IBM Form Number SC26–4348–0 (1987).

[IBM 1988] IBM Corporation, *SQL/Data System: Interactive SQL User's Reference for VSE*, IBM Form Number SH09–8035–01 (1988).

[Jaeschke and Schek 1982] G. Jaeschke and H. J. Schek, "Remarks on the Algebra of Non First Normal Form Relations," *Proceedings of the ACM SIGACT-SIGMOD Symposium on Principles of Database Systems* (1982), pages 124–138.

[Jajodia and Mutchler 1987] S. Jajodia and D. Mutchler, "Dynamic Voting," *Proceedings of the ACM SIGMOD International Conference on Management of Data* (1987), pages 227–238.

[Jajodia and Mutchler 1990] S. Jajodia and D. Mutchler, "Dynamic Voting Algorithms for Maintaining the Consistency of a Replicated Database," *ACM Transactions on Database Systems*, Volume 15, Number 2 (June 1990), pages 230–280.

[Jajodia and Sandhu 1990] S. Jajodia and R. Sandhu, "Polyinstantiation Integrity in Multilevel Relations," *Proceedings of the IEEE Symposium on Research in Security and Privacy* (1990), pages 104–115.

[Jardine 1977] D. A. Jardine (Editor), *The ANSI/SPARC DBMS Model*, North Holland, Amsterdam, The Netherlands (1977).

[Jarke and Koch 1984] M. Jarke and J. Koch, "Query Optimization in Database Systems," *ACM Computing Surveys*, Volume 16, Number 2 (June 1984), pages 111–152.

[Kaiser 1990] G. Kaiser, "A Flexible Transaction Model for Software Engineering," *Proceedings of the International Conference on Data Engineering* (1990).

[Kam and Ullman 1977] J. B. Kam and J. D. Ullman, "A Model of Statistical Databases and Their Security," *ACM Transactions on Database Systems*, Volume 2, Number 1 (January 1977), pages 1–10.

[Kambayashi et al. 1982] Y. Kambayashi, M. Yoshikawa, and S. Yajima, "Query Processing for Distributed Databases Using Generalized Semi-joins," *Proceedings of the ACM SIGMOD International Conference on the Management of Data* (1982), pages 151–160.

[Kanellakis and Preparata 1986] P. C. Kanellakis and F. P. Preparata, (Editors), *Advances in Computing Research — The Theory of Databases*, Jai Press Inc., London, England (1986).

[Kapp and Leben 1978] D. Kapp and J. Leben, *IMS Programming Techniques*, Van Nostrand Reinhold, New York, NY (1978).

[Katz and Weiss 1984] R. Katz and S. Weiss, "Design Transaction Management," *Proceedings of the Design Automation Conference* (1984).

[Katz and Wong 1982] R. H. Katz and E. Wong, "Decompiling CODASYL DML into Relational Queries," *ACM Transactions on Database Systems*, Volume 7, Number 1 (March 1982), pages 1–23.

[Kedem and Silberschatz 1979] Z. M. Kedem and A. Silberschatz, "Controlling Concurrency Using Locking Protocols," *Proceedings of the Annual IEEE Symposium on Foundations of Computer Science* (1979), pages 275–285.

[Kedem and Silberschatz 1983] Z. M. Kedem and A. Silberschatz, "Locking Protocols: From Exclusive to Shared Locks," *Journal of the ACM*, Volume 30, Number 4 (October 1983), pages 787−804.

[Keller 1982] A. M. Keller, "Updates to Relational Database Through Views Involving Joins," in **[Scheuermann 1982]**, pages 363−384.

[Keller 1985] A. M. Keller, "Updating Relational Databases Through Views," Ph.D. thesis, Department of Computer Science, Stanford University, Stanford, CA (1985).

[Kerschberg et al. 1976] L. Kerschberg, A. Klug, and D. C. Tsichritzis, "A Taxonomy of Data Models," in **[Lockemann and Neuhold 1976]**, pages 43−64.

[Kerschberg et al. 1982] L. Kerschberg, P. D. Ting, and S. B. Yao, "Query Optimization in Star Computer Networks," *ACM Transactions on Database Systems*, Volume 7, Number 4 (December 1982), pages 678−711.

[Khoshafian and Copeland 1990] S. Khoshafian and G. P. Copeland, "Object Identity," in **[Zdonik and Maier 1990]**, pages 37−46.

[Kim 1982] W. Kim, "On Optimizing an SQL-like Nested Query" *ACM Transactions on Database Systems*, Volume 3, Number 3 (September 1982), pages 443−469.

[Kim 1984] W. Kim, "Query Optimization for Relational Database Systems," in **[Unger et al. 1984]**.

[Kim 1989] W. Kim, "A Model of Queries for Object-Oriented Databases," *Proceedings of the International Conference on Very Large Data Bases* (1989).

[Kim 1990a] W. Kim, "Architectural Issues in Object-Oriented Databases," *Journal of Object-Oriented Programming* (March/April 1990).

[Kim 1990b] W. Kim, *Introduction to Object-Oriented Databases*, MIT Press, Cambridge, MA (1990).

[Kim 1990c] W. Kim, "Object-Oriented Databases: Definition and Research Directions," *IEEE Transactions on Knowledge and Data Engineering* (June 1990).

[Kim 1990d] W. Kim, "Research Directions in Object-Oriented Databases," *Proceedings of the ACM SIGACT-SIGMOD-SIGART Symposium on Principles of Database Systems* (1990), pages 1−15.

[Kim and Lochovsky 1989] W. Kim and F. Lochovsky (Editors), *Object-Oriented Concepts, Databases, and Applications*, Addison-Wesley, Reading, MA (1989).

[Kim et al. 1984] W. Kim, R. Lorie, D. McNabb, and W. Plouffe, "Transaction Mechanism for Engineering Design Databases," *Proceedings of the International Conference on Very Large Data Bases*, (August 1984), pages 355-362.

[Kim et al. 1985] W. Kim, D. S. Reiner, and D. S. Batory (Editors), *Query Processing in Database Systems*, Springer-Verlag, Berlin, Germany (1985).

[Kim et al. 1988a] H. J. Kim, H. F. Korth, and A. Silberschatz, "PICASSO: A Graphical Query Language," *Software−Practice and Experience*, Volume 18, Number 3 (March 1988), pages 169−203.

[Kim et al. 1988b] W. Kim, N. Ballou, J. Banerjee, H. T. Chou, J. F. Garza, and D. Woelk, "Integrating an Object-Oriented Programming System with a Database System," *Proceedings of the International Conference on Object-Oriented Programming Systems, Languages, and Applications* (1988).

[Kim et al. 1989] W. Kim, K. C. Kim, and A. Dale, "Indexing Techniques for Object-Oriented Databases," in [Kim and Lochovsky 1989], pages 371−394.

[King 1981] J. J. King, "QUIST: A System for Semantic Query Optimization in Relational Data Bases," *Proceedings of the International Conference on Very Large Data Bases* (1981), pages 510−517.

[King et al. 1983] R. P. King, H. F. Korth, and B. E. Willner, " Design of a Document Filing and Retrieval Service," *Proceedings of the ACM SIGMOD-SIGBDBD Database Week* (1983).

[Klimbie and Koffeman 1974] J. W. Klimbie and K. L. Koffeman (Editors), *Data Base Management*, North Holland, Amsterdam, The Netherlands (1974).

[Klug 1982] A. Klug, "Equivalence of Relational Algebra and Relational Calculus Query Languages Having Aggregate Functions," *Journal of the ACM*, Volume 29, Number 3 (July 1982), pages 699−717.

[Knapp 1987] E. Knapp, "Deadlock Detection in Distributed Databases," *ACM Computing Surveys*, Volume 19, Number 4 (December 1987).

[Knuth 1973] D. E. Knuth, *The Art of Computer Programming, Volume 3: Sorting and Searching*, Addison-Wesley, Reading, MA (1973).

[Kogan and Jajodia 1990] B. Kogan and S. Jajodia, "Concurrency Control in Multilevel-secure Databases Using Replicated Architecture," *Proceedings of the ACM SIGMOD International Conference on the Management of Data* (1990), pages 153−162.

[Kohler 1981] W. H. Kohler, "A Survey of Techniques for Synchronization and Recovery in Decentralized Computer Systems," *ACM Computing Surveys*, Volume 13, Number 2 (June 1981), pages 149−183.

[Korth 1981] H. F. Korth, "The Optimal Locking Problem in a Directed Acyclic Graph," Technical Report STAN-CS-81−847, Department of Computer Science, Stanford University, Stanford, CA (March 1981).

[Korth 1982] H. F. Korth, " Deadlock Freedom Using Edge Locks," *ACM Transactions on Database Systems*, Volume 7, Number 4 (December 1982), pages 632−652.

[Korth 1983] H. F. Korth, "Locking Primitives in a Database System," *Journal of the ACM*, Volume 30, Number 1 (January 1983), pages 55–79.

[Korth 1986] H. F. Korth, "Extending the Scope of Relational Languages," *IEEE Software*, Volume 3, Number 1 (January 1986), pages 19–28.

[Korth and Peltier 1990] H. F. Korth and X. Peltier, "Query Processing Issues in Knowledge Bases," *Proceedings of the Conference on Artificial Intelligence in Petroleum Exploration and Production* (1990).

[Korth and Roth 1989] H. F. Korth and M. A. Roth, "Query Languages for Nested Relational Databases," in **[Abiteboul et al. 1989]**, pages 190–204.

[Korth and Silberschatz 1985] H. F. Korth and A. Silberschatz, "ROSI: A User-Friendly Operating System Interface Based on the Relational Data Model," *Proceedings of the International Symposium on New Directions in Computing* (1985), pages 302–310.

[Korth and Speegle 1988] H. F. Korth and G. Speegle, "Formal Model of Correctness Without Serializability," *Proceedings of the ACM SIGMOD International Conference on Management of Data* (1988), pages 379–386.

[Korth and Speegle 1990] H. F. Korth and G. Speegle, "Long Duration Transactions in Software Design Projects," *Proceedings of the International Conference on Data Engineering* (1990), pages 568–575.

[Korth et al. 1984] H. F. Korth, G. M. Kuper, J. Feigenbaum, A. Van Gelder, and J. D. Ullman, "System/U: A Database System Based on the Universal Relation Assumption," *ACM Transactions on Database Systems*, Volume 9, Number 3 (September 1984), pages 331–347.

[Korth et al. 1988] H. F. Korth, W. Kim, and F. Bancilhon, "On Long Duration CAD Transactions," *Information Science*, Volume 46 (October 1988), pages 73–107.

[Korth et al. 1990a] H. F. Korth, E. Levy, and A. Silberschatz, "A Formal Approach to Recovery by Compensating Transactions," *Proceedings of the International Conference on Very Large Data Bases* (1990), pages 95–106.

[Korth et al. 1990b] H. F. Korth, N. Soparkar, and A. Silberschatz, "A Triggered Real-Time Databases with Consistency Constraints," *Proceedings of the International Conference on Very Large Data Bases* (1990), pages 71–82.

[Kroenke and Dolan 1988] D. Kroenke and K. Dolan, *Database Processing*, Third Edition, Science Research Associates, Chicago, IL (1988).

[Kumar and Stonebraker 1988] A. Kumar and M. Stonebraker, "Semantics Based Transaction Management Techniques for Replicated Data," *Proceedings of the ACM SIGMOD International Conference on Management of Data* (1988), pages 117–125.

[Kung and Lehman 1980] H. T. Kung and P. L. Lehman, "Concurrent Manipulation of Binary Search Trees," *ACM Transactions on Database Systems*, Volume 5, Number 3 (September 1980), pages 339−353.

[Kung and Robinson 1981] H. T. Kung and J. T. Robinson, " Optimistic Concurrency Control," *ACM Transactions on Database Systems*, Volume 6, Number 2 (June 1981), pages 312−326.

[Kwong and Wood 1982] Y. S. Kwong and D. Wood, "Method for Concurrency in B^+-trees," *IEEE Transactions on Software Engineering*, Volume SE-8, Number 3 (March 1982), pages 211−223.

[Lacriox and Pirotte 1977] M. Lacriox and A. Pirotte, "Domain-Oriented Relational Languages," *Proceedings of the International Conference on Very Large Data Bases* (1977).

[Lai and Wilkinson 1984] M. Y. Lai and W. K. Wilkinson "Distributed Transaction Management in JASMIN," *Proceedings of the International Conference on Very Large Data Bases* (1984), pages 466−472.

[Lamport 1978] L. Lamport, "Time, Clocks, and the Ordering of Events in a Distributed System," *Communications of the ACM*, Volume 21, Number 7 (July 1978), pages 558−565.

[Lampson and Sturgis 1976] B. Lampson and H. Sturgis "Crash Recovery in a Distributed Data Storage System," Technical Report, Computer Science Laboratory, Xerox, Palo Alto Research Center, Palo Alto, CA (1976).

[Langefors 1963] B. Langefors, "Some Approaches to the Theory of Information Systems," *BIT*, Volume 3 (1963), pages 229−254.

[Langefors 1977] B. Langefors, "Information Systems Theory," *Information Systems*, Volume 2 (1977), pages 207−219.

[Langefors 1980] B. Langefors, "Infological Models and Information User Views," *Information Systems*, Volume 5 (1980), pages 17−32.

[Langerak 1990] R. Langerak, "View Updates in Relational Databases with an Independent Scheme," *ACM Transactions on Database Systems*, Volume 15, Number 1 (March 1990), pages 40−66.

[Larson 1978] P. Larson, "Dynamic Hashing," *BIT*, 18 (1978).

[Larson 1982] P. Larson, "Performance Analysis of Linear Hashing with Partial Expansions," *ACM Transactions on Database Systems*, Volume 7, Number 4 (December 1982), pages 566−587.

[Larson 1988] P. Larson, "Linear Hashing with Separators — A Dynamic Hashing Scheme Achieving One-Access Retrieval," *ACM Transactions on Database Systems*, Volume 19, Number 3 (September 1988), pages 366−388.

[Lecluse et al. 1988] C. Lecluse, P. Richard, and F. Velez, "O2: An Object-Oriented Data Model," *Proceedings of the ACM International Conference on the Management of Data* (1988), pages 424−433.

[Leiss 1982a] E. Leiss, *Principles of Data Security*, Plenum Press, New York, NY (1982).

[Leiss 1982b] E. Leiss, "Randomizing, A Practical Method for Protecting Statistical Databases Against Compromise," *Proceedings of the International Conference on Very Large Data Bases* (1982), pages 189−196.

[Lehman and Yao 1981] P. L. Lehman and S. B. Yao, "Efficient Locking for Concurrent Operations on B-trees," *ACM Transactions on Database Systems*, Volume 6, Number 4 (December 1981), pages 650−670.

[Lempel 1979] A. Lempel, "Cryptography in Transition," *ACM Computing Surveys*, Volume 11, Number 4 (December 1979), pages 286−303.

[Lenzerini and Santucci 1983] M. Lenzerini and C. Santucci, "Cardinality Constraints in the Entity Relationship Model," in **[Davis et al. 1983]**.

[Levesque and Mylopoulos 1979] H. J. Levesque and J. Mylopoulos, "A Procedural Semantics for Semantic Networks," in **[Findler 1979]**, pages 93−120.

[Lien and Weinberger 1978] Y. E. Lien and P. J. Weinberger, "Consistency, Concurrency and Crash Recovery," *Proceedings of the ACM SIGMOD International Conference on Management of Data* (1978), pages 9−14.

[Lilien and Bhargava 1985] L. Lilien and B. Bhargava, "Database Integrity Block Construct: Concepts and Design Issues," *IEEE Transactions on Software Engineering*, Volume SE-11, Number 9 (September 1985), pages 865−885.

[Lindsay 1981] B. G. Lindsay, "Object Naming and Catalog Management for a Distributed Database Manager," *Proceedings of the International Conference on Distributed Computing Systems* (1981).

[Lindsay et al. 1980] B. G. Lindsay, P. G. Selinger, C. Galtieri, J. N. Gray, R. A. Lorie, T. G. Price, G. R. Putzolu, I. L. Traiger, and B. W. Wade, "Notes on Distributed Databases," in [**Draffen and Poole 1980**], pages 247−284.

[Lindsay et al. 1984] B. G. Lindsay, L. M. Haas, C. Mohan, P. F. Wilms, and R. A. Yost, "Computation and Communication in R*: A Distributed Database Manager," *ACM Transactions on Computer Systems*, Volume 2, Number 1 (February 1984), pages 24−38.

[Litwin 1978] W. Litwin, "Virtual Hashing: A Dynamically Changing Hashing," *Proceedings of the 4th International Conference on Very Large Data Bases* (1978), pages 517−523.

[Litwin 1980] W. Litwin, "Linear Hashing: A New Tool for File and Table Addressing," *Proceedings of the International Conference on Very Large Data Bases* (1980), pages 212−223.

[Litwin 1981] W. Litwin, "Trie Hashing," *Proceedings of the ACM SIGMOD International Conference on Management of Data* (1981), pages 19–29.

[Litwin and Abdellatif 1986] W. Litwin and A. Abdellatif, "Multidatabase Interoperability," *IEEE Computer,* Volume 12, Number 19 (1986), pages 10–18.

[Liu 1985] J. Liu (Editor), *Proceedings of the International Conference on Entity-Relationship Approach* (1985).

[Lockemann and Neuhold 1976] P. C. Lockemann and E. J. Neuhold (Editors), *Systems for Large Data Bases,* North Holland, Amsterdam, The Netherlands (1976).

[Lomet 1981] D. G. Lomet, "Digital B-trees," *Proceedings of the International Conference on Very Large Data Bases* (1981), pages 333–344.

[Lorie 1977] R. A. Lorie, "Physical Integrity in a Large Segmented Database," *ACM Transactions on Database Systems,* Volume 2, Number 1 (March 1977), pages 91–104.

[Lorie and Plouffe 1983] R. A. Lorie and W. Plouffe, "Complex Objects and Their Use in Design Transactions," *Proceedings of the ACM SIGMOD International Conference on Management of Data, Engineering Design Applications* (1983), pages 115–122.

[Lorie and Wade 1979] R. A. Lorie and B. W. Wade, "The Compilation of a High Level Data Language," Research Report RJ2598, IBM Research Laboratory, San Jose, CA (1979).

[Lorie et al. 1985] R. Lorie, W. Kim, D. McNabb, W. Plouffe, and A. Meier, "Supporting Complex Objects in a Relational System for Engineering Databases," in [Kim et al. 1985], pages 145–155.

[Lum 1974] V. Y. Lum, "On the Selection of Secondary Indexes," *Proceedings of the ACM Conference* (1974).

[Lum and Ling 1970] V. Y. Lum and H. Ling, "Multi-Attribute Retrieval With Combined Indices," *Communications of the ACM,* Volume 13, Number 11 (November 1970), pages 660–665.

[Lunt et al. 1990] T. F. Lunt, D. E. Denning, R. R. Schell, M. Heckman, and W. R. Shockley, "The SeaView Security Model," *IEEE Transactions on Software Engineering,* Volume SE-16, Number 6 (June 1990), pages 593–607.

[Lusk et al. 1980] E. L. Lusk, P. A. Overbeek, and B. Parrello, "A Practical Design Methodology for the Implementation of MS Databases, Using the Entity-Relationship Model," *Proceedings of the ACM SIGMOD International Conference on Management of Data* (1980), pages 9–21.

[Lynch 1983] N. A. Lynch, "Multilevel Atomicity–A New Correctness Criterion for Database Concurrency Control," *ACM Transactions on Database Systems,* Volume 8, Number 4 (December 1983), pages 484–502.

[Lynch 1986] N. A. Lynch, "Concurrency Control for Resilient Nested Transactions," in **[Kanellakis and Preparata 1986]**, pages 335−373.

[Lynch and Merritt 1986] N. A. Lynch and M. Merritt, "Introduction to the Theory of Nested Transactions," *Proceedings of the International Conference on Database Theory* (1986).

[Lynch et al. 1988] N. A. Lynch, M. Merritt, W. Weihl, and A. Fekete, "A Theory of Atomic Transactions," *Proceedings of the International Conference on Database Theory* (1988), pages 41−71.

[Lyngbaek and Vianu 1987] P. Lyngbaek and V. Vianu, "Mapping a Semantic Database Model to the Relational Model," *Proceedings of the ACM SIGMOD International Conference on the Management of Data* (1987), pages 132−142.

[Mahmoud and Riordon 1976] S. Mahmoud and J. S. Riordon, "Optimal Allocation of Resources in Distributed Information Networks," *ACM Transactions on Database Systems*, Volume 1, Number 1 (January 1976), pages 66−78.

[Maier 1983] D. Maier, *The Theory of Relational Databases*, Computer Science Press, Rockville, MD (1983).

[Maier and Stein 1986] D. Maier and J. Stein, "Indexing in an Object-Oriented DBMS," *Proceedings of the International Workshop on Object-Oriented Database Systems* (1986).

[Maier et al. 1982] D. Maier, D. Rozenshtein, S. Salveter, J. Stein, and D. S. Warren, "Towards Logical Data Independence: A Relational Query Language without Relations," *Proceedings of the ACM SIGMOD International Conference on the Management of Data* (1982), pages 51−60.

[Maier et al. 1986] D. Maier, J. Stein, A. Otis, and A. Purdy, "Development of an Object-Oriented DBMS," *Proceedings of the International Conference on Object-Oriented Programming Systems, Languages, and Applications* (1986), pages 472−482.

[Makinouchi 1977] A. Makinouchi, "A Consideration of Normal Form on Not-necessarily Normalized Relations in the Relational Data Model," *Proceedings of the International Conference on Very Large Data Bases* (1977), pages 447−453.

[Malamud 1989] C. Malamud, *Ingres: Tools for Building an Information Architecture*, Van Nostrand Reinhold (1989).

[Malley and Zdonick 1986] C. Malley and S. Zdonick, "A Knowledge-Based Approach to Query Optimization," *Proceedings of the International Conference on Expert Database Systems* (1986), pages 329−344.

[Manber and Ladner 1984] U. Manber and R. E. Ladner, "Concurrency Control in a Dynamic Search Structure," *ACM Transactions on Database Systems*, Volume 9, Number 3 (September 1984), pages 439−455.

[March et al. 1981] S. T. March, D. G. Severance, and M. Wilens, "Frame Memory: A Storage Architecture to Support Rapid Design and Implementation of Efficient Databases," *ACM Transactions on Database Systems*, Volume 6, Number 3 (September 1981), pages 441−463.

[Markowitz and Raz 1983] V. Markowitz and Y. Raz, "ERROL: An Entity-Relationship, Role Oriented, Query Language," in **[Davis et al. 1983]**.

[Markowitz and Shoshani 1989] V. Markowitz and A. Shoshani, "On the Correctness of Representing Extended Entity-Relationship Structures in the Relational Data Model," *Proceedings of the ACM SIGMOD International Conference on the Management of Data* (1989), pages 430−439.

[Martin 1973] J. Martin, *Security, Accuracy, and Privacy in Computer Systems*, Prentice-Hall, Englewood Cliffs, NJ (1973).

[Martin and Norman 1970] J. Martin and A. R. D. Norman, *The Computerized Society*, Prentice-Hall, Englewood Cliffs, NJ (1970).

[Martin et al. 1989] J. Martin, K. K. Chapman, and J. Leben, *DB2: Concepts, Design, and Programming*, Prentice-Hall, Englewood Cliffs, NJ (1989).

[McCune and Henschen 1989] W. W. McCune and L. J. Henschen, "Maintaining State Constraints in Relational Databases: A Proof Theoretic Basis," *Journal of the ACM*, Volume 36, Number 1 (January 1989), pages 46−68.

[McFadyen and Kanabar 1991] R. McFadyen and V. Kanabar, *An Introduction to Structured Query Language*, Wm. C. Brown, Dubuque, IA (1991).

[McGee 1977] W. C. McGee, "The Information Management System IMS/VS Part I: General Structure and Operation," *IBM Systems Journal*, Volume 16, Number 2 (June 1977), pages 84−168.

[Menasce and Muntz 1979] D. A. Menasce and R. R. Muntz, "Locking and Deadlock Detection in Distributed Databases," *IEEE Transactions on Software Engineering*, Volume SE-5, Number 3 (May 1979), pages 195−202.

[Menasce et al. 1980] D. A. Menasce, G. Popek, and R. Muntz, "A Locking Protocol for Resource Coordination in Distributed Databases," *ACM Transactions on Database Systems*, Volume 5, Number 2 (June 1980), pages 103−138.

[Mendelzon and Maier 1979] A. O. Mendelzon and D. Maier, "Generalized Mutual Dependencies and the Decomposition of Database Relations," *Proceedings of the International Conference on Very Large Data Bases* (1979), pages 75−82.

[Mikkilineni and Su 1988] K. Mikkilineni and S. Su, "An Evaluation of Relational Join Algorithms in a Pipelined Query Processing Environment," *IEEE Transactions on Software Engineering*, Volume SE-14, Number 6 (November 1988), pages 838−848.

[Minker 1988] J. Minker, *Foundations of Deductive Database and Logic Programming,* Morgan-Kaufmann, San Mateo, CA (1988).

[Minoura and Wiederhold 1982] T. Minoura and G. Wiederhold, "Resilient Extended True-Copy Token Scheme for a Distributed Database," *IEEE Transactions on Software Engineering,* Volume SE-8, Number 3 (May 1982), pages 173–189.

[Mohan 1990] C. Mohan, "Commit-LSN: A Novel and Simple Method for Reducing Locking and Latching in Transaction Processing Systems," *Proceedings of the International Conference on Very Large Data Bases* (1990), pages 406–418.

[Mohan and Lindsay 1983] C. Mohan and B. Lindsay, "Efficient Commit Protocols for the Tree of Processes Model of Distributed Transactions," *Proceedings of the Second ACM SIGACT-SIGOPS Symposium on the Principles of Distributed Computing* (1983).

[Mohan et al. 1986] C. Mohan, B. Lindsay, and R. Obermarck, "Transaction Management in the R* Distributed Database Management System," *ACM Transactions on Database Systems,* Volume 11, Number 4 (December 1986), pages 378–396.

[Mohan et al. 1991] C. Mohan, D. Haderle, B. Lindsay, H. Pirahesh, and P. Schwarz, "ARIES: A Transaction Recovery Method Supporting Fine-Granularity Locking and Partial Rollback Using Write-Ahead Logging," *ACM Transactions on Database Systems* (1991).

[Morgan and Levin 1977] H. L. Morgan and J. D. Levin, "Optimal Program and Data Locations in Computer Networks," *Communications of the ACM,* Volume 20, Number 5 (May 1977), pages 315–322.

[Morris et al. 1986] K. Morris, J. D. Ullman, and A. Van Gelder, "Design Overview of the NAIL! System," *Proceedings of the Third International Conference on Logic Programming* (1986), pages 554–568.

[Moss 1982] J. E. B. Moss, "Nested Transactions and Reliable Distributed Computing," *Proceedings of the Symposium on Reliability in Distributed Software and Database Systems* (1982).

[Moss 1985] J. E. B. Moss, *Nested Transactions: An Approach to Reliable Distributed Computing,* MIT Press, Cambridge, MA (1985).

[Moss 1987] J. E. B. Moss, "Log-Based recovery for Nested Transactions," *Proceedings of the International Conference on Very Large Data Bases* (1987), pages 427–432.

[Motro 1987] A. Motro, "Superviews: Virtual Integration of Multiple Databases," *IEEE Transactions on Software Engineering,* Volume SE-13, Number 7 (July 1987), pages 785–798.

[MRI 1974] MRI Systems Corporation, "System 2000 Reference Manual," Document UMN-1 (1974).

[MRI 1979] MRI Systems Corporation, "Language Specification Manual: The DEFINE Language," Document LSM-DEF-10 (1979).

[Mylopoulos et al. 1975] J. Mylopoulos, S. A. Schuster, and D. Tsichritzis, "A Multilevel Relational System," *Proceedings of the National Computer Conference* (1975), pages 403−408.

[Mylopoulos et al. 1976] J. Mylopoulos, A. Borgida, P. Cohen, N. Roussopoulos, J. Tsotsos, and H. K. T. Wong, "TORUS: A Step towards Bridging the Gap between Data Bases and the Casual User," *Information Systems*, Volume 2 (1976), pages 71−77.

[Ng 1981] P. A. Ng, "Further Analysis of the Entity-Relationship Approach to Database Design," *IEEE Transactions on Software Engineering*, Volume SE-7, Number 1 (January 1981), pages 85−98.

[Nievergelt 1974] J. Nievergelt, "Binary Search Trees and File Organization," *ACM Computing Surveys*, Volume 6, Number 3 (September 1974), pages 195−207.

[Nievergelt et al. 1984] J. Nievergelt, H. Hinterberger, and K. C. Sevcik, "The Grid File: An Adaptable Symmetric Multikey File Structure," *ACM Transactions on Database Systems*, Volume 9, Number 1 (March 1984), pages 38−71.

[Nijssen 1976] G. M. Nijssen (Editor), *Modeling in Data Base Management Systems*, North Holland, Amsterdam, The Netherlands (1976).

[Obermarck 1980] R. Obermarck "IMS/VS Program Isolation Feature," Research Report RJ2879, IBM Research Laboratory, San Jose, CA (1980).

[Obermarck 1982] R. Obermarck, "Distributed Deadlock Detection Algorithm," *ACM Transactions on Database Systems*, Volume 7, Number 2 (June 1982), pages 187−208.

[Olle 1978], T. W. Olle, *The CODASYL Approach to Data Base Management*, John Wiley and Sons, New York, NY (1978).

[Orestein 1982] J.A. Orestein, "Multidimensional Tries Used for Associative Searching," *Information Processing Letters*, Volume 14, Number 4 (June 1982), pages 150−157.

[Ozsoyoglu and Yuan 1987] G. Ozsoyoglu and L. Yuan, "Reduced MVDs and Minimal Covers," *ACM Transactions on Database Systems*, Volume 12, Number 3 (September 1987), pages 377−394.

[Ozsoyoglu et al. 1987] G. Ozsoyoglu, Z. M. Ozsoyoglu, and V. Matos, "Extending Relational Algebra and Relational Calculus with Set-Valued Attributes and Aggregate Functions," *ACM Transactions on Database Systems*, Volume 12, Number 4 (December 1987), pages 566−592.

[Papadimitriou 1979] C. H. Papadimitriou, "The Serializability of Concurrent Database Updates," *Journal of the ACM*, Volume 26, Number 4 (October 1979), pages 631–653.

[Papadimitriou 1982] C. H. Papadimitriou, "A Theorem in Database Concurrency Control," *Journal of the ACM*, Volume 29, Number 5 (October 1982), pages 998–1006.

[Papadimitriou 1986] C. H. Papadimitriou, *The Theory of Database Concurrency Control*, Computer Science Press, Rockville, MD (1986).

[Papadimitriou et al. 1977] C. H. Papadimitriou, P. A. Bernstein, and J. B. Rothnie, "Some Computational Problems Related to Database Concurrency Control," *Proceedings of the Conference on Theoretical Computer Science* (1977), pages 275–282.

[Parent and Spaccapietra 1985] C. Parent and S. Spaccapietra, "An Algebra for a General Entity-Relationship Model," *IEEE Transactions on Software Engineering*, Volume SE-11, Number 7 (July 1985), pages 634–643.

[Paris 1986] J. Paris, "Voting with Witnesses: A Consistency Scheme for Replicated Files," *Proceedings of the IEEE International Conference on Data Engineering* (1986).

[Patterson et al. 1988] D. A. Patterson, G. Gibson, and R. H. Katz, "A Case for Redundant Arrays of Inexpensive Disks (RAID)," *Proceedings of the ACM SIGMOD International Conference on the Management of Data* (1988), pages 109–116.

[Pecherer 1975] R. M. Pecherer, "Efficient Evaluation of Expressions in a Relational Algebra," *Proceedings of the ACM Pacific Conference* (1975), pages 17–18.

[Peckham and Maryanski 1988] J. Peckham and F. Maryanski, "Semantic Data Models," *Computing Surveys*, Volume 20, Number 3 (September 1988), pages 153–189.

[Penney and Stein 1987] J. Penney and J. Stein, "Class Modification in the GemStone Object-Oriented DBMS," *Proceedings of the International Conference on Object-Oriented Programming Systems, Languages, and Applications* (1987).

[Peterson 1987] G. E. Peterson, *Object-Oriented Computing*, IEEE Computer Society Press (1987).

[Pistor and Andersen 1986] P. Pistor and F. Andersen, "Designing a Generalized NF2 Model with an SQL-type Language Interface" *Proceedings of the International Conference on Very Large Data Bases* (1986), pages 278–285.

[Pistor and Dadam 1989] P. Pistor and P. Dadam, "The Advanced Information Management Prototype," in **[Abiteboul et al. 1989]**, pages 3–26.

[Pistor and Traunmueller 1986] P. Pistor and R. Traunmueller, "A Database Language for Sets, Lists and Tables," *Information Systems*, Volume 11, Number 4 (1986), pages 323–336.

[Pu 1987] C. Pu, "Superdatabases: Transactions Across Database Boundaries," *IEEE Data Engineering* (1987).

[Pu et al. 1988] C. Pu, G. Kaiser, and N. Hutchinson, "Split-transactions for Open-Ended Activities," *Proceedings of the International Conference on Very Large Data Bases* (1988), pages 26–37.

[Rabitti et al. 1988] F. Rabitti, D. Woelk, and W. Kim, "A Model of Authorization for Object-Oriented and Semantic Databases," *Proceedings of the International Conference on Extending Database Technology* (1988), pages 231–250.

[Ramakrisha and Larson 1989] M. V. Ramakrishna and P. Larson, "File Organization Using Composite Perfect Hashing," *ACM Transactions on Database Systems*, Volume 14, Number 2 (June 1989), pages 231–263.

[Ramesh et al. 1989] R. Ramesh, A. J. G. Babu, and J. P. Kincaid, "Index Optimization: Theory and Experimental Results," *ACM Transactions on Database Systems*, Volume 14, Number 1 (March 1989), pages 41–74.

[Ranft et al. 1990] M. Ranft, S. Rehm, and K. Dittrich, "How to Share Work on Shared Objects in Design Databases," *Proceedings of the International Conference on Data Engineering* (1990).

[Reed 1978] D. Reed, "Naming and Synchronization in a decentralized Computer System," Ph.D. thesis, Department of Electrical Engineering, MIT, Cambridge, MA (1978).

[Reed 1983] D. Reed, "Implementing Atomic Actions on Decentralized Data," *ACM Transactions on Computer Systems*, Volume 1, Number 1 (February 1983), pages 3–23.

[Reisner 1977] P. Reisner, "Use of Psychological Experimentation as an Aid to Development of a Query Language," *IEEE Transactions on Software Engineering*, Volume SE-3, Number 3 (May 1977), pages 218–229.

[Reisner et al. 1975] P. Reisner, R. F. Boyce, and D. D. Chamberlin, "Human Factors Evaluation of Two Data Base Query Languages: SQUARE and SEQUEL," *Proceedings of the AFIPS National Computer Conference* (1975), pages 447–452.

[Reuter 1980] A. Reuter, "A Fast Transaction-Oriented Logging Scheme for UNDO Recovery," *IEEE Transactions on Software Engineering*, Volume SE-6, Number 4 (July 1980), pages 348–356.

[Ries 1979] D. R. Ries, "The Effect of Concurrency Control on the Performance of a Distributed Database Management System," *Proceedings of the Berkeley*

Workshop on Distributed Data Management and Computer Networks (1979), pages 75−112.

[Ries and Stonebraker 1977] D. R. Ries and M. Stonebraker, "Effects of Locking Granularity in a Database Management System," *ACM Transactions on Database Systems*, Volume 2, Number 3 (September 1977), pages 233−246.

[Rissanen 1979] J. Rissanen, "Theory of Joins for Relational Databases - A Tutorial Survey," *Proceedings of the Symposium on Mathematical Foundations of Computer Science*, Springer-Verlag, Berlin, Germany (1979), pages 537−551.

[Rivest 1976] R. L Rivest, "Partial Match Retrieval Via the Method of Superimposed Codes," *Siam Journal of Computing*, Volume 5, Number 1 (1976), pages 19−50.

[Rivest et al. 1978] R. L. Rivest, A. Shamir, and L. Adelman, "On Digital Signatures and Public Key Cryptosystems," *Communications of the ACM*, Volume 21, Number 2 (February 1978), pages 120−126.

[Rosenkrantz et al. 1978] D. J. Rosenkrantz, R. E. Stearns, and P. M. Lewis II, "System Level Concurrency Control For Distributed Data Base Systems," *ACM Transactions on Database Systems*, Volume 3, Number 2 (March 1978), pages 178−198.

[Roth and Korth 1987] M. A. Roth and H. F. Korth, "The Design of ¬1NF Relational Databases into Nested Normal Form," *Proceedings of the ACM SIGMOD International Conference on Management of Data* (1987), pages 143−159.

[Roth et al. 1987] M. A. Roth, H. F. Korth, and D. S. Batory, "SQL/NF: A Query Language for ¬1NF Relational Databases," *Information Systems*, Volume 12, Number 1 (1987), pages 99−114.

[Roth et al. 1988] M. A. Roth, H. F. Korth, and A. Silberschatz, "Extended Algebra and Calculus for Nested Relational Databases," *ACM Transactions on Database Systems*, Volume 13, Number 4 (December 1988), pages 389−417.

[Roth et al. 1989] M. A. Roth, H. F. Korth, and A. Silberschatz, "Null Values in Nested Relational Databases," *Acta Informatica*, Volume 26 (1989), pages 615−642.

[Rothnie and Goodman 1977] J. B. Rothnie, Jr. and N. Goodman, "A Survey of Research and Development in Distributed Database Management," *Proceedings of the International Conference on Very Large Data Bases* (1977), pages 48−62.

[Roussopoulos and Mylopoulos 1975] N. Roussopoulos and J. Mylopoulos, "Using Semantic Networks for Data Base Management," *Proceedings of the International Conference on Very Large Data Bases* (1975), pages 144−172.

[RTI 1983] Relational Technology, "Ingres Reference Manual," Relational Technology, Inc. (1983).

[Rustin 1972] R. Rustin (Editor), *Data Base Systems*, Prentice-Hall, Englewood Cliffs, NJ (1972).

[Sadri and Ullman 1982] F. Sadri and J. Ullman, "Template Dependencies: A Large Class of Dependencies in Relational Databases and Its Complete Axiomatization," *Journal of the ACM*, Volume 29, Number 2 (April 1982), pages 363–372.

[Sagiv and Yannakakis 1981] Y.Sagiv and M. Yannakakis, "Equivalence among Relational Expressions with the Union and Difference Operators," *Journal of the ACM*, Volume 27, Number 4 (November 1981).

[Sakai 1980] H. Sakai, "Entity-Relationship Approach to the Conceptual Schema Design," *Proceedings of the ACM SIGMOD International Conference on Management of Data* (1980), pages 1–8.

[Salem and Garcia-Molina 1986] K. Salem and H. Garcia-Molina, "Disk Striping," *Proceedings of the International Conference on Data Engineering* (1986), pages 336–342.

[Schek and Scholl 1989] H. J. Schek and M. H. Scholl, "The Two Roles of Nested Relations in the DASDBS Project," in **[Abiteboul et al. 1989]**, pages 50–68.

[Schenk 1974] K. L. Schenk, "Implementational Aspects of the CODASYL DBTG Proposal," *Proceedings of the IFIP Working Conference on Data Base Management Systems* (1974).

[Scheuermann 1982] P. Scheuermann (Editor), *Improving Database Usability and Responsiveness*, Academic Press, New York, NY (1982).

[Scheuermann et al. 1979] P. Scheuermann, G. Schiffner, and H. Weber, "Abstraction Capabilities and Invariant Properties Modeling Within the Entity-Relationship Approach," *Proceedings of the International Conference on Entity-Relationship Approach* (1979), pages 121–140.

[Schiffner and Scheuermann 1979] G. Schiffner and P. Scheuermann, "Multiple View and Abstractions with an Extended Entity-Relationship Model," *Journal of Computer Languages*, Volume 4 (1979), pages 139–154.

[Schlageter 1981] G. Schlageter, "Optimistic Methods for Concurrency Control in Distributed Database Systems," *Proceedings of the International Conference on Very Large Data Bases* (1981), pages 125–130.

[Schmid and Swenson 1975] H. A. Schmid and J. R. Swenson, "On the Semantics of the Relational Model," *Proceedings of the ACM SIGMOD International Conference on the Management of Data* (1975), pages 211-223.

[Schneider 1982] H. J. Schneider, "Distributed Data Bases," *Proceedings of the International Symposium on Distributed Databases* (1982).

[Schneiderman 1976] B. Schneiderman, "Reduced Combined Indexes for Efficient Multiple Attribute Retrieval," *Information Systems*, Volume 2, Number 4 (1976).

[Schneiderman 1978] B. Schneiderman (Editor), *Database: Improving Usability and Responsiveness*, Academic Press, New York, NY (1978).

[Scholl 1986] M. H. Scholl, "Theoretical Foundation of Algebraic Optimization Utilizing Unnormalized Relations," *Proceedings of the International Conference on Database Theory* (1986), pages 380–396.

[Scholl et al. 1989] M. Scholl, S. Abiteboul, F. Bancilhon, N. Bidoit, S. Gamerman, D. Plateau, P. Richard, and A. Verroust, "VERSO: A Database Machine Based on Nested Relations," in **[Abiteboul et al. 1989]**, pages 27–49.

[Sciore 1982] E. Sciore, "A Complete Axiomatization for Full Join Dependencies," *Journal of the ACM*, Volume 29, Number 2 (April 1982), pages 373–393.

[Sciore 1983] E. Sciore, "Improving Database Schemes by Adding Attributes," *ACM SIGACT-SIGMOD Symposium on the Principles of Database Systems* (1983), pages 379–382.

[Sciore et al. 1983] E. Sciore, D. S. Warren, and P. B. Henderson, "A Relational Model of Operating System Environments," Technical Report 83/060, Department of Computer Science, State University of New York at Stony Brook, Stony Brook, NY (1983).

[Selinger and Adiba 1980] P. G. Selinger and M. E. Adiba, "Access Path Selection in Distributed Database Management Systems," Research Report RJ2338, IBM Research Laboratory, San Jose, CA (1980).

[Selinger et al. 1979] P. G. Selinger, M. M. Astrahan, D. D. Chamberlin, R. A. Lorie, and T. G. Price, "Access Path Selection in a Relational Database System," *Proceedings of the ACM SIGMOD International Conference on the Management of Data* (1979), pages 23–34.

[Sellis 1988] T. K. Sellis, "Multiple Query Optimization," *ACM Transactions on Database Systems*, Volume 13, Number 1 (March 1988), pages 23–52.

[Senko 1975] M. E. Senko, "Information Systems: Records, Relations, Sets, Entities, and Things," *Information Systems*, Volume 1 (1975), pages 3–13.

[Senko 1977] M. E. Senko, "Data Structures and Data Accessing in Database Systems Past, Present and Future," *IBM Systems Journal*, Volume 16 (1977), pages 208–257.

[Sha et al. 1988] L. Sha, J. Lehoczky, and D. Jensen, "Modular Concurrency Control and Failure Recovery," *IEEE Transactions on Computing*, Volume 37, Number 2 (February 1988), pages 146−159.

[Shapiro 1986] L. D. Shapiro, "Join Processing in Database Systems with Large Main Memories," *ACM Transactions on Database Systems*, Volume 11, Number 3 (September 1986), pages 239−264.

[Shasha and Goodman 1988] D. Shasha and N. Goodman, "Concurrent Search Structure Algorithms," *ACM Transactions on Database Systems*, Volume 13, Number 1 (March 1988), pages 53−90.

[Sheard and Stemple 1989] T. Sheard and D. Stemple, "Automatic Verification of Database Transaction Safety," *ACM Transactions on Database Systems*, Volume 14, Number 3 (September 1989), pages 322−368.

[Shipman 1981] D. Shipman, "The Functional Data Model and the Data Language DAPLEX," *ACM Transactions on Database Systems*, Volume 6, Number 1 (March 1981), pages 140−173.

[Shoshani 1978] A. Shoshani, "CABLE: A Language Based on the Entity-Relationship Model," Technical Report, Computer Science and Applied Mathematics Department, Lawrence Berkeley Laboratory, Berkeley, CA (1978).

[Sibley 1976] E. Sibley, "The Development of Database Technology," *ACM Computing Surverys*, Volume 8, Number 1 (March 1976), pages 1−5.

[Sibley and Kerschberg 1977] E. Sibley and L. Kerschberg, "Data Architecture and Data Model Considerations," *Proceedings of the AFIPS National Computer Conference* (1977).

[Silberschatz and Kedem 1980] A. Silberschatz and Z. Kedem, "Consistency in Hierarchical Database Systems," *Journal of the ACM*, Volume 27, Number 1 (January 1980), pages 72−80.

[Silberschatz 1982] A. Silberschatz, "A Multi-Version Concurrency Control Scheme With No Rollbacks," *ACM SIGACT-SIGOPS Symposium on Principles of Distributed Computing* (1982), pages 216−223.

[Silberschatz et al. 1990] A. Silberschatz, M. R. Stonebraker, and J. D. Ullman (Editors), "Database Systems: Achievements and Opportunities," *ACM SIGMOD Record,* Volume 19, Number 4 (1990).

[Silberschatz et al. 1991] A. Silberschatz, J. Peterson, and P. Galvin, *Operating System Concepts,* Third Edition, Addison Wesley, Reading, MA (1991).

[Simmons 1979] G. J. Simmons, "Symmetric and Asymmetric Encryption," *ACM Computing Surveys,* Volume 11, Number 4 (December 1979), pages 304−330.

[Skarra and Zdonik 1986] A. Skarra and S. Zdonik, "The Management of Changing Types in an Object-Oriented Database," *Proceedings of the International Conference on Object-Oriented Programming Systems, Languages, and Applications* (1986).

[Skarra and Zdonik 1989] A. Skarra and S. Zdonik, "Concurrency Control in Object-Oriented Databases," in **[Kim and Lochovsky 1989]**, pages 395−421.

[Skeen 1981] D. Skeen, "Non-blocking Commit Protocols." *Proceedings of the ACM SIGMOD International Conference on the Management of Data* (1981), pages 133−142.

[Smith and Barnes 1987] P. Smith and G. Barnes, *Files and Databases: An Introduction,* Addison Wesley, Reading, MA (1987).

[Smith and Chang 1975] J. M. Smith and P. Chang, "Optimizing the Performance of a Relational Algebra Interface," *Communications of the ACM,* Volume 18, Number 10 (October 1975).

[Smith and Smith 1977] J. M. Smith and D. C. P. Smith, "Database Abstractions: Aggregation and Generalization," *ACM Transactions on Database Systems,* Volume 2, Number 2 (March 1977), pages 105−133.

[Snodgrass 1987] R. Snodgrass, "The Temporal Query Language TQuel," *ACM Transactions on Database Systems,* Volume 12, Number 2 (March 1987), pages 247−298.

[Snodgrass and Ahn 1985] R. Snodgrass and I. Ahn, "A Taxonomy of Time in Databases" *Proceedings of the ACM SIGMOD International Conference on the Management of Data* (1985), pages 236−246.

[Software AG 1978] "ADABAS *Introduction,*" Software AG of North America, Reston, VA (1978).

[Soisalon-Soininen and Wood 1982] E. Soisalon-Soininen and D. Wood, "An Optimal Algorithm for Testing Safety and Detecting Deadlocks," *Proceedings of the ACM SIGACT-SIGMOD Symposium on Principles of Database Systems* (1982), pages 108−116.

[Spector and Schwarz 1983] A. Z. Spector and P. M. Schwarz, "Transactions: A Construct for Reliable Distributed Computing," *ACM SIGOPS Operating Systems Review,* Volume 17, Number 2 (1983), pages 18−35.

[Sperry Univac 1973] *UNIVAC 1100 series, Data Management System (DMS 1100)* publications: *Schema Definition, Data Administrator Reference, American National Standard Cobol (Fielddata), Data Manipulation Language, Programmer Reference,* Sperry Rand Corporation (1973).

[Stachour and Thuraisingham 1990] P. D. Stachour and B. Thuraisingham, "Design of LDV: A Multilevel Secure Relational Database Management System," *IEEE Transactions on Knowledge and Data Engineering*, Volume 2, Number 2 (June 1990), pages 190–209

[Stefik and Bobrow 1986] M. Stefik and D. G. Bobrow, "Object-Oriented Programming: Themes and Variations," *The AI Magazine* (January 1986), pages 40–62.

[Stonebraker 1974] M. R. Stonebraker, "A Functional View of Data Independence," *Proceedings of the ACM SIGMOD Workshop on Data Description, Access and Control* (1974), pages 63–81.

[Stonebraker 1975] M. Stonebraker, "Implementation of Integrity Constraints and Views by Query Modification," *Proceedings of the ACM SIGMOD International Conference on the Management of Data* (1975), pages 65–78.

[Stonebraker 1980] M. Stonebraker, "Retrospection on a Database System," *ACM Transactions on Database Systems*, Volume 5, Number 2 (March 1980), pages 225–240. Also in **[Stonebraker 1986b]**, pages 46–62.

[Stonebraker 1981] M. Stonebraker, "Operating System Support for Database Management," *Communications of the ACM*, Volume 24, Number 7 (July 1981), pages 412–418. Also in **[Stonebraker 1986b]**, pages 172–182.

[Stonebraker 1986a] M. Stonebraker, "Inclusion of New Types in Relational Database Systems," *Proceedings of the International Conference on Data Engineering* (1986), pages 262–269.

[Stonebraker 1986b] M. Stonebraker (Editor), *The Ingres Papers*, Addison Wesley, Reading, MA (1986).

[Stonebraker 1987] M. Stonebraker, "The Design of the POSTGRES Storage System," *Proceedings of the International Conference on Very Large Data Bases* (1987).

[Stonebraker 1988] M. Stonebraker (Editor), *Readings in Database Systems*, Morgan Kaufmann Publishers, Inc., San Mateo, CA (1988).

[Stonebraker and Hearst 1988] M. Stonebraker, and M. Hearst, "Future Trends in Expert Database Systems," *Proceedings of the International Conference on Expert Database Systems*, Benjamin Cummings, Redwood City, CA (1988), pages 3–20.

[Stonebraker and Rowe 1986] M. Stonebraker and L. Rowe, "The Design of POSTGRES," *Proceedings of the ACM SIGMOD International Conference on the Management of Data* (1986).

[Stonebraker and Wong 1974] M. Stonebraker and E. Wong, "Access Control in a Relational Database Management System by Query Modification," *Proceedings of the ACM National Conference* (1974), pages 180–187.

[Stonebraker et al. 1976] M. Stonebraker, E. Wong, P. Kreps, and G. D. Held, "The Design and Implementation of INGRES," *ACM Transactions on Database Systems*, Volume 1, Number 3 (September 1976), pages 189−222. Also in **[Stonebraker 1986b]**, pages 1−45.

[Stonebraker et al. 1987a] M. Stonebraker, J. Anton, and E. Hanson, "Extending a Database System with Procedures," *ACM Transactions on Database Systems*, Volume 12, Number 3 (September 1987), pages 350−376.

[Stonebraker et al. 1987b] M. Stonebraker, E. Hanson, and C. H. Hong, "The Design of the POSTGRES Rule System," *Proceedings of the International Conference on Data Engineering* (1987), pages 356−374.

[Stroustrup 1988] B. Stroustrup, "What Is Object-Oriented Programming?," *IEEE Software* (May 1988), pages 10−20.

[Stuart et al. 1984] D. G. Stuart, G. Buckley, and A. Silberschatz, "A Centralized Deadlock Detection Algorithm," Technical Report, Department of Computer Sciences, University of Texas, Austin, TX (1984).

[Sundgren 1974] B. Sundgren, "Conceptual Foundation of the Infological Approach to Data Bases," in **[Klimbie and Koffeman 1974]**, pages 61−96.

[Sundgren 1975] B. Sundgren, *Theory of Data Bases*, Mason/Charter, New York, NY (1975).

[Tanenbaum 1981] A. S. Tanenbaum, *Computer Networks*, Prentice-Hall, Englewood Cliffs, NJ (1981).

[Taylor and Frank 1976] R. W. Taylor and R. L. Frank, "CODASYL Data Base Management Systems," *ACM Computing Surveys*, Volume 8, Number 1 (March 1976), pages 67−103

[Teorey and Fry 1982] T. J. Teorey and J. P. Fry, *Design of Database Structures*, Prentice-Hall, Englewood Cliffs, NJ (1982).

[Teorey et al. 1986] T. J. Teorey, D. Yang, and J. P. Fry, "A Logical Design Methodology for Relational Databases Using the Extended Entity-Relationship Model," *ACM Computing Surveys*, Volume 18, Number 2 (June 1986), pages 197−222.

[Thomas 1979] R. H. Thomas, "A Majority Consensus Approach to Concurrency Control," *ACM Transactions on Database Systems*, Volume 4, Number 2 (June 1979), pages 180−219.

[Todd 1976] S. J. P. Todd, "The Peterlee Relational Test Vehicle - A System Overview," *IBM Systems Journal*, Volume 15, Number 4 (1976), pages 285−308.

[Traiger 1982] I. L. Traiger, "Virtual Memory for Database Systems," *ACM SIGOPS Operating Systems Review*, Volume 16, Number 4 (1982), pages 26−48.

[Traiger 1983] I. L. Traiger, "Trends in Systems Aspects of Database Management," Research Report RJ3845, IBM Research Laboratory, San Jose, CA (1983).

[Traiger et al. 1982] I. L. Traiger, J. N. Gray, C. A. Galtieri, and B. G. Lindsay, "Transactions and Consistency in Distributed Database Management Systems," *ACM Transactions on Database Systems*, Volume 7, Number 3 (September 1982), pages 323–342.

[Tremblay and Sorenson 1985] J.-P. Tremblay and P. G. Sorenson, *The Theory and Practice of Compiler Writing*, McGraw-Hill, New York, NY (1985).

[Trivedi et al. 1980] K. S. Trivedi, R. A. Wagner, and T. M. Sigmon, "Optimal Selection of CPU Speed, Device Capacities and File Assignment," *Journal of the ACM*, Volume 7, Number 3 (July 1980), pages 457–473.

[Tsichritzis and Klug 1978] D. C. Tsichritzis and A. Klug (Editors), *The ANSI/X3/SPARC Framework*, AFIPS Press, Montvale, NJ (1978).

[Tsichritzis and Lochovsky 1976] D. C. Tsichritzis and F. H. Lochovsky, "Hierarchical Data-base Management: A Survey," *ACM Computing Surveys*, Volume 8, Number 1 (March 1976), pages 67–103.

[Tsichritzis and Lochovsky 1977] D. C. Tsichritzis and F. H. Lochovsky, *Data Base Management Systems*, Academic Press, New York, NY (1977).

[Tsichritzis and Lochovsky 1982] D. C. Tsichritzis and F. H. Lochovsky, *Data Models*, Prentice-Hall, Englewood Cliffs, NJ (1982).

[Tsou and Fischer 1982] D. -M. Tsou and P. Fischer, "Decomposition of a Relation Scheme into Boyce-Codd Normal Form," *ACM SIGACT News*, Volume 14, Number 3 (1982), pages 23–29.

[Tsur and Zaniolo 1986] S. Tsur and C. Zaniolo, "LDL: A logic-Based Data-Language," *Proceedings of the International Conference on Very Large Data Bases* (1986), pages 33–41.

[Tuzhilin and Clifford 1990] A. Tuzhilin and J. Clifford, "A Temporal Relational Algebra as a Basis for Temporal Relational Completeness," *Proceedings of the International Conference on Very Large Data Bases* (1990), pages 13–23.

[U.S. Dept. of Commerce 1977] United States Department of Commerce, *Data Encryption Standard*, National Bureau of Standards Federal Information Processing Standards Publication 46 (1977).

[U.S. Dept. of Defense 1985] United States Department of Defense, "Department of Defense Trusted Computer System Evaluation Criteria," National Computer Security Center (1985).

[Uhrowczik 1973] P. P. Uhrowczik, "Data Dictionary/Directories," *IBM System Journal*, Volume 12, Number 4 (December 1973), pages 332–350.

[Ullman 1982] J. D. Ullman, "The U. R. Strikes Back," *Proceedings of the ACM SIGACT-SIGMOD Symposium on Principles of Database Systems* (1982), pages 10–22.

[Ullman 1985] J. D. Ullman, "Implementation of Logical Query Languages for Databases," *ACM Transactions on Database Systems*, Volume 10, Number 3 (September 1985).

[Ullman 1988] J. D. Ullman, *Principles of Database and Knowledge-base Systems*, Volumes I and II, Computer Science Press, Rockville, MD (1988).

[Unger et al. 1984] E. A. Unger, P. S. Fisher, and J. Slonim (Editors), *Advances in Data Base Management*, Volume 2, John Wiley and Sons, New York, NY (1984).

[Valduriez and Gardarin 1989] P. Valduriez and G. Gardarin, *Analysis and Comparison of Relational Database Systems*, Addison Wesley, Reading, MA (1989).

[Valduriez and Khoshafian 1989] P. Valduriez and S. Khoshafian "Parallel Evaluation of the Transitive Closure of a Database Relation," *International Journal of Parallel Programming*, Volume 17, Number 1 (March 1989).

[Van Gucht 1987] D. Van Gucht, "On the Expressive Power of the Extended Relational Algebra for the Unnormalized Relational Model," *Proceedings of the ACM SIGACT-SIGMOD-SIGART Symposium on Principles of Database Systems* (1987), pages 302–312.

[Vassiliou et al. 1985] Y. Vassiliou, J. Clifford, and M. Jarke, "Database Access Requirements of Knowledge-Based Systems," in **[Kim et al. 1985]**, pages 156–170.

[Verhofstad 1978] J. S. M. Verhofstad, "Recovery Techniques for Database Systems," *ACM Computing Surveys*, Volume 10, Number 2 (June 1978), pages 167–195.

[Vorhaus and Mills 1967] A. Vorhaus and R. Mills, *The Time-Shared Data Management System: A New Approach to Data Management*, Technical Memo SP-2634, System Development Corporation, Santa Monica, CA (1967).

[Wang 1984] S. Wang, "Normal Entity-Relationship Model — A New Method to Design Enterprise Schema," *Proceedings of the IEEE International Conference on Computers and Applications* (1984).

[Weihl and Liskov 1990] W. Weihl and B. Liskov, "Implementation of Resilient, Atomic Data Types," in **[Zdonik and Maier 1990]**, pages 332–344.

[Weikum and Schek 1984] G. Weikum and H. J. Schek, "Architectural Issues of Transaction Management in Multi-Level Systems," *Proceedings of the International Conference on Very Large Data Bases* (1984), pages 454–465.

[Weikum et al. 1990] G. Weikum, C. Hasse, P. Broessler, and P. Muth, "Multi-Level Recovery," *Proceedings of the ACM SIGACT-SIGMOD-SIGART Symposium on Principles of Database Systems* (1990), pages 109−123.

[Weldon 1981] J. Weldon, *Data Base Administration*, Plenum Press, New York, NY (1981).

[Whang and Krishnamurthy 1990] K. Whang and R. Krishnamurthy, "Query Optimization in a Memory-Resident Domain Relational Calculus Database System," *ACM Transactions on Database Systems,* Volume 15, Number 1 (March 1990), pages 67−95.

[Whang et al. 1982] K. Whang, G. Wiederhold, and D. Sagalowicz, "Physical Design of Network Model Databases Using the Property of Separability," *Proceedings of the International Conference on Very Large Data Bases* (1982), pages 98−107.

[Wiederhold 1983] G. Wiederhold, *Database Design*, Second Edition, McGraw-Hill, New York, NY (1983).

[Wiederhold et al. 1983a] G. Wiederhold, J. Milton, and D. Sagalowicz, "Applications of Artificial Intelligence in the Knowledge-Based Management Systems Project," *IEEE Database Engineering Bulletin*, Volume 6, Number 4 (December 1983), pages 75−82.

[Wiederhold et al. 1983b] G. Wiederhold, J. Milton, and D. Sagalowicz, "Artificial Intelligence in the Knowledge-Based Management Systems Project," *ACM-SIGART Newsletter* (1983), pages 59−63.

[Williams et al. 1982] R. Williams, D. Daniels, L. Haas, G. Lapis, B. Lindsay, P. Ng, R. Obermarck, P. Selinger, A. Walker, P. Wilms, and R. Yost, "R*: An Overview of the Architecture," in **[Scheuermann 1982]**, pages 1−27.

[Wilms et al. 1983] P. F. Wilms, B. G. Lindsay, and P. Selinger, "I Wish I Were Over There: Distributed Execution Protocols for Data Definition in R*," *Proceedings of the ACM SIGMOD International Conference on the Management of Data* (1983), pages 238−242.

[Wolfson and Silberschatz 1988] O. Wolfson and A. Silberschatz, "Distributed Processing of Logic Programs," *Proceedings of the ACM SIGMOD International Conference on Management of Data* (1988), pages 329−336.

[Wolfson and Ozeri 1990] O. Wolfson and A. Ozeri, "A New Paradigm for Parallel and Distributed Rule-Processing," *Proceedings of the ACM SIGMOD International Conference on Management of Data* (1990), pages 133−142.

[Wong 1977] E. Wong, "Retrieving Dispersed Data from SDD-1: A System for Distributed Databases," *Proceedings of the Berkeley Workshop on Distributed Data Management and Computer Networks* (1977), pages 217−235.

[Wong 1983] E. Wong, "Dynamic Rematerialization-Processing Distributed Queries Using Redundant Data," *IEEE Transactions on Software Engineering*, Volume SE-9, Number 3 (May 1983), Pages 228–232.

[Wong and Mylopoulos 1977] H. K. T. Wong and J. Mylopoulos, "Two Views of Data Semantics: A Survey of Data Models in Artificial Intelligence and Database Management," *INFOR*, Volume 15 (1977), pages 344–383.

[Wong and Youssefi 1976] E. Wong and K. Youssefi, "Decomposition-A Strategy for Query Processing," *ACM Transactions on Database Systems*, Volume 1, Number 3 (September 1976), pages 223–241.

[Woods 1975] W. A. Woods, "What's in a Link? Foundations for Semantic Networks," in **[Bobrow and Collins 1975]**, pages 35–82.

[Yannakakis 1981] M. Yannakakis, "Issues of Correctness in Database Concurrency Control by Locking," *Proceedings of the ACM Symposium on the Theory of Computing* (1981), pages 363–367.

[Yannakakis et al. 1979] M. Yannakakis, C. H. Papadimitriou, and H. T. Kung, "Locking Protocols: Safety and Freedom from Deadlock," *Proceedings of the IEEE Symposium on the Foundations of Computer Science* (1979), pages 286–297.

[Yao 1979a] A. C. Yao, "A Note on a Conjecture of Kam and Ullman Concerning Statistical Databases," *Information Processing Letters* (1979).

[Yao 1979b] S. Yao, "Optimization of Query Evaluation Algorithms," *ACM Transactions on Database Systems*, Volume 4, Number 2 (June 1979), pages 133–155

[Zaniolo 1976] C. Zaniolo, "Analysis and Design of Relational Schemata for Database Systems," Ph.D. thesis, Department of Computer Science, University of California, Los Angeles, CA (1976).

[Zaniolo 1979a] C. Zaniolo, "Design of Relational Views over Network Schemas," *Proceedings of the ACM SIGMOD International Conference on the Management of Data* (1979), pages 179–190.

[Zaniolo 1979b] C. Zaniolo, "Multimodel External Schemas for CODASYL Data Base Management Systems," in **[Bracchi and Nijssen 1979]**, pages 157–176.

[Zaniolo 1983] C. Zaniolo, "The Database Language GEM," *Proceedings of the ACM SIGMOD International Conference on the Management of Data* (1983), pages 207–218.

[Zaniolo 1989] C. Zaniolo, "Object Identity and Inheritance in Deductive Databases: An Evolutionary Approach," *Proceedings of the International Conference on Deductive and Object-Oriented Databases* (1989).

[Zdonik and Maier 1990] S. Zdonik and D. Maier, *Readings in Object-Oriented Database Systems*, Morgan Kaufmann Publishers, Inc., San Mateo, CA (1990).

[Zhang and Mendelzon 1983] Z. Q. Zhang and A. O. Mendelzon, "A Graphical Query Language for Entity-Relationship Databases," in **[Davis et al. 1983]**, pages 441−448.

[Zloof 1977] M. M. Zloof, "Query-by-Example: A Data Base Language," *IBM Systems Journal*, Volume 16, Number 4 (1977), pages 324−343.

[Zloof 1978] M. M. Zloof, "Security and Integrity Within the Query-by-Example Data Base Management Language," IBM Research Report RC6982, IBM T. J. Watson Research Center, Yorktown Heights, NY (1978).

[Zook et al. 1977] W. Zook, K. Youssefi, N. Whyte, P. Rubinstein, P. Kreps, G. Held, J. Ford, R. Berman, and E. Allman, *INGRES Reference Manual*, Department of EECS, University of California, Berkeley, CA (1977).

Index